# AMERICA BECOMING

## Racial Trends and Their Consequences

## Volume I

Neil J. Smelser, William Julius Wilson, and Faith Mitchell, *Editors*

Commission on Behavioral and Social Sciences and Education

National Research Council

NATIONAL ACADEMY PRESS
Washington, D.C.

NATIONAL ACADEMY PRESS   2101 Constitution Avenue, N.W.   Washington, D.C. 20418

NOTICE: The project that is the subject of this report was approved by the Governing Board of the National Research Council, whose members are drawn from the councils of the National Academy of Sciences, the National Academy of Engineering, and the Institute of Medicine.

The study was supported by Grant No. SBR-9709489 between the National Academy of Sciences and the National Science Foundation through interagency agreements with the Office of the Assistant Secretary for Planning and Evaluation/U.S. Department of Health and Human Services, Bureau of Transportation Statistics/U.S. Department of Transportation, U.S. Department of Defense, U.S. Department of Energy, U.S. Department of Education, U.S. Department of Labor, Environmental Protection Agency, Economic Research Service/U.S. Department of Agriculture, U.S. Department of Housing and Urban Development, U.S. Department of the Interior, National Institute of Justice/U.S. Department of Justice, President's Initiative on Race, Social Security Administration, U.S. Department of Treasury, and the U.S. Department of Veterans Affairs. The Mellon and Mott foundations provided additiona support. Any opinions, findings, conclusions, or recommendations expressed in this publication are those of the author(s) and do not necessarily reflect the view of the organizations or agencies that provided support for this project.

Suggested citation: National Research Council (2001). *America Becoming: Racial Trends and Their Consequences*. Volume I. Neil J. Smelser, William Julius Wilson, and Faith Mitchell, Editors. Commission on Behavioral and Social Sciences and Education. Washington, DC: National Academy Press.

**Library of Congress Cataloging-in-Publication Data**

America becoming : racial trends and their consequences / Commission on Behavioral and Social Sciences and Education, National Research Council ; Neil Smelser, William Julius Wilson, and Faith Mitchell, editors.
     p. cm.
Includes bibliographical references and index.
   ISBN 0-309-06495-3 (v. 1) — ISBN 0-309-06838-X (v. 1 : pbk.)
    1. United States—Race relations—Research—Congresses. 2. United States—Ethnic relations—Research—Congresses. 3. United States—Population—Statistics—Congresses. 4. Minorities—United States—Social conditions—Research—Congresses. 5. Minorities—United States—Economic conditions—Reasearch—Congresses. I. Smelser, Neil J. II. Wilson, William J., 1935- III. Mitchell, Faith. IV. National Research Council (U.S.). Commission on Behavioral and Social Sciences and Education.
   E184.A1 A497 2000
   305.8'00973—dc21

                                           00-010549

Additional copies of this report are available from National Academy Press, 2101 Constitution Avenue, N.W., Washington, D.C. 20418

Call (800) 624-6242 or (202) 334-3313 (in the Washington metropolitan area)

This report is also available online at **http://www.nap.edu**

Printed in the United States of America

# THE NATIONAL ACADEMIES

National Academy of Sciences
National Academy of Engineering
Institute of Medicine
National Research Council

The **National Academy of Sciences** is a private, nonprofit, self-perpetuating society of distinguished scholars engaged in scientific and engineering research, dedicated to the furtherance of science and technology and to their use for the general welfare. Upon the authority of the charter granted to it by the Congress in 1863, the Academy has a mandate that requires it to advise the federal government on scientific and technical matters. Dr. Bruce M. Alberts is president of the National Academy of Sciences.

The **National Academy of Engineering** was established in 1964, under the charter of the National Academy of Sciences, as a parallel organization of outstanding engineers. It is autonomous in its administration and in the selection of its members, sharing with the National Academy of Sciences the responsibility for advising the federal government. The National Academy of Engineering also sponsors engineering programs aimed at meeting national needs, encourages education and research, and recognizes the superior achievements of engineers. Dr. William A. Wulf is president of the National Academy of Engineering.

The **Institute of Medicine** was established in 1970 by the National Academy of Sciences to secure the services of eminent members of appropriate professions in the examination of policy matters pertaining to the health of the public. The Institute acts under the responsibility given to the National Academy of Sciences by its congressional charter to be an adviser to the federal government and, upon its own initiative, to identify issues of medical care, research, and education. Dr. Kenneth I. Shine is president of the Institute of Medicine.

The **National Research Council** was organized by the National Academy of Sciences in 1916 to associate the broad community of science and technology with the Academy's purposes of furthering knowledge and advising the federal government. Functioning in accordance with general policies determined by the Academy, the Council has become the principal operating agency of both the National Academy of Sciences and the National Academy of Engineering in providing services to the government, the public, and the scientific and engineering communities. The Council is administered jointly by both Academies and the Institute of Medicine. Dr. Bruce M. Alberts and Dr. William A. Wulf are chairman and vice chairman, respectively, of the National Research Council.

## COMMISSION ON BEHAVIORAL AND SOCIAL SCIENCES AND EDUCATION

# Foreword

*Christopher Edley, Jr.*

T he President's Race Initiative was launched in June 1997 in the
belief that no challenge facing the nation as it enters the new century is as critical and daunting as the challenge of color. Around
the world and throughout human history, there have been countless trag-
edies born of our seemingly innate tendencies toward misunderstanding,
distrust, resentment, prejudice, hatred, and even violence—all triggered
by racial, ethnic, tribal, and religious differences. It would be hubris to
believe that Americans have somehow escaped this human condition,
miraculously healed and henceforth immune from our own color-based
brand of tribalism. We are unlikely in the next few years to face the
upheavals of ethnic cleansing familiar from the Balkans and Central Africa, or the slow burn of ethnicity-based conflict and even terrorism we
have witnessed in Sri Lanka, Indonesia, Northern Ireland, Spain, Mexico,
and countless other places. The growth of America's diversity is breath-
taking. However, unless we in the United States do better to confront and
bind our racial and ethnic divisions, the powerful legacy of racial caste
will shackle our progress and rend our communities.

Our secular catechism of equality and justice for all, authored at the
nation's birth, was belied by practices at the time. Yet these remain the
powerful ideals to which we aspire, at least in our nobler moments, and
without regard to political party or social status. One could even argue
that the essence of being an American has much more to do with allegiance to our conceptions of justice and fairness than it does to proficiency in a common language or devotion to some vague set of cultural
practices. (Baseball? Apple pie? Some religion? Television?) When Ameri-

cans express patriotic pride, we may mention our relative prosperity or some iconic character trait such as self-reliance. But more likely, we boast about our civic institutions and, especially, civic values such as equality and tolerance.

Racial caste in this land is more than twice as old as the nation itself. It began with the campaigns of displacement, killing, and subjugation of native peoples by European settlers, and then expanded to the chattel slavery of imported Africans. Because the roots of American prejudice and racism are some 250 years deeper than the bedrock of our constitutional ideals, it would be yet another form of hubris to believe that the legacy can be undone in a mere generation or two, and the wounds healed. Nonetheless, healing with unflagging determination is precisely what we must be about. The first step must be a better understanding of our history and our present condition. This is where the leaders of the social sciences have an indispensable contribution to make. The Race Initiative asked the National Research Council of the National Academies to provide the nation with an authoritative assessment of where we are. *America Becoming: Racial Trends and Their Consequences* is the result.

*America Becoming* details demographic changes that have moved America beyond Black and White into a complex multiethnic environment that we still do not understand. Disparities, discrimination, progress, and retrogression within this multilayered economic and social environment demonstrate that the color question is pervasive in our lives, and it is an explicit tension or at least subtext in countless policy debates. These debates range from K-12 school improvement, to criminal justice, to reinvention of the health care system.

The premise is that rational explication, based in research, can make a difference in the pursuit of our ideals. There is, unfortunately, substantial evidence to the contrary when it comes to race and ethnicity. The difficulties are of many sorts. These volumes amply illustrate that there is no shortage of factual, methodological, and conceptual challenges in studying "race"—itself a contingent social construct, rather than a fixed biological or anthropological one. They also illustrate that the research enterprise, try as we might, is almost inextricably tied to our politics—to the currents of public values, interests, and debates. There are contestable judgments implicit in the choice of data we decide to keep, the subjects scholars choose to investigate (and that can attract funding), the questions and variables researchers select, the interpretations and application of the research findings, and so forth. All of this means that research related to race has been the victim of the public's decreased interest in civil rights in the past 25 years, and that even sound research results have often been viewed through lenses shaped by political or ideological agendas.

In the complex agenda of color and ethnicity, it is vital that researchers contribute to a reengagement of both the public and the research community, despite the difficulties and risks. In these papers, researchers repeatedly identify important questions requiring further research. The greatest success of *America Becoming* will be in providing the impetus for a reinvigoration of the social scientific commitment to the cause of racial and ethnic justice: to answer and raise questions, to guide and critique policy actors, to take stock, and, especially, to teach.

*America Becoming* will be instrumental in feeding thoughtful debate. There is ample nourishment here, to be sure, and one can find in the media and countless communities and institutions reason to hope that the appetite for serious civic discourse on the matter of race is on the rise. In colleges and universities, to take one example, dialogues on race have proliferated, and one must hope that a resurgence of sophisticated course offerings in this field will be a signal achievement of this decade. As we prepare students to live and lead in increasingly diverse communities, it is education malpractice if we fail to provide an understanding of where America is and has been on these troubling matters.

Race is not rocket science; it is harder than rocket science. Race demands an intellectual investment equal to the task. It also demands relentlessness in research and teaching that will overwhelm the human tendency to let our differences trigger the worst in our natures.

# Acknowledgments

T he editors would like to acknowledge the role that many people and agencies played in contributing to the success of the Research Conference on Racial Trends in the United States and the report based on that conference, *America Becoming: Racial Trends and Their Consequences.*

The conference grew out of discussions between the National Research Council (NRC) and the President's Initiative on Race. Judith Winston, the executive director of the Initiative, and her staff, including Lin Liu and John Goering, were engaged and helpful throughout the process. The additional support of Christopher Edley, Jr. (special adviser to the Initiative), Rebecca Blank (Council of Economic Advisers), Peter Rundlet (White House), and Katherine Wallman (Office of Management and Budget), was indispensable. Their ability to demonstrate the importance of the documentation of racial trends persuaded many agencies to support the conference. An advisory committee, made up of representatives of the sponsoring agencies and chaired by Rebecca Blank, met several times with NRC staff during the conference planning period. This committee provided the NRC with very helpful feedback and advice.

The sponsors of the conference included the Bureau of Transportation Statistics of the U.S. Department of Transportation, the Economic Research Service of the U.S. Department of Agriculture, the Environmental Protection Agency, the National Institute of Justice of the U.S. Department of Justice, the Office of the Assistant Secretary for Planning and Evaluation of the U.S. Department of Health and Human Services, the

President's Initiative on Race, the U.S. Department of Defense, the U.S. Department of Education, the U.S. Department of Energy, the U.S. Department of Housing and Urban Development, the U.S. Department of the Interior, and the U.S. Department of Labor. A generous Mellon Foundation grant provided support for the dissemination of *America Becoming*. Thanks to the paper authors, discussion leaders, and other presenters, the intellectual content and tone of the conference were of the highest quality from beginning to end. We would like to thank: Bruce Alberts, chairman of the National Research Council and president of the National Academy of Sciences, Richard Alba, Marcus Alexis, Rebecca Blank, Alfred Blumstein, Lawrence Bobo, Frank Bonilla, Thomas Boston, John Sibley Butler, Albert Camarillo, Ken Chay, Beverly Coleman-Miller, Cecilia Conrad, Christopher Edley, Jr., Reynolds Farley, Ronald Ferguson, Roberto Fernandez, Rodolfo de la Garza, Peter Gottschalk, Darnell Hawkins, Jennifer Hochschild, Harry Holzer, James S. Jackson, Paul Jargowsky, Gerald Jaynes, Renée Jenkins, James Jones, Thomas Kane, Randall Kennedy, Raynard Kington, Sanders Korenman, Betsy Lozoff, Anthony Marx, Douglas Massey, Vonnie McLoyd, Robert Moffitt, Charles Moskos, Don Nakanishi, the late Herbert Nickens, Eugene Oddone, Michael Omi, Manuel Pastor, Laura Petersen, Sharon Robinson, Gary Sandefur (with Molly Martin, Jennifer Eggerling-Boeck, Susan E. Mannon, and Ann M. Meier), Thomas Shapiro, Daryl Smith, James Smith, Matthew Snipp, Carol Swain, Russell Thornton, Mary Waters, Morris Weinberger, David Williams, and Min Zhou.

This report was reviewed in draft form by individuals chosen for their diverse perspectives and technical expertise, in accordance with procedures approved by the NRC's Report Review Committee. The purpose of this independent review was to provide candid and critical comments that assist the institution in making the published report as sound as possible and to ensure that the report meets institutional standards for objectivity, evidence, and responsiveness to the study charge. To protect the integrity of the deliberative process, the review comments and draft manuscript remain confidential.

We are indebted to the following individuals for their helpful comments on a previous draft of *America Becoming*: Robert Bates (Harvard University), Lawrence Friedman (Stanford University), Jack Geiger (CUNY Medical School), Robert M. Hauser (University of Wisconsin), Christopher S. Jencks (Harvard University), Eleanor E. Maccoby (Stanford University), Cora B. Marrett (University of Massachusetts), Robert A. Moffitt (Johns Hopkins University), T. Paul Schultz (Yale University), Tim Smeeding (Syracuse University), and Kenneth I. Wolpin (University of Pennsylvania). However, responsibility for the final content of this report rests entirely with the editors and the National Academy of Sciences.

We would like to thank the Committee on National Statistics of the Commission on Behavioral and Social Sciences and Education for their involvement in this project. In addition, many commission staff either volunteered their time during the conference or worked on bringing the report to completion. Margo Cullen, Myrna McKinnon, Brenda McLaughlin, Janet Overton, and Ronné Wingate from the Commission's Division on Social and Economic Studies all contributed to finalizing the manuscript, under the masterful guidance of CBASSE reports editor Christine McShane.

Finally, Barbara Boyle Torrey, executive director of CBASSE, has been an essential player throughout, contributing her fine intelligence, humor, and insight to the planning and execution of this enormous endeavor.

Neil J. Smelser
William Julius Wilson
Faith Mitchell

# Contents

# NEIGHBORHOOD AND GEOGRAPHIC TRENDS

## TABLES AND FIGURES

### Tables

# Figures

# Contents
# Volume II

## HEALTH TRENDS

# APPENDIXES

# Terminology Used in This Report

As many of the authors point out, the term "race" as used to categorize ethnic origins of human beings is a social construct and has no biological basis. Nevertheless, we have come to identify certain terms and names with certain groups of people. The variety of those terms was reflected in the various authors' usage choices; often, more than one term was used for the same group in the same paper. For the purposes of these volumes, we will use the terms as recommended by the U.S. Office of Management and Budget (OMB) in 1999: it coded race into five single-race groups: White, Black, American Indian or Alaska Native, Asian or Pacific Islander, and Other. These terms are defined the terms as follows:

*American Indian or Alaska Native.* A person having origins in any of the original peoples of North and South America (including Central America), and who maintains tribal affiliation or community attachment.

*Asian.* A person having origins in any of the original peoples of the Far East, Southeast Asia, or the Indian subcontinent including, for example, Cambodia, China, India, Japan, Korea, Malaysia, Pakistan, the Philippine Islands, Thailand, and Vietnam.

*Black or African American.* A person having origins in any of the black racial groups of Africa. Terms such as "Haitian" or "Negro" can be used in addition to "Black or African American."

*Native Hawaiian or Other Pacific Islander.* A person having origins in any of the original peoples of Hawaii, Guam, Samoa, or other Pacific Islands.

*White.* A person having origins in any of the original peoples of Europe, the Middle East, or North Africa.

*Hispanic or Latino.* With respect to ethnicity, is defined as: Hispanic or Latino. A person of Cuban, Mexican, Puerto Rican, South or Central American, or other Spanish culture or origin, regardless of race. The term "Spanish origin" can be used in addition to "Hispanic or Latino." (Note: A Hispanic person can be Black or White.)

Again, for the purposes of brevity and consistency, the terms used throughout these volumes are those recommended by OMB—American Indian or Alaska Native, Asian or Pacific Islander, Black, Hispanic, and White. Where necessary to distinguish, non-Hispanic Black and non-Hispanic White are used.

SOURCE: Tabulation Working Group, Interagency Committee for the Review of Standards for Data on Race and Ethnicity. 1999. Draft Provisional Guidance on the Implementation of the 1997 Standards for the Collection of Federal Data on Race and Ethnicity (3-5,65; February 17, 1999). Washington, D.C.: Executive Office of the President, Office of Management and Budget.

# AMERICA BECOMING

# 1

# Introduction

*Neil J. Smelser, William Julius Wilson, and Faith Mitchell*

T he United States is, perhaps more than any other industrialized country, distinguished by the size and diversity of its racial and ethnic populations; and current trends promise that these features will endure. In fact, demographers project that by the year 2050 the United States will likely have no single majority group. Considerable behavioral and social science research has chronicled the remarkable evolution of our multiracial society, its patterns of discrimination, and its progress in reducing racial bias.

To pull together this large body of research, the National Research Council (NRC) convened the Research Conference on Racial Trends in the United States on October 15-16, 1998. The conference was convened in response to a request from the President's Initiative on Race (PIR) and the President's Council of Economic Advisers, and gained support from 15 federal sponsors. It was co-chaired by Neil J. Smelser, Director of the Center for Advanced Study in the Behavioral Sciences at Stanford University, and William Julius Wilson, Lewis P. and Linda L. Geyser University Professor at Harvard University.

The conference was an historic gathering of the nation's leading scholars on racial and ethnic relations, assembled to assess past and current trends for America's Blacks, Hispanics, Asians, and American Indians—and all their multiple and varied national groupings—in regard to several key institutional arenas. Topics of discussion included demographics, education, employment, income and wealth, housing and neighborhood characteristics, health access and status, and the criminal justice system.

These are all essential aspects of American life, and all have been shown to have a racialized component.

It is unfortunate that other equally important topics were not discussed. For example, there is no paper on race and politics because the author who agreed to address that topic had to withdraw from the conference. Other important topics not discussed, that nevertheless evince relevant racial and ethnic nuances, include transportation, rural communities, and disability. None of these yet has a strong enough research base to warrant the commissioning of papers.

Nonetheless, the scholarly papers produced for discussion covered a wide range of issues. They summarized key trends, described gaps in research and data, and suggested research directions for the next decade. These volumes contain updated versions of selected conference papers and, in the case of criminal justice, two discussants' comments.

At the end of this introduction, the key findings are briefly summarized. Preceding that summarization, however, there is a discussion of two issues that are important to bear in mind in any overall assessment of racial trends in America: (1) the methodological considerations affecting the study of race and ethnicity, and (2) the complexity of the different social and cultural foundations of inequalities and other racial and ethnic group outcomes.

## METHODOLOGICAL CONSIDERATIONS

### Definition of "Race" and "Ethnicity"

Some incipient idea of race goes back as far in history as ethnocentrism itself. For our times, the most relevant heritage is found in the concept of "race" produced by nineteenth-century colonialism and anthropology. Human classifications varied, but were largely associated with the world's regional distribution of populations; in some cases races were named for skin color—white, black, yellow, brown, and red. The widely accepted definitional basis was biological—skin color, distinctive facial characteristics, height, build, hair texture, and other physical features, as well as temperamental and psychological traits. Above all, this concept of race connoted that groups could be arrayed on a scale from biologically superior to biologically inferior; consequently, the biological basis for race has an ugly and tragic past, invoked as it has been to justify racial discrimination, colonial domination, slavery, genocide, and holocaust.

One of the great accomplishments of the behavioral and social sciences in the twentieth century has been to logically discredit the nineteenth-century conception of race by amassing evidence on millennia of human migration, contact, and genetic diversification through cross-reproduction. As a result, a more realistic, sociocultural conceptualization of race has developed. Although continuing to acknowledge the genetic, demographic, and geographic dimensions of human diversity, most social scientists now give prominence to the principle that both race and ethnicity derive from *sociocultural* categories that are produced, sustained, and reproduced. Moreover, these categories are, from the standpoint of any given group, to some degree imposed by others and to some degree self-selected. Instead of representing race as a simple biological-physical crosshatch, social scientists now define race as a multidimensional mixture, hence, *"race" is a social category based on the identification of (1) a physical marker transmitted through reproduction and (2) individual, group, and cultural attributes associated with that marker.* Defined as such, race is, then, a form of ethnicity, but distinguished from other forms of ethnicity by the identification of distinguishing *physical* characteristics, which, among other things, make it more difficult for members of the group to change their identity.

Care should be taken, however, not to push this insight to its constructionist extreme and claim that race is merely a social contrivance and therefore not "real." In this connection, we take our lead from the classic insight of W.I. Thomas that if things are defined as real, they are real in their consequences. The concepts of race and ethnicity are social realities because they are deeply rooted in the consciousness of individuals and groups, and because they are firmly fixed in our society's institutional life. Further, these concepts are sustained by several mechanisms that frame the categories of race and ethnicity in terms of kinship and descent, group intermarriage and reproduction, distinctive geographical location and residence, specification in law and policies, discrimination and prejudice, and self-identification. These facts steer us toward a conclusion that is at once true and paradoxical—i.e., "while biological notions of race have little meaning, the society itself is extremely racialized" (Smith, 1998:3).

Because race and ethnicity contain such a complex array of sustaining mechanisms and overlapping connotations, consistent definitions are hard to come by. Even the great sociology master, Max Weber, was frustrated in his efforts to deal with them. In attempting to identify the essence of ethnicity, he invoked a very inclusive definition (Weber, 1968:I, 389):

> [T]hose human groups that entertain a subject belief in their common descent because of similarities of physical type or of customs or both, or because of memories of colonization and migration; this belief must be important for the propagation of a group; conversely, it does not matter whether or not an objective blood relationship exists.

In the end, however, he concluded that the term "ethnic" is too inclusive to be helpful sociologically; for if it were disaggregated into all its component parts and influences, it would be "abandoned" as "unsuitable for a really rigorous analysis" (Weber, 1968:I, 395). The modern student of race might well come to the same conclusion.

Without necessarily fully embracing Weber's pessimistic conclusion, we must nevertheless acknowledge that the terms "race" and "ethnicity" comprise such complex social phenomena that they pose enormous problems of both description and measurement. With respect to description, what is the principal identifying characteristic: physical marker? attributed physical marker? common descent? legal definition? others' attribution? self-identification? With respect to measurement, a similarly confusing array of choices exists—how do we measure race and ethnicity: on the basis of assignment by administrators (e.g., staff at the Office of Management and Budget, officials at the Census Bureau)? social investigators (census officials, survey conductors)? by some legal definition (perhaps, from the Congress)? by a group's "culture"? by their self-reported identification? And how do we deal with those of mixed racial and ethnic parentage?

To appreciate the anomalous consequences of different measures, consider the fact that most "Hispanics," often identified, both popularly and by some social scientists, as a separate racial category, identify themselves as "White" (see Raynard Kington and Herbert Nickens, Volume II, Chapter 11). Or consider the fact that, by self-report, the population of American Indians *tripled* between the 1960 and 1990 censuses, a rate far exceeding any increase based on migration or due to births (see Gary Sandefur et al., Volume I, Chapter 3).

The methodological lessons to be derived from these observations are that, for race and ethnicity (1) there is no single master descriptor or measurement; (2) different descriptors and measures should be used according to the analytic purpose at hand; (3) whatever descriptor or measure (or whatever combination) is used, it should be regarded as a contingent analytic strategy rather than a reflection of some fixed social reality; and (4) because of the essential fluidity of racial categories and measures, we must regard with caution all future projections about racial composition that are based on current measures, because the categories and measures themselves will no doubt change over time.

## Classification and Aggregation

The major racial categories used by the U.S. Bureau of the Census, by other government agencies, and by survey researchers—and to a significant degree lodged in the public mind—are White (or Caucasian or

Anglo), Black (or African American), Hispanic (or Latino), Asian, and Native American (or American Indian). Because these categories are now acknowledged, to varying degrees, by group members themselves and in the eyes of outsiders, a legitimate case can be made for representing them in such aggregated form. In that form, it is easier to see the enormous differences among these major groups with respect to income, health, education, welfare, crime, and legal disadvantage, and, thereby, reveal the pervasive and systematic inequalities among them.

At the same time, to represent these racial and ethnic categories in aggregated terms exacts several costs:

• *Aggregated categories are imprecise.* They conceal the great heterogeneity found within every general grouping. There are approximately 500 identifiable tribal groups in the American Indian population. "White" as a category includes Scandinavians; Eastern, Western, Northern, and Southern Europeans; North Africans; most Hispanics; and others. "Asian" includes not only the major groups of Chinese, Japanese, and Filipino, but also groups from Southeast and South Asia and the Pacific Islands, and others. "Black" includes U.S.-born African Americans as well as those born in the many countries of the African continent, West Indians, Haitians, some Hispanics, and others. As for Hispanics, the minimal internal divisions are Mexican, Cuban, Puerto Rican, and Central and South American, with further divisions possible. Noting these Hispanic subgroup differences, Albert Camarillo and Frank Bonilla conclude simply that "Hispanics in the United States at the dawn of the twenty-first century defy generalizations as a single group" (see Camarillo and Bonilla, Volume I, Chapter 4). As reflected in the pages of this report, all racial and ethnic subcategories manifest enormous differences in income, wealth, education, health, and almost all other social measures. To persist in aggregating the subgroups hides that variation and makes for a reification of social reality that does not correspond to the life situations of the subgroups.

• *Analyzing aggregates obscures data.* Analyzing the circumstances of racial groupings in gross, aggregated terms often obscures the causal significance of race as a variable. Consider these statements from the paper by Renée Jenkins (Volume II, Chapter 13): "Whites were more likely than Blacks and Hispanics to live in families with no minor children"; and "Black and Hispanic youth were more likely to carry a weapon, be involved in fights, and be victimized by others." Taken by themselves, unless disaggregated by subgroups and adjusted, at a minimum, for socioeconomic class, such statements are misleading because they imply that the operative independent variable is racial or ethnic membership.

## Other Methodological Issues

### Multiple Causation

In most cases, the causes of apparent racial differences also have to be disaggregated. In other words, racial correlations are almost inevitably found to conceal the presence of operative variables other than race. Eugene Oddone et al. (Volume II, Chapter 15), for example, note that differences in health care outcomes usually attributed to race can arise from differences in clinical factors affecting underlying disease patterns, patients' ability to pay, and patient preferences, as well as racial bias. Similarly, Harry Holzer's analysis (Volume II, Chapter 5) of Black-White wage differentials since 1975 breaks down into a mix of both nonracial and racial influences, including rising economic returns on skills, declining industrialization and unionism, social/spatial factors, persistent discrimination, and expectations, alternative income, and illegal activity. The dramatic increase, since the 1980s, in the percentage of Blacks in prisons is traceable in large part to the criminal justice system's intensive crackdown on drug activity—which may or may not (see Randall Kennedy, Alfred Blumstein, and Darnell Hawkins, Volume II, Chapters 1, 2, and 3) have been motivated, in part, by racial considerations. In a word, almost all causal statements involving race, when thoroughly analyzed and broken down, reveal a complex interaction of many causes, only some of which are explicitly racial in nature.

### Racial Data as Obscured Data

One of America's great advances in the past two centuries is that it has moved away from the historical situation in which prejudice, discrimination, and subjugation—manifested by extermination of American Indian populations, slavery, Jim Crow laws, restrictive laws and policies against immigrant Chinese, and signs such as "No Irish Need Apply"—were not only legal, but largely regarded as "normal." Relative to past social arrangements, this nation has moved toward a collective realization of the social and economic values of equality and justice. Despite these advances, however, a great deal of prejudice and discrimination persists, even though in many cases discriminatory practices are against the law.

This combination of circumstances has produced situations in which some people who retain racist proclivities are motivated to conceal or distort their prejudices and discriminatory behavior. Audit surveys, especially with respect to housing discrimination, have proved to be an effective mechanism in uncovering those landlords and employers who, while proclaiming fair rental and employment practices, continue to discriminate (see Douglas Massey, Volume I, Chapter 13). The methodological consequence of covert racist practices is that they tend to conceal and distort the very data that we, as social-science investigators, wish to discover, analyze, and explain. The arena of racism—like crime, corruption, scandal, and marital infidelity—is one in which the subject matter, in the nature of the case, remains partially obscured.

In other cases racial data are obscured by the research techniques themselves. Surveys tapping racial and ethnic attitudes often rely on dichotomous (yes or no) or scaled (one-to-five as to strength of attitude) responses. Such responses fail to represent situational variabilities of reported attitudes, to say nothing of their complexity and ambivalence. In some cases, surveys ask for single, forced-choice responses to questions regarding racial or ethnic status, distorting the fact that vast numbers of respondents are "mixed" or do not regard their race or ethnic status as particularly important in their lives. Recent changes introduced by the Census Bureau permit people to chose multiple categories in response to the question of racial identity; but even this change in measurement will not capture the full complexity of group membership.

## The Omnipotence of Relative Deprivation in Race and Ethnic Relations

Committed as we are to tracking the progress of racial and ethnic groups toward conditions of equity and justice, as well as tracking the persisting advantages of others, we often make judgments and assertions about the absolute progress of groups. A simple example is a statement such as: "Over the course of the century, the life expectancy for Blacks more than doubled, and for Whites it increased by 60 percent; yet in spite of improvements, a gap between Blacks and Whites remained and even increased in the 1980s." Such a statement, being tied to a specific measure, is relatively nonproblematical, yet care must be taken to assure that the measures for the categories of "Blacks," "Whites," and "life expectancy" have remained the same over time and are thus comparable with one another at different times.

When it comes to questions of group expectations and attitudes about progress, such statements are difficult to assess because of the phenomenon of relative deprivation. This concept refers to the fact that individuals and groups are continuously shifting their self-assessments because, over time, both their frames of reference—to other groups and to benchmarks in their own history—are also continuously changing. History is replete with examples of groups that experience extreme deprivation measured by absolute standards, but manifest little discontent, and groups that have experienced advances, yet express extreme dissatisfaction because they have not improved more or faster. Understanding the logic of relative deprivation demystifies findings of groups simultaneously experiencing both progress and increased resentment.

In this section, a formidable array of methodological issues and obstacles concerning the study of race and ethnic relations has been outlined. It should be clearly understood, however, that we in no way mean to strike a posture of hopelessness or pessimism. As social scientists, we believe it is important to lay out explicitly all relevant issues and obstacles and to cope with them openly as challenges. This seems the only viable strategy for making our knowledge more reliable and valid.

## Effects of Social Structure and Culture on Racial Group Outcomes

Social and cultural outcomes will differ for racial groups as a result of three kinds of causal mechanisms:

1. those that arise from individual attributes and individual choices;
2. those that originate in direct social actions based on racial considerations, notably discrimination; and
3. those that result from social and cultural changes transpiring elsewhere in society—i.e., changes that are not driven by racial considerations, but nonetheless have an impact on the fortunes of racial groups.

These causal mechanisms do not operate in isolation; they interact and act in concert. Consequently, each has to be included in any effort to understand fully racial trends in the United States.

## Individual Attributes and Choices

Differences in individual skills, motivation, attitudes, and self-selecting "out"—i.e., not taking advantage of opportunities—are some of the individual attributes and choices that can cause stratified racial outcomes. However, these individual factors, although they are definitely operative causal factors, are themselves shaped by larger structural and cultural forces.

## Direct Social Actions

Forces that operate directly to advantage or disadvantage individuals and groups on the basis of race, and thus contribute to racial inequality, include two types—social acts and structural processes. Among the social acts are discrimination in hiring and promotion, housing, and admission to educational institutions, as well as exclusion from unions, employers' associations, and clubs. Systematic structural factors in this category of direct causes are laws, policies, and institutional practices that exclude people on the basis of race or ethnicity. These range from explicit arrangements, such as Jim Crow segregation laws, voting restrictions, and targeted policies, to more subtle institutional processes—e.g., school tracking along racial lines, racial profiling, etc.—whereby ideologies about group differences are embedded in organizational arrangements.

## Indirect Structural and Cultural Factors

*Structural Factors*

The third causal mechanism—indirect structural and cultural factors—is not adequately represented either in the literature on race relations or in any of the following chapters. Social science researchers, themselves being sensitive to (and often outraged by) direct causal factors such as discrimination, have paid more attention to them than to indirect causal factors. In reality the indirect causal factors are often so massive in their impact on the social position and experiences of minorities that they deserve full consideration in understanding the forces leading to differential outcomes along racial lines. We would like to take this opportunity to discuss briefly those causes of stratified racial outcomes that advantage or disadvantage people even though there is no deliberate aim or intended effort to do so.

We assert that these causal mechanisms are "indirect" because they are mediated by the racial group's position in the social stratification system (the extent to which the members of the group occupy positions of power, influence, prestige, and privilege). Take, for example, the effects of changes in the economy or the situation of low-skilled Black workers.

The demand for different kinds of labor skills in recent years has been created by the computer revolution, the spread of new technologies that reward more highly trained workers, and the growing internationalization of economic activity (Katz, 1996). In general, highly skilled or highly educated workers have benefited from these trends, while lower skilled workers face the growing threat of eroding wages and job displacement. The number of skilled Black managers, professionals, and technicians has increased significantly since the 1950s; however, the percentage of unskilled Black workers is still disproportionately large. Accordingly, the decreased relative demand for low-skilled labor has had a greater impact on Black communities. Low-skilled workers in all racial and ethnic groups are likely to be adversely affected by the changes in the relative demand for labor, but the severest dislocations will be felt in the racial minority communities.

The decreased demand for low-skilled labor is also among the factors contributing to the growth of wage inequality in the United States. Also, slow wage growth over the past several years has resulted in annual decreased inflation-adjusted earnings for most workers; and the steepest decreases occurred among the least skilled. The slow growth in real wages is related most fundamentally to the overall decrease in productivity growth between the early 1970s and the mid-1990s. But it is also related to factors that include the accelerated growth of the part-time and temporary work industries, the decrease in national income caused by "raw labor" and the increase caused by human capital (Krueger, 1997),[1] the drop in the real value of the minimum wage, and the dramatic decline of union membership in the private sector.

Given the relatively large percentage of low-skilled Black workers, the effect of the economy's slow real wage growth, like the impact of the decreased relative demand for low-skilled labor, is strongly felt in the Black community and in other relatively disadvantaged racial minority communities (Wilson, 1999). Absent the existing system of economic stratification, these changes in the economy would have no differential impact by race.

Another instance of an indirect structural effect causing a racialized outcome is welfare provisions that specify family factors—e.g., marital status—as conditions for receiving welfare payments. These policies are not explicitly racial in character but they may have had different effects on those racial minorities with high percentages of fragile family structures.

Another example of an indirect structural effect is the college education entitlement of the 1944 G.I. Bill, which, although available to all veterans, imparted an unintended advantage along racial lines. At the time of enactment many minority veterans had not achieved a high school education, a requirement for college eligibility.

Likewise, hospital policies requiring patients to pay before they receive medical services are not specifically directed at minorities, but they have the effect of differentially disadvantaging them because minorities, being most predominant in the low-income bracket, are less able to pay for these services. Related to this problem, private insurance companies' "race-neutral" determinations of uninsurable or risky categories indirectly

---

[1]In a recent paper, Alan Krueger (1999) decomposes labor's compensation into a component due to "raw labor" and a component due to human capital. He finds that only 5 percent of national income is due to raw labor, down from 15 percent in the 1960s.

affect racial outcomes because high-risk categories frequently include disproportionate numbers of racial minorities. An example is the rejection of an applicant because of health history. Racial minorities are more likely to have experienced health problems because of greater exposure to high-risk environments that are not as conducive to physical well-being.

Furthermore, government policies that pertain to taxation, interest rates, the labor market, international trade, criminal justice, and investment and redistribution, as well as corporate decisions involving the mobility and location of industries, affect economic-class groups in different ways. Because minorities are more concentrated in low-income positions, some of these policies have distinctly racial implications.

Finally, the system of racial segregation or social isolation in poor neighborhoods creates mechanisms that affect race-neutral processes that ultimately influence minority group outcomes. Consider the problem of differential flows of information to urban neighborhoods. In order to make wise decisions, one must have good information. However, the more segregated or isolated a neighborhood, the less likely it is that the residents will have easy access to information concerning schools, apprenticeship programs, the labor market, financial markets, and so on.

## Cultural Factors

Indirect *cultural* factors that affect racial group outcomes are in the domain of social interaction and collective experiences within a community—shared outlooks, shared modes of behavior, traditions, belief systems, world views, values, skills, preferences, styles, and linguistic patterns. Several factors determine the extent to which communities differ in outlook and behavior. These factors include the degree to which the community is socially isolated from the broader society; the material assets or resources controlled by members of the community; the benefits and privileges they derive from these resources; their accumulated cultural experiences from current as well as historical, political, and economic arrangements; and the influence members of the community wield because of these arrangements (Wilson, 1996).

Culture is closely intertwined with social relations in the sense of providing tools and creating constraints in patterns of social interaction (Tilly, 1998), including social interaction that results in different racial outcomes. Culture's effects on stratified racial outcomes are therefore indirect, filtered through social relational and collective processes. Voluntary or imposed restrictions on the actions of members of the community enhance differences in outlook and behavior and may result in limited opportunities for social and economic advancement. This creates situations in which social factors, such as the level of economic well-being,

interact with cultural factors in the formation of observable group characteristics and traits over time. As pointed out previously, these group characteristics and traits often shape the attributes of individual members of
the community, including their skills, motivations, and attitudes, which
in turn affect their patterns of social mobility. One of the effects of living
in racially segregated neighborhoods is exposure to group-specific cultural traits (particular skills, styles of behavior, habits, orientations, and
world views) that emerged from patterns of racial exclusion and that may
not be conducive to scoring well on the standard or conventional measures of performance, such as the Scholastic Aptitude test (SAT).

Thus, exposure to different cultural influences—including culturally
shaped habits, styles, skills, values, and preferences—has to be taken into
account and related to different forms of social relations to explain fully
the divergent social trends and outcomes of racial groups (Wilson, 1996).

The most comprehensive analysis of racial trends will include measures and research strategies that capture the unintended racial effects of
organizational, relational, and collective processes embodied in the social
structure of racial inequality. An important aspect of this analysis is a
study of the impact of culture as it is integrated into a broader discussion
of social relations. We note the absence of a discussion of indirect or
unintended causes of stratified racial outcomes among the excellent papers in this volume.

## RACIAL TRENDS IN AMERICA:
## AN OVERVIEW OF THIS VOLUME

### Attitudes and Institutions

As Lawrence Bobo points out, "If one compares the racial attitudes
prevalent in the 1940s with those commonly observed today, it is easy to
be optimistic" (Volume I, Chapter 9). Indeed, Bobo's data indicate that the
United States now enjoys a fairly high degree of consensus about the
ideals of integration and racial equality. Similarly, contrary to the assumption that Blacks and Whites are hopelessly divided over affirmative
action, Carol Swain (Volume I, Chapter 11) finds that ambiguity about the
meaning of "affirmative action" and confusion about affirmative-action
policies mask considerable cross-race agreement on the need to level the
playing field to enhance opportunities for minorities and women. Nonetheless, Bobo concludes that consensus on the ideals of racial equality and
integration founders on different groups' beliefs about the prevalence of
discrimination and on the persistence of negative racial stereotypes.

Ronald Ferguson's research on the impact of racial perceptions on
school performance confirms the role of stereotypes (Volume I, Chapter

12). His work suggests that teachers do not expect Black and Hispanic children to achieve at levels comparable to non-Hispanic Whites, that they subconsciously—and sometimes consciously—convey this belief in their instruction of children, and that this expectation lowers Black and Hispanic children's cognitive test scores. He further points out that lower performance may also be a function of popular minority-group culture, which sets achievement levels for Blacks and Hispanics below those set in White and Asian communities.

The different social and cultural perceptions of racial group achievement, as well as the persistence of racial stereotyping described by Bobo, are clear indications that race continues to be an important social construct in America. However, as Michael Omi argues (Volume I, Chapter 8), merely asserting that race is socially constructed does not uncover the ways in which specific concepts of race emerge, reveal the fundamental determinants of racialization, or show how race articulates with class, gender, and other major axes of stratification. Omi underlines the importance of examining how specific concepts of race are conceived and deployed in public-policy initiatives, political discourse, social-science research, and cultural representations. He maintains that the massive, recent influx of new immigrants has "destabilized specific concepts of race, led to a proliferation of identity positions, and challenged prevailing modes of political and cultural organization" (p. 243).

Omi's article demonstrates the importance of an historical perspective in trying to understand the meaning of race and the impact of changing social, political, and economic situations on racial identity, attitude formation, and racial discourse. On the other hand, Anthony Marx's paper (Volume I, Chapter 10) clearly shows the value of a cross-cultural perspective. Comparing the United States with South Africa and Brazil, he finds that, historically, relations between African and European descendants fell along a continuum of legal racial domination. At one extreme, twentieth-century South Africa encoded pervasive discrimination and imposed severe nationwide political and economic restrictions on its Black majority population. At the other extreme, Brazil legally encoded neither apartheid nor Jim Crow segregation; nevertheless, Afro-Brazilians did experience pervasive informal discrimination and prejudice. Between these two extremes, the United States featured uneven and locally encoded policies of racial domination over its Black minority population, amid what Marx calls "social discrimination." In all three countries, race relations have been significantly contested, "with the enactment of rules of relations (or debates thereof) focusing on the treatment of Blacks." Any analysis of racial trend data in the three countries has to take into account the long-term effects of these differently codified systems of racial domination.

## Economics: Labor, Employment, Wealth, and Welfare

If any institutional force were to be singled out as differentially affecting the fortunes of ethnic and racial groups in the United States, it would be the labor market. We are fortunate to be able to include several chapters bearing on different facets of labor markets, employment, and race. James Smith's paper (Volume II, Chapter 4) provides a general overview of long-term and short-term trends. It shows that significant wage differentials along racial lines are a permanent feature in the American economy. However, several groups have experienced very different fortunes. Quite remarkable progress has been made in narrowing the wage gap for Black workers since 1950, but that trend has slowed since the 1970s. Hispanics, as an aggregate, have not fared so well, and some actual deterioration in their market position is shown in the 1980s and 1990s. It is difficult to give a literal reading of such a statement, however, because the composition of the Hispanic population has changed so much. A significant part of the Hispanic story is the special labor-market disadvantages experienced by recent immigrants from Mexico and other Latin American countries. Unscrambling the factors responsible for the stagnation is a formidable, uncertain task, but Smith makes an effort to assess the relative impacts of changing schooling, quality of students, affirmative action, and rising wage inequality.

The articles by Harry Holzer (Volume II, Chapter 5) and Cecilia Conrad (Volume II, Chapter 6) focus on the differential labor-market fortunes of minority men and women, respectively. The findings presented by Holzer confirm the general picture drawn by Smith: a period of labor-market progress for minorities, with dramatic results in the 1960s, then a slowing in relative earnings since the 1970s. Among the causal factors he cites are education, language proficiency and differences (affecting Hispanic and Asian immigrants), declining industrialization and unionism, and discrimination. Conrad's portrait for women is similar. Relative earnings of White and Black women workers reveal a dramatic convergence between 1960 and 1975—likely traceable to schooling, declining discrimination, and shifts in occupational distribution—and an apparent reversal since then. The causal picture is less clear for the latter period, but some scholars suspect that increased labor-market discrimination and characteristics such as differential schooling seem to have been significant. In addition, the changing composition of the White female labor force—now including larger numbers of the very highly skilled—may also have contributed to the trends. The decline of relative wages for Asian and Hispanic women workers since 1990 is traceable to productivity-related characteristics such as education, and the immigrant status of many Hispanic women workers plays a role. Looking ahead, Conrad foresees the possibility of even greater wage inequality for younger Hispanic and Black women in the labor force.

Minority-owned businesses, as analyzed by Thomas Boston (Volume II, Chapter 9), have shown a decided shift from small-scale personal service and retail—i.e., "mom and pop"—establishments, to firms involved in finance, insurance, real estate, business services, and wholesale industries. This shift mirrored the broader economic transitions in this direction; and minority involvement in small business was facilitated by advances in their educational attainment and by affirmative-action efforts in the areas of contracting and business procurement.

John Butler and Charles Moskos (Volume II, Chapter 8) trace the history of minorities—especially Blacks—in the military, an institution that involves more minority participation than any other. They attempt to tease out some of the factors that may have contributed to the "success story" of this institution. Among the lessons to be learned from the military experience, they suggest, is that organizations should focus on opportunity channels rather than on changing racial attitudes, and that affirmative-action policies should be linked to consistent performance standards and the pool of qualified potential participants.

The chapter by Melvin Oliver and Thomas Shapiro (Volume II, Chapter 10) shifts the level of analysis from participation and income to wealth as a source of inequality. Inequality, as measured by wealth—disposable assets—is always more extreme than income inequality, and that generalization holds when applied to racial differences in wealth. The picture is most extreme for Blacks, and can be traced to factors such as exclusion from wealth-generating opportunities made available through government policies, disadvantages in real-estate ownership, lesser participation in wealth-creating business activities, and cumulative disadvantages at the lower end of the income scale.

Robert Moffitt and Peter Gottschalk (Volume II, Chapter 7) turn to the welfare system. They find very great differences in receipt of welfare benefits, with American Indians and Aleutian Eskimos having the highest probability of receiving receipts, and Black and Hispanic households having very high rates as well. Most of these differences trace to "risk factors" such as differences in income, family structure, employment, and education of head of household—all of which are race-associated. Moffitt and Gottschalk conclude by recommending policy attacks on these risk factors, which presumably will reduce racial disparities, rather than race-specific welfare policies.

## Demography and Geography

Gary Sandefur et al. (Volume I, Chapter 3) provide a valuable survey of racial and ethnic differences and trends in population composition, including growth, fertility, family formation, mortality, and migration since the 1950s. The differences among the major groups in the country are striking. Extrapolating from these trends, the authors confirm the now-familiar estimate that the percentage of Whites will decrease dramatically by 2050 and thereafter. Further analysis of the trends and differences also suggests the possibility that Whites and Asians may converge toward one racial/ethnic cluster and that American Indians, Blacks, and Hispanics may converge toward another.

Three additional articles focus on demographic and related characteristics of Hispanics, American Indians, and Asians, respectively. The case of Hispanics is perhaps most dramatic, inasmuch as some projections suggest that by 2050 nearly one-quarter of the U.S. population will be of Hispanic origin. Albert Camarillo and Frank Bonilla (Volume I, Chapter 4) qualify this claim by insisting on the heterogeneity of the Hispanic subpopulations. They outline the distinctive economic, occupational, and educational aspects of the Hispanic experience, and focus closely on the prospects for an increase in Hispanic political power. They locate a double tendency, one suggesting a pattern of conventional assimilation to mainstream U.S. life, another suggesting a pattern of continued poverty, insulation, and possible cultural alienation.

For the American Indian population, a group holding special interest because of its traumatic past relationship to the U.S. government, Russell Thornton (Volume I, Chapter 5) traces the group's demographic (including strikingly high rates of intermarriage), geographic, and related fortunes. Thornton also addresses problems associated with the legal status of tribes, tribal identity, and recent trends in economic development, as well as the anomalous situation of American Indian studies and the politically thorny issue of the repatriation of American Indian human remains and other cultural objects to their tribal sources.

In his essay on the Asian Pacific American population, Don Nakanishi (Volume I, Chapter 6) takes special note of the "demographic revolution" occurring among these historically small minorities—a revolution sending their numbers from 1.5 million in 1970 to nearly 12 million in 1998, with predictions of nearly 20 million by 2020. This group has increased greatly in internal heterogeneity as a result of the diversification of sources of immigration since the 1970s. Nakanishi gives special attention to the issue of political participation and electoral power of this group, now only partially crystallized on account of its cultural diversity, but promising to become a significant force in the American polity.

Immigration, and the dramatically increased levels since the 1960s, are the focus of Min Zhou's chapter (Volume I, Chapter 7). Interestingly, although immigration continues to bring enormous numbers of people to American shores, the current rate of immigration is slightly lower than previous inflows because of America's much larger current population base. The "new immigration" is notable for its heterogeneity, with Latin and Asian countries being the primary contributors; for large numbers of undocumented immigrants; and for the large streams of refugees and asylees among them. The impact of the recent wave has been greatest in urban centers, effecting permanent changes in the ethnic demography of cities like Los Angeles, Miami, and San Francisco. Zhou also turns her attention to special issues such as economic mobility of the new immigrants, prospects for their second generation, and the impact of new immigrants on the Black minority.

Two papers look at the spatial distribution of racial and ethnic groups and how location affects access to social and economic opportunity. First, Douglas Massey (Volume I, Chapter 13) examines long-term trends in the segregation of Blacks, Hispanics, and Asians. He finds that extreme geographical segregation is unique to Blacks, and is largely unrelated to economic status; and he argues further that it is not explained by residential preferences. Housing is probably one of those areas in which the persistence of White prejudice and discrimination is still most alive. Massey concludes that residential segregation of Blacks contributes directly and indirectly to high concentrations of poverty, educational failure, joblessness, unwed parenthood, crime, and mortality. In a related treatment (Volume I, Chapter 14), Manuel Pastor, Jr., argues that suburbanization has taken resources and economic dynamism from central cities and led to a diminished community life and buildups of hazardous waste. He suggests further that the increasing importance of suburbs in national voting has contributed to a declining political will to deal with poverty, race, and urban decline. Pastor notes the possibility that the emergent "new regionalism" and changes in how inner-ring suburbs and inner cities operate regionally may reduce the city-suburb divide.

## Health

One unhappy aspect of racial and ethnic life in the United States is that many differences in health by race and ethnicity persist, with the members of many, but not all, racial and ethnic minorities experiencing worse health than the majority population. Raynard Kington and Herbert Nickens (Volume II, Chapter 11) document this persistence. They develop an overview of causal factors that contribute to the differences, including socioeconomic position, health-risk behaviors, access to health care, culture and acculturation, genetic factors, and environmental and occupational exposures. David Williams (Volume II, Chapter 14) looks at the health of adults, and documents racial differences and trends in chronic diseases, infectious diseases, and homicide and suicide, and offers a number of methodological cautions in reading and interpreting these data. He examines a variety of institutional factors, such as economic discrimination, residential segregation, differential education, and differential access to the health system, that work to produce the differences.

The case of racial differences in veterans' health and health care is taken up by Eugene Oddone et al. (Volume II, Chapter 15). This category is special because of the federal government's unique commitment to attend to the health of war veterans. Oddone et al. explore a number of factors that may contribute to racial and ethnic differences in health (including veterans' health): economic variables, patient perceptions of their own health, patient preferences, differential trust in the health system, and differential behavior of the providers of medical care.

Two articles focus on children's and adolescents' health. Vonnie McLoyd and Betsy Lozoff (Volume II, Chapter 12) note racial differences in such diverse health disorders as iron deficiency, elevated lead levels, low birth weight, prenatal alcohol exposure, adolescent homicide and assaultive violence, suicide, and drug use. Throughout the article, the authors track the mixed record of public policies and programs in dealing with these problems. In a closely related treatment (Volume II, Chapter 13), Renée Jenkins addresses the changes in health indicators from the federal government's Healthy People 2000 project, concentrating on racial differences in infant mortality, immunizations, teen births, and violent deaths, and assessing a variety of national and local policies designed to reduce the disparities.

## Crime and Justice

As Randall Kennedy points out in introducing his chapter (Volume II, Chapter 1), racial aspects of the administration of criminal law constitute one of the most sensitive and volatile features of American life. This fact is symbolized by the extremely high incarceration rates for minorities, especially Black and Hispanic males. Kennedy reviews three flash points of tension in the justice system—the use of race as a criterion in the surveillance, questioning, searching, and arresting of suspects; jury selection; and differential punishment of minorities. The record of accomplishment in all three areas is decidedly mixed and in need of reform. In his commentary on Kennedy's paper (Volume II, Chapter 3), Darnell Hawkins confirms the importance of these problem areas, and suggests three historical and demographic trends that have contributed to the rising racial imbalance of levels of imprisonment. These are the mainstreaming and integration of White ethnics and southerners into American economic, political, and social structures, thus reducing arrest rates among them; Black migration from the South, which increased their risk of involvement with the criminal justice system; and the increasing geographic marginalization of very poor Whites, which may insulate them from some forms of crime detection and social control found in large cities. Finally, Alfred Blumstein's remarks (Volume II, Chapter 2) provide even more stunning evidence of the differential incarceration rates among Blacks and Hispanics. In his search for contributing factors, he examines acts of discrimination on the part of law enforcement agents, and policies that have intended or unintended racial effects. He also addresses differential involvement (by race) in certain types of crimes.

## CONCLUDING REMARKS

From the outset of this project to provide a comprehensive review of racial trends in the United States, the organizers and editors, and all our colleagues at the National Research Council, have been keenly aware of the great importance of this scientific survey and assessment—both for the nation and for its abiding problems of racial and ethnic inequality. Recognizing this importance, we have been correspondingly enthusiastic through all of the project's phases: conceiving, planning, organizing, executing, compiling, and, now, making public the results of the project. We conclude this introduction with the hope that readers in all quarters will share this sense of importance and enthusiasm, and that the scientific base we have constructed will be one of the many ingredients that contribute to enlightened and effective policies affecting race in America.

## REFERENCES

Fischer, C., M. Sanchez-Jankowski, S. Lucas, A. Swidler, and K. Voss
   1996   *Inequality and Design: Cracking the Bell-Curve Myth*. Princeton: Princeton University Press.
Katz, L.
   1996   Wage Subsidies for the Disadvantaged. National Bureau of Economic Research, Inc., Working Paper 5679. Cambridge, Mass.
Krueger, A.
   1997   What's Up With Wages? Mimeo, Industrial Relations Section, Princeton University.
   1999   Measuring Labor's Share. Working Paper No. 413, Industrial Relations Section, Princeton University.
Smith, D.
   1998   *Racial Trends in Higher Education*. Paper delivered at the National Research Council's Research Conference on Racial Trends in the United States, October 15-16, 1998, Washington, D.C.
Tilly, C.
   1998   *Durable Inequality*. Berkeley: University of California Press.

Weber, M.
  1968   *Economy and Society: An Outline of Interpretive Sociology*, G. Roth and C. Wittich, eds. New York: Bedminster Press.
Wilson, W.
  1996   *When Work Disappears: The World of the New Urban Poor*. New York: A. Knopf.
  1999   *The Bridge Over the Racial Divide: Rising Inequality and Coalition Politics*. Berkeley, Calif.: University of California Press.

# 2

# An Overview of Trends in Social and Economic Well-Being, by Race

*Rebecca M. Blank*

This country's progress on race-related issues is often measured by trends in the economic and social well-being of the various racial and ethnic groups. During the first part of 1998, I headed an effort to pull together information on these trends from a wide variety of sources, as part of the work of the President's Initiative on Race, launched by President Clinton in 1997. This chapter offers a very brief overview of those data, providing an introduction to topics that other authors address in greater detail in later chapters of this report.

## INTRODUCTION

In general, there are many signs of improvement across all racial and ethnic groups in a wide variety of measures of well-being, such as educational achievement, health status, and housing quality. In some cases, disparities between different racial groups have narrowed, as all groups have experienced improvements. But in too many cases, overall improvement in well-being among all groups has brought about no lessening of racial or ethnic disparities. In a few key measures, disparities have actually widened. The primary conclusion of this paper is that race and ethnicity continue to be salient predictors of well-being in American society. To understand what is happening in America today and what will be happening in America tomorrow, one must understand the role of race.

## Indicators of Well-Being

This chapter discusses trends in seven areas:

1. population/demographic change,
2. education,
3. labor markets,
4. economic status,
5. health status,
6. crime and criminal justice, and
7. housing and neighborhoods.

Wherever possible, trends over time are presented for key variables, focusing on five major population groups: non-Hispanic Whites, non-Hispanic Blacks, Hispanics, Asian and Pacific Islanders, and American Indians and Alaska Natives. These data are taken almost entirely from U.S. government sources. In many cases, however, data for all groups are not available, or not available for the entire time period. Data available for as many groups as possible are presented in the 14 figures. The term "minority" is used to refer to a group that composes a minority of the total population. Although these five groups are currently minorities in the population, current trends project they will, together, constitute more than half the U.S. population by 2050.

This brief introduction does not attempt to provide anything like a comprehensive discussion of the available data.[1] Provided here is an overview of some of the more interesting trends, particularly focusing on issues that introduce key topics that will be addressed in this book. One particular limitation of these data is that they present averages across very large aggregate categories of racial and ethnic classification. This hides much of the rather important information about subgroups. For instance, although data for Dominican and Cuban Americans might show very different trends, they are both combined within the Hispanic category. Similarly, Japanese and Laotian Americans are grouped together in the Asian and Pacific Islanders category; Italian and Norwegian Americans are grouped together as non-Hispanic Whites.

## An Increasingly Diverse Population

The U.S. population is becoming increasingly diverse. Hispanics, non-Hispanic Blacks, Asian and Pacific Islanders, and American Indians and

---

[1]See Council of Economic Advisers (1998) for a more comprehensive discussion of all data presented here, as well as other related data. Data and trends discussed in this paper are all documented and discussed in greater detail in this publication.

Alaska Natives currently constitute 27 percent of the population. By 2005, Hispanics will be the largest of these groups within the United States, surpassing non-Hispanic Blacks. These changes will present this nation with a variety of social and economic opportunities and challenges.

Recent high levels of immigration are also increasing diversity within these groups. At present, 38 percent of Hispanics are foreign-born; 61 percent of Asian and Pacific Islanders are foreign-born. This raises questions of assimilation and generational change. Will the second generation among these groups show a narrowing of the disparities that distinguish their foreign-born parents from the U.S.-born population?

Based on 1990 Census data, Figure 2-1 provides one view of this diversity, plotting projections of the minority composition of the population by region for 1995. Where people live and who they live next to is important in determining how individuals experience racial and ethnic diversity. The projections shown in Figure 2-1 indicate that the population in the West is the most diverse, with more than one-third of the population composed of racial and ethnic minorities. The West is also the

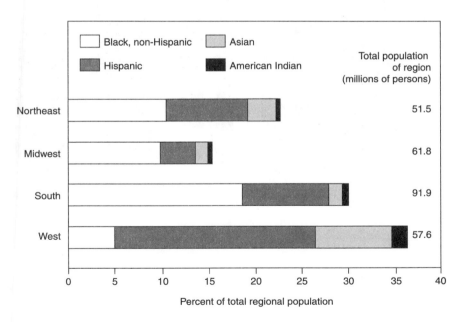

FIGURE 2-1 Minority population by region, 1995. Data for Asians exclude Hispanic Asians, and data for American Indians exclude Hispanic American Indians. Data are projections based on the 1990 census. SOURCE: Council of Economic Advisers (1998).

region where a higher percentage of Hispanics, Asian and Pacific Islanders, and American Indians and Alaska Natives reside. The South is the second most diverse region and has the largest percentage of non-Hispanic Blacks. The Midwest is the region with the least population diversity; 85 percent of its population is non-Hispanic Whites.

The household structure of these different groups varies greatly, as shown in Figure 2-2. Household structure, based here on data for 1970 and 1996, correlates with a variety of other variables, particularly variables relating to economic well-being. More adults in a family means

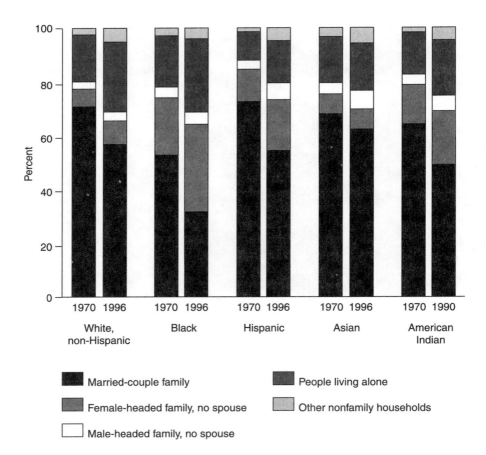

FIGURE 2-2  Household structure.  In 1970, data for Whites include Hispanic Whites.  In 1970, data for Asians are for Japanese, Chinese, and Filipinos.  Data for 1996 are not available for American Indians.  SOURCE:  Council of Economic Advisers (1998).

more potential earnings as well as more available adults to care for children. Single-parent households are among the poorest groups in the country. Individuals who live alone are also often more economically vulnerable than are persons who live with other family members.

All groups show significant increases in the number of people living alone or in single-parent families between 1970 and 1996, but the percentage living in single-parent families is much larger among Blacks, Hispanics, and American Indians and Alaska Natives. In fact, the biggest recent percentage increases are in single-father families, rather than single-mother families, although single-father families continue to be a small percentage of all families. The reasons for these trends—and why some groups have much larger percentages of single-parent families in particular—are much debated.

Household structure is closely related to age distribution as well. Minority populations have a significantly larger percentage of children under the age of 17 than do non-Hispanic Whites, whereas Whites have a much larger percentage of elderly persons. The result is that the school-aged population—persons aged 5 to 17—is more racially and ethnically diverse than the population as a whole, so that today's schools reflect tomorrow's more diverse adult population—and also mirror some of the conflicts and the benefits that accompany growing diversity.

## EDUCATIONAL ATTAINMENT

In a society growing increasingly complex, educational skills are key to future life opportunities. Disparities in education are fundamental because they can determine lifetime earning opportunities and influence an individual's ability to participate in civic activities as well.

The labor market of the twenty-first century will rely increasingly on computers; thus, obtaining computer skills is fundamental. Figure 2-3 shows how children's access to computers has changed over time, both in their schools and in their homes. Clearly, more and more children have access to computers, particularly in their schools; but there is an ongoing gap in computer use between White children versus Black and Hispanic children. Between 1984 and 1993, the years for which these data are available, this gap increased for computer use at home, leaving children in minority groups further behind.

Other more conventional measures of achievement in elementary and secondary schooling have generally shown narrowing gaps across racial groups. Mathematics proficiency scores, as measured among children of different ages by the National Assessment of Educational Progress, have shown ongoing gains, particularly by Black children. High school completion continues to inch up among both Whites and Blacks, with substan-

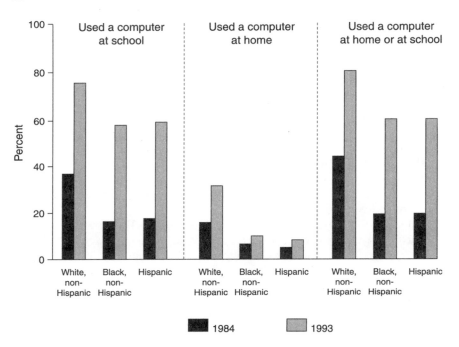

FIGURE 2-3 Computer use by children in first through sixth grades. SOURCE: Council of Economic Advisers (1998).

tially greater progress among Blacks; so that the White-Black high school dropout rates are slowly converging over time. Among Hispanics, high school completion has been stagnant at approximately 60 percent since the early 1980s. Hence, the gap between Hispanics and other groups in terms of educational achievement is widening.

Figure 2-4 shows trends in attainment of college degrees, through 1997, among Whites, Blacks, and Hispanics. Economic returns to a college education have increased dramatically in recent years, and college degrees continue to be an important credential for entry into many white-collar jobs. Although college completion has increased steeply among Whites, it has increased only modestly among Blacks, leading to a widening gap since the early 1990s. Among Hispanics, college completion rates are not much higher now than they were in the mid-1980s.

The more stagnant educational trends among Hispanics reflect, in part, the growing immigrant percentage of that population. Immigrants are less likely to hold high school or college degrees. U.S.-born Hispanics are making progress in increasing both their high school and college completion levels, but this progress is being diluted by the growing pool

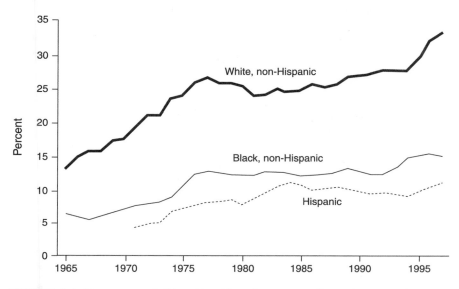

FIGURE 2-4  Persons aged 25 to 29 with a four-year college degree or higher. Prior to 1971, data for Whites include Hispanic Whites, and data for Blacks include Hispanic Blacks.  Data for non-Hispanic Blacks and Hispanics are three-year centered averages.  Prior to 1992, data are for persons having completed four or more years of college.  SOURCE:  Council of Economic Advisers (1998).

of less-educated immigrants. This re-emphasizes the question of how second-generation Hispanic children will fare. If they follow the trends of other U.S.-born populations, Hispanic educational attainment will start to increase over time.

## LABOR-MARKET INVOLVEMENT

Involvement in the labor force means integration with the mainstream U.S. economy. Earnings are the primary source of income for most persons. Although job-holding may create some stress, it also produces economic rewards. Access to jobs is key for economic progress.

Figure 2-5 plots the labor-force participation rates from the 1950s to 1997 for Whites, Blacks, and Hispanics, by gender. The chart shows rapidly increasing convergence in labor-force participation rates, as men's rates have slowly decreased while women's rates have increased steadily. White women, who used to be much less likely to work than Black women, are now just as likely to be in the labor force. In fact, both White women's and Black women's labor-force participation rates are rapidly

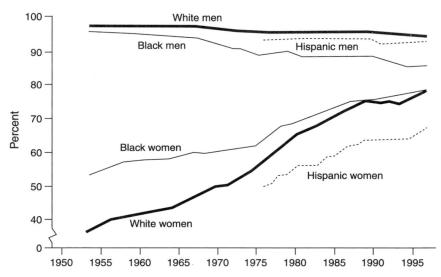

FIGURE 2-5  Labor force participation rates of persons aged 25 to 54.  Prior to 1972, data for Blacks include all non-Whites.  SOURCE:  Council of Economic Advisers (1998).

converging with those of Black men, who have experienced steady decreases in work involvement.

Hispanic women also have shown increases in labor-force participation, but remain much less likely to work than other women. A major question for the Hispanic population is whether adult women will show rapid increases in labor-force participation, to the level of women from other groups. Such changes in women's labor-market involvement not only mean changes in the economic base of families—and probably in the economic security and decision-making power of husbands versus wives—but may also mean substantial changes in family functioning and in child-rearing practices.

Along with labor-force participation, unemployment is another measure of access (or lack of access) to jobs. After two decades of higher unemployment rates, unemployment in the late 1990s was at 25-to-30-year lows among all groups. The differentials between groups, however, remained quite large. For instance, unemployment rates among Blacks have consistently been at least twice as high as those of Whites.

The labor-market issue that has received the most attention in recent years is wage opportunities. Figure 2-6 plots median weekly earnings among male and female full-time workers from 1965 through the first two quarters of 1998. Among all groups, men's wages decreased steadily

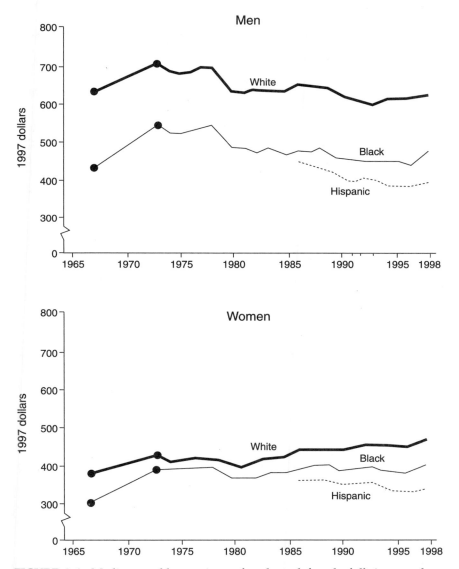

FIGURE 2-6 Median weekly earnings of male and female full-time workers. Straight line between dots indicates data are not available for intervening years. Prior to 1979, data for Blacks include all non-Whites. Data for 1998 are from the first two quarters. SOURCE: Council of Economic Advisers (1998).

from 1980 until 1995, when there was evidence of an upturn. The pay gap between White and Black men changed little, however, with no sign of relative progress in wages for Black men. Hispanic men have actually seen decreases in both absolute and relative wages, compared with White and Black men. Again, this pattern is at least partially the result of the growing percentage of less-educated immigrants in the Hispanic population.

In contrast, women have not experienced wage decreases. In fact, White women's wages have grown slowly since the 1980s, so that they now earn more than both Hispanic and Black men. Black women's wages have been largely stagnant, although they show a recent upturn; and Hispanic women's wages have decreased slightly. Thus, the wage gap between White women and both Black and Hispanic women has increased.

## ECONOMIC STATUS

Continued and even growing gaps in earnings imply that the economic situation is not improving for minority populations relative to the White population. Other measures of family economic well-being reinforce this conclusion. Figure 2-7 shows median family income for Asian and Pacific Islanders, non-Hispanic Whites, Hispanics, and Blacks through 1996. Family income is probably the most widely used measure

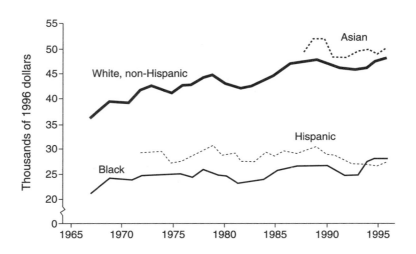

FIGURE 2-7 Median family income. Prior to 1972, data for Whites include Hispanic Whites. SOURCE: Council of Economic Advisers (1998).

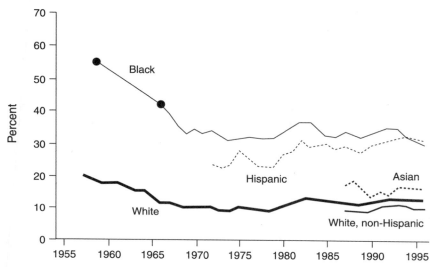

FIGURE 2-8 Poverty rates for individuals. Straight line between dots indicates data not available for intervening years. SOURCE: Council of Economic Advisers (1998).

of overall economic well-being. Among non-Hispanic Whites, family income has been rising steadily. Essentially, the growth in female labor-force participation and increases in White women's wages have resulted in more family income, even though men's earnings have deteriorated somewhat. Asian families earn even more than Whites. Black family income has been relatively stagnant since the 1970s, although there were signs of increase after 1993. Hispanic family income decreased in the 1990s.

This means that income differentials have widened between Whites and Asian and Pacific Islanders on the upper end of the income brackets and Blacks and Hispanics on the lower end. American Indians and Alaska Natives, for whom we only have data from the 1990 Census, show lower income than Blacks in that year.

These median family income numbers hide very different experiences at different points in the income distribution. Households headed by less-skilled workers—particularly those headed by single parents—have generally experienced income decreases over the past several decades. Households headed by a person with a college degree have generally experienced income increases.

One might be particularly concerned with the number of families at very low income levels. Figure 2-8 shows poverty rates among individuals by racial group, indicating the percentage of the population in each group living in families with incomes below the official U.S. poverty line, which was less than $8,000 per year in the late 1990s. In general, poverty rates have been relatively flat since the early 1970s. About 10 percent of the White population has been poor over this period. Asian and Pacific Islanders show a slightly higher poverty rate, underscoring the diversity within the Asian and Pacific Islander populations—they have both higher median incomes than Whites as well as higher poverty rates, reflecting the fact that at least some Asian groups are experiencing economic difficulties.

Black poverty has also been relatively constant, but at nearly 30 percent—three times the White poverty rate. Hispanic poverty has increased somewhat since the mid-1980s; Hispanic poverty rates are now higher than Black poverty rates. Poverty rates among subgroups, such as children or the elderly, show similar differentials between racial and ethnic groups.

## HEALTH STATUS

Economic well-being is often closely linked to other aspects of well-being, such as health status. Interestingly, health differences do not necessarily show the same patterns as economic differences. Infant-mortality rates provide a primary indicator of both health status and access to health care in a population. Figure 2-9 plots infant-mortality rates by race from

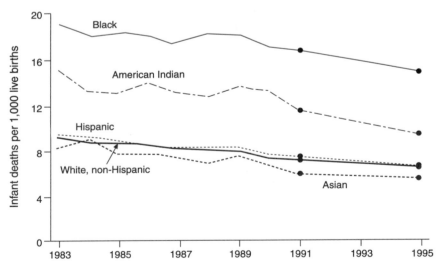

FIGURE 2-9 Infant mortality rates. Straight line between dots indicates data not available for intervening years. SOURCE: Council of Economic Advisers (1998).

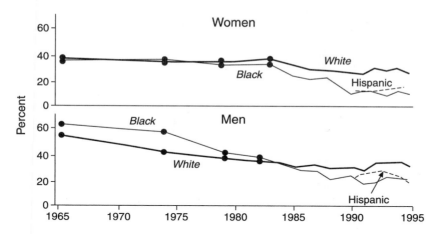

FIGURE 2-10 Prevalence of smoking among persons aged 18 to 24. Straight line between dots indicates data not available for intervening years. Data for Hispanics are for 1990-1991, 1992-1993, and 1994-1995. SOURCE: Council of Economic Advisers (1998).

the early 1980s through 1995. Infant mortality has been steadily decreasing among all groups, indicating major health improvements within all populations. The disparities between groups, however, have remained largely constant. Black infant-mortality rates are about two-and-a-half times White rates. American Indian and Alaska Native rates have fallen a bit faster than other groups, but remain well above White rates.

Figure 2-9 also shows a pattern visible in much health data—namely, although Hispanics show substantial educational and economic differentials, they show far fewer health differentials. Hispanic infant-mortality rates are almost identical to White and Asian and Pacific Islander infant-mortality rates.

Figure 2-10 shows smoking prevalence for people aged 18 to 24, from 1965 through 1995. Clearly, smoking is a health issue that emerges in adolescence. Smoking is correlated with shorter life expectancy and greater health risks. In general, smoking rates have fallen for both young women and men over the past 30 years; and this is one of the few indicators where Blacks and Hispanics do better than Whites. Black smoking rates have fallen faster than White rates, so that young Blacks, who used to be more likely to smoke than Whites, are now less likely to smoke.

In contrast, Figure 2-11 shows death rates among 15- to 34-year-olds in the mid-1990s. There are very large differences in death rates by cause among different racial groups. American Indians and Alaska Natives are far more likely to die as a result of unintentional injuries—typically auto-

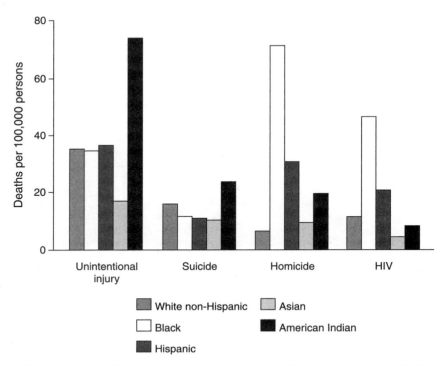

FIGURE 2-11 Death rates by cause, for persons aged 15 to 34, 1994 to 1995. Data for 1994 and 1995 are averaged to provide more reliable estimates. HIV data for American Indians are for 1993-1995. SOURCE: Council of Economic Advisers (1998).

mobile accidents—and suicide. Blacks are far more likely to die as a result of homicide and HIV infection. These differences emphasize that living conditions and health-risk factors are quite different among different populations.

## CRIME AND CRIMINAL JUSTICE

There is no single aggregate measure of the likelihood of being a victim of crime. Figure 2-12 plots homicide rates, which constitute a small percentage of all crimes but are among the best measured crime statistics (few homicides go unnoticed or unreported). Figure 2-12 shows that Blacks are far more likely to be homicide victims than is any other group. The homicide victimization rate of Blacks is more than twice that of Hispanics and six times that of non-Hispanic Whites and Asian and Pacific Islanders. American Indian and Alaska Native homicide rates are about

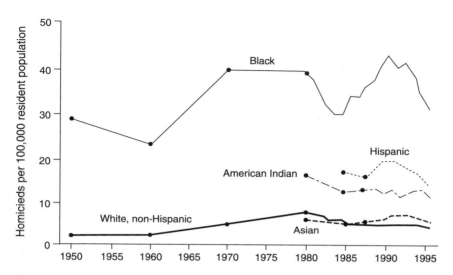

FIGURE 2-12 Victims of homicide. Straight line between dots indicates data not available for intervening years. Data include deaths from "legal intervention" (use of police force). Prior to 1985, data for Whites include Hispanic Whites. Prior to 1970, data include nonresidents. SOURCE: Council of Economic Advisers (1998).

twice those of Whites and Asian and Pacific Islanders, and slightly below those of Hispanics. Although public discussion often focuses on the higher likelihood that Blacks will be arrested for crimes, there is little discussion of the fact that Blacks are also much more likely to be victims. There are large disparities by race in both the likelihood of being a victim of a crime, as well as in the likelihood of being arrested and incarcerated by the criminal justice system. Although other crime statistics, such as property crimes, show smaller racial disparities, they also show higher victimization among minority groups.

Data on experiences within the criminal justice system are largely tabulated only for Whites and Blacks, and hence provide less comprehensive measures across racial groups. Blacks are far more likely to be arrested and incarcerated than are Whites. Some of these differences reflect differences in the crimes for which Blacks are disproportionately arrested, and some may reflect discriminatory behavior on the part of police and other persons within the criminal justice system. In 1995, more than 9 percent of the Black population was under correctional supervision, either on probation or parole, or in jail or prison, compared to 2 percent of the White population. Among young Black men 20 to 29 years old, more than 25 percent are under correctional supervision. Because arrests and prison stays often fracture families and reduce future labor-market opportunities, these high rates of involvement with the criminal justice system are correlated with the reduced economic opportunities of Black families.

## HOUSING AND NEIGHBORHOODS

Where people live, and the housing they live in, is correlated with their health and economic status. Increasing concern among social scientists about "neighborhood effects"—the influence of peers and of neighborhood characteristics on individual health and behavior—has raised interest in housing and neighborhood issues. Figure 2-13 shows the percentage of  populations living in housing units with physical problems, such as substandard plumbing or heating as well as electrical and other serious upkeep problems. All groups for which we have data, from the mid-1970s to the mid-1990s, show substantial improvement in housing quality; but, as in other areas, large disparities remain across groups. Non-Hispanic Blacks, Hispanics, and American Indians and Alaska Natives are far more likely to live in substandard housing than are Whites or

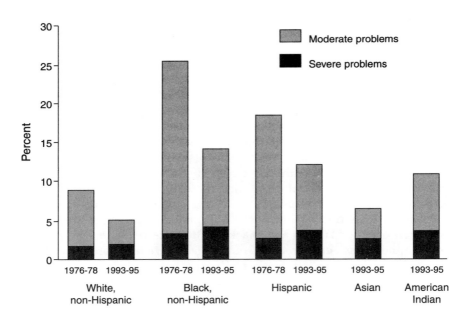

FIGURE 2-13  Housing units with physical problems.  Data for 1976 and 1978, or 1993 and 1995, are averaged to provide more reliable estimates.  Data for Asians exclude Hispanic Asians, and data for American Indians exclude Hispanic American Indians.  SOURCE:  Council of Economic Advisers (1998).

Asian and Pacific Islanders. Other measures of housing adequacy, such as crowding, show similar trends, with overall improvement among all groups, but continuing large disparities between groups.

Information about neighborhoods raises again the question of where people live and who they live next to. The diversity of a person's neighborhood can affect his or her overall sense of national diversity and knowledge of members of other races or ethnicities. Figure 2-14 shows the neighborhood composition of different groups in the United States. At the top is the overall population composition of Whites, Blacks, Hispanics, Asian and Pacific Islanders, and American Indians and Alaska Natives. If all people lived in a randomly chosen location, the composition of neighborhoods would reflect the composition of the overall population. The bot-

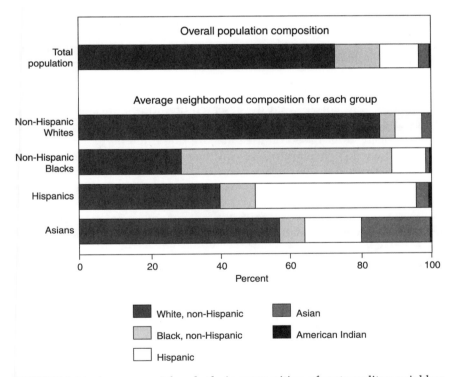

FIGURE 2-14 Average racial and ethnic composition of metropolitan neighborhoods, 1990. Data for Asians exclude Hispanic Asians, and data for American Indians exclude Hispanic American Indians. The American Indian category includes individuals classified as "other." SOURCE: Council of Economic Advisers (1998).

tom of the figure shows what the average neighborhood composition looks like for persons of each racial group.

Whites are by far the most segregated population, even more than their larger population percentage would justify. The average White person lives in a neighborhood that is more than 80 percent White. Blacks are the next most segregated, living in neighborhoods that are, on average, about 60 percent Black and 30 percent White.

Hispanics live in neighborhoods that have close to equal amounts (about 40 percent each) of Whites and Hispanics. Asian and Pacific Islanders live in the most diverse neighborhoods, composed of a mix of Whites, Blacks, Hispanics, and other Asian and Pacific Islanders. This suggests that these two population groups are experiencing and living in the midst of diversity in this country to a much greater degree than Whites or Blacks.

## WHAT DO THESE DISPARITIES MEAN?

This very quick and quite limited review of some of the key indicators of economic and social well-being underscores the ongoing importance of disparities by race and by Hispanic origin in U.S. society. Of course, there are multiple reasons behind these disparities. Many of the other chapters in this book summarize what the research literature indicates about the causes and effects of racial disparities in key areas of society. Three overarching conclusions, based on the data, are presented here.

First, race and Hispanic origin continue to be defining characteristics for many Americans. They are correlated with educational and economic opportunities, with health status, and with where people live and who they live next to. The magnitude of these differences, especially for Blacks and Hispanics, is extremely significant on average, suggesting that these disparities are widely experienced. Relative to the White and Asian populations, the Black population on average has only two-fifths as many college graduates, three-fourths as much earnings, and only slightly more than one-half as much income. The Hispanic population fares even worse. Although we do not have as much comparable information for American Indians and Alaska Natives, their data tend to be closer to those of Blacks and Hispanics than to those of Whites. Whatever their causes, these are substantial differentials; they shape our life opportunities and they shape our opinions about and behaviors toward each other. To repeat the point I started with at the beginning of this chapter, race continues to be a salient predictor of well-being in American society.

Second, the growing presence of Hispanic and Asian and Pacific Islander populations is fundamentally changing the face of America. The displacement of Blacks as the largest minority group in the population in the early 2000s may cause some political and social tension. High numbers of immigrants within the Hispanic and Asian and Pacific Islander groups make questions of assimilation and second-generation progress particularly important in the years ahead. If second-generation Hispanic women behave more like other U.S.-born women, there will be many more Hispanic families with wives in the labor market two decades from now. If second-generation Hispanics acquire education at the rate of other U.S.-born populations, the education levels within the Hispanic community will rise substantially.

Third, Whites may be less aware of the changes and the challenges of growing population diversity than any other group. In part, there is often a "blindness" among the majority to the situation of other groups, because their own situation is typically taken as the norm. This "blindness" is reinforced by locational patterns and neighborhood choice. Whites are much more likely to live in the Midwest than other groups, the least diverse part of the nation; and they tend to live in the most segregated neighborhoods in the other regions. In contrast, Asian and Pacific Islanders—who do as well as Whites on many measures of well-being—live in much more diverse neighborhoods and are almost surely more aware of issues relating to diversity and difference, even when these issues do not translate into personal economic differentials. In short, the growing populations of Hispanics and Asian and Pacific Islanders, as well as many Blacks, may be better prepared to address the challenges, and to take advantage of the benefits, of an increasingly diverse population than are Whites.

This introduction has provided a set of data-based "snapshots" of diversity and differentials by race and Hispanic origin in some key areas. The rest of this book provides in-depth examinations of these same key areas. The chapters that follow look beneath the averages and the aggregate snapshots and disclose a nuanced sense of how and why racial differentials continue to exist, and how they have been influenced by policy choices.

## ACKNOWLEDGMENTS

The opinions expressed in this paper reflect the personal views of the author and not the official position of the Council of Economic Advisers. I thank all my staff at the CEA who worked on putting together the information summarized here.

## REFERENCE

Council of Economic Advisers
1998 *Changing America: Indicators of Social and Economic Well-Being by Race and Hispanic Origin*. Washington, D.C.: U.S. Government Printing Office.

# 3

# An Overview of Racial and Ethnic Demographic Trends

*Gary D. Sandefur, Molly Martin, Jennifer Eggerling-Boeck,*
*Susan E. Mannon, and Ann M. Meier*

Provided here is an overview of major demographic trends for racial and ethnic groups in the United States over the past 50 or so years—a daunting undertaking for one paper, given the variety of groups and topics addressed. Consequently, this overview is selective, covering what we feel are the most important trends—population composition and growth, fertility, family, mortality, and migration. Racial and ethnic categories are the ones used by the federal government.

To enumerate racial and ethnic groups, demographers rely on the U.S. decennial census and annual Current Population Surveys (CPS). To estimate marriage, fertility, and mortality rates, demographers use the national vital statistics records of births, marriages, and deaths. Estimates of internal migration come from the U.S. Bureau of the Census (USBC), and estimates of international migration come from the Immigration and Naturalization Services and USBC.

## THE LIMITATIONS OF PUBLIC DATA
## FOR STUDYING TRENDS

The U.S. Census has classified people by "race" since its inception in 1790. In spite of this long practice of differently defining groups, prior to the 1970s (in some cases, even later), tables of population characteristics and other official statistics, including vital statistics, often list only "Whites" and "non-Whites." One factor complicating the analysis of historical trends for Blacks is the use of different racial and ethnic categories in different years. Initially, slave status was used as a proxy for a racial category for Black Americans. Classification options for race were only "free White persons, slaves, or all other free persons." Later a category for "free colored persons" was added. In 1870, "mulatto" was added; census enumerators were instructed to " . . . be particularly careful in reporting the class *Mulatto*. The word is here generic, and includes quadroons, octoroons, and all persons having any perceptible trace of African blood" (U.S. Bureau of the Census, 1989). The 1890 Census divided Blacks thus: Black described those who had "three-fourths or more Black blood"; mulatto, those who had "three-eighths to five-eighths Black blood"; quadroon, "one-fourth Black blood"; and octoroon, "one-eighth or any trace of Black blood." Terms used for a Black person changed from "slave," to "colored person," to "Negro," to "Black." The 2000 Census used "Black/African American."

For Asians, the history of classification is as complicated. In censuses of the late 1800s and early 1900s, three Asian groups were typically represented—Chinese, Japanese, and Filipino. Other Asian categories were added along the way—Korean in 1940 and Vietnamese and Asian Indian in 1980. By 1990, nine ethnic groups were listed under Asians and Pacific Islanders (API)—Chinese, Japanese, Filipino, Asian Indian, Hawaiian, Samoan, Korean, Guamanian, and Vietnamese—as well as an "Other API" option with a blank for identifying "Other." Trend analysis is further complicated by the fact that statistics released by USBC do not always mirror actual census classification; USBC combines some categories for ease of reporting. For example, most published tabulations of 1990 data on race report for the umbrella category of Asian and Pacific Islander, not each of the nine ethnic groups. Another complication for analysis is the fact that Asians do not appear in vital statistics publications until recently.

The 1870 Census included American Indians as a separate racial group. Prior to that, only Indians who paid taxes were enumerated, but they were not distinguished racially from the rest of the population. Currently, the census asks those who identify themselves as American Indians to write in their tribal affiliation. Published information on American Indians from 1970 onward sometimes includes data for Eskimo and Aleut populations as Alaska Natives. An issue that has a pronounced impact on the analysis of trends among American Indians is the USBC change to self-identification. Between 1970 and 1990, the size of the American Indian population tripled (Nagel, 1996; Eschbach, 1993), an increase far beyond what was generated by either migration or births. Renewed pride in American Indian heritage among many who earlier had identified themselves with some group other than American Indian (often White) led to the increased numbers of American Indians.

The 1970 Census introduced self-identification for persons of Spanish origin. The "Hispanic" population includes Mexicans, Puerto Ricans, Cubans, and those of other Hispanic origin or descent (U.S. Bureau of the Census, 1989). In the past, census methods to identify respondents of Spanish origin included identification based on Spanish surname, use of Spanish language at home, and respondent's birthplace or birthplace of parents (Bean and Tienda, 1987). These identifiers were less than satisfactory. Surnames often change after marriage, some Spanish surnames are indistinguishable from Italian and Portuguese surnames, questions about one's birthplace or birthplace of parents only capture first- and second-generation Hispanics, and identification by the use of Spanish at home excludes Hispanics who do not use Spanish at home. In fact, the 1980 Census found that of the 14.6 million Hispanics identified, only 11.1 million reported speaking Spanish at home (Davis et al., 1983). In the 2000 Census, the ethnicity question was only slightly different, asking respondents whether they are of "Hispanic or Latino" origin or descent rather than "Spanish/Hispanic" origin or descent (Office of Management and Budget, 1997).

Perhaps the most important development in racial and ethnic group definitions also came in 1970; that year the census was distributed by mail rather than having enumerators go door-to-door. This made enumerator identification of race obsolete. The 1960 Census was primarily self-identification, but enumerator identification was used in some rural areas where census forms were not mailed. Thus, since 1970, racial identification is no longer the province of census enumerators. Respondents now classify their own race and that of the members of their households.

Although the ethnicity question has remained relatively consistent in the past two censuses, USBC continues to grapple with racial classification. Most recently the issue is the classification of individuals of multiracial parentage who eschew single-race classification. The 2000 Census allowed respondents to identify with as many racial groups as they wished in a "check all that apply" list of options (Office of Management and Budget, 1997). This could prove extremely complicated when attempting to tabulate the composition of the nation by race.

A final limitation of the data to be mindful of is that decennial censuses have been plagued by a differential undercount problem. It is estimated that the 1990 Census missed 8.5 percent of Black males and 3.0 percent of Black females, compared to 2 percent of non-Black males and 0.6 percent of non-Black females (Robinson et al., 1993). Other hard-to-reach populations, such as American Indians on reservations, are undercounted as well.

The heterogeneity of the major racial and ethnic groups in the United States creates a final problem. All racial and ethnic groups discussed in this book are composed of subgroups that vary widely in characteristics.

Nevertheless, there is value in looking at trends for the broader groups. Federal, state, and local programs and funding allocations are often based on broad group membership rather than narrowly defined racial and ethnic groups. Also, most of the racial or ethnic groups within broader classifications share some cultural or historical experiences.

## POPULATION SIZE, HISTORICAL TRENDS, AND PROJECTIONS

Population size is determined by three principal components of demography: fertility, mortality, and migration. Racial and ethnic differences in rates of one or more of these components cause the racial composition of the nation to shift. Recently, international migration and higher fertility rates among some racial and ethnic groups have been the primary contributors to the nation's population growth and changing composition.

### Historical Trends

The racial and ethnic composition of the more than 265 million U.S. residents is 1 percent American Indian, 3 percent Asian, 11 percent Hispanic, 12 percent Black, and 73 percent White (Deardorff and Hollmann, 1997)—quite different than it was 50 years ago, and projected to be different 50 years from now. Figure 3-1 shows historical trends in racial composition from 1900 to 1990, with projections to 2050.

Until 1940, Whites are shown as constituting more than 80 percent of the population; since then, the percentage of the population that is White has been declining. Hispanic and Asian percentages have increased significantly. The percentage of Blacks—10 to 12 percent—has remained relatively stable. The percentage of American Indians has grown dramatically, but is still only 1 percent at the end of this century.

### Projected Trends

From 2000 to 2050 (Figure 3-1), the Black population is projected to increase only slightly, while the Hispanic and Asian populations are projected to increase dramatically. By 2010, Hispanics are expected to surpass Blacks as the largest minority group in the United States. Whites are projected to comprise 53 percent of the population by 2050.

One must take such projections with a huge grain of salt. Immigration rates may change. Fertility or mortality regimes could change significantly. The way Americans think and talk about racial and ethnic distinc-

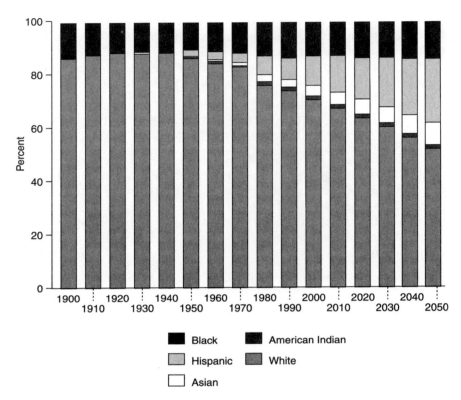

FIGURE 3-1 Racial and ethnic composition of the United States: 1900 to 2050.
SOURCES: Adapted from Day (1996:Table 1); Davis et al. (1983:Table 3); Garcia
and Montgomery (1991:Table 1); Thornton and Marsh-Thornton (1981:Tables 1
and 4); Barringer et al. (1993:Table 2.4A); Elben (1974:Table 2); Coale and Rives
(1973:Table 4); Hollmann (1993:Tables 1 and 2); Bogue (1985:Tables 2 and 3);
Coale and Zelnik (1963:Tables 16 and 17); Siegel (1974:Table 2); and McDaniel
(1995:Figure 1).

tions, as well as the racial and ethnic categories used by the federal government, may change in fundamental ways, as they have in the past.

### Age Structure of Racial and Ethnic Groups

Figure 3-2, a through f, illustrates the age composition of U.S. populations over time. Figure 3-2a shows that the population as a whole has
aged from 1950 to 1996. The most notable shifts are the decreases in the
younger groups and increases in the middle-age groups. In 1950, the

youngest age group comprised the largest percentage of the population—the beginning of the baby-boom era.  The dent in the 1950 age composition, at the 15- to-19-year-old segment, can be attributed, in part, to low fertility during the Depression.  In 1950, almost half of the population was less than 30 years old; by 1996, only about 40 percent of the population was less than 30 years old.  In the 1996 data, the bulge at the middle-age groups represents the aging of the baby-boomers, and the percentages of the population at the oldest ages are greater than they were in 1950, indicating the aging of the population.

   In Figure 3-2, b through f, the population pyramids illustrate changes in relative age structures for racial and ethnic groups and indicate future trends.  Logically, because they are the most populous group, Whites (Figure 3-2b) most closely mirror age structure trends for the total United States, with a lower and stabilizing birth rate, the baby-boomer bulge around the middle-age groups in 1996, and an aging population.

   The pyramid for the Black population (Figure 3-2c) shows an older

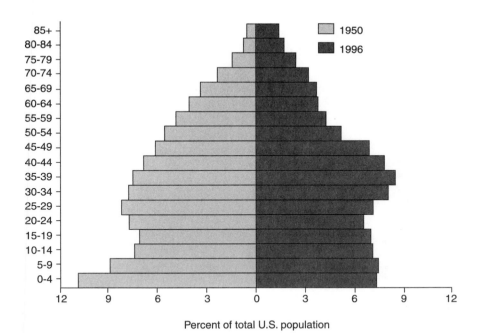

Percent of total U.S. population

FIGURE 3-2a  1950 and 1996 U.S. total age composition.  SOURCES: Adapted from U.S. Bureau of the Census (1965:Table 1); Deardorff and Hollmann (1997:Table 1).

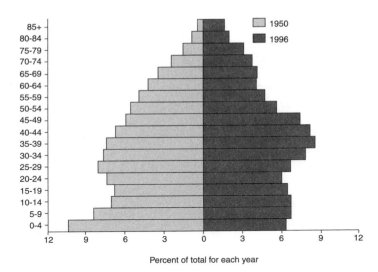

FIGURE 3-2b  1950 White (including Hispanic) and 1996 non-Hispanic White age composition.  SOURCES:  Adapted from U.S. Bureau of the Census (1965:Table 1); Deardorff and Hollmann (1997:Table 1).

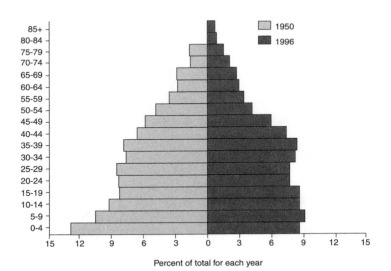

FIGURE 3-2c  1950 Black (including Hispanic) and 1996 non-Hispanic Black age composition.  75-79 represents 75+ for the 1950 data, the highest age group tabulated for this group in 1950. SOURCES:  Adapted from U.S. Bureau of the Census (1953f:Table 2); Deardorff and Hollmann (1997:Table 1).

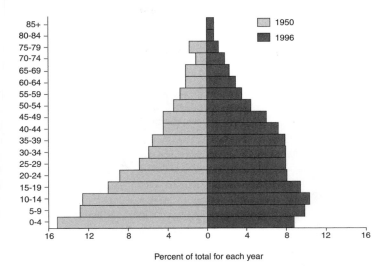

FIGURE 3-2d  1950 and 1996 American Indian age composition.  SOURCES: Adapted from U.S. Bureau of the Census (1953f:Table 2); Deardorff and Hollmann (1997:Table 1).

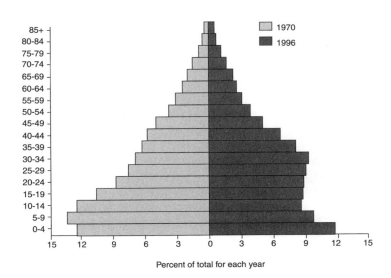

FIGURE 3-2e  1970 and 1996 Hispanic age composition. SOURCES:  Adapted from U.S. Bureau of the Census (1973c:Table 2); Deardorff and Hollmann (1997:Table 1).

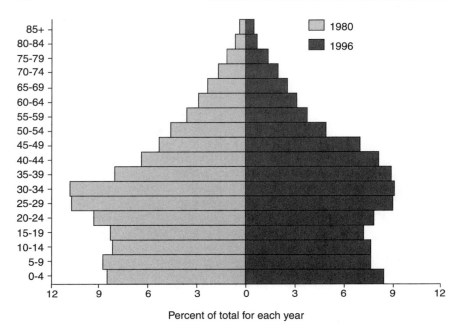

FIGURE 3-2f  1980 and 1996 Asian age composition. SOURCES:  Adapted from U.S. Bureau of the Census (1983:Table 2); Deardorff and Hollmann (1997:Table 1).


population in 1996 than in 1950, but one that is still younger than that of the United States overall and Whites specifically.

The pyramid for American Indians (Figure 3-2d) suggests that that population has undergone dramatic changes in age composition since 1950; however, changes in self-identification probably influenced changes in age composition as well.  In 1950, more than 15 percent of the American Indian population were less than 5 years old; by 1996, the percentage was almost half that, at just over 8 percent; at this time, data are also included for Alaska Natives.  Even with the decline, this percentage is still higher than that for the total United States or Whites, but comparable to percentages for Blacks and Asians.  Despite their aging population, in 1996 well over 50 percent of the American Indian population was less than 30 years old.

Hispanics (Figure 3-2e) are currently the youngest population of all major U.S. racial and ethnic groups.  Nearly 60 percent of the Hispanic population is less than 30 years old; 12 percent are less than 5 years old, at least 3 percentage points more than Blacks, Asians, or American Indians/

Alaska Natives. Higher percentages in the young age groups in 1970[1] may be a reflection of immigration of young children under the Immigration Act of 1965, which emphasized family reunification. The young age of the Hispanic population, coupled with current high rates of immigration, support projections that the Hispanic population will surpass Blacks as the largest minority group by the year 2010.

In the pyramid for the Asian population (Figure 3-2f), 1980, rather than 1950, data are used because 1980 was the first year complete data for Asians are available. Earlier information reported only on selected Asian subgroups. The pyramid on the 1996 side is wider at the younger ages through the middle-age groups and more narrow at the older age groups. This is, in part, the result of the high rate of immigration among Asians. Together, Asians and Hispanics comprised 85 percent of all U.S. immigrants during the 1980s (Martin and Midgley, 1994). The relatively young age structure and high rates of immigration indicate rapid growth for Asians in the future; projected growth rates exceed 2.5 percent per year through 2020 (Day, 1996).

## POPULATION DISTRIBUTION AND MIGRATION

### Historical Trends

The dramatic growth in major U.S. racial and ethnic populations owes much to immigration. In addition to legal immigration, substantial numbers of undocumented immigrants have entered the United States since the mid-1960s; estimates have been a source of controversy, but the most widely accepted is between 2 and 4 million (Bean and Tienda, 1987; see also, Passel and Woodrow, 1984). The 1965 Immigration Act, which replaced the national-origins system, increased the total number of immigrants allowed into the United States, and caused the number of immigrants entering the country to skyrocket.

### Regional Distribution

USBC distinguishes between four major census regions: the Northeast, Midwest, South, and West. Nearly one-half of the White population lives in the Northeast and Midwest, compared to less than one-third for all other racial and ethnic groups. Regional concentrations are shown in Table 3-1.

---

[1]1970 data are used rather than 1950 data because 1970 is the first time complete data on Hispanic ethnicity were gathered in the Census. Earlier information is based on surname or language spoken at home, or it is only for selected states.

TABLE 3-1 Population Percentage by Region, 1950 to 1990

| Race/Ethnicity | Region | Year | | | | |
|---|---|---|---|---|---|---|
| | | 1950 | 1960 | 1970 | 1980 | 1990 |
| Total U.S. | | | | | | |
| | Northeast | 26.2 | 24.91 | 24.13 | 21.69 | 20.43 |
| | Midwest | 29.5 | 28.79 | 27.84 | 25.99 | 23.99 |
| | South | 31.32 | 30.66 | 30.9 | 33.28 | 34.36 |
| | West | 13.4 | 15.64 | 17.14 | 19.06 | 21.22 |
| White | | | | | | |
| | Northeast | 27.54 | 25.95 | 24.69 | 22.47 | 21.07 |
| | Midwest | 31.01 | 30 | 28.77 | 27.71 | 26.04 |
| | South | 27.13 | 27.17 | 28.09 | 31.3 | 32.84 |
| | West | 13.68 | 16.14 | 17.48 | 18.52 | 20.05 |
| Black | | | | | | |
| | Northeast | 13.42 | 16.04 | 19.24 | 18.3 | 18.73 |
| | Midwest | 14.81 | 18.26 | 20.25 | 20.14 | 19.05 |
| | South | 67.98 | 59.94 | 53.01 | 53.02 | 52.83 |
| | West | 3.8 | 5.75 | 7.51 | 8.54 | 9.39 |
| Hispanic[a] | | | | | | |
| | Northeast | —[b] | 18.8[d] | 20.89 | 17.83 | 16.61 |
| | Midwest | — | 5 | 11.55 | 8.74 | 7.58 |
| | South | — | 32.2 | 30.44 | 30.63 | 30.42 |
| | West | — | 44.1 | 37.12 | 42.81 | 45.39 |
| Asian | | | | | | |
| | Northeast | 12.17[c] | 8.97[c] | 13.57[e] | 15.99 | 18.26 |
| | Midwest | 9.88 | 6.5 | 7.96 | 11.14 | 10.47 |
| | South | 14.4 | 5.22 | 6.64 | 13.42 | 15.23 |
| | West | 63.55 | 79.23 | 71.83 | 59.45 | 56.01 |
| American Indian | | | | | | |
| | Northeast | 4.6 | 6.41 | 5.99 | 5.56 | 6.15 |
| | Midwest | 22.4 | 19.23 | 18.89 | 17.49 | 17.42 |
| | South | 20.05 | 24.36 | 25.46 | 26.2 | 29.28 |
| | West | 52.96 | 50.18 | 49.66 | 50.74 | 47.15 |

[a]Includes persons of Spanish origin of any race.

[b]Statistics on Hispanic population limited to persons of Spanish origin in only five southwestern states during this year.

[c]Includes Japanese, Chinese, Filipino, and other Asians (Koreans, Asian Indians, and Malayans) for 1950 and 1960.

[d]Hispanic population figures for 1960 based on Bean and Tienda (1987:Table 5.1).

[e]Includes Japanese, Chinese, and Filipino for 1970.

SOURCES: Adapted from U.S. Bureau of the Census (1953f:Tables 3-7; 1963i:Tables 2-6; 1973e:Tables 1, 16, 31; 1973c:Table 1; 1973d:Table 1; 1975:Series A172-194; 1991:Table E; 1993a:Table 135); Bean and Tienda (1987:Table 5.1).

Despite the dramatic migration of Blacks from the South during much of the past century, more than half continued to live in the South in 1990. Return migration of Blacks to the South in the past few decades, however, contributes to this regional concentration, despite the fact that the overall percentage has been declining. The West had the lowest percentage of Blacks in 1990. Nonetheless, this percentage has steadily increased since the 1950s.

The Hispanic population experienced its most dramatic boost in the late 1960s as a result of immigration reform, refugee movements, and illegal immigration (Bean and Tienda, 1987). Since the 1960s, approximately three-fourths of the Hispanic population has settled in either the West or the South (Table 3-1). Underlying this general pattern are significant variations by Hispanic origin. Mexicans, for example, live primarily in the West and Southwest, Puerto Ricans in the Northeast, and Cubans in Florida.

The Asian population experienced a dramatic increase in the 1980s, more than doubling their numbers (Barringer et al., 1993). With changing immigration laws in the 1960s, and recent refugee movements, immigration is clearly the most important factor leading to the concentration of Asians in Hawaii and the West. As with Hispanics, distribution varies considerably among Asian ethnic groups. Chinese, Koreans, Asian Indians, Pakistanis, Sri Lankans, and Bangladeshis were more likely to reside in the Northeast than other Asian Americans in 1980 and 1990. Filipinos, Japanese, Okinawans, and, to a lesser extent, Cambodians and Indonesians, were more concentrated in the West than all other Asians in 1980 and 1990. Malayans and Hmong were largely living in the Midwest in 1980 and 1990, and Laotians were primarily residing in the Midwest in 1980 (Barringer et al., 1993). Table 3-1 indicates that although the percentage of Asians living in the West dropped since the 1950s, more than half continued to reside in the West in 1990.

The vast majority of the American Indian population resides in the West and South. Although the percentage has decreased slightly since the 1950s, close to one-half continue to reside in the West alone. By 1990, almost 30 percent of American Indians lived in the South, an increase from 20 percent in 1950.

## Metropolitan Areas

Harrison and Bennett (1995) argue that the geography of minority concentration is more related to states and metropolitan areas than to regions. In fact, minority groups are represented in large numbers in only a few states, most notably California, Texas, Florida, New York, New Jersey, and Illinois. In these states, the vast majority of racial and ethnic groups are concentrated in a few key cities, such as Miami, New York City, and Chicago. The USBC's Standard Metropolitan Statistical Areas (SMSAs) include both metropolitan (metro) areas and nonmetro areas. SMSAs are further divided as inside and outside central cities. Tables 3-2 and 3-3 provide data for racial and ethnic distribution in SMSAs and central cities.

## Blacks

The percentage of Blacks living in rural areas declined from 47 percent to 16 percent between 1950 and 1990, which contrasts with the steady deconcentration of the White population from cities to rural areas for the past 20 years (Long, 1981). The majority of Blacks moving to metro areas during this time relocated to central cities, where the percentage of the Black population increased from 41 to 57 percent from 1950 to 1990 (Table 3-3). This pattern should not disguise, however, the trend toward Black suburbanization. By 1980, Blacks had begun to migrate to the suburbs, causing the overall proportion of Blacks living in central cities to decline for the first time (Long and DeAre, 1981). In fact, the percentage of the Black population in the suburbs more than doubled between 1950 and 1980, with a 70 percent increase in the 1970s alone. A great deal of variation exists in the rates of Blacks moving to suburbs, however, by city and by region. In the 1970s, for example, the rate in the South was almost double the rate in the North (Nelson, 1980). Of the 21 metro areas to which more than 5,000 Blacks moved during 1985 to 1990, 15 are located in the South Atlantic region. Both the large size of the pre-existing southern Black population, and their net in-migration to the South beginning in the 1970s, account for this. At the same time, Blacks are more likely than Whites and American Indians, but less likely than Asians and Hispanics, to reside in metro areas. As Table 3-3 indicates, Blacks have been increasingly well represented in the nation's largest metro areas. In addition to South Atlantic metro areas, Blacks have historically settled in Philadelphia, Detroit, and Baltimore.

## Hispanics

Since the 1950s, the Hispanic population has moved in substantial numbers to metro areas, their percentages in metro areas exceeding that of Whites since the 1960s and reaching 90 percent in 1990 (Table 3-1). The Hispanic population has generally been more concentrated in central cities; however, the percentage of this population residing in central cities has declined since 1960. Hispanics are less concentrated in central cities than Blacks, but more so than all other racial/ethnic groups. Neverthe-

TABLE 3-2 Population Percentage Inside/Outside Metropolitan Areas and Central Cities, 1950 to 1990

| Race/Ethnicity | | Year | | | | |
|---|---|---|---|---|---|---|
| | | 1950 | 1960 | 1970 | 1980 | 1990 |
| Total U.S. | Inside Metro Areas | 56.07 | 62.95 | 68.60 | 75.80 | 77.49 |
| | Inside Central Cities | 32.79 | 32.35 | 31.39 | 32.00 | 31.30 |
| | Outside Central Cities | 23.28 | 30.60 | 37.21 | 43.80 | 46.19 |
| | Outside Metro Areas | 43.93 | 37.05 | 31.40 | 24.20 | 22.51 |
| White | Inside Metro Areas | 56.14 | 62.30 | 67.18 | 74.40 | 75.56 |
| | Inside Central Cities | 31.66 | 29.78 | 27.54 | 27.00 | 25.78 |
| | Outside Central Cities | 24.48 | 32.52 | 39.64 | 47.40 | 49.79 |
| | Outside Metro Areas | 43.86 | 37.70 | 32.82 | 25.60 | 24.43 |
| Black | Inside Metro Areas | 52.73 | 64.68 | 74.27 | 82.00 | 83.77 |
| | Inside Central Cities | 41.18 | 51.42 | 58.19 | 59.70 | 57.34 |
| | Outside Central Cities | 11.55 | 13.27 | 16.08 | 22.30 | 26.43 |
| | Outside Metro Areas | 47.27 | 35.32 | 25.73 | 18.00 | 16.23 |
| Hispanic | Inside Metro Areas | — | 79.70[a] | 86.8[a] | 87.70 | 90.39 |
| | Inside Central Cities | — | 72.60 | 64.80 | 52.90 | 51.50 |
| | Outside Central Cities | — | 7.10 | 22.00 | 34.80 | 38.89 |
| | Outside Metro Areas | — | 20.30 | 13.20 | 12.30 | 9.61 |
| Asian | Inside Metro Areas | — | — | 87.70[b] | 91.70 | 93.81 |
| | Inside Central Cities | — | — | 54.10 | 48.10 | 46.45 |
| | Outside Central Cities | — | — | 33.50 | 43.60 | 47.36 |
| | Outside Metro Areas | — | — | 12.30 | 8.30 | 6.19 |
| American Indian | Inside Metro Areas | — | — | 38.80[b] | 48.20 | 51.36 |
| | Inside Central Cities | — | — | 19.90 | 22.30 | 23.33 |
| | Outside Central Cities | — | — | 18.90 | 25.90 | 28.04 |
| | Outside Metro Areas | — | — | 61.20 | 51.80 | 48.64 |

[a]Figures for the Hispanic population in 1960 and 1970 based on Bean and Tienda (1987:Table 5.5-5.6).
[b]Figures for the Asian and American Indian populations in 1970 based on Harrison and Bennett (1995:Table 4A.1).

SOURCES: Adapted from U.S. Bureau of the Census (1984d:Table J; 1975:Series A276-287; 1991:Table E; 1993a:Table 5); Bean and Tienda (1987:Tables 5.5-5.6); Harrison and Bennett (1995:Table 4A.1).

TABLE 3-3 Population Percentage by Selected Metropolitan Areas, 1950 to 1990

| Metropolitan Area | Group | Year | | | | |
|---|---|---|---|---|---|---|
| | | 1950 | 1960 | 1970 | 1980 | 1990 |
| Los Angeles | Black | 5 | 6.9 | 10.8 | 9.2[d] | 8.5[d] |
| | Hispanic | 7.5[a] | 9.3[a] | 13.3 | 24 | 32.9 |
| | Asian | 1.3[b] | 1.7[b] | 2.3 | 4.9 | 9.2 |
| | American Indian | [c] | 0.1 | 0.3 | 0.7 | 0.6 |
| Miami | Black | 13.1 | 14.7 | 15 | 14.9[d] | 18.5[d] |
| | Hispanic | — | — | 22.1 | 23.5 | 33.3 |
| | Asian | [c] | 0.1 | 0.2 | 0.6 | 1.4 |
| | American Indian | [c] | [c] | [c] | 0.1 | 0.2 |
| Houston | Black | 19.8 | 19.8 | 19.3 | 18.2[d] | 17.9[d] |
| | Hispanic | 4.2 | 5.3 | 8 | 14.7 | 20.8 |
| | Asian | — | 0.2 | 0.3 | 1.7 | 3.6 |
| | American Indian | — | [c] | 0.2 | 0.2 | 0.3 |
| San Francisco | Black | 6.6 | 8.6 | 10.6 | 8.7[d] | 8.6[d] |
| | Hispanic | 4.4 | 6.4 | 7.6 | 12.3 | 15.5 |
| | Asian | 2.9 | 1.4 | 5.3 | 8.5 | 14.8 |
| | American Indian | [c] | 0.2 | 0.4 | 0.6 | 0.7 |
| San Antonio | Black | 6.5 | 6.6 | 6.9 | 6.8 | 6.8 |
| | Hispanic | 33.7 | 35.9 | 36.6 | 44.9 | 47.6 |
| | Asian | — | 0.2 | 0.3 | 0.8 | 1.2 |
| | American Indian | — | [c] | 0.1 | 0.3 | 0.4 |
| New York | Black | 8.6[d] | 11.5[d] | 16.3[d] | 16.1[d] | 18.2[d] |
| | Hispanic | — | — | 11.1 | 11.7 | 15.4 |
| | Asian | 0.3 | 0.5 | 0.7 | 2.1 | 4.8 |
| | American Indian | [c] | [c] | [c] | 0.1 | 0.3 |
| Honolulu | Black | [c] | 1 | 1.2 | 2.2 | 3.1 |
| | Hispanic | — | — | — | 7.2 | 6.8 |
| | Asian | 54.6[d] | 46.8 | 44 | 59.8 | 63 |
| | American Indian | [c] | 0.1 | 0.2 | 0.3 | 0.4 |

less, they, too, are part of the national trend toward suburbanization; the possible exception to this trend is Mexicans (Bean and Tienda, 1987). In 1980, Puerto Ricans were the most highly concentrated group in the central cities, whereas Cubans were the least concentrated (Bean and Tienda, 1987). In the past few decades, the Hispanic population has gravitated toward a few key metro areas, including Los Angeles, New York, Miami, San Antonio, and Houston. The metro areas with the highest number of Hispanics are Los Angeles and San Antonio, where Hispanics made up 33 and 47 percent, respectively, of the total populations in 1990. Recent immigration by Hispanics has contributed to this concentration.

TABLE 3-3 *Continued*

| Metropolitan Area | Group | Year | | | | |
|---|---|---|---|---|---|---|
| | | 1950 | 1960 | 1970 | 1980 | 1990 |
| Washington, DC | Black | 23.1 | 24.3 | 24.6 | 26.8 | 26.6 |
| | Hispanic | — | — | 1.9 | 2.9 | 5.7 |
| | Asian | 0.3$^e$ | 0.3 | 0.6 | 2.6 | 5.2 |
| | American Indian | $c$ | $c$ | 0.1 | 0.2 | 0.3 |
| Chicago | Black | 10.3$^d$ | 14.3$^d$ | 17.6$^d$ | 19.6$^d$ | 19.2$^d$ |
| | Hispanic | — | — | 5 | 8 | 11.1 |
| | Asian | 0.3 | 0.4 | 0.5 | 1.8 | 3.2 |
| | American Indian | $c$ | $c$ | 0.1 | 0.2 | 0.2 |
| Dallas-Fort Worth | Black | 13.4$^f$ | 14.3$^f$ | 15.9$^f$ | 14.3$^d$ | 14.3$d$ |
| | Hispanic | 2.8 | 3.3 | 4.6 | 8.5 | 13.4 |
| | Asian | $c$ | $c$ | 0.1 | 0.8 | 2.5 |
| | American Indian | $c$ | 0.2 | 0.3 | 0.4 | 0.5 |

$^a$White with Spanish surname for 1950 and 1960.
$^b$Japanese, Chinese, and Filipino for 1950 and 1960.
$^c$Less than 0.1 percent of the metropolitan area population.
$^d$Metropolitan area represents Consolidated Statistical Metropolitan Area.
$^e$Japanese and Chinese only.
$^f$Dallas only for 1950-1970.

SOURCES: Adapted from U.S. Bureau of the Census (1953f:Tables 15-19; 1953g:Table 8; 1953c:Table 47; 1953b:Table 14; 1953e:Table 47; 1953f:Table 47; 1953g:Table 29; 1963b: Tables 50-54; 1963c:Table 9; 1963d:Table 21; 1963e:Table 21; 1963g:Table 21; 1963a:Table 21; 1963c: Table 21; 1963d:Table 21; 1963b:Table 21; 1963k:Table 1; 1971:Table 1; 1972c: Table 67; 1972b: Table 32; 1973d:Table 11; 1973e:Tables 11, 26, 41; 1973f:Table 11; 1973c: Table 13; 1984d: Tables1, 3, 4); Harrison and Bennett (1995:Figure 4.3); Reddy (1993a:Table 94; 1993b:Table 146).

## Asians

Asians are the most urbanized group of the total U.S. population, with almost 94 percent residing in metro areas in 1990. Of all the Asian groups, Chinese have been most prone to settle in urban areas (Barringer et al., 1993). The percentages for Asians are between those for Whites and Hispanics, in terms of central-city/suburban concentration, but their central-city concentration showed a slight decline from 1980 to 1990. Chinese showed the highest levels of central-city concentration, whereas Asian Indians exhibited the lowest levels. An interesting point is that U.S.-born Asians are more concentrated in metro areas than recent Asian immigrants (Barringer et al., 1993). Although some immigrant groups followed unique settlement patterns, such as the Hmong who settled in Minnesota and Wisconsin, most recent Asian immigrants tend to concentrate in traditional port-of-entry metros. Vietnamese and Indochinese refugees are more geographically dispersed throughout the country as a result of federal government efforts to spread the impact of incoming refugees (see Barringer et al., 1993; Gordon, 1984). In 1990, more than half the U.S. Asian population lived in Los Angeles, San Francisco, and New York, where Asian populations have steadily increased since the 1950s (Table 3-3). Asians also made up 63 percent of the Honolulu population in 1990, another metro area traditionally attracting a large proportion of Asians.

### American Indians

American Indians' rapid urbanization in the 1950s and 1960s significantly altered their metro/nonmetro distribution, although it did not change the fact that they are one of the least urbanized groups in the United States. In 1990, a little more than half of the American Indian population resided in metro areas, compared to 77 percent of all Americans. Reservations continue to be a feature of life that sets American Indians apart from other racial and ethnic groups. In 1990, approximately 438,000 American Indians resided on the 279 American Indian reservations throughout the United States. Although in absolute numbers the reservation population is the largest it has ever been, in terms of percentages, there has been a decline, from 27 percent in 1980 to 22 percent in 1990 (Snipp, 1989).

Almost half of all American Indians living in urban settings live in only 16 cities. The urban relocation programs after World War II primarily directed American Indians to San Francisco, Dallas, Seattle, Los Angeles, Oklahoma City, Tulsa, and Chicago. As a percentage of these cities' total populations, that of American Indians is small.

### Internal Migration

Migration patterns of the U.S. population overall have been southward and westward in recent decades; however, substantial variation underlies migration streams for each group. USBC classifies U.S. citizens who resided in a different location five years prior to the census year as internal migrants.

After World War II, during the wave of industrialization in the North and West in the 1950s and 1960s, Blacks migrated to metro areas in the North and West, away from the rural South. During the 1950s, their growth in the Midwest was almost five times their growth rate in the

South (Johnson and Campbell, 1981). Beginning in 1970, however, Blacks began to migrate back to small and large metros in the South. During the 1970s, the Black population in the South grew by 17.3 percent—a rate that exceeded growth rates in both the Midwest and Northeast regions (Johnson and Campbell, 1981). In their return migration, Blacks have tended to move to areas with substantial pre-existing Black populations. The most popular destinations have been small and large metro areas in Georgia, North Carolina, and Maryland (Harrison and Bennett, 1995).

Because there was no Hispanic category on the U.S. census until the 1970 Census, internal migration data for the Hispanic population are lacking prior to the 1970s. Since then, however, regional migration of Hispanics has followed the trend South and West. The Northeast and Midwest experienced net losses of Hispanics, whereas the South and West gained substantially. In some cases, the rates at which Hispanics migrated to the South and West far exceeded those of the non-Hispanic White population (Bean and Tienda, 1987). They have tended to migrate to growth areas where there are pre-existing high concentrations of Hispanics. A great deal of variation underlies this trend with respect to national origin. Cubans, for example, have generally tended toward further regional concentration, whereas both Mexicans and Puerto Ricans have become more geographically dispersed (Bean and Tienda, 1987).

Although foreign-born Hispanics are more likely to settle in traditional port-of-entry metro areas, such as Los Angeles and Miami, U.S.-born Hispanics have tended to migrate outward (McHugh, 1989; Bartel, 1989). From 1985 to 1990, U.S.-born Hispanic migrants moved to metropolitan areas such as Orlando, Las Vegas, and Sacramento (Harrison and Bennett, 1995).

According to the 1860 Census, 100 percent of the U.S. Asian population resided in the West. Beginning in 1940, less than 90 percent lived in the West, and the percentage has decreased ever since. Despite this trend, Asian populations did not exceed 20 percent in any other region in 1990. Net migration flows during the 1970s and 1980s indicate that the six largest Asian ethnic groups tended to migrate to both the South and West in patterns similar to the overall U.S. population, but regional patterns differed among the various groups. The Vietnamese, for example, showed the highest migration from the Northeast and Midwest to the West (Barringer et al., 1993). Asians disperse from traditional immigrant metros even more so than Hispanics, in patterns related to their diverse origins and higher levels of education (Frey, 1995). As in the case of Hispanics, Asians tend to move outward to metro areas in high-growth regions; thus, during the late 1980s, there was a net migration of Asians out of such traditional Asian immigrant metro areas as New York, Chicago, and Honolulu. Los Angeles attracts both immigrants and internal migrants;

but in addition to Los Angeles, Asian migrants are moving to Sacramento, Atlanta, Orlando, and Las Vegas (Harrison and Bennett, 1995). Like Blacks and Hispanics, most Asians are moving to communities with high concentrations of their own groups.

Largely because of centuries of U.S. policies forcing American Indians westward, this group is primarily concentrated in the West. The most significant demographic trend in the second half of the twentieth century, however, has been rapid urbanization brought about by federal urban relocation programs aimed at moving reservation populations into cities as a way to address deteriorating economic conditions on reservations (Sorkin, 1971; Fixico, 1986). Some portion of this demographic shift can also be attributed to changing self-identification, rather than the actual relocation of individuals (Snipp, 1989); nevertheless, Sorkin (1971) estimates that from 1952 to 1972, approximately 100,000 American Indians migrated to cities such as Los Angeles, San Francisco, and Chicago. Unfortunately, migration data provided by USBC are potentially problematic for American Indians. The census does not track residential relocations of less than five-years' duration; yet, case studies suggest there is a good deal of short-term mobility between reservations and metropolitan areas. From 1985 to 1990, approximately 45 percent living in nonmetro areas moved, and about 65 percent in metro areas moved. Snipp (1989) argues that this mobility most likely represents movement to and from reservations as opposed to intra-reservation movement. In any case, the movement did not lead to significant changes in the distribution of the American Indian populations in metro and nonmetro areas (Snipp, 1989).

## Understanding the Trends

After World War II, White and Black migration closely followed changes in national and regional economies. The push/pull factors, including mechanization of agriculture in the South and opportunities in the North's manufacturing sectors, contributed to individual decisions to migrate (Fligstein, 1981, 1983; Dillingham and Sly, 1966; Johnson and Campbell, 1981; Raymond, 1972). Most Blacks first migrated to urban areas in the South (Dillingham and Sly, 1966). As competition for unskilled work in southern metro areas intensified, however, many Blacks migrated to northern metro areas, where incomes were higher, employment opportunities more plentiful, and educational opportunities promised upward advancement both socially and economically. Further, substantial Black communities in key northern metros offered physical protection, social acclimation, and economic assistance (Johnson and Campbell, 1981).

More recently, however, growth of industries such as agribusiness, defense, technology, real estate and construction, and tourism was concentrated in southern and western states, reflecting the larger geographic decentralization of economic activity and sparking a massive redistribution of people and resources out of the Northeast and Midwest and into the South and West (Sale, 1975). For Whites, this population redistribution has involved not only movement to the South and West, but also a deconcentration of the population and dispersal to nonmetro areas of the South.

The reversal of the South-to-North pattern in Black internal migration was largely a response to the deindustrialization process and the concomitant decline in blue-collar jobs in manufacturing (Pettigrew, 1980; Long and Hansen, 1975). Blacks, like Whites, gravitated toward the growing economies, manufacturing communities, and university towns of the South Atlantic region. Disillusionment with the lack of economic and social ascendancy, as well as rising discontent with northern cities in general, were also compelling reasons for many Blacks to flee the inner cities of the North. The network of kinship ties throughout the South facilitated this return migration. Whether this southern migration reflects an increased assimilation into national labor markets for Blacks is debatable. As noted, most Blacks moved to metro areas in the South, not to nonmetro areas, which is where employment opportunities are actually expanding. Although there has been a lower net migration of Blacks into metro areas in each subsequent decade, their redistribution to nonmetro areas of the South has progressed more slowly. At the same time, the increase in the suburban Black population might reflect an ascendancy of more Blacks into the middle class (Frey, 1995); because many Blacks have moved to less affluent suburbs, however, this view is contentious.

Immigration and assimilation complicate this overall picture. Many metro areas and regions experienced a dramatic influx of internal migrants, but other areas grew primarily as a result of immigration from abroad. In port-of-entry cities such as Los Angeles, San Francisco, New York, and Chicago, migration from abroad was the total source of gains in population from 1985 to 1990 (Harrison and Bennett, 1995).

Most recent immigrants rely on social networks of family and friends to aid in the settlement process. For Hispanic populations, geographic concentration is much more pronounced among foreign-born Hispanics than U.S.-born Hispanics (Bean and Tienda, 1987); thus, newly arrived Hispanic immigrants have generally settled in large port-of-entry metros in the Northeast and South following historic immigration patterns. As Bean and Tienda (1987) note, this pattern also mirrors that of European immigrants who typically settled in large cities in the Northeast. The one exception to this trend is the early Mexican immigrants, who were employed in mining and agriculture and, therefore, drawn to rural areas.

Since World War II, however, Mexicans have urbanized at a rapid rate. Current internal Hispanic migration streams suggest that Hispanics are in fact following larger national migration flows; however, they are moving to growth areas with substantial pre-existing Hispanic populations (Harrison and Bennett, 1995).

Asians appear to respond to the same forces as other groups in terms of geographic distribution and migration (Barringer et al., 1993). Recent immigrants, such as Koreans and Asian Indians, have tended to follow the migration stream of the U.S. population overall, responding to economic opportunities. The larger, older Asian groups have, nevertheless, tended to remain in the West and Hawaii. In both cases, economic opportunities and the location of family and friends are important motivating factors behind location decisions (De Jong and Fawcett, 1981).

Barringer et al. (1993) argue that as Asians become more assimilated, it is likely that their distribution patterns will come to more closely resemble those of the larger U.S. population, as in the case of Hispanics. Length of residence, generational effects, and identity formation all contribute to this process, which is apparently occurring at the regional level; evidence at the metro level is less indicative of this process. Bartel (1989) argues that because most Asians are moving to metro areas where high concentrations of Asians already live, the pattern does not suggest greater assimilation.

Historical distribution of the American Indian population was primarily determined by the migration of White settlers and U.S. policy (Snipp, 1989). In the North, disease and warfare destroyed many tribes after contact with Europeans; in the South and the Ohio River Valley, Indians were forced to move westward beginning in the early nineteenth century. Forced migrations continued under Andrew Jackson's Indian Removal Act of 1830, leading to removal of the entire American Indian population from eastern homelands onto reservations or into Indian Territory, what is now Oklahoma.

American Indians and Indian reservations are concentrated in rural areas because of another aspect of removal policies—an attempt to locate Indians in remote areas, separate from mainstream U.S. society. The rapid urbanization occurring in the second half of the twentieth century was brought about by federal urban relocation programs, primarily as a means to address deteriorating economic conditions on reservations by moving reservation populations into cities (Sorkin, 1971; Fixico, 1986). Such federal policies contributed to the trend of urbanization that had begun among the American Indian population with the start of World War II, which drew significant numbers into military service and into urban-based war-related industries (Hagan, 1979; Bernstein, 1991). Many American Indians chose to remain in metro areas for improved job opportunities (Fixico, 1986; Bernstein, 1991). A large percentage also returned to the reservations, however. Those who remained in metro areas tended to be younger, with higher levels of education, and of mixed blood. Motivating factors for returnees included lack of economic success in the city and difficulties in adjusting to urban life (Sorkin, 1971). Decreased emphasis on the relocation policies in the late 1960s and early 1970s slowed urbanization considerably, which is why almost half the American Indian population continues to live outside metro areas. The absence of any significant interregional shifts and high rates of mobility by this population in recent decades suggest less involvement in national labor markets (Harrison and Bennett, 1995).

## Possible Future Trends

Short- (1993 to 2000) and long-term (1993 to 2020) trends suggest that the size of the population in the West and South regions will continue to increase. Whereas the West will receive a major portion of its growth from international migration, the South will experience growth from both international and internal migration. Net internal migration from both the Northeast and Midwest will account for slower growth in these regions (Campbell, 1993). The Black population is expected to be the second fastest growing group in the South, Northeast, and Midwest; Whites are expected to be the slowest-growing group in the long term.

Blacks are projected to continue being concentrated in the South, which will experience the largest gains in Black population of any region. Although growth of the Hispanic population is expected to be substantial in all four regions, the greatest absolute increase is expected to occur in the West. In all regions, Hispanics are projected to comprise a larger share of the population. Asians are projected to be the fastest growing group in all four regions. More than half of the 8 million Asians projected to be added to the total U.S. population will reside in the West. Finally, the American Indian population is projected to be the second fastest growing group in the West.

Despite the growing significance of all groups, in terms of their share of the overall U.S. population, regional- and metro-level disparities are likely to remain. Census data on five-year migration patterns show these patterns differ in magnitude and tend to involve migration to areas with pre-existing concentrations of the subject racial/ethnic group—South and West for Whites, South Atlantic states for Blacks, Florida for Hispanics, and California for Asians. American Indians tend to remain within regions rather than migrate across regional boundaries. Further, immigration will continue to largely concentrate groups in traditional port-of-entry metros. If White flight from high-immigration metro areas and states continues, a few immigrant ports-of-entry will continue to gain minority populations while losing Whites to more prosperous areas. These developments may result in a more pronounced racial and ethnic balkanization pattern in the United States (Frey, 1995). As a result, minorities may continue to be virtually absent from many parts of the United States, and relatively disconnected to national labor markets (Harrison and Bennett, 1995). Furthermore, in those metropolitan areas or states with large Hispanic and White populations, race- and age-based political interests may begin to interact as the Hispanic population remains young and the White population grows increasingly older.

## FERTILITY RATES AND FAMILY PATTERNS

Fertility rates and family patterns are two key elements of a population's demography. Rates of marriage (same-race and interracial), divorce, and single-parenthood influence the population's fertility rate, socioeconomic status, and sense of well-being. Fertility among couples, singles, and teenagers also affects a group's rate of growth and age structure. Racial and ethnic groups differ significantly in their family patterns and fertility rates; these differences provide valuable clues to the rates of assimilation between and among the groups and into the mainstream, cultural differences, and possible reasons for socioeconomic differences.

In the United States, fertility rates rose after World War II, from 1950 to 1960—the baby-boom years—and then began a decline that lasted until 1975. From 1975 to 1990, fertility rates gradually increased, but declined slightly in the 1990s. The teenage childbearing rate also rose during the baby-boom years and then began a decline that lasted until 1985; the rate rose slightly in the late 1980s and has declined since. The rate of out-of-wedlock childbearing more than tripled from 1950 to 1995. Marriage trends also changed dramatically in this period. The median age at first marriage rose for both men and women, and divorce rates more than doubled, which led to a dramatic increase in single-parent families. Trends for racial and ethnic groups vary significantly within these overall trends in fertility rates and family patterns.

## Fertility

### Measuring Fertility

Three techniques for measuring fertility will be discussed in this chapter. The first technique counts the number of children ever born per 1,000 women of a certain age range as a rough indicator of fertility. The information for this measure is collected via the census. However, the number of children ever born is an imperfect indicator because it is not limited to recent years—i.e., the births counted have been occurring over the entire childbearing period of women of different ages prior to the census. To have estimates of more recent fertility, the data must be limited to only young women, who have had their children in the few years before the census.

The second technique is the fertility rate (or general fertility rate). This rate computes the births per 1,000 women ages 15 to 44 for one year, thus gauging recent fertility data while including women of all ages. However, the age structure of females ages 15 to 44 differs from population to population, with some populations having more females at the younger end of this range and still in prime childbearing years, and others having females more concentrated at the older end of the range when females have usually completed their childbearing.

The third technique—total fertility rate—controls for these differences. This rate is a calculation of the number of children a woman would bear throughout her life if the rates for a given year for each age range were to remain stable. This technique requires the most information and therefore is not always available. Table 3-4 shows trends in the total fertility rate for racial and ethnic groups; we also discuss data on children ever born and the general fertility rate.

## Fertility Trends Among Racial and Ethnic Groups

### Blacks

U.S. census data show that Black women have, since data were collected, had higher fertility rates than White women (Farley and Allen, 1987). In 1950, the total fertility rate for non-Whites was 3,579 per 1,000 women or 3.6 children per woman, compared to 2.9 for Whites (Farley and Allen, 1987). Rates for both groups rose sharply in the post-war baby boom. Total fertility rates peaked in 1960 for both Blacks (4,542) and Whites (3,510). Black fertility then declined to 1985, rose in the late 1980s, and declined in the early 1990s.

Between 1960 and 1996, the absolute difference between Black and White total fertility rates dropped from 1,032 children to 408 children per 1,000 women, a 40 percent decline. In 1960, total fertility rates for Blacks were approximately 30 percent higher than those of Whites, while in 1996 they were 23 percent higher. Both ways of looking at the trends in fertility suggest a convergence over time. Others have found a clear convergence between Blacks and Whites regarding the percent of women who remain childless and the birthrate for married women (Farley and Allen, 1987; Jaynes and Williams, 1989).

TABLE 3-4 Total Fertility Rates (births per 1,000 women), 1950 to 1996

| | 1950 | 1955 | 1960 | 1965 | 1970 | 1975 | 1980 | 1985 | 1990 | 1996 |
|---|---|---|---|---|---|---|---|---|---|---|
| Total U.S. | 3,028 | 3,498 | 3,606 | 2,882 | 2,432 | 1,770 | 1,840 | 1,844 | 2,081 | 2,027 |
| White | 2,945 | 3,405 | 3,510 | 2,764 | 2,338 | 1,685 | 1,773 | 1,787 | 1,851[d] | 1,796[d] |
| Non-White | 3,579 | 4,126 | — | — | — | — | — | — | — | — |
| Black | — | — | 4,542 | 3,829 | 3,099 | 2,243 | 2,177 | 2,109 | 2,548[d] | 2,204[d] |
| Hispanic | — | — | — | — | — | — | 2,534 | — | 2,960 | 3,048 |
| Asian | — | — | — | 2,399[a] | 2,179[b] | 1,948[c] | 1,954 | 1,885 | 2,003 | 1,908 |
| American Indian | — | — | — | 3,398[a] | 2,722[b] | 2,409[c] | 2,163 | 2,128 | 2,183 | 2,030 |

NOTE:—, Data not collected or separated by groups.

[a]Data for 1965 to 1969.
[b]Data for 1970 to 1974.
[c]Data for 1975 to 1979.
[d]Data are for non-Hispanic Whites and Blacks.

SOURCES: Adapted from U.S. Bureau of the Census (1997:Table 93); Taffel (1977:Table 13); National Center for Health Statistics (1994:Table 1-9); Barringer et al. (1993:Table 3.3); Ventura et al. (1998).

*Hispanics*

Fertility data for Hispanics are more limited than data for Blacks (see Darabi, 1987), but since 1980, the total fertility rate for Hispanic women has been the highest of any group (Table 3-4). In addition, although other groups experienced a decline in the 1990s, the Hispanic fertility rate continued to increase. Among Hispanics in 1996, the total fertility rate was highest for the Mexican population (3,354) and lowest for the Cuban population (1,775) (National Center for Health Statistics, 1998). In relation to non-Hispanic Whites, the total fertility rate of the Mexican population was 87 percent higher and the total fertility rate of the Cuban population was slightly lower. This illustrates one of the many dimensions of heterogeneity within the Hispanic population.

Calculating the number of children ever born for Hispanics enhances the discussion of fertility. (This information is available for Hispanics from 1950, but it should be noted that 1950 and 1960 data are based on Spanish surname, and that the published data from census reports for 1950 included data for White Hispanics with data for Whites, and for Black Hispanics with data for Blacks; 1970 and 1980 data are based on Spanish origin.) Hispanic fertility was almost 30 percent higher than that of both Whites and Blacks in 1950. Higher fertility rates may be due in part to the desire for larger families among Hispanics (Darabi, 1987). Following the overall baby-boom trend, the number of children ever born increased for all age groups of Hispanic women in 1960.

*American Indians*

The U.S. census did not begin to collect data on the number of children ever born to American Indian women until 1960. Thus, information about fertility rates of American Indians is even more limited than that for Hispanics. Table 3-4 shows that the total fertility rate of American Indians has been lower than that of Hispanics since the first data shown for that group, 1980, but above that of Whites since 1970. In 1996, the total fertility rate of American Indians (2,030) was 13 percent higher than that of Whites, compared to 23 percent higher in 1965.

Birth rates rose during the baby boom after being at notably low levels in the early part of the century. According to Snipp (1996), 1960 Census data show that American Indian women had the highest number of children ever born of any racial or ethnic group. Older American Indian women had more children than both older Whites and Blacks. Census data show American Indian fertility levels declined in 1970 and again in 1980, except for births among teenagers. Snipp (1996) theorizes that key factors contributing to these higher levels of fertility are the younger ages at which American Indian women begin bearing children and their contribution beyond the ages at which other groups suspend childbearing. Snipp (1996) also notes significant differences in American Indian fertility patterns relative to urban or rural residence, same-race or interracial marriage, and tribal affiliation.

## Asians

The first available census-based data for Asian fertility are from the 1960 Census, which collected information on children ever born to Japanese and Chinese women. These data show that Asian fertility rates were the lowest of all racial/ethnic groups. In 1970, the number of children ever born had decreased for both Japanese and Chinese women for all age groups except Chinese women ages 35 to 44, for whom the rate had risen.

Table 3-4 shows that the total fertility rate for Asians was lower than that for Whites in 1965, but 6 percent higher than that for Whites in 1996. It is important to remember, however, that the care with which data are gathered for the Asian population has improved since 1965; so, the safest thing to say is that the evidence indicates that Asian fertility rates are lower than those for Hispanics, Blacks, and American Indians, but higher than those for Whites.

It is clear that there are distinct differences among Asian groups. Barringer et al. (1993) analyzed data from the 1980 Census and found that Vietnamese women had much higher fertility levels than other Asian women; Asian Indians had the second highest fertility rates, followed by Filipinos, Koreans, and Chinese; Japanese women had the lowest fertility levels.

## Teenage Childbearing

Both historically and recently, there are important differences among racial and ethnic groups regarding teenage childbearing. In 1950, the teenage fertility rate—births per 1,000 women ages 15 to 19—for non-Whites was more than twice that of Whites (Table 3-5). According to Taylor et al. (1997), currently 21 percent of White adolescent girls, as opposed to 40 percent of minority adolescent girls, become pregnant by age 18. Historically, the overall teenage fertility rate followed the same pattern as the general fertility rate, rising quickly between 1940 and 1960 (although teenage childbearing seems to have peaked slightly earlier than overall fertility), falling through 1985, rising through 1990, and falling between 1990 and 1995.

There are substantial differences between childbearing of Black and White teens. In 1960, the teenage fertility rate for Blacks was almost twice that of Whites; by 1995, this gap had widened and Black teens were more than two and one-half times more likely to give birth than their White counterparts. More Black teens than White teens are sexually active, and in general, Blacks engage in sexual activity at younger ages than Whites, therefore increasing the numbers of those at risk for pregnancy (Farley and Allen, 1987). Black teens also use contraception and abortion at lower rates than Whites. More positive attitudes toward motherhood among young Black women than among Whites may contribute to these differences (Taylor et al., 1997).

The American Indian population has also had a high teenage birth rate. In 1995, the general fertility rate for American Indian teenagers was 78, roughly twice that for Whites. Data from the census on the number of children ever born show that the childbearing rates for American Indian teens were close to those of Black teens and very similar to Hispanic teens from 1960 through 1990. As Snipp (1996) points out, American Indians begin bearing children early, 45.2 percent having their first child by age 20, whereas 20.6 percent of White women had their first child by this age in 1990.

Table 3-5 shows that Hispanic teens also had higher fertility rates than Whites, and slightly higher rates than Blacks, in 1995. However, data on children ever born suggest that fertility rates for Hispanic teens are dropping at a faster rate in the last 20 years than those of Blacks and American Indians. For the three main Hispanic groups, teen birth rates mirror the pattern of overall fertility: Cubans have lower teen fertility rates than non-Hispanic Whites, rates for Puerto Ricans range in the middle, and Mexican rates are significantly higher. In 1980, the teenage fertility rate for Mexicans was more than five and one-half times that of non-Hispanic Whites (Bean and Tienda, 1987). There are few studies on sexual activity among Hispanic teenagers, but Darabi (1987) suggests that Hispanic teenagers may begin sexual activity later than Blacks and Whites and may be more likely to postpone sex until after marriage. As it has for Blacks, the relative difference in teenage fertility rates from that of Whites has widened for Hispanics and American Indians.

Table 3-5 shows that Asian teenagers had the lowest general fertility rates of any of the groups in 1995.

## Out-of-Wedlock Childbearing

Out-of-wedlock childbearing is an aspect of fertility that changed dramatically in the United States over the past 50 years. The fertility rate for unmarried women of all races more than tripled from 1950 to 1995 (Table 3-6). This is in large part a result of the declining tendency of unmarried pregnant women to marry before the birth of the child. Had

TABLE 3-5 General Fertility Rates (births per 1,000 women) for Teenagers Ages 15-19, 1950 to 1995

| | 1950 | 1955 | 1960 | 1965 | 1970 | 1975 | 1980 | 1985 | 1990 | 1995 |
|---|---|---|---|---|---|---|---|---|---|---|
| Total U.S. | 81.6 | 90.3 | 89.1 | 70.5 | 68.3 | 55.6 | 53.0 | 51.0 | 59.1 | 56.8 |
| White | 70.0 | 79.1 | 79.4 | 60.6 | 57.4 | 46.4 | 44.7 | 42.5 | 49.3 | 39.3 |
| Non-White | 163.5 | 167.2 | 158.2 | 138.4 | 133.4 | 106.4 | 94.6 | 88.9 | 102.4 | — |
| Black | — | — | 156.1 | 144.6 | 140.7 | 111.8 | 100.0 | 97.9 | 118.3 | 99.3 |
| Hispanic | — | — | — | — | — | — | — | — | — | 106.7 |
| Asian | — | — | — | — | — | — | — | — | — | 26.1 |
| American Indian | — | — | — | — | — | — | — | — | — | 78.0 |

SOURCES: Adapted from National Center for Health Statistics (1994:Tables 1-9); Ventura et al. (1997:Table A); Ventura et al. (1998).

marriage rates remained steady from 1960 to the present, the increase in nonmarital births would have been greatly reduced (Taylor et al., 1997). Because women in general are spending less time married (marrying later and divorcing more often), they spend more time at risk for unmarried pregnancy; this fact, combined with lower birth rates among married women, produces a higher proportion of unmarried births (Farley and Allen, 1987; U.S. Department of Health and Human Services, 1995).

The increase in unmarried childbearing has been especially sharp among White women, whose out-of-wedlock childbearing rate in 1995 was more than six times higher than that for 1950. The rate for non-Whites increased just 12 percent from 1950 to 1990. Although a large gap remains, these figures illustrate a convergence between unmarried fertility rates for Whites and non-Whites.

Farley and Allen (1987) report that out-of-wedlock childbearing rates for Black women had been increasing before 1970. At that time, unmarried Black women were almost seven times more likely to bear a child than unmarried White women. Since 1970, however, fertility rates for unmarried Blacks fell from 95.5 to 75.9. This drop and the corresponding increase among White women led to a partial convergence of Black and White rates, to the point that fertility rates for unmarried Black women were approximately double those for Whites. The fact that Black women are still less likely than Whites to marry because of pregnancy, and are only about half as likely to end a nonmarital pregnancy in abortion, contributes to their higher rates of unmarried fertility (Farley and Allen, 1987). Despite the significant drop in out-of-wedlock childbearing for unmarried Black women, these births are an increasing proportion of all births to Black women (Farley and Allen, 1987; U.S. Department of Health and Human Services, 1995; Taylor et al., 1997). In 1995, approximately seven of ten births to Black women were out of wedlock.

Few data are available concerning out-of-wedlock childbearing among Hispanics. According to Table 3-6, unmarried fertility rates for Hispanics in 1995 were much higher than those for both Whites (153 percent higher) and Blacks (25 percent higher). This primarily reflects the presence of higher rates for Hispanic women older than age 25 (U.S. Department of Heath and Human Services, 1995). Since fertility rates are also higher for married Hispanic women, however, less than one-third of Hispanic babies were born out of wedlock in 1996.

Data are similarly sparse for American Indian women. John (1998) notes that evidence suggests rising nonmarital fertility rates for American Indians, but explains that out-of-wedlock childbearing is relatively common among this group and is not met with particularly negative attitudes, although childbirth within marriage is still the norm. In 1996, 58 percent of American Indian births were to unmarried women. As with

TABLE 3-6 Fertility Rates (births per 1,000 women) for Unmarried Women, Ages 15 to 44, 1950 to 1990; All Ages, 1995

| | 1950 | 1955 | 1960 | 1965 | 1970 | 1975 | 1980 | 1985 | 1990 | 1995 |
|---|---|---|---|---|---|---|---|---|---|---|
| Total U.S. | 14.1 | 19.3 | 21.6 | 23.4 | 26.4 | 24.5 | 28.4 | 32.8 | 43.8 | 45.1 |
| White | 6.1 | 7.9 | 9.2 | 11.6 | 13.8 | 12.6 | 17.6 | 21.8 | 31.8 | 37.5 |
| Non-White | 71.2 | 87.2 | 98.3 | 97.6 | 89.9 | 80.4 | 77.2 | 72.4 | 79.7 | — |
| Black | — | — | — | — | 95.5 | 84.2 | 82.9 | 79.0 | 90.5 | 75.9 |
| Hispanic | — | — | — | — | — | — | 52.0 | — | 89.6 | 95.0 |
| Asian | — | — | — | — | — | — | — | — | — | — |
| American Indian | — | — | — | — | — | — | — | — | — | — |

SOURCES: U.S. Bureau of the Census (1977:Table 87; 1996:Table 98); Ventura (1980:Table 11); Ventura et al. (1997:Table 14); National Center for Health Statistics (1994: Table 1-77); U.S. Department of Health and Human Services (1995:Table II-1).

other fertility behaviors, there is most likely tribal and residential (rural/urban) variation.

Although there is little information available about out of wedlock childbearing among Asian and Pacific Islander women, in 1996, 17 percent of babies in this group were born out of wedlock (National Center for Health Statistics, 1998).

## Family Patterns

### Marriage, Divorce, Intermarriage, and Single-Parent Households

Marital patterns have moved away from traditional models in the last half-century. The median age at first marriage is one of the changing aspects. Since 1950, it has risen 21 percent for women and 17 percent for men for all race groups. This delay in marriage has been offset by a rise in rates of cohabitation. Young couples are still living together, but there has been a decrease in the legalization of these unions (Taylor et al., 1997).

Table 3-7 shows the percentage distribution of marital status from 1950 to 1995. Although this measure is influenced by a population's age structure, it reveals some general trends. The percent of persons married in 1995 had fallen 9 percent from 1950 levels; the percent divorced had risen substantially. Despite a slight decrease after 1980, there were more than three and one-half times as many persons divorced in 1995 than there were in 1950. Cherlin (1992) points out that divorce rates have been rising steadily since 1860. The rate of increase slowed in the 1950s only to pick up again in the early 1960s and rise to historic highs by the early 1980s, when rates began to level off.

For Blacks, the median age at first marriage is roughly parallel to that of Whites, according to 1980 census data. Historically, Blacks have married at younger ages than Whites, but more recently the groups have traded places and now Blacks marry at somewhat older ages than Whites. Throughout their lives, Black women spend less time married than do their White counterparts. According to 1975 to 1980 rates, Black women could expect to spend 16 years of a 73-year life span married, whereas White women could expect to spend 33 out of their 77 years married. This 17-year difference increased from an 11-year difference based on 1955 to 1960 rates (Jaynes and Williams, 1989).

Jaynes and Williams (1989) suggest that Black women may feel less pressure than White women to marry or to stay married for financial support because of the poor economic status of Black men. It is also possible that the inner-city environment in which a larger portion of Blacks reside may exert less social pressure to enter, or remain in, marital situations; most of the increase in the percentage of unmarried people

TABLE 3-7 Percent Distribution of Marital Status, 1950 to 1995

| | 1950 | 1960 | 1965 | 1970 | 1975 | 1980 | 1985 | 1990 | 1995 |
|---|---|---|---|---|---|---|---|---|---|
| **Total U.S.** | | | | | | | | | |
| Single | 22.8 | 22.0 | 14.9 | 16.2 | 17.5 | 20.3 | — | 22.2 | 22.9 |
| Married | 67.0 | 67.3 | 73.2 | 71.7 | 69.6 | 65.5 | — | 61.9 | 60.9 |
| Separated/divorced | 1.9 | 2.3 | 2.9 | 3.2 | 4.6 | 8.0 | — | 7.6 | 7.0 |
| Widowed | 8.3 | 8.4 | 9.0 | 8.9 | 8.3 | 6.2 | — | 8.3 | 9.2 |
| **White** | | | | | | | | | |
| Single | — | — | — | 15.6 | — | 18.9 | 19.8 | 20.3 | 20.6 |
| Married | — | — | — | 72.6 | — | 67.2 | 65.0 | 64.0 | 63.2 |
| Separated/divorced | — | — | — | 3.1 | — | 7.8 | 7.5 | 7.5 | 7.0 |
| Widowed | — | — | — | 8.7 | — | 6.0 | 7.7 | 8.1 | 9.1 |
| **Black** | | | | | | | | | |
| Single | 23.9 | 29.6 | 31.9 | 24.3 | 27.2 | 30.5 | 34.6 | 35.1 | 38.4 |
| Married | 63.5 | 63.3 | 61.1 | 66.9 | 62.7 | 51.4 | 46.3 | 45.8 | 43.2 |
| Separated/divorced | — | 2.4 | 3.1 | 3.6 | 5.1 | 9.8 | 9.5 | 8.5 | 7.6 |
| Widowed | 12.6[a] | 4.6 | 3.9 | 5.2 | 5.0 | 8.4 | 9.6 | 10.6 | 10.7 |
| **Hispanic** | | | | | | | | | |
| Single | 31.6 | 27.9 | — | 29.3 | 31.6 | 24.1 | 25.5 | 27.2 | 28.6 |
| Married | 59.0 | 61.9 | — | 62.4 | 60.3 | 65.6 | 62.7 | 61.7 | 59.3 |
| Separated/divorced | — | 4.8 | — | 3.4 | 4.1 | 4.4 | 6.7 | 4.0 | 4.2 |
| Widowed | 9.4[a] | 5.4 | — | 4.9 | 4.1 | 5.8 | 5.1 | 7.0 | 7.9 |

| | | | | | | | | | | | | |
|---|---|---|---|---|---|---|---|---|---|---|---|---|
| **Asian** | | | | | | | | | | | | |
| Single | 32.1[b] | 34.2[c] | 27.3[b] | 29.8[c] | — | 25.4[b] | 32.4[c] | — | 29.6[d] | — | 31.8 | — |
| Married | 58.0[b] | 60.1[c] | 65.3[b] | 62.2[c] | — | 64.9[b] | 60.0[c] | — | 60.8[d] | — | 58.6 | — |
| Separated/divorced | — | — | 1.9[b] | 2.9[c] | — | 3.4[b] | 2.5[c] | — | 4.9[d] | — | 5.4 | — |
| Widowed | 9.8[a,b] | 5.7[a,c] | 5.5[b] | 5.0[c] | — | 6.4[b] | 5.4[c] | — | 4.8[d] | — | 4.3 | — |
| **American Indian** | | | | | | | | | | | | |
| Single | 32.1 | | 34.7 | | — | 26.8 | | — | 36.9[e] | — | 32.4 | — |
| Married | 57.4 | | 52.7 | | — | 57.8 | | — | 46.9[e] | — | 46.6 | — |
| Separated/divorced | — | | 5.7 | | — | 8.1 | | — | 9.3[e] | — | 15.5 | — |
| Widowed | 10.6[a] | | 6.9 | | — | 7.3 | | — | 6.7[e] | — | 5.5 | — |

[a] Includes widowed and divorced respondents.
[b] Japanese.
[c] Chinese.
[d] For states and Standard Metropolitan Statistical Areas with 25,000 or more Asians and Pacific Islanders.
[e] For identified reservations.

SOURCES: U.S. Bureau of the Census (1953f:Tables 8-13; 1953g:Table 6; 1963h:Table 3; 1963i:Tables 10-12; 1966b:Table1; 1972a:Table 1; 1973d:Table 5; 1973c:Tables 5 and 20; 1977:Tables 48-50; 1984b:Table 10; 1986:Table 3; 1993b:Table 1; 1994:Table 3; 1997:Table 58); Schick and Schick (1991:Table C1-4).

among Blacks can be attributed to those who have never married. In contrast, for Whites, the increase is primarily the result of rising rates of divorce and decreasing rates of remarriage (Taylor et al., 1997). Blacks are also less likely than Whites to remarry after a divorce. Only one-third of Black women remarry within 10 years of a separation (Taylor et al., 1997). As with the general population, the number of Blacks cohabiting has increased, as have rates of divorce and separation.

In spite of the similarities, there has been a growing divergence between Blacks and Whites in marital behaviors (Cherlin, 1992), with regard to age at first marriage, rate of separation and divorce, and amount of time spent separated/divorced before remarriage. This has led to a marriage gap that grew from a 5 percent difference between Blacks versus Whites and Hispanics in 1950, to an almost 30 percent difference in 1995, when 60.9 percent of Whites and Hispanics were married versus 43.2 percent of Blacks (Table 3-7).

As regards trends in intermarriage, Black women are slightly more likely than White women to marry outside their race. The percentage of Black women married to non-Black men increased from 0.9 percent in 1960 to 3.2 percent in 1994. In 1960, the number of Black men married to Black women was approximately equal to the number of Black women married to Black men; since then, interracial marriages among Black men increased relatively sharply. In 1994, 6.6 percent of Black men were married to someone of a different race (Table 3-8).

As with other topics, fewer data on Hispanic marital trends are available than for Whites and Blacks, although it has traditionally been assumed that marriage and family relationships are more important and therefore more stable for Hispanics relative to non-Hispanics (Bean and Tienda, 1987). Bean and Tienda (1987) found that marital patterns for Cubans were much like those of non-Hispanic Whites by 1980, but that Mexicans married earlier and in higher percentages than Whites. However, among Hispanics in general they found no evidence of lower rates of marital instability, and concluded that the assumption of stronger familial importance among Hispanics was probably not valid. Rather, Hispanics have followed the general trend away from traditional marriage patterns.

The rate of interracial marriage among Hispanics has traditionally been far above that of Whites or Blacks. Jaffe et al. (1976) examined interracial marriage among Hispanics and found that most were to non-Hispanic Whites. Cubans have the highest rate of intermarriage, followed by Mexicans, with Puerto Ricans being the least likely to marry non-Hispanics. Hispanic women have intermarried more than Hispanic men; however, unlike Blacks and Whites, levels of interracial marriage for Hispanics have changed little since 1970 and, if anything, have decreased.

TABLE 3-8 Percent of Wives and Husbands in Same-Race Marriages, 1960 to 1994

| | 1960 | 1970 | 1980 | 1985 | 1990 | 1994 |
|---|---|---|---|---|---|---|
| White | | | | | | |
| Wives | 99.8 | 99.7 | 99.0 | 98.6 | — | 98.8 |
| Husbands | 99.8 | 99.6 | 98.9 | 98.8 | — | 98.7 |
| Black | | | | | | |
| Wives | 99.1 | 99.2 | 98.8 | 97.2 | — | 96.8 |
| Husbands | 99.0 | 98.5 | 96.4 | 93.7 | — | 93.4 |
| Hispanic | | | | | | |
| Wives | — | 82.3[a] | 81.3 | — | 81.5[b] | 83.9 |
| Husbands | — | 82.5[a] | 82.2 | — | 85.3[b] | 86.9 |
| Asian | | | | | | |
| Wives | 76.3[c] 89.2[d] | 66.8[c] 87.8[d] | 59.4[c] 83.2[d] | — | 75.8 | — |
| Husbands | 93.9[c] 85.8[d] | 88.6[c] 86.5[d] | 81.4[c] 86.9[d] | — | 87.7 | — |
| American Indian | | | | | | |
| Wives | 75.8 | 61.0 | 46.3 | — | 39.8 | — |
| Husbands | 82.5 | 64.2 | 47.6 | — | 41.2 | — |

[a]Includes Mexican, Puerto Rican, and Other Spanish.
[b]Data for 1989.
[c]Japanese.
[d]Chinese.

SOURCES: U.S. Bureau of the Census (1966b:Table 10; 1972a:Table 12; 1985:Table 11); Schick and Schick (1991:Table C1-7); Saluter (1996:Table C); Sandefur and Liebler (1996:Figure 9.3); Shinagawa and Jang (1998:page 53).

Although data on the marital patterns of American Indians are limited, some conclusions can be drawn. In 1980, the median age at first marriage for both men and women was slightly lower than that for Whites. Throughout the past 50 years, American Indians have had a higher percentage of single persons and a lower percentage of married persons than the total U.S. population. The gap for percentage of persons married has widened since 1950. The percent married has dropped 9 percent for all races but 18 percent for American Indians. However, it is difficult to draw conclusions from these data because of changes in the self-identification patterns of American Indians. The general trends of higher rates of never-married and divorced persons have probably been reflected in the American Indian population, as well as the rise in the age at first marriage (Sandefur and Liebler, 1996). The 1980 to 1990 percentages of American Indians divorced indicate a slower rate of increase relative to the total United States, but absolute differences grew simply because American Indians started with a higher percent of divorced persons.

American Indians have a long history of intermarriage with Whites (Sandefur and Liebler, 1996; John, 1998) and have had the highest rate of interracial marriage of all the groups, at almost all times over the last half-century; more women have married non-American Indians than men. The rates of intermarriage among American Indians increased substantially from 1960 to 1990. In 1970, American Indians were involved in 27 percent of all intermarriages (Sandefur and Liebler, 1996). In 1990, almost 60 percent of married American Indians had non-American Indian spouses; but this increase, too, may be partially the result of shifting self-identification.

The 1980 Census data show that Asian men and women marry much later than the general U.S. population, and Japanese and Chinese men and women marry later than other Asians (Barringer et al., 1993). Data in Table 3-7 show that for 1980 and 1990, a larger percentage of Asians were single than was the case for the overall population. Although changing racial definitions make trends difficult to read, the percentage of single Asian persons appears to have remained fairly constant. Asians historically have had lower divorce rates than the general population, and rates for Asian immigrants are lower than for U.S.-born Asians (Barringer et al., 1993); however, trends show increasing percentages of persons divorced.

Rates of interracial marriage for Asians are quite high, closer to those of Hispanics than Blacks and Whites. Among Asians, Japanese women have had especially high rates of marriage to non-Asian men. It appears that most Asian groups have had increasing rates of intermarriage over time, although rates for Chinese men have declined. Again, changes in racial classifications make trends difficult to interpret.

**Single-Parent Families**

Increasing rates of divorce and out-of-wedlock childbearing have resulted in a proliferation of children living with only one parent, usually the mother. The data in Table 3-9 show that for the total population, the percentage of children younger than age 18 living with both parents declined from 88.5 percent in 1960 to only 69 percent in 1995. The percentage of children living with only their mother more than tripled during this time period. Cherlin (1992) points out that divorced mothers had historically moved in with other family members, but this trend has declined in recent decades. Cherlin (1992) and McLanahan and Sandefur (1994) note that single parents frequently do not have enough time or resources for their children. McLanahan and Sandefur (1994) find evidence that children from single-parent homes are at increased risk for dropping out of high school, and girls are more likely to become teen mothers. The consequences are somewhat less harmful for Blacks and Hispanics than for Whites, however (McLanahan and Sandefur, 1994).

Black children are much more likely to reside in a single-parent home than White children, as has been the case throughout the last 50 years. The percentage of Black children living with both parents decreased by half, from 67 percent in 1960 to 33 percent in 1995. Between 1970 and 1995, the percentage of White children living with both parents also fell, but by 15 percent, compared to 43 percent for Black children. By 1995, a little more than half of Black children lived with their mother only.

Some sociologists, such as E. Franklin Frazier, have theorized that Black family structure is a pathological result of forced family disorganization during slavery and the subsequent marginalization of Blacks in America (see, e.g., Frazier, 1968; see also Farley and Allen, 1987; and Cherlin, 1992, for a discussion of Frazier's theory). Cherlin (1992), however, concludes that differing family patterns result from differential experiences of Black and White families in cities. Farley and Allen (1987) conclude that economic status and cultural values influence the Black family structure.

The percentages of Hispanic children living with both parents range between the rates for Black and White children, with the percentages of single-parent families having increased by 19 percent between 1970 and 1995. Within Hispanic ethnic groups, Bean and Tienda (1987) find that Cubans have the lowest rates of families headed by single females, with Mexicans at a slightly higher rate. Puerto Rican rates are much higher, approximately double those of Cubans and Mexicans, and similar to those of Blacks.

American Indians have also experienced an increase of single-parent families. Their rates are higher than for Hispanic but lower than for Black children. The rate of decrease of children with both parents has paralleled that of Hispanics. Sandefur and Liebler (1996) point out that there is significant variation among American Indian tribes as regards single-parent families, but rates on all reservations are higher than those for Whites.

Asian populations have also experienced increases in the number of single-parent families, but not to the same degree as other racial and ethnic groups. In 1970, the percentage of Asian (Japanese) children living with both parents was similar to that of Whites; but there was an 8 percent drop over the next 25 years, compared to a 15 percent drop for non-Hispanic Whites. Barringer et al. (1993) note that, within the Asian population, the levels of single-female heads of household are very low for Asian Indians and highest (higher than non-Hispanic Whites) for the Vietnamese population.

In sum, fertility rates and family structure have undergone significant

TABLE 3-9 Percent Distribution of Children Younger Than Age 18 Living in Both- or Single-Parent Households, 1960 to 1995

| | 1960[a] | 1970 | 1975 | 1980 | 1985 | 1990 | 1995 |
|---|---|---|---|---|---|---|---|
| Total U.S. | | | | | | | |
| Both parents | 88.5 | 84.9 | 80.3 | 77 | 74 | 73 | 69 |
| Mother only | 7.5 | 10.8 | 15.5 | 18 | 21 | 22 | 23 |
| Father only | 1 | 1.1 | 1.5 | 2 | 3 | 3 | 4 |
| White | | | | | | | |
| Both parents | — | 89.2 | 85.4 | 83 | 80 | 79 | 76 |
| Mother only | — | 7.8 | 11.3 | 14 | 16 | 16 | 18 |
| Father only | — | 0.9 | 1.5 | 2 | 2 | 3 | 3 |
| Non-White | | | | | | | |
| Both parents | 67.7 | — | — | — | — | — | — |
| Mother only | 19.6 | — | — | — | — | — | — |
| Father only | 1.8 | — | — | — | — | — | — |
| Black | | | | | | | |
| Both parents | 67 | 58.1 | 49.4 | 42 | 40 | 38 | 33 |
| Mother only | — | 29.4 | 41 | 44 | 51 | 51 | 52 |
| Father only | — | 2.2 | 1.8 | 2 | 3 | 4 | 4 |

| | | | | | | | |
|---|---|---|---|---|---|---|---|
| Hispanic | | | | | | | |
| Both parents | 77.6[b] | — | — | 75 | 68 | 67 | 63 |
| Mother only | — | — | — | 20 | 27 | 27 | 28 |
| Father only | — | — | — | 2 | 2 | 3 | 4 |
| Asian | | | | | | | |
| Both parents | 89.3[c] | 90.1[d] | — | 89.3 | — | 83.6 | 82.4[f] |
| Mother only | — | — | — | — | — | — | 10.9[f] |
| Father only | — | — | — | — | — | — | 3.0[f] |
| American Indian | | | | | | | |
| Both parents | 68.6[c] | — | — | 57.6[e] | — | 55.4 | — |
| Mother only | — | — | — | — | — | — | — |
| Father only | — | — | — | — | — | — | — |

[a]Data are for children younger than age 14.
[b]Respondents of Spanish origin.
[c]Japanese.
[d]Chinese.
[e]For identified reservations.
[f]Data for 1994.

SOURCES: U.S. Bureau of the Census (1964c:Table 1; 1973c:Table 4; 1973d:Table 3; 1973e:Tables 3 and 18; 1977:Table 66; 1984b:Table 8; 1986:Table 6 and 15; 1993b:Table 2; 1994:Table 2; 1997:Table 81); Russell (1996:page 18); Shinagawa and Jang (1998:page 32).

changes within the last half-century. There has been a move away from traditional fertility and family behaviors; out-of-wedlock childbearing, divorce, single-parent families, and later marriage have all increased; and differences in fertility rates and family patterns between racial and ethnic groups persist.

## MORTALITY

Racial and ethnic mortality differences are determined by calculating life expectancies and death rates. These measures give information about the average length of life, but not the average quality of life. To help explicate reasons behind mortality patterns, researchers analyze infant mortality and causes of death.

### Data and Their Limitations

Many researchers question the accuracy of the racial and ethnic identity items on vital statistics records (Hahn, 1992; Hahn et al., 1992; Palloni, 1978) because of the data problems mentioned previously. In addition, death registration data have shown problems of misclassification. Asians and American Indians are frequently misclassified as Whites on death certificates, which minimizes their groups' mortality and exaggerates White mortality (Hahn, 1992). Furthermore, census underestimation also affects statistics on racial and ethnic group mortality. Infant mortality statistics are derived from two vital statistics registration forms—birth and death certificates. Inconsistencies in coding of race and ethnicity have been found across forms, and greater inconsistencies are found for Asians, American Indians, and Hispanics. When the group identification does not match, most misassignments code the individual as White (Hahn et al., 1992). Thus, rates presented below are probably underestimates of actual rates for Blacks, Asians, and American Indians and should be considered a lower bound of the true rates.

### Life Expectancy

Life expectancy at birth is a commonly used indicator of the intrinsic mean health of a group. Life expectancies represent the mean number of years left to live, based on then-current mortality rates (Péron and Strohmenger, 1985:112). Since the 1950s, life expectancies for all Americans have increased through the elimination of many premature deaths (Wright, 1997). Whites have historically had the highest life expectancy, but their relative advantages are declining (Kitagawa and Hauser, 1973).

In 1950, the gap between White and non-White life expectancies was 8 years; by 1995 the gap had narrowed to 4.5 years (Table 3-10).

Blacks consistently have the lowest life expectancy among major U.S. racial and ethnic groups. A Black person born in 1970 could expect to live 64 years; by 1995, Black life expectancy had increased to 70 years. The 1990 life expectancy of Blacks is 7 years less than the 1990 life expectancy of Whites. American Indians also have lower life expectancies. An American Indian born in 1950 could expect to live, on average, 60 years; by 1990, the average was 74 years. The 1990 life expectancy for American Indians is 2 years less than the 1990 life expectancy of Whites.

Little historical information is available for the life expectancies of Hispanics and Asians. Life expectancies at birth for Asians and various Asian subgroups are only available for persons born in 1992 for seven selected states—California, Hawaii, Illinois, New Jersey, New York, Texas, and Washington. These seven states, combined, accounted for 73 percent of the Asian population in 1990 (Hoyert and Kung, 1997) (see Table 3-10, column for 1990). The 1992 life expectancies for Asian subgroups vary greatly, but generally remain longer than life expectancy for Blacks. Hawaiians and Samoans had the lowest life expectancies; and Guamanians, Asian Indians, and Koreans had the highest, although estimates for Samoans, Guamanians, and Asian Indians should be viewed with caution because their small population sizes limit the reliability of results. Chinese and Japanese life expectancies were estimated at 82 years.

Females generally live longer than males, given their different mortality rates. This is true across all racial and ethnic groups. As seen in Figure 3-3, non-White females have made the greatest gains in life expectancy since 1950.

## Death Rates and Age-Adjusted Death Rates

Death rates for racial and ethnic groups are calculated based on the number of deaths for that group per 1,000 persons. To account for the different age compositions of any population group, demographers calculate *age-adjusted* or *standardized* death rates. U.S. rates are calculated using direct age standardization, adopting the 1940 total U.S. population age structure as the standard population (for information on calculation methodologies, see Péron and Strohmenger, 1985; Curtin and Klein, 1995). Thus, the age-adjusted rate shows what the death rate would be in an actual population with the same age distribution as the standard population (Zopf, 1992). Table 3-11 shows historical patterns for age-adjusted death rates, and reveals that they have dropped dramatically. Standardized death rates for all males dropped more than the standardized death rates for all females, primarily because males started at much higher rates.

TABLE 3-10 Life Expectancy at Birth, 1950 to 1995

|  | 1950 | 1955 | 1960[a] | 1965 | 1970[c] |
|---|---|---|---|---|---|
| **Both Sexes** |  |  |  |  |  |
| Total U.S. | 68.2 | 69.6 | 69.7 | 70.2 | 70.9 |
| White | 69.1 | 70.5 | 70.6 | 71.0 | 71.7 |
| Non-White | 60.8 | 63.7 | 63.6 | 64.1 | 65.3 |
|   Black | — | — | — | — | 64.1 |
|   Hispanic | — | — | — | — | — |
|   Asian | — | — | 77.4[b] | — | — |
|   American Indian | 60.0 | — | 61.7 | — | 65.1 |
| **Males** |  |  |  |  |  |
| Total U.S. | 65.6 | 66.7 | 66.6 | 66.8 | 67.1 |
| White | 66.5 | 67.4 | 67.4 | 67.6 | 68.0 |
| Non-White | 59.1 | 61.4 | 61.1 | 61.1 | 61.3 |
|   Black | — | — | — | — | 60.0 |
|   Hispanic | — | — | — | — | — |
|   Asian | — | — | — | — | — |
|   American Indian | 58.1 | — | 60.0 | — | 60.7 |
| **Females** |  |  |  |  |  |
| Total U.S. | 71.1 | 72.8 | 73.1 | 73.7 | 74.7 |
| White | 72.2 | 73.7 | 74.1 | 74.7 | 75.6 |
| Non-White | 62.9 | 66.1 | 66.3 | 67.4 | 69.4 |
|   Black | — | — | — | — | 68.3 |
|   Hispanic | — | — | — | — | — |
|   Asian | — | — | — | — | — |
|   American Indian | 62.2 | — | 65.7 | — | 71.2 |

[a]Prior to 1960, data exclude Alaska and Hawaii.

[b]Data for only the Japanese population.

[c]Beginning in 1970, tabulations exclude nonresidents of the United States.

[d]Data for 1992 and for only those in California, Hawaii, Illinois, New Jersey, New York, Texas, and Washington.

[e]Data for years 1990-1992 for the population in areas served by the Indian Health Service.

After adjusting for their age composition, Whites have lower standardized death rates and have rates closer to those of Asians and Hispanics. Blacks have the highest age-adjusted death rates across all points in time for both the total group population and by sex, followed by American Indians, and then Whites. Hispanics have the second lowest age-adjusted death rates across time and for both sexes in the years in which data are available. Finally, Asians show the lowest age-adjusted death rates across time. The lower age-adjusted rates for Asians and Hispanics reflect misreporting of race on death certificates and population underestimation.

| 1975 | 1980 | 1985 | 1990 | 1995 |
|------|------|------|------|------|
| 72.6 | 73.7 | 74.7 | 75.4 | 75.8 |
| 73.4 | 74.4 | 75.3 | 76.1 | 76.5 |
| 68.0 | 69.5 | 71.0 | 71.2 | 71.9 |
| 66.8 | 68.1 | 69.3 | 69.1 | 69.6 |
| — | — | — | — | — |
| — | — | — | 75.2[d] | — |
| — | 71.1 | — | 73.5[e] | — |
| | | | | |
| 68.8 | 70.0 | 71.1 | 71.8 | 72.5 |
| 69.5 | 70.7 | 71.8 | 72.7 | 73.4 |
| 63.7 | 65.3 | 67.0 | 67.0 | 67.9 |
| 62.4 | 63.8 | 65.0 | 64.5 | 65.2 |
| — | — | — | — | — |
| — | — | — | — | — |
| — | 67.1 | — | — | — |
| | | | | |
| 76.6 | 77.4 | 78.2 | 78.8 | 78.9 |
| 77.3 | 78.1 | 78.7 | 79.4 | 79.6 |
| 72.4 | 73.6 | 74.8 | 75.2 | 75.7 |
| 71.3 | 72.5 | 73.4 | 73.6 | 73.9 |
| — | — | — | — | — |
| — | — | — | — | — |
| — | 71.1 | — | — | — |

SOURCES: National Center for Health Statistics (1996:Table 6-5); Anderson et al. (1997:Table 5); Kochanek et al. (1994:Table 5); Hoyert and Kung (1997:Table B); Reddy (1993b:Table 398); Snipp (1989:Table 3.1); Indian Health Service (1995:Table 4.33); Barringer et al. (1993:Table 3.5).

The low standardized death rates for Hispanics and Asians mask the great diversity within these two groups. Immigrants and refugees usually have higher death rates than U.S.-born groups (Bradshaw and Liese, 1991; Barringer et al., 1993; Gardner et al., 1985). In 1992, among Asian groups, age-adjusted death rates were the lowest for Asian Indians, Koreans, and Japanese, respectively, and highest for Hawaiians and Samoans (Hoyert and Kung, 1997). For 1979 to 1981, and among Hispanic groups, Cubans had the lowest standardized death rates, and Mexicans ranged between Cubans and Puerto Ricans, who had the highest rates (Maurer et

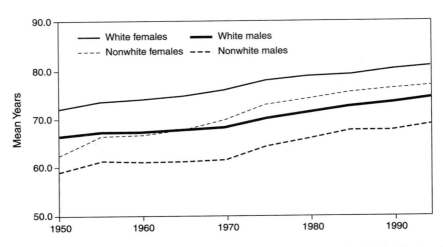

FIGURE 3-3  Life expectancy at birth by sex, 1950 to 1995.  SOURCE: National Center for Health Statistics (1996:Table 5).

al., 1990).[2]  This same pattern held for foreign-born Hispanics in 1979 to 1981 (Shai and Rosenwaike, 1991).

The relationship between male and female standardized death rates varies among groups.  For both Whites and Blacks, female age-adjusted death rates are a little less than half the age-adjusted rates of males.  The differences are smaller for Hispanics, Asians, and American Indians.

### Infant Mortality

Like life expectancy, infant mortality is a general indicator of a group's overall well-being or, conversely, deprivation (Cramer, 1987).  Infant mortality is defined as the number of deaths in the first 11 months of life per 1,000 live births.  Infant mortality can be broken down into neonatal mortality (rate of deaths in the first 28 days of life per 1,000 live births) and postneonatal mortality (the rate of deaths in the 1st through 11th month of life per 1,000 live births).  Deaths in the neonatal period often result from congenital anomalies and problems associated with preg-

---

[2]For this group, data are derived from 15 states (Arizona, Colorado, Georgia, Hawaii, Illinois, Indiana, Kansas, Mississippi, Nebraska, New York, North Dakota, Ohio, Texas, Utah, and Wyoming). During 1979-1981, 20 states had a census question about Hispanic or ethnic origin, but only these 15 had comparable wording on the origin question and at least 90 percent completion for that question.

nancy. Deaths in the postneonatal period more likely result from environmental causes (Bertoli et al., 1984).

Particular data problems arise for infant mortality statistics. First, as discussed previously, the race coded on an infant's death certificate may or may not match that which the mother indicates on the birth certificate. This problem is especially important for children of mixed racial/ethnic couples, and, thus, the infant mortality of groups with higher rates of intermarriage. Babies of mixed ethnicity tend to be more often classified as White at death than at birth, leading to an underestimate of the infant mortality for non-Whites (Barringer et al., 1993).

Second, in 1989, the National Center for Health Statistics changed the way it calculated the race of live births. Before 1989, the Center determined the race of a child using an algorithm of the mother's and father's race:

- if both parents were of the same race, the child was coded as that race;
- if one parent was White and one parent was non-White, the child was classified as the non-White race;
- when neither parent was White, the child was assigned the race of the father with one exception—if the mother was of Hispanic origin, the child was always determined by the Hispanic status of the mother;
- if one parent was Hawaiian, then the child was considered Hawaiian;
- if race was only reported for one parent, the race of the child was coded as the race of that parent (Hoyert, 1994).

Since 1989, the race, for all births, is classified as the race of the mother.

On a death certificate, the race of a child is not determined by any uniform rules, but by the next of kin or an official local or state recorder. The change in race coding of live births led to significant increases in the rates of infant mortality for racial and ethnic minority groups, especially for American Indians, Japanese, and Hawaiians (Hoyert, 1994); and this change limits our ability to compare rates before and after 1989.

Despite these additional data limitations, overall trends in infant mortality, as presented in Table 3-12, reveal dramatic declines in the U.S. infant mortality rate since 1950. The decrease results from significant reductions in neonatal mortality (MacDorman and Rosenberg, 1993; Singh and Yu, 1995); it falls short, however, of declines experienced in other industrialized countries. The slower pace of declines in infant mortality in the United States is largely the result of racial and socioeconomic inequalities in U.S. infant mortality rates (Singh and Yu, 1995).

TABLE 3-11 Death Rates and Age-Adjusted Death Rates Reported, 1950 to 1995 (per 1,000 persons)

| Death Rates | 1950 | 1955 | 1960 | 1965 |
|---|---|---|---|---|
| Both Sexes | | | | |
| Total U.S. | 9.6 | 9.3 | 9.5 | 9.4 |
| White | 9.5 | 9.2 | 9.5 | 9.4 |
| Non-White | 11.2 | 10.0 | 10.1 | 9.6 |
| Black | 11.3 | — | 10.4 | 10.4 |
| Hispanic | — | — | — | — |
| Asian | — | — | — | — |
| Chinese | 9.0 | — | 6.8 | — |
| Japanese | 6.1 | — | 5.1 | — |
| American Indian | — | — | — | — |
| Age Adjusted for Both Sexes[a] | | | | |
| Total U.S. | 8.4 | 7.6 | 7.6 | 7.4 |
| White | 8.0 | 7.3 | 7.3 | 7.0 |
| Non-White | 12.3 | 10.4 | 10.5 | 10.1 |
| Black | — | — | 10.7 | 10.5 |
| Hispanic | — | — | — | — |
| Asian | — | — | — | — |
| Chinese | — | — | — | — |
| Japanese | — | — | — | — |
| American Indian | — | — | — | — |
| Age Adjusted for Males[a] | | | | |
| Total U.S. | 10.0 | 9.3 | 9.5 | 9.5 |
| White | 9.6 | 9.1 | 9.2 | 9.1 |
| Non-White | 13.6 | 11.9 | 12.1 | 12.2 |
| Black | — | — | 12.5 | 12.7 |
| Hispanic | — | — | — | — |
| Asian | — | — | — | — |
| American Indian | — | — | — | — |
| Age Adjusted for Females[a] | | | | |
| Total U.S. | 6.9 | 6.1 | 5.9 | 5.6 |
| White | 6.5 | 5.7 | 5.6 | 5.3 |
| Non-White | 11.0 | 9.1 | 8.9 | 8.3 |
| Black | — | — | 9.2 | 8.6 |
| Hispanic | — | — | — | — |
| Asian | — | — | — | — |
| American Indian | — | — | — | — |

[a]1940 U.S. Population used for the standardization.
[b]Data an average of 1979 through 1981 cohorts and from 15 states.

| 1970 | 1975 | 1980 | 1985 | 1990 | 1995 |
|------|------|------|------|------|------|
| 9.5 | 8.8 | 8.8 | 8.8 | 8.6 | 8.8 |
| 9.5 | 8.7 | 8.9 | 9.0 | 8.9 | 9.1 |
| 9.4 | 8.2 | 7.9 | 7.4 | 7.4 | |
| 10.0 | 8.8 | 8.8 | 8.5 | 8.7 | 8.6 |
| — | — | $3.7^b$ | — | — | 3.5 |
| — | — | 3.0 | 2.8 | 2.8 | 3.0 |
| 4.7 | — | 3.7 | — | — | — |
| 4.2 | — | 4.0 | — | — | — |
| — | — | 4.9 | 4.2 | 4.0 | 4.5 |
| 7.1 | 6.2 | 5.9 | 5.5 | 5.2 | 5.0 |
| 6.8 | 6.0 | 5.6 | 5.2 | 4.9 | 4.8 |
| 9.8 | 8.4 | 7.7 | 7.1 | 6.9 | — |
| 10.4 | 8.9 | 8.4 | 7.9 | 7.9 | 7.6 |
| — | — | $4.6^b$ | — | — | 3.9 |
| — | — | 3.2 | 3.1 | 3.0 | 3.0 |
| 4.9 | — | 3.5 | — | — | — |
| 3.3 | — | 2.9 | — | — | — |
| — | — | 5.6 | 4.7 | 4.5 | 4.7 |
| 9.3 | 8.2 | 7.8 | 7.2 | 6.8 | 6.5 |
| 8.9 | 8.0 | 7.5 | 6.9 | 6.4 | 6.1 |
| 12.3 | 10.9 | 10.1 | 9.3 | 9.1 | — |
| 13.2 | 11.6 | 11.1 | 10.5 | 10.6 | 10.1 |
| — | — | $6.12^b$ | — | — | 5.2 |
| — | — | 4.2 | 4.0 | 3.8 | 3.8 |
| — | — | 7.3 | 6.0 | 5.7 | 5.8 |
| 5.3 | 4.6 | 4.3 | 4.1 | 3.9 | 3.9 |
| 5.0 | 4.4 | 4.1 | 3.9 | 3.7 | 3.6 |
| 7.7 | 6.3 | 5.8 | 5.4 | 5.1 | — |
| 8.1 | 6.7 | 6.3 | 5.9 | 5.8 | 5.7 |
| — | — | $3.3^b$ | — | — | 2.7 |
| — | — | 2.2 | 2.3 | 2.3 | 2.3 |
| — | — | 4.1 | 3.5 | 3.4 | 3.7 |

SOURCES: National Center for Health Statistics (1996:Tables 1-2 and 1-3); Anderson et al. (1997:Tables 1 and 14); Maurer et al. (1990:Table 2); Barringer et al. (1993:Table 3.4).

TABLE 3-12 Infant Mortality (percent reported per 1,000 live births), 1950 to 1995

| | 1950 | 1955 | 1960 | 1965 | 1970 | 1975 | 1980 | 1985 | 1990[d] | 1995 |
|---|---|---|---|---|---|---|---|---|---|---|
| **Infant (0 to 11 months of age)** | | | | | | | | | | |
| Total U.S. | 29.2 | 26.4 | 26.0 | 24.7 | 20.0 | 16.1 | 12.6 | 10.6 | 9.2 | 7.6 |
| White | 26.8 | 23.6 | 22.9 | 21.5 | 17.8 | 14.2 | 11.0 | 9.3 | 7.6 | 6.3 |
| Non-White | 44.5 | 42.8 | 43.2 | 40.3 | 30.9 | 24.2 | 19.1 | 15.8 | 15.5 | 12.6 |
| Black | 43.9 | 43.1 | 44.3 | 41.7 | 32.6 | 26.2 | 21.4 | 18.2 | 18.0 | 15.1 |
| Hispanic | — | — | — | — | — | — | 10.9[b] | 8.5[c] | 7.9[c] | 6.3 |
| Asian | — | — | — | — | — | — | — | 7.8 | — | 5.3 |
| American Indian[a] | — | 62.7 | 48.0 | 38.5 | 24.6 | 18.7 | 13.8 | 9.7 | 9.7[f] | 9.0 |
| **Neonatal (less than 1 month of age)** | | | | | | | | | | |
| Total U.S. | 20.5 | 19.1 | 18.7 | 17.7 | 15.1 | 11.6 | 8.5 | 7.0 | 5.8 | 4.9 |
| White | 19.4 | 17.7 | 17.2 | 16.1 | 13.8 | 10.4 | 7.5 | 6.1 | 4.8 | 4.1 |
| Non-White | 27.5 | 27.2 | 26.9 | 25.4 | 21.4 | 16.8 | 12.5 | 10.3 | 9.9 | 8.1 |
| Black | 27.8 | 27.8 | 27.8 | 26.5 | 22.8 | 18.3 | 14.1 | 12.1 | 11.6 | 9.8 |
| Hispanic | — | — | — | — | — | — | 7[b] | 5.5[c] | 5[e] | 4.1 |
| Asian | — | — | — | — | — | — | — | 4.8 | — | 3.4 |
| American Indian[a] | — | 23.1 | — | 16.1 | 12.2 | 9.2 | 6.6 | 4.4 | 4.6[f] | 3.9 |

| Postneonatal (1 to 11 months of age) | | | | | | | | | |
|---|---|---|---|---|---|---|---|---|---|
| Total U.S. | 8.7 | 7.3 | 7.3 | 7.0 | 4.9 | 4.5 | 4.1 | 3.7 | 3.4 | 2.7 |
| White | 7.4 | 5.9 | 5.7 | 5.4 | 4.0 | 3.8 | 3.5 | 3.2 | 2.8 | 2.2 |
| Non-White | 16.9 | 15.6 | 16.4 | 14.9 | 9.5 | 7.5 | 6.6 | 5.5 | 5.7 | 4.5 |
| Black | 16.1 | 15.3 | 16.5 | 15.2 | 9.9 | 7.9 | 7.3 | 6.1 | 6.4 | 5.3 |
| Hispanic | — | — | — | — | — | — | 3.9[b] | 3.0[c] | 2.9[e] | 2.1 |
| Asian | — | — | — | — | — | — | — | 3.0 | — | 1.9 |
| American Indian[a] | — | 39.7 | — | 20.7 | 12.3 | 9.5 | 7.2 | 5.2 | 5.1[f] | 5.1 |

[a]Data an average of three years, centering on the year given, except where noted.
[b]Data an average of 1979 through 1981 cohorts and from 15 states.
[c]Data for 1985 and 1987 cohorts from 20 states and Washington, D.C.
[d]After 1989, the race of births is tabulated by the race of the mother. Before 1989, births were tabulated by the race of the child as determined by an algorithm of the mother's and father's race.
[e]Data for 1987 from 18 states and the District of Columbia.
[f]Data an average of 1987 and 1988 cohorts.

SOURCES: National Center for Health Statistics (1996:Table 2-2); MacDorman and Rosenberg (1993:Table 2); Pastore and MacDorman (1995:Table J); MacDorman and Atkinson (1998:Tables A and C); Maurer et al. (1990:Table C); Schick and Schick (1991:Table E1-14); Anderson et al. (1997:Table 25); Reddy (1993b:Tables 415, 448 and 449); Gall and Gall (1993:Table 439).

## Current Rates

In 1995, Asians had the lowest infant mortality rates. Hispanics and Whites had the next lowest rates. American Indians had the second highest infant mortality rate, and Blacks had the highest. The low rates for Asians and Hispanics mask the variability within these groups. Among Hispanics, Mexicans, Cubans, and Central and South Americans have similar rates, but Puerto Ricans have significantly higher rates (MacDorman and Atkinson, 1998). Among Asians, Chinese have the lowest rates; Japanese, Filipino, and "Other Asians" have median rates; and Hawaiians have the highest rate. For neonatal mortality, Blacks have an astonishingly high rate; Puerto Ricans, Whites, and Hawaiians have the next highest rates; and Chinese, Japanese, and Filipinos have the lowest rates. Cubans have the lowest Hispanic neonatal mortality rate. Postneonatal mortality rates remain especially high for American Indians and Blacks.

## Trends

American Indians have experienced larger decreases in infant mortality than have Whites. Between 1955 and 1995, White infant mortality fell by 73 percent while American Indian infant mortality fell by 86 percent. Most of the declines in infant mortality for American Indians occurred between 1955 and 1980, and the decline results from reductions in postneonatal mortality. Black infant mortality rates have declined the least since 1955, by 65 percent. For Blacks, both neonatal and postneonatal mortality-rate declines contributed equally to the overall reduction in infant mortality rates since 1955; but declines in neonatal mortality rates have not kept pace with that of Whites. Since the 1970s, the gap between White and Black infant mortality rates has actually widened. Since 1985, Asian infant mortality rates have declined by 32 percent and Hispanic infant mortality rates have declined by 26 percent. Reductions in postneonatal mortality account for the overall attenuation of infant mortality rates for Asians and Hispanics since 1985.

### Explaining Mortality Trends

The reduction in infectious and parasitic diseases largely accounts for the lower death rates and longer life expectancies reported here. This reduction occurred as a result of progress made in medicine and sanitation, as well as improvements in nutrition and health awareness (Zopf, 1992). Reductions in infant mortality have been associated with increased and improved prenatal care and better maternity health habits. Improved living standards for all groups, especially for minorities in the last half century, reduced child and adult mortality from diseases and environmental causes. Employment and higher education and income status are associated with lower mortality for all groups (Kitagawa and Hauser, 1973; Bertoli et al., 1984; Sorlie et al., 1995). Also, the concentrated efforts of public health organizations, for the population as a whole and for various racial and ethnic groups, have helped improve health standards for everyone. The Indian Health Service and tribal health clinics, for example, greatly improved the health conditions of American Indians in areas of infant mortality, tuberculosis, gastrointestinal disease, and accidents (Indian Health Service, 1995). One of the three broad goals of the Presidential Healthy People 2000 Plan included targeted efforts to reduce health disparities for racial and ethnic groups, especially along the lines of infant mortality and certain causes of death (Plepys and Klein, 1995; also see the discussion in Volume II, Chapter 13). Also, because foreign-born members of Asian and Hispanic groups tend to be healthier than their U.S.-born counterparts, the better mortality conditions of Asians and Hispanics could be related to the higher proportions of Asian and Hispanic immigrants. The reason for better immigrant health might be that those Hispanics and Asians able to migrate are healthier than the general homeland populations (Barringer et al., 1993).

Discrepancies between the White and non-White mortality regimes continue to exist, despite advances, for several reasons. First, socioeconomic differences persist between Whites and non-Whites. Higher death and infant mortality rates, and higher instances of certain causes of disease, are associated with lower education and income levels (Kitagawa and Hauser, 1973; Cramer, 1987); and non-Whites, with the exception of Asians, have lower education and income levels (Harrison and Bennett, 1995). Asians have better-than-average socioeconomic status and, concurrently, lower mortality rates. Second, racial and ethnic groups have lower rates of health insurance coverage and receive lower-quality medical care than do Whites (U.S. General Accounting Office, 1992; Zopf, 1992). Finally, diet and health practices vary by racial and ethnic group and influence certain causes of disease, such as heart disease, stroke, and lung cancer (Gardner et al., 1985; Rogers, 1991). There is additional discussion of mortality differentials in Volume II, Chapter 14.

### Possible Future Trends

Few projected estimates are calculated for mortality statistics, but one such projection was made for infant mortality. Singh and Yu (1995) projected neonatal and postneonatal mortality rates for Blacks and Whites through the year 2010. Based on their projections, the overall Black-White disparity is not expected to diminish. These forecasts, however, do not take into account political, social, behavioral, demographic, or medical influences on future mortality changes.

One such future political influence is the President's Healthy People 2010 plan, which includes the goal of reducing infant mortality by 22 percent for Blacks with the eventual goal of eliminating this racial disparity for Blacks, American Indians, and Puerto Ricans. Other Healthy People 2010 goals include increased screening and management for cancer; reductions in stroke and heart disease mortality; the elimination of disparities in diabetes, especially for Blacks and American Indians; equal access to life-enhancing therapies for low-income HIV-infected persons; and increased access to immunizations for minorities (U.S. Department of Health and Human Services, 1998). Each of these measures will help eliminate important differences among racial and ethnic groups and break down barriers to increased life chances. These measures could help bring our population one step closer to a convergence in infant mortality and life expectancy.

Racial and ethnic minority groups suffer disproportionately from higher mortality rates and, thus, lower life expectancies and unequal chances for survival. Most of the gaps between Whites and non-Whites have narrowed over the years, but continue to be significant. Especially disturbing is the continued, and increasing, gap between Black and White infant mortality.

The United States has experienced a great reduction in the leading causes of death during this century, from suffering and dying primarily from infectious and parasitic diseases to degenerative diseases. Racial and ethnic groups have experienced this reduction in leading cause of death later than Whites, and still suffer more from infectious diseases than do Whites. The leading causes of death differ greatly, depending on age groups, but for both age-specific and overall causes of death, mortality rates are generally higher for Blacks and American Indians.

Additional difficulties arise for interpreting racial and ethnic mortality statistics because of multiple data problems. Combined, these data problems tend to underestimate the mortalities of non-Whites. Regardless of whether these estimates are lower bounds of the true discrepancies between racial and ethnic groups and Whites, clearly more attention needs to be devoted to the health conditions of minorities.

## SUMMARY

The United States has witnessed significant demographic shifts in its racial and ethnic composition over the past 50 years, and still greater change is anticipated in the twenty-first century. Historically, Blacks constituted the largest racial and ethnic minority group; Hispanics, Asians, and American Indians comprise smaller proportions of the population; but Hispanic and Asian populations are growing at a rapid rate. Hispanics are expected to surpass Blacks as the largest minority group, and the Asian population is expected to increase more rapidly than any other group.

Projected increases in the Hispanic and Asian populations can be partially explained by the influx of immigrants in the past several decades. The regional and metropolitan distribution of different racial and ethnic groups in the United States often reflects patterns of international migration. Foreign-born immigrants traditionally cluster on the coasts in port-of-entry cities such as Los Angeles, Miami, and New York; however, substantial numbers of the second generation move to inland metropolitan areas. In spite of all this movement, for both internal migrants and immigrants, racial and ethnic minority groups tend to migrate to areas with existing concentrations of coethnics or members of their racial or ethnic group.

Another aspect of the growing Hispanic population is fertility rates. Hispanic women have traditionally had much higher fertility rates than Whites and slightly higher rates than Blacks. In 1996, American Indian women had higher fertility rates than White, Black, and Asian women, for whom the rate was lowest, mostly because American Indian women start childbearing earlier and continue to have children much later than women in other racial and ethnic groups.

Blacks, Hispanics, and American Indians had the highest rates of teenage childbearing, in 1995, while Asians had the lowest. Out-of-wedlock childbearing, at any age, increased for all groups, but especially for Whites. Researchers attribute the particular increase among Whites to a decline in marriage rates. Despite the largest increase in out-of-wedlock childbearing being among Whites, Blacks maintained a rate twice that of Whites in this category, and American Indian women had out-of-wedlock childbearing rates similar to Blacks.

Blacks historically married at younger ages than Whites, but in 1995, Blacks married later than Whites. As the proportion of children born out of wedlock increased, as the average age at first marriage increased, and as the divorce rate increased, single-parent families became increasingly common. The proportion of children living in single-parent families was highest among Blacks in 1995, followed by American Indians, Hispanics, Whites, and finally Asians.

Life expectancies in 1995 were lowest at birth for Blacks and American Indians. These two groups also had the highest infant mortality rates and age-adjusted death rates.

As data collection for specific U.S. populations has improved, and continues to improve, our understanding of specific-population characteristics has improved substantially. The quantity and quality of information on the major racial and ethnic groups—Blacks, Whites, American Indians, Asians and Pacific Islanders, and Hispanics—is better now than ever before. Furthermore, we are accumulating better and better data on specific subgroups such as the Hmong, Vietnamese, and Mexican populations. Nonetheless, severe data limitations remain, especially in the area of vital statistics. The future of data collection and analysis will be even more complicated if patterns of immigration and intermarriage continue.

## ACKNOWLEDGMENTS

This paper was prepared for the Research Conference on Racial Trends in the United States sponsored by the National Research Council, October 15-16, 1998. Work on this paper was carried out at the Center for Demography and Ecology, University of Wisconsin, Madison, which receives financial support from the National Institute for Child Health and Human Development.

## REFERENCES

Anderson, R., K. Kochanek, and S. Murphy
    1997    Advance report of final mortality statistics, 1995. *Monthly Vital Statistics Report* 45(11S).
Barringer, H., R. Gardner, and M. Levin
    1993    *Asians and Pacific Islanders in the United States.* New York: Russell Sage Foundation.
Bartel, A.
    1989    Where do the new U.S. immigrants live? *Journal of Labor Economics* 7:371-391.
Bean, F., and M. Tienda
    1987    *The Hispanic Population of the United States.* New York: Russell Sage Foundation.
Bernstein, A.
    1991    *American Indians and World War II: Toward a New Era in Indian Affairs.* Norman, Okla.: University of Oklahoma Press.
Bertoli, F., C. Rent, and G. Rent
    1984    Infant mortality by socio-economic status for Blacks, Indians, and Whites: A longitudinal analysis of North Carolina, 1968-1977. *Sociology and Social Research* 68(3):364-377.
Bogue, D.
    1985    *Population of the United States: Historical Trends and Future Projections.* New York: The Free Press.
Bradshaw, B., and K. Liese
    1991    Mortality of Mexican-origin persons in the southwestern United States. Ch. 5 in *Mortality of Hispanic Populations*, I. Rosenwaike, ed. New York: Greenwood Press.

Campbell, P.
  1993  *Population Projections for States, by Age, Sex, Race, and Hispanic Origin: 1993 to 2020.* U.S. Bureau of the Census, Current Population Reports P25-1111. Washington, D.C.: U.S. Government Printing Office.
Cherlin, A.
  1992  *Marriage Divorce Remarriage,* Revised and Enlarged Edition. Cambridge, Mass.: Harvard University Press.
Coale, A., and N. Rives
  1973  A statistical reconstruction of the Black population of the United States, 1880-1970: Estimates of the numbers by age and sex, birth rates and total fertility. *Population Index* 39:3-35.
Coale, A., and M. Zelnik
  1963  *New Estimates of Fertility and Population in the United States.* Princeton: Princeton University Press.
Cramer, J.
  1987  Social factors and infant mortality: Identifying high-risk groups and proximate causes. *Demography* 24(3):299-322.
Curtin, L., and R. Klein
  1995  Direct standardization (age-adjusted death rates). *Healthy People 2000: Statistical Notes* (10):1-10.
Darabi, K.
  1987  *Childbearing among Hispanics in the United States: An Annotated Bibliography.* New York: Greenwood Press.
Davis, C., C. Haub, and J. Willette
  1983  U.S. Hispanics: Changing the face of America. *Population Bulletin* 38(3).
Day, J.
  1996  *Population Projections of the United States by Age, Sex, Race, and Hispanic Origin: 1995 to 2050.* U.S. Bureau of the Census, Current Population Reports, P25-1130. Washington, D.C.: U.S. Government Printing Office.
Deardorff, K., and F. Hollmann
  1997  *U.S. Population Estimates by Age, Sex, Race and Hispanic Origin: 1990 to 1996.* U.S. Bureau of the Census, PPL-57, Washington, D.C.: U.S. Government Printing Office.
De Jong, G. and J. Fawcett
  1981  Motivations for migration: An assessment and a value-expectancy research model. In G. De Jong and R. Gardner, eds., *Migration Decision Making: Multidisciplinary Approaches to Microlevel Studies in Developed and Developing Countries.* New York: Pergamon Press.
Dillingham, H., and D. Sly
  1966  The mechanical cotton picker, Negro migration and the integration movement. *Human Organization* 25(Winter):346.
Elben, J.
  1974  New estimates of vital rates of the United States Black population during the nineteenth century. *Demography* 11:301-319.
Eschbach, K.
  1993  Changing identification among American Indians and Alaska Natives. *Demography* 30:635-652.
Farley, R., and W. Allen
  1987  *The Color Line and the Quality of Life in America.* New York: Russell Sage Foundation.

Fixico, D.
    1986    *Termination and Relocation: Federal Indian Policy, 1945-1960.* Albuquerque: University of New Mexico Press.
Fligstein, N.
    1981    *Going North, Migration of Blacks and Whites from the South, 1900-1950.* New York: Academic Press.
    1983    The transformation of southern agriculture and the migration of Blacks and Whites, 1930-40. *International Migration Review* 17:268-290.
Frazier, E.
    1968    The Negro Family in America. Pp. 191-209 in *E. Franklin Frazier on Race Relations.* Chicago: University of Chicago Press.
Frey, W.
    1995    The new geography of population shifts. In *State of the Union: America in the 1990s. Vol. II: Social Trends,* R. Farley, ed. New York: Russell Sage Foundation.
Gall, S.B., and T.L. Gall, editors
    1993    *Statistical Record of Asian Americans.* Detroit: Gale Research, Inc.
Garcia, J., and P. Montgomery
    1991    *The Hispanic Population in the United States: March 1990.* U.S. Bureau of the Census. Current Population Reports, P20-449. Washington, D.C.: Government Printing Office.
Gardner, R., B. Robey, and P. Smith
    1985    Asian Americans: Growth change and diversity. *Population Bulletin* 40(4):1-44.
Gordon, L.
    1984    Migration of refugees within the United States: New data sources and findings. Paper presented at the Annual Meeting of the Population Association of Geographers.
Hagan, W.
    1979    *American Indians.* Chicago: University of Chicago Press.
Hahn, R.
    1992    The state of federal health statistics on racial and ethnic groups. *Journal of the American Medical Association* 267(2):268-271.
Hahn, R., J. Mulinare, and S. Teutsch
    1992    Inconsistencies in coding of race and ethnicity between birth and death in U.S. infants. *Journal of the American Medical Association* 267(2):259-263.
Harrison, R., and C. Bennett
    1995    Racial and ethnic diversity. Ch. 4 in *State of the Union: America in the 1990s. Vol. II: Social Trends,* R. Farley, ed. New York: Russell Sage Foundation.
Hollmann, F.
    1993    *U.S. Population Estimates by Age, Sex, Race and Hispanic Origin: 1980 to 1991.* U.S. Bureau of the Census, Current Population Reports, P25-1127. Washington, D.C.: Government Printing Office.
Hoyert, D.
    1994    Effect on mortality rates of the 1989 change in tabulating race. National Center for Health Statistics. *Vital and Health Statistics,* Series 20(25).
Hoyert, D., and H. Kung
    1997    Asian or Pacific Islander mortality, selected states, 1992. *Monthly Vital Statistics Report* 46(1), (S).
Indian Health Service
    1979    *Selected Vital Statistics For Indian Health Service Areas and Service Units, 1972 to 1977.* Washington, D.C.: U.S. Department of Health, Education and Welfare.

1995    *Trends in Indian Health, 1995.* Washington, D.C.: U.S. Department of Health and Human Services.

Jaffe, A., R. Cullen, and T. Boswell
    1976    *Spanish Americans in the United States: Changing Demographic Characteristics.* New York: Research Institute for the Study of Man.

Jaynes, G., and R. Williams, Jr., eds.
    1989    *A Common Destiny: Blacks and American Society.* Washington, D.C.: National Academy Press.

John, R.
    1998    American Indian families. Pp. 382-421 in *Ethnic Families in America: Patterns and Variations,* 4th edition, C. Mindel, R. Habenstein, and R. Wright, Jr., eds. Upper Saddle River, N.J.: Prentice Hall.

Johnson, D., and R. Campbell
    1981    *Black Migration in America—A Social Demographic History.* Durham, N.C.: Duke University Press.

Kitagawa, E., and P. Hauser
    1973    *Differential Mortality in the United States.* Cambridge, Mass.: Harvard University Press.

Kochanek, K.D., J.D. Maurer, and H.M. Rosenberg
    1994    *Causes of Death Contributing to Changes in Life Expectancy: United States, 1984-1989.* Hyattsville, MD: National Center for Health Statistics.

Lieberson, S., and M. Waters
    1988    *From Many Strands: Ethnic and Racial Groups in Contemporary America.* New York: Russell Sage Foundation.

Long, J.
    1981    *Population Deconcentration in the United States.* Special Demographics Analysis. CDES-81-5US. U.S. Bureau of the Census. Washington, D.C.: Government Printing Office.

Long, L.
    1988    *Migration and Residential Mobility in the United States.* New York: Russell Sage Foundation.

Long, L., and D. DeAre
    1981    The suburbanization of Blacks. *American Demographics* (September):16.

Long, L., and K. Hansen
    1975    Trends in return migration to the South. *Demography* 12(4):501-514.

MacDorman, M., and J. Atkinson
    1998    Infant mortality statistics from the linked birth/infant death data set, 1995 period data. *Monthly Vital Statistics Report* 46(6), (S2).

MacDorman, M., and H. Rosenberg
    1993    Trends in infant mortality by cause of death and other characteristics: 1960-1988. National Center for Health Statistics. *Vital and Health Statistics,* Series 20(20).

Martin, P., and E. Midgley
    1994    Immigration to the United States: Journey to an uncertain destination. *Population Bulletin* 49(2).

Maurer, J., H. Rosenberg, and J. Keemer
    1990    Deaths of hispanic origin, 15 reporting states, 1979-1981. National Center for Health Statistics. *Vital and Health Statistics,* Series 20(18).

McDaniel, A.
    1995    The dynamic racial composition of the United States. *Daedalus* 124:179-199.

McHugh, K.
    1989    Hispanic migration and population redistribution in the United States. *Profes-sional Geographer* 41:429-439.
McLanahan, S., and G. Sandefur
    1994    *Growing Up With a Single Parent: What Hurts, What Helps?* Cambridge, Mass.: Harvard University Press.
Nagel, J.
    1996    *American Indian Ethnic Renewal: Red Power and the Resurgence of Identity and Culture.* New York: Oxford University Press.
National Center for Health Statistics
    1994    *Vital Statistics of the United States, 1990. Volume I, Natality.* Washington, D.C.: Public Health Service.
    1996    *Vital Statistics of the United States, 1991. Vol. II, Mortality, Part A.* Washington, D.C.: Public Health Service.
    1998    *Monthly Vital Statistics Report.* June 30.
Nelson, K.
    1980    Recent suburbanization of Blacks. *Journal of the American Planning Association* (July):287-300.
Office of Management and Budget
    1997    Revisions to the standards for the classification of federal data on race and ethnicity. *Federal Register.* Washington, D.C.: U.S. Government Printing Office.
Palloni, A.
    1978    Application of an indirect technique to study group differentials in infant mortality. Ch. 12 in *The Demography of Racial and Ethnic Groups,* F. Bean and W. Frisbie, eds. New York: Academic Press.
Passel, J., and K. Woodrow
    1984    Geographic distribution of undocumented immigrants: Estimates of undocumented aliens counted in the 1980 Census by state. *International Migration Review* 18:642-671.
Pastore, L., and M. MacDorman
    1995    Infant mortality by Hispanic origin of mother: 20 states, 1985-1987 birth cohort. National Center for Health Statistics. *Vital and Health Statistics,* Series 20(27).
Péron, Y., and C. Strohmenger
    1985    *Demographic and Health Indicators.* Ottawa: Statistics Canada.
Pettigrew, T.
    1980    Racial change and the intrametropolitan distribution of Black Americans. In *The Prospective City: Economic, Population, Energy and Environmental Developments,* A. Soloman, ed. Cambridge, Mass.: MIT Press.
Plepys, C., and R. Klein
    1995    Health status indicators: Differentials by race and Hispanic origin. *Healthy People 2000: Statistical Notes* (10):1-8.
Raymond, R.
    1972    Determinants of non-White migration during the 1950s. *The American Journal of Economics and Sociology* 31:9-20.
Reddy, M., ed.
    1993a   *Statistical Record of Hispanic Americans.* Washington, D.C.: Gale Research.
    1993b   *Statistical Record of Native North Americans.* Washington, D.C.: Gale Research.
Robinson, J., B. Ahmed, P. Das Gupta, and K. Woodrow
    1993    Estimation of population coverage in the 1990 United States Census based on demographic analysis. *Journal of the American Statistical Association* 88:1061-1071.

Rogers, R.
  1991   Health-related lifestyles among Mexican-Americans, Puerto Ricans, and Cubans in the United States. Ch. 9 in *Mortality of Hispanic Populations*, I. Rosenwaike, ed. New York: Greenwood Press.
Russell, C.
  1996   *Racial and Ethnic Diversity: Asians, Blacks, Hispanics, American Indians, and Whites.* Ithaca, N.Y.: New Strategist Publications, Inc.
Sale, K.
  1975   *Power Shift: The Rise of the Southern Rim and Its Challenge to the Eastern Establishment.* New York: Random Press.
Saluter, A.
  1996   Marital status and living arrangements: March 1994. *Current Population Reports.* Series P20(484).
Sandefur, G., and C. Liebler
  1996   The demography of American Indian families. Pp. 196-217 in *Changing Numbers, Changing Needs*, G. Sandefur, R. Rindfuss, and B. Cohen, eds. Washington, D.C.: National Academy Press.
Schick, F., and R. Schick
  1991   *Statistical Handbook on U.S. Hispanics.* Phoenix: The Oryx Press.
Shai, D., and I. Rosenwaike
  1991   An overview of age-adjusted death rates among three Hispanic populations in their home countries and in the United States. Ch. 13 in *Mortality of Hispanic Populations*, I. Rosenwaike, ed. New York: Greenwood Press.
Shinagawa, L., and M. Jang
  1998   *Atlas of American Diversity.* Walnut Creek, Calif.: AltaMira Press.
Siegel, J.
  1974   Estimates of coverage of the population by sex, race, and age in the 1970 Census. *Demography* 11:1-23.
Singh, G., and S. Yu
  1995   Infant mortality in the United States: Trends, differentials, and projections, 1950 through 2010. *American Journal of Public Health* 85(7):957-964.
Snipp, C.
  1989   *American Indians: The First of This Land.* New York: Russell Sage Foundation.
  1996   The size and distribution of the American Indian population: Fertility, mortality, migration, and residence. Pp. 17-52 in *Changing Numbers, Changing Needs*, G. Sandefur, R. Rindfuss, and B. Cohen, eds. Washington, D.C.: National Academy Press.
Sorkin, A.
  1971   *American Indians and Federal Aid.* Washington, D.C.: Brookings Institution.
Sorlie, P., E. Backlund, and J. Keller
  1995   U.S. mortality by economic, demographic, and social characteristics: The national longitudinal mortality study. *American Journal of Public Health* 85(7):949-956.
Taffel, S.
  1977   Trends in fertility in the United States. National Center for Health Statistics. *Vital and Health Statistics*, Series 20(28).
Taylor, R., M. Tucker, L. Chatters, and R. Jayakody
  1997   Recent demographic trends in African American family structure. Pp. 14-62 in *Family Life in Black America*, R. Taylor, J. Jackson, and L. Chatters, eds. Thousand Oaks, Calif.: Sage Publications.

Thornton, R., and J. Marsh-Thornton
    1981    Estimating prehistoric American Indian population size for the United States area:
            Implication of the nineteenth century population decline and nadir. *American
            Journal of Physical Anthropology* 55:47-53.
U.S. Bureau of the Census (USBC)
    1953a   *1950 Census of Population, Characteristics of the Population, Vol. II. Part 5: California.*
            Washington, D.C.: U.S. Government Printing Office.
    1953b   *1950 Census of Population, Characteristics of the Population, Vol. II. Part 9: Washing-
            ton D.C.* Washington, D.C.: U.S. Government Printing Office.
    1953c   *1950 Census of Population, Characteristics of the Population, Vol. II. Part 10: Florida.*
            Washington, D.C.: U.S. Government Printing Office.
    1953d   *1950 Census of Population, Characteristics of the Population, Vol. II. Part 43: Texas.*
            Washington, D.C.: U.S. Government Printing Office.
    1953e   *1950 Census of Population, Characteristics of the Population, Vol. II. Part 52: Hawaii.*
            Washington, D.C.: U.S. Government Printing Office.
    1953f   *1950 Census of Population, Special Reports, PE-3B, NonWhite Population by Race.*
            Washington, D.C.: U.S. Government Printing Office.
    1953g   *1950 Census of Population, Special Reports, PE-3C8, Persons of Spanish Surname.*
            Washington, D.C.: U.S. Government Printing Office.
    1963a   *1960 Census of Population, Characteristics of the Population, Vol. 1. Part 6: California.*
            Washington, D.C.: U.S. Government Printing Office.
    1963b   *1960 Census of Population, Characteristics of the Population, Vol. 1. Part 10: Washing-
            ton D.C.* Washington, D.C.: U.S. Government Printing Office.
    1963c   *1960 Census of Population, Characteristics of the Population, Vol. 1. Part 11: Florida.*
            Washington, D.C.: U.S. Government Printing Office.
    1963d   *1960 Census of Population, Characteristics of the Population, Vol. 1. Part 13: Hawaii.*
            Washington, D.C.: U.S. Government Printing Office.
    1963e   *1960 Census of Population, Characteristics of the Population, Vol. 1. Part 15: Illinois.*
            Washington, D.C.: U.S. Government Printing Office.
    1963f   *1960 Census of Population, Characteristics of the Population, Vol. 1. Part 34: New York.*
            Washington, D.C.: U.S. Government Printing Office.
    1963g   *1960 Census of Population, Characteristics of the Population, Vol. 1. Part 45: Texas.*
            Washington, D.C.: U.S. Government Printing Office.
    1963h   *1960 Census of Population, Subject Reports, PC(2)-1B, Persons of Spanish Surname.*
            Washington, D.C.: U.S. Government Printing Office.
    1963i   *1960 Census of Population, Subject Reports, PC(2)-1C, NonWhite Population by Race.*
            Washington, D.C.: U.S. Government Printing Office.
    1963j   *1960 Census of Population, Subject Reports, PC(2)-2B, Mobility for States and State
            Economic Areas.* Washington, D.C.: U.S. Government Printing Office.
    1963k   *1960 Census of Population, Subject Reports, PC(3)-1D, Standard Metropolitan Statisti-
            cal Areas.* Washington, D.C.: U.S. Government Printing Office.
    1964a   *1960 Census of Population, Subject Reports, PC(2)-3A, Women by Number of Children
            Ever Born.* Washington, D.C.: U.S. Government Printing Office.
    1964b   *1960 Census of Population, Subject Reports, PC(2)-4B Persons by Family Characteris-
            tics.* Washington, D.C.: U.S. Government Printing Office.
    1964c   *1960 Census of the Population, Characteristics of the Population, Vol. 1. Part 1: United
            States Summary.* Washington, D.C.: U.S Government Printing Office.
    1965    *Current Population Reports, Series P25-310, Estimates of the Population of the United
            States and Components of Change, by Age, Color, and Sex, 1950-1960.* Washington,
            D.C.: U.S. Government Printing Office.

1966a *1960 Census of Population, Subject Reports, PC(2)-4D, Age at First Marriage.* Washington, D.C.: U.S. Government Printing Office.

1966b *1960 Census of Population, Subject Reports, PC(2)-4E, Marital Status* Washington, D.C.: U.S. Government Printing Office.

1971 *1970 Census of Population, Subject Reports, PHC(2)-1, General Demographic Trends for Metropolitan Areas, 1960 to 1970.* Washington, D.C.: U.S. Government Printing Office.

1972a *1970 Census of Population, Subject Reports, PC(2)-4C, Marital Status.* Washington, D.C.: U.S. Government Printing Office.

1972b *1970 Census of Population, Supplementary Reports, PC(S1)-15, Race of the Population for SMSAs, Urbanized Areas, and Places of 50,000 or More: 1970.* Washington, D.C.: U.S. Government Printing Office.

1972c *1970 Census of Population, Supplementary Reports, PC(S1)-7, Population of Standard Metropolitan Statistical Areas: 1950 to 1970.* Washington, D.C.: U.S. Government Printing Office.

1973a *1970 Census of Population, Characteristics of the Population, Vol. 1. Part 1: United States Summary.* Washington, D.C.: U.S. Government Printing Office.

1973b *1970 Census of Population, Subject Reports, PC(2)-1B, The Negro Population.* Washington, D.C.: U.S. Government Printing Office.

1973c *1970 Census of Population, Subject Reports, PC(2)-1C, Persons of Spanish Origin.* Washington, D.C.: U.S. Government Printing Office.

1973d *1970 Census of Population, Subject Reports, PC(2)-1F, American Indian Population.* Washington, D.C.: U.S. Government Printing Office.

1973e *1970 Census of Population, Subject Reports, PC(2)-1G, Japanese, Chinese, and Filipinos in the United States.* Washington, D.C.: U.S. Government Printing Office.

1973f *1970 Census of Population, Subject Reports, PC(2)-2B Mobility for States and the Nation.* Washington, D.C.: U.S. Government Printing Office.

1973g *1970 Census of Population, Subject Reports, PC(2)-3A, Women by Number of Children Ever Born.* Washington, D.C.: U.S. Government Printing Office.

1973h *1970 Census of Population, Subject Reports, PC(2)-4D, Age at First Marriage.* Washington, D.C.: U.S. Government Printing Office.

1975 *Historical Statistics of the United States: Colonial Times to 1970.* Part 1, Bicentennial Edition. Washington, D.C.: U.S. Government Printing Office.

1977 *Statistical Abstract of the United States: 1977.* (98th edition.) Washington, D.C.: U.S. Government Printing Office.

1983 *1980 Census of Population, PC-80-1-B1, General Social and Economic Characteristics, U.S. Summary.* Washington, D.C.: U.S. Government Printing Office.

1984a *1980 Census of Population, Characteristics of the Population, PC80-1-D1-A, Detailed Population Characteristics, Part I: United States Summary.* Section A: United States. Washington, D.C.: U.S. Government Printing Office.

1984b *1980 Census of Population, Subject Reports, PC80-2-1E, Asian and Pacific Islander Population in the United States: 1980.* Washington, D.C.: U.S. Government Printing Office.

1984c *1980 Census of Population, Supplementary Reports, PC80-S1-16, Residence in 1975 by Age, Sex, Race, and Spanish Origin: 1980.* Washington, D.C.: U.S. Government Printing Office.

1984d *1980 Census of Population, Supplementary Reports, PC80-S1-18, Metropolitan Statistical Areas* Washington, D.C.: U.S. Government Printing Office.

1984e *Statistical Abstract.* 104th edition. Washington, D.C.: U.S. Government Printing Office.

1985   *1980 Census of Population, Subject Reports, PC80 24C, Marital Characteristics.* Washington, D.C.: U.S. Government Printing Office.

1986   *1980 Census of Population, Subject Reports, PC80-2-1D, American Indians, Eskimos, and Aleuts on Identified Reservations and in the Historic Areas of Oklahoma (Excluding Urbanized Areas).* Washington, D.C.: U.S. Government Printing Office.

1989   *200 Years of U.S. Census Taking: Population and Housing Questions, 1790-1990.* Washington, D.C.: U.S. Government Printing Office.

1991   *State and Metropolitan Area Data Book.* 4th edition. Washington, D.C.: U.S. Government Printing Office.

1992   *1990 Census of Population, General Characteristics, U.S. Summary.* 1990 CP-1-1. Washington, D.C.: U.S. Government Printing Office.

1993a  *1990 Census of Population, Social and Economic Characteristics, United States.* 1990 CP-2-1. Washington, D.C.: U.S. Government Printing Office.

1993b  *1990 Census of Population. Subject Reports, CP-3-5, Asians and Pacific Islanders in the United States.* Washington, D.C.: U.S. Government Printing Office.

1993c  *Statistical Abstract.* 113th edition. Washington, D.C.: U.S. Government Printing Office.

1994   *1990 Census of Population, Subject Reports, Characteristics of American Indians by Tribe and Language.* CP-3-7. Washington, D.C.: U.S. Government Printing Office.

1996   *Statistical Abstract of the United States: 1996.* 116th edition. Washington, D.C.: U.S. Government Printing Office.

1997   *Statistical Abstract of the United States: 1997.* 117th edition. Washington, D.C.: U.S. Government Printing Office.

U.S. Department of Health and Human Services (USDHHS)
1995   *Report to Congress on Out-of-Wedlock Childbearing.* Hyattsville, Md.

1998   President Clinton announces new racial and ethnic health disparities initiative. *White House Fact Sheet*, February 20.

U.S. General Accounting Office (GAO)
1992   *Hispanic Access to Health Care: Significant Gaps Exist.* Report to Congressional Requesters, PEMD-92-6.

Ventura, S.
1980   Births of Hispanic parentage, 1980. *Monthly Vital Statistics Report* 32(6S). Hyattsville, Md.: National Center for Health Statistics.

1988   Births of Hispanic parentage, 1985. *Monthly Vital Statistics Report* 36(11S). Hyattsville, Md.: National Center for Health Statistics.

Ventura, S., J. Martin, S. Curtin, and T. Mathews
1997   Report of final natality statistics, 1995. *Monthly Vital Statistics Report* 45(11S). Hyattsville, Md.: National Center for Health Statistics.

1998   Report of final natality statistics, 1996. *Monthly Vital Statistics Report* 46(11S). Hyattsville, Md.: National Center for Health Statistics.

Wright, R.
1997   *Life and Death in the United States.* Jefferson, N.C.: McFarland Press.

Zopf, P., Jr.
1992   *Mortality Patterns and Trends in the United States.* Westport, Conn.: Greenwood Press.

# 4

# Hispanics in a Multicultural Society: A New American Dilemma?

*Albert M. Camarillo and Frank Bonilla*

As the twenty-first century dawns, and as the U.S. Bureau of the Census (USBC) prepares for another decennial snapshot of demographic change in American society, the population enumeration for the year 2000 is certain to reveal the continuation of dramatic shifts in U.S. ethnic and racial group makeup. The multiethnic and multiracial character of the nation is accelerating at a pace even more rapid than many demographers had projected. The most recent projections from USBC confirm the population increases of American minority groups, in particular that of Hispanics. Indeed, the term "minority," as a useful population classification, will become increasingly outmoded with each passing decade.

Much is being made of the projection that Hispanics will constitute the nation's largest minority population by 2050. High birth rates and continual immigration from Mexico, Central and South America, and the Caribbean are pushing Hispanics' numbers higher than those of Blacks'. But what will it mean for this highly diverse group to become the largest minority in the United States? In the early twenty-first century, will patterns of residential, occupational, educational, and other measures of mobility resemble those of the great waves of immigrants from Europe and their offspring in the early twentieth century? Or will large numbers of Hispanics, midway through the next century, be described as a "new American dilemma," members of the nation's largest ethnic group and economically isolated from mainstream American society? In 1944, in *An American Dilemma: The Negro Problem and Modern Democracy* (1944),

Gunnar Myrdal identified a central tension. In this landmark study, he outlined the moral dilemma between the "American Creed . . . [a value system] . . . where the American thinks, talks, and acts under the influence of high national and Christian precepts"—and the discriminatory treatment of Blacks. Will a new American dilemma characterize growing sectors of the Hispanic and Black populations, cut off from economic opportunity and meaningful participation in the civic life of the nation in the twenty-first century (Bonilla, 1988)?

The status of Hispanics is a mixed bag, with signs of group progress matched by signs of decline and stagnation. Some Hispanics are achieving impressive upward socioeconomic gains, having successfully climbed the ladder of occupational and geographic mobility to better jobs and better homes in safer neighborhoods. Others languish in deepening chasms of poverty and despair, seemingly trapped in urban *barrios* increasingly isolated geographically from opportunities in the larger society. The changing dynamics of U.S. and global economies are altering labor markets in fundamental ways that will have important consequences for Hispanic workers. Will the legions of today's Hispanic youngsters be incorporated fully into the body politic and institutional life of the nation in the next century, or will too many of them remain outside a "gated" American community? Will fears about the "Balkanization" of American society and identity politics result in a "Quebec-type" situation for Hispanics?

## HISTORICAL LEGACIES AND HISPANIC AMERICA

Any starting point for discussion of the contemporary status or future prospects of Hispanics must begin with consideration of critical historical legacies—developments of the past that continue to indelibly stamp the contemporary reality of Hispanic subgroups. Among the many benchmarks that have influenced the course of history for Hispanics in the United States, two stand out as being particularly important—the Mexican-American War in 1848 and the Spanish-American War in 1898. These events set the stage for the incorporation of Spanish-speaking peoples from Mexico, Puerto Rico, and Cuba into the United States, and, at the same time, established economic, political, and international diplomatic relations that later played a great role in the migration and immigration of millions of Spanish-surnamed people to the United States.

The Treaty of Guadalupe Hidalgo, between the United States and Mexico, resulted in the annexation of nearly half of Mexico's territory and the incorporation of a new regional minority—Mexican Americans of the Southwest (Camarillo, 1993; Griswold del Castillo, 1990). During the early twentieth century, growing instability in the Republic of Mexico, and a heavy-handed dictatorship, gave rise to the first modern revolution—a civil war that unleashed the first great wave of Mexican immigrants to venture north to the United States. Throughout the past 100 years, U.S. dependence on workers from south of U.S. borders, coupled with Mexico's economic instability and inability to absorb its expanding work-force, resulted in many millions of Mexican immigrants settling in the United States. With the exception of the Great Depression years, immigration from Mexico was continuous throughout the twentieth century, swelled the ranks of existing Mexican American communities, and spawned the development of newer communities in the Southwest and elsewhere (Gutierrez, 1995).

Although the manner of incorporation into the United States was different for both Puerto Ricans and Cubans, a war—the Spanish-American War—also set in motion forces that later propelled millions of people from those islands to U.S. shores. The United States acquired Puerto Rico from Spain in 1898 and established a colonial relationship with the island. Puerto Ricans were not accorded the status of U.S. citizenship, however, until 1917, just in time to make them eligible for military service in World War I. In 1947, Puerto Rico was accorded commonwealth status, a development that did not appreciably change the status of the island and its people as possessions of the United States. Numerous factors—interdependency, U.S. domination of the island's economy, unemployment, poverty, and lack of opportunity, combined with cheap transportation costs to the United States—resulted in Puerto Ricans migrating to the U.S. mainland; and the movement gained momentum in the decades after World War II. Steady migration streams of Puerto Ricans arrived in mainland cities, especially New York City, where a highly segregated urban experience unfolded (Sánchez-Korrol, 1983).

The Cubans' experience was quite different. A few years after military occupation of the island in 1898, the United States turned over control to the Cubans. Though a small Cuban immigrant community had developed in Florida, especially in Miami, mass migration did not occur until after Castro's socialist revolution in 1959 (Portes and Bach, 1985). Successive migrations followed.

With the exception of the first wave of immigrants from Cuba, the historical legacies of the wars in 1848 and 1898—conquest, racial and class subordination, colonialism, and economic interdependency—created political, economic, and social patterns for Mexicans and Puerto Ricans that persisted into the late twentieth century. As racialized minorities in American society, most Hispanics share a dubious distinction with other U.S. citizens of color. Generalizations of this type, however, must be considered in light of significant differences between each Hispanic subgroup. Because of the enormous diversity within this broadly defined group, any demographic profile of Hispanics must consider the particulars of each nationality.

## CONTEMPORARY TRENDS

### Demographic Profile

The increasing national attention on, and concern about, Hispanics in U.S. society has been driven, in large part, by the spectacular growth of this population, especially since the 1960s. That Hispanics will soon become the nation's largest minority—a demographic shift frequently noted in the media, and one that causes consternation for many Americans—is testimony to the dramatic growth of this diverse group. The expansion of Hispanic America must be considered one of the fundamental demographic trends that is sure to continue in the future. Thus, when one considers projections for the future, the question of whether this group will constitute an essential component of a "new" American dilemma turns basically on the issue of numbers.

Though the specific numbers may be imprecise (because of such factors as census undercounting, different ways used by USBC to identify Hispanics over time, and undocumented immigration), the general patterns are clear. Between 1960 and 1996, the total population of Hispanics soared from about 6.9 million to more than 25.3 million (Table 4-1); and the Hispanic percentage of the total U.S. population more than doubled, increasing from less than 4 percent to 11 percent. There is no end in sight for this population growth. USBC projections estimate a total of 31.4 million Hispanics in 2000, increasing to 95.5 million by 2050. Nearly a quarter

TABLE 4-1  Hispanic Population in the United States 1960 to 1996 with Projections for 2000 to 2050 (millions)

|  | 1960 | 1970 | 1980 | 1996 | 2000 | 2030 | 2050 |
|---|---|---|---|---|---|---|---|
| Total Hispanic population | 6.9 | 9.1 | 14.6 | 25.3 | 31.4 | 65.6 | 95.5 |
| Hispanics as percent of total U.S. population | 3.9 | 4.5 | 6.4 | 10.7 | 11.4 | 18.9 | 24.5 |

SOURCES: Adapted from Bean and Tienda (1987:59, Table 3.1); U.S. Bureau of the Census (1996:12, Table 1); del Pinal and Singer (1997:6, Table 1).

of the entire U.S. population in 2050 is projected to be of Hispanic origin. The driving force of this population expansion is the high fertility rate among Hispanic women (with the exception of Cuban women), but nearly as important is the constant stream of both documented and undocumented immigrants from Latin American nations (especially Mexico) and the ongoing circulation of Puerto Ricans from the island to the mainland (del Pinal and Singer, 1997; Torre, 1992).

Among the different Hispanic subgroups, Mexicans have always constituted the largest contingent. In 1970, the Mexican-origin population comprised about half of the Hispanic people enumerated in the census. The percentage increased to 64 percent by the mid-1990s. Puerto Ricans made up the second largest Hispanic subgroup, between 15 and 11 percent of the total Hispanic population between 1970 and 1996. Cubans have accounted for 4 percent to 6 percent of the Hispanic population since 1970, and Central and South Americans, and a category labeled by USBC as "Other Hispanic" (including immigrants from Spain and people of mixed Hispanic heritage from other countries), constitute sizable proportions of the total Hispanic population (Figure 4-1) (Bean and Tienda, 1987; del Pinal and Singer, 1997).

The historical legacy of regionally concentrated Hispanic subgroups is still plainly visible today (Table 4-2). Mexican-origin people continue to be overwhelmingly concentrated in the five states of the American Southwest, especially California and Texas, whereas most Puerto Ricans are located in New York and other Northeastern states, and Cubans are clustered primarily in Florida. Since the 1970s, Central and South American immigrants have gravitated to particular cities, especially port-of-entry cities, such as New York, Los Angeles, San Francisco, and Miami. Central Americans also form substantial communities in Chicago, Washington, D.C., and New Orleans; and Spanish-speaking Caribbean people are concentrated in New York City and other Atlantic seaboard cities (Ueda, 1994). With few exceptions, all Hispanic subgroups are highly urbanized (more than 80 percent lived in cities in 1980), one of the defining demographic patterns of Hispanic America since before World War II (Bean and Tienda, 1987).

City life for Hispanics since the 1950s has gone hand in hand with residential segregation, both in long-established *barrios* and in newer urban localities. Only since 1960 have scholars attempted to assess the levels of residential isolation of various Hispanic subgroups from Whites, and the picture that has emerged fits somewhere between the extremely high levels of residential segregation experienced by Blacks and the patterns of neighborhood formation and dispersal experienced by many European groups.

The analysis of the spatial characteristics of Hispanics, conducted by

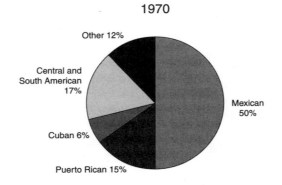

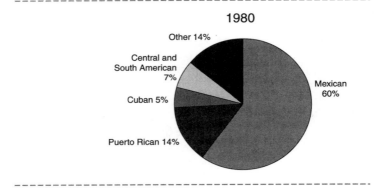

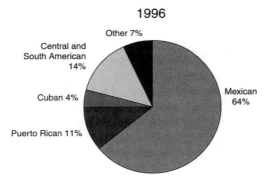

FIGURE 4-1  Hispanic population in the United States, by national origin, 1970 to 1996.  The decrease in the number and percentage of people of Central and South American origin between 1970 and 1980 is likely due to changes in self-reporting for Mexicans made by the U.S. Bureau of the Census during the 1970s.  SOURCE: Adapted from the U.S. Bureau of the Census (1974: 2, 9:Tables 1-1 and 1-3); del Pinal and Singer (1997: 7:Figure 1); Bean and Tienda (1987: 60).

TABLE 4-2 Hispanic Population in Selected States, 1970 to 1990 with Projections to 2020 (millions)

| State | 1970 | | 1980 | | 1990 | | 2020 | |
|---|---|---|---|---|---|---|---|---|
| | n | % of State Population | n | % of State Population | n | % of State Population | n | % of State Population |
| California | 2.0 | 12 | 4.5 | 19 | 7.7 | 26 | 17.5 | 36.5 |
| Texas | 1.8 | 16 | 3.0 | 21 | 4.3 | 25 | 10.3 | 40.3 |
| New York | 1.2 | 7 | 1.7 | 9 | 2.2 | 12 | 3.0 | 15.9 |
| Florida | 0.4 | 6 | 0.6 | 6 | 1.6 | 12 | 4.2 | 21.5 |
| Illinois | 0.5 | 4 | 0.6 | 6 | 0.9 | 8 | 2.1 | 15.7 |
| Arizona | 0.3 | 15 | 0.4 | 16 | 0.7 | 18 | 1.8 | 31.7 |
| New Jersey | 0.3 | 5 | 0.5 | 7 | 0.7 | 10 | 1.5 | 17.0 |
| New Mexico | 0.3 | 30 | 0.5 | 37 | 0.6 | 38 | 1.3 | 55.4 |
| Colorado | 0.2 | 10 | 0.3 | 12 | 0.4 | 13 | 1.0 | 20.0 |

SOURCES: Adapted from Bean and Tienda (1987:77-81); U.S. Bureau of the Census (1996); Horner (1997:12-15, 17-18).

Frank Bean and Marta Tienda (1987), using 1980 Census data, also revealed that substantial variety exists among Hispanics regarding residential segregation. Hispanics concentrated in the largest metropolitan areas—i.e., Los Angeles, New York, and Chicago—had the highest levels of residential segregation from Whites, while only moderate levels of segregation characterized the smaller metropolitan areas in which Hispanics reside. Among the various Hispanic subgroups, Puerto Ricans had much higher levels of residential segregation from Whites—an historical pattern that continues to define the group's urban experiences—than both Mexicans and Cubans. Ongoing immigration has increased levels of residential isolation, especially for Mexicans in the largest metropolitan areas where they reside in great numbers. If this trend continues through the 21st century, we may see sprawling urban *barrios* that look increasingly like the inner-city ghettos inhabited by Blacks.

## Economic, Occupational, and Educational Status

However one chooses to characterize the socioeconomic restructuring of the United States since the mid-1970s, the impact of these changes on Hispanics has been felt most directly through major labor-market shifts. These changes have contributed to increasing the segmentation of Hispanic workers at the lower end of the occupational ladder. General trends of growing inequality and absolute poverty have weighed heavily on substantial Hispanic working sectors, especially Hispanics born outside the United States. A large body of research now tracks the main forces, domestic and transnational, defining the magnitude, composition, and circuits of labor-force movement and the distinctive patterns shaping the incorporation of Hispanics in the regions and principal cities to which they have gravitated.

Because they are the largest and fastest growing sector of the Hispanic population, and because of their particular modes of entry and accommodation within the United States, both U.S.-born and foreign-born Mexicans dramatically illustrate some of the most fundamental changes taking place in the United States. In addition, their large numbers make possible a more refined analysis of the dynamics of these processes and their impacts on youth and women, and on particular occupations and sectors of the economy. Nevertheless, this summary account can only point to general characteristics of the present labor force and its ethnic and racial composition.

Unemployment rates in 1996 for Hispanics, put at 10 percent for both men and women, hovered at double the rates for Whites. Rates for Hispanics had been between those for Whites and Blacks for decades; but the gap between Hispanics and Blacks seemed to be closing, with "Other

Hispanics" apparently adding to the ranks of Hispanic unemployed and pushing the joblessness rates closer to those for Black males. Puerto Ricans and most other Hispanics, except Cubans (whose unemployment rates tended to be closer to those for Whites than for other Hispanics), were all clustered around the 10 percent rate, though other analyses suggest that patterns of labor-market participation and exclusion for the larger subgroups vary considerably. Mexicans generally remain longer in low-wage jobs; Puerto Ricans are more likely to step out of, or lose connection to, low-end job markets; and Cubans, constituting a special case, are moving, in the present generation, toward patterns long shared by other disadvantaged groups.

Occupational patterns from 1996 Census data point to the sustained segmentation of job-market access, with White males about evenly divided between professional, administrative, and sales positions, as opposed to jobs in the service, skilled, and unskilled labor market (Table 4-3). By contrast, two-thirds of Blacks were in service and low-skilled jobs, and almost three-fourths of all Hispanic males held these types of jobs. Slightly more than one-half of Cuban males were also employed in these job categories. Fully four-fifths of Hispanics born outside the United States remain at the bottom of the occupational hierarchy. It is interesting to note, however, that Hispanic women manifest a markedly superior capacity to break through into the professional and managerial sectors, especially the U.S.-born.

Poverty rates and family incomes closely match labor-force participation and placement (Table 4-4). About 25 percent of Black and Hispanic families are estimated to be living below poverty levels, whereas only 6 percent of White families are in that income group. Among Hispanics, 36 percent of Puerto Rican families and 30 percent of those born outside the United States stand out as the most deprived; the rate of poverty for Cubans (16 percent) is closest to the figure for all American families. Cubans and U.S.-born Hispanics, as a group, stand out among Hispanic families with annual incomes of $25,000 or more, an indication of the modest inroads that some have made into the ranks of middle- and higher income classes. Median family income by race and ethnicity since the 1970s reveals that great disparities still characterize annual income levels between Whites and Asians at the higher end and Blacks and Hispanics at the lower end (Figure 4-2). Hispanic and Black family income, relative to that of White families, has decreased since the mid-1970s. Hispanic median family income has actually dropped substantially, in fact; but much of this decrease is attributed to large-scale immigration of people who are relatively unskilled and who do not possess much formal education. In a report prepared by the Council of Economic Advisers (1998a), which President Clinton transmitted to Congress in February 1998, important

TABLE 4-3 Percentages of Unemployed and Employed Persons (16 years and older) and Employment Categories by Race and Ethnicity, 1996

| Race/Ethnic Group | % Unemployed[a] Men | % Unemployed[a] Women | Employed Workers — Men: Professional, Administrative, Sales | Employed Workers — Men: Service, Skilled/ Unskilled Labor | Employed Workers — Women: Professional, Administrative, Sales | Employed Workers — Women: Service, Skilled/ Unskilled Labor |
|---|---|---|---|---|---|---|
| Total | 7 | 5 | 48 | 52 | 72 | 28 |
| Non-Hispanic | 6 | 5 | 50 | 50 | 74 | 26 |
| White | 5 | 4 | 51 | 49 | 76 | 24 |
| Black | 14 | 9 | 34 | 66 | 61 | 39 |
| Other Non-Hispanic[b] | 7 | 5 | 58 | 42 | 67 | 33 |
| Hispanic | 10 | 10 | 27 | 73 | 56 | 44 |
| Mexican | 10 | 10 | 23 | 77 | 55 | 45 |
| Puerto Rican | 10 | 11 | 37 | 63 | 64 | 36 |
| Cuban | 6 | 6 | 44 | 56 | 72 | 28 |
| Central/South American | 8 | 10 | 29 | 71 | 48 | 52 |
| Other Hispanic | 16 | 7 | 45 | 55 | 60 | 40 |
| Born in U.S. | 10 | 9 | 41 | 59 | 72 | 28 |
| Born outside United States[c] | 9 | 11 | 18 | 82 | 40 | 60 |

[a]Persons age 16 or older in the labor force.
[b]Includes Asians, Pacific Islanders, American Indians, Eskimos, Aleuts, and other non-Hispanics.
[c]Includes Puerto Ricans born outside the contiguous states.

SOURCE: del Pinal and Singer (1997:38, Table 8). Reprinted with permission from the Popualation Reference Bureau, Washington, D.C.

TABLE 4-4 Family Income and Poverty Rates, by Race and Ethnicity, 1995

| Race/Ethnic Group | Number of Families (1000s) | Family Income (%) | | | Percent Below Poverty | | |
|---|---|---|---|---|---|---|---|
| | | Under $10,000 | $10,000-24,999 | $25,000 or more | All Families | Female-headed | Elderly[a] |
| Total | 69,597 | 7 | 21 | 72 | 11 | 32 | 6 |
| Non-Hispanic | 63,311 | 7 | 20 | 74 | 9 | 30 | 5 |
| White | 52,861 | 5 | 18 | 77 | 6 | 22 | 4 |
| Black | 7,871 | 19 | 29 | 51 | 26 | 45 | 17 |
| Other Non-Hispanic[b] | 2,579 | 10 | 20 | 70 | 15 | 33 | 10 |
| Hispanic | 6,287 | 16 | 35 | 49 | 27 | 49 | 18 |
| Mexican | 3,815 | 15 | 37 | 47 | 28 | 50 | 18 |
| Puerto Rican | 742 | 26 | 29 | 45 | 36 | 64 | 19 |
| Cuban | 312 | 10 | 28 | 62 | 16 | 29 | 12 |
| Central/South American | 929 | 11 | 35 | 54 | 22 | 35 | 19 |
| Other Hispanic | 489 | 20 | 26 | 54 | 25 | 50 | 20 |
| Born in U.S. | 2,466 | 15 | 29 | 56 | 22 | 47 | 16 |
| Born outside United States[c] | 3,821 | 17 | 38 | 45 | 30 | 51 | 20 |

aHouseholders age 65 or older.

bNon-Hispanic American Indian, Eskimo, Aleuts, Asian, and Pacific Islander.

cIncludes Puerto Rican householders born outside the 50 contiguous states.

Note: Percentages may not add to 100 because of rounding.

SOURCE: del Pinal and Singer (1997:40, Table 9). Reprinted with permission from the Popualation Reference Bureau, Washington, D.C.

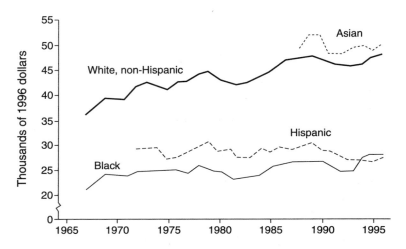

FIGURE 4-2  Median family income by race.  Prior to 1972, data for Whites include Hispanic Whites.  SOURCE:  Council of Economic Advisers (1998b).

explanations were offered regarding the growth of income inequality among ethnic and racial minorities.

> Thirty-four years ago the signing of the Civil Rights Act of 1964 set the Nation on a course toward racial equality. As the economy surged, income differences narrowed for a full decade. The sharp recessions of the mid-1970s and early 1980s hit Black and Hispanic Americans particularly hard, however. And in the expansion of the 1980s, economic growth was accompanied by sharp increases in overall income inequality. As a result, despite the economic growth of this period, income differences between Black and Hispanic families on the one hand, and non-Hispanic White families on the other, did not diminish. The recession of the early 1990s brought further economic hardship, as the poverty rate climbed to a new 30-year high (p. 119).

Educational attainment is, of course, an essential key to job access and improved incomes. Among the many factors that promote success, adequate schooling remains a serious obstacle to Hispanic progress. Hispanics' educational attainment rates are significantly lower than those for both Whites and Blacks, although, again, U.S.-born Hispanics of every national origin have made some gains in the number of years of high school education completed. For example, the median number of years of schooling attained by native born Mexicans (age 25 and over) went from a low of 6.4 years in 1960 to 9.1 years in 1980. For other Hispanic groups, between 1960 and 1980, the median number of school years increased

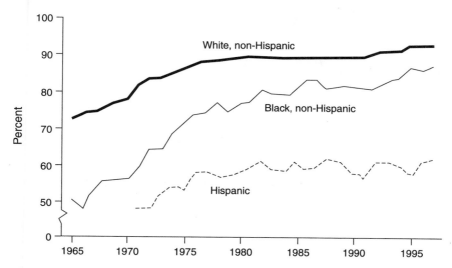

FIGURE 4-3 Persons aged 25 to 29 with a high school degree or equivalent. SOURCE: Council of Economic Advisers (1998b).

from 7.5 to 10.0 years for Puerto Ricans and from 8.0 to 11.7 years for Cuban-Americans. By contrast, the median school years attained by Blacks during these years increased markedly from 8.0 in 1960 to 12.0 years in 1980 (Bean and Tienda, 1987), a figure that matched those of non-Hispanic Whites (11.0 years attained in 1960 and 12.0 years in 1980). Comparing high school completion rates also reveals a similar pattern of educational disadvantage among Hispanics. Figure 4-3 illustrates how the gap between Hispanics, Whites, and Blacks, with regard to high school completion (and equivalency), has actually increased since the 1980s; only about 60 percent of Hispanics completed four years of high school in 1997.

The relatively low rates of high school completion for Hispanics is, to a substantial degree, attributable to the large percentage of immigrants who generally have lower levels of educational attainment. Indeed, the rather dismal educational profile of Hispanics brightens when one compares the rates between U.S. born and foreign born. Figure 4-4 compares the educational attainment rates among the various Hispanic groups by nativity. In 1996, about 70 percent of all U.S.-born Hispanics had completed high school or some higher education level; Cubans and Central and South Americans achieved the highest levels of educational attainment (86 percent and 84 percent, respectively); Mexican-Americans had the lowest rate (67 percent). Across the board, foreign-born Hispanics

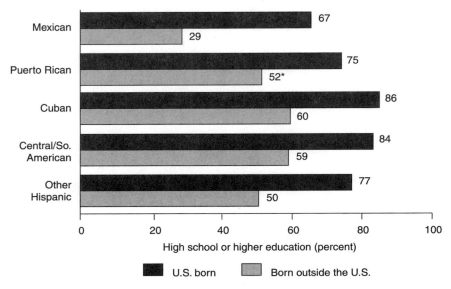

FIGURE 4-4 Educational attainment of Hispanics by national origin and by nativity, 1996. Sample includes persons ages 25 or older. Puerto Ricans born in Puerto Rico or outside the 50 states and the District of Columbia. SOURCE: del Pinal and Singer (1997:p.33, Figure 11). Reprinted with permission from the Population Reference Bureau, Washington, D.C.

were less educated, especially immigrants from Mexico. Although second-generation Hispanics have narrowed the educational gap, compared with Whites and Blacks, large numbers of them are still disadvantaged educationally—a fact that continues to have great influence on individual and group socioeconomic status.

A pattern of under-education for Hispanics is also illustrated when one considers institutions of higher learning. Since the 1960s, the percentage of Americans aged 25 to 29 who completed a four-year college education has steadily increased. The percentage of Hispanic and non-Hispanic Blacks who completed four years of higher education also increased, but at a disproportionately lower rate than that for non-Hispanic Whites. In 1997, about 33 percent of Whites had completed college, compared with about 11 percent for Hispanics and 14 percent for Blacks. As is indicated in Figure 4-5, Hispanics and Blacks continue to fall significantly behind Whites in attaining four or more years of college (Council of Economic Advisors, 1998b), and this higher-education gap actually widened rather than narrowed in the 1990s.

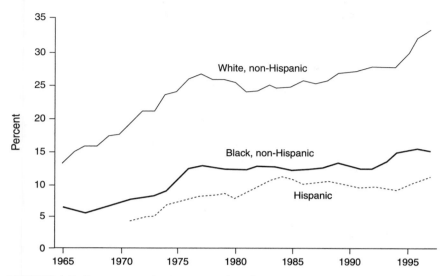

FIGURE 4-5 Persons aged 25 to 29 with a four-year college degree or higher.
SOURCE: Council of Economic Advisers (1998b:22).

The identification of groups by race and ethnicity reported here with respect to jobs, incomes, and formal schooling, though drawn from "official" sources, provides only a broad overview of a volatile and complex process that can elude observation or obscure the actual dynamics shaping outcomes (del Pinal and Singer, 1997). Unemployment rates, for example, generally reported in recent years as close to a "full-employment" standard, omit millions of part-time workers who would like full-time jobs, and millions of additional "discouraged workers" who need jobs but no longer actively pursue opportunities. School drop-out rates similarly reflect a multifaceted dynamic of school readiness among pupils, family conditions, and institutional readiness, especially in public schools confronted with unprecedented levels of ethnic and racial diversity.

## Political Participation and Group Identity

Looking back to the 1950s, at the participation of Hispanics in American political institutions at the local, state, or national levels, one cannot help but be impressed by gains that have occurred. Fifty years ago, with the exception of New Mexico, the number of Hispanic elected officials at the state or federal level could be counted on one hand. Though Hispanics were able to help elect a few of their own kind to local public offices, for the most part discriminatory practices such as poll taxes, gerrymandering, and English language-literacy provisions excluded Hispanics from the political process. These historical legacies, when combined with high poverty and low naturalization rates, effectively disenfranchised huge numbers of Hispanics.

By the 1970s and 1980s, however, more and more political commentators and prospective candidates—including those attached to the national political parties—began to take notice of the growing Hispanic influence. Significantly, the Voting Rights Act of 1965, intended to help unlock the ballot box for Blacks, also helped to make the political process more open to Hispanics (Moore and Pachon, 1985). Characterizations of a "sleeping brown giant" beginning to show political awakening in the late 1960s and 1970s were reinforced by signs that, indeed, Hispanics were emerging as a political force to be reckoned with in the 1980s, the so-called "Decade of the Hispanic."

Clearly, Hispanics have come a long way in the past generation with regard to flexing their growing political muscle. Hispanic elected officials at all levels now number more than 5,000; and there are hundreds of Spanish-surnamed persons who have been elected to state and federal positions. But although these gains are impressive, Hispanics are still grossly underrepresented, based on their percentage of the U.S. population (DeSipio, 1996). Greater political participation of Hispanics in electoral politics may take a long time, and may be difficult to achieve. One must raise the question of whether Hispanics will follow the political paths of other ethnic and racial minorities—Eastern and Southern European immigrants and their children in the earlier decades of the twentieth century and Blacks since the Civil Rights era—toward ever-increasing inclusion in the American political system.

Some political pundits and politicians point to the low voter registration and voting rates of Hispanics as indications of less interest in things political. In the 1992 and 1994 elections, Hispanic voter turnout ranged between 20 percent and 28 percent of registered voters, whereas the rate for Whites hovered around 64 to 65 percent, and that for Blacks ranged from 37 to 54 percent (DeSipio, 1996; del Pinal and Singer, 1997). In rebuttal, Hispanic advocacy organizations and ethnic political leaders argue that ongoing voter registration and education drives will result in more and more Hispanics who will exercise the franchise, ensuring greater and greater Hispanic political influence at all levels of government, especially at the local levels where they are currently more concentrated (Hero, 1992).

Several factors will help determine the eventual outcome of Hispanics as a powerful political force in the United States. First, it is commonly understood that low socioeconomic and educational status have a huge bearing on political participation rates; on this count, Hispanics have a long way to go. This factor is particularly important for the Mexican-American and Puerto Rican populations, which are disproportionately represented among the ranks of the poorer working classes and who continue to have lower rates of higher education attainment. Second, the Hispanic population is one of the youngest in the nation; one-third of all Hispanics are younger than 18 years old, and more than one-fifth of all Hispanics of voting age are between the ages of 18 and 24. It is a fact that younger voters simply do not participate as actively in the political process as older voters. Third, immigrants and their children comprise about two-thirds of all Hispanics; and naturalization rates among them, especially among Mexican immigrants, is one of the lowest of any group in U.S. history. In 1996, for example, more than 40 percent of Hispanics older than age 18 were not naturalized citizens of the United States and, therefore, were ineligible to register to vote (del Pinal and Singer, 1997; Young, 1991). Finally, Hispanics do not constitute an ethnic voting bloc; they are composed of diverse constituencies with different political attitudes and are unlikely to combine their political power in the near future.

Scholars who analyzed data from the Latino National Political Survey of 1990 concluded that the various Hispanic subgroups do not view themselves in common. There are, however, issues of importance—such as increased government action to support education, especially bilingual education, to fight crime, and to provide child care services—that cut across national-origin group interests. It would, nevertheless, be misleading to describe an "Hispanic partisanship," because the political differences between Mexicans, Puerto Ricans, and Cubans are too great to lend themselves to a vision of a united Hispanic electorate (de la Garza et al., 1992). In some specific locales, however, historical circumstances have converged, bringing together different Hispanic subgroups for concerted political action. Chicago is a case in point (Padilla, 1985).

To no one's surprise, the Latino National Political Survey also revealed that Hispanics overwhelmingly prefer to use national-origin terms as primary ethnic identifiers—i.e., Mexican, Puerto Rican, Cuban, etc.—although U.S.-born Hispanics use these terms less than the foreign born, as one would expect (de la Garza et al., 1992). The pan-ethnic labels, Hispanic or Latino, are used as secondary terms of identification; and here, again, the U.S. born are more likely to use the pan-ethnic terms than the foreign born. Among those who use the pan-ethnic labels, a 1996 USBC survey found, a majority—58 percent—use the term Hispanic rather than Latino, the term used by only 12 percent (Pinal and Singer, 1997).

Ethnic or national-origin identity for Hispanics raises some interesting questions about race and ethnicity in America, not only about how the different subgroups view themselves, but also how the larger society views Hispanics. The U.S. government classifies Hispanics as an ethnic group; yet, Hispanics can be of any race (most classify as White, a minority as Black, and a growing percentage as "Other"). In the minds of the majority population, and in the minds of many Hispanics, there is ambiguity about racial or ethnic categories—an ambiguity that has indeed characterized Americans' preoccupation with skin color, national origin, and other sociocultural/religious differences that have separated Americans from other Americans for hundreds of years. This ambiguity is aptly reflected in the many confusing ways USBC has categorized Hispanics over the past century. For example, with the exception of the 1930 Census, when Mexicans were classified as a separate "race," Hispanics have been identified by foreign parentage, birthplace, "Spanish mother tongue," "Spanish surname," "Spanish origin," and, beginning in 1980, Spanish/Hispanic origin (Bean and Tienda, 1987). Given the diverse makeup of the nation's Hispanic populations—in terms of immigrant cohorts, national origins, cultural roots, distinct local and regional concentrations, and socioeconomic status—it is clear that any attempt to categorize them as a distinct, homogeneous group is counterproductive. Consequently, the catch-all term "Hispanic," as the preferred label of the federal government, includes the foreign born with the native born of many generations in the United States, political refugees, undocumented and legal immigrants, and people from many national origins. Yes, they derive from common Spanish-language origins and Roman Catholic religious traditions, and can trace their heritage to Spain's colonial legacies in the New World, but Hispanics in the United States at the dawn of the twenty-first century defy generalizations as a single group. The diversity that distinguishes Hispanics will surely continue to be one of the main characteristics of the group, a diversity that exists not only across but within each national-origin group.

## PROBLEMS AND PROSPECTS

It may seem ironic to many that one of the thorniest intellectual and social-policy challenges presented by the surging number of Hispanics on the U.S. mainland today is identifying and counting them. The problem is far from new but is now at the center of heated controversy with respect to the 2000 Census and the related prescriptions for federal data-keeping mandated by the Office of Management and Budget ( 1997). There has been a growing furor about where and how the color line will be drawn in the twenty-first century, which has clearly displaced the complacency on this issue reflected in a 1983 report to the U.S. Department of Health and Human Services. That report (Davis et al., 1983) stated:

> Prior to the 1970 census, the concept of Hispanics as a group barely existed. Information on some components of the population, such as

Mexicans, could be obtained from the usual census questions on a person's country of birth or that of parents, use of a language other than English at home, and ancestry. . . . But none of the identifiers used prior to 1970 could satisfy the need for a definition which could be applied nationwide and with reasonable consistency over time (p. 5).

Beyond the problem of accuracy in population counts, until recently seen as safely anchored in mutually exclusive racial categories and thorough enumeration, lies a dawning awareness of the multiracial character of Hispanic peoples and the potential significance of the growing pace of interethnic and interracial marriages, which adds yet more ambiguity to existing racial classifications. In fact the catalytic power of Hispanics in stimulating racial mixing in the rigidly divided United States of the 1940s was noted at the time by Myrdal (1944) in his study of more than 400 industrial plants. He noted:

> The most frequently encountered policy was one based on the belief that 'Negro and White workers will not mix.' They did "mix", however, in over 50 of the plants studied. In certain plants where Mexicans were regarded as White, Negroes were not allowed to "mix" with them; where Mexicans were classed as colored, Negroes not only worked with them but were given positions over them. In certain plants Mexicans and Whites worked together; in some others White workers accepted Mexicans and objected to Japanese. Mexicans and Negroes worked under a White foreman; Italians and Mexicans under a Negro foreman (p. 393).

It is worth noting that at about that same time, Puerto Ricans in New York were configured together with Blacks in the first "minority/majority" senatorial district for the state legislature in what are today parts of Harlem and "el barrio." A 1935 pamphlet (The Tragedy of the Puerto Ricans and Colored Americans) delineated the obstacles in that setting to effective transracial/ethnic coalition-building in terms that have considerable resonance today (Martinez, 1935). Clearly, efforts to link the resources and capabilities of Hispanics with other marginalized communities to contest subordination are hardly new; there is, however, much to be done to pin down key elements of the present conjuncture in this regard as well as to critically revisit key historical experiences.

As discussed regarding Hispanics' demographic profile, despite the acknowledged constraints on the range and precision of public data gathering on Hispanics since the 1960s, a fairly consensual depiction of the dramatic shifts in the size, composition, location, and basic conditions of that population has been assembled by both official bodies and independent scholars, much of it by Hispanics themselves. On this front, public discourse on these questions has been decisively transformed. Still, in recent years, USBC's insistence on the qualifying proviso in every tabulation that "Hispanics may be of any race" has hammered home the idea of

Hispanic communities as multiracial social formations, without seriously addressing the challenges and enigmas for research methods.

Present quandaries, and the need for pertinent inquiry, thus cluster on both of these fronts. The decision to combine data on ethnicity with race, and perhaps to allow more than one self-designation in both categories, generates complexities in the collection and manipulation of these identifiers as well as their linkages to other variables. The alternatives in data collection now under discussion all confront difficulties, especially when coupled with the added dimension of adjustments being considered to remedy a troubling growth in census undercounts that disproportionately affect minorities. Expert opinions range from those who consider any such assignations unnecessary, and, perhaps, absurd and wasteful, to others bent on fully charting the rich mosaic of U.S. society, even if it means radically enlarging the number of racial categories and allowing multiple options per respondent. Some of the latter voices are, of course, psychometricians and geneticists determined to track "race" links to "capacities" and behaviors, though the task of unraveling these from developmental and environmental conditions, and deciding which genes are at work in any instance, may be effectively moot in present circumstances. At least one member of the citizens' board advising USBC insisted that with 95 percent of Americans still checking only one race, the essential racial order remains firmly in place and all the brouhaha is pointless (Holmes, 1998).

Significant population growth is sure to increase the role of Hispanics in the American political system; and more-or-less "official" readings of the most recent data confirm protracted demographic growth, continued diversification, and potential assimilation (notably via intermarriage with non-Hispanic Whites). Recent economic slippage for most Hispanics and barriers to increased political participation likely reflect the limiting constraints of newness to the society, noncitizenship, language barriers, education lags, and class factors, rather than racial discrimination. Hispanic newcomers are said to bring positive work, gender, family, and community values (social capital) into the troubled milieus to which they gravitate. Thus, whatever the evolving dynamics in the immediate future, Hispanics are expected to play an important role in transforming the United States. Ensuring their well-being is manifestly in the national interest (Davis et al., 1983).

But the emergence of Hispanics as strategic actors in major processes of social change within the United States has even more far-reaching implications. In the context of expanding transnational interdependence and international migration, Hispanic communities in the United States are integral to the economic and political restructurings that are redefining identities, citizenship, democracy, and human rights. As millions of individuals are obliged to maintain viable lives simultaneously in more than one society, and as formal legal structures to accommodate these realities—e.g., dual citizenship—begin to be brought into place, every arena of policy formulation and implementation is impacted. It is into this essentially uncharted terrain that Hispanics are now called on to play an important role (Bonilla et al., 1998).

## CONTEMPORARY POLICIES, ISSUES, AND CHALLENGES

### The Problem of Inequality and Exclusion

Since the 1960s, a number of key public policies have helped to open doors of opportunity for Hispanics and other minorities who were historically cut off from avenues of educational, occupational, and political mobility. Affirmative action-oriented admissions policies and new financial-aid opportunities facilitated access to institutions of higher learning that had been out of reach of the great majority of Hispanics. In addition, employment policies that provided protections against discriminatory practices in the workplace (e.g., those overseen by the Equal Employment Opportunity Commission) and policies that promoted the growth of minority-owned businesses (e.g., those overseen by the Office of Federal Contract Compliance Programs) helped to establish a beachhead for economic progress in Hispanic communities.

Similarly, fair-housing statutes, voting-rights laws, and bilingual-education programs were efforts orchestrated by the federal government to combat discrimination as well as attempts to create new paths for individual and group advancement. These laws and policies, and others, were important for three principal reasons. (1) They acknowledged the contemporary effects of historical discrimination that were embedded in the institutions of society. (2) They represented proactive federal-government intervention and allocation of resources required to turn American society in a direction where all citizens of the nation—regardless of race, ethnicity, national origin, sex, age, or disabilities—could have a fair chance to pursue opportunities as far as their individual capabilities would permit. (3) These policies contributed to the burgeoning Hispanic middle class and served as proof that new policies made a difference in the life chances of hundreds of thousands of Mexican-Americans, Puerto Ricans, and other Hispanic Americans.

Just as important, many of the policies of the past generation were evidence that the American "creed of opportunity"—sewn into the fabric of democratic society and culture—though narrowly conceived originally, could expand and change over time. During the course of U.S. history, citizens have sacrificed and struggled to reconceive this creed so that women, racial and ethnic minorities, disabled people, the poor, and others historically outside the gates of opportunity could enter. For those Americans who, over many generations, were denied opportunity, the legacies of exclusion and inequality are still painfully visible at the dawn of the twenty-first century. For many Hispanics and other minorities, history weighs heavily on their contemporary reality. To be sure, socioeconomic and educational group progress was achieved in the last quarter of the 1900s, in ways unimaginable to previous generations of Hispanics; but the modest gains made must be sustained and accelerated if members of the nation's soon-to-be largest ethnic group have a chance to become full shareholders in American society.

The current public-policy discourse and acerbic debates about programs such as affirmative action in employment and education (admission to colleges and universities), bilingualism and educational reform (English-only state laws, bilingual education curricula, and voucher programs), immigration (services to documented and undocumented immigrants), and welfare reform (consequences for the poor as a result of the welfare reform policies of 1996) tend to exacerbate the racial and ethnic divides in society. A more productive policy discourse about these and other existing policies—most of which were developed by lawmakers to promote opportunity—should center on a fundamental question critical to the well-being of all Americans: As U.S. and global economies move toward ever-increasing interdependence, and as the nature of the American economic system shifts in the postindustrial era, which existing policies should be amended and which new policies should be envisioned that will sustain and improve opportunities for all Americans?

Any consideration of future public policies that does not take into account the human and economic costs of large sectors of society who are undereducated, underemployed, impoverished, and in ill health will surely undermine the foundations of American civilization. If the demographic projections are correct, and if the disturbing trends that characterize so many Hispanics today continue into the mid-twenty-first century, when Hispanics will constitute a quarter of the entire population, it may well be impossible to change the course of history for such a huge sector of the citizenry. For the well-being of American society in general, improving the life chances and opportunities for disadvantaged Hispanics and other poor Americans may indeed be one of the challenges that will determine the course of American democracy in the present century.

## Hispanics in the Postindustrial Order

The Hispanic condition, as we look ahead, reflects, in stark ways, an overarching contraposition of social promise and denial in the contemporary relations of nation-state and market, both within the most advanced postindustrial U.S. setting and in the countries of origin of Hispanic peoples. As a major living link in the playing out of economic restructuring in the hemisphere, Hispanics confront massive shortfalls in the capacity of market and state to provide employment at a living wage or adequate social infrastructures for all. As the global rush to embrace free markets surges ahead, along with the ascendancy of the need to privilege capital and its freedom of movement, two key questions emerge: (1) When and how will some new forms of state control or legal norms be brought into place in response to the deepening social crises generated by the untrammeled movement of transnational capital? (2) What voice can workers, themselves trying to balance attachments to multiple national and cultural identities, have in shaping whatever social pact will undergird the emergent transnational global order, and protect their rights to work and decent living standards (Morales and Bonilla, 1993)?

Having become an overwhelmingly urban population, Hispanics now also stand at the epicenter of social transformations that dramatize the social pathologies of big-city decline. For these communities, the bad news continues. Inner-city Hispanics are now reported to be the most discriminated-against group in housing markets across the country. Their neighborhoods are awash with environmental perils, just as their workplaces are exposed to the severest job hazards (Yinger, 1995; Goldman, 1991). Yet, we begin to hear, as well, that newness to the society and social isolation may temporarily shield some Hispanics, especially those freshly arrived, from the perverse effects of urban poverty. For example, despite more modest human-capital endowments, Mexican immigrants are perceived by some employers as more willing and disciplined low-wage workers than Blacks. New immigrants have been hailed not only for their willingness to fill the demand for low-wage service workers, but also for their entrepreneurial energies in the informal economy and small enterprise. Thus, recent immigrants, in contrast to long-time resident Blacks and Puerto Ricans, are now credited with producing for New York City a "low cost equivalent of gentrification" (Sassen, 1991).

## Cultural Citizenship

Historically, both indigenous groups and immigrant populations, including Hispanics, were expected to shed their cultural and ethnic baggage and conform to Anglo-Saxon norms as a condition for inclusion into mainstream American society. A host of social, institutional, political, and cultural forces together weighed heavily on efforts by groups to maintain some semblance of their ethnic or cultural identity. Indeed, society's expectation for assimilation was pervasive for any group identified as culturally or ethnically different. For many groups, this expectation was internalized, thus hastening the processes of assimilation and acculturation. But despite the so-called "Anglo conformity" or "one-way" model of group assimilation, certain racial and immigrant minorities remained outside the gates of the American community. This has been the experience for large numbers of Hispanics.

In the second half of the twentieth century, recognition that many groups had maintained distinctive elements of their ethnic and cultural heritage, and others had insisted on preserving the integrity of their social and cultural differences, gave rise to ideas about the United States as an ethnically diverse democracy that did not have to force assimilation on all its citizens. These ideas are best reflected in the pluralism and multiculturalism models of group relations in a diverse society. In contrast to the dominant paradigm of assimilation, these two approaches help explain how different groups are able to maintain their cultural distinctiveness and how society benefits from an understanding and appreciation of the many cultures that constitute the larger society. Though pluralistic and multicultural models promote cultural democracy in the United States and encourage celebration of contributions to society from many different groups, neither explains satisfactorily how groups can change society—its social, cultural, and political norms.

The idea of "cultural citizenship" has been developed by a team of Hispanic scholars (Flores and Benmayor, 1997) exploring ways to understand how Hispanics and other groups not only make cultural contributions to a plural society, but also alter society. By the sheer size of the Hispanic population and the myriad ways they are influencing society, this idea of cultural citizenship provides some valuable insights into how Hispanics, now and in the future, are bound up in dynamic interaction in American society, a dialectical process in which both the group and the society at large are constantly changing one another. "In our opinion," the authors state, "what makes cultural citizenship so exciting is that it offers us an alternative perspective to better comprehend cultural processes that result in community building and in political claims raised by marginalized groups in the broader society" (Flores and Benmayor, 1997:15). Using the idea of citizenship as a concept that extends universal rights to members of a society, cultural citizenship broadens the concept to include groups historically positioned, in the legal sense, as "second class" or "noncitizens." This concept helps account for how these and other groups build communities and develop identities, how they lay claim to cultural "spaces," and how they claim rights in society. These spaces and claims have the potential not only to reform society—e.g., the Civil Rights era reforms and reaffirmation of Black identity—but also to elevate various subcultures to a level where no one culture dominates. Thus, the idea of cultural citizenship, by logical extension, may form the basis on which Americans see themselves not in contentious ways, but as cultural citizens of a nation with connected and interdependent cultural communities that constitute the whole.

As the Hispanic population continues to grow, and thus leaves American society with no "majority" population, the idea of cultural citizenship in a heterogeneous society may serve as a useful way to envision society and cultural change as a key component of American democracy in the twenty-first century.

## Country of Origin Linkages

To complicate matters, the growing importance given to Hispanics in the United States by governments in their countries of origin has not escaped worried observers. In 1987, for example, the Mexican government established an outreach program for its citizens, and their offspring, in the United States. Components of this program proliferated and took on new dimensions as the North American Free Trade Agreement between the United States, Mexico, and Canada took shape. Components now include several newspapers geared to community interests; sponsorship of cultural and sports events and organizations; academic exchanges; networking among labor, feminist, environmental, and religious entities; and so on. In 1997, the Mexican legislature, with unanimous support from all major parties, legalized dual citizenship, permitting immigrants who chose to become naturalized U.S. citizens to also retain their full rights as Mexican citizens. Parallel developments, especially with respect to absentee voting in presidential elections, are being pursued by numerous other countries—e.g., Peru, Colombia, the Dominican Republic, and some Central American nations. In every instance, a major consideration stimulating this outreach to the millions in the diaspora is, of course, the millions in dollars and other remittances channeled homeward by immigrant communities.

In the late 1980s, Puerto Rico's Commonwealth government similarly moved to establish a cabinet-level Department of Community Affairs for Puerto Ricans in the United States. This agency soon mounted major voter mobilization campaigns in several states, thus raising major questions about "cross-state" political interference—i.e., using public monies from one state for political action in another. The repeated calls for binding referendums on the island's political status also highlight concerns about the rights of Puerto Rican mainland dwellers to a formal voice in such crucial matters. The intensifying debate about the island's status brings sharply into focus the fluidity and paradoxes of the waning powers of nation-states, of whatever order, to sustain the economic and social rights of their citizens within the emergent hemispheric and global context.

An official "dialogue" between the Cuban government and its nationals in exile in the United States was also mounted in 1987, and consultations involving the United States and other governments and international bodies along with Cuban-American organizations continue apace. Even the Spanish government has forthrightly declared its interest in U.S. "Hispanics" as a function of their "increasing political, social, and economic weight" (Cortina and Moncada, 1988). In brief, new kinds of transnational political relations are being pieced together, strengthened by the historic, existential ties of family, locality, culture, and other networks that have maintained immigrants' connections to their countries of origin over generations. Parallel efforts by federal agencies to engage Hispanic interests and political energies in support of U.S. foreign policy objectives further enhance the opportunities for Hispanic communities to assert independent perspectives in this terrain, rather than passively bowing to home-country or U.S. objectives.

## Coalition Building

The record of misfires, divisive contention, and deliberate interventions by established power wielders to disrupt coalitions of Hispanics, especially with Blacks, goes back a long way. Mainstream apprehensions in this connection have peaked recently as part of the broad backlash against "big" government and social spending. Lance Liebman, a Harvard law professor, put the matter as succinctly and coldly as anyone in the early 1980s (Liebman, 1982):

> . . . we should hope for a Supreme Court wise enough and ingenious enough to uphold legislative decisions that assist Blacks but refuse to uphold, because the justifications are weaker and the costs to the social fabric so great, extensions of those arrangements to other groups (p. 173).

"Other groups" here means, of course, chiefly Hispanics and especially new arrivals among them, whatever their immigrant status. As a matter of fact, despite these intimations of hardening resistance to any moves to unify racial and ethnic interests, the 1990s opened on a very positive note in this connection with a major conference at the Lyndon B. Johnson School of Public Affairs (University of Texas at Austin), bringing together notables from local communities and from outside the communities—politicians, academics, policy analysts, and community organizers. Present at the forum, launched by the Inter-University Program for Latino Research (IUPLR) and the Joint Center for Policy Studies, were such figures as David Dinkins, Barbara Jordan, Henry Cisneros, Nicholas Katzenbach, and Robert Reischauer. A landmark volume, *Hispanics and Blacks in the Cities: Policies for the 1990s* (Romo, 1990) provided a solid grounding for continued initiatives that are stretching into the present.

Taking stock of progress during the 1990s, there was the positioning of a critical mass of information, organizational capacity, and leadership resources backing minority coalitions that nevertheless confront serious reversals, determined opposition, shallow supports, and systemic challenges (Betancurt and Gills, 2000). For example, what early in the 1990s appeared as major electoral breakthroughs for Blacks and Hispanics in major cities—New York, Chicago, Los Angeles, San Francisco—soon gave way to conservative counterattacks and a crumbling disarray under the pressures of deepening inequality and poverty, budget deficits, and waning federal social infrastructure supports. Locally, there was contention at municipal and state levels over minimal resources. Competition for jobs, especially in the public sector, also surfaced as a divisive issue. Growing political apathy and withdrawal from partisan and electoral activity have also put a chill on efforts to mobilize coalitions within and across ethnic and racial lines. Still, newly articulated visions of comprehensive social development, with enhanced democratic participation and recognition of the social value of diversity, continue to propel scattered initiatives and "model" programs around the country (Hartman, 1997; Pacific Coast Council on International Policy, 1998). Many of these must manage to overcome entrenched obstacles to effective action—individualism, elitism, and the challenges to giving a genuine voice in decisions to marginalized participants. An encouraging development is the increasing recognition and practical implementation of transnational perspectives and organizational strategies in many of these undertakings (Brecher and Castello, 1994).

## Responses to Public-Policy Initiatives

Shared empowerment pursued through coalition-building may remain elusive. Nevertheless, a critical advantage is gained through intensified communication and collaboration across groups, however limited. The amplification of horizons and synergizing impact of the give and take about policy perspectives on common issues enhances and strengthens communication and mutual empowerment. In this connection, IUPLR, mentioned earlier, has been a driving force among Hispanic academics and has fostered collaboration for scholarly research, policy formulation, and community mobilization around matters crucial to all disadvantaged Hispanics and the nation at large. The more pertinent point is the virtual explosion of parallel endeavors validating and implementing, in new venues, IUPLR's approach to overcoming the barriers between the academic world, public-policy arenas, and communities in need. Numerous such entities come to mind; one in particular, the National Jobs for All Coalition (NJFAC), can serve as exemplar here.

NJFAC, in operation since the mid-1990s, joined forces with an IUPLR working group on "Hispanics in a Changing U.S. Economy" to create a model advocacy forum in New York City to prepare a diverse group of Hispanic and other agencies to have a voice in municipal and state policies bearing on jobs and welfare rights. The nature of their contribution is well conveyed in their statement of task (Hernandez and Torres-Saillant, 1998):

> We will develop and disseminate economic and political analyses in formats appropriate for reaching the target audiences. These include new issues of our "Uncommon Sense" publications, written by experts on specific dimensions of the employment-unemployment area. The coalition has published more than 20 in this series; they are used by a wide range of organizations. The Coalition will also develop materials suitable for dissemination on the web, and in the form of video cassettes appropriate to school, university, and general audiences. We will expand our speakers' bureau for talks and appearances in universities and schools, on public forums, radio and television interviews and commentary, community and religious groups and other appropriate occasions (pp. 20-21).

NJFAC has a score of distinguished individuals on its executive committee and nearly 80 specialists, advocates, and important organizations on its national advisory board. Thus, as Hispanics move into the policy arena, they will have opportunities to draw on exceptional resources in bringing informed and responsible perspectives into this discourse. Parallel groups exist or are being formed to address many other issue areas—immigration, language, education, health, environmental conditions, youth, the roles and needs of women, community revitalization, and so on. The full inclusion of well-articulated minority perspectives and voices continues to be an aspiration rather than an accomplished fact; but the stage is set for a transformation of the coordination of research, explorations of policy alternatives, and community-driven political initiatives in which Hispanics may make creative contributions.

## CONCLUSION

In many ways, Hispanics at the beginning of the twenty-first century stand at a crossroads in American society. On one level of analysis—especially if one examines the growing ranks of the emergent middle class—Hispanic families seem to be doing just fine. They have, in ever-increasing numbers, accessed opportunities in education and employment and have carved out a niche of American prosperity for themselves and their children. They tend to live in integrated neighborhoods and appear in so many ways to have achieved the "American dream," if one measures that aspiration by a standard of material possessions and economic stability. To the casual observer, tens of thousands of second- and third-generation Mexican Americans (predominantly a people with immigrant roots in the twentieth century) as well as Puerto Ricans and Cubans (who have lived on the mainland for dozens of years) seem to be following a stair-step rise in status, as each successive wave of migrants and immigrants settles in the United States.

If one looks deeper and more critically, however, at the diverse Hispanic population, there is cause for real concern—in some cases, cause for alarm. Below the thin ranks of the Hispanic middle class lies a much larger group. They are not thriving. They are increasingly falling into the new categories of the "working poor" or, worse, are seemingly trapped as a class of severely impoverished people living in urban *barrios*. They are the Hispanic underclass. Given the current size of the Hispanic population, the great diversity that characterizes the group, and the sustained projected growth, Hispanics themselves and the society and its institutions must search for explanations for why some are faring well and others are faring so poorly. It is this latter group of Hispanics, particularly the great numbers of young people, who stand at a crossroads in American society. If the path can lead to educational achievement that ends with good jobs that pay a decent wage and provide hope, Hispanics in the twenty-first century will be productive citizens who will contribute in significant ways to society. But if these disturbing trends persist or increase, the potential for a "new" American dilemma seems frighteningly real.

The challenge is for Hispanics to muster a unified response, drawing on all their resources and capabilities, and become an integral part of the movement to uncover the complex forces intensifying inequality, poverty, political passivity, exploitation, and social isolation, not only within their own ranks but in the United States as a whole. This means reaching out and grasping every opportunity to share in the scholarly debate, policy assessment, and organized movement to restore priority to human rights objectives, despite the limitations under which all such initiatives now operate. These limitations, and their accompanying enigmas, have thrown disciplines, institutions, and even social philosophy into disarray. We must remember that the societal transformations affecting the dynamics of race, ethnicity, class, and gender demand patience and commitment and unconditional resistance to any tendencies toward withdrawal or self-isolation.

# REFERENCES

Bean, F., and M. Tienda
    1987    The Hispanic Population of the United States. New York: Russell Sage Foundation.
Betancurt, J., and D. Gills
    2000    The Collaborative City: Opportunities and Challenges for Blacks and Latinos. New York:
            Garland Publishing.
Bonilla, F.
    1988    From Racial Justice to Economic Rights: The New American Dilemma. Washington,
            D.C.: Smithsonian Institution.
Bonilla, F., E. Melendez, R. Morales, and M. de los Angeles Torres
    1998    Borderless Borders: U.S. Latinos, Latin Americans, and the Paradox of Interdependence.
            Philadelphia: Temple University Press.
Brecher, J., and T. Castello
    1994    Global Village or Global Pillage: Economic Reconstruction from the Bottom Up. Boston:
            South End Press.
Camarillo, A.
    1993    Latin Americans. In Encyclopedia of American Social History, Vol. 1, M. Kupiec
            Cayton, E. Gorn, and P. Williams, eds. New York: Charles Scribner's Sons.
Cortina, R., and A. Moncada
    1988    Hispanos en los Estados Unidos. Madrid: Ediciones de la Cultura Hispanica.
Council of Economic Advisers
    1998a   Economic Report of the President. Washington, D.C.: U.S. Government Printing Of-
            fice.
    1998b   Changing America: Indicators of Social and Economic Well-Being by Race and Hispanic
            Origin. Washington, D.C.: U.S. Government Printing Office.
Davis, C., C. Haub, and J. Willette
    1983    U.S. Hispanics: Changing the face of America. Population Bulletin (38)3. Washing-
            ton, D.C.: Population Reference Bureau.
de la Garza, R., L. DeSipio, F. Garcia, J. Garcia, and A. Falcon
    1992    Latino Voices: Mexican, Puerto Rican and Cuban Perspectives on American Politics.
            Boulder, Colo.: Westview Press.
del Pinal, J., and A. Singer
    1997    Generations of diversity: Latinos in the United States. Population Bulletin (52):3.
            Washington, D.C.:  Population Reference Bureau.
DeSipio, L.
    1996    Counting on the Latino Vote: Latinos as a New Electorate. Charlottesville, Va.: Uni-
            versity of Virginia Press.
Flores, W., and R. Benmayor, eds.
    1997    Latino Cultural Citizenship: Claiming Identity, Space, and Rights. Boston: Beacon
            Press.
Goldman, B.
    1991    The Truth About Where You Live. New York: Random House.
Griswold del Castillo, R.
    1990    The Treaty of Guadalupe Hidalgo: A Legacy of Conflict. Norman: University of Okla-
            homa Press.
Gutiérrez, D.
    1995    Walls and Mirrors: Mexican Americans, Mexican Immigrants, and the Politics of
            Ethnicity. Berkeley: University of California Press.
Hartman, C., ed.
    1997    Double Exposure: Poverty and Race in America. Armonk, N.Y.: M.E. Sharpe.

Hernandez, R., and S. Torres-Saillant
    1998    An advocacy forum for Latino empowerment. Unpublished paper. New York: City College of New York, CUNY Dominican Studies Institute.
Hero, R.
    1992    *Latinos and the U.S. Political System: Two-Tiered Pluralism.* Philadelphia: Temple University Press.
Holmes, S.
    1998    U.S. officials are struggling to measure multiracial marriages. *New York Times* June 13.
Horner, L., ed.
    1997    *Hispanic Americans: A Statistical Sourcebook.* Palo Alto, Calif.: Information Publications.
Liebman, L., ed.
    1982    *Ethnic Relations in America.* Englewood Cliffs, N.J.: Prentice-Hall.
Martinez, F.
    1935    The Tragedy of the Puerto Ricans and the Colored Americans. New York: n.p.
Moore, J., and H. Pachon
    1985    *Hispanics in the United States.* Englewood Cliffs, N.J.: Prentice-Hall.
Morales, R., and F. Bonilla
    1993    *Latinos in a Changing U.S. Economy: Comparative Perspectives on Growing Inequality.* Newbury Park, Calif.: Sage Publications.
Myrdal, G.
    1944    *An American Dilemma: The Negro Problem and Modern Democracy*, Vol. 1. New York: Harper and Row.
Office of Management and Budget
    1997    Revisions to the standards for the classification of federal data on race and ethnicity, Part II. *Federal Register* (62):210.
Pacific Coast Council on International Policy
    1998    *Advancing the International Interests of African-Americans, Asian-Americans and Latinos.* Los Angeles: Pacific Coast Council.
Padilla, F.
    1985    *Latino Ethnic Consciousness: The Case of Mexican Americans and Puerto Ricans in Chicago.* Notre Dame: University of Notre Dame Press.
Portes, A., and R. Bach
    1985    *Latin Journey: Cuban and Mexican Immigrants in the United States.* Berkeley: University of California Press.
Romo, H., ed.
    1990    *Latinos and Blacks in the Cities: Policies for the 1990s.* Austin: University of Texas Press.
Sánchez-Korrol, V.
    1983    *From Colonia to Community.* Westport, Conn.: Greenwood Press.
Sassen, S.
    1991    *The Global City: New York, London, Tokyo.* Princeton: Princeton University Press.
Torre, C., ed.
    1992    *The Commuter Nation: Perspectives on Puerto Rican Migration.* Rio Piedras, Puerto Rico: Editorial Universitaria.
Ueda, R.
    1994    *Postwar Immigrant America: A Social History.* Boston: St. Martin's Press.
U.S. Bureau of the Census
    1974    Americans of Spanish Origin. *A Study of Selected Socio-Economic Characteristics of Ethnic Minorities Based on the 1970 Census*, Vol. I. Washington, D.C.: U.S. Department of Health, Education, and Welfare.

1973   *1970 Census of the Population, Subject Reports: Persons of Spanish Origin.* PC-92-1C. Washington, D.C.: U.S. Bureau of the Census.

1996   Current Population Reports. *Population Projections of the United States by Age, Sex, Race, and Hispanic Origin: 1995-2050.* P25-1130 (February). Washington, D.C.: U.S. Bureau of the Census.

Yinger, J.
1995   *Closed Doors, Opportunities Lost: The Continuing Costs of Housing Discrimination.* New York: Russell Sage Foundation.

Young, W.
1991   *Unlocking the Golden Door: Hispanics and the Citizenship Process.* Washington, D.C.: National Council of La Raza.

# 5

# Trends Among American Indians in the United States[1]

*Russell Thornton*

S cholars debate the size of the aboriginal population north of present-day Mexico, and the magnitude of population decline beginning sometime after A.D. 1500 and continuing to about 1900. Early in the twentieth century, for the region north of the Rio Grande, James Mooney estimated individual indigenous tribal population sizes at first European contact, summed them by regions, then totaled them, arriving at an estimate of 1,152,950 aboriginal people in that region of what would become North America (Mooney, 1910, 1928). Subsequent scholars generally accepted Mooney's estimate, although one—Alfred L. Kroeber—suggested the number was excessive and lowered it.

In 1966, however, Henry Dobyns used depopulation ratios to assert an aboriginal population size, for this area, of between 9 and 12 million people (Dobyns, 1966). In 1983, Dobyns used depopulation ratios from epidemics along with possible carrying capacities to assert some 18 million native Americans for North America—i.e., northern Mexico as well as the present-day United States, Canada, and Greenland (Dobyns, 1983).

Most scholars now agree that Mooney's population estimate significantly underestimated aboriginal population size for the area north of the Rio Grande and, thus, the baseline from which the area's aboriginal popu-

---

[1]The sections of this paper on demography, education, and repatriation were drawn freely from my chapters on the same topics in Thornton (1998).

TABLE 5-1 Twentieth Century Estimates of the Aboriginal
Population of North America

| North America[a] | United States | Researcher (Date) |
|---|---|---|
| 1,148,000 | 846,000 | Mooney (1910) |
| 1,148,000 | — | Rivet (1924) |
| 2-3,000,000 | — | Sapper (1924) |
| 1,153,000 | 849,000 | Mooney (1928) |
| 1,002,000 | — | Wilcox (1931) |
| 900,000 | 720,000 | Kroeber (1939) |
| 1,000,000 | — | Rosenblatt (1945) |
| 1,000,000 | — | Steward (1949) |
| 2-2,500,000 | — | Ashburn (1947) |
| 1,001,000 | — | Steward (1949) |
| 2,240,000 | — | Aschmann (1959) |
| 1-2,000,000 | — | Driver (1961) |
| 9.8-12,500,000 | — | Dobyns (1966) |
| 3,500,000 | 2,500,000 | Driver (1969) |
| 2,171,000 | — | Ubelaker (1976) |
| 4,400,000 | — | Denevan (1976) |
| — | 1,845,000 | Thornton (1981) |
| 18,000,000 | — | Dobyns (1983) |
| 5-10,000,000 | — | Hughes (1983) |
| 12,000,000 | — | Ramenofsky (1987) |
| 7,000,000 | 5,000,000 | Thornton (1987) |
| 1,894,000 | — | Ubelaker (1988) |
| 2-8,000,000 | — | Zambardino (1989) |

[a]North of Mesoamerica.

lation decline may be assessed.[2] By the same token, most scholars consider Dobyns's estimates to be excessive.[3] Other contemporary estimates, some of which are shown in Table 5-1, have varied from around 2 million to somewhat more than 7 million. The 7+ million estimate for north of present-day Mexico (Thornton, 1987) includes more than 5 million people in the present-day United States area and more than 2 million for present-day Canada, Alaska, and Greenland. Despite dissension about earlier

---

[2]Dates for Mooney's regional estimates, from which his overall estimate was derived, varied from A.D. 1600 to A.D. 1845, depending on the region in question. A reason for his underestimate, scholars now realize, was Mooney's assumption that little population decline had occurred prior to his dates for the beginning of an extended European presence in a region. In fact, it seems that prior depopulation had occurred in most, if not all, regions.

[3]There have been various criticisms of Dobyns's methodologies, particularly those in his 1983 book but also those in his 1966 paper.

population levels, there is no argument that substantial depopulation did occur after European arrival. The native population of the United States, Canada, and Greenland reached a nadir of perhaps 375,000 by 1900 (Thornton, 1987), although a somewhat larger nadir population has been argued (Ubelaker, 1988).

Trends in demographics, as well as in tribal sovereignty, economic development, education, and repatriation will be discussed here, with emphasis on change since the 1950s.

## DEMOGRAPHIC AND RELATED TRENDS

### Population Recovery

At the beginning of the twentieth century, the American Indian population of the United States and Canada began to increase. For the United States, census enumerations suggest almost continuous increase since 1900 (Table 5-2), a result of both decreases in mortality rates and increases in fertility rates. In fact, fertility has remained higher for American Indians than for the U.S. population as a whole (see Thornton et al., 1991). The increase has also been a result of changes in the number of individuals self-identifying as "Indian" on recent U.S. censuses. Not including Inuits (Eskimo) and Aleuts, the American Indian population increased from 524,000 in 1960, to 793,000 in 1970, to 1.4 million in 1980, to more than 1.8 million in 1990, largely because of changing racial definitions from one

TABLE 5-2 American Indian and Alaska Native[a] Population in the United States, 1900-1990

| Year | Population |
| --- | --- |
| 1900 | 237,000 |
| 1910 | 291,000 |
| 1920 | 261,000 |
| 1930 | 362,000 |
| 1940 | 366,000 |
| 1950 | 377,000 |
| 1960 | 552,000 |
| 1970 | 827,000 |
| 1980 | 1,420,000 |
| 1990 | 1,959,000 |

[a]Note: American Indian, Inuit, and Aleut.

SOURCE: U.S. Bureau of the Census (1993).

census to another. It has been estimated that about 25 percent of the change from 1960 to 1970, about 60 percent of the change from 1970 to 1980, and about 35 percent of the change from 1980 to 1990 resulted from these changing identifications (Passel, 1976; Passel and Berman, 1986; Harris, 1994). Changing self-identification has generally been attributed to racial and ethnic consciousness-raising during the 1960s and 1970s, as well as American Indian political mobilization during the period.[4]

If Inuits and Aleuts are added to the more than 1.8 million American Indians enumerated in the 1990 Census, there was a total of more than 1.9 million native Americans in the United States in 1990 (U.S. Bureau of the Census, 1994). Adding in natives of Canada, the total in 1990 was approximately 2.75 million native Americans. This is obviously a significant increase over the 375,000 estimated for 1900 (Thornton, 1987); however, it is far less than the 7+ million in 1492. It is also only a very small fraction of the total population of the United States (more than 250 million in 1990) and Canada (more than 25 million in 1990).

U.S. census enumerations also provide self-reported tribal affiliations and ancestries. According to the 1990 Census, the 10 largest tribal affiliations in the United States are Cherokee, 308,000; Navajo, 219,000; Chippewa (Ojibwe), 104,000; Sioux, 103,000; Choctaw, 82,000; Pueblo, 53,000; Apache, 50,000; Iroquois, 49,000; Lumbee, 48,000; and Creek, 44,000 (U. S. Bureau of the Census, 1993: Figure 5-1).[5]

## Tribal Enrollment

There are 317 American Indian tribes in the United States that are "recognized" by the federal government and receive services from the U.S. Bureau of Indian Affairs (BIA). There are also some 217 Alaska Native Village Areas identified in the 1990 Census, with populations of 9,807 American Indians, 32,502 Inuits, and 4,935 Aleuts (U.S. Bureau of the Census, 1992), some 125 to 150 tribes that are seeking federal recognition, and dozens of other groups who might do so in the future.

In 1990, some 437,079 American Indians, 182 Inuits, and 97 Aleuts

[4]Changing self-identification was perhaps also a result of individuals of mixed ancestry who formerly did not identify as American Indian because of the stigma attached to such an identity by the larger society. Clearly, however, some individuals with minimal, or no, Native American ancestry may have identified as American Indian because of the desire to affirm a marginal, or establish a nonexistent, ethnic identity.

[5]It should be noted that about 11 percent of those individuals identifying as Native American in the 1990 Census did not report a tribal affiliation.

TABLE 5-3 The 10 Largest Reservations and Trust Lands

| | |
|---|---|
| Navajo Reservation and Trust Lands | 143,405 |
| Pine Ridge Reservation and Trust Lands | 11,182 |
| Fort Apache Reservation | 9,825 |
| Gila River Reservation | 9,116 |
| Papago Reservation | 8,480 |
| Rosebud Reservation and Trust Lands | 8,043 |
| San Carlos Reservation | 7,110 |
| Zuni Pueblo | 7,073 |
| Hopi Pueblo and Trust Lands | 7,061 |
| Blackfeet Reservation | 7,025 |

SOURCE: U.S. Bureau of the Census (1993).

TABLE 5-4 Blood-Quantum Requirements by Reservation Basis and Membership Size

| | More than $1/4$ | $1/4$ or Less | No Minimum Requirement |
|---|---|---|---|
| Number of tribes | 21 | 183 | 98 |
| Reservation based | 85.7% | 83.1% | 63.9% |
| Median number of individual members | 1,022 | 1,096 | 1,185 |

Note: Information not available for 15 tribes.

SOURCES: Thornton (1987); U.S. Bureau of Indian Affairs (unpublished tribal constitutions and tribal enrollment data obtained by the author).

lived on 314 reservations and trust lands; half of these—218,290 American Indians, 25 Inuits, and 5 Aleuts—lived on the 10 largest reservations and trust lands (Table 5-3; U.S. Bureau of the Census, 1993).

BIA has, generally, required a one-fourth degree of American Indian "ancestry" (blood quantum) and/or tribal membership to recognize an individual as American Indian.

Tribal membership requirements are typically set forth in tribal constitutions, approved by BIA. Each tribe also has a set of requirements for membership (enrollment) of individuals, generally including a blood-quantum requirement, and requirements vary widely (Table 5-4). The Walker River Paiute require at least a one-half Indian (or tribal) blood quantum, while many tribes—e.g., Navajo—require a one-fourth blood quantum. Some tribes, generally in Oklahoma or California, require a one-eighth or one-sixteenth or one-thirty-second blood quantum. Many tribes have no minimum blood-quantum requirement, but do require some degree of American Indian lineage (Thornton, 1997). American Indian tribes on reservations tend to have higher blood-quantum requirements for membership than those not on reservations, as indicated in Table 5-4; and those with higher blood-quantum requirements tend to be slightly smaller than tribes with lower blood-quantum requirements.

The total membership of the more than 300 federally recognized tribes in the late 1980s was slightly more than 1 million; hence, only about 60 percent of the more than 1.8 million individuals self-identified as American Indian on the 1990 Census were actually enrolled in a federally recognized tribe (Thornton, 1997). Differences in self-identification and tribal enrollment varied considerably from tribe to tribe. For example, most of the more than 219,000 Navajo in the 1990 Census were enrolled in the Navajo Nation, but only about one-third of the more than 300,000 Cherokee were enrolled in one of the three Cherokee tribes—Cherokee Nation of Oklahoma, Eastern Band of Cherokee Indians, and United Keetoowah Band of Cherokee Indians.[6]

### Redistribution and Urbanization

By the beginning of the twentieth century, American Indian groups that survived European contact had been redistributed (Figure 5-1). Much of this redistribution occurred during the nineteenth century with American Indian "removals," the establishment of the reservation system, and the subsequent elimination and allotment of some reservations. According to the 1990 Census, the 10 states with the largest American Indian populations were: Oklahoma, 252,000; California, 242,000; Arizona, 204,000; New Mexico, 134,000; Alaska, 86,000; Washington, 81,000; North Carolina, 80,000; Texas, 66,000; New York, 63,000; and Michigan, 56,000 (U.S. Bureau of the Census, 1993).

A redistribution of American Indians also occurred through urban-

---

[6]The situation in Canada is somewhat different. In Canada one must be registered under the Indian Act of Canada to be an "official" Indian. Categories of Canadian Indians include: (1) status (or registered) Indians, those recognized under the Act; and (2) nonstatus (or nonregistered) Indians, those never registered under the Act or those who gave up their registration (and became "enfranchised"). Status Indians are subdivided into treaty and nontreaty Indians, depending on whether the group ever entered into a treaty relationship with the Canadian government. There are also the *Métis*—individuals of Indian and White ancestry not legally recognized as Indians. Some 500,000 of the 575,000 Canadian Indians in the mid-1980s were registered. About 70 percent of Canadian Indians live on one of the 2,272 reserves. There were 578 bands of Canadian Indians in the early 1980s, most containing fewer than 500 members. Only three bands had more than 5,000 members: Six Nations of the Grand River, 11,172; Blood, 6,083; and Kahnawake, 5,226.

FIGURE 5-1   Native American populations according to the 1990 census. U.S. Bureau of the Census (2000).   URL:  http://tiger.census.gov/cgi-bin/map browse.tbl.

ization in the United States and Canada. As shown in Table 5-5, only 0.4 percent of the American Indians in the United States lived in urban areas in 1900. By 1950, the number had increased to 13.4 percent; in 1990, 56.2 percent of American Indians lived in urban areas (U.S. Bureau of the Census, 1992; Thornton, 1997).

Important in this urbanization was the migration to cities and towns, some of which occurred under the BIA relocation program, which began in 1950 to assist American Indians in moving from reservations and rural areas to selected urban areas (Thornton, 1994). U.S. cities with the largest American Indian populations are New York City, Oklahoma City, Phoenix, Tulsa, Los Angeles, Minneapolis-St. Paul, Anchorage, and Albuquerque (Thornton, 1994).[7]

---

[7]Canadian provinces with the largest number of Native Americans are Ontario, British Columbia, Saskatchewan, and Manitoba. Approximately 40 percent of Canadian Native Americans lived in cities in the mid-1980s, particularly Vancouver, Edmonton, Regina, Winnipeg, Toronto, and Montreal. This was an increase from the 30 percent who lived in cities in the early 1970s, and the mere 13 percent who lived in cities in 1961. However, still only about 20 percent of Canadian Inuits live in cities, while only about 30 percent of the status Indians do.

TABLE 5-5 Percentage Urban of
American Indian Population of the
United States, 1900 to 1990

| Year | Percentage Urban |
|------|------------------|
| 1900 | 0.4 |
| 1910 | 4.5 |
| 1920 | 6.1 |
| 1930 | 9.9 |
| 1940 | 7.2 |
| 1950 | 13.4 |
| 1960 | 27.9 |
| 1970 | 44.5 |
| 1980 | 49.0 |
| 1990 | 56.2 |

## Issues in the Twenty-First Century

New demographic threats will be faced by American Indians in the twenty-first century because of urbanization and its partner, intermarriage. As populations of American Indians declined, and as they came into increased contact with Whites, Blacks, and others, American Indians increasingly married non-Indians, and this pattern has accelerated with the recent increase in urbanization. In the United States today, almost 60 percent of all American Indians (as defined by the Office of Management and Budget) are married to non-Indians (Sandefur and McKinnell, 1985; Eschbach, 1995). It has also been argued that those "Native Americans" by way of self-identification—or "'new' Native Americans" (Thornton, 1997)—are more likely to be intermarried (Eschbach, 1995; Nagel, 1995).

Urbanization has also created some decreased sense of tribal identity. In the 1970 Census, about 20 percent of American Indians overall reported no tribal affiliation. Only about 10 percent of those on reservations reported no affiliation, whereas 30 percent of those in urban areas reported no affiliation (Thornton, 1987). The 1980 and 1990 Censuses report no comparable urban/reservation data; however, 25 percent of the American Indians in the 1980 Census and 15 percent of those in the 1990 Census reported no tribal affiliation (Thornton, 1994; U.S. Bureau of the Census, 1994). The 1990 Census also indicates that only about one-fourth of all American Indians speak an Indian language at home (U.S. Bureau of the Census, 1992); census enumerations indicate also that urban residents are far less likely than reservation residents to speak an Indian language or participate in cultural activities (Thornton, 1987).

If these trends continue, both the genetic and tribal distinctiveness of the total American Indian population will be greatly lessened. An American Indian population comprised primarily of "'old' Native Americans" strongly attached to their tribes will change to a population with a predominance of "'new' Native Americans" who may or may not have tribal attachments or even tribal identities. It may even make sense at some point in the future to speak mainly of Native American ancestry or ethnicity (Thornton, 1997).

## SOVEREIGNTY AND POLITICAL PARTICIPATION

The idea of American Indian tribal sovereignty within the United States and the related issue of political participation within the larger American society have long been important issues for American Indians. They have, however, achieved new prominence in recent decades.

### Sovereignty: Myth or Reality?

Chief Justice John Marshall described American Indian tribes as "domestic dependent nations" with "aspects of sovereignty" (Strickland, 1998). As Strickland pointed out (Strickland, 1998):

[F]rom the beginning of the Republic, the courts have acknowledged that Native American government is rooted in an established legal and historical relationship between the United States and Native American tribes or nations. This is at the heart of Native American constitutionalism and grows from precontact tribal sovereignty. [Moreover] the rights and obligations of Native Americans, unique to Indian law, derive from a legal status as members or descendants of a sovereign Indian tribe, not from race. [Nevertheless] for the Native American, law and the courts have been seen alternatively as shields of protection and swords of extermination, examples of balanced justice and instruments of a conquering empire (p. 248).

The federal government has a long history of defining, and thereby determining, the tribal status of both American Indian groups and American Indian individuals (Thornton, 1987). In 1871, Congress enacted legislation that basically destroyed tribal sovereignty, by ending the rights of American Indian groups to negotiate treaties with the United States. It said, "Hereafter no Indian Nation or Tribe within the Territory of the United States shall be acknowledged or recognized as an independent nation, tribe, or power with whom the United States may contract by treaty" (Blackwell and Mehaffey, 1983:53). Between then and 1934, American Indian tribes "became increasingly disorganized, in part because of other legislation passed in the late 1800s calling for the allotment of tribal lands" (Thornton, 1987:195). In 1934, the Indian Reorganization Act was passed, allowing that an American Indian group had "rights to organize for its common welfare," and delineated steps whereby this might occur (Cohen, 1982). Subsequently, though, "the U.S. government adopted policies more or less aimed at ending the special legal status of American Indian tribes, and in fact, 61 tribes were officially terminated" (Thornton, 1987:195)—i.e., no longer recognized by the federal government for the purposes of having relations.

## Self-Determination Since Nixon

President Richard Nixon rejected the idea of terminating American Indian tribes, and in 1976 the Federal Acknowledgment was created, specifying seven mandatory criteria for an American Indian group to achieve federal recognition. It also placed the "burden of proof" on the American Indian group itself (Thornton, 1987). The seven criteria are:

1. A statement of facts establishing that the petitioner has been identified from historical times until the present on a substantially continuous basis, as "American Indian," or "aboriginal."

2. Evidence that a substantial portion of the petitioning group inhabits a specific area or lives in a community viewed as American Indian and distinct from other populations in the area, and that its members are descendants of an Indian tribe which historically inhabited a specific area.

3. A statement of facts which establishes that the petitioner has maintained tribal political influence or other authority over its members as an autonomous entity throughout history until the present.

4. A copy of the group's present governing document, or in the absence of a written document, a statement describing in full the membership criteria and the procedures through which the group currently governs its affairs and its members.

5. A list of all known current members of the group and a copy of each available former list of members based on the tribe's own defined criteria.

6. The membership of the petitioning group is composed principally of persons who are not members of any other North American tribe.

7. The petitioner is not, nor are its members, the subject of congressional legislation which has expressly terminated or forbidden the federal relationship (U.S. Bureau of Indian Affairs, 1978).

Given that a tribe is federally recognized, however, "the courts have consistently recognized that one of an Indian tribe's most basic powers is the authority to determine questions of its own membership. A tribe has power to grant, revoke, and qualify membership" (Cohen, 1982).

## Legal Status Today

Today, American Indian tribes as entities are healthy, if not thriving. Both tribes and individuals, however, are dominated by a maze of laws and their interpretation. Strickland (1998) notes:

> Much contemporary confusion results from the duality of traditional tribal law and federally enforced regulations. . . . The courts have powers of life-and-death proportion over tribal existence. The nature of U.S. constitutional law and public policy is such that legal issues loom large in even the smallest details of Native American cultural, economic, and political life. More than four thousand statutes and treaties controlling relations with Native Americans have been enacted and approved by Congress. Federal regulations and guidelines implementing these are even more numerous. The tribe's own laws, and some state statutes dealing with Indians, further complicate this legal maze (p. 252).

Importantly, American Indian tribes and individuals are unique in American society—they are the only segment of the U.S. population with a separate legal status, both as groups and as individuals.

> As Native American peoples prepare to move into the twenty-first century, the issues facing tribes are not substantially different from those faced over the last five centuries . . . . The miracle of the past 500 years is that Native American people and their values have survived in the face of the most unbelievable onslaughts. There is little question that the law and the courts have been, and will continue to be, a major battlefield in the struggle for sovereign survival (Strickland, 1998:255).

## Increased Political Participation

Until the late nineteenth century, American Indians were the dominant "minority group" the U.S. government had to deal with on the national, political scene. From the Civil War until the 1980s, however, American Indians were a "moral" but not "powerful" minority political group.

With the reaffirmation and reestablishment of American Indian tribes as legal entities since the 1970s, and the accompanying economic well-being of some of these tribes, however, American Indian tribes are becoming increasingly important and increasingly sophisticated political actors, something we have not seen since the subjugation of the great Sioux Nations around 1890.

## ECONOMIC DEVELOPMENT AND ECONOMIC WELL-BEING

One of the most intriguing developments since the 1970s is the increased economic development of American Indian tribes and the increased control of American Indian tribes over this development. As Snipp (1988) noted,

> Historically, American Indians have been one of the most economically deprived segments of American society. Joblessness and the accouterments of poverty, such as high infant-mortality rates and alcoholism, have been a traditional plague among Indian people (p. 1). . . . [A]s internal colonies, Indian lands are being developed primarily for the benefit of the outside, non-Indian economy (p. 3). [Thus] the tribes have been relatively unsuccessful in capturing the material benefits of development, and some observers claim that Indians are now exposed to subtle forms of economic exploitation, in addition to the political dominance they have experienced as captive nations.

Since Snipp made his arguments, the situation has changed partially; certainly not totally.

## What Is Tribal Economic Development?
## Does It Translate to Tribal and Individual Well-Being?

Tribal economic development is generally conceived of as an increase in economic activities, particularly successful ones, on the part of the tribe itself as an entity, rather than increased economic well-being of tribal members per se. Individual economic well-being, nevertheless, is an important objective of tribal economic development; and American Indian tribes and individuals engage in virtually the entire spectrum of economic activities available in modern society, ranging from small service industries to manufacturing to extraction of natural resources—fishing, logging, hunting, etc. In some instances, the ability to exploit such resources has involved extensive legal issues engendered by American Indians' unique legal status in American society (Olson, 1988).

Tribes are also engaged in activities more specifically related to American Indian culture and themselves as American Indian peoples or peoples in rural areas. As is the case with many indigenous peoples worldwide, American Indian tribes are often involved in tourism, as objects of tourism or providers of facilities for tourists in tribal areas or both. Activities related to tourism on tribal lands include running museums, gift shops, gas stations, hotels, and restaurants; providing transportation and other direct services; and performing cultural plays, pow wows, dances, and, sometimes, ceremonies.

American Indian tribes have also engaged in economic activities available to them because of (rather than in spite of) their unique legal status in American society. First and foremost is legal gambling. In some instances, tribes have built and/or operate large, successful casinos that have brought some degree of prosperity to them and their members. Some of the more successful ones are operated by the Mississippi Choctaw in Philadelphia and Mississippi and by the Pequot in Connecticut.

Generally, tribal and individual economic well-being go hand in hand. It is not, however, always a simple, straightforward matter. For example, it is typically an issue of some discussion—and often dissension—as to how much of the "profits" from economic activities are to be either turned back into the business in question; used for tribal activities involving health, education, and welfare programs; distributed to tribal members individually; or used to fund other tribal activities. "Other activities" might include buying sacred tribal sites back from state governments (the Mississippi Choctaw considered buying their sacred mound from Mississippi), or giving donations to the National Museum of the American Indian (as did the Pequot), or making direct political campaign contributions (as was the case with the Southern Cheyenne of Oklahoma).

### Conflicting Values and Traditions

Important in the decision to engage in economic activities is the issue of the type of activity to engage in and how chosen activities may or, typically, may not fit into the traditional cultural values of the tribe. Nowhere does more conflict occur than in considering the issue of gambling. Some tribes have explicitly decided not to engage in such activities—as profitable as they might be—because they conflict with important values. Wilma Mankiller, the former principal chief of the Cherokee Nation of Oklahoma, said that one of the most difficult decisions she made as principal chief was the decision that the Nation would not engage in gaming. "I literally cried when I made the decision," she said (personal conversation with the author). Gaming could have been very profitable for the Cherokee Nation and could have improved the economic well-being of tribal members, but it is also against Cherokee values.

There are American Indian communities who see economic development either as a return to old subsistence practices or as simply a reaffirmation of such practices. The attempt by the Makah Nation of Neah Bay, Washington, to return to traditional whaling practices is a case in point. Similarly, there are Inuit communities in Alaska who still cherish their traditional, subsistence lifestyles and are determined to preserve them.

## EDUCATION OF AMERICAN INDIANS

Europeans sought to convert to Christianity and educate ("civilize," as they defined it) the native peoples of this hemisphere since, virtually, their first arrival. In 1568, in present-day Havana, Cuba, the Jesuits established a school to educate the Indians of La Florida, which extended far north of present-day Florida (Berry, 1969; Thompson, 1957). Spanish, French, and English efforts to "civilize" native people expanded as European colonization progressed.

In the seventeenth century, there were French schools along the St. Lawrence River and educational communities of "praying Indians" in New England. More missions were planned, and some actually established, in La Florida and Virginia and elsewhere by both Catholics and Protestants. The efforts were very much a part of European colonization: "Indians could not be Christians until they first abandoned native habits and accepted 'civilized' customs. . . . 'Civilization and salvation' was the credo of nearly every North American missionary, which often proved to be a euphemism for cultural invasion and tribal decline" (Ronda and Axtell, 1978:30). Europeans' plans for the education of American Indians included not only mission schools but also colleges. The objectives were basically the same—train an elite group of natives who would then teach their own people "civilization and salvation."

The Charter of 1650 for Harvard College states it is for "the education of the English and Indian youth of this country in knowledge and godliness" (Elliott and Chambers, 1934). Virginians founded The College of William and Mary so that their "Youth may be piously educated in good Letters and Manners, and that the Christian Faith may be propagated amongst the Western Indians, to the Glory of Almighty God," as its 1693 charter states (Knight, 1949). Few natives enrolled, and considerably fewer graduated.

American Indians did not necessarily see the benefits of such an education. According to Benjamin Franklin, to a 1744 invitation from the Virginia government to send six young men to William and Mary, the Iroquois responded:

> Several of our young people were formerly brought up at the Colleges . . . ; but, when they came back to us, they were bad Runners, ignorant of every means of living in the Woods, unable to bear either Cold or Hunger, knew neither how to build a Cabin, take a Deer, or kill an Enemy, spoke our Language imperfectly, . . . were totally good for nothing. . . . However, . . . if the Gentlemen of Virginia will send us a Dozen of their Sons, we will take great Care of their Education, instruct them in all we know, and make *Men* of them (Smyth, 1907:98-99).

Nor did American Indians given a Christian education in early colleges necessarily stay Christian (though they may have stayed "educated"). William Byrd wrote of American Indian students educated at William and Mary, "They have been taught to read and write, and have been carefully Instructed in the Principles of the Christian Religion, till they came to be men. Yet after they return'd home, instead of civilizing and converting the rest, they have immediately Relapt into Infidelity and Barbarism themselves" (Byrd, 1929:118).

After some 250 years of higher education, Dartmouth is the college best known for having a commitment to the education of Indian youth. Its 1769 charter states it is "for the education and instruction of Youth of the Indian Tribes in this land in reading, writing, and all parts of Learning which shall appear necessary and expedient for civilizing and chris-tianizing Children of Pagans as well as in all liberal Arts and Sciences; and also of English Youth and any others" (Elliott and Chambers, 1934:179). Few American Indians enrolled or graduated from Dartmouth in the ensuing two centuries, however.[8]

## Government Schools

As Whites struggled with the idea of the new country they were creating, they sought to place American Indians within it. It became im-portant for enlightened thinkers, like the revolutionary founding fathers, to believe that American Indians could attain equality with Whites through proper training. Their success would demonstrate to the world that America was carrying out its announced mission as a "New World" for all. Henry Knox, an early architect of U.S. federal Indian policy, wrote in 1792 to Anthony Wayne "If our modes of population and War destroy the tribes the disinterested part of mankind and posterity will be apt to class the effects of our Conduct and that of the Spaniards in Mexico and Peru together" (Knopf, 1960:165).

Thomas Jefferson advocated intermarriage as well as the adoption of White lifestyles through training. After telling a gathering of Indians to adopt farming and private property, he predicted to them, "you will be-come one people with us; your blood will mix with ours, and will spread with ours over this great island" (Jefferson). Thus, intermarriage with Whites would "uplift" the entire American Indian race. The problem was those American Indians who insisted on being "Indians" and living un-"White" lifestyles. The solution became mandatory training and educa-tion for all American Indians.

Often education was incorporated into treaties. The first mention of education in a treaty between American Indians and the U.S. government was in the 1794 treaty with the Oneida, Tuscarora, and Stockbridge tribes.

---

[8]In 1969, Dartmouth reaffirmed its commitment to the education of Native Americans; it began to enroll more American Indian students and created a Native American studies program.

Others treaties incorporating education followed with the Creek Confederacy in 1801, the Kaskaskia (an Illinois group) in 1803, and the Delaware in 1804 (Berry, 1969). Soon, other groups began to establish their own schools—particularly the Five Tribes (Choctaw, Chickasaw, Cherokee, Creek, and Seminole). At some schools, manual art was taught as well as regular academics and, of course, Christianity. Typically, students were required to work in the fields to produce food. By the mid-1800s, there were 37 Indian schools run by the U.S. government (Prucha, 1975).

Schools included the Presbyterian Union among the Osage in Indian Territory; the Methodist Episcopal Society school for the Shawnee at Leavenworth, Kansas; the Methodist New Hope Academy (women) and Fort Coffee (men) in Indian Territory for Choctaw; and the Presbyterian school for Winnebagos in Minnesota. By 1881, there were 106 schools run by the U.S. government (Prucha, 1975).

## Boarding and Other Schools

When one thinks of the history of the education of American Indians, one thinks first of the American Indian boarding and day schools provided by the U.S. government primarily for elementary and secondary education and vocational and technical training. The schools began generally after the Civil War, with many established in the 1870s through 1890s. Several were on reservations.

In 1878, a group of American Indian students were sent to Hampton Normal and Agricultural Institute (now Hampton University) in Virginia, established in 1868 for former slaves. The Indians were some of the Kiowa, Comanche, and Cheyenne former prisoners, members of southern plains tribes, involved in the "Outbreak of 1874" during the winter of 1874-1875. They had been imprisoned at Fort Marion, Florida.[9] Other American Indian students soon followed, and American Indians continued to attend Hampton until 1923.

Carlisle Indian School, of football and Jim Thorpe fame, established at Carlisle, Pennsylvania, in 1879, under Richard H. Pratt, was the first American Indian off-reservation boarding school. It restricted students' access to their families and gave them half a day of education and half a day of work. It also had an outing system, whereby students were placed

---

[9]This event is represented in the Dohasan Kiowa Winter Count with a picture of Big Meat, who was killed by soldiers. Above his head is a drawing of Fort Sill, Indian Territory (I.T., now Oklahoma), where some Kiowa were also imprisoned. (See *A Chronicle of the Kiowa Indians (1832-1892)*. Berkeley: R.H. Lowie Museum of Anthropology, University of California, Berkeley, pp. 10, 18, footnote O.)

TABLE 5-6  Schools Under the Auspices of the Five Tribes

| | Schools | | Orphan Homes/ | |
| | Day | Boarding | Academies | Others |
|---|---|---|---|---|
| Cherokee Nation | 140 | 1 | 1 | 1 colored high school 2 seminaries |
| Creek Nation | 52 | 6 (2 colored) | 1 (1 colored) | |
| Choctaw Nation | 190 | | 5 | |
| Chickasaw Nation | 16 | 3 | 1 | |
| Seminole Nation | Unknown number of schools | | | |

Note: "Colored" denotes schools for former slaves of the Cherokee and Creek nations.

SOURCE: U.S. Bureau of Indian Affairs (1903).

with a White family to work for three years. Other boarding schools included Chilocco Industrial School in Oklahoma (1884), Albuquerque Indian School (1886), Santa Fe School (1890), Phoenix School (1892), Pipestone Indian Training School in Minnesota (1893), Chamberlain School in South Dakota (1898), and Riverside School in California (1902).

A 1903 report (U.S. Bureau of Indian Affairs, 1903) describes 221 government schools on reservations, 93 boarding schools, and 128 day schools, in addition to schools provided by states and schools in Indian Territory under the auspices of the Five Tribes (Table 5-6). Also listed are 26 off-reservation boarding schools and five off-reservation day schools.

A quarter-century later, it was realized that such schools were not providing the appropriate type of education. The Meriam Report of 1928 noted "that the whole Indian problem is essentially an educational one" (Meriam, 1928:348), and called for the redirection of the education of American Indians. As a result, the 1930s became a turning point, with educational objectives becoming more sympathetic to American Indians. Slowly, schools established for American Indians began to incorporate aspects of American Indian history and culture into their curricula. Following the Meriam Report, the number of boarding schools decreased, as students were increasingly channeled to day schools and, especially, public schools.

By the 1950s, public school education for American Indians had become more prevalent, following legislation terminating federal relationships with tribes and the relocation of American Indians to urban areas, "thus dumping many thousands of additional Indian students into the *public* school system" (Noriega, 1992:386). There were still, however, well over 200 American Indian schools run by the U.S. government. By 1968, the education of American Indians in the United States was, in the words of the U.S. Senate Special Subcommittee on Indian Education, "a national tragedy" (Prucha, 1975). The solution was greater involvement of American Indians in their own schools. Specific federal legislation was passed—the Indian Education Act of 1972 and the Indian Self-Determination and Educational Assistance Act of 1975. Also "survival schools" were established by the American Indian Movement, in urban areas primarily (Heart of the Earth in Minneapolis and The Red Schoolhouse in St. Paul, Minnesota), but also on reservations.

In 1999, there were almost 100 American Indian day and boarding schools.

## Colleges

The first all-American Indian college in North America was Bacone College in Muskogee, Oklahoma, founded in 1880 by the Baptist Home Mission Board. Several academies were then established to provide students for Bacone—the Cherokee Academy, the Choctaw Academy, the Seminole Female Academy, the Waco Baptist Academy for the Wichita (at Anadarko), and The Lone Wolf Mission among the Kiowa (Prucha, 1975).

Pembroke State University was established in 1887 at Lumberton, North Carolina, it, too, solely for the education of American Indians. Originally an elementary and secondary school, Pembroke became a two-year, then four-year college, then a university in 1969, and was the only four-year, state-supported university in the United States exclusively for American Indians. Both Bacone and Pembroke State eventually expanded their mandate to include non-American Indians.

Haskell Indian Nations University (formerly Haskell Institute) in Lawrence, Kansas, was first established as the U.S. Indian Industrial Training School in 1884 as a boarding school focused on agricultural education. A decade later it changed its name to Haskell Institute as it expanded its training. In 1970, it became Haskell Indian Junior College; its current name was taken in 1993, after receiving accreditation to offer a bachelor's degree in education. It is still only for American Indians, and provides higher education to federally recognized tribal members. In 1995, it had the full-time equivalent of 890 students, representing some 147 tribes.

Since 1969, 29 tribal colleges have been established, either solely or primarily for American Indians. The first was the Navajo Community College in Tsaile, Arizona (1969). Typically, these schools are two-year community colleges offering associate degrees in academic, vocational, and technical areas; they also have programs in American Indian studies, frequently focused on their own tribe. As of 1996, there were three four-year colleges and one offering a master's degree (National Research Council, 1996:56). There are also other two-year community colleges, not wholly tribally run, that offer instruction in American Indian studies.

## American Indian Studies

The Civil Rights Movement emerged fully in the 1960s. Accompanying it was heightened ethnic consciousness; not only Black became beautiful, any shade became beautiful and any ethnic origin became meaningful. Against these forces, the American academic system was changed. Students became important decision makers in their own education and educational institutions. Formerly all-male colleges became co-ed; and colleges and universities became more racially and ethnically integrated. As increasing numbers of minority students entered higher education, ethnic studies developed organizationally, if not intellectually. Ethnic studies courses found their way into curricula; and ethnic studies programs, departments, and degrees were created. A main driving force was the increased number of Black students calling for Black studies programs. Other groups followed their lead.

The impetus for the development of "Native American" studies was increased numbers of American Indian students. They formed organizations and associations and lobbied university faculties and administrators for academic programs to accompany the student support programs that were developing, and to receive their share of the ethnic studies impetus.

By the mid-1970s, 76 of 100 colleges and universities surveyed had courses dealing with American Indian concerns (Locke, 1974). When American Indian studies entered the academic system, however, it did so primarily as a reaction to the way American Indians were usually studied, rather than as a positive, worthy body of knowledge in its own right. Of particular concern, and inciting particular opposition, was the type of research conducted under the aegis of anthropology, and the "all inclusiveness" of anthropology as the discipline encompassing American Indian studies. An important problem had been anthropology's focus on American Indians at the point of the "ethnographic present," as if frozen in time with little prior history—and certainly no significant subsequent history—as "real" American Indians. In no small way, American Indian studies were also a protest against the technique of researchers establishing "friendships" with American Indians solely for research purposes.

American Indian studies also reacted against the history curriculum's lack of inclusion of American Indians as part of mainstream American history. What American Indian history was included, focused all too frequently on wars, battles, and American Indian warriors, and too little on American Indian views, philosophies, or the oral record. American Indian history was virtually limited to literature covering American Indian-White relationships, as though American Indians had no other history as a group or individually as nations. And, finally, American Indian studies reacted against the almost total lack of study of American Indian societies and cultures by other disciplines, such as sociology, political science, psychology, art, music, literature, religion, or philosophy. The main emphasis of the new area became American Indian history, a topic seemingly present in every American Indian studies program. Focusing on ethnic history was a means of going beyond the traditional anthropological approach, recognizing that American Indians were real people with significant pasts and futures.

Other disciplines were important, but had little foundation; they merely sought to present the American Indian view, whatever that might be. The newly emerging American Indian literature became important. As Washburn (1975) phrased it, the "sophisticated melding of anthropology and history in these books can be deemed the distinguishing characteristic of Indian studies as it is now emerging" (p. 270). There was interest in presenting and describing native cultures, religions, art, music, customs, and practices; and a consideration of contemporary issues was ever-present. Other subjects included federal Indian law (typically not "Native American law," as traditionally practiced), the education of American Indians, and American Indian languages and linguistics.

There is the same mix of topics 30 years later, although some have been added—e.g., economic development. "Native American" literature is at the forefront of the humanities facet of American Indian studies. American Indian history in the form of "ethnohistory" remains at the forefront of the social science component.[10]

American Indian literature is hybrid literature, developed in and around American Indian studies. Literary invention has occurred within it; the subfield is alive and well and productive. Fiction, however, is a form unknown in traditional American Indian societies; so it suffers from not being truly American Indian in this limited sense. Many traditional,

---

[10]The repatriation of American Indian human remains, grave goods, sacred objects, and objects of cultural patrimony from museums, colleges, universities, and elsewhere as mandated by the Native American Graves Protection and Repatriation Act (NAGPRA) of 1990 as well as the National Museum of the American Indian (NMAI) Act of 1989 (which limited its provisions to the Smithsonian Institution) has greatly expanded the importance of ethnohistory, particularly to native peoples but also to museums and educational institutions. Critical to the repatriation process under both NAGPRA and the NMAI Act is the establishment of cultural affiliation between contemporary groups and historic groups represented by the remains or objects. Thus, American Indian groups may, and often must, present different types of evidence to establish cultural affiliation—archaeological evidence, including physical anthropology, written history, oral traditions, ethnography, etc. For repatriation, archaeology and physical anthropology are important components of ethnohistory, along with anthropology and history. The archaeological record and the written record may be eventually reconciled with American Indian memories, in oral traditions, or otherwise.

tribal American Indians even think some of the writings are insulting to them. Accompanying this fiction has been a rapid increase in biographies and autobiographies of native people, which is an important development.

Despite all the activity, American Indian studies as a separate intellectual entity in higher education is underdeveloped. This does not mean that acceptable courses are not offered (though little innovation may be shown in the courses), that important community service and applied activities are not performed, that students are not adequately advised, or even that important research and writings have not been accomplished. All have, to one degree or another.[11] However, the full potential of American Indian studies is unrealized in most American Indian studies programs, in whatever fashion they are organized.

## REPATRIATION, HEALING THE TRAUMA OF HISTORY, AND TRIBAL RENAISSANCE

The repatriation of American Indian human remains as well as the repatriation of funerary objects and other cultural objects, identified as "objects of patrimony"—i.e., something owned by the entire people—such as wampum belts, or sacred objects such as medicine bundles, is occurring today because of determined efforts by American Indians to achieve legal changes in American society.

### Collecting Human Remains as Objects of Study

It has been estimated that objects obtained from graves and other sacred sites, and skeletal remains of "hundreds of thousands" of American Indians are held in various universities, museums, historical societies, and even private collections in the United States and in other countries (Price, 1991). Whatever the actual figure, the estimates indicate a sizeable problem. It is also estimated that the skeletons, or more typically pieces of them, of several hundred American Indians and countless objects buried with them are uncovered every year in highway, housing, and other types of construction (Price, 1991).

American Indian remains and artifacts have been objects of study and intrigue to non-American Indians for centuries. Reported excavations of American Indian burial sites and mounds date from the eighteenth century. American Indian crania have been objects of particular scientific

---

[11]There are journals devoted to Native American studies—e.g., *American Indian Quarterly, Northeast Indian Studies, American Indian Culture and Research Journal*, and *Wicazo Sa Review.*

interest since the early nineteenth century. Various scholars actively collected American Indian remains, seeking to explain possible migration from Asia by comparing American Indians with Asians (Bieder, 1986). They also sought to explain physical and cultural differences between and among native peoples and others; often cultural differences were seen as a result of racial ones. In 1839, Morton published *Crania Americana*, reporting that Caucasians had larger brain capacities and therefore higher intelligence than American Indians, and the "science" of phrenology soon developed. Collecting crania became more widespread, as scholars attempted to relate intelligence, personality, and character to skulls and brains.

The Smithsonian Institution opened in 1846 and provided further impetus for the development of American archaeology, physical anthropology, and ethnology. On May 21, 1862, Surgeon General William Hammond suggested that an Army Medical Museum be established for "the study of military medicine and surgery and that the proposed museum house a collection of specimens of morbid anatomy, surgical or medical, which may be regarded as valuable; together with projectiles and foreign bodies removed" (Hammond, 1862:2). Collecting would be done by U.S. Army medical officers, concurrent with the U.S. Civil War. After the Civil War, as the former Union Army turned its attention westward to confront American Indians on the plains, the Army Medical Museum sought to update its collections in light of the new conflict, as well as obtain other types of specimens. The U.S. Army also became involved as their mandate to handle the "Indian problem" expanded. On April 4, 1867, Surgeon General J.K. Barnes requested that medical officers also collect:

1. Rare pathological specimens from animals, including monstrosities.
2. Typical crania of Indian tribes; specimens of their arms, dress, implements, rare items of their diet, medicines, etc.
3. Specimens of poisonous insects and reptiles, and their effects on animals (Lamb, n.d.:43).

Over time, more than 4,000 American Indian skulls were collected from burial scaffolds, graves, and ossuaries, and battlefields and sites of massacres, and sent to the Army Medical Museum.[12]

---

[12]Many other museums also participated in the endeavor of collecting American Indian skeletal remains, including the Peabody Museum at Harvard University, the American Museum of Natural History in New York, and the Field Museum of Chicago, which obtained some remains sent originally to Chicago for the 1893 World's Columbian Exposition.

Some of the human remains and objects subject to legal repatriation were obtained appropriately, with the permission if not actual support of American Indians at the time. Many, however, were not. The fact that many of the human remains and objects were obtained by grave robbing, theft, and fraudulent acts adds to American Indian discomfort and further legitimates claims for repatriation.

Virtually all of the 4,000 crania at the Army Medical Museum were eventually transferred to the Smithsonian's National Museum of Natural History, to be added to the remains of approximately 14,500 other American Indians, along with non-American Indians. This, supposedly, represents the largest single collection of American Indian remains in the United States, followed by some 13,500 held by the Tennessee Valley Authority. The University of California also has a very large collection. The Hearst (formerly Lowie) Museum at its Berkeley campus has "the third largest number of catalogued skeletal entries in the United States (more than 11,000), representing many more individuals. The majority of remains are those of California Indians from the Northern California coast and the Sacramento Valley (representing more than 8,000 individuals). . . . [and there are] roughly 1 million or more pieces [of artifacts at Berkeley]."[13]

## Important Research Findings

Research on American Indians' skeletal remains has generated much important knowledge about such diverse topics as population size and composition, cultural patterns of tooth mutilation, diseases among populations and customs of treatments for the diseases, life expectancies, growth patterns, population affinities, origins and migrations, and diets, including dates when corn was introduced into the diets of the native peoples of North America (Buikstra, 1992). From studying human remains of American Indians we now know, for example, that tuberculosis was present in this hemisphere prior to European contact, as were some other infectious diseases, especially treponema infections; that certain native groups had serious iron deficiencies from a diet heavily dependent on corn;[14] and that among some groups, males with more social prestige—as reflected by burial objects—were physically larger than males with less social prestige (perhaps because they had better diets, perhaps because bigger men were simply given more prestige).

---

[13]"Summary description of UC collections of human skeletal remains and artifacts," unpublished statement, University of California, n.d.

[14]These and other topics are discussed in Verano and Ubelaker (1992).

American Indian skeletal remains will become even more important as objects of study, scholars assert, given recent advances in scientific technology (Ubelaker and Grant, 1989). Benefits of these advances include the detection of immunoglobulin and DNA from bone. The study of immunoglobulins from the skeletons could enable scholars to establish explicit past disease experiences; deciphering the DNA from skeletons could enable scholars to establish genetic relationships among historical populations. This is no small issue, and much of the knowledge gained could benefit both American Indians and peoples of the world.

Some scholars and others assert that the scientific knowledge to be gained from the remains and cultural objects outweigh claims American Indians may have on them. They argue that the scientific value is important not only to native peoples themselves but to the public at large as scholars attempt to reconstruct histories of American Indians. A related view is that the remains and objects now housed in museums and educational institutions belong not only to American Indians, but to all Americans, even to all peoples of the world, as part of the heritage of all humanity. Yet another view is that scholars are keeping and studying the remains because American Indians do not know what they are doing when requesting repatriation. Perhaps they think that someday American Indians will want this knowledge, and it is up to science to preserve it for them.

## The Repatriation Movement

Many American Indians believe repatriation must occur despite any scholarly or general public good that may be derived from the study or display of the remains and objects. They assert that cultural and spiritual factors outweigh science and education. Furthermore, they point out that society and the government have already placed all sorts of restrictions on research deemed inappropriate. Particularly important, American Indians contend, is that Americans have been resolute in regard to returning to the United States the remains of American soldiers who died on foreign shores defending this country. American Indian skeletons obtained from battlefields, as many of those in the Army Medical Museum were, are remains of American Indians who died defending their homelands. It is felt that refusal to return the remains of American Indian warriors killed in battle implies that these fighters—and civilians killed in battles and massacres—are less deserving of an honorable burial than American servicemen and -women who died for the United States.

American Indians have attempted to legally prevent the collection of their human remains and cultural objects for more than a century (Cole, 1985). In the 1970s and 1980s, they increasingly demanded that ancestral remains and sacred objects be returned to them for proper disposal or care. National American Indian leaders, such as Walter Echo-Hawk of the American Indian Rights Fund and Susan Shown Harjo of the National Congress of American Indians, continued to seek the repatriation of human skeletal remains, from the Smithsonian and elsewhere. Professional associations such as the Council for Museum Anthropology, Society for American Archaeology, American Anthropological Association, and American Association of Museums became involved and issued position papers. Various universities also debated the issues, forming committees and panels to develop policies.

One idea considered but discarded was to "create a national memorial where bones 'which are not useful for scientific inquiry' would be buried, 'giving due regard to the religious and ceremonial beliefs and practices of those Indians, Aleuts and Eskimos whose ancestors may be included in the Smithsonian collection'" (*New York Times*, 1987).

The private sector also became involved in the repatriation movement, just as it did in the Civil Rights Movement. A major turning point was when Elizabeth Sackler purchased for $39,050 three Hopi and Navajo ceremonial masks in 1991. Her intent was to return them to the tribes. She then established the American Indian Ritual Object Repatriation Foundation to assist native groups in retrieving important cultural objects from private individuals and organizations.[15] The Foundation continues to be active in repatriation.

During the 1980s, the Pan-Indian Repatriation Movement began to experience some success through the passage of federal and state laws not only calling for the repatriation of human remains and objects to descendants, but also preventing the further disenfranchisement of remains and objects. Not only has the success of the repatriation movement revitalized Native America by providing new-found self-esteem, the task of actually repatriating human remains and cultural objects has also revitalized communities by bringing members together in the struggle as well as reaffirming important knowledge about many cultural and sacred objects. It is not always an easy undertaking, however; but the end result is worth it.

## State and Federal Laws

Repatriation legislation has been enacted at both the state and federal levels. Some laws simply reiterate and reapply existing laws against grave robbing, trespass, and vandalism, or general public health and cemetery laws; nevertheless, 11 states have laws addressing the disposition of pre-

---

[15]The Foundation has recently published *Mending the Circle* to assist native groups with their repatriation efforts; it is distributed free of charge to them.

historic aboriginal remains and grave goods (Price, 1991:43). The land-mark state legislation was probably Nebraska's 1989 Unmarked Human Burial Sites and Skeletal Remains Protection Act. In passing the Act, Ne-braska became the first state with a general repatriation statute. It pro-vides for the protection of unmarked burial sites throughout the state and the repatriation to relatives or American Indian tribes, within one year of a request, of human remains and associated "burial goods" held in state-sponsored or state-recognized public bodies (Peregoy, 1992; for a survey of state laws, see Price, 1991).

The federal government has increasingly enacted legislation aimed at protecting the rights of American Indian groups vis-à-vis ancestral re-mains and sacred objects. Twentieth-century legislation may be dated from the Antiquities Act of 1906, which granted the federal government jurisdiction over all aboriginal remains and artifacts on federal property. Other important legislation followed.

Specific federal legislation on repatriation that has been enacted since the 1980s began with Public Law 101-185 in November 1989, which estab-lished the National Museum of the American Indian (NMAI) as part of the Smithsonian Institution. A component of this law mandated the re-turn of American Indian human remains and funerary objects held by the Smithsonian to appropriate individuals and groups. NMAI also man-dates a repatriation review committee "to monitor and review the inven-tory, identification, and return of Indian human remains and Indian funerary objects." The committee is composed of five individuals, at least three of whom are selected from individuals nominated by American Indian groups. The amendment to NMAI added two members to the committee, both of whom are to be "traditional religious leaders."

In October 1990, Public Law 101-601, the Native American Grave Protection and Repatriation Act (NAGPRA), was enacted. NAGPRA con-cerns the disposition of American Indian human remains and artifacts in federal agencies (other than the Smithsonian) *as well as* in institutions receiving federal support (McManamon, 1994). It increases the protection of American Indian graves on federal and tribal land, proscribes commer-cial trafficking in American Indian remains, requires the inventory and repatriation to culturally affiliated tribes or descendants of all collections of American Indian remains and associated funerary objects held by fed-eral agencies and federally funded museums (and universities), and also requires the repatriation of American Indian sacred objects and cultural patrimony.[16]

---

[16]Public Law 101-601, Sec. 7, Pt. a. For a history of this law see Trope and Echo-Hawk (1992). "Cultural affiliation" as defined in NAGPRA, means, "there is a relationship of shared group identity which can be reasonably traced historically or prehistorically be-

NAGPRA gave institutions five years to complete inventories of human remains and funerary objects, with a possible extension of time, and three years to provide summaries of unassociated funerary objects, sacred objects, and objects of cultural patrimony. After the inventory, six months are allowed for notifying tribes of affiliated remains and funerary objects. Full repatriation efforts under NAGPRA are only now really commencing, with the Smithsonian ahead of many other museums and institutions in actual repatriations. Nevertheless, many important issues remain to be settled in implementing NAGPRA. Two are (1) whether nonfederally recognized tribes are entitled to repatriated remains and objects (they are by the Smithsonian), and (2) what to do about remains or objects when cultural affiliation cannot be established.

The Smithsonian Institution made the decision to adhere to Public Law 101-601 as well as Public Law 101-185, thereby extending the mandate of repatriation to include not only human remains and funerary objects but also sacred objects and objects of cultural patrimony. In 1996, an amendment to NMAI was passed by the U.S. Congress, amending the Act along the lines of the NAGPRA legislation, whereby a strict time schedule is set for repatriation of objects of cultural patrimony, sacred objects, and human remains and funerary objects.

The repatriation process has great potential for bridging the gap between native worlds and larger society. As it developed, repatriation of human remains polarized advocates of reburial and advocates of study and preservation in repositories. Little compromise occurred between American Indian repatriation activists and researchers; yet, some degree of compromise is not only desirable, it is necessary. Science and scholarship have much to offer to American Indians, as American Indians attempt to recapture their lost histories. American Indians are no longer powerless in American society, but are important actors in shaping their own destinies. American Indian values, wishes, and perspectives must be respected by scholars. Although some disciplines such as anthropology have histories of applied work with American Indians, the repatriation process is providing new challenges for the application of scholarly disciplines to real-life concerns of American Indians.

---

tween a present-day Indian tribe or Native Hawaiian organization and an identifiable earlier group." Under the provisions of NAGPRA, a seven-person review committee was established to monitor and review the law's mandated repatriation activities. Three of the members are appointed from nominations of Native American groups and religious leaders, at least two of whom must be "traditional Indian religious leaders"; three members are appointed from nominations of museum and scientific organizations; and one member is appointed from a list suggested by the other six members.

## HEALING THE WOUNDS FROM THE TRAUMA OF HISTORY

On the morning of Friday, October 9, 1993, a small group of Northern Cheyenne arrived at the Smithsonian Institution's National Museum of Natural History. They had come for their dead. Almost 115 years earlier, on January 9, 1879, at least 83 members of Dull Knife's (a.k.a. Morning Star's) band of 149 Northern Cheyenne had been massacred by U.S. government soldiers near Fort Robinson, Nebraska, after the Cheyenne's final, desperate attempt for freedom. They had been removed to a reservation in Oklahoma to live with the Southern Cheyenne in 1877, and now had fled toward their homelands in Montana. They were captured, however. They were then held in the stockade at Fort Robinson with little food, water, or even heat. After two weeks, they attempted to escape. During the attempt, at least 57 Northern Cheyenne were killed; 32 others escaped but were trapped on January 22 at the edge of Antelope Creek. In the massacre that followed, 26 were killed. Most of those killed in the escape attempt were buried near the fort; those killed at Antelope Creek were buried nearby in a mass grave. The bones of 17 of the Northern Cheyenne dead were collected for scientific study by the U.S. Army Medical Examiner. In 1880, the mass grave at Antelope Creek was exhumed, and the bones of 9 more Cheyenne dead were obtained. The bones—mostly crania—were later transferred to the Smithsonian's National Museum of Natural History. The bones were from Cheyenne ranging in age from a 49-year-old adult to a 3-year-old child; the child was one of those massacred at Antelope Creek. In October 1993, all were being returned to their people in a joint repatriation effort made by the Smithsonian and the Peabody Museum of Archaeology and Ethnology at Harvard, which had obtained skeletal remains from Antelope Creek.

At the ceremony, the bones were officially turned over to an impressive Northern Cheyenne delegation, represented by the tribal chair, the Crazy Dogs society of warriors, the Elk Horn society, Sun Dance priests, four women who were fourth-generation descendants of Dull Knife, and, most important, James Black Wolf, Keeper of the Sacred Buffalo Hat. The remains were carefully arranged on small Pendleton blankets; a pipe ceremony was performed, words and prayers were said, a drum was played, and songs were sung. Each person's bones were then wrapped in the blanket and interred in cedar boxes for the journey home to Montana and final rest.

During the ceremony, it was discovered that a shattered lower part of a skull from the Harvard museum matched an upper part of a woman's skull from the Smithsonian. Either at death 115 years earlier or afterward, the young woman's head had been shattered into two pieces, each piece taken to a different location. She had been collected as two different people; but on October 9, 1993, was reunited not only with her people, her skull itself was reunited.

(After the ceremony, a young native man from the Smithsonian came up to me and told me about the 3-year-old's skull. "The child was a little girl. I saw her. She was dressed in white and had yellow ribbons in her hair. I told the Cheyenne I had seen her, and that she was now happy. They were very pleased. They thanked me for telling them."[17])

On the way to Busby, Montana, for burial of the remains, a stop was made at Fort Robinson, Nebraska. The journey then continued to Montana. A small teddy bear was given to the little girl and placed in the cedar box with her remains. She and the other Cheyenne were buried on a hill near Two Moon Monument. A permanent memorial near the graves will be established.

It is theorized by some (Duran et al., 1998; Duran and Duran, 1995) that events in the history of a people can cause a trauma to that group much in the same way catastrophic events in an individual's life may cause lasting trauma. Psychologists have stated that "if a person is traumatized, the trauma must be resolved for the person to be psychologically healthy" (e.g., Duran et al., 1998:62). Similarly, when a people are traumatized, the trauma must also be resolved; if not, the group psyche remains wounded. Without resolution, some have even argued that the effects of historical trauma are "intergenerationally cumulative, thus compounding the mental health problems of succeeding generations" (e.g., Duran et al., 1998:64).

Many of the arguments for historical trauma, and its need for resolution come from studies of the Nazi Holocaust (Bergman and Jucovy, 1990). According to Duran et al., effects of historical trauma include "difficulty in mourning over a mass grave, the dynamics of collective grief, and the importance of community memorialization" (Duran et al., 1998:66). European Jews live "among the perpetrators and murderers of their families" (Fogelman, 1991:94), which has not allowed them the more healthy griev-

---

[17]As chairman of the Smithsonian Institution's Native American Repatriation Review Committee, I attended the ceremony in Washington, D.C. It was even more meaningful for me because my mother had died a few days before. I had stopped in Washington to attend the ceremony before continuing on to Vian, Oklahoma, for her funeral the following day. At the Washington ceremony, I kept thinking that my mother would be laid to rest only a few days after her death; these Northern Cheyenne had waited in museums for more than a century before they could be buried. I also thought that my mother had had a long, full life and had died peacefully; these Northern Cheyenne men, women, and children had lived foreshortened lives that ended violently, cruelly. Nevertheless, the return of their ancestors appeared to have brought some measure of healing to the attendees. As they said, "Naevahoo'ohtseme" (We are going back home).

ing process of American Jews (Fogelman, 1991; Duran et al., 1998). Likewise, "Native Americans live in a colonized country where similar patterns of grief have emerged" (Fogelman, 1991), and which also has hindered a healthy grieving process.

Other American Indian groups in the United States have attempted various ways to heal the historical traumas they experienced. The Dakota Sioux uprising of 1862 in southern Minnesota resulted in numerous Sioux deaths. It also resulted in the largest single, formal execution in U.S. history—the mass hanging of 38 Sioux at Mankato, Minnesota, on December 26, 1862 (Thornton, 1987). One hundred twenty-five years later, the Dakota Sioux established a "year of reconciliation," whereby they attempted to deal with the events of 1862, and "come to terms with what happened, and move on with our lives, but not forget" (personal conversation with the author).

The forced removal of the Cherokee Indians from the Southeast into Indian Territory during the late 1830s is well known in U.S. history. It was such a tragic event and caused so much pain and death that it was named literally "the trail where we cried" and has become known as the "Trail of Tears," in Cherokee "Nunna daul Tsuny." An estimated 4,000 men, women, and children died on the thousand-mile trek. The event stands as the single most significant event in the history of the Cherokee Nation. In an effort to deal with this trauma and confront the pain it caused, the Cherokee established a Trail of Tears Association, whereby the event is commemorated annually and the graves of those who were removed are marked with a special medallion—our attempt to heal the wounds of the trauma of history.[18]

On December 29, 1890, several hundred Sioux men, women, and children were massacred by soldiers of the Seventh Cavalry[19] at Wounded Knee Creek. Earlier, a band of 350 Sioux had fled their reservation in order to practice their new religion—the Ghost Dance. The massacre occurred when the troops were attempting to disarm the escaped Sioux and prepare them for shipment back to their reservation. After the massacre, the Cavalry left with their dead and wounded. A burial detail was sent out a few days later to bury the Indians. In the meantime, other Sioux

---

[18]I said, at a presentation to the 1998 meeting of the Trail of Tears Association, "We are lucky in this regard. We have confronted this sad part of our history, have recognized it, and have been able to heal some of the hurt it caused us as a people. Other Indian groups are not so fortunate."

[19]The Seventh Calvary was the regiment commanded by General George A. Custer, who was defeated by the Sioux, Northern Cheyenne and other tribes on June 25, 1876, in the Battle of Greasy Grass, or, as more well-known, the Battle of the Little Big Horn.

learned of the massacre and collected some of the dead. When the burial detail arrived January 1, 1891, a heavy blizzard had covered the remaining dead bodies. One hundred and forty-six men, women, and children were collected and buried in a mass grave. Seven generations after the massacre, the Sioux "undertook a communal memorialization through the *Tatanka Iyotake* (Sitting Bull) and *Wokiksuye* (Bigfoot) Ride, which traced the path of the Hunkpapa and Miniconju massacred at Wounded Knee" (Duran et al., 1998). It was time for them, they said, to put the event behind them and go on with their lives, but not forget.

## Repatriation and Healing the Trauma of History

The repatriation process has helped American Indian groups to achieve some closure on traumatic events of their histories. For example, some of the Sioux massacred at Wounded Knee wore sacred Ghost Dance shirts; they were stripped of these shirts before being dumped into the grave. Six of these shirts ended up at the National Museum of Natural History; one was displayed in a museum exhibit with the caption that it was taken from the Wounded Knee "Battlefield."[20] The Smithsonian officially had 29 "objects" from those massacred including a blanket from "a dead body," a pair of boy's moccasins, and baby jackets and caps. The return of the objects to the descendants of those killed occurred in September 1998.

## SUMMARY AND CONCLUSIONS

Trends in demographics, tribal sovereignty, economic development, education, and repatriation are extremely important for American Indians in American society. Demographically, American Indians are now not only surviving in society, but also increasing in numbers. However, the ways American Indians define themselves, and are defined by our society, are changing; and this may have far-reaching implications for American Indians in the twenty-first century.

American Indian tribal sovereignty is alive if not well, and numerous court cases will continue to emerge as the legal relationships between

---

[20]In the fall of 1986, I was a fellow at the National Museum of Natural History. I remember vividly a trip one afternoon with a curator into the attic of the National Museum of Natural History building to examine some of their North American Indian collections. He volunteered to show me these shirts. He pulled out a drawer from a large cabinet. There they were; almost 100 years after it occurred, I was a witness to a remaining legacy of the massacre at Wounded Knee. The shirts have bullet holes and are stained with blood; some still have medicine bags attached.

American Indians and society continue to be debated, refined, and changed. Important, however, is the fact that American Indians may once again emerge as powerful political players on the national scene—not just as moral entities, but also as significant economic entities. This is in part because of the newly possible economic development of American Indian tribes. The twenty-first century holds much promise for American Indians in this regard.

Educationally, American Indians have gained some measure of control over the education of their youth, a trend unlikely to reverse itself in the new century. Also important, educationally, is the emergence of American Indian studies. It has the potential to fundamentally alter American conceptions about American Indians and bring important new knowledge bases within the realm of academe; unfortunately, that potential is largely unfilled.

Finally, the legally mandated repatriation of American Indian human remains and objects back to the native communities from which they came—and to which many would say they belong—is fundamentally altering the relationships of American Indians with society and academe. Important in this is the movement toward alleviating the traumas of history many American Indians experienced with colonialism and still find unresolved.

## REFERENCES

Bergman, M., and M. Jucovy, eds.
    1990   *Generations of the Holocaust*. New York: Columbia University Press.
Berry, B.
    1969   *The Education of American Indians: A Survey of the Literature*. Washington, D.C.:
          U.S. Government Printing Office.
Bieder, R.
    1986   *Science Encounters the Indian, 1820-1880: The Early Years of American Ethnology*.
          Norman: University of Oklahoma Press.
Blackwell, C., and J. Mehaffey
    1983   American Indians, trust and recognition. In *Nonrecognized American Indian Tribes:
          An Historical and Legal Perspective*, F. Porter, III, ed. Occasional Papers Series, no.
          7. Chicago: The Newberry Library.
Buikstra, J.
    1992   Diet and disease in late prehistory. Pp. 87-101 in *Disease and Demography in the
          Americas*, J. Verano and D. Ubelaker, eds. Washington, D.C.: Smithsonian Institu-
          tion Press.
Byrd, W.
    1929   *Histories of the Dividing Line Betwixt Virginia and North Carolina*. Raleigh, N.C.: The
          North Carolina Historical Commission.
Cohen, F.
    1982 [1942]  *Handbook of Federal Indian Law* (reprint). New York: AMS Press.

Cole, D.
   1985   *Captured Heritage: The Scramble for Northwest Coast Artifacts*. Seattle: University of Washington Press.
Dobyns, H.
   1966   Estimating Aboriginal American population: An appraisal of techniques with a new hemispheric estimate. *Current Anthropology* 7:395-416.
   1983   *Their Number Become Thinned: Native American Population Dynamics in Eastern North America*. Knoxville: University of Tennessee Press.
Duran, B., E. Duran, and M. Yellow Horse Brave Heart
   1998   Native Americans and the trauma of history. In *Studying Native America: Problems and Prospects*, R. Thornton, ed. Madison: University of Wisconsin Press.
Duran, E., and B. Duran
   1995   *Native American Postcolonial Psychology*. Albany: State University of New York Press.
Elliott, E., and M. Chambers, eds.
   1934   *Charters and Basic Laws of Selected American Universities and Colleges*. New York: The Carnegie Foundation for the Advancement of Teaching.
Eschbach, K.
   1995   The enduring and vanishing American Indian. *Ethnic and Racial Studies* 18:95.
Fogelman, E.
   1991   Mourning without graves. In *Storms and Rainbows: The Many Faces of Death*, A. Medvene, ed. Washington, D.C.: Lewis Press.
Hammond, W.
   1862   Surgeon General's Office, Washington, D.C., Circular No. 2, May 21. In *A History of the United States Army Medical Museum, 1862 to 1917*, D. Lamb, compiler. Washington, D.C.: n.p.
Harris, D.
   1994   The 1990 Census count of American Indians: What do the numbers really mean? *Social Science Quarterly* 15:583.
Jefferson, T.
   n.d.   Thomas Jefferson address, War Department, National Archives.
Kaeppler, A.
   1985   Letter to tribal representatives. Chairman, Department of Anthropology, National Museum of Natural History, November 22.
Knight, E., ed.
   1949   *A Documentary History of Education in the South Before 1860, Volume 1*. Chapel Hill, N.C.: The University of North Carolina Press.
Knopf, R., ed.
   1960   *Anthony Wayne: A Name in Arms*. Pittsburgh: University of Pittsburgh Press.
Lamb, D., compiler
   n.d.   *A History of the United States Army Medical Museum, 1862 to 1917*. Washington, D.C.: n.p.
Locke, P.
   1974   *A Survey of College and University Programs for American Indians*. Boulder, Colo.: Western Interstate Commission for Higher Education.
McManamon, F.
   1994   Memorandum to Universities, Colleges, Departments of Anthropology, Schools of Medicine. National Park Service, United States Department of the Interior, August 15, Washington, D.C.

Meriam, L.
    1928    *The Problem of Indian Administration*. Baltimore: The Johns Hopkins Press.
Mooney, J.
    1910    Population. In *Handbook of American Indians North of Mexico*, F. Hodge, ed. Washington, D.C.: U.S. Government Printing Office.
    1928    The aboriginal population of America north of Mexico. In *Smithsonian Miscellaneous Collections*, Vol. 80, J. Swanton, ed. Washington, D.C.: U.S. Government Printing Office.
Nagel, J.
    1995    Politics and the resurgence of American Indian ethnic identity. *American Sociological Review* 60:953.
National Research Council
    1996    *Colleges of Agriculture at the Land Grant Universities: Public Service and Public Policy*. Washington, D.C.: National Academy Press.
*New York Times*
    1987    December 8.
Noriega, J.
    1992    American Indian education in the United States: Indoctrination for subordination to colonialism. In *The State of Native America: Genocide, Colonization, and Resistance*, M. Jaimes, ed. Boston: South End Press.
Olson, M.
    1988    The legal road to economic development: Fishing rights in western Washington. Pp. 77-112 in *Public Policy Impacts on American Indian Economic Development*, C. Snipp, ed. Albuquerque: Institute for Native American Development, Development Series No. 4, University of New Mexico.
Passel, J.
    1976    Provisional evaluation of the 1970 Census count of American Indians. *Demography* 13:397-409.
Passel, J., and P. Berman
    1986    Quality of 1980 Census data for American Indians. *Social Biology* 33:986.
Peregoy, R.
    1992    The legal basis, legislative history, and implementation of Nebraska's landmark reburial legislation. *Arizona State Law Journal* 24:329-389.
Price, H., III
    1991    *Disputing the Dead: U.S. Law on Aboriginal Remains and Grave Goods*. Columbia: University of Missouri Press.
Prucha, F., ed.
    1975    *Documents of United States Indian Policy*. Lincoln: University of Nebraska Press.
Ronda, J., and J. Axtell
    1978    *Indian Missions: A Critical Bibliography*. Bloomington: Indiana University Press.
Sandefur, G., and T. McKinnell
    1985    Intermarriage among Blacks, Whites and American Indians. Paper presented at the meetings of the American Sociological Association, Washington, D.C.
Smyth, A., ed.
    1907 [1784] *The Writings of Benjamin Franklin, Volume X, 1789-1790*. New York: The Macmillan Co.
Snipp, C.
    1988    Public policy impacts and American Indian economic development. In *Public Policy Impacts on American Indian Economic Development*, C. Snipp, ed. Albuquerque: Institute for Native American Development, Development Series No. 4, University of New Mexico.

Strickland, R.
   1998   The eagle's empire. In *Studying Native America: Prospects and Problems*, R. Thornton, ed. Madison: University of Wisconsin Press.
Thompson, H.
   1957   Education among American Indians: Institutional aspects. *The Annals of the American Academy of Political and Social Science* 311:95.
Thornton, R.
   1987   *American Indian Holocaust and Survival: A Population History since 1492*. Norman: University of Oklahoma Press.
   1994   Urbanization. Pp. 670-671 in *Native Americans in the Twentieth Century: An Encyclopedia*, M. Davis, ed. New York: Garland.
   1997   Tribal membership requirements and the demography of "old" and "new" Native Americans. *Population Research and Policy Review* 7:9.
   1998   *Studying Native America: Problems and Prospects*. Thornton, R. ed. Madison: University of Wisconsin Press.
Thornton, R., G. Sandefur, and C. Snipp
   1991   American Indian fertility history. *American Indian Quarterly* 15:359-367.
Trope, J., and W. Echo-Hawk
   1992   The Native American Graves Protection and Repatriation Act: Background and legislative history. *Arizona State Law Journal* 24:35-77.
U.S. Bureau of the Census
   1992   *1990 Census of Population: General Population Characteristics: American Indian and Alaska Native Areas*. Washington, D.C.: U. S. Government Printing Office.
   1993   *We the . . . First Americans*. Washington, D.C.: U.S. Government Printing Office.
   1994   *1990 Census of the Population: Characteristics of American Indians by Tribe and Language*. Washington, D.C.: U.S. Government Printing Office.
U.S. Bureau of Indian Affairs
   1903   *Statistics of Indian Tribes, Agencies, and Schools, 1903*. Washington, D.C.: U.S. Government Printing Office.
   1978   Guidelines for Preparing a Petition for Federal Acknowledgment as an Indian Tribe. Washington, D.C., photocopy:3, 8-11, 17.
Ubelaker, D.
   1988   North American Indian population size, A.D. 1500 to 1985. *American Journal of Physical Anthropology* 77:289-294.
Ubelaker, D., and L. Grant
   1989   Human skeletal remains: Preservation or reburial? *Yearbook of Physical Anthropology* 32:249-287.
Verano, J., and Ubelaker, D., eds.
   1992   *Disease and Demography in the Americas*. Washington, D.C.: Smithsonian Institution Press.
Washburn, W.
   1975   American Indian studies: A status report. *American Quarterly* XXVII:270.

# 6

# Political Trends and Electoral Issues of the Asian Pacific American Population

*Don T. Nakanishi*

M any Asian Pacific American, or Asian and Pacific Islander,[1] leaders had worked for years to ensure that the November 1996 elections would be considered a major defining moment for Asians and Pacific Islanders in American electoral politics and public-policy participation. The elections were intended to herald a highly successful, first-ever, nationwide Asian and Pacific Islander voter-registration campaign that enfranchised thousands of new Asian and Pacific Islander voters; 75,000 registered by organized grassroots organizations were added to the approximately 1.2 million registered Asian and Pacific Islander voters across the country (Ong and Nakanishi, 1996). In California alone, the more than 3 million Asians and Pacific Islanders represented 1 in 10 residents. The idea that the state's electorate might someday reflect this demographic profile, and Asians and Pacific Islanders perhaps become an important future swing vote, no longer seemed unrealistic (Nakanishi, 1998).

The November 1996 elections also were supposed to be viewed as historically significant because of the number of Asians and Pacific Is-

---

[1]In this paper, Asians and Pacific Islanders are defined in a manner similar to that of Asian Pacific American, so named by a fact-finding report issued by the Asian Pacific American Education Advisory Committee of the Office of the Chancellor of the California State University (1990): "Asian Pacific Americans are defined as immigrants, refugees, and the U.S.-born descendants of immigrants from Asia, including Pakistan and the countries lying east of it in South Asia, East Asia, and the Pacific Islands" (p. 1).

landers elected to major political offices throughout the country. Most notable was the election of Gary Locke, Governor of the state of Washington, the first Chinese American to capture a governorship, and the first Asian and Pacific Islander elected governor outside of Hawaii. In addition, the election of Martha Choe to the Seattle City Council and, in California, the election of Mike Honda to the California Assembly and Leland Yee and Michael Yaki to the San Francisco Board of Supervisors provided further credence that the November 1996 elections were groundbreaking for Asian and Pacific Islander electoral empowerment.

Asian and Pacific Islander political leaders had expected recognition of a strong Asian and Pacific Islander presence, especially among Democrats, when exit polls conducted by the *Los Angeles Times* and the National Asian Pacific American Legal Consortium (NAPALC) showed that Asian and Pacific Islander voters strongly favored President Bill Clinton over Bob Dole and Ross Perot. Also, there were expectations of recognition of Asian and Pacific Islander political voice in light of exit polls in California, which showed that Asian and Pacific Islander voters, despite their portrayal by conservative pundits and politicians as being just like the majority of White voters in the state in opposing affirmative action, voted against the antiaffirmative action Proposition 209 ballot initiative by a substantial margin (61 percent, according to *Los Angeles Times* exit polls, and more than 75 percent according to NAPALC), and at levels nearly comparable to those of other voters of color (Ha, 1996; Nakanishi and Lai, 1998). Indeed, there was anxious speculation by many Asian and Pacific Islander community leaders that the Democratic Party might now become the party of choice for Asians and Pacific Islanders, who usually registered in nearly equal percentages as Democrats, Republicans, and "no-party" independents (Nakanishi, 1998).

In regard to campaign fund-raising, Asian and Pacific Islander political leaders of both political parties expected that, as had been the case in each presidential election since the 1970s, Asians and Pacific Islanders would set new fund-raising records. At one gala fund-raising event in July 1996, nearly 1,000 Asians and Pacific Islanders contributed $1,000 each to hear President Clinton speak (Nakanishi, 1975). The event raised nearly $1 million.[2] Asian and Pacific Islander political leaders hoped that maybe this time around, President Clinton, in assembling a cabinet that "looks like America," would make sure to appoint at least one Asian and

---

[2]This was a particularly memorable, and now somewhat controversial, fund-raising event. It was organized by John Huang and attended by James Riady, Maria Hsia, Ted Sioeng, and others who since gained notoriety as result of the subsequent campaign finance controversy.

Pacific Islander. University of California, Berkeley, Chancellor Chang-lin Tien and former Congressman Norman Mineta were prominently mentioned as viable contenders for the positions of Secretaries of Energy and Transportation, respectively. With the decisive electoral and monetary support Clinton received from Asians and Pacific Islanders, the prospects for the nation's first-ever Asian and Pacific Islander cabinet-level appointment seemed almost assured.

That is how Asian and Pacific Islander leaders wanted their participation in the November 1996 elections to be portrayed. And for more than a year after those elections, Asians and Pacific Islanders did occupy center stage in American electoral politics; however, the attention they received from the mass media, Senate and House committees, and federal agencies did not focus on their milestones during those elections, but instead on allegations and innuendoes of improper or illegal campaign finance activities by some Asian and Pacific Islander donors and fund-raisers. Indeed, some Asian and Pacific Islander leaders felt that the unprecedented media and partisan focus on campaign violations by a few Asians and Pacific Islanders had a "chilling effect" on present and future involvement of Asians and Pacific Islanders in electoral politics (Akaka, 1998). Many were disappointed when the anticipated nominations of Tien and Mineta did not materialize, and that the President again constructed a cabinet that did not include any Asians and Pacific Islanders. A few Asian and Pacific Islander leaders felt that this "Asian-bashing" controversy was the worst thing that had happened to Asians and Pacific Islanders since the incarceration of 120,000 Japanese Americans during World War II, when similarly unsubstantiated accusations of disloyalty were aired by many of the nation's highest ranking officials (Lin, 1997).

## THE TREND OF INCREASED ASIAN PACIFIC AMERICAN POLITICAL REPRESENTATION

Fortunately, there is considerable evidence to suggest that the political growth and maturation of Asians and Pacific Islanders did not come to an abrupt end with the controversy during the months after the November 1996 elections, nor has it stopped or prevented Asians and Pacific Islanders from running for, and winning, political office. In 1998, there were more than 2,000 Asian and Pacific Islander elected and appointed officials across the nation (Nakanishi and Lai, 1998). Since the release of the May 1996 edition of *National Asian Pacific American Political Almanac* (Nakanishi and Lai, 1996), there has been an approximate 10 percent increase in the number of Asians and Pacific Islanders elected to public office—in 33 states—with most having been elected after the November 1996 elections. Like Gary Locke and Mike Honda, the majority of these new officials were elected in jurisdictions that did not have a majority of Asian and Pacific Islander voters and had to appeal to a diverse elector-ate. It is not clear whether many of them—or those who did not win elections—were handicapped by the campaign-finance scandal. What is evident is that the elected officials are part of a visible trend of increased Asian and Pacific Islander political representation.

Since the mid-1990s, groups like the Asian Pacific Planning and Policy Council of Southern California, an umbrella organization of more than 50 Asian and Pacific Islander social services and civil rights groups in Los Angeles, have escalated their campaigns to naturalize and register re-cently arrived Asians and Pacific Islanders. These groups have placed voter registration at the top of their leadership agendas. At the same time, a number of individuals who previously restricted their contributions solely to electing political candidates have begun to make donations in support of voter-registration campaigns in Asian and Pacific Islander com-munities (Ha, 1997).

Regardless of the controversy surrounding the November 1996 elec-tions, there is little question that issues of political participation and pub-lic-policy representation have become increasingly salient and compel-ling for the Asian and Pacific Islander population. At the same time, there has been considerable speculation by the mainstream media about the current status and future impact of the Asian and Pacific Islander elector-ate on American politics (Arax, 1986; Tachibana, 1986; Stokes, 1988; Gurwitt, 1990; Karnow, 1992; Skelton, 1993; Miller, 1995; Purdum, 1997).

This heightened electoral participation and political potential of Asians and Pacific Islanders is all the more remarkable in the context of the historical legacy of disenfranchisement of Asians and Pacific Island-ers, evidenced by the plethora of discriminatory laws and policies rang-ing from the Chinese Exclusion Act of 1882 to *Ozawa v. United States* (1922), which forbade Asian immigrants from becoming naturalized citi-zens (Chuman, 1976; Ichioka, 1977; Takaki, 1989; Chan, 1991). These legal barriers prevented early Asian immigrants from becoming involved in electoral politics in any form—from the type of ward politics practiced by European immigrants in the Atlantic and Midwest states to simply vot-ing—and substantially delayed the development of political participation and representation by Asians and Pacific Islanders in Hawaii, California, and elsewhere until the second generation after World War II—more than 100 years after their initial period of immigration.

Even though the national news media have often, since the mid-1960s, touted Asians and Pacific Islanders as America's "model minority"—a label that Asian and Pacific Islander leaders and scholars have disputed because of its simplistic implication that other minority groups can over-come racial and other discriminatory barriers by following the example of

Asians and Pacific Islanders—their reputed success has disguised their historic lack of access and influence in the nation's most significant political and social decision-making arenas and institutions (Suzuki, 1977; Chun, 1980; Miller, 1992; Woo, 1994; Walker-Moffat, 1995). At the same time, Asian and Pacific Islander civil rights groups have remained vigilant in seeking the elimination of "political structural barriers" such as unfair redistricting plans and the lack of Asian-language bilingual ballots, which many leaders believe have prevented Asian and Pacific Islanders from fully exercising their voting rights (Bai, 1991; Kwoh and Hui, 1993).

Asian and Pacific Islander's participation in electoral and other forms of political activities deserves special focus because the topic has received far less scholarly and public-policy attention than other forms of individual and group-level societal involvement by Asians and Pacific Islanders. Indeed, in contrast to their purported "over-representation," or success, in some sectors of American society such as higher education or small-business enterprises, Asians and Pacific Islanders appear to be "under-represented," or, at least, less represented than many other ethnic and racial groups, in the political arena. This appears to be the case despite the fact that the Asian and Pacific Islander population exhibits seemingly high educational and socioeconomic attainment levels, which are usually associated with above-average political participation (Nakanishi, 1986a). Nonetheless, clearly increased political participation provides a number of special vantage points from which to understand the ramifications of the extraordinary recent demographic growth and diversification of the Asian and Pacific Islander population in the broader context of changing race relations in America, as well as increasingly important international processes and events.

## THE NEW ASIAN PACIFIC AMERICAN POPULATION: A DEMOGRAPHIC REVOLUTION

The Asian and Pacific Islander population has undergone a series of dramatic demographic transformations since the 1960s that have greatly augmented their numbers and led to their extraordinary levels of internal heterogeneity. These trends have had, and will continue to have, a significant impact on issues dealing with their access, representation, and influence in both public and private institutions and sectors. To begin with, Asians and Pacific Islanders are the fastest growing group, their population having doubled from 1.5 million in 1970 to 3.5 million in 1980, reaching 7.2 million in 1990. Recent projections estimate that Asians and Pacific Islanders will continue to increase to 12 million by 2000 and nearly 20 million by 2020 (Fawcett and Carino, 1987; LEAP Asian Pacific American Public Policy Institute and the UCLA Asian American Studies Center,

1993; *Rafu Shimpo*, 1995). The increase can be attributed, in large measure, to the Immigration Act of 1965, which eliminated the discriminatory quota provisions of the Immigration Act of 1924; the Indochinese Refugee Resettlement Program Act of 1975; and the Refugee Act of 1980. The latter two legislative measures permitted the migration and entry of nearly 1 million refugees from Southeast Asia (Hing, 1993; Hing and Lee, 1996).

## Effects of Immigration

Reversing a four-decade trend begun in the 1930s, Asians and Pacific Islanders now represent one of the largest groups of legal immigrants in the United States. Between 1931 and 1960, when the provisions of the 1924 National Origins Act were in effect, 58 percent of legal U.S. immigrants were from Europe, 21 percent from North America, 15 percent from Latin America, and the smallest portion, 5 percent, from Asia. By 1980 to 1984, however, Europe represented 12 percent of the total population of legal U.S. immigrants and North America, 2 percent; conversely, Latin American countries accounted for 35 percent, and Asian countries, 48 percent of the United States total legal immigrant populations (United Way Asian Pacific Research and Development Council, 1985). Indeed, from 1981 to 1996, the top 10 sending nations were Latin American and Asian.[3]

From 1970 to 1980, and continuing into the 1990s, the Asian and Pacific Islander population also dramatically shifted from being largely U.S.-born to predominantly foreign-born, as a result of the surge in migration. In the 1990 Census, 65.6 percent of all Asians and Pacific Islanders were foreign-born: 79.9 percent of the Vietnamese, 72.7 percent of the Koreans, 64.4 percent of the Filipinos, 75.4 percent of the Asian Indians, and 69.3 percent of the Chinese populations were born outside the United States. Of all Asian and Pacific Islander groups, with 32.4 percent foreign-born, only the Japanese had more U.S-born in its population. In marked contrast, 8.7 percent of White, 7.2 percent of Black, and 38.5 percent of Hispanic populations were foreign-born (U.S. Department of Commerce, 1993b). In California in 1994, 64.5 percent of Asians and Pacific Islanders were foreign-born, compared with 44.3 percent of Hispanics, 20.8 percent of Whites, and 3.7 percent of Blacks (U.S. Department of Commerce, 1993a). Recent population projections estimate that foreign-born Asians and Pacific Islanders will remain in the majority for several decades to

---

[3]From 1981 to 1996, there were 13,484,275 immigrants to the United States. The top 10 sending nations were  Mexico (3,304,682), Philippines (843,741), Vietnam (719,239), China (539,261), Dominican Republic (509,902), India (498,309), and Korea (453,018) (Immigration and Naturalization Service, 1998).

come (LEAP Asian Pacific American Public Policy Institute and the UCLA Asian American Studies Center, 1993; Shinagawa, 1996).

Since the 1960s, there have also been significant changes in the relative representation of ethnic and national groups within the Asian and Pacific Islander population. In 1970, the Japanese were the largest Asian and Pacific Islander ethnic group, representing nearly 40 percent of all Asians and Pacific Islanders. By 1980, however, both Chinese (812,178) and Filipino (781,894) surpassed the Japanese (716,331); and other Asian and Pacific Islander groups, like Asian Indians (387,223), Koreans (357,393), and Vietnamese (245,025) grew rapidly through immigration. By 1990, both Chinese (1,645,472) and Filipino (1,406,770) populations had grown to nearly twice the size of the Japanese population (847,562), which had experienced relatively little immigration from Japan and a gradually declining birth rate. The other three major Asian and Pacific Islander groups—Asian Indians (815,447), Koreans (798,849), and Vietnamese (614,547)—also recorded substantial population gains by 1990. It is projected that in 2000 the Japanese group will fall further down the population scale, with practically all other major Asian and Pacific Islander groups outnumbering them, and Filipinos will replace Chinese as the largest Asian and Pacific Islander ethnic group (LEAP Asian Pacific American Public Policy Institute and the UCLA Asian American Studies Center, 1993).

In 1990, California, with approximately 3 million, had the largest Asian and Pacific Islander population—40 percent of the total U.S. Asian and Pacific Islander population, outnumbering the state's Black population, and second only to the rapidly growing Hispanic population, which continues to be California's single largest population of color (Bouvier and Martin, 1985; California Department of Finance, 1985). In 2000, it is estimated that more than 5 million of the nation's projected 12.1 million population of Asians and Pacific Islanders will be Californians (*Rafu Shimpo*, 1995). At the same time, other non-Western states and cities also experienced considerable growth in their Asian and Pacific Islander populations. In 1997, New York had the second largest Asian and Pacific Islander population (952,736), followed by Hawaii (748,748), Texas (532,972), and New Jersey (423,738) (U.S. Department of Commerce, 1999).

## Diversity of the Asian Pacific American Population

The Asian and Pacific Islander population clearly is not a single, monolithic group (U.S. Commission on Civil Rights, 1979; Chun, 1980; Endo et al., 1980; Gardner et al., 1985; United Way Asian Pacific Research and Development Council, 1985; Fawcett and Carino, 1987; U.S. Commission on Civil Rights, 1992; U.S. Department of Commerce, 1993b; Tam,

1995; Min, 1995; Espiritu, 1997; Lee, 1998). It is an extremely heterogeneous population, with respect to ethnic and national origins, cultural
values, generation, social class, religion, multiracial background, sexual
orientations, and other socially differentiating characteristics (Root, 1992;
Leong, 1995; Gall and Natividad, 1995; Nash, 1997; Stanfield, 1997; Lee,
1998).

> The most evident fact about Asian and Pacific immigration is its diversi-
> ty. Whether one looks at the political and economic status of the coun-
> tries of origin, the characteristics of the immigrants themselves, or their
> modes of adaptation in the host society, differences are more striking
> than similarities. Sending countries include socialist Vietnam, capitalist
> South Korea, and colonial American Samoa—each having quite differ-
> ent economic resources and strategies for development. Significant
> groups of immigrants include Hmong hill farmers, Indian scientists and
> engineers, Chinese businessmen, and Filipino service workers—as well
> as Thai, Filipino, and Korean women immigrating as marriage partners
> (Fawcett and Arnold, 1987:453).

Even within any particular Asian and Pacific Islander group, like the
Chinese, within-group differences can be quite pronounced, reflecting
different historical waves of immigration and different segments of a
class hierarchical structure (Nee and Nee, 1974; Zhou, 1992; Fong, 1994;
Horton, 1995; Kwong, 1996; see also, for Indo-Americans, Kar, 1995/96;
for Koreans, Kim, 1997; Park, 1998). Hirschman and Wong (1981) use
census data to illustrate significant within-group differences in socioeconomic achievement among foreign-born versus U.S.-born Chinese, Japanese, and Filipinos.

It is highly likely that the terms "Asian American" and "Asian Pacific
American," which have been imbued with constantly changing strategic,
ideological, and tactical connotations since they were first articulated in
the 1960s, will undergo further reconsideration in the future (Espiritu,
1992).

## Technical and Methodological Problems Facing Researchers

In contrast to the study of other, larger racial and ethnic populations,
a common problem facing researchers studying Asian and Pacific Islander
populations is that empirical data are not routinely collected or reported
for Asians and Pacific Islanders in toto or, more important, with respect to
the different ethnic groups of the population. Until recently, the decennial
census represented one of the few quantitative data sources providing
such ethnic breakdowns for 13 different major Asian and Pacific Islander
groups—Asian Indians, Chinese, Hmongs, Cambodians, Laotians, Thais,
Guamanians, Hawaiians, Japanese, Koreans, Filipinos, Samoans, and Viet-

namese, among others. Decennial census data, however, have assorted technical and substantive limitations, especially in terms of the restricted set of individual-level characteristics surveyed, the long delay between collection and public dissemination of data, and the special sampling problems resulting in substantial undercounting, which persistently have hampered the gathering of data from Asians and Pacific Islanders and other racial and ethnic populations (U.S. Commission on Civil Rights, 1979; Yu, 1982). Further, it was not until 1989 that the periodic Current Population Surveys (CPS), also conducted by the U.S. Bureau of the Census, separated Asians and Pacific Islanders from the category of "Other," and reported data on their voter registration and voting patterns, as had been done for many years for Blacks, Whites, and Hispanics.

Although data from these surveys are highly useful in interpreting patterns in national and regional trends (indeed, they will be a focus of analysis later in this paper), because of the shortcomings noted, researchers studying Asian and Pacific Islander populations must often devise tailored data-collection strategies. To investigate topics such as the extent of interracial marriages, usage rates of mental health facilities, conditions of poverty, or levels of political involvement for specific Asian and Pacific Islander groups, a sufficiently large sample of empirical data is needed prior to the application of rigorous data analysis tools (Kikumura and Kitano, 1973; Yu, 1982; Nakanishi, 1986b; Ong, 1993; Ong and Hee, 1993; National Asian Pacific American Legal Consortium, 1996). Yet, public records of marriage licenses and voter registrations do not contain information about the ethnicity, national origin, generation, or racial background; and there is, presently, no reliable computer-based dictionary of Asian and Pacific Islander surnames for identifying members of the different ethnic and national groups.

To research interracial marriage rates or voter-registration trends among Asians and Pacific Islanders, scholars have had to assemble and train panels of bilingual and bicultural researchers to identify and locate Asian and Pacific Islander-surnamed individuals who obtained marriage licenses or registered to vote. What would seem to be a simple data-collection exercise in a municipality like Los Angeles County involves, for Asian and Pacific Islanders, analyzing tens of thousands of marriage licenses, or listings of millions of registered voters. Reliability of the overall identification processes is controlled through multiple verification of names in which two or three professionally trained, and linguistically or culturally knowledgeable readers, examine and verify the same records.

Such added attention to the gathering of reliable and valid data is crucial to researching topics dealing with the diverse Asian and Pacific Islander ethnic groups and analyzing within-group differences and similarities. Both academic and public-policy inquiries of the political participation and behavior of Asian and Pacific Islander populations should be guided by similar data-gathering considerations, and thus avoid common pitfalls that result from not being fully informed or appreciative of the complexities of this growing sector of the nation's population. Grant Din (1984) provides a revealing example of such a faux pas:

> A *San Francisco Examiner* analysis of the 1984 California presidential primary discussed the results of the ABC News exit polling in California and New Jersey. According to these results, in California, "Mondale carried the Asian vote with 40 percent, Hart trailed with 33 percent (and Jackson had 20 percent)." A closer examination, however, reveals that only 2 percent of the 1,125 voters surveyed, or 23, were Asian American. This translates into 9 votes for Mondale, 8 for Hart, and 5 for Jackson! The poll claimed an overall margin of error of 3 percent, but it must have been higher for such a small population (p. 21).

## Educational Attainment

Understanding between- and within-group differences in educational attainment among Asians and Pacific Islanders has long been a subject of interest to researchers.[4] For Asians and Pacific Islanders, Blacks, American Indians, Hispanics, non-Hispanic Whites, and "Others," Table 6-1 provides 1990 Census data on levels of educational attainment for males and females, 25 years old and older, targeted for voter-registration campaigns. Asians and Pacific Islanders and Hispanics appear to be at polar extremes of the educational continuum, with Asians and Pacific Islanders having a seemingly unrivaled percentage of college graduates, and Hispanics exhibiting a disturbingly unmatched percentage of individuals with less than eight years of formal schooling. Previous studies have made similar observations (Brown et al., 1980; Duran, 1983; Davis et al., 1985; Sue and Padilla, 1986).

However, Table 6-2, which differentiates the Asian and Pacific Islander category among 11 ethnic groups, illustrates the need to recognize and analyze the internal heterogeneity of this population. Several Asian and Pacific Islander groups, for example Cambodians, Hmongs, and Laotians, do not reflect high educational attainment levels, and generally have far fewer college graduates and proportionately more non-high

---

[4]There have been a growing number of studies on Asian and Pacific Islander educational issues and institutions. At the K-12 levels, see Sue and Padilla (1986), Kiang and Lee (1993), Kao (1995), Lee (1996), Asian Americans/Pacific Islanders in Philanthropy (1997), and Zhou (1998). For higher educational issues and trends, see Hsia (1988a, 1988b), Asian and Pacific American Education Advisory Committee (1990), Escueta and O'Brien (1991), and Hune and Chan (1997). For an overview of Asian Pacific American educational topics, see Nakanishi and Yamano Nishida (1995).

TABLE 6-1 Education-Attainment Levels (percentage) for Males and Females, 25 Years and Older, California, 1990

|  | Eight Years or Less of Schooling | Non-High School Graduate | College Graduate |
|---|---|---|---|
| Asian Pacific Americans |  |  |  |
| Males | 11 | 19 | 39 |
| Females | 17 | 26 | 31 |
| Blacks |  |  |  |
| Males | 7 | 25 | 15 |
| Females | 7 | 24 | 14 . |
| American Indians |  |  |  |
| Males | 9 | 27 | 12 |
| Females | 9 | 30 | 10 |
| Hispanics |  |  |  |
| Males | 35 | 55 | 8 |
| Females | 35 | 55 | 6 |
| Non-Hispanic Whites |  |  |  |
| Males | 4 | 13 | 33 |
| Females | 4 | 15 | 23 |
| Others |  |  |  |
| Males | 39 | 60.4 | 6 |
| Females | 41 | 61 | 4 |
| Total Population |  |  |  |
| Males | 11 | 23 | 27 |
| Females | 11 | 25 | 20 |

SOURCE: 1990 Census of Population, Social and Economic Characteristics, California (1993).

school graduates (and those with less than eight years of schooling) than Asians and Pacific Islanders, as a whole, and other ethnic and racial populations. At the same time, other Asian and Pacific Islander groups with stronger group-level academic profiles, like the Chinese, Koreans, Thais, and Asian Indians, also show significant percentages of individuals with limited educational backgrounds. Approximately 25 percent of the women in these four groups had not completed high school, and more than 10 percent had less than eight years of schooling. Such between- and within-group differences, as well as other quality-of-life indicators, are expected to continue among Asians and Pacific Islanders in the future

TABLE 6-2  Education-Attainment Levels (percentage) for Asian Pacific American Males and Females, 25 Years and Older, California, 1990

|  | Eight Years or Less of Schooling | Non-High School Graduate | College Graduate |
|---|---|---|---|
| Asian Indians |  |  |  |
| Males | 2 | 15 | 72 |
| Females | 16 | 27 | 42 |
| Cambodians |  |  |  |
| Males | 45 | 56 | 8 |
| Females | 66 | 77 | 3 |
| Chinese |  |  |  |
| Males | 14 | 23 | 44 |
| Females | 21 | 31 | 32 |
| Hmongs |  |  |  |
| Males | 49 | 60 | 7 |
| Females | 65 | 85 | 2 |
| Japanese |  |  |  |
| Males | 3 | 8 | 44 |
| Females | 5 | 11 | 30 |
| Koreans |  |  |  |
| Males | 5 | 11 | 45 |
| Females | 13 | 24 | 27 |
| Laotians |  |  |  |
| Males | 45 | 57 | 7 |
| Females | 65 | 76 | 6 |
| Pacific Islanders |  |  |  |
| Males | 8 | 24 | 12 |
| Females | 10 | 28 | 9 |
| Filipinos |  |  |  |
| Males | 8 | 14 | 35 |
| Females | 11 | 18 | 41 |
| Thais |  |  |  |
| Males | 6 | 15 | 43 |
| Females | 18 | 28 | 27 |

SOURCE: 1990 Census of Population, Social and Economic Characteristics, California (1993).

(LEAP Asian Pacific American Public Policy Institute and the UCLA Asian American Studies Center, 1993).

## Finding Common Ground

The combination of significant demographic growth, along with extraordinary internal diversification, has had a number of implications for Asians and Pacific Islanders. They have come to represent an increasingly sizable percentage of the populations in some states, most notably California, and in  urban areas like Los Angeles and San Francisco counties. As a result, such topics as redistricting, bilingual ballots, and fair political representation have become critical policy issues for Asians and Pacific Islanders involved in electoral politics. Indeed, a number of Asian and Pacific Islander communities—from Silicon Valley in Northern California to Queens and Chinatown in New York City—expressed deep concern about potential gerrymandering practices, and the possible dilution of Asian and Pacific Islander electoral strength during reapportionment hearings at the beginning of the 1990s. As never before, Asian and Pacific Islander leaders participated actively in these deliberations, and they will likely continue to do so (Saito, 1998).

At the same time, their unusual internal heterogeneity will challenge leaders and organizers of different Asian and Pacific Islander sectors and communities—often separated by both real and symbolic boundaries of national origin, language, culture, social class, religion, and other characteristics—to find common ground on key policy issues, to cope with the uneven political development and maturation of different ethnic groups, and to seek effective mechanisms for pursuing shared interests in a unified manner on both continuous and ad hoc bases (LEAP Asian Pacific American Public Policy Institute and the UCLA Asian American Studies Center, 1993; Ong, 1994). Although this may appear visionary, there are examples of such unifying issues since the 1970s, including opposition to university admissions quotas, anti-Asian violence, glass ceilings, and unfair immigration policy legislation. (Nakanishi, 1989; Tsuang, 1989; Takagi, 1992; U.S. Commission on Civil Rights, 1992; Woo, 1994; Chi et al., 1996; National Asian Pacific American Legal Consortium, 1996; Lin, 1997; Prashad, 1998).

## THE EMERGING ASIAN PACIFIC AMERICAN ELECTORATE

. . . [A]lthough Asian Pacific Americans as a whole currently reflect a majority preference for the Democratic party, it should be obvious that the large and growing pool of non-registered voters could have a profound impact on the overall partisan identification of Asian Pacific

Americans, and especially among groups like Koreans and Vietnamese, which are overwhelmingly composed of recent immigrants. Therefore, the extent to which the two major parties further cultivate their relations with, and address the specific concerns of, the Asian Pacific American community will greatly determine the future partisan direction of the Asian Pacific American electorate (Nakanishi, 1986b:10).

In recent years, a number of political commentators and scholars have speculated about whether Asians and Pacific Islanders will become a major force in American electoral politics, perhaps akin to the Jewish population, because of their dramatic demographic growth and concentration in certain key electoral states like California, New York, and Texas (Tachibana, 1986; Cain, 1988; Stokes, 1988; Nakanishi, 1986a; Karnow, 1992; Miller, 1995). Many believe that if Asians and Pacific Islanders, like Jewish voters, come to represent a percentage of the electorate that is comparable to, or greater than, their share of the total population, then they could become a highly influential "swing vote" in critical local, state, and presidential elections. For example, if Asians and Pacific Islanders, who represent 10 percent of California residents, also became 10 percent of the California electorate—which will continue to control the nation's largest number of Congressional seats and presidential electoral college votes—then they could play a strategically important role in national and local elections. Indeed, their voting potential, coupled with other attractive aspects of their political infrastructure, like their proven record of campaign fund-raising, could elevate Asians and Pacific Islanders to the status of important actors in American electoral politics (*Asianweek*, 1984; Miller, 1995; Purdum, 1997).

Since the 1970s, there has been an unmistakable increase in the representation of Asians and Pacific Islanders in electoral politics. In 1978, when the first edition of the *Asian Pacific American Political Almanac* was published, it listed several hundred elected officials, who held offices primarily in Hawaii, California, and Washington (Nakanishi, 1978); almost all were second- and third-generation Asians and Pacific Islanders, and the vast majority were Japanese. In contrast, as mentioned earlier, the eighth edition of the almanac, published in 1998, lists more than 2,000 Asian and Pacific Islander elected and appointed officials in 33 states, as well as the federal government (Nakanishi and Lai, 1998). Although most are second or third generation, a growing number are immigrants, such as Jay Kim of Walnut, California, the first Korean elected to Congress; David Valderrama, the first Filipino elected as a Delegate to the Assembly of Maryland; and City Councilman Tony Lam of Westminster, California, the first Vietnamese elected to public office. At the same time, in the 1990s, Asian and Pacific Islander candidates have run well-financed, professional campaigns for mayor in some of the nation's largest cities, including Los Angeles, San Francisco, and Oakland.

Beyond this seemingly optimistic and glowing assessment of Asian and Pacific Islander electoral achievements, however, is the reality of an immigrant-dominant population that has yet to reach its full electoral potential, especially in transforming its extraordinary population growth into comparable percentages of registered voters, and actual voters during elections. In California, for example, Asians and Pacific Islanders may represent 10 percent of all residents, but it is estimated that Asians and Pacific Islanders are no more than 5 percent of the state's registered voters and 3 percent of those who actually vote (The Field Institute, 1992).

## Voter Registration

Previous studies have found that rates of voter registration vary markedly; Japanese Americans have the highest percentage of registered voters and Southeast Asians have the lowest (Nakanishi, 1986b). The discussion here is based on the 1990, 1992, and 1994 CPS data, which included information on voter registration and voting for Asians and Pacific Islanders. These data allow examination of both national and regional trends, with a sufficiently large sample of Asians and Pacific Islanders,[5] and analysis of potential differences in registration and voting rates in relation to U.S.-born and naturalized citizens, which has rarely been examined rigorously (Din, 1984; Nakanishi, 1986b; Horton, 1995; Shinagawa, 1995; Tam, 1995). The 1994 CPS data were particularly useful because they provided detailed information, similar to the decennial census, about the citizenship status of individuals. It was therefore possible to differentiate between both foreign-born and U.S.-born Asians and Pacific Islanders as well as between naturalized and non-naturalized immigrant and refugee Asians and Pacific Islanders. Unfortunately, this data source does not allow analysis of differences in electoral participation among the array of Asian ethnic communities.

The major findings are that foreign-born Asians and Pacific Islanders have lower rates of voter registration than U.S.-born Asians and Pacific Islanders; however, naturalized Asians and Pacific Islanders who have been in this country for more than 20 years have rates of registration that are comparable to or exceed those of U.S.-born Asians and Pacific Islanders, while those who arrived more than 30 years ago have higher rates of

---

[5]The 1994 CPS included 3,317 Asians and Pacific Islanders out of a total sample of 102,197. The 1990 survey included 2,914 of 105,875; and the 1992 CPS had 3,443 of 102,901. Both weighted and unweighted data were analyzed for this report.

both registration and voting. As was the case in a separate analysis of naturalization rates (Ong and Nakanishi, 1996), multiple-regression analysis revealed that year of entry was the single most important factor in determining voter-registration rates. In terms of actual voting, two other factors along with year of entry—educational attainment and age— were found to be the best predictors. Finally, the characteristics of Asian and Pacific Islander voters as a whole, as well as between U.S.-born and foreign-born, are reflective of an ethnic electorate that is far from being monolithic with respect to political party affiliations, ideological preferences, and voting preferences. Rather, it has many dimensions of diversity, which are influencing its continued development.

## Rates of Voter Registration

The Asian and Pacific Islander population in the United States has the largest percentage of individuals over the age of 18 (hereafter, adult) who cannot take the first step toward participating in American electoral politics because they are not citizens. In 1994, 55 percent of adult Asians and Pacific Islanders were not citizens, compared with 44 percent of Hispanics, 5 percent of Blacks, and 2 percent of non-Hispanic Whites. By geographic region, percentages of non-citizens among the adult Asian and Pacific Islander populations showed that Honolulu had the lowest (21 percent), New York had the highest (73 percent), Los Angeles County followed closely (63 percent), and the Oakland-San Francisco region also had a substantial percentage (52 percent).

According to CPS data for 1994, nationwide, 1,165,000 Asians and Pacific Islanders were registered voters, of whom 58 percent (680,190) were U.S.-born and 42 percent (485,710) were naturalized citizens (Table 6-3). California's Asian and Pacific Islander electorate, which accounted for 42 percent of the country's Asian and Pacific Islander registered voters, mirrored the nation's composition of U.S.-born (58 percent) to foreign-born (42 percent) voters. Hawaii, on the other hand, which has far less Asian and Pacific Islander immigration than many mainland states, had an overwhelmingly U.S.-born Asian and Pacific Islander electorate (88 percent). Hawaii's Asian and Pacific Islander voter profile was similar to that of other racial and ethnic populations, which had substantially higher percentages of U.S.-born voters: 87 percent of Hispanic, 99 percent of Black, and 98 percent of non-Hispanic White voters.

Asians and Pacific Islanders (by birth or naturalization) exhibited low overall rates of voter registration. Nationally, 1994 CPS data estimated that 56 percent of all Asians and Pacific Islanders were registered, compared with 61 percent of Blacks and 69 percent of non-Hispanic Whites (Table 6-4). The level of Hispanic voter registration (53 percent) was simi-

TABLE 6-3 Distribution of Naturalized and U.S.-Born Asian Pacific American Registered Voters, 1994

|  | California | Hawaii | Rest of Nation | National Total |
|---|---|---|---|---|
| U.S.-born | 271,820 (58%) | 218,580 (88%) | 189,790 (42%) | 680,190 (58%) |
| Naturalized | 194,840 (42%) | 29,170 (12%) | 261,680 (58%) | 485,710 (42%) |
| Total | 466,660 | 247,750 | 451,470 | 1,165,900 |
| Percent of national total | 40% | 21% | 39% | 100% |

SOURCE: Current Population Survey (1994).

TABLE 6-4 Voter Registration and Turnout Rates (percentage) for Asian Pacific Americans and Others, 1994

|  | Registered to Vote | Voted in 1994 Elections |
|---|---|---|
| Asian Americans |  |  |
|   U.S. born | 56 | 78 |
|   Foreign born | 49 | 74 |
|   Overall | 53 | 76 |
| Hispanics |  |  |
|   U.S. born | 53 | 62 |
|   Foreign born | 53 | 74 |
|   Overall | 53 | 64 |
| Blacks |  |  |
|   U.S. born | 61 | 63 |
|   Foreign born | 58 | 78 |
|   Overall | 61 | 63 |
| Non-Hispanic Whites |  |  |
|   U.S. born | 69 | 73 |
|   Foreign born | 68 | 78 |
|   Overall | 69 | 73 |

SOURCE: Current Population Survey (1994).

lar to that of Asians and Pacific Islanders. Similar patterns for these population groups were observed in 1992 in Los Angeles, Oakland-San Francisco, New York, and Honolulu. Indeed, in some regions, the differences
in voter-registration rates between Asians and Pacific Islanders and non-
Hispanic Whites, who usually have the highest rates of registration, were
quite substantial. In 1992, in the Oakland-San Francisco region, 56 percent
of all adult Asians and Pacific Islanders were registered to vote, compared with 86 percent of non-Hispanic Whites, 73 percent of Blacks, and
63 percent of Hispanics. At the same time, voter-registration rates for
Asian and Pacific Islander communities were highest in Los Angeles (64
percent) and lowest in New York (54 percent). Previous studies found
that Asians and Pacific Islanders have lower rates of voter registration
than Blacks and non-Hispanic Whites, and usually the same or somewhat
lower rates than that of Hispanics. Although this is a consistent finding, it
is nonetheless an extremely puzzling one because of Asians and Pacific
Islanders' relatively high attainment levels in education and other socioeconomic variables, which has, in political science research, long been
associated with active electoral participation (Nakanishi, 1986a; Cain,
1988; The Field Institute, 1992; Erie and Brackman, 1993; Lien, 1994).

Among Asians and Pacific Islanders, those who were U.S. born had a
higher overall rate of voter registration than did those who were born
abroad and had become naturalized. In 1994, as Table 6-4 illustrates, 56
percent of all U.S.-born Asians and Pacific Islanders were registered compared with 49 percent of those who were naturalized. Indeed, foreign-
born Asians and Pacific Islanders had among the lowest rates of any
group, including naturalized Hispanics (53 percent). However, in terms
of electoral participation beyond registration, both Asians and Pacific Islander naturalized and U.S.-born voters had among the highest rates of
voting during the 1994 elections. Therefore, Asian and Pacific Islander
immigrants appear to reflect a provocative series of discrete, nonlinear
trends from becoming citizens to becoming registered voters and then to
becoming actual voters: they have one of the highest rates of naturalization after immigrating, but one of the lowest rates of voter registration
after becoming citizens. Once they register to vote, however, naturalized
Asians and Pacific Islanders have among the highest rates of voting of
any group (Ong and Nakanishi, 1996).

A closer and more detailed examination of naturalized Asians and
Pacific Islanders indicates that those who immigrated prior to 1975 had
rates of voter registration comparable to, if not higher than, those who
were born in this country (Table 6-5). Indeed, this was the case for practically all age groups, all educational attainment levels, and for women. On
the other hand, those who immigrated since the late 1970s had rates of
registration substantially lower than U.S.-born citizens and naturalized

TABLE 6-5 Registration and Voting (percentage) by
Year of Immigration for Naturalized and U.S.-Born
Asian Pacific American Citizens, 1994

| Year of Immigration | Registered to Vote | Voted |
|---|---|---|
| Pre-1965 | 77 | 92 |
| 1965-1974 | 57 | 66 |
| 1975-1985 | 43 | 71 |
| 1986-1994 | 26 | 81 |
| Overall | 49 | 74 |
| U.S.-born | 56 | 78 |

SOURCE: Current Population Survey (1994).

citizens who arrived before 1975. This was consistent for practically all age and educational attainment levels, as well as for men and women. As in the case of naturalization, year of entry was the best predictor of voter registration in a multiple-regression analysis. For voting, by contrast, year of entry, educational attainment, and age were the strongest explanatory variables.

Like the process of naturalization, the importance of time-dependent variables for electoral participation is consistent with the view that immigrants and refugees must often undergo a prolonged and multifaceted process of social adaptation and learning before fully participating in their newly adopted country. To become actively involved in American electoral politics, and to become politically acculturated, may be one of the most complex, lengthy, and least understood learning experiences. Foreign-born Asians and Pacific Islanders, like other groups of immigrants (Gittleman, 1982), largely acquired their core political values, attitudes, and behavioral orientations in sociopolitical systems that were different in a variety of ways from that of the United States. Some of their countries of origin did not have universal suffrage, others were dominated by a single political party (which made voting nearly inconsequential), and still others were in extreme political upheaval as a result of civil war or international conflict. Indeed, one of the major reasons why many Asian and Pacific Islander refugees left their homelands was to escape horrendous political situations. As a result, previously learned lessons and orientations toward government and political activities may not be easily supplanted or supplemented. For example, adult education classes in American civics and government, which immigrants usually take to prepare for their naturalization examinations, expose them to the most rudimentary facts about American government, but probably have little or no impact on their preexisting political belief systems, their general sense of political efficacy and trust toward government, or their knowledge of the traditions, current policy debates, and political party agendas of American politics. Learning about and, more important, becoming actively involved in politics "American style" through registering to vote and voting in elections, probably takes place through a range of personal and group experiences that go beyond citizenship classes, and evolve over time and in conjunction with other aspects of acculturating to American life and society.

The Asian and Pacific Islander electorate is clearly in the process of transformation and change. Its future characteristics and impact will be largely determined by the extent to which newly naturalized, foreign-born Asians and Pacific Islanders are incorporated into the political system, and encouraged to register to vote and to cast their ballots. An electorate that "looks like Asian and Pacific Islander America," in all of its dimensions of diversity, especially in being predominantly foreign-born rather than reflecting its current U.S.-born majority profile, may have far different partisan preferences and public-policy priorities.

The changing electorate in the City of Monterey Park in Los Angeles County, where Asians and Pacific Islanders constituted 56 percent of all residents in 1990, is illustrative of trends in political partisanism (Table 6-6). In 1984, among Chinese voters, there was a plurality of Democrats (43 percent) over Republicans (31 percent), but also an extremely high percentage of individuals who specified no party affiliation (25 percent), and considered themselves to be independents.[6] By 1997, Chinese voters (with most probably being recently naturalized), who accounted for the vast majority of new registered voters in Monterey Park since 1984, were nearly evenly divided among Democrats (34 percent), Republicans (33 percent), and no-party independents (30 percent) (Nakanishi, 1998). In contrast, the Japanese, who experienced far less population growth, reflected a different electoral profile, showing a preference for the Democratic party and a greater likelihood of declaring a party affiliation rather than registering as an independent. Moreover, the total Asian and Pacific Islander electorate in Monterey Park changed its overall partisan orientation through the addition of these new, largely Chinese, registered voters. In 1984, Asian and Pacific Islander voters as a whole in Monterey

---

[6]Din (1984) and Chen et al. (1989) found that some groups of Asian and Pacific Islander voters register in higher percentages than expected as having no party affiliation or as independents.

TABLE 6-6  Asian Pacific American Registered Voters, Monterey Park, California, 1984 and 1997

| | Number Registered | Democrats | Republicans | Other Parties | No Party |
|---|---|---|---|---|---|
| **Citywide** | | | | | |
| 1984 | 22,021 (100.0%) | 13,657 (62.0%) | 5,564 (25.0%) | 368 (1.7%) | 2,290 (10.4%) |
| 1997 | 23,849 (100.0%) | 12,861 (53.9%) | 6,553 (27.5%) | 676 (2.8%) | 3,759 (15.8%) |
| 1984-1997 net gain/loss | +1,828 | -796 | +989 | +308 | +1,469 |
| **Asian Pacific Americans Total** | | | | | |
| 1984 | 6,441 (100.0%) | 3,265 (50.7%) | 1,944 (30.2%) | 54 (0.8%) | 1,178 (18.3%) |
| 1997 | 10,495 (100.0%) | 4,051 (38.6%) | 3,533 (33.7%) | 318 (3.0%) | 2,593 (24.7%) |
| 1984-1997 net gain/loss | +4,054 | +786 | +1,589 | +264 | +1,415 |
| **Non-Asian Pacific Americans Total** | | | | | |
| 1984 | 15,438 (100.0%) | 10,392 (67.3%) | 3,620 (23.4%) | 314 (2.0%) | 1,112 (7.2%) |
| 1997 | 13,354 (100.0%) | 8,810 (65.9%) | 3,020 (22.6%) | 358 (2.7%) | 1,166 (8.7%) |
| 1984-1997 net gain/loss | -2,084 | -1,582 | -600 | +44 | -146 |
| **Chinese Americans** | | | | | |
| 1984 | 3,152 (100.0%) | 1,360 (43.1%) | 972 (30.8%) | 23 (0.7%) | 797 (25.3%) |
| 1997 | 5,935 (100.0%) | 2,028 (34.0%) | 1,983 (33.4%) | 164 (2.7%) | 1,760 (29.7%) |
| 1984-1997 net gain/loss | +2,783 | +668 | +1,011 | +144 | +963 |
| **Japanese Americans** | | | | | |
| 1984 | 2,586 (100.0%) | 1,429 (55.3%) | 838 (32.4%) | 21 (0.8%) | 298 (11.5%) |
| 1997 | 2,647 (100.0%) | 1,329 (50.2%) | 891 (33.7%) | 44 (1.6%) | 383 (14.5%) |
| 1984-1997 net gain/loss | +61 | -100 | +53 | +23 | +85 |

Note: In 1997, Asian Pacific Americans were 44 percent of all voters in Monterey Park; 32 percent of all Democrats; 54 percent of all Republicans; and 69 percent of all individuals who registered as No Party. In 1990, 56 percent of the residents of Monterey Park were Asian Pacific American.

SOURCE: Nakanishi (1986b).

Park showed a slight majority preference for the Democrats. By 1997, with an increase of more than 4,000 new registered voters, it was no longer possible to characterize the Asian and Pacific Islander electorate in the city in this manner. In an analogous fashion, on a larger national scale, the Asian and Pacific Islander electorate at both the grassroots and leadership levels have been undergoing, and will continue to undergo, significant changes with the increased political participation of foreign-born Asians and Pacific Islanders.

## CONCLUSION

Although there has been a visible increase in political involvement and representation by Asians and Pacific Islanders during the past decade, it would be highly remiss to conclude that they have now become a powerful and unified political entity. It would also be incorrect to conclude that they are now capable of competing equally with other political actors, be they other immigrant and minority groups or special interests, in realizing their specific political goals. Compared with other, more established political actors, like Jews and Blacks, Asians and Pacific Islanders still have not fully developed and used the wide array of real and symbolic resources that are needed to compete on an equal basis in major electoral and policy arenas with other groups. Their various levels of internal diversity have often prevented them from being the unified political actor suggested by their overarching umbrella label of Asian and Pacific Islanders. In some of the smaller California suburban cities like Torrance, Cerritos, and Monterey Park, and to a lesser extent in the big cities like San Francisco, Seattle, and Los Angeles, Asians and Pacific Islanders have become increasingly viable and recognized political participants. In most areas aside from Hawaii and at higher levels of state and federal decision-making, however, Asians and Pacific Islanders remain largely ignored and underrepresented. Indeed, as a result of both structural and group-specific constraints, they have not been able to sufficiently cultivate a statewide or national political presence. Also, they have yet to develop an explicit set of national priorities that could, at least, be recognized when major policy issues dealing with the poor, the elderly, health care, or even United States relations with Asia are legislated and implemented. At best, their present impact on American politics and public-policy deliberations has been regional and sporadic rather than national and continuous; and their reputed success as a model minority continues to disguise their lack of influence and representation in many of the most significant decision-making arenas and social institutions of American society.

The political incorporation of both U.S.-born and naturalized Asians and Pacific Islanders into the American electoral system needs to be accelerated. The contemporary remnants of the political exclusion and isolation that Asians and Pacific Islanders experienced in the past must be fully confronted and eliminated not only by Asian and Pacific Islander groups, but also by the two major political parties and others who believe that citizens should be able to fully exercise their right of franchise. Unfair redistricting of Asian and Pacific Islander communities, lack of bilingual voter-registration application forms and ballots, restrictions on campaign contributions from permanent residents, and opposition to the implementation of legislation like the National Voter Registration Act of 1993 (a.k.a. Motor Voter Act) perpetuate "political structural barriers" that must be challenged and replaced by fair and inclusive political practices and policies. Asians and Pacific Islanders, both foreign-born and U.S.-born, have much to contribute to all aspects of American political life—as voters, campaign workers, financial donors, policy experts, and elected officials—and must be allowed, and encouraged, to participate fully.

In recent years, the incentive and necessity for Asians and Pacific Islanders to become more involved in electoral politics has been greatly enhanced in both obvious and unexpected ways. Politicians and the major political parties, which had long neglected to address the unique public-policy interests and quality-of-life concerns of Asians and Pacific Islanders, have become increasingly responsive and attentive, especially to the growing sector of the Asian and Pacific Islander population that contributes sizable amounts to political campaign coffers. Less interest, however, has been shown toward augmenting the long-term voting potential of Asians and Pacific Islanders, and few attempts have been made by the Democratic or Republican parties to finance voter-registration and education campaigns in Asian and Pacific Islander communities. However, the increasing number of Asians and Pacific Islanders, especially those of immigrant background, who are seeking public office appears to be stimulating greater electoral participation among Asians and Pacific Islanders at the grassroots level. For example, it is becoming a common practice for Asian and Pacific Islander candidates to make special efforts in seeking monetary donations and in registering new voters among Asians and Pacific Islanders in the jurisdictions in which they are running for office. These activities provide Asian and Pacific Islander immigrants with important and direct vantage points from which to understand the workings of the American political system, thereby facilitating their political acculturation. At the same time, a wide array of advocacy and social services groups have formed in Asian and Pacific Islander communities across the nation, and a number of different outreach campaigns have been launched to promote citizenship and to register individuals, particularly those who have just become citizens at naturalization ceremonies.

And finally, disastrous events like the civil unrest in Los Angeles in 1992, in which more than 2,000 Korean and Asian and Pacific Islander-owned businesses were destroyed, have underscored the need for immigrant-dominant communities to place greater organizational and leadership emphasis on augmenting their access to and influence in local government and other policy arenas, as well as to increase their representation in voter-registration rolls.

The start of the new century, widely viewed optimistically because of seemingly positive demographic trends, will be an important period to witness and analyze because of the extraordinary challenges and opportunities that will undoubtedly be presented to Asians and Pacific Islanders in realizing their full potential as citizens and electoral participants. However, the level of success that they will achieve in the political arena as well as other sectors of American society will not be solely determined by the Asian and Pacific Islander population, or its leaders and organizations. It will undoubtedly require the assistance and intervention of a wide array of groups, leaders, and institutions in both the private and public sectors. Whether Asians and Pacific Islanders become a major new political force in the American electoral system is nearly impossible to predict with any precision; however, our ability to raise and seriously entertain such a question in the context of the historical disenfranchisement and exclusion of Asians and Pacific Islanders is quite revealing in itself.

## REFERENCES

Akaka, D.
  1998    From the Senate floor: Asian Americans and the political fundraising investigation. Pp. 22-28 in *The 1998-99 National Asian Pacific American Political Almanac*, D. Nakanishi and J. Lai, eds. Los Angeles: UCLA Asian American Studies Center.
Arax, M.
  1986    Group seeks to reverse voter apathy by Asians. *Los Angeles Times* (March 3):1-3.
Asian Americans/Pacific Islanders in Philanthropy (AAsian and Pacific IslanderP)
  1997    *An Invisible Crisis: The Educational Needs of Asian Pacific American Youth.* New York: Asian Americans/Pacific Islanders in Philanthropy.
Asian and Pacific American Education Advisory Committee
  1990    *Enriching California's Future: Asian/Pacific Americans in the CSU.* Long Beach, Calif.: Office of the Chancellor.
*Asianweek*
  1984    Asians called a "major national force" in political fund-raising. *Asianweek* (June 1):5.
Bai, S.
  1991    Affirmative pursuit of political equality for Asian Pacific Americans: Reclaiming the Voting Rights Act. *University of Pennsylvania Law Review* 139(3):731-767.

Bouvier, L., and P. Martin
    1985    *Population Change and California's Future.* Washington, D.C.: Population Reference
            Bureau.
Brown, G., et al.
    1980    *The Condition of Hispanic Americans.* Washington, D.C.: National Center for Edu-
            cational Statistics.
Bunzel, J., and J. Au
    1987    Diversity or discrimination? Asian Americans in college. *Public Interest* 87:49-62.
California Department of Finance
    1985    *Projected Total Population of California Counties.* Sacramento: Department of Fi-
            nance.
Cain, B.
    1988    Asian-American electoral power: Imminent or illusory? *Election Politics* 5:27-30.
Carmody, D.
    1989    Secrecy and tenure: An issue for high court. *New York Times* (December 6):B8.
Chan, S.
    1991    *Asian Americans: An Interpretive History.* Boston: Twayne.
Chen, M., W. New, and J. Tsutakawa
    1989    Empowerment in New York Chinatown: Our work as student interns. *Amerasia
            Journal* 15:299-206.
Chi, G., S. Cho, J. Kang, and F. Wu
    1996    *Beyond Self-Interest: Asian Pacific Americans Toward a Community of Justice.* Los
            Angeles: UCLA Asian American Studies Center.
Chuman, F.
    1976    *The Bamboo People: Japanese Americans and the Law.* Del Mar, Calif.: Publisher's Inc.
Chun, K.
    1980    The myth of Asian American success and its educational ramifications. *IRCD
            Bulletin* 15:1-12.
Davis, C., C. Haub, and J. Willette
    1985    U.S. Hispanics: Changing the face of America. Pp. 464-489 in *Majority and Minor-
            ity,* N. Yetman, ed. Boston: Allyn and Bacon.
Din, G.
    1984    An analysis of Asian/Pacific American registration and voting patterns in San
            Francisco. M.A. thesis. Claremont Graduate School.
Duran, R.
    1983    *Hispanics' Education and Background: Predictors of College Achievement.* New York:
            College Entrance Examination Board.
Endo, R., S. Sue, and N. Wagner, eds.
    1980    *Asian Americans: Social and Psychological Perspectives, Vol. 2.* Palo Alto, Calif.: Sci-
            ence and Behavior.
Erie, S., and H. Brackman
    1993    *Paths to Political Incorporation: Hispanics and Asian Pacifics in California.* Berkeley:
            The California Policy Seminar.
Escueta, E., and E. O'Brien
    1991    *Asian Americans in Higher Education: Trends and Issues.* Washington, D.C.: Ameri-
            can Council on Higher Education.
Espiritu, Y.
    1992    *Asian American Panethnicity: Bridging Institutions and Identities.* Philadelphia:
            Temple University Press.
    1997    *Asian American Women and Men: Labor, Laws, and Love.* Thousand Oaks, Calif.:
            Sage Publications.

Fawcett, J., and F. Arnold
    1987   Explaining diversity: Asian and Pacific immigration systems. Pp. 453-473 in *Pacific Bridges*, J. Fawcett and B. Carino, eds. Staten Island, N.Y.: Center for Migration Studies.
Fawcett, J., and B. Carino, eds.
    1987   *Pacific Bridges*. Staten Island, N.Y.: Center for Migration Studies.
The Field Institute
    1992   *A Digest on California's Political Demography*. Newsletter from the Field Institute, San Francisco.
Fong, T.
    1994   *The First Suburban Chinatown*. Philadelphia: Temple University Press.
Gall, S., and I. Natividad
    1995   *The Asian American Almanac*. Detroit: Gale Research.
Gardner, R., B. Robey, and P. Smith
    1985   Asian Americans: Growth, change, diversity. *Population Bulletin* 4(4).
Gittleman, Z.
    1982   *Becoming Israelis: Political Resocialization of Soviet and American Immigrants*. New York: Praeger.
Gurwitt, R.
    1990   Have Asian Americans arrived politically? Not quite. *Governing* (November):32-38.
Ha, J.
    1996   APAs voted overwhelmingly against Prop. 209. *Rafu Shimpo* (Nov. 8):1.
    1997   PSA say 'get out the vote'—This time for local elections. *Rafu Shimpo* (February 28):1.
Hing, B.
    1993   *Making and Remaking Asian America Through Immigration, 1850-1990*. Stanford, Calif.: Stanford University Press.
Hing, B., and R. Lee, eds.
    1996   *The State of Asian Pacific America: Reframing the Immigration Debate*. Los Angeles: LEAP Asian Pacific American Public Policy Institute and UCLA Asian American Studies Center.
Hirschman, C., and M. Wong
    1981   Trends in socioeconomic achievement among immigrant and native-born Asian-Americans, 1960-1976. *Sociological Quarterly* 22(4):495-514.
Horton, J.
    1995   *The Politics of Diversity*. Philadelphia: Temple University Press.
Hsia, J.
    1988a  Limits of affirmative action: Asian American access to higher education. *Educational Policy* 2:117-136.
    1988b  *Asian Americans in Higher Education and Work*. Hillsdale, N.J.: Lawrence Erlbaum Associates.
Hune, S.
    1998   *Asian Pacific Women in Higher Education: Claiming Visibility and Voice*. Washington, D.C.: Association of American Colleges and Universities.
Hune, S., and K. Chan
    1997   Special focus: Asian Pacific American demographic and education trends. In *Minorities in Higher Education, Vol. 15*, D. Carter and R. Wilson, eds. Washington, D.C.: American Council on Education.

Ichioka, Y.
  1977   The early Japanese quest for citizenship: The background of the 1922 Ozawa case. *Amerasia Journal* 4:1-22.

Kao, G.
  1995   Asian Americans as model minorities? A look at their academic performance. *American Journal of Education* 103(2):121-160.

Kar, S., et al.
  1995/96 Invisible Americans: An exploration of Indo-American quality of life. *Amerasia Journal* 21(3):25-52.

Karnow, S.
  1992   Apathetic Asian Americans? Why their success hasn't spilled over into politics. *Washington Post* (November 29):C1, C2.

Kiang, P., and V. Wai-Fun Lee
  1993   Exclusion or contribution?  Education K-12 policy. In *The State of Asian Pacific America: Policy Issues to the Year 2020*. Los Angeles: LEAP Asian Pacific American Public Policy Institute and the UCLA Asian American Studies Center.

Kikumura, A., and H. Kitano
  1973   Interracial marriages. *Journal of Social Issues* 29(2):570-582.

Kim, E.
  1997   Korean Americans in U.S. race relations: Some considerations. *Amerasia Journal* 23(2):69-78.

Kwoh, S., and M. Hui
  1993   Empowering our communities: Political policy. Pp. 189-197 in *The State of Asian Pacific America: Policy Issues to the Year 2020*. Los Angeles: LEAP Asian Pacific American Public Policy Institute and the UCLA Asian American Studies Center.

Kwong, P.
  1996   *The New Chinatown*. New York: HarperCollins.

LEAP Asian Pacific American Public Policy Institute and the UCLA Asian American Studies Center
  1993   *The State of Asian Pacific America: Policy Issues to the Year 2020*. Los Angeles: LEAP Asian Pacific American Public Policy Institute and the UCLA Asian American Studies Center.

Lee, S.J.
  1996   *Unraveling the Model Minority Stereotype*. New York: Teachers College Press.

Lee, S.M.
  1998   Asian Americans: Diverse and growing. *Population Bulletin* 53(2).

Leong, R.
  1995   *Asian American Sexualities*. New York: Routledge.

Lien, P.
  1994   Ethnicity and political participation: A comparison between Asian and Mexican Americans. *Political Behavior* 16(2):237-264.

Lin, S.
  1997   Commission on Civil Rights to hear Asian-bashing complaints. *Rafu Shimpo* (December 4):1, 4.

Miller, J.
  1995   Asian Americans head for politics. *The American Enterprise* 6:56-58.

Miller, S.
  1992   Asian-Americans bump against glass ceiling. *Science* 258:13.

Min, P.
  1995   *Asian Americans: Contemporary Trends and Issues*. Thousand Oaks, Calif.: Sage Publications.

Nakanishi, D.
   1975   Japanese Americans in the city of smog. Pp. 223-257 in *Mutual Images: Essays in American-Japanese Relations*, A. Iriye, ed. Cambridge, Mass.: Harvard University Press.
   1978   The national Asian American roster, 1978: A listing of Asian American elected officials at the federal, state, and local levels. Pp. 156-176 in *Political Participation of Asian Americans: Problems and Strategies*, Y. Jo, ed. Chicago: Pacific/Asian American Mental Health Research Center.
   1986a  Asian American politics: An agenda for research. *Amerasia Journal* 12:1-27.
   1986b  *The UCLA Asian Pacific American Voter Registration Study*. Los Angeles: Asian Pacific American Legal Center.
   1989   A quota on excellence? The debate on Asian American admissions. *Change* (November/December):38-47.
   1998   When numbers do not add up: Asian Pacific Americans and California politics. Pp. 3-43 in *Racial and Ethnic Politics in California. Vol. 2*, M. Preston, B. Cain, and S. Bass, eds. Berkeley: Institute of Governmental Studies Press.
Nakanishi, D., and J. Lai
   1996   *National Asian Pacific American Political Almanac and Resource Guide*. Los Angeles: UCLA Asian American Studies Center.
   1998   *1998/1999 National Asian Pacific American Political Almanac and Resource Guide*. Los Angeles: UCLA Asian American Studies Center.
Nakanishi, D., and T. Yamano Nishida, eds.
   1995   *The Asian American Educational Experience*. New York: Routledge.
Nash, P.
   1997   Will the Census go multiracial? *Amerasia Journal* 23(1):17-27.
National Asian Pacific American Legal Consortium (NAPALC)
   1996   *Audit of Violence Against Asian Pacific Americans*. Washington, D.C.: National Asian Pacific American Legal Consortium.
Nee, B., and V. Nee
   1974   *Longtime Californ': A Documentary Study of an American Chinatown*. Boston: Houghton Mifflin.
Ong, P.
   1993   *Beyond Asian American Poverty*. Los Angeles: LEAP Asian Pacific American Public Policy Institute and UCLA Asian American Studies Center.
   1994   Ed. *The State of Asian Pacific America: Economic Diversity, Issues and Policies*. Los Angeles: LEAP Asian Pacific American Public Policy Institute and UCLA Asian American Studies Center.
Ong, P., and S. Hee
   1993   The growth of the Asian Pacific American population: 20 million in 2020. Pp. 11-24 in *The State of Asian Pacific America: Policy Issues to the Year 2020*. Los Angeles: LEAP Asian Pacific American Public Policy Institute and the UCLA Asian American Studies Center.
Ong, P., and D. Nakanishi
   1996   Becoming citizens, becoming voters: The naturalization and political participation of Asian immigrants. Pp. 275-305 in *Reframing the Immigration Debate*, B. Hing and R. Lee, eds. Los Angeles: LEAP and UCLA Asian American Studies Center.
Park, E.
   1998   Competing visions: Political formation of Korean Americans in Los Angeles, 1992-1997. *Amerasia Journal* 24(1):41-58.
Prashad, V.
   1998   Anti-D'Souza: The ends of racism and the Asian American. *Amerasia Journal* 24(1):23-40.

Purdum, T.
    1997    Asian-Americans set to flex political muscle made large. *New York Times* (November 15):A1, A9.
*Rafu Shimpo*
    1995    Asian Americans better educated but earn less. *Rafu Shimpo* (December 12):1.
Root, M., ed.
    1992    *Racially Mixed People in America*. Newbury Park: Sage.
Saito, L.
    1998    *Race and Politics: Asian Americans, Hispanics, and Whites in a Los Angeles Suburb*. Urbana: University of Illinois Press.
Shinagawa, L.
    1995    *Asian Pacific American Electoral Participation in the San Francisco Bay Area*. Final Report. (June 15). San Francisco: Asian Law Caucus.
    1996    The impact of immigration on the demography of Asian Pacific Americans. In. *The State of Asian Pacific America: Reframing the Immigration Debate*, B. Hing and R. Lee, eds. Los Angeles: LEAP Asian Pacific American Public Policy Institute and UCLA Asian American Studies Center.
Skelton, G.
    1993    Voters of Asian heritage slow to claim voice. *Los Angeles Times* (August 19):A3.
Stanfield, R.
    1997    Multiple choice. *National Journal* (November 22):2353-2355.
Stokes, B.
    1988    Learning the game. *National Journal* 43(October 22):2649-2654.
Sue, S., and A. Padilla
    1986    Ethnic minority issues in the United States: Challenges for the educational system. Pp. 35-72 in *Beyond Language*, S. Sue and A. Padilla, eds. Sacramento, Calif.: Bilingual Education Office, California Department of Education.
Suzuki, B.
    1977    Education and socialization of Asian Americans. *Amerasia Journal* 4:23-51.
Tachibana, J.
    1986    California's Asians: Power from a growing population. *California Journal* 17:534-543.
Takagi, D.
    1992    *Retreat from Race*. New Brunswick, N.J.: Rutgers University Press.
Takaki, R.
    1989    *Strangers from a Different Shore*. Boston: Little, Brown, and Company.
Tam, W.
    1995    Asians—A monolithic voting bloc? *Political Behavior* 17(2):223-249.
Tsuang, G.
    1989    Assuring equal access of Asian Americans to highly selective universities. *Yale Law Journal* 98:659-678.
U.S. Commission on Civil Rights
    1979    *Civil Rights Issues of Asian and Pacific Americans: Myths and Realities*. Washington, D.C.: U.S. Commission on Civil Rights.
    1992    *Civil Rights Issues Facing Asian Americans in the 1990s*. Washington, D.C.: U.S. Government Printing Office.
U.S. Department of Commerce
    1993a   *1990 Census of the Population: Social and Economic Characteristics. California*. Washington, D.C.: U.S. Bureau of the Census.
    1993b   *We the Americans . . . Asians*. Washington, D.C.: U.S. Bureau of the Census.
    1999    *Today's Asian Pacific Americans: Population Snapshots*. Washington, D.C.: Bureau of the Census.

United Way Asian Pacific Research and Development Council
  1985   *Pacific Profiles: A Demographic Study of the Asian Pacific Population in Los Angeles County*. Los Angeles: United Way.
Walker-Moffat, W.
  1995   *The Other Side of the Asian-American Success Story*. San Francisco: Jossey-Bass.
Woo, D.
  1990   The "overrepresentation" of Asian Americans: Red herrings and yellow perils. *Sage Race Relations Abstracts* 15(2):1-36.
  1994   *The Glass Ceiling and Asian Americans*. Washington, D.C.: U.S. Department of Labor, Glass Ceiling Commission.
Yu, E.
  1982   Koreans in Los Angeles: Size, distribution, and composition. Pp. 23-48 in *Koreans in Los Angeles*, Eui-Young et al., eds. Los Angeles: Korean and Korean American Studies Program, California State University, Los Angeles.
Zhou, M.
  1992   *Chinatown: The Socioeconomic Potential of an Urban Enclave*. Philadelphia: Temple University Press.
  1998   *Growing Up American: How Vietnamese Children Adapt to Life in the United States*. New York: Russell Sage Foundation.

# 7

# Contemporary Immigration and the Dynamics of Race and Ethnicity

*Min Zhou*

T his article examines three interrelated questions: (1) To what extent does contemporary immigration differ from immigration at the turn of the century, and how may these differences affect our approach to the issues of, and concerns about, immigration? (2) How have settlement patterns of new immigrants transformed America's urban centers and the nature of racial and ethnic relations in these centers? (3) What opportunities and challenges have new immigrants and their offspring faced as they converge in America's largest urban centers, and will they be able to advance socioeconomically if they follow the path taken by earlier European immigrants?

## IMMIGRATION THEN AND NOW

### General Trends

Contemporary immigration refers to the period of large-scale, non-European immigration to the United States from the time immigration began to accelerate in the late 1960s through the mid-1990s, following a long hiatus of restricted immigration (Massey, 1995). Between 1971 and 1995, the United States admitted approximately 17.1 million immigrants, including 1.6 million formerly unauthorized aliens and 1.1 million Special Agricultural Workers[1] (SAW) who were granted permanent-resident sta-

---

[1]The Immigration Reform and Control Act (IRCA) of 1986 (Public Law 99-603; Act of 11/6/86), was passed to control and deter illegal immigration to the United States. Its major

tus under the provisions of the Immigration Reform and Control Act of 1986 (hereafter IRCA). The scale of contemporary immigration almost matched that during the first quarter of the century (17.2 million admissions between 1901 and 1925), when immigration to the United States was at its peak. Although similar in number, the annual admission trends in these two peak periods looked quite different, as shown in Figure 7-1. From 1901 to 1925, annual admission numbers fluctuated, with several noticeable ebbs and flows. In contrast, from 1971 to 1995, the inflow was fairly steady. Annual admission numbers were less than 500,000 from 1971 to 1978, then gradually increased from 1978 to 1988. Then in 1989, annual admission numbers suddenly surged above the 1 million mark in a spurt that lasted until 1992. Afterward, the admission flow subsided, but fell to a level higher than the pre-1989 mark; and it has since remained steady and substantially large.

The upsurge in the late 1980s impressed the media and the public, who mistook it for an increase in the overall size of the flow. In fact, the 1989-1992 increase (reflected in the triangular peak in Figure 7-1) was almost entirely the result of legalization, permitted by IRCA, of formerly undocumented immigrants. In theory, all the IRCA legalizees should have been residing in the country for a considerable period of time prior to 1989, though a substantial portion of those whose status was legalized by the SAW program turned out to be relatively recent arrivals. Nonetheless, the more accurate description of trends in legal admission separates the legalizees from other legal immigrants, as shown in Figure 7-1. Clearly, had it not been for IRCA, immigration trends would have been stable, though heading in a gradual, upward direction.

---

provisions stipulate legalization of undocumented aliens, legalization of certain agricultural workers, sanctions for employers who knowingly hire undocumented workers, and increased enforcement at U.S. borders. Special Agricultural Workers (SAW) are aliens who performed labor in perishable agricultural commodities for a specified period of time and were admitted for temporary, and then permanent, residence under a provision of IRCA. Up to 350,000 aliens who worked at least 90 days in each of the three years preceding May 1, 1986, were eligible for Group I temporary resident status. Eligible aliens who qualified under this requirement but applied after the 350,000 limit was met, and aliens who performed labor in perishable agricultural commodities for at least 90 days during the year ending May 1, 1986, were eligible for Group II temporary resident status. Adjustment to permanent resident status is essentially automatic for both groups; however, aliens in Group I were eligible on December 1, 1989, and those in Group II were eligible one year later on December 1, 1990.

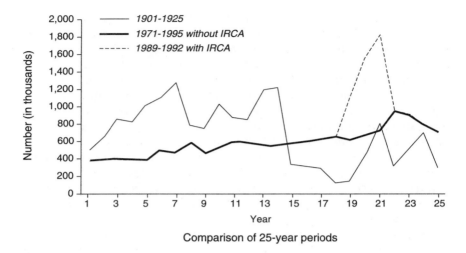

Comparison of 25-year periods

FIGURE 7-1  Immigration to the United States: 1901 to 1925 versus 1971 to 1995.
SOURCE: U.S. Immigration and Naturalization Service (1997).

## Contemporary Immigration in Historical Perspective

From a historical standpoint, the trend of contemporary immigration differs from the earlier trend in five significant ways. First, despite the absolute numbers, the rate of contemporary immigration relative to the total U.S. population is much lower than that of the earlier period, simply because the U.S. population more than tripled during the course of the twentieth century (Smith and Edmonston, 1997). The average rate from 1986 to 1995 was 3.9 immigrants per 1,000 U.S. residents, as opposed to 11.1 from 1905 to 1914 (U.S. Immigration and Naturalization Service, 1997:17). The comparatively low rate of contemporary immigration implies a more modest overall impact on the U.S. population today than in the past, though such an impact is disproportionately localized in areas of high immigration.

Second, the rate of contemporary emigration is also considerably lower today than in the past. It was estimated that for every 100 immigrants who arrived from 1901 through the early twenties, 36 returned to their homelands. Between 1971 and 1990, in contrast, less than 25 returned. This trend suggests a more steady rate of growth today than in the past, and indicates that contemporary immigrants are more likely than their earlier counterparts to stay in the United States permanently (Warren and Kraly, 1985; U.S. Immigration and Naturalization Service, 1997).

Third, unlike immigration then, today's immigration is accompanied by a much larger number of undocumented immigrants. Before the Nationality Act of 1924 established the national-origins quota system, immigration to the United States was relatively open, with legal restrictions only on immigrants from Asia—a small fraction of total U.S. immigration. Thus, the number of undocumented immigrants before 1924 was not at issue. Today, various immigration laws are in place to regulate front-door entrants; but historical patterns of labor's reliance on Mexican migration, especially in agriculture, as well as migration networks, have facilitated undocumented immigration through back-door channels (Massey, 1995).

Net trends in undocumented immigration have fluctuated since the 1980s. On the one hand, IRCA "dried up" a large portion of the undocumented population because former illegals were no longer illegal. Moreover, the employer-sanctions provisions of IRCA exercised an initial deterrent effect on illegal flows of laborers across the Mexican border. Fairly quickly, however, conditions returned to the status quo ante, as undocumented workers and their employers learned to circumvent new restrictions; and the inertial effect of long-established migrant networks facilitated the inflows. Consequently, the number of undocumented immigrants grew to 5 million as of October 1996, up from an estimated 3.9 million in October 1992, indicating an average annual growth of 275,000 during the 1994 to 1996 period. About 60 percent of undocumented immigrants enter across land borders. Undocumented immigrants from Mexico alone account for 54 percent of the total, eight times the number from El Salvador, the second largest source. California's share is 40 percent of all undocumented immigrants (U.S. Immigration and Naturalization Service, 1997:185). Because of the high visibility of so many immigrants of Mexican origin, and because of the geographic concentration, undocumented immigration has become a highly publicized and contested policy issue in California.

Fourth, compared to immigration then, today's inflows are made up of a higher proportion of refugees and those seeking asylum.[2] From 1946 to 1995—i.e., in the 50 years after World War II ended—more than 3 million refugees and people seeking asylum were granted lawful permanent-resident status through various legislation. Unlike post-WWII refugees, more than 90 percent of whom were from war-torn countries in

---

[2]Refugees and people seeking asylum can be anyone with a well-founded fear of prosecution on the basis of race, religion, membership in a social group, political opinion, or national origin. Refugees are those seeking protection from outside the United States; those seeking asylum are seeking protection once already in the United States.

Europe, contemporary refugees reflect more numerous and diverse national origins, with most coming from the Caribbean, Central America, Southeast Asia, and the former Soviet Union. From 1961 to 1995, the number of refugees admitted annually averaged 68,150, compared to 47,000 over the 15-year span immediately after the War (1946 to 1961). The admission of refugees today implies a much larger base for later immigration through family reunification.

Last but not least, the all-time high presence of nonimmigrants arriving in the United States temporarily each year also bears a broad implication for potential immigration, both legal and illegal. According the Immigration and Naturalization Service (INS), of 22.6 million nonimmigrant visas issued in 1995, 17.6 million (78 percent) were for tourists who came for short visits, business or pleasure; the rest were for long-term nonimmigrants, including 395,000 foreign students along with their spouses and children, 243,000 temporary workers or trainees along with their immediate relatives, and a smaller number of traders and investors. These groups contain a significant pool of potential immigrants. The majority of those who initially entered as students can freely seek employment in the United States after the completion of their studies, which in turn increases the probability of later moving to permanent-resident status. Among those who entered as tourists, the great majority will depart on time; however, a relatively small proportion, but a quantitatively large number, of those who might qualify for family-sponsored immigration, may overstay their visas and wait here to have their status adjusted. In 1995, almost one-half of the legal immigrants admitted were originally nonimmigrants who had their visas adjusted here in the United States. About 40 percent of the total undocumented immigrant population were "nonimmigrant overstays" (U.S. Immigration and Naturalization Service, 1997).

In sum, lower rates of emigration, higher numbers of undocumented immigrants and refugees or people seeking asylum, and the larger pool of potentially permanent immigrants among nonimmigrants suggests the complexity of contemporary immigration. Another significant implication for immigration to America is that it is a more challenging task than ever to accurately measure the scale and impact of immigration and to manage or control the inflows.

## HETEROGENEITY OF CONTEMPORARY IMMIGRANTS

Compared with the turn-of-the-century immigrants, contemporary immigrants are markedly heterogeneous in national origins, types of admission, spatial distribution, and socioeconomic characteristics. The newcomers come predominantly from non-European countries. Since the

1980s, 88 percent of the immigrants admitted to the United States come from the Americas (excluding Canada) and Asia, and only 10 percent from Europe, compared to more than 90 percent at the earlier peak. In particular, the percentage of immigrants from the Americas, as a proportion of total legal immigrant admissions, has risen substantially from its 1950 base of 25 percent, moving to 39 percent in the 1960s, and jumping up to 50 percent since the 1980s. Similarly, the percentage of immigrants from Asia, as a proportion of the total admissions, grew from a tiny 5 percent in the 1950s, to 11 percent in the 1960s, to 33 percent in the 1970s, and has stayed at 35 percent since 1980, except for 1991 when the Asian share dropped to 18 percent because of the sudden increase in the legalizees under IRCA, most of whom were Mexicans or Central Americans (U.S. Immigration and Naturalization Service, 1997).[3] The top five sending countries from 1981 through 1995 were Mexico, the Philippines, China/Taiwan, the Dominican Republic, and India, compared to Italy, Austria/Hungary, the Soviet Union, Canada, and the United Kingdom during the first two decades of the century. Mexico alone accounted for more than one-fifth of the total legal admissions since the 1980s. In fact, Mexico was on the INS list of the top five countries of last residence from 1921 through 1960, and was number one after 1960 (U.S. Immigration and Naturalization Service, 1997:14).

The size and composition of immigration has a lasting effect on the size and composition of the general U.S. population. During the past 30 years, immigration accounted for more than one-third of total U.S. population growth. Asian- and Hispanic-origin populations grew particularly fast, in both absolute and relative sizes. Some groups—Salvadorans, Guatemalans, Dominicans, Haitians, Jamaicans, Asian Indians, Koreans, Vietnamese, Cambodians, and Laotians—grew at spectacular rates, mainly as a result of immigration. It is estimated that, at the current rates of net immigration, intermarriage, and ethnic affiliation, the size of the Asian population will increase from 9 to 34 million by 2050 (growing from 3 to 8 percent of the population) and the Hispanic population will rise from 27 million in 1995 (about 9 percent of the population) to 95 million (or 25 percent of the population) in 2050 (Smith and Edmonston, 1997).

Spatially, the turn-of-the-century immigrants were highly concentrated along the Northeastern seaboard and in the Midwest. For them, the top five most preferred state destinations were New York, Pennsylvania, Illinois, Massachusetts, and New Jersey; and the most preferred immigrant urban destinations were New York, Chicago, Philadelphia, St. Louis, and Boston (Waldinger and Bozorgmehr, 1996). In contrast, today's

---

[3]Not including immigrants from Iran, Israel, and Turkey.

newcomers are highly concentrated not simply in states or urban areas traditionally attracting most immigrants but also in states or urban areas in the West, Southwest, and Southeast. Since 1971, the top five states of immigrant intended residence have been California, New York, Florida, Texas, and New Jersey, accounting for almost two out of every three newly admitted immigrants. California has been the leading state of immigrant destination since 1976. In 1995, the five leading urban areas of high immigrant concentration were New York, Los Angeles-Long Beach, Chicago, Miami-Hialeah, and Orange County, California (U.S. Immigration and Naturalization Service, 1997).

The new immigrants also differ from the turn-of-the-century inflows in their diverse socioeconomic backgrounds. The image of the poor, uneducated, and unskilled "huddled masses," used to depict the turn-of-the-century European immigrants, does not apply to today's newcomers. The 1990 Census attests to the vast differences in demographic characteristics, levels of education, occupation, and income by national origins (Table 7-1). The sex ratio was nearly balanced, with a slightly higher proportion of females coming from the former Soviet Union, the Dominican Republic, Jamaica, the Philippines, and Korea. Most of the immigrants were of prime age, between 27 and 35, except for the Chinese, who were slightly older, and the Russians, who were comparably much older. For all other groups listed in Table 7-1, except the Russians, the majority of the immigrants arrived after 1980.

These new immigrants also varied drastically in socioeconomic status. For example, more than 60 percent of foreign-born persons (age 25 years or older) from India reported having attained college degrees, three times the percentage for average Americans; but less than 5 percent of those from El Salvador and Mexico so reported. Among employed foreign-born workers (age 16 years or older), more than 45 percent of the Indians held managerial or professional occupations, more than twice the percentage of average American workers; but less than 7 percent of the Salvadorans, Guatemalans, and Mexicans held comparable jobs. Moreover, for immigrants from India a median household annual income of $48,000 was reported, compared to a $30,000 average for American households; those from the Dominican Republic and the Soviet Union reported median annual household incomes of less than $20,000. Percentages varied for those reporting poverty-level annual incomes (less than $16,500 per year), ranging from a low of 5 percent of Asian Indians and Filipinos to a high of 33 percent of Dominicans, compared to about 10 percent of American families.

## SOURCES AND PERPETUATION OF
## CONTEMPORARY IMMIGRATION

### Immigration Legislation

Contemporary immigration is often referred to as "post-1965" immigration. The use of the term is not arbitrary, because immigration from the Americas and Asia surged after the passage of the 1965 amendments to the Immigration and Nationality Act (the Hart-Cellar Act). However, it is debatable whether the Hart-Cellar Act was the principal cause of the major shift in today's immigration. The Hart-Cellar Act, which took effect in 1968, had a humanitarian goal of reunifying families and an economic goal of bringing in needed labor. It abolished the national-quotas system that restricted immigration from Southern and Eastern Europe, lifted the ban on immigration from Asia, and established the seven preference categories. The act set an annual numerical cap of 290,000 (spouses and minor children of U.S. citizens were exempt from numerical limitations), allocating 170,000 to the Eastern Hemisphere, with a 20,000-per-country limit, and 120,000 to the Western Hemisphere, with no per-country limit.

The abolition of national quotas was intended to spur immigration from countries in Eastern and Southern Europe and, to a lesser extent, from Asian countries. In fact, the 1965 Act and its subsequent amendments set the first-ever cap on immigration from the Western Hemisphere, restricting immigration from the Americas, especially Mexico, which had been under way since the 1920s (Massey, 1995). Figure 7-2 shows that immigration from the Americas (not including Canada), as a percentage of total inflow, was notably large (16 percent) in the 1920s; decreased to 10 percent in the 1930s, mainly because of the Great Depression; then grew substantially in the 1940s (18 percent) and 1950s (25 percent). Immigration from Asia, by contrast, was relatively insignificant prior to 1970 (less than 6 percent) but surged rapidly after the enactment of the Hart-Cellar legislation. In the decades after passage, there has been a continuous surge in immigration, and the new arrivals have been disproportionately from the Americas and Asia—a development facilitated, but not caused, by the 1965 shift in immigration policies. Rather the national-origins composition reflects broader changes in the United States and around the world.

### Globalization

The globalization of the U.S. economy since the 1960s has forged extensive economic, cultural, and ideological ties among the United States

TABLE 7-1  Socioeconomic Characteristics of Immigrants from Selected
Countries, 1990

|  | Soviet Union | Mexico | El Salvador | Guatemala | Dominican Republic |
|---|---|---|---|---|---|
| Female, % | 54.8 | 44.9 | 48.4 | 48.7 | 54.6 |
| Median age, yrs. | 50 | 29.3 | 27.9 | 28.7 | 32.5 |
| Immigrated after 1980, % | 39.4 | 50.0 | 75.3 | 68.2 | 53.2 |
| Poor English,[a] % | 51.9 | 70.7 | 72.4 | 70.7 | 68.7 |
| College degrees,[b] % | 26.5 | 3.5 | 4.7 | 5.8 | 7.4 |
| Professional Occupations,[c] % | 30.9 | 5.8 | 5.8 | 7.0 | 10.9 |
| Household income, $ | 19,125 | 21,926 | 23,533 | 24,362 | 19,996 |
| Poverty % | 18.5 | 27.4 | 22.5 | 21.5 | 33.4 |
| Total (1,000s) | 334 | 4,298 | 465 | 226 | 348 |

[a]Age 5 and older.
[b]Age 25 and older.
[c]Age 16 and older

SOURCE: U.S. Census of Population (1990).

and many developing countries in Latin America and Asia. Direct U.S.-
capital investments in developing countries have transformed those countries' economic and occupational structures. Foreign investment disproportionately targets production for export, taking advantage of raw
material and cheap labor in developing countries. Such development
results in tremendous internal rural-urban migration, predominantly of
low-skilled and female laborers coming from the rural economy to urban
industrial centers, which in turn causes underemployment and displacement of the urban work force. Robust but unstable employment in the
growing export manufacturing sector, combined with unemployment and
underemployment in national economies, has created an enormous pool
of potential emigrants (Sassen, 1989).

On the other hand, economic development following the American
model has stimulated consumerism and consumption and raised expecta-

| Haiti | Jamaica | China | Philippines | India | Korea | Vietnam | Total |
|-------|---------|-------|-------------|-------|-------|---------|-------|
| 50.2 | 55.1 | 49.6 | 56.6 | 45.1 | 57.0 | 47.5 | 51.1 |
| 34.8 | 34.5 | 44.6 | 38.4 | 36.9 | 33.8 | 29.2 | 35.3 |
| 58.7 | 46.2 | 54.5 | 49.1 | 55.8 | 56.2 | 62.9 | 43.8 |
| 55.2 | 1.7 | 72.2 | 32.0 | 27.2 | 61.9 | 66.2 | 46.9 |
| 11.8 | 15.0 | 30.9 | 45.6 | 63.0 | 34.4 | 15.9 | 20.5 |
| 13.8 | 21.2 | 29.0 | 28.3 | 48.1 | 25.5 | 16.9 | 22.2 |
| 25,454 | 30,599 | 30,597 | 45,419 | 48,320 | 30,147 | 30,039 | 28,314 |
| 20.9 | 10.4 | 12.5 | 4.6 | 5.1 | 15.1 | 23.8 | 14.9 |
| 225 | 334 | 530 | 913 | 450 | 568 | 543 | 19,767 |

tions regarding the standard of living. The widening gap between consumption expectations and the available standards of living within the structural constraints of the developing economies, combined with easy access to information and migration networks, has in turn created tremendous pressure for emigration (Portes, 1979; Portes and Rumbaut, 1996). Thus, U.S. foreign-capital investments in developing countries have resulted in the paradox of rapid economic growth and high emigration from these countries to the United States.

On the U.S. side, unprecedented growth in capital-intensive, high-tech industries and services has created a severe shortage of skilled workers. American businesses and policy makers believe that importing skilled labor is the quickest solution, as opposed to training American workers. Since the 1980s, about one-third of the engineers and medical personnel in the U.S. labor market have come from abroad. The needs of business,

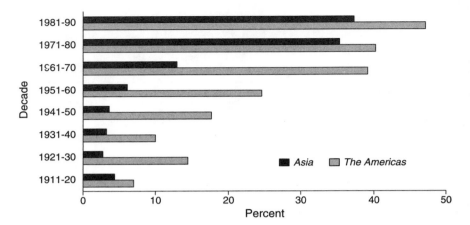

FIGURE 7-2 Immigration from the Americas (not including Canada) and Asia, as a proportion of the total immigration to the United States, 1911 to 1990. SOURCE: U.S. Immigration and Naturalization Service (1997).

however, are not sufficient explanation of the trends in high-skill migration; a disproportionate percentage, almost 60 percent, of the total skilled immigration in 1995 originated from selected countries in Asia. It is the global integration of higher education in many of the sending countries and advanced training in the United States, interacting with the opportunity structure in the homelands, that have set in motion the high-skill immigration.

The infusion of the educational systems with globalization in many developing countries—notably India, Korea, the Philippines, and Taiwan—has given rise to a sizeable professional class. Many members of this emerging middle class are frustrated by uneven economic development and rigid opportunity structures in their homelands that devalue their human capital worth; in addition, many feel powerless to make changes because of repressive political systems. They therefore aggressively seek emigration as the most preferred alternative, and the change in U.S. immigration policy facilitated their move (Liu and Cheng, 1994). The emergence of the United States as the leading place for training international students has also been instrumental in supplying the U.S. economy with needed skilled labor (Ong et al., 1992). Many foreign students found permanent employment in the United States after completing their studies or practical training. For example, in fiscal year 1995, close to 40 percent of the immigrants from mainland China were admitted under employment-based preferences. Almost all of them had received higher education or training in the United States.

## Global Refugee Movement

The world refugee phenomenon is another macrostructural factor facilitating human movement, and is also beyond the control of U.S. immigration policy. The word "refugee" denotes someone in flight from persecution or war. The United States has received a substantial number of refugees throughout its history; however, the system of refuge and asylum is a product of the post-WWII period. Therefore, immigrants admitted as refugees or asylees are, by definition, distinguished from earlier major migration waves.

Since WWII, the United States has accepted tens of thousands of refugees. Table 7-2 lists the top 10 countries from which refugees or people seeking asylum were admitted to the United States from 1946 to 1995. During the first 15 years immediately after WWII, 705,718 refugees were granted permanent-resident status. Among them, 95 percent came from war-torn countries in Europe. Later waves of refugees, however, were more diverse, with less than 25 percent coming from Europe. Many refugees were pushed out of their homelands as a result of revolutions, civil wars, or U.S. political, military, and economic involvements in originating countries. For example, the Cuban Revolution and U.S. anti-Commu-

TABLE 7-2 Top 10 Countries of National Origin for Refugees and Asylees Granted Permanent Resident Status, 1946 to 1995

| 1946-1960 | | | 1961-1995 | | |
|---|---|---|---|---|---|
| Country of Birth | Number | % of Total | Country of Birth | Number | % of Total |
| Poland | 159,852 | 22.7 | Vietnam | 560,888 | 23.5 |
| Germany | 99,493 | 14.1 | Cuba | 532,394 | 22.3 |
| Hungary | 61,826 | 8.8 | Soviet Union | 209,953 | 8.8 |
| Italy | 61,299 | 8.7 | Laos | 179,047 | 7.5 |
| Yugoslavia | 54,571 | 7.7 | Cambodia | 123,436 | 5.2 |
| Soviet Union | 44,131 | 6.2 | Iran | 54,501 | 2.3 |
| Latvia | 38,205 | 5.4 | Romania | 49,213 | 2.1 |
| Greece | 28,692 | 4.1 | Poland | 44,278 | 1.9 |
| Lithuania | 27,263 | 3.9 | Thailand | 41,260 | 1.7 |
| Romania | 16,237 | 2.3 | Yugoslavia | 35,247 | 1.4 |
| Top 10 countries | 591,569 | 83.8 | Top 10 countries | 1,830,217 | 76.7 |
| European countries | 668,129 | 94.7 | European countries | 543,443 | 22.8 |
| All countries | 705,718 | 100.0 | All countries | 2,385,267 | 100.0 |

SOURCE: U.S. Immigration and Naturalization Service (1997: Table 32).

nist foreign policy led to the admission of more than 500,000 Cubans since the late 1950s. U.S. military involvement in Southeast Asia brought 700,000 refugees from Vietnam since the end of the Vietnam War, along with 135,000 Cambodians and 210,000 Laotians (almost one-half were Hmongs), and some 200,000 ethnic Chinese from Southeast Asia. Refugees from the former Soviet Union, mostly Jews, formed the third largest post-WWII refugee group to the United States. About 103,615 Russian refugees were granted permanent-resident status between 1971 and 1990. The collapse of the former Soviet Union in the early 1990s contributed a surge of refugees, 45,000 annually, between 1991 and 1995 (U.S. Immigration and Naturalization Service, 1997).

Though a large refugee population emerged in Europe in the aftermath of WWII, the United States simultaneously shut its doors to the very groups most affected by displacement. Not only were rights of refuge and asylum a product of the immediate postwar period; they were heavily influenced by the politics of the time, in particular, the anti-Communist orientation of U.S. foreign policy. Hence, there has often been divergence between the sociological and bureaucratic or official criteria for refugee or eligibility status, which has in turn produced great conflict. The admission of Cubans, Southeast Asians, Russians, and Nicaraguans as refugees, and the simultaneous exclusion of Haitians, Guatemalans, and Salvadorans, are perfect examples. The civil wars in El Salvador and Guatemala, with increased U.S. intervention and military assistance in the early 1980s, led to the influx of almost half a million refugees and people seeking asylum into the United States. At the same time that Nicaraguans fleeing Sandinista "totalitarianism" were welcomed, Salvadorans and Guatemalans fleeing political violence and extreme economic hardship were treated unfavorably. They were permitted into the United States only temporarily; many of them applied for political asylum but became undocumented in the late 1980s when their applications were denied (Lopez et al., 1996). The fate of 34,000 Haitian detainees at the Guantanamo base in the early 1990s was similar to that of Salvadorans and Guatemalans (Stepick, 1992). Many Salvadorans, Guatemalans, and Haitians who arrived in the United States and applied for political asylum have not been granted permanent-resident status, and thus have been forced into a legal limbo.

A variety of factors limit the ability of the United States to exercise control over refugee inflows: (1) the extension and consolidation of the worldwide human-rights regime; (2) the increase in conflicts at the subnational level in the wake of the break-up of the Soviet Union, which has produced growing refugee populations throughout the world; and (3) globalization, which facilitates the inflow of potential asylum seekers under other auspices (e.g., the special legislation granting permanent residency to thousands of Chinese students and their families as a result of the 1989 Tienanmen incident).

## Migration Networks

Once set in motion, international migration is perpetuated by extensive and institutionalized migration networks (Massey et al., 1987). Networks are formed by family, kinship, and friendship ties. They facilitate and perpetuate international migration because they lower the costs and risks of movement and increase the expected net returns on such movement (Massey et al., 1993). More than two-thirds of the legal immigrants admitted to the United States since the 1970s are family-sponsored immigrants. Even among employer-sponsored migrants, the role of networking is crucial. Family, kin, and friendship networks also tend to expand exponentially, serving as a conduit to additional and thus potentially self-perpetuating migration. For example, a recent poll showed that about one-half of the Dominican Republic population (7.5 million) reported having relatives in the United States, and two-thirds of them would move to the United States if they could (cited in Rumbaut, 1999). In Mexico, about one-half of all adult Mexicans have some kind of relationship with someone living in the United States, and more than one-third have been in the United States at some point in their lives (Massey and Espinosa, 1997). Similarly, at least one-third of Cuba's population (11 million) has relatives in the United States and Puerto Rico, despite nearly four decades of hostile relations (cited in Rumbaut, 1999). These microstructural ties and potentially vast social networks have become a powerful force perpetuating migration. Networks are also established by legitimate institutions that assist migrants and potential migrants, by underground organizations that emerge to reap profits from a lucrative black market, and by humanitarian organizations established to aid both legal and undocumented immigrants (Massey et al., 1993).

U.S. immigration policy has been instrumental in sustaining and expanding family migration networks. The Hart-Cellar Act and its subsequent amendments give preference to family reunification, providing immediate relatives of U.S. citizens with unlimited visa numbers; the majority of the remaining visa allocations go to other relatives, subject to the numerical cap. In 1995, 64 percent of the total 720,461 admissions were family-sponsored immigrants (U.S. Immigration and Naturalization Service, 1997). U.S. policies have also been crucial in establishing employment networks for unskilled-labor migration and, to a lesser extent, for skilled-labor migration. For example, the Bracero Program, aimed at easing the labor shortage of U.S. agriculture in the Southwest, set a key link in the chain of agricultural labor from Mexico. With the end of the program in 1964, labor migration from Mexico became institutionalized, as a result of both a black market that reorganized the flow of undocumented immigration and a humanitarian-organization presence that arose simultaneously to protect the rights of undocumented immigrants (Massey and Liang, 1989; Massey and Espinosa, 1997). The enactment of IRCA, intended to curb illegal immigration through a carrot (amnesty) and stick (employer sanction) approach, not only suddenly increased the volume of immigration but also induced more seasonal migrant workers to stay in the United States permanently, while raising a false sense of hope encouraging undocumented immigrants to stay.

Overall, contemporary immigration has been influenced and perpetuated by the interplay of a complex set of macro- and microstructural forces. Understanding its dynamics requires a reconceptualized framework that takes into account the effects of globalization, uneven political and economic developments between developing and developed countries, the role of the United States in world affairs, as well as the social processes of international migration.

## THE SPATIAL IMPACT OF IMMIGRATION ON THE URBAN LANDSCAPE

Contemporary immigrants are overwhelmingly urban bound. About 94 percent of Asian and close to 90 percent of Hispanic immigrants live in urban areas, compared to slightly more than 70 percent of the U.S.-born population. New immigrants, like their fellow Americans, are spatially distributed not only by social class and race, but also by social networks and family or kinship ties. As discussed previously, today's immigrants are highly concentrated in just a few states; and, within these states, they are highly concentrated in just a few metropolitan areas. Next, describe patterns of spatial concentration in five of the largest metropolitan regions—New York, Los Angeles, Miami, San Francisco, and Chicago.[4] As the different national-origin groups converge in particular urban centers, these urban centers are in turn impacted by the arrival of newcomers.

## OLD AND NEW "ELLIS ISLANDS"

Ellis Island in New York, where the Statue of Liberty stands, is the historic gateway for millions of European immigrants, who made New York City their new home in the late nineteenth and early twentieth

---

[4]These are Census Bureau designated PMSAs (Primary Metropolitan Statistical Areas) rather than cities proper.

centuries. Since the 1970s, immigration has transformed old "Ellis Islands" and given rise to new ones. New York remains the most popular immigrant receiving center; however, Los Angeles has surpassed it as the largest immigrant metropolis in absolute and relative terms. In absolute numbers, Los Angeles is home to 600,000 more foreign-born persons than New York, as of 1990. Approximately 33 percent of Los Angeles' residents are immigrants, compared to 27 percent in New York, a decrease for New York from 40 percent at the turn of the century (Waldinger and Bozorgmehr, 1996). Miami and San Francisco, which are much smaller metropolises, have become more densely populated by new immigrants than any other U.S. metropolitan areas; 34 percent and 27 percent of their populations, respectively, are foreign born. In contrast, Chicago, the second largest immigrant metropolis in 1910, dropped a few places down the list by 1990, with immigrants comprising 13 percent of the total population.

Moreover, new immigrant centers bring together a much larger share of the country's immigrant population than old ones. In 1910, immigrants were 15 percent of the total U.S. population. About a quarter lived in the top five largest metropolises—New York, Chicago, Philadelphia, St. Louis, and Boston (Waldinger and Bozorgmehr, 1996). In 1990, immigrants constituted less than 9 percent of the total population; however, a much higher proportion (37 percent) were concentrated in the five largest metropolitan areas—Los Angeles, New York, San Francisco, Miami, and Chicago. Also, the majority of urban immigrants lived in the central city.

## WHO GOES WHERE?

Different urban centers attract immigrants from different countries. Table 7-3 lists statistics for the top 10 national origins of immigrant groups in five metropolitan areas. New York, which received primarily European immigrants at the turn of the century, has now become the center for Caribbean immigrants. Dominicans, Haitians, and Jamaicans comprise almost one-fifth of New York's immigrant population, yet none of these groups outnumbered other groups by an overwhelming margin; and none ranked in the national top-10 list (see Table 7-3). In all, two-thirds of Dominican immigrants, 36 percent of Haitian immigrants, and 39 percent of Jamaican immigrants in the United States lived in New York.

In Los Angeles, Mexican immigrants are the largest immigrant group, comprising 40 percent of the area's immigrant population, 5.5 times more than the second largest group on the metropolis' top-10 list and on the national top-10 list. Also noticeable are immigrants from El Salvador and Guatemala, making up 11 percent of the area's immigrant population. Although these two Central American groups are not on the national top-

TABLE 7-3 Top 10 Immigrant Groups by Selected PMSAs, Listed by National Origin, 1990 (1,000s)

| Rank | United States | n | New York | n | Los Angeles | n |
|------|---------------|---|----------|---|-------------|---|
| 1 | Mexico | 4,298 | Dominican Republic | 232 | Mexico | 1,167 |
| 2 | Philippines | 913 | China[a] | 166 | El Salvador | 213 |
| 3 | China[a] | 774 | Jamaica | 129 | Philippines | 161 |
| 4 | Canada | 745 | Italy | 122 | China[a] | 136 |
| 5 | Cuba | 737 | Soviet Union | 84 | Korea | 114 |
| 6 | Germany | 712 | Haiti | 80 | Guatemala | 108 |
| 7 | United Kingdom | 640 | Guyana | 77 | Vietnam | 76 |
| 8 | Italy | 580 | Colombia | 71 | Iran | 67 |
| 9 | Korea | 568 | Poland | 66 | Soviet Union | 51 |
| 10 | Vietnam | 543 | Ecuador | 64 | Japan | 40 |
| Totals | | | | | | |
| Top 10 | | 10,510 | | 1,092 | | 2,102 |
| All immigrants | | 19,767 | | 2,286 | | 2,895 |

[a]Includes Hong Kong and Taiwan.

SOURCE: U.S. Census of Population (1990).

10 list, they are disproportionately concentrated in Los Angeles, which is home to 48 percent of Guatemalan immigrants and 46 percent of Salvadoran immigrants in the United States. Compared to the immigrant population in New York, Los Angeles' appears to be less diverse ethnically, though it may have as many national-origins groups as one can count. It is also less diverse in class status because of the strong correlation between national origins and skill levels of the newcomers.

The dominance of Cubans in Miami is a different story. Though Miami is a much smaller metropolitan area, it not only has the highest proportion of immigrants of all, it is also a metropolis with the largest presence of Cubans. More than one-half of Miami's immigrant population is of Cuban origin—a percentage 6.5 times larger than that of Miami's

| Miami | *n* | San Francisco | *n* | Chicago | *n* |
|---|---|---|---|---|---|
| Cuba | 429 | China[a] | 95 | Mexico | 238 |
| Nicaragua | 67 | Philippines | 60 | Poland | 76 |
| Haiti | 45 | Mexico | 48 | Philippines | 43 |
| Colombia | 43 | El Salvador | 26 | India | 34 |
| Jamaica | 31 | Vietnam | 17 | Italy | 28 |
| Dominican Republic | 16 | Nicaragua | 14 | Germany | 28 |
| Honduras | 16 | United Kingdom | 11 | Korea | 25 |
| Peru | 15 | Germany | 11 | China[a] | 24 |
| Mexico | 10 | Soviet Union | 9 | Greece | 18 |
| Spain | 10 | Canada | 9 | Yugoslavia | 18 |
| | 682 | | 300 | | 532 |
| | 875 | | 441 | | 797 |

second largest immigrant group, Nicaraguans. Unlike Mexicans in Los Angeles, Cubans in Miami are not simply the largest foreign-born group in size, they are also socioeconomically diverse with a significantly large middle class and strong influence in the area's political and economic matters.

Like Miami, San Francisco is also a much smaller metropolitan area. Though no single national-origin group is dominant, the Asian presence is impressive, making up more than 40 percent of the immigrant population. In contrast, Chicago is a much larger metropolis but its foreign-born population is relatively small (13 percent). Interestingly, Mexican immigrants form the largest foreign-born group, three times larger than Polish immigrants, the second group on Chicago's top-10 list. However, their visibility is blurred by the area's relatively large native born population.

## DEMOGRAPHIC TRANSFORMATION IN
## URBAN PORTS-OF-ENTRY

The diversity of contemporary immigrants, and their geographic concentrations, have a profound effect on both old and new "Ellis Islands" with significant bearing on the changing dynamics of racial and ethnic relations. Just 30 years ago, America's urban landscape, including the areas with high immigrant density, was predominantly White and culturally homogeneous. The racial hierarchy was dictated by a Black-White dichotomy, with a White dominance. Although various immigrant groups coexisted in the urban social structure, these immigrants were expected to eventually become assimilated—i.e., become "White." Immigrant enclaves or ghettos did exist, mostly in the central city, but they did not constitute a permanent problem because they were considered transitional stops or springboards and were expected to eventually disappear in time. Indeed, within the span of only two to three generations, and a long hiatus of low immigration, the once "inferior races"—Jews and Italians—have become indistinguishably "White" (Alba and Nee, 1997). Meanwhile, the majority of second- and third-generation Americans of Asian and Hispanic origin also quietly dispersed into White middle class without much public notice because they represented only a tiny fraction of the population.

In the past three decades, however, the continuously high immigration has rapidly transformed the racial composition in American cities, making it less "White," but no more "Black"—i.e., more "brown" and/or "yellow" than ever before. Figure 7-3 illustrates the racial composition of five selected metropolises by generation using the 1994-to-1997 data from the U.S. Current Population Survey (CPS). The top graph illustrates the racial composition of the foreign-born population, which reflects the patterns of contemporary immigrant settlement noted. It is not surprising that Los Angeles and Miami have become remarkable Hispanic centers. The middle graph shows the racial composition of the children of immigrants. Only Los Angeles contains a Hispanic-dominant second generation, with the same shift in Miami, slowed down by its large concentration of White second-generation retirees, making Miami's second-generation population an ethnically diverse group. New York and Chicago contain a predominantly White second-generation population, a reflection of the impact of these areas' earlier immigration histories. San Francisco, the singularly Asian-dominant region, stands out as different,

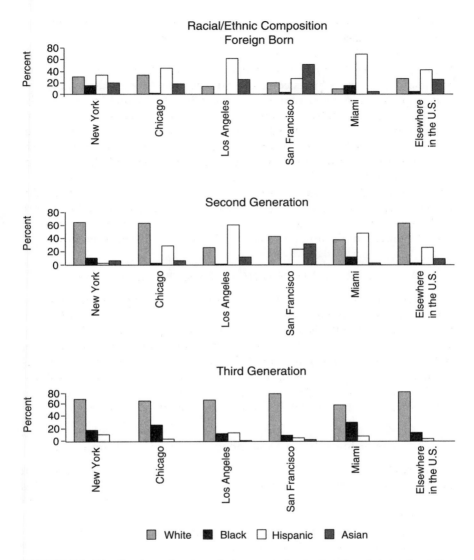

FIGURE 7-3 Distribution of major ethnic groups by generational status in major metropolitan areas with large immigrant populations. SOURCE: Current Population Survey (1994 to 1997). Foreign born refers to first generation; second generation refers to U.S.-born persons with at least one foreign-born parent; and third generation refers to U.S.-born persons with U.S.-born parents.

boasting the greatest variety in the ethnic composition of its second generation, as well as the most pronounced Asian tilt.

As for the third-plus generation illustrated by the lower graph, this turns out to be the one characteristic around which there is the least regional variation. Whites comprise 60 percent of the third-plus generation population in every region, and the White-Black dichotomy is quite striking, while other ethnic groups are barely visible across regions. Noteworthy is the absence of third-generation Asians in San Francisco. Because of various Asian exclusion acts that barred immigration from Asia from the 1880s through much of the twentieth century, only the Japanese-ancestry group (and Chinese to a lesser extent) has a noticeable third generation. Nonetheless, third-generation non-Mexican Hispanics (mostly Puerto Ricans who have citizenship rights by birth) in New York and Mexicans (who are mostly descendants of U.S.-born Mexicans rather than Mexican immigrants) in Los Angeles are visibly represented.

## THE CHANGING DYNAMICS OF RACE AND ETHNICITY

A more critical aspect of these demographic changes is the effect the arrival of non-European immigrants has on racial and ethnic relations in the various new "Ellis Islands." Since the 1970s, a massive influx of non-White immigrants into America's largest urban centers, and a concurrent out-migration of non-Hispanic Whites from these areas, has made ethnicity more salient, posing new challenges to all Americans—White, Black, and U.S.-born of Asian or Hispanic ancestry—and to the newcomers themselves who are striving to become accepted as Americans.

### A Crisis of Identity for Descendants of European Immigrants

Non-Hispanic Whites are, primarily, descendents of earlier European immigrants. Decreasing numbers notwithstanding, U.S.-born Whites have continued to hold dominant political and economic power, even in cities where they are a numerical minority; and the shift of the Black-White paradigm does not change this dominance. How then have the descendants of European immigrants been affected by new immigration? Perhaps the most significant impact has involved notions of an "American" identity and "American" ways. Although America's White middle class can afford to avoid the urban poor, by retreating into suburban communities, it is confronted with the "invasion" of "unacculturated," but nonetheless well-to-do, newcomers who have not set foot in an inner-city immigrant neighborhood—i.e., did not gradually work their way out through acculturation, as European parents or grandparents did. The new mode of incorporation into the middle class—moving immediately to the suburbs—has disrupted the customary ways. Those who tend to judge new immigrants by standards established in the "good old days," fear that newcomers will overtake America and Americans will be un-Americanized by them.

In affluent suburban communities with a large and sudden influx of middle-class newcomers, such fears are more pronounced. For example, in Monterey Park, California, Whites used to be able to drop their hyphens as unqualified Americans, distinct from ethnic or racial minority groups. But in the wake of the large influx of affluent Asian immigrants, they find themselves on the defensive, without an ethnic culture of resistance and empowerment to express their fears and anxiety (Horton, 1995).

The residential concentration of poor, low-skilled immigrants has also created a threat, but not so much to poor Whites who remain in urban ghettos as to suburban Whites. The hotly contested issues of multiculturalism, bilingualism, and immigration reform in the political arena reflect some of these deeply rooted fears. These fears, however, manifest themselves differently in different metropolitan settings. For example, in Los Angeles, the Spanish language is stigmatized and is being banned from instruction in schools; whereas in Miami, the same language is considered an important marketable skill, and bilingualism is celebrated as the American way. In many ways, non-Hispanic Whites, especially those in areas of immigrant concentration, are pressured to negotiate out of a new dilemma of becoming a minority with a majority mentality in a multiethnic society (Horton, 1995).

## The Shrunken Territory of Blacks

Blacks, also a predominantly U.S.-born group, have been culturally, socially, and economically affected by the influx of "colored" immigrants. In the wake of the contemporary surge of immigrants, U.S.-born Blacks have experienced increasing differentiation in socioeconomic characteristics at the individual level and bifurcation between the middle class and the poor (Oliver and Shapiro, 1995; Grant et al., 1996). These patterns of differentiation and bifurcation are primarily caused by the drastic economic restructuring of America's urban labor markets simultaneously with rapid growth in immigration. Uneducated and poor Blacks have been trapped in the inner city, where ladders of social mobility have disappeared and where entry to low-skilled jobs is barred by employer discrimination and immigrant employment networks (Waldinger, 1996; Wilson, 1996). Middle-class Blacks have experienced unprecedented social mobility; yet, many have continued to face racial discrimination, especially in the housing market, which constrains their residential mobility (Massey and Denton, 1987; Clark, 1996).

The arrival of large numbers of non-White immigrants has significantly changed the racial composition of the urban population, rendering the Black-White paradigm outdated. However, the change has not moved Blacks up the racial hierarchy. Instead, Blacks' racial caste status has been further pushed down by the unfortunate incorporation of the new colored immigrants into the "moral problem in the hearts and minds of Americans" (Myrdal, 1944). For example, the widely publicized Black-Korean conflicts in America's inner cities and the 1994 Los Angeles urban unrest were not caused so much by economic competition as by the realignment of racial relations, manifested in tensions over "turf," which has constrained Blacks in virtually every aspect of their lives (Morrison and Lowry, 1994; Min, 1996). In their struggle for racial equality, many U.S.-born Blacks are confronted with a daunting dilemma—how to deal with being a U.S.-born minority competing with foreign-born minorities whose members have come from different backgrounds, many with a majority mentality, and heading in different directions.

U.S.-born Blacks also face fierce economic competition from new immigrants. Although a direct-replacement effect is inconclusive, the large and readily available pool of immigrants may have contributed, at least indirectly, to exacerbating the economic situation of urban Blacks. The oversupply of labor allows employers to lower wages for qualified workers and to discriminate against U.S.-born Blacks. In addition, immigrant-employee networks, developed initially to help coethnic members find jobs, erect entry barriers against Blacks who are outside these networks (Scott, 1996). What is more threatening is that Blacks, especially the educated class, suddenly find their hard-won occupational niche suddenly shared by immigrant minorities (Waldinger, 1996).

## "Foreigners" in Their Own Land—Americans of Asian and Hispanic Ancestry

U.S.-born children and grandchildren of Asian and Hispanic ancestry have also felt the intense cultural and social impact of contemporary immigration, especially those already "assimilated." Suddenly they are confronted with the renewed image of themselves as "foreigners." Their American identity is now questioned because they look like these newcomers who do not fit the old characterization of "American" as "an European or the descendant of an European" (De Crevecoeur, 1782[1904]) or an "immaculate, well-dressed, accent-free Anglo" (Zangwill, 1914). Such characterizations, widely and often unconsciously held, make it harder for many Americans who do not fit those characterizations to feel fully American, even those who are actually native-born—i.e., American Indians or Mexican Americans, whose ancestors settled on this land long before it came to be called "America."

Stereotypical images of "American" create both psychological and practical problems for U.S.-born Americans who phenotypically resemble the new arrivals. Harassment of a Mexican American accused of being an undocumented immigrant, or comments about a third-generation Japanese American's "good English" are frequently reported. These ethnic Americans suffer persistent disadvantages merely because they look "foreign" (U.S. Commission on Civil Rights, 1988, 1992).

Although infuriated by the unfair treatment as foreigners, U.S.-born Asians and Hispanics are also caught in a dilemma of inclusion versus exclusion in their struggle for racial equality. U.S.-born Asians and Hispanics and their foreign-born counterparts often hold contradictory values and standards about labor rights, individualism, civil liberty, and, ultimately, the ideology of assimilation. These differences, intertwined with the acculturation gap between immigrant and U.S.-born generations, have impeded ethnic coalition-building, ideological consensus, and collective action. For example, the picketing of restaurants in New York's Chinatown in 1994 and Los Angeles's Koreatown in 1998, an effort mostly by second-generation Asian Americans fighting for immigrant rights, was perceived by the ethnic community as a group of "Whitened" kids trying to "destroy their parents' businesses" and the ethnic community. Ironically, the parent generation consciously struggles to push children to become "White" by moving their families to White neighborhoods, sending their children to White schools, and discouraging their children from playing basketball and mimicking hip-hop culture. For Afro-Caribbean immigrants, the parents even push their children to adopt strategies, such as invoking their accents or other references to French or British colonial culture, to differentiate themselves from U.S.-born Blacks and avoid the stigma of "Blackness" (Waters, 1994, 1996; Portes and Stepick, 1993). But becoming "White" is politically incorrect, and thus unacceptable for the U.S.-born generation.

## New Immigrants at the Crossroads

The social, cultural, and economic impacts of contemporary immigration are perhaps most profound on the newcomers themselves. Unlike earlier labor migrants of Asian or Hispanic origin, who were mostly sojourners with every intention of eventually returning to their homelands, the new immigrants tend to regard America as their permanent home and make concerted efforts to assimilate socioeconomically. However, new immigrants, middle class and working class alike, are almost always regarded as "foreigners," sometimes even rejected by U.S.-born coethnics as "FOB" (fresh-off-the-boat—a derogatory term referring to newcomers from third-world countries). Many encounter a skeptical and hostile public that keeps questioning their willingness to assimilate and casting doubts on their ability to assimilate. Meanwhile, they face the unrealistically high expectation that they should assimilate quickly. It took the early European immigrants two to three generations to integrate into the middle class, and their transition was facilitated by economic expansion, industrialization, and a long hiatus of restricted immigration (Alba, 1985; Alba and Nee, 1997; Perlmann and Waldinger, 1997). Today the second generation of contemporary immigrants is just coming of age, and predictions about their future assimilation are only estimates.

### Economic Incorporation

Aside from assimilation, immigrants must deal with the issue of economic survival. New immigrants have arrived in cities where economic restructuring and globalization have created bifurcated labor markets. There are numerous labor-intensive, low-paying jobs that do not require much education or skill, and do not provide a living wage, on the one end; and a growing sector of knowledge-intensive, good-paying jobs that require extensive educational credentials and proficiency with the English language, on the other. This bifurcated labor market renders many immigrants underemployed with substandard wages or occupational overqualification (Zhou, 1997a).

Table 7-4 shows patterns of labor-force participation and underemployment rates for working-age (25 to 64 years old) immigrants by ethnicity and gender, compared to U.S.-born non-Hispanic Whites. Except for Southeast Asians, male immigrants had high rates of labor-force participation (more than 90 percent). Southeast Asian workers were more than twice as likely as other workers to be economically inactive; the higher rate of nonparticipation in the labor force among Southeast Asian refugees was the result of their lack of education, English proficiency, job skills, measurable economic resources, and access to employment networks through preexisting ethnic communities (Rumbaut, 1995; Zhou and Bankston, 1998).[5] However, Mexican workers who were most handicapped of all immigrant groups by the lack of skills and English proficiency had the highest labor-force participation rate (95.7 percent). This, however, was because most Mexican immigrant workers arrived through extensive employment and migrant networks (Massey, 1996). Of those in the labor force, all male immigrants, except Europeans, were more likely

---

[5]The African immigrant group also includes a significant component of refugees from Ethiopia who had a high labor-force participation rate. Unlike Southeast Asian refugees, African refugees, as well as refugees from Europe, tend to have attained higher educational levels, more fluent English proficiency, and better access to community-based employment networks.

than U.S.-born White workers to be underemployed, with more than 50 percent of the immigrants (more than 60 percent of the Asians) experiencing underemployment.

Among underemployed males, Mexicans and other Asians showed the lowest proportions in the sub-unemployment category; other Asians showed the lowest rate of unemployment. Partial employment seemed to be the modal category among underemployed males of all groups; percentages ranged from 38.4 percent among other Asians to about 48 percent among West Indians and Hispanics other than Mexicans, whose rate was 55.6 percent. For the low-wage employment and overqualified categories, there were significant intergroup differences. Among underemployed male workers, Mexicans were almost twice as likely as other groups to be in the low-wage category and least likely to be in the overqualified category. By contrast, Africans, Asians, and Europeans were more likely to be educationally overqualified for the jobs they held. Clearly, disadvantages in labor-market status do not necessarily affect immigrant groups in the same manner.

Patterns of labor-force participation among female workers also showed significant intergroup differences. Only 10 percent of West Indian working-age (25 to 64 years old) women stayed out of the labor force, but more than 33 percent of Mexican and Southeast Asian women did. Among those in the labor force, the majority were underemployed, regardless of race/ethnicity; however, West Indian women had a much lower rate of underemployment than all other groups. Relative to their male counterparts, all female workers were generally less likely to participate in the labor force; when they did, they were more disproportionately underemployed.

Among underemployed women, the intergroup patterns were quite similar to those among underemployed men. Sub-unemployed women appeared to be more severely affected than their male counterparts, even after accounting for education or age. However, sub-unemployed males may be assumed to be discouraged workers who have detached themselves from the labor market involuntarily; sub-unemployed females, on the other hand, may be in that category voluntarily, having withdrawn from the labor force because of marriage or childbearing. Partial employment among men may be viewed as an imposed disadvantage; partial employment among women may be voluntary or a strategy for supplementing a husband's low-wage employment.

## Prospects of Economic Mobility

Whether all forms of underemployment yield comparable economic disadvantages is a matter of debate. Unemployment is an absolute disad-

TABLE 7-4 Labor Force Participation and Underemployment Among
Immigrant Workers Ages 25 to 64 by Ethnicity and Gender, 1990

| Characteristics | African | West Indian | Mexican |
|---|---|---|---|
| All Males (n) | 3,484 | 8,341 | 72,485 |
| Not in the labor force (%) | 6.7 | 5.1 | 4.3 |
| In the labor force (%) | 93.3 | 94.9 | 95.7 |
| Underemployed (%) | 57.5 | 49.5 | 57.3 |
| All Underemployed | | | |
| Sub-unemployment (%) | 9.0 | 11.1 | 8.8 |
| Unemployment (%) | 8.5 | 18.0 | 14.9 |
| Partial employment (%) | 44.1 | 48.6 | 55.6 |
| Low-wage employment (%) | 5.7 | 8.2 | 17.2 |
| Overqualified employment (%) | 32.6 | 14.2 | 3.5 |
| | | | |
| All Females (n) | 1,893 | 9,890 | 60,229 |
| Not in the labor force (%) | 17.6 | 10.1 | 35.2 |
| In the labor force (%) | 82.4 | 89.9 | 64.8 |
| Underemployed (%) | 73.9 | 55.9 | 83.7 |
| All Underemployed | | | |
| Sub-unemployment (%) | 16.9 | 15.2 | 21.9 |
| Unemployment (%) | 12.6 | 13.4 | 15.9 |
| Partial employment (%) | 51.0 | 54.1 | 47.2 |
| Low-wage employment (%) | 5.7 | 10.4 | 13.8 |
| Overqualified employment  (%) | 13.9 | 7.0 | 1.2 |

aUndersampled (1/10 of the 5% PUMS).

SOURCE: U.S. Census of Population and Housing (1990), PUMS (5%).

vantage. Partial employment, or low-wage employment, is usually inadequate for sustaining a decent living, much less for moving up the socioeconomic ladder. These two types of underemployment affect Mexican immigrants disproportionately. Although Mexican immigrants have relatively easy access to the U.S. labor market, their employment stability is heavily affected by the uncertain demands of the highly competitive, volatile industries in which they work, such as the agricultural and apparel industries. These conditions, in turn, constrain Mexican immigrants' ability to achieve economic success commensurate with their high rate of labor-force participation.

Immigrants who arrive with strong human capital—a good education or highly marketable skills—may be able to overcome labor-market disadvantages. Those who arrive with weak human capital are likely to be employed at low wages in dead-end jobs; coupled with this disadvan-

| Other Hispanic | Southeast Asian | Other Asian | European | U.S.-Born Non-Hispanic[a] |
|---|---|---|---|---|
| 65,070 | 10,411 | 51,897 | 61,833 | 78,704 |
| 7.9 | 16.2 | 5.6 | 5.0 | 6.2 |
| 92.1 | 83.8 | 94.4 | 95.0 | 93.8 |
| 52.8 | 56.8 | 60.4 | 47.3 | 43.8 |
| | | | | |
| 12.0 | 11.4 | 8.3 | 12.0 | 13.8 |
| 14.4 | 12.4 | 5.9 | 8.3 | 10.2 |
| 48.8 | 46.1 | 38.4 | 39.4 | 39.5 |
| 11.5 | 8.4 | 8.5 | 6.6 | 9.6 |
| 13.4 | 21.7 | 38.9 | 33.7 | 27.0 |
| | | | | |
| 72,516 | 10,797 | 62,896 | 78,661 | 82,141 |
| 28.5 | 34.9 | 23.9 | 25.0 | 20.8 |
| 71.5 | 65.1 | 76.1 | 75.0 | 79.2 |
| 74.4 | 72.3 | 72.1 | 70.8 | 67.6 |
| | | | | |
| 18.5 | 17.5 | 17.1 | 22.2 | 20.8 |
| 13.6 | 12.1 | 6.9 | 6.2 | 6.0 |
| 49.9 | 50.8 | 48.3 | 56.3 | 58.0 |
| 12.7 | 11.6 | 9.6 | 7.1 | 8.3 |
| 5.2 | 7.9 | 18.0 | 8.2 | 6.9 |

tage, they usually have few economic resources and cannot afford the time or cost for the kind of reeducation and retraining that could possibly advance them in the labor market. Those who initially hold entry-level, low-wage jobs are not necessarily trapped at the bottom of the labor market, however. As immigrants gain labor-market experience, many are able to advance within and across industries to better-paying positions and even to self-employment (Portes and Zhou, 1992, 1996; Zhou, 1992). Thus, the long-term scenarios of underemployment being either an alternative means to upward social mobility or a dead-end job trapping immigrants at the starting point, or pushing them further toward the bottom, are not mutually exclusive. Whether one can successfully move out of underemployment depends not simply on individual human capital or incentive, however; the effects of human capital may be circumvented by factors beyond the control of individuals.

## "Will Money Whiten?"

While the new immigrants are transforming America, their options are, in turn, being constrained by the changing dynamics of race and ethnicity.  Once in the United States, non-Whites are racialized into a highly stratified system that imposes a minority status, with all its accrued disadvantages.  Descendents of European immigrants became White as they shed their imposed "racial" minority status and "melted" into the middle-class mainstream. If becoming "White" means convergence toward the middle class, some highly skilled immigrants achieved that shortly after arriving in the United States.  Those from the working class face more obstacles in climbing the social ladder, but they too are expected to eventually make it, if not in this generation, then surely in succeeding generations.  In reality, the likelihood that "money will Whiten" seems likely for some immigrant groups, but not for others.

Mexican immigrants and their offspring, for example, have to bear the double burden of "race."  They come, primarily, from the lower segment of Mexican society, which is stratified on the basis of color and class, and their incorporation into the host society further reinforces and stigmatizes the disadvantaged status they carried with them from Mexico.  Moreover, their initial low socioeconomic status impedes economic mobility, which further reinforces their placement in the preexisting highly stratified and racialized hierarchy.  Though not nearly as despised or disliked as Blacks, Mexicans suffer from a stigma that adversely affects the schooling of their U.S.-born children, which, in turn, may produce some downward movement into the "underclass" (Lopez and Stanton-Salazar, forthcoming).  Most Asian immigrants, by contrast, do not have to bear the double burden of home-country stratification and host-country ascribed racism, because the U.S. contemporary norm tends to treat Asians as the "model minority."  Whether money will "Whiten" this "other colored" group, however, is still too early to conclude.

## THE NEW SECOND GENERATION

The settlement patterns and modes of incorporation of new immigrants affect not only them, but their children as well.  Because of the recency of contemporary immigration, a new generation of immigrant children and children of immigrant parentage is just coming of age.  This new second generation is not only disproportionately young but also ethnically diverse.  Recent national survey data show that almost 40 percent of the second generation are under 18 years of age, in contrast to 28 percent of the U.S. population.  In the second generation, 35 percent are of Latin American ancestry and 7 percent of Asian ancestry, compared with

14 percent and 3 percent, respectively, in the total U.S. population (Current Population Survey, 1994-1997). If it were distributed randomly across America's urban landscape, the new second generation would not be of great interest since it is relatively small in absolute numbers. As in the past, however, the second generation is highly concentrated in just a handful of metropolitan regions. For example, California alone accounted for some 45 percent of the nation's immigrant student population. More than 1 out of 10 school-aged children in the state were foreign born, and over one-third of the state's school-aged children spoke a language other than English at home (Cornelius, 1995). In major immigrant-receiving cities, such as Los Angeles, San Francisco, New York, and Miami, more than one-third of the students in the entire school system speak a language other than English at home (Zhou, 1997b).

As I have discussed earlier, the structural changes associated with massive immigration during the past three decades, along with the shifts in the economy, local cultures, and neighborhoods, create diverse receiving contexts quite different from the ones taken for granted by classical assimilation theorists. Differing from their immigrant parents, immigrant children lack meaningful connections to their "old" world. They are thus unlikely to consider a foreign country as a place they will return to. Instead, they are prone to evaluate themselves or to be evaluated by others by the standards of their new country (Gans, 1992; Portes, 1995; Portes and Zhou, 1993).

Nonetheless, the encounter in any metropolitan context is likely to invoke one of the following scenarios: the child either succeeds in school and moves ahead, or falls behind (or remains the same as), the modest, often low, status of the parents' generation. The latter scenario is labeled by Herbert Gans (1992) as "second-generation decline." Thus, a more pressing issue is whether or not the new second generation will be able to incorporate into middle-class America, following the path taken by the "old" second generation arriving at the turn of the century, and to advance beyond their parents' generation. Next, I provide a brief demographic profile of the new second generation and highlight some prominent issues about second-generation adaptation and the ways in which the nature and consequences of immigration affect the prospect of immigrant children.

## The Age Structure of the Second Generation

Figure 7-4 presents the second generation's distinctive age profile. Unlike the foreign born (in broken lines), whose population tends to peak in the early adult years, the age distribution among the children of the immigrants takes a distinctive U-shaped curve, with the largest second-

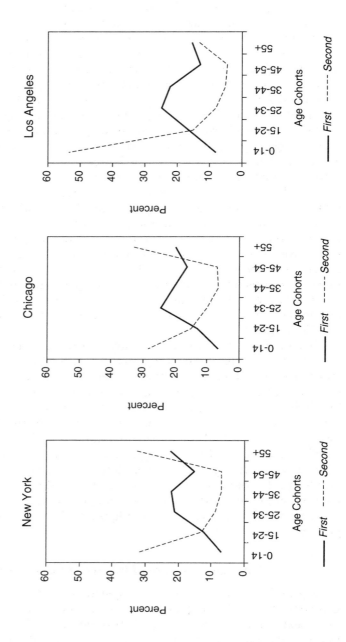

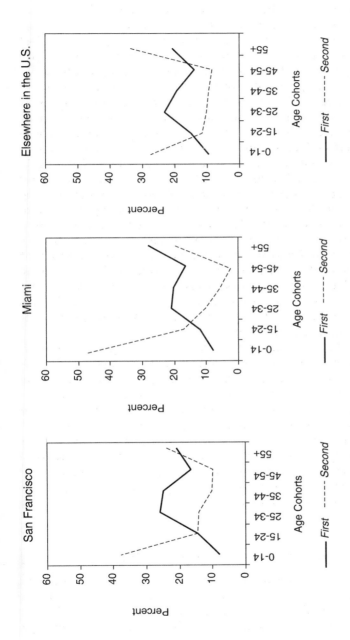

FIGURE 7-4 Distribution of age cohorts in major metropolitan areas with large immigrant populations. First generation (foreign born) versus second generation (U.S. born with at least one foreign-born parent). SOURCE: Current Population Survey (1994 to 1997).

generation contingents either under 15 or over 55, and relatively small cohorts resting in between.  The U-curve not only implies a high level of variation among the second generation, but it also indicates that the relative weight of this population differs greatly across the age cohort.  Most importantly, the second-generation presence is of relative importance among the youngest and oldest groups.  Among prime-age adults, however, immigrant offspring are still a relatively inconspicuous minority.

The U-curve, though always observable, nonetheless assumes a different form in each of the immigration regions.  Los Angeles looks especially distinct, with a disproportionately large population of second-generation children, and a disproportionately low population of second-generation elders, making for a very peculiar looking "U."  Miami again resembles Los Angeles, differing only in the relative weight of elderly immigrant offspring, most of whom are undoubtedly migrants from the colder climates of the Northeast and the Midwest.  Though the fissure point obviously varies from place to place, splitting the second-generation population into those born before and after 1960 highlights the ethnic contrast between the old and the new second generation.  Immigrant offspring born before 1960 are predominately White in all five regions, and almost exclusively so in New York, Los Angeles, and even Miami.  By contrast, those born after 1960 are a far more varied lot, with Whites topping out at 40 percent in New York and Chicago, and not quite reaching the 20 percent mark in Los Angeles.

The age and ethnic structures of various immigrant regions are linked, and consequentially so.  Whereas the shift from old to new second generation can be seen in the youngest cohort in every place, nowhere has the majority of the new second generation yet come of age.  But within age cohorts, the shift from old to new is considerably more advanced in some places than in others.  In Chicago, only the youngest cohort has seen the White second-generation group change from a quantitative majority to a quantitative minority; in New York the same transition has already transpired among adolescents and the youngest of adults, but not among any other cohorts.  By contrast, the ethnic origins of younger, but prime-aged, second-generation adults have already tipped in Los Angeles, San Francisco, and Miami.

## Second-Generation Progress or Decline?

The demographic patterns discussed above suggest that the new second generation is still in the making, but is expected to come of age rapidly in the next decade or so.  This new second generation is highly concentrated in regions of first-generation settlement, yet extraordinarily diverse in national origins. The central question of concern is whether this second generation will decline or eventually converge toward the mean. Analyses of CPS data yield several important findings about the second generation in America's major immigrant receiving centers—New York, Chicago, Los Angeles, San Francisco, and Miami (Zhou, 1999). First, there is a consistent trend of significant second-generation progress beyond that of the first generation, across regions and ethnic groups. Members of the second generation generally fare as well as, and in many cases better than, members of the third generation. The second generation also tends to do better in immigrant centers than elsewhere in the United States. Once important demographic and socioeconomic factors are controlled, the second generation's progress beyond the third generation's becomes even more pronounced.

Second, foreign birth does not exert as severe a penalty as generally expected; compared to the status of the third generation, the second generation's initial disadvantages become insignificant, once measurable demographic and socioeconomic factors are controlled for. This finding indicates that first-generation disadvantages are strongly associated with ethnicity, spatial concentration of ethnic groups, and major socioeconomic factors, and that controlling for these factors reduces the negative impact of foreign birth.

Third, the effects of ethnicity are consistent with prior research, in that they consistently favor Asian-origin groups and penalize other minority groups. And in the third generation, there is a clear convergence of Asian Americans toward the socioeconomic status of non-Hispanic Whites and a persistent gap between Mexican and other Hispanic groups and non-Hispanic Whites, which resembles the Black-White gap.

Fourth, immigrant centers that are distinct from other major urban areas are also distinct from each other. These urban centers offer opportunities as well as disadvantages for immigrants and their offspring. The broader inter-regional variations bear on ethnicity. Specifically, Asians fare better in Chicago than their coethnics elsewhere; but Blacks, Mexicans, and other Hispanics suffer most in the same region. Miami is clearly favorable for the adaptation of non-Mexican Hispanics (most of whom are Cuban), but Los Angeles does not seem to provide similar advantages for Mexicans.

Although my analyses do not directly test the hypothesis of "second-generation decline," the findings clearly show that the second generation is advancing in big strides. More troubling are the significant intergroup differences in the rate of progress and the trend toward third-generation decline, both of which reflect the enduring influence of the U.S. system of ethnic stratification.

## Determinants of Social Mobility for Immigrant Children

The intergenerational mobility of immigrants has been empirically measured by the extent to which immigrant groups achieve parity with the society's dominant group in education, occupation, income and wealth, and political power—as Gordon puts it, "secondary structural assimilation" (Gordon, 1964). The experiences of the children and grandchildren of the European immigrants who arrived in the early twentieth century appear to confirm assimilationist predictions. Between 1920 and 1950, when America experienced a long hiatus of restricted immigration, the earlier waves of immigrants were absorbed. They experienced significant upward mobility across generations, as measured by length of stay, mastery of the English language, acquisition of human capital, and increasing exposure to American cultures (Alba, 1985; Chiswick, 1977; Greeley, 1976; Sandberg, 1974; Wytrwal, 1961).

The question is open as to whether new immigrants and their offspring will follow the path of their European predecessors. In terms of the direction of intergenerational mobility, the distinctions between the earlier European immigrants and the contemporary newcomers may not be as sharp as they appear. With regard to the rate of structural assimilation, the classical assimilationist paradigm shows its constraints. The historiography of the turn-of-the-century European immigrants and studies of new immigrants reveal divergent rather than convergent outcomes across national-origin groups (Landale and Oropesa, 1995; Model, 1991; Perlmann, 1988; Tienda and Lii, 1987; Zhou and Kamo, 1994). These studies suggest that the direction and the rate of social mobility are two distinct dimensions of the adaptational outcomes and that what determines the direction may not necessarily determine the rate.

### Class

Socioeconomic status shapes the immediate social conditions for adaptation, because it determines the type of neighborhood in which children live, the quality of the schools they attend, and the group of peers with whom they associate. Immigrant children from middle-class backgrounds benefit from financially secure families, good schools, safe neighborhoods, and supportive formal and informal organizations, which ensure better life chances for them. Children of poorly educated and unskilled parents, by contrast, generally grow up in neighborhoods subject to poverty, poor schools, violence, drugs, and a generally disruptive social environment.

Clearly, outcomes of adaptation vary according to whether immigrants settle in affluent middle-class suburbs or in impoverished inner-city ghettos. Although the emergence of a middle-class population is a distinctive aspect of contemporary immigration, a disproportionately large number of immigrant children converge in underprivileged and linguistically distinctive neighborhoods. There, the immigrants and their children come into direct daily contact with the poor rather than with the middle class; they are also apt to encounter members of native minorities and other immigrants rather than members of the dominant majority. At school, many immigrant children find themselves in classrooms with other immigrant children speaking a language other than English, or with native minority children who either have problems keeping up with schoolwork or consciously resist academic achievement. These adversarial circumstances have been found to be detrimental to second-generation adaptation (Ogbu, 1974; Perlmann and Waldinger, 1997; Portes, 1995; Portes and Zhou, 1993).

### Race/Ethnicity

The effect of race/ethnicity is intertwined with class. As immigrant children are absorbed into different segments of American society, becoming American may not always be an advantage. When immigrants enter middle-class communities directly, or after a short transition, they may find it advantageous to acculturate and assimilate. If the social environment surrounding immigrant children is rich in resources, and if its goals are consistent with those of the immigrant family, then ethnic resources may be relatively less important, but they may still count. For example, many middle-class immigrant parents move into affluent White neighborhoods, send their children to schools attended primarily by White students from similarly or more affluent socioeconomic backgrounds, and still insist on enrolling their children in weekend or after-school ethnic schools, or involving them in ethnic, religious, or cultural activities. The children then benefit both from privileged socioeconomic contacts with the dominant group in mainstream America and from the group-specific expectations of and opportunities for intellectual development.

Different outcomes are possible where the social environment is not so rich. Many immigrant children have moved to central cities with few socioeconomic resources and live in inner-city ghettos among the most disadvantaged segments of the native minority and immigrant populations. The problem of poverty concentration has been exacerbated by the disappearance of industrial jobs in these urban areas, reducing the demand for low- and semi-skilled labor and trapping the working poor in underemployment and unemployment (Wilson, 1987). The flight of the middle class has worsened the situation, removing opportunities for immigrants to integrate into mainstream society and causing severe social isolation—similar to that commonly faced by U.S.-born minorities in the most impoverished stratum of society.

### Contextual Factors

Changes in social and economic conditions in the host society create structural constraints for second-generation mobility. Economic restructuring has eliminated most of the well-paying, blue-collar jobs in manufacturing that enabled less-skilled European immigrants to climb the social ladder. With the hourglass economy taking shape, as Gans (1992: 173-174) predicts,

> [S]ome members of the second generation, especially those whose parents did not themselves escape poverty, could in adulthood finish in persistent poverty because they will either not be asked, or be reluctant to work at immigrant wages and hours as their parents did but will lack the job opportunities, skills, and connections to do better.

Moreover, American popular culture, with its emphasis on materialism, consumption, and individualism, and its anti-intellectual streak, powerfully influences all children. The effects of exposure to popular culture, however, vary also by class and race. Many inner-city children who feel oppressed and excluded from the American mainstream are also frustrated by the hypocrisy of a culture that highly values freedom and materialism and offers only a dwindling economic future. Many respond to their social isolation and their constrained opportunities with resentment toward middle-class America, rebelling against all forms of authority and rejecting the goals of achievement and upward mobility. Because students in schools shape one another's attitudes and expectations, such an oppositional culture negatively affects educational outcomes. School achievement seems unlikely to lead to upward mobility, and high achievers are seen as sell-outs to oppressive authority.

Although there is a strong anti-intellectual streak in American youth culture at all socioeconomic levels, the rejection of academic pursuits is especially intense among members of minority groups, who are more likely than members of the majority to identify school administrations with oppressive authority, to perceive their entry into the middle class as almost impossible, and to be in schools where learning is strongly discouraged by peers. Lowered chances for mobility create frustration and pessimism for all American youth, but these emotions are most strongly felt by those at the bottom of the economic hierarchy. When those at the bottom are also members of historically oppressed minority groups, frustration is mixed with the need to maintain self-esteem, so that rejection of middle-class mores and opposition to authority become important strategies for psychological survival. In underprivileged neighborhoods, in particular, immigrant children meet U.S.-born peers with little hope for the future and are thus likely to be pressured by their peers to resist assimilation into the middle class, as expected by their parents. These trends pose a challenge to all parents, but the challenge is especially daunting for immigrant parents with limited educational backgrounds, frequently limited English skills, and few resources (Zhou, 1997b).

Thus, when immigrant children enter American society at the bottom of the ethnic hierarchy, acculturation and assimilation are likely to be tinged with distinct disadvantages, viewed as maladjustment by both mainstream society and the ethnic community. Immigrant children from less fortunate socioeconomic backgrounds have a much harder time succeeding in school than do middle-class children, and a significant number of the children of poor, especially dark-skinned, immigrants can be trapped in permanent poverty in an era of stagnant economic growth, and in the process of rapid Americanization. The prospects facing children of the less fortunate may be high rates of unemployment, crime, alcoholism, drug use, and other pathologies associated with poverty and the frustration of diminishing expectations. In this case, young immigrants or children of immigrants may benefit from cultivating social ties within ethnic communities to develop forms of behavior likely to break the cycle of disadvantage. The extent to which young people are integrated into this immigrant community also becomes a major determinant of school adaptation, especially when the social environment otherwise places children at risk (Zhou and Bankston, 1998).

## CONCLUSION

The significant differences between contemporary immigration and turn-of-the-century European immigration necessitate a reconceptualization of the phenomenon and the development of alternative theories of immigration and immigrant adaptation. Contemporary immigration in the United States has resulted from the interplay of macro- and microstructural factors operating cross-nationally, rather than unilaterally. The new immigration has transformed America's major immigrant-receiving centers through a dialectical process, creating opportunities and constraints for immigrant incorporation as well as for a realignment of racial and ethnic relations. For new immigrants and their children, the path to integration into American society may be rugged and segmented because of the diverse socioeconomic backgrounds of new immigrants. Many new immigrants continue to follow the traditional route, starting from the bottom rungs of the socioeconomic ladder and gradually working their way up. A visible proportion of the immigrants, however, have managed to bypass that bottom step, incorporating directly into mainstream professional occupations and dispersing into suburban middle-class communities. Still, a significant number may be permanently "trapped" at the bottom, either unable to find work or working at "dead-end" jobs with little hope for social mobility.

Increasing diversity has posed challenges for all Americans—U.S. born and immigrant—as they are pressured to negotiate the culture of diversity and redefine themselves in the new racial/ethnic stratification system. The old framework of assimilation has become outmoded. In multiethnic urban centers today, all U.S.-born racial/ethnic groups are facing the challenge of adjustment to the new reality. There are growing tensions arising from an urgent need to negotiate the culture of diversity and redefine oneself in the new racial/ethnic stratification system.

Furthermore, the future of the new second generation is intrinsically linked to the diversity of immigration and to the current system of social stratification into which today's immigrant children are assimilating. The American public still seems to assume that all immigrant children should move up and melt into the middle class. As there are poor Whites who have never attained middle class, it should not be a surprise that some immigrant children may not make it either. Certainly, we cannot expect all immigrant children to excel equally in a society as unequal as ours. As Gans (1992) argues, it is time to question the American faith in the inevitability of immigrant success. Children of middle-class immigrants have a better chance for success; their poorer counterparts, especially the darker-skinned ones, may not fare equally well. Consequently, assimilation as a widespread outcome for contemporary immigrant groups is possible for some but questionable for others. It is too early to reach a definite conclusion about assimilation, with scenarios of second-generation decline still a matter of speculation; it seems clear, however, that assimilation no longer means that everybody eventually succeeds.

## ACKNOWLEDGMENTS

The original version of this article was presented at the Research Conference on Racial Trends in the United States, National Research Council, Washington, D.C., October 15-16, 1998. The author wishes to thank Roger Waldinger and Mary Waters for their helpful comments and Vincent Fu and Diana Lee for their research assistance.

# REFERENCES

Alba, R.
1985 *Italian Americans: Into the Twilight of Ethnicity.* Englewood Cliffs, N.J.: Prentice-Hall.
Alba, R., and V. Nee
1997 Rethinking assimilation theory for a new era of immigration. *International Migration Review* 31(4):826-874.
Chiswick, B.
1977 Sons of immigrants: Are they at an earnings disadvantage? *American Economic Review* 67(February):376-380.
Clark, W.
1996 Residential patterns: Avoidance, assimilation, and succession. Pp. 109-138 in *Ethnic Los Angeles,* R. Waldinger and M. Bozorgmehr, eds. New York: Russell Sage Foundation.
Cornelius, W.
1995 Educating California's immigrant children: Introduction and overview. Pp. 1-16 in *California's Immigrant Children: Theory, Research, and Implications for Educational Policy,* R. Rumbaut and W. Cornelius, eds. La Jolla, Calif.: Center for U.S.-Mexican Studies, University of California, San Diego.
De Crevecoeur, J.H. St. John
1782 [1904] *Letters from An American Farmer.* New York: Fox, and Duffield.
Gans, H.
1992 Second-generation decline: Scenarios for the economic and ethnic futures of the post-1965 American immigrants. *Ethnic and Racial Studies* 15(2):173-192.
Gordon, M.
1964 *Assimilation in American Life: The Role of Race, Religion, and National Origins.* New York: Oxford University Press.
Grant, D., M. Oliver, and A. James
1996 African Americans: Social and economic bifurcation. Pp. 379-411 in *Ethnic Los Angeles,* R. Waldinger and M. Bozorgmehr, eds. New York: Russell Sage Foundation.
Greeley, A.
1976 The ethnic miracle. *The Public Interest* 45:20-36.
Horton, J.
1995 *The Politics of Diversity: Immigration, Resistance, and Change in Monterey Park, California.* Philadelphia: Temple University Press.
Landale, N., and R. Oropesa
1995 Immigrant children and the children of immigrants: Inter- and intra-group differences in the United States. Research paper 95-02, Population Research Group, Michigan State University.
Liu, J., and L. Cheng
1994 Pacific Rim development and the duality of post-1965 Asian immigration to the United States. Pp. 74-99 in *The New Asian Immigration in Los Angeles and Global Restructuring,* P. Ong, E. Bonacich, and L. Cheng, eds. Philadelphia: Temple University Press.
Lopez, D., E. Popkin, and E. Tells
1996 Central Americans: At the bottom, struggling to get ahead. Pp. 279-304 in *Ethnic Los Angeles,* R. Waldinger and M. Bozorgmehr, eds. New York: Russell Sage Foundation.

240    IMMIGRATION AND THE DYNAMICS OF RACE AND ETHNICITY

Lopez, D., and R. Stanton-Salazar
Forth-    In *Ethnicities: Coming of Age in Immigrant America*, R. Rumbaut and A. Portes, eds.
coming    Berkeley and New York: University of California Press and Russell Sage Foundation.
Massey, D.
    1995    The new immigration and ethnicity in the United States. *Population and Development Review* 21(3):631-652.
    1996    The age of extremes: Concentrated affluence and poverty in the twenty-first century. *Demography* 33(4):395-412.
Massey, D., and N. Denton
    1987    Trends in residential segregation of Blacks, Hispanics, and Asians: 1970-1980. *American Sociological Review* 52:802-825.
Massey, D., and K. Espinosa
    1997    What's driving Mexico-U.S. migration? A theoretical, empirical, and policy analysis. *American Journal of Sociology* 102(4):939-999.
Massey, D., and Z. Liang
    1989    The long-term consequences of a temporary worker program: The U.S. Bracero experience. *Population Research and Policy Review* 8:199-226.
Massey, D., R. Alarcon, J. Durand, and H. Gonzalez
    1987    *Return to Aztlan: The Social Process of International Migration from Western Mexico.* Berkeley: University of California Press.
Massey, D., J. Arango, G. Hugo, A. Kouaouci, A. Pellegrino, and J. Taylor
    1993    Theories of international migration: A review and appraisal. *Population and Development Review* 19(3):431-466.
Min, P.
    1996    *Caught in the Middle: Korean Communities in New York and Los Angeles.* Berkeley: University of California Press.
Model, S.
    1991    Caribbean immigrants: A Black success story? *International Migration Review* 25:248-276.
Morrison, P., and I. Lowry
    1994    A riot of color: The demographic setting. Pp. 19-46 in *The Los Angeles Riot*, M. Baldassare, ed. Boulder, Colo.: Westview Press.
Myrdal, G.
    1944/1962 *An American Dilemma: The Negro Problem and Modern Democracy.* New York: Harper and Row.
Ogbu, J.
    1974    *The Next Generation: An Ethnography of Education in an Urban Neighborhood.* New York: Academic Press.
Oliver, M., and T. Shapiro
    1995    *Black Wealth/White Wealth: A New Perspective on Racial Inequality.* New York: Routledge.
Ong, P., L. Cheng, and L. Evans
    1992    Migration of highly educated Asians and global dynamics. *Asian and Pacific Migration Journal* 1(3-4):543-567.
Perlmann, J.
    1988    *Ethnic Differences: Schooling and Social Structure among the Irish, Jews, and Blacks in an American City, 1880-1935.* New York: Cambridge University Press.
Perlmann, J., and R. Waldinger
    1997    Second generation decline? Immigrant children past and present—A reconsideration. *International Migration Review* 31(4):893-922.

Portes, A.
1979 Illegal immigration and the international system, lessons from recent legal Mexican immigrants to the United States. *Social Problems* 26:425-438.
1995 Economic sociology and the sociology of immigration: A conceptual overview. Pp. 1-41 in *The Economic Sociology of Immigration: Essays on Networks, Ethnicity, and Entrepreneurship*, A. Portes, ed. New York: Russell Sage Foundation.

Portes, A., and R. Rumbaut
1996 *Immigrant America: A Portrait.* Second edition. Berkeley, Calif.: University of California Press.

Portes, A., and A. Stepick
1993 *City on the Edge: The Transformation of Miami.* Berkeley, Calif.: University of California Press.

Portes, A., and M. Zhou
1992 Gaining the upper hand: Economic mobility among immigrant and domestic minorities. *Ethnic and Racial Studies* 15:491-522.
1993 The new second generation: Segmented assimilation and its variants among post-1965 immigrant youth. *Annals of the American Academy of Political and Social Science* 530(November):74-98.
1996 Self-employment and the earnings of immigrants. *American Sociological Review* 61:219-230.

Rumbaut, R.
1995 Vietnamese, Laotian, and Cambodian Americans. Pp. 232-270 in *Asian Americans: Contemporary Trends and Issues*, P. Min, ed. Thousand Oaks, Calif.: Sage Publications.
1999 Assimilation and its discontents: Ironies and paradoxes. Pp. 172-199 in *Becoming American, America Becoming*, C. Hirschman, P. Kasinitz, and J. DeWind, eds. New York: Russell Sage Foundation.

Sandberg, N.
1974 *Ethnic Identity and Assimilation: The Polish-American Community.* New York: Praeger Publishers.

Sassen, S.
1989 America's immigration problems. *World Policy Journal* 6(4).

Scott, A.
1996 The manufacturing economy: Ethnic and gender division of labor. Pp. 215-244 in *Ethnic Los Angeles*, R. Waldinger and M. Bozorgmehr, eds. New York: Russell Sage Foundation.

Smith, J., and B. Edmonston, eds.
1997 *The New Americans: Economic, Demographic and Fiscal Effects of Immigration.* Washington, D.C.: National Academy Press.

Stepick, A., III
1992 The refugees nobody wants: Haitians in Miami. In *Miami Now! Immigration, Ethnicity, and Social Change*, G. Grenier and A. Stepick III, eds. Gainesville: University Press of Florida.

Tienda, M., and D. Lii
1987 Minority concentration and earnings inequality: Blacks, Hispanics and Asians compared. *American Journal of Sociology* 2:141-165.

U.S. Bureau of the Census (USBC)
1993 *1990 Census of the Population: The Foreign Born Population in the United States.* Washington, D.C.: U.S. Government Printing Office.

U.S. Commission on Civil Rights
  1988   *The Economic Status of Americans of Asian Descent: An Exploratory Investigation.*
         Washington, D.C.: Clearing House Publications.
  1992   *Civil Rights Issues Facing Asian Americans in the 1990s. A Report.* Washington,
         D.C.: U.S. Government Printing Office.
U.S. Immigration and Naturalization Service (USINS)
  1997   *Statistical Yearbook of the Immigration and Naturalization Service, 1995.* Washington,
         D.C.: U.S. Government Printing Office.
Waldinger, R.
  1996   *Still the Promised City? African-Americans and New Immigrants in Postindustrial New
         York.* Cambridge: Harvard University Press.
Waldinger, R., and M. Bozorgmehr
  1996   The making of a multicultural metropolis. Pp. 3-37 in *Ethnic Los Angeles*, R.
         Waldinger and M. Bozorgmehr, eds. New York: Russell Sage Foundation.
Warren, R., and E. Kraly
  1985   The elusive exodus: Emigration from the United States. Population Trends and
         Public Policy Occasional Paper #8, March. Washington, D. C.: Population Refer-
         ence Bureau.
Waters, M.
  1994   Ethnic and racial identities of second-generation Black immigrants in New York
         City. *International Migration Review* 28(4):795-820.
  1996   Immigrant families at risk: Factors that undermine chances of success. In *Immi-
         gration and the Family: Research and Policy on U.S. Immigrants*, A. Booth, A. Crouter,
         and N. Landale, eds. Hillsdale, N.J.: Lawrence Erlbaum Associates.
Wilson, W.
  1987   *The Truly Disadvantaged: The Inner City, the Underclass, and Public Policy.* Chicago:
         University of Chicago Press.
  1996   *When Work Disappears: The World of the New Urban Poor.* New York: Alfred A.
         Knopf.
Wytrwal, J.
  1961   *America's Polish Heritage: A Social History of Poles in America.* Detroit: Endurance
         Press.
Zangwill, I.
  1914   *The Melting Pot: Drama in Four Acts.* New York: MacMillan.
Zhou, M.
  1992   *Chinatown: The Socioeconomic Potential of an Urban Enclave.* Philadelphia: Temple
         University Press.
  1997a  Employment patterns of immigrants in the U.S. Economy. Presented at the con-
         ference International Migration at Century's End: Trends and Issues, Interna-
         tional Union for Scientific Study of the Population, Barcelona, Spain, May 7-10.
  1997b  Growing up American: The challenge confronting immigrant children and chil-
         dren of immigrants. *Annual Review of Sociology* 23:3-95.
  1999   Second-generation prospects: Progress, decline, stagnation? Presented at the 1999
         Annual Meeting of the American Sociological Association, Chicago, August 6-10.
Zhou, M., and C. Bankston III
  1998   *Growing up American: The Adaptation of Vietnamese Adolescents in the United States.*
         New York: Russell Sage Foundation.
Zhou, M., and Y. Kamo
  1994   An analysis of earnings patterns for Chinese, Japanese and non-Hispanic Whites
         in the United States. *The Sociological Quarterly* 35(4):581-602.

# 8

# The Changing Meaning of Race

*Michael A. Omi*

The 1997 President's Initiative on Race elicited numerous comments regarding its intent and focus. One such comment was made by Jefferson Fish, a psychologist at St. John's University in New York, who said: "This dialogue on race is driving me up the wall. Nobody is asking the question, 'What is race?' It is a biologically meaningless category" (quoted in Petit, 1998:A1).

Biologists, geneticists, and physical anthropologists, among others, long ago reached a common understanding that race is not a "scientific" concept rooted in discernible biological differences. Nevertheless, race is commonly and popularly defined in terms of biological traits—phenotypic differences in skin color, hair texture, and other physical attributes, often perceived as surface manifestations of deeper, underlying differences in intelligence, temperament, physical prowess, and sexuality. Thus, although race may have no biological meaning, as used in reference to human differences, it has an extremely important and highly contested *social* one.

Clearly, there is an enormous gap between the scientific rejection of race as a concept, and the popular acceptance of it as an important organizing principle of individual identity and collective consciousness. But merely asserting that race is socially constructed does not get at how specific racial concepts come into existence, what the fundamental determinants of racialization are, and how race articulates with other major axes of stratification and "difference," such as gender and class. Each of these topics would require an extensive treatise on possible variables shaping our collective notions of race. The following discussion is much more modest.

I attempt to survey ways of thinking about, bringing into context, and interrogating the changing meaning of race in the United States. My intent is to raise a series of points to be used as frames of reference, to facilitate and deepen the conversation about race.

My general point is that the meaning of race in the United States has been and probably always will be fluid and subject to multiple determinations. Race cannot be seen simply as an objective fact, nor treated as an independent variable. Attempting to do so only serves, ultimately, to emphasize the importance of critically examining how specific concepts of race are conceived of and deployed in areas such as social-science research, public-policy initiatives, cultural representations, and political discourse. Real issues and debates about race—from the Federal Standards for Racial and Ethnic Classification to studies of economic inequality—need to be approached from a perspective that makes the concept of race problematic.

A second point is the importance of discerning the relationship between race and racism, and being attentive to transformations in the nature of "racialized power." The distribution of power—and its expression in structures, ideologies, and practices at various institutional and individual levels—is significantly racialized in our society. Shifts in what "race" means are indicative of reconfigurations in the nature of "racialized power" and emphasize the need to interrogate specific concepts of racism.

## GLOBAL AND NATIONAL RACIAL CHANGE

The present historical moment is unique, with respect to racial meanings. Since the end of World War II, there has been an epochal shift in the global racial order that had persisted for centuries (Winant and Seidman, 1998). The horrors of fascism and a wave of anticolonialism facilitated a rupture with biologic and eugenic concepts of race, and challenged the ideology(ies) of White supremacy on a number of important fronts. Scholarly projects in genetics, cultural anthropology, and history, among others, were fundamentally rethought, and antiracist initiatives became a crucial part of democratic political projects throughout the world.

In the United States, the Civil Rights Movement was instrumental in challenging and subsequently dismantling patterns of Jim Crow[1] segrega-

---

[1]The original "Jim Crow" was a character in a nineteenth-century minstrel act, a stereotype of a Black man. As encoded in laws sanctioning ethnic discrimination, the phrase refers to both legally enforced and traditionally sanctioned limitations of Blacks' rights, primarily in the U.S. South.

tion in the South. The strategic push of the Movement in its initial phase was toward racial integration in various institutional arenas—e.g., schools, public transportation, and public accommodations—and the extension of legal equality for all regardless of "color." This took place in a national context of economic growth and the expansion of the role and scope of the federal government.

Times have changed and ironies abound. Domestic economic restructuring and the transnational flow of capital and labor have created a new economic context for situating race and racism. The federal government's ability to expand social programs, redistribute resources, and ensure social justice has been dramatically curtailed by fiscal constraints and the rejection of liberal social reforms of the 1960s. Demographically, the nation is becoming less White and the dominant Black-White paradigm of race relations is challenged by the dramatic growth and increasing visibility of Hispanics and Asians.

All these changes have had a tremendous impact on racial identity, consciousness, and politics. Racial discourse is now littered with confused and contradictory meanings. The notion of "color-blindness" is now more likely to be advanced by political groups seeking to dismantle policies, such as affirmative action, initially designed to mitigate racial inequality. Calls to get "beyond race" are popularly expressed, and any hint of race consciousness is viewed as racism.

In this transformed political landscape, traditional civil rights organizations have experienced a crisis of mission, political values, and strategic orientation. Integrationist versus "separate-but-equal" remedies for persistent racial disparities have been revisited in a new light. More often the calls are for "self-help" and for private support to tackle problems of crime, unemployment, and drug abuse. The civil rights establishment confronts a puzzling dilemma—formal, legal equality has been significantly achieved, but substantive racial inequality in employment, housing, and health care remains, and in many cases, has deepened.

All this provides an historical context in which to situate evolving racial meanings. Over the past 50 years, changes in the meaning of race have been shaped by, and in turn have shaped, broader global/epochal shifts in racial formation. The massive influx of new immigrant groups has destabilized specific concepts of race, led to a proliferation of identity positions, and challenged prevailing modes of political and cultural organization.

## DEMOGRAPHIC CHANGE AND RACIAL TRANSFORMATION

In a discussion of Asian American cultural production and political formation, Lowe (1996) uses the concepts of *heterogeneity, hybridity,* and *multiplicity* to disrupt popular notions of a singular, unified Asian American subject. Refashioning these concepts, I use them to assess the changes in, and issues relevant to, racial meaning created by demographic shifts.

## Heterogeneity

Lowe defines heterogeneity as "the existence of differences and differential relationships within a bounded category" (1996:67). Over the past several decades, there has been increasing diversity among so-called racial groups. Our collective understanding of who Blacks, Hispanics, and Asians are has undergone a fundamental revision as new groups entered the country. The liberalization of immigration laws beginning in 1965, political instability in various areas of the world, and labor migration set in motion by global economic restructuring all contributed to an influx of new groups—Laotians, Guatemalans, Haitians, and Sudanese, among others.

In the United States, many of these immigrants encounter an interesting dilemma. Although they may stress their national origins and ethnic identities, they are continually racialized as part of a broader group. Many first-generation Black immigrants from, for example, Jamaica, Ethiopia, or Trinidad, distance themselves from, subscribe to negative stereotypes of, and believe that, as ethnic immigrants, they are accorded a higher status than, Black Americans (Kasinitz, 1992). Children of Black immigrants, who lack their parents' distinctive accents, have more choice in assuming different identities (Waters, 1994). Some try to defy racial classification as "Black Americans" by strategically asserting their ethnic identity in specific encounters with Whites. Others simply see themselves as "Americans."

Panethnic organization and identity constitute one distinct political/ cultural response to increasing heterogeneity. Lopez and Espiritu define panethnicity as "the development of bridging organizations and solidarities among subgroups of ethnic collectivities that are often seen as homogeneous by outsiders" (1990:198); such a development, they claim, is a crucial feature of ethnic change, "supplanting both assimilation and ethnic particularism as the direction of change for racial/ethnic minorities" (1990:198).

Omi and Winant (1996) describe the rise of panethnicity as a response to racialization, driven by a dynamic relationship between the group being racialized and the state. Elites representing panethnic groups find it advantageous to make political demands backed by the numbers and resources panethnic formations can mobilize. The state, in turn, can more easily manage claims by recognizing and responding to large blocs, as opposed to dealing with specific claims from a plethora of ethnically defined interest groups. Different dynamics of inclusion and exclusion are continually expressed. Conflicts often occur over the precise definition and boundaries of various racially defined groups and their adequate representation in census counts, reapportionment debates, and minority set-aside programs. The increasing heterogeneity of racial categories raises several questions for research to answer.

- How do new immigrant groups negotiate the existing terrain of racial meanings? What transformations in racial self-identity take place as immigrants move from a society organized around one concept of race, to a new society with a different mode of conceptualization? Oboler (1995), for example, explores how Latin Americans "discover" the salience of race and ethnicity as a form of social classification in the United States.
- Under what conditions can we imagine panethnic formations developing, and when are ethnic-specific identities maintained or evoked? Conflicts over resources within presumed homogeneous racial groups can be quite sharp and lead to distinctive forms of political consciousness and organization.
- Under what conditions does it make sense to talk about groups such as Asians and Pacific Islanders, American Indians and Alaska Natives, Hispanics, Blacks, etc., and when is it important to disaggregate the various national-origin groups, ethnic groups, and tribes that make up these panethnic formations?

Researchers and policy makers need to be attentive to the increasing heterogeneity of racial/ethnic groups and assess how an examination of "differences" might help us rethink the nature and types of questions asked about life chances, forms of inequality, and policy initiatives.

## Hybridity

Crouch, in his essay "Race Is Over" (1996), speculates that in the future, race will cease to be the basis of identity and "special-interest power" because of the growth in mixed-race people. It has been a long-standing liberal dream, most recently expressed by Warren Beatty in the film *Bulworth*, that increased "race mixing" would solve our racial problems. Multiraciality disrupts our fixed notions about race and opens up new possibilities with respect to dialogue and engagement across the color line. It does not, however, mean that "race is over."

Although the number of people of "mixed-racial descent" is unclear, and contingent on self-definition, the 1990 census counted two million children (under the age of 18) whose parents were of different races (Marriott, 1996). The demographic growth and increased visibility of "mixed-race" or "multiracial" individuals has resulted in a growing literature on multiracial identity and its meaning for a racially stratified society (Root, 1992; Zack, 1994).

In response to these demographic changes, there was a concerted effort from school boards and organizations such as Project RACE (Reclassify All Children Equally) to add a "multiracial" category to the 2000 Census form (Mathews, 1996). This was opposed by many civil rights organizations (e.g., Urban League, National Council of La Raza) who feared a reduction in their numbers and worried that such a multiracial category would spur debates regarding the "protected status" of groups and individuals. According to various estimates, 75 to 90 percent of those who now check the "Black" box could check a multiracial one (Wright, 1994). In pretests by the Census Bureau in 1996, however, only 1 percent of the sample claimed to be multiracial (U.S Bureau of the Census, 1996).

In October 1997, the Office of Management and Budget (OMB) decided to allow Americans the option of multiple checkoffs on the census with respect to the newly modified racial and ethnic classifications (Holmes, 1997). Initial debate centered on how to count people who assigned themselves to more than one racial/ethnic category. At issue is not only census enumeration, but also its impact on federal policies relevant to voting rights and civil rights.

It remains to be seen how many people will actually identify themselves as members of more than one race. Much depends on the prevailing consciousness of multiracial identity, the visibility of multiracial people, and representational practices. As Reynolds Farley notes, "At the time of the 2000 census, if we have another Tiger Woods . . . those figures could up to 5 percent—who knows?" (quoted in Holmes, 1997:A19).

The debate over a multiracial category reveals an intriguing aspect about our conceptualizations of race. The terms "mixed race" or "multiracial" in themselves imply the existence of "pure" and discrete races. By drawing attention to the socially constructed nature of "race," and the meanings attached to it, multiraciality reveals the inherent fluidity and slipperiness of our concepts of race. Restructuring concepts of race has a number of political implications. House Speaker Newt Gingrich (1997), for example, used the issue of multiraciality to illustrate the indeterminacy of racial categories and to vigorously advocate for their abolition in government data collection, much as advocates of color-blindness do.

In her definition of hybridity, Lowe refers to the formation of material culture and practices "produced by the histories of uneven and unsynthetic power relations" (Lowe, 1996:67). Indeed, the question of power cannot be elided in the discussion of multiraciality because power is deeply implicated in racial trends and in construction of racial meanings. The rigidity of the "one-drop rule,"[2] long-standing fears of racial "pollution," and the persistence (until the *Loving* decision in 1967) of antimiscegenation laws demonstrate the ways in which the color line has been policed in the United States. This legacy continues to affect trends in interracial marriage. Lind (1998) suggests that both multiculturalists and nativists have misread trends, and that a new dichotomy between Black and non-Blacks is emerging. In the 21st century, he envisions "a White-Asian-Hispanic melting-pot majority—a hard-to-differentiate group of beige Americans—offset by a minority consisting of Blacks who have been left out of the melting pot once again" (p. 39). Such a dire racial landscape raises a number of troubling political questions regarding group interests, the distribution of resources, and the organization of power.

Simultaneously, racial hybridity reveals the fundamental instability of all racial categories, helps us discern particular dimensions of racialized power, and raises a host of political issues.

- How, when, and under what conditions, do people choose to identify as "mixed race"? According to the Bureau of the Census the American Indian population increased 255 percent between 1960 and 1990 as a result of changes in self-identification. What factors contributed to this shift?
- What effects do multiracial identity and classification have on existing "race-based" public policies? Although most forms of race-based policies are under attack, a vast structure of bureaucracies, policies, and practices exists within government, academic, and private sectors that relies on discrete racial categories. Who, for example, would be considered an "underrepresented minority" and under what circumstances?
- Although there has been a significant growth in the literature on multiraciality, much of it has not deeply examined the racial meanings that pervade distinctive "combinations" of multiracial identity. The experience of being White-Asian in most college/university settings is significantly different from being Black-Asian. Some groups, such as Black Cubans in Miami, encounter marginalization from both Black and Hispanic American communities (Navarro, 1997). We need to deconstruct multiraciality and understand the racial meanings that correspond to specific types of multiracial identities and classifications.

The repeal of antimiscegenation laws, the marked lessening of social distance between racial groups, and interracial marriage among specific

---

[2]A person was legally Negroid, regardless of actual physical appearance, if there were any proof of African ancestry—i.e., one drop of African blood.

groups have contributed to the growth and increased visibility of a multi-racial population. Studies thus far have focused on "cultural conflict" and psychological issues of individual adjustment. We need to assess more deeply how multiraciality affects the logic and organization of data on racial classification, and the political and policy issues that emanate from this.

## Multiplicity

It is, by now, obvious that the racial composition of the nation has been radically changing. In seven years, Hispanics will surpass Blacks as the largest "minority group" in the United States (Holmes, 1998). Trends in particular states and regions are even more dramatic. In 1970, Whites constituted 77 percent of the San Francisco Bay Area's population. Hispanics and Asians constituted 11 and 4 percent, respectively, of the population (McLeod, 1998). In 1997, Whites constituted 54 percent, and Hispanics and Asians each comprised nearly 20 percent of the population.

Much has been made in the popular literature about the "changing face of America," but little has been said about how the increasing multiplicity of groups shapes our collective understanding about race. Specifically, how are the dominant paradigms of race relations affected by these demographic realities?

At the first Advisory Board meeting of the President's Initiative on Race (July 14, 1997), a brief debate ensued among the panelists. Linda Chavez-Thompson argued that the "American dilemma" had become a proliferation of racial and ethnic dilemmas. Angela Oh argued that the national conversation needed to move beyond discussions of racism as solely directed at Blacks. Advisory Board chairman John Hope Franklin, by contrast, affirmed the historical importance of Black-White relations and stressed the need to focus on unfinished business. Although the Board members subsequently downplayed their differences, their distinct perspectives continued to provoke debate within academic, policy, and community activist settings regarding the Black-White race paradigm.

How we think about, engage, and politically mobilize around racial issues have been fundamentally shaped by a prevailing "Black-White" paradigm of race relations. Historical accounts of other people of color in the United States are cast in the shadows of the Black-White encounter. Contemporary conflicts between a number of different racial/ethnic groups are understood in relationship to Black-White conflict, and the media uses the bipolar model as a master frame to present such conflicts.

Such biracial theorizing misses the complex nature of race relations in post-Civil Rights Movement America. Complex patterns of conflict and accommodation have developed among multiple racial/ethnic groups.

In many major U.S. cities, Whites have fled to suburbia, leaving the inner city to the turf battles among different racial minorities for housing, public services, and economic development.

The dominant mode of biracial theorizing ignores the fact that a range of specific conditions and trends—such as labor-market stratification and residential segregation—cannot be adequately studied by narrowly assessing the relative situations of Whites and Blacks. Working within a "two-nations" framework of Black and White, Hacker (1992) needs to consider Asians in higher education at some length in order to address the issue of race-based affirmative action.

In suggesting that we get beyond the Black-White paradigm, I'm conscious of the consequences of such a move. On the one hand, I do not mean to displace or decenter the Black experience, which continues to define the fundamental contours of race and racism in our society. On the other hand, I do want to suggest that the prevailing Black-White model tends to marginalize, if not ignore, the experiences, needs, and political claims of other racialized groups. The challenge is to frame an appropriate language and analysis to help us understand the shifting dynamic of race that all groups are implicated in.

We would profit from more historical and contemporary studies that look at the patterns of interaction between, and among, a multiplicity of groups. Almaguer (1994), in his study of race in nineteenth-century California, breaks from the dominant mode of biracial theorizing to illustrate how American Indians, Mexicans, Chinese, and Japanese were racialized and positioned in relation to one another by the dominant Anglo elite. Horton (1995) takes a look at distinct sites of political and cultural engagement between different groups in Monterey Park, California—a city where Asians constitute the majority population. Such studies emphasize how different groups shape the conditions of each other's existence.

Research needs to consider how specific social policies (e.g., affirmative action, community economic development proposals) have different consequences for different groups. The meaning and impact of immigration reforms for Hispanics, for example, may be quite distinct from its meaning and impact for Asians. In line with an eye toward heterogeneity, different ethnic groups (e.g., Cubans and Salvadorans) within a single racial category (Hispanic) may be differentially affected by particular policy initiatives and reforms. All this is important because politics, policies, and practices framed in dichotomous Black-White terms miss the ways in which specific initiatives structure the possibilities for conflict or accommodation among different racial minority groups.

The multiplicity of groups has transformed the nation's political and cultural terrain, and provoked a contentious debate regarding multiculturalism. New demographic realities have also provided a distinctive context in which to examine the changing dynamics of White racial identity. Both the debate over multiculturalism and the increasing salience of White racial identity are tied to changes in the meaning of race as a result of challenges to the logic and organization of White supremacy.

## MULTICULTURALISM AND WHITENESS

Controversies over the multiculturalism have been bitter and divisive. Proponents claim that a multicultural curriculum, for example, can facilitate an appreciation for diversity, increase tolerance, and improve relations between and among racial and ethnic groups. Opponents claim that multiculturalists devalue or relativize core national values and beliefs, shamelessly promote "identity politics," and unwittingly increase racial tensions.

One of problems of the multicultural debate is the conflation of "race" and "culture." I take seriously Hollinger's (1995) claim that we have reified what he calls the American "ethno-racial pentagon." Blacks, Hispanics, American Indians/Alaska Natives, Asians/Pacific Islanders, and Whites are now seen as the five basic demographic blocs we treat as the subjects of multiculturalism. The problem is that these groups do not represent distinct and mutually exclusive "cultures." American multiculturalism, Hollinger claims, has accomplished, in short order, a task that centuries of British imperial power could not complete: the making of the Irish as indistinguishable from English. Such a perspective argues for the need to rethink what we mean by the terms "race" and "culture," and to critically interrogate the manner in which we articulate the connection between the two in research and policy studies.

Another issue is how forms of multiculturalist discourse elide the organization and distribution of power. Multiculturalism is often posed as the celebration of "differences" and unique forms of material culture expressed, for example, in music, food, dance, and holidays. Such an approach tends to level the important differences and contradictions within and among racial and ethnic groups. Different groups possess different forms of power—the power to control resources, the power to push a political agenda, and the power to culturally represent themselves and other groups. In a recent study of perceived group competition in Los Angeles, Bobo and Hutchings (1996) found, among other things, that Whites felt least threatened by Blacks and most threatened by Asians, while Asians felt a greater threat from Blacks than Hispanics. Such distinct perceptions of "group position" are related to, and implicated in, the organization of power.

Some scholars and activists have defined racism as "prejudice plus power." Using this formula, they argue that people of color can't be racist because they don't have power. But things aren't that simple. In the post-Civil Rights era, some racial minority groups have carved out a degree of power in select urban areas—particularly with respect to administering social services and distributing economic resources. This has led, in cities like Oakland and Miami, to conflicts between Blacks and Hispanics over educational programs, minority business opportunities, and political power. We need to acknowledge and examine the historical and contemporary differences in power that different groups possess.

Dramatic challenges to ideologies and structures of White supremacy in the past 50 years, have caused some Whites to perceive a loss of power and influence. In 25 years, non-Hispanic Whites will constitute a minority in four states, including two of the most populous ones, and in 50 years, they will make up barely half of the U.S. population (Booth, 1998:A18). Whiteness has lost its transparency and self-evident meaning in a period of demographic transformation and racial reforms. White racial identity has recently been the subject of interrogation by scholars (Roediger, 1991; Lott, 1995; Ignatiev, 1995), who have explored how the social category of "White" has evolved and been implicated with racism and the labor movement. Contemporary works look at how White racial identities are constructed, negotiated, and transformed in institutional and everyday life (Hill, 1997).

Research on White Americans suggests that they do not experience their ethnicity as a definitive aspect of their social identity (Alba, 1990; Waters 1990). Rather, they perceive it dimly and irregularly, picking and choosing among its varied strands that allow them to exercise an "ethnic option" (Waters, 1990). Waters found that ethnicity was flexible, symbolic, and voluntary for her White respondents in ways that it was not for non-Whites.

The loose affiliation with specific European ethnicities does not necessarily suggest the demise of any coherent group consciousness and identity. In the "twilight of ethnicity," White racial identity may increase in salience. Indeed, in an increasingly diverse workplace and society, Whites experience a profound racialization.

The racialization process for Whites is evident on many college/university campuses as White students encounter a heightened awareness of race, which calls their own identity into question. Focus group interviews with White students at the University of California, Berkeley, reveals many of the themes and dilemmas of White identity in the current period: the "absence" of a clear culture and identity, the perceived "disadvantages" of being White with respect to the distribution of resources, and the stigma of being perceived as the "oppressors of the nation" (Institute for the Study of Social Change, 1991:37). Such comments underscore the new problematic meanings attached to "White," and debates about the meanings will continue, and perhaps deepen, in the years to come, fueled by such social issues as affirmative action, English-only initiatives, and immigration policies.

Racial meanings are profoundly influenced by state definitions and discursive practices. They are also shaped by interaction with prevailing forms of gender and class formation. An examination of both these topics reveals the fundamental instability of racial categories, their historically contingent character, and the ways they articulate with other axes of stratification and "difference." Extending this understanding, it is crucial to relate racial categories and meanings to concepts of racism. The idea of "race" and its persistence as a social category is only given meaning in a social order structured by forms of inequality—economic, political, and cultural—that are organized, to a significant degree, along racial lines.

## FEDERAL STANDARDS FOR
## RACIAL AND ETHNIC CLASSIFICATION

State definitions of race and ethnicity have inordinately shaped the discourse of race in the United States. OMB Statistical Directive 15 (Office of Management and Budget, 1977) was initially issued to create "compatible, nonduplicated, exchangeable racial and ethnic data by Federal agencies" for three reporting purposes—statistical, administrative, and civil rights compliance. The directive has become the de facto standard for state and local agencies, the private and nonprofit sectors, and the research community. Social scientists use Directive 15 categories because data are organized and available under these rubrics.

Since its inception, the Directive has been the subject of debate regarding its conceptual vagueness and the logical flaws in its categorization (Edmonston and Tamayo-Lott, 1996). Some of the categories are racial, some are cultural, and some are geographic. Some groups cannot neatly be assigned to any category. In addition, little attention is given to the gap between state definitions and popular consciousness. Given the social construction of race and its shifting meaning, administrative definitions may not be meaningful to the very individuals and groups they purport to represent (Omi, 1997).

Some politicians and political commentators have seized on the difficulty of establishing coherent racial categories as a reason to call for the abolition of all racial classification and record keeping. Such a move, they argue, would save federal dollars and minimize racial/ethnic distinctions, consciousness, and divisive politics. In 1997, the American Anthropological Association counseled the federal government to phase out use of the term "race" in the collection of data because the concept has no scientific justification in human biology (Overbey, 1997). The problem is, social concepts of race are still linked to forms of discrimination. Abolishing data-collection efforts that use racial categories would make it more difficult for us to track specific forms of discrimination with respect to financial loan practices, health-care delivery, and prison-sentencing patterns among other issues (Berry et al., 1998). The current debate about police "profiling" of Black motorists illustrates the issues involved in racial record keeping (Wilgoren, 1999).

Wishing to preserve racial and ethnic data, some demographers and social scientists argue for categories that are more precise, conceptually valid, exclusive, exhaustive, measurable, and reliable over time. I believe this is an impossible task because it negates the fluidity and transformation of race and racial meanings, and definitions, over time.

The strange and twisted history of the classification of Asian Indians in the United States is instructive. During and after the peak years of immigration, Asian Indians were referred to and classified as "Hindu," though the clear majority of them were Sikh. In *United States v. B.S. Thind* (1923), the U.S. Supreme Court held that Thind, as a native of India, was indeed "Caucasian," but he wasn't "White" and therefore was ineligible to become a naturalized citizen (p. 213). "It may be true," the court declared, "that the blond Scandinavian and the brown Hindu have a common ancestor in the dim reaches of antiquity, but the average man knows perfectly well that there are unmistakable and profound differences between them today" (p. 209). Their status as non-White was reversed after World War II when they became "White" in part as reward for their participation in the Pacific war and as a consequence of the postwar climate of anticolonial politics. In the post-Civil Rights era, Asian Indian leaders sought to change their classification in order to seek "minority" group status. In 1977, OMB agreed to reclassify immigrants from India and their descendants from "White/Caucasian" to "Asian Indian." Currently, many Asian Indians self-identify as "South Asian" to foster panethnic identification with those from Pakistan and Bangladesh, among other countries.

The point of all this is that racial and ethnic categories are often the effects of political interpretation and struggle, and that the categories in turn have political effects. Such an understanding is crucial in the ongoing debates around the federal standards for racial and ethnic classification.

## INTERSECTIONALITY

In a critique of racial essentialism, Hall (1996:444) states that "the central issues of race always appear historically in articulation, in a formation, with other categories and divisions and are constantly crossed and recrossed by categories of class, of gender and ethnicity." Although this may seem obvious, most social-science research tends to neglect an examination of the connections between distinct, yet overlapping, forms of stratification and "difference." The result is a compartmentalization of inquiry and analysis. Higginbotham (1993:14) notes that, "Race *only* comes up when we talk about African Americans and other people of color, gender *only* comes up when we talk about women, and class *only* comes up when we talk about the poor and working class."

Analyses that do grapple with more than one variable frequently reveal a crisis of imagination. Much of the race-class debate, for example, inspired by the work of Wilson (1978), suffers from the imposition of rigid categories and analyses that degenerate into dogmatic assertions of the primacy of one category over the other. In fairness, more recent work has examined the interactive effects of race and class on residential segregation (Massey and Denton, 1993) and inequalities in wealth accumulation (Oliver and Shapiro, 1995). Still, most work treats race and class as discrete and analytically distinct categories.

A new direction is reflected in scholarship that emphasizes the "intersectionality" of race, gender, and class (Collins, 1990). Such work does not simply employ an additive model of examining inequalities (e.g., assessing the relative and combined effects of race and gender "penalties" in wage differentials), but examines how different categories are constituted, transformed, and given meaning in dynamic engagement with each other. Glenn's (1992, 1999) work on the history of domestic and service work, for example, reveals how race is gendered and gender is raced. Frankenberg (1993) explores the ways in which White women experience, reproduce, and/or challenge the prevailing racial order. In so doing, she reveals how the very notion of racial privilege is experienced and articulated differently by women and men.

In institutional and everyday life, any clear demarcation of specific forms of "difference" is constantly being disrupted. This suggests the importance of understanding how changes in racial meaning are affected by transformations in gender and class relations. New research promises a break with the conception of race, class, and gender as relatively static categories, and emphasizes an approach that looks at the multiple and mutually determining ways that they shape each other. Such a framework of analysis is, however, still tentative, incomplete, and in need of further elaboration and refinement.

## RACE AND RACISM

Blauner (1994) notes that in classroom discussions of racism, White and Black students tend to talk past one another. Whites tend to locate racism in color consciousness and find its absence in color-blindness. In so doing, they see the affirmation of difference and racial identity among racially defined minority students as racist. Black students, by contrast, see racism as a system of power, and correspondingly argue that they cannot be racist because they lack power. Blauner concludes that there are two "languages" of race, one in which members of racial minorities, especially Blacks, see the centrality of race in history and everyday experience, and another in which Whites see race as a peripheral, nonessential reality.

Such discussions remind us of the crucial importance of discerning and articulating the connections between the changing meaning of race and concepts of racism. Increasingly, some scholars argue that the term "racism" has suffered from conceptual inflation, and been subject to so many different meanings as to render the concept useless (Miles, 1989). Recently, John Bunzel, a former member of the U.S. Commission on Civil Rights and current senior research fellow at Stanford's Hoover Institution, argued that the President's Advisory Board on Race should call for a halt to the use of the term "racism" because it breeds "bitterness and polarization, not a spirit of pragmatic reasonableness in confronting our difficult problems" (Bunzel, 1998:D-7).

In academic and policy circles, the question of what racism is continues to haunt discussions. Prior to World War II, the term "racism" was not commonly used in public discourse or in the social-science literature. The term was originally used to characterize the ideology of White supremacy that was buttressed by biologically based theories of superiority/inferiority. In the 1950s and 1960s, the emphasis shifted to notions of individual expressions of prejudice and discrimination. The rise of the Black power movement in the 1960s and 1970s fostered a redefinition of racism that focused on its institutional nature. Current work in cultural studies looks at the often implicit and unconscious structures of racial privilege and racial representation in daily life and popular culture.

All this suggests that more precise terms are needed to examine racial consciousness, institutional bias, inequality, patterns of segregation, and the distribution of power. Racism is expressed differently at different levels and sites of social activity, and we need to be attentive to its shifting meaning in different contexts. As Goldberg (1990:xiii) states, "the presumption of a single monolithic racism is being displaced by a mapping of the multifarious historical formulations of *racisms*."

This intellectual task is wrapped up with, indeed, intrinsically connected to, surveying the changing meaning(s) of race. In a period when major social policies with respect to race are being challenged and rethought, it is crucial to consider how different meanings of race are shaped by, and in turn help shape, different concepts of racism. Being clear about what we do and do not mean by *racism* is essential to future dialogues on race—dialogues that need to interrogate the nature of past and present forms of inequality, and the meaning of social justice.

## LOOKING BACK, THINKING AHEAD

It is important to consider how unique the current racial context is, and its meaning for theorizing about race. Alba (1998) argues that many commentators and social scientists seize on the increasing complexity of race to reject, in blanket fashion, prior and existing understandings of racial transformation. He urges critical restraint, and states that "the conceptual models we have from the past should not be so quickly eclipsed by the seeming novelty of the present" (p. 7). To buttress his remarks, Alba suggests that we consider a "more refined conception of assimilation" to understand the trajectory of immigrant group incorporation over succeeding generations. Processes of assimilation render demographic projections, and the significance we impute to them, problematic because they rest on the assumption that racial and ethnic categories are stable enclosures. Rather than speak of the decreasing White population, Alba suggests that our collective notion of "majority group" might undergo a profound redefinition as "some Asians and Hispanics join what has been viewed as a 'White,' European population" (p. 10).

There is much here to consider. First, clearly there are historical continuities in patterns of relevance to race in the United States. The color line was rigidly enforced throughout much of America's history, and racial inequalities have been stubbornly persistent in the face of political reforms. But I believe the current historical moment is a relatively unique one with respect to racial meanings. Over the past 50 years, White supremacy has been significantly challenged, not only in the United States but on a global scale. Since the end of World War II, there has been an epochal shift in the logic, organization, and practices of the centuries-old global racial order. Opposition to fascism, anticolonial struggles in Africa, Asia, and Latin America, and the Civil Rights Movement in the United States facilitated the rupture with biologic and eugenic concepts of race. In the United States and South Africa, particularly, antiracist initiatives have become crucial elements of an overall project to extend political democracy. These developments provide a unique historical context for understanding the meaning we impart to race.

Second, while older paradigms of race can help us understand what's going on today, it is important to historically situate various models of race and ethnicity, and see them as reflective of historically specific concerns. The vast influx of different groups of European immigrants at the turn of the century stimulated sociological thinking regarding assimilation and group incorporation into the mainstream of American life. In a similar manner, the current influx of immigrant groups from Asia, Latin America, the Caribbean, and the former Soviet Union, and elsewhere, provides an opportunity to rethink the nature of immigration, identity, and community formation; but the jury is still out on whether older models need to be modified to capture new realities, or if new and radically different models are called for.

Old theories, of course, are often revisited and remodeled. Traditional theories of assimilation, for example, have been substantially revised. No longer is assimilation posed and envisioned as a zero-sum game; the more "assimilated" one is, does mean that one is less "ethnic." Assimilation is also no longer read as "Anglo conformity"; there is no clearly discernible social and cultural "core" that immigrant groups gravitate toward. Forms of what Portes and Zhou (1993) label "segmented assimilation" are occurring, and they involve complex patterns of accommodation and conflict between increasingly diverse racial and ethnic groups.

That said, it is important to critically examine racial trends and their interpretation through a conceptual framework such as assimilation. What is missing is sufficient attentiveness to the processes of *racialization*— the ways racial meanings are constructed and imparted to social groups and processes. From an assimilationist vantage point, one could examine the intermarriage patterns among Asians to support the idea of their incorporation into the White mainstream. Indeed some social scientists (Hacker, 1992) believe that increasing Asian-White marriage rates, along with positive trends in income, education, and residential patterns, suggest that Asian Americans are becoming "White" as the very category of "Whiteness" is being expanded.

Such a conclusion draws on a troublesome aspect of the traditional assimilationist paradigm, namely, its lack of attention to differences in group *power*. Interracial marriage has been seen as a crucial subprocess of assimilation (Gordon, 1964). Increasing rates of marriage between minority and majority groups were read as an important indicator of narrowing of social distance, a reduction in group prejudice and discrimination, and the lessening of strict group boundaries. But increasing intermarriage could also illustrate inequalities in racial power and the complex articulation of race, gender, and sexuality (Shinagawa and Pang, 1996). Asian women, for example, are construed as desirable spouses/partners drawing on specific racial and gender representations (Marchetti, 1993). These ideas and images circulate in a variety of settings—in popular films, pornography, and "mail-order bride" services. Given the pervasiveness of these representations, can increased rates of intermarriage between Asian women and White men simply be read as an indicator of assimilation? I think not.

What it does suggest is the need to look at the cultural representations and discursive practices that shape racial meanings. This has crucial implications for the examination and interpretation of racial trends. By looking at levels of educational attainment, residential patterns, median family incomes, and poverty rates, Asians, as one group, do not appear to be structurally disadvantaged by race. But there lurks beneath these glowing social indicators a repertoire of ideologies and practices that can be evoked in particular moments to render Asians foreign, subversive, and suspect. The Asian campaign finance controversy (Wang, 1998; Nakanishi, 1998) and the recent Chinese spy scandal provide illustrations of this. Popular interpretations of these events have had a chilling effect on both Asian American political participation and employment in scientific research settings.

The point of all this is to underscore the necessity of an interdisciplinary, multidimensional approach to the study of race and its changing meaning. Social scientists often treat the category of race in an unproblematic fashion. Seeing it as an independent variable, correlations are established between a host of other variables, and trends are discerned with respect to life chances. But we need to problematize race in our work; to look more closely and critically at the connections between structures and discursive practices—linking, for example, labor-market stratification with cultural representations. In focusing on such dynamic relationships, we can more fully appreciate how racial meanings change, and what those changes mean to our collective identity as a people.

## REFERENCES

Alba, R.
   1990   *Ethnic Identity: The Transformation of White America.* New Haven: Yale University Press.
   1998   On the possibility of continuities between the American past and future. Unpublished comments prepared for the National Research Council Conference on Racial Trends in the United States. National Academy of Sciences, Washington, D.C., October 15-16.
Almaguer, T.
   1994   *Racial Fault Lines: The Historical Origins of White Supremacy in California.* Berkeley: University of California Press.
Berry, M., Y. Lee, C. Reynoso, and L. Higginbotham
   1998   Closing our eyes to discrimination. *San Francisco Chronicle* (September 8):A21.
Blauner, B.
   1994   Talking past each other: Black and White languages of race. In *Race and Ethnic Conflict: Contending Views on Prejudice, Discrimination, and Ethnoviolence,* F. Pincus and H. Ehrlich, eds. Boulder, Colo.: Westview Press.
Bobo, L., and V. Hutchings
   1996   Perceptions of racial group competition: Extending Blumer's theory of group position to a multiracial social context. *American Sociological Review* 61(6):951-972.

Booth, W.
  1998   One nation, indivisible: Is it history? *The Washington Post* (February 22):A1.
Bunzel, J.
  1998   Words that smear, like "racism," provoke polarization. *San Francisco Sunday Examiner and Chronicle* (July 26):D-7.
Collins, P.
  1990   *Black Feminist Thought: Knowledge, Consciousness, and the Politics of Empowerment.* New York: Routledge.
Crouch, S.
  1996   Race is over: Black, White, Red, Yellow—same difference. *New York Times Magazine* (Sept. 29):170.
Edmonston, B., J. Goldstein, and J. Tamayo-Lott, eds.
  1996   *Spotlight on Heterogeneity: The Federal Standards for Racial and Ethnic Classification.* Washington, D.C.: National Academy Press.
Frankenberg, R.
  1993   *White Women, Race Matters: The Social Construction of Whiteness.* Minneapolis: University of Minnesota Press.
Gingrich, N.
  1997   Testimony of speaker Newt Gingrich. Pp. 661-662 in House of Representatives, Committee on Government Reform and Oversight, Subcommittee on Government Management, Information, and Technology Hearings, *Federal Measures of Race and Ethnicity and the Implications for the 2000 Census,* 105th Congress, First Session, 25 July.
Glenn, E.
  1992   From servitude to service work: Historical continuities in the racial division of paid reproductive labor. *Signs: Journal of Women in Culture & Society* 18:1-43.
  1999   Social construction and institutionalization of gender and race: An integrative framework. In *Revisioning Gender,* M. Ferree, J. Lorber, and B. Hess, eds. Thousand Oaks, Calif.: Sage Publications.
Goldberg, D., ed.
  1990   *Anatomy of Racism.* Minneapolis: University of Minnesota Press.
Gordon, M.
  1964   *Assimilation in American Life.* New York: Oxford University Press.
Hacker, A.
  1992   *Two Nations: Black and White, Separate, Hostile, Unequal.* New York: Charles Scribner's Sons.
Hall, S.
  1996 [1986] Gramsci's relevance for the study of race and ethnicity. In *Stuart Hall: Critical Dialogues in Cultural Studies,* D. Morley and K. Chen, eds. New York: Routledge.
Higginbotham, E.
  1993   Sociology and the multicultural curriculum: The challenges of the 1990s and beyond. *Race, Sex, and Class* 1:13-24.
Hill, M., ed.
  1997   *Whiteness: A Critical Reader.* New York: New York University Press.
Hollinger, D.
  1995   *Postethnic America: Beyond Multiculturalism.* New York: Basic Books.
Holmes, S.
  1997   People can claim more than one race on federal forms. *New York Times* (October 30):A1.
  1998   Figuring out Hispanic influence. *New York Times: Week 3* (August 16).

Horton, J.
    1995    The Politics of Diversity: Immigration, Resistance, and Change in Monterey Park, California. Philadelphia: Temple University Press.
Ignatiev, N.
    1995    How the Irish Became White. New York: Routledge.
Institute for the Study of Social Change
    1991    The Diversity Project: The Final Report. Berkeley: University of California.
Kasinitz, P.
    1992    Caribbean New York: Black Immigrants and the Politics of Race. Ithaca, N.Y.: Cornell University Press.
Lind, M.
    1998    The beige and the Black. The New York Times Magazine (August 18):38-39.
Lopez, D., and Y. Espiritu
    1990    Panethnicity in the United States: A theoretical framework. Ethnic and Racial Studies 13:198-224.
Lott, E.
    1995    Love and Theft: Blackface Minstrelsy and the American Working Class. New York: Oxford University Press.
Lowe, L.
    1996    Immigrant Acts: On Asian American Cultural Politics. Durham and London: Duke University Press.
Marchetti, G.
    1993    Romance and the "Yellow Peril": Race, Sex, and Discursive Strategies in Hollywood Fiction. Berkeley: University of California Press.
Marriott, M.
    1996    Multiracial Americans ready to claim their own identity. New York Times (July 20):A1.
Massey, D., and N. Denton
    1993    American Apartheid: Segregation and the Making of the Underclass. Cambridge, Mass.: Harvard University Press.
Mathews, L.
    1996    More than identity rides on a new racial category. New York Times (July 6):Y7.
McLeod, R.
    1998    "Minority majority" well on way in state. San Francisco Chronicle (Sept. 4):A22.
Miles, R.
    1989    Racism. New York: Routledge.
Nakanishi, D.
    1998    Beyond the campaign finance controversy: Trends and issues of the new Asian Pacific American population. Paper prepared for the National Research Council Conference on Racial Trends. National Academy of Sciences, Washington, D.C., October 15-16.
Navarro, M.
    1997    Black and Cuban-American: Bias in 2 worlds. New York Times (September 13):Y7.
Oboler, S.
    1995    Ethnic Labels, Latino Lives: Identity and the Politics of (Re)presentation in the United States. Minneapolis: University of Minnesota Press.
Office of Management and Budget
    1977    Statistical Directive No. 15: Race and Ethnic Standards for Federal Statistics and Administrative Reporting (May 12). Washington, D.C.: Government Printing Office.
Oliver, M., and T. Shapiro
    1995    Black Wealth/White Wealth: A New Perspective on Racial Inequality. New York: Routledge.

Omi, M.
  1997 Racial identity and the State: The dilemmas of classification. *Law & Inequality* XV(1):7-23.
Omi, M., and H. Winant
  1996 Contesting the meaning of race in the post-civil rights movement era. In *Origins and Destinies: Immigration, Race, and Ethnicity in America*, S. Pedraza and R. Rumbaut, eds. Belmont, Calif.: Wadsworth Publishing.
Overbey, M.
  1997 AAA tells feds to eliminate 'race'. *Anthropology Newsletter* (American Anthropological Association) 38(7):1.
Petit, C.
  1998 No biological basis for race, scientists say. *San Francisco Chronicle* (February 23):A1.
Portes, A., and M. Zhou
  1993 The new second generation: Segmented assimilation and its variants. *The Annals* 530:74-96.
Roediger, D.
  1991 *The Wages of Whiteness: Race and the Making of the American Working Class*. New York: Verso.
Root, M., ed.
  1992 *Racially Mixed People*. Newbury Park, Calif.: Sage Publications.
Shinagawa, L., and G. Pang
  1996 Asian American panethnicity and intermarriage. *Amerasia Journal* 22(2):127-152.
U.S. Bureau of the Census
  1996 Results of the 1996 race and ethnic targeted test. Population Division Working Paper No. 18.
United States v. B.S. Thind
  1923 261 U.S. 204.
Wang, L.
  1998 Race, class, citizenship, and extraterritoriality: Asian Americans and the 1996 campaign finance scandal. *Amerasia Journal* 24(1):1-22.
Waters, M.
  1990 *Ethnic Options: Choosing Identities in America*. Berkeley and Los Angeles: University of California Press.
  1994 Ethnic and racial identities of second-generation Black immigrants in New York City. *International Migration Review* 28:795-820.
Wilgoren, J.
  1999 Police profiling debate: Acting on experience, or on bias. *New York Times* (April 9):A21.
Wilson, W.
  1978 *The Declining Significance of Race: Blacks and Changing American Institutions*. Chicago: University of Chicago Press.
Winant, H., and G. Seidman
  1998 The modern world racial system in transition. Paper presented at the 93rd Annual Meeting of the American Sociological Association, San Francisco, August 21-25.
Wright, L.
  1994 One drop of blood. *The New Yorker* (July 25):47.
Zack, N.
  1994 *Race and Mixed Race*. Philadelphia: Temple University Press.

# 9

# Racial Attitudes and Relations at the Close of the Twentieth Century

*Lawrence D. Bobo*

The color-line is not static; it bends and buckles and sometimes breaks.
(Drake and Cayton, 1945:101)

Throughout the 1990s, assessments of racial and ethnic relations in the United States suggested that we have become increasingly racially polarized. Essayist and political scientist Andrew Hacker declared that, "a huge racial chasm remains, and there are few signs that the coming century will see it closed" (1992:219). Civil rights activist and legal scholar Derrick Bell offered the bleak analysis that, "racism is an integral, permanent, and indestructible component of this society" (1992:ix). These statements, it seemed, only set the stage for even more dramatic declarations from both Hispanics (Delgado, 1996) and other Blacks (Rowan, 1996). Reaction against such pessimistic analyses seemed inevitable.

In 1997, conservative analysts Stephan and Abigail Thernstrom argued that, "the foundation of progress for many Blacks is no longer fragile. Progress is real and solid" (Thernstrom and Thernstrom, 1997:535). This sentiment was echoed by the eminent historical sociologist Orlando Patterson, who maintained that "being Afro-American is no longer a significant obstacle to participation in the public life of the nation. What is more, Afro-Americans have also become full members of what may be called the nation's moral community and cultural life" (1997:17). Indeed, journalist Jim Sleeper goes so far as to deride the analyses offered by Hacker, Bell, Rowan, Delgado, and others as so much "liberal racism" (1997).

The empirical social science literature examining racial attitudes and relations is no less divided. Sociologist Joe Feagin (1997) recently argued that, "the basic racial problem in the United States is White racism. White racism is a social disease that afflicts the minds, emotions, behaviors, and institutions of Whites. White racism pervades every nook and cranny of U.S. society" (p. 29). Political psychologist David Sears developed a densely argued and analytically detailed critique of the claim that race-neutral political values, as opposed to anti-Black animus, lay at the base of many Whites' discontent with social policies developed on the basis of race. After examining data from three national surveys and one Los Angeles-based survey, Sears and his colleagues concluded:

> The strength of the findings here will lay to rest the notion that White opposition to racially targeted policies is primarily motivated by nonracial considerations, or that any racially based motivation is limited to a few poorly educated ethnocentrics or believers in White supremacy. Racism is considerably more widespread in American society than that, it cannot be reduced to the older forms of prejudice familiar in the pre-civil rights era, and it continues to have quite pervasive effects. It is not a pleasant aspect of our society, but it is not one that should be swept under the carpet, either (Sears et al., 1997:49).

Yet, other students of public opinion vehemently disagree. Sears and colleagues' conclusion is directly antithetical to that reached by Sniderman and Carmines (1997). On the basis of a series of experiments embedded in large-scale surveys examining Whites' views about affirmative action, they argued that, "it is simply wrong to suppose that racial prejudice is a primary source of opposition to affirmative action . . . racism turns out to be just one of a string of explanations offered for opposition to affirmative action that don't cash out" (Sniderman and Carmines, 1997:144). Likewise, some analysts of trend data have also ventured broad generalizations about a decline in racism. According to public-opinion researchers Niemi et al., "without ignoring real signs of enduring racism, it is still fair to conclude that America has been successfully struggling to resolve its Dilemma and that equality has been gaining in ascendancy over racism" (1989:168).

And so the battle is joined. This great debate, whether waged at the level of public intellectuals or between empirical social scientists, raises serious questions about racial attitudes and relations, as well as about the success and health of American democracy, as we enter a new century.

## DEVELOPING THE EMPIRICAL ASSESSMENT

The paramount question is whether America is moving toward becoming a genuinely "color-blind" society or stagnating as a society deeply polarized by race. As is by now obvious, studies of racial attitudes in the United States present a difficult dilemma. On the one hand, several recent studies emphasize steadily improving racial attitudes of Whites, especially in terms of their attitudes toward Blacks. These attitudinal trends are reinforced by many more tangible indicators, most notably the size, relative security, and potentially growing influence of the Black middle class. On the other hand, there is evidence of persistent negative stereotyping of racial minorities, evidence of widely divergent views of the extent and importance of racial discrimination to modern race relations, and evidence of deepening feelings of alienation among Blacks (and possibly among members of other minority groups as well). These more pessimistic attitudinal trends are reinforced by such tangible indicators as the persistent problem of racial segregation of neighborhoods and schools, discrimination in access to housing and employment, innumerable everyday acts of racial bias, and numerous signs of the gulf in perception that often separates Blacks and Whites.

Empirical assessment here focuses on five aspects of the research: (1) the predominant trend toward positive change concerning the goals of integration and equal treatment; (2) the evident difficulty of moving from these goals to concrete support for change in social policy and individual living conditions; (3) the problem of persistent stereotyping; (4) the differing views of racial discrimination; and (5) the possible deepening of Black alienation. Wherever possible, trends are emphasized. It is essential to have a sense of whether and how much things have changed if we are to make sense of where we stand today or might head in the future. Although this analysis will emphasize what is known about the views of Whites toward Blacks, at several important points a multiracial perspective will be incorporated.

By way of foreshadowing what is to come, it is important to note that we now have a deeply rooted national consensus on the ideals of racial equality and integration. These high ideals founder, however, on racial differences in preferred levels of integration, they founder on sharp racial differences in beliefs about racial discrimination, they founder on the persistence of negative racial stereotypes, and they result in policy stagnation and mutual misunderstanding. Although America has turned away from Jim Crow racism, it heads into an uncertain future. With specific regard to the Black-White divide, journalist David Shipler comes as close as anyone has to understanding the special character of this cleavage:

> [T]he fountainhead of injustice has been located between Blacks and Whites, and that legacy remains the country's most potent symbol of shame. Nothing tests the nation, or takes the measure of its decency, quite like the rift between Black and White . . . . I have sought and found common denominators at a level of attitude that transcends boundaries

of place. Everywhere I have looked, I have seen a country where Blacks and Whites are strangers to each other (1997:x).

Before proceeding, it seems prudent to provide some anchorage for the terms "race" and "ethnicity," "attitude," "prejudice," and "racism." There is no settled consensus on how to define and use race and ethnicity (Petersen, 1982; Alba, 1992). Common usage tends to associate "race" with biologically based differences between human groups, differences typically observable in skin color, hair texture, eye shape, and other physical attributes. "Ethnicity" tends to be associated with culture, pertaining to such factors as language, religion, and nationality. There may be quite real differences in physical features that come to be understood as indicia for racial group membership. Yet, it is widely agreed by social scientists that both race and ethnicity are, fundamentally, social constructions (Jones, 1972; Omi and Winant, 1986; Stone, 1985; See and Wilson, 1989).

Some have argued vigorously for discontinuing use of the term "race." Early forceful proponents of this position were Ashley Montagu (1964) and Gordon Allport (1954). More recent advocates are Thernstrom and Thernstrom (1997) and Patterson (1997). "Race" is retained here for two reasons. (1) It still comports with prevailing social usage and understanding. The core mission here is to convey the state of public opinion on these matters; therefore, to introduce new vocabulary inconsistent with what much of the public readily comprehends introduces a distraction. (2) As Petersen eloquently explained, "Whether the removal of a word would also eradicate group antipathies is doubtful; one suspects that with another classification Jews and Gypsies would have been murdered just as beastially. In any case, deleting the term does not remove the need for some designation" (1982:7).

Although perceived racial distinctions often result in sharper and more persistent barriers than ethnic distinctions, this is not invariably the case, and both terms share elements of presumed common descent or ascriptive inheritance. The broad census categories of Asian and Pacific Islander, Hispanic, Black, and White conceal important subgroup differences defined along lines of nativity, national origin, class, gender, and other dimensions.

Social psychologists have long understood "attitudes" to involve "a favorable or unfavorable evaluation of an object" (Schuman, 1995:68). In this case, the objects of attitude are racial and ethnic groups and their attributes, aspects of relations between groups, public policies relevant to race, contact between those groups, and assessments of the character of intergroup relations.[1] Attitudes are, therefore, important guides to likely

---

[1]Thus, we rely on a multidimensional conception of attitudes about race and ethnicity (Jackman, 1977; Bobo, 1983). Although some social scientists still defend the usefulness of

patterns of social behavior. Racial attitudes, however, are not automatically indicative of racial prejudice or of racism. Both prejudice and racism are themselves complex, internally differentiated concepts. Therefore, it would be inappropriate to interpret patterns revealed by any single racial attitude question, even in relation to a major conceptual grouping, as indicating a fundamental or global change in the level of either prejudice or racism. Such generalizations and interpretations should be made with great caution because social phenomena may remain powerfully "racialized" even as one way of understanding prejudice or racism is undergoing major change (Bonilla-Silva, 1996).

Social psychologist Thomas Pettigrew suggested that prejudice involved "irrationally based negative attitudes against certain ethnic groups and their members" (1981:2). Prejudice thus involved an "antipathy accompanied by a faculty generalization" (Pettigrew, 1981:3). Sociologists Katherine O'Sullivan See and William Julius Wilson suggest that the term "prejudice" be reserved for the "attitudinal dimension of intergroup relations, to the processes of stereotyping and aversion that may persist even in the face of countervailing evidence" (See and Wilson, 1989:227). Prejudice is thus distinct from racism. See and Wilson suggested that

> [R]acism is a more complex belief system that prescribes and legitimates a minority group's or an out-group's subordination by claiming that the group is either biogenetically or culturally inferior . . . . There are two components to racism that are not present in prejudice: an ideology that justifies social avoidance and domination by reference to the 'unalterable' characteristics of particular groups and a set of norms that prescribe differential treatment for these groups (See and Wilson, 1989:227).

Many analysts recognize forms of racism that exist at the level of individual attitudes and beliefs (Pettigrew, 1981; Gaertner and Dovidio, 1986; Jones, 1988; Sears, 1988), but there are also good reasons why distinction between the two should be maintained. (1) There is value in clearly differentiating individual and societal levels of analysis. Using the term "prejudice" to speak to the individual level and "racism" to speak to the cultural and societal levels helps to maintain greater conceptual clarity. (2) In a larger social context, where the term "racism" has become

---

thinking of racial attitudes in terms of points along a single prejudice-to-tolerance continuum (Kleinpenning and Hagendoorn, 1993), most analysts acknowledge the usefulness of perceiving racial attitudes as having several broad conceptual types. To be sure, some critics argue that examinations of racial attitudes are intrinsically static and destined simply to show declining prejudice (Bonilla-Silva, 1996; Steinberg, 1998); this view is easily refuted, however, once one adopts a multidimensional framework and devotes even the most cursory attention to empirical studies of change over time (Schuman et al., 1997).

heavily loaded with potential to alienate as well as to stigmatize, and given that it has often been used carelessly, there is some value to insisting on delimited and careful use of the term.

## MAJOR PATTERNS IN RACIAL ATTITUDES AND BELIEFS

### New Principles of Equality and Integration

The single clearest trend shown in studies of racial attitudes has involved a steady and sweeping movement toward general endorsement of the principles of racial equality and integration. The data charted in Figures 9-1, 9-2, and 9-3 show much of this trend. When major national assessments of racial attitudes were first conducted in the early 1940s, 68

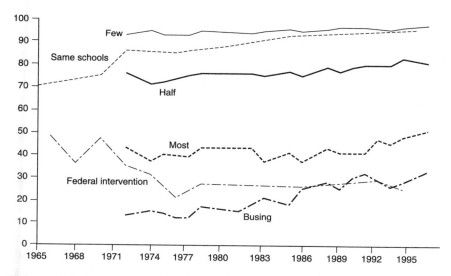

FIGURE 9-1 Trends in Whites' attitudes about school integration. SOURCE: Adapted from Schuman et al. (1997). *Few*: Would you have any objection to sending your children to a school where a few of the children are Blacks? *Half*: [If "no" or don't know to *FEW*] Where half of the children are Blacks? *Most*: [If "no" or don't know to *HALF*]: Where more than half of the children are Blacks? *Same Schools*: Do you think White students and Black students should go to the same schools or to separate schools? *Federal Intervention*: Do you think the federal government should see to it that White and Black children go to the same schools, or should federal officials stay out of this area, as it is not their business? *Busing*: In general, do you favor or oppose the busing of Black and White school children from one school district to another?

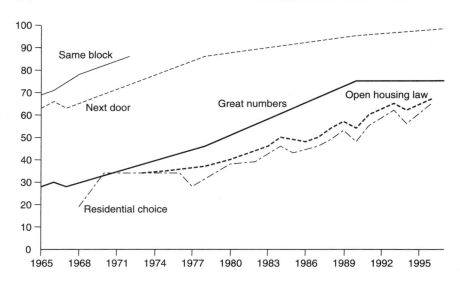

FIGURE 9-2  Trends in Whites' attitudes about residential choice. SOURCE: Adapted from Schuman et al. (1997). *Same Block*: If a Black family with the same income and education as you have moved into your block, would it make any difference to you? *Next Door*: If Blacks came to live next door, would you move? *Great Numbers*: Would you move if Blacks came to live in great numbers in your neighborhood? *Open Housing Law*: Suppose there is a community-wide vote on the general housing issue. One law says that a homeowner can decide for himself who to sell his house to, even if he prefers not to sell to Blacks. The second law says that a homeowner cannot refuse to sell to someone because of their race or color. Which law would you vote for? *Residential Choice*: Do you agree with this statement? White people have a right to keep Blacks out of their neighborhoods if they want to, and Blacks should respect that right.

percent of Whites expressed the view that Black and White school children should go to separate schools, 54 percent felt that public transportation should be segregated, and 54 percent felt that Whites should receive preference over Blacks in access to jobs. By the early 1960s, percentages of Whites advocating segregation and discrimination had decreased substantially, so much so that the questions on public transportation and access to jobs were dropped from national surveys in the early 1970s (Figure 9-3). By then, virtually all Whites endorsed the idea that transportation should be integrated and that access to jobs should be equal without regard to race. The issue of integrated schools remained more divided; however, the trend was equally steady. By 1995, fully 96 percent of

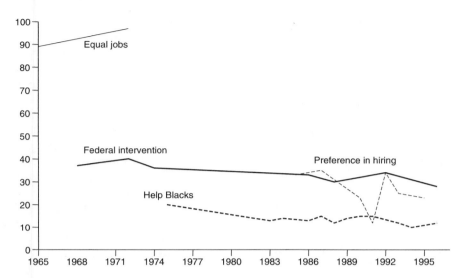

FIGURE 9-3 Trends in Whites' attitudes about race and employment. SOURCE: Adapted from Schuman et al. (1997). *Equal Jobs*: Do you think Blacks should have as good a chance as White people to get any kind of job, or do you think White people should have the first chance at any kind of job? *Federal Intervention*: Should the federal government see to it that Black people get fair treatment in jobs, or should the federal government leave these matters to the states and local communities? *Preference in Hiring*: Are you for or against preferential hiring and promotion of Blacks? [If For] Do you favor preference in hiring and promotion strongly or not strongly [If Against] Do you oppose preference in hiring and promotion strongly or not strongly? *Help Blacks*: Some people think that Blacks have been discriminated against for so long that the government has a special obligation to help improve their living standards. Others believe that the government should not be giving special treatment to Blacks. Where would you place yourself on this scale [1. I strongly agree the government is obligated to help Blacks. 3. I agree with both answers. 5. I strongly agree that government shouldn't give special treatment], or haven't you made up your mind on this?

Whites expressed the view that White and Black school children should go to the same schools (Figure 9-1). Three points about this transformation of basic principles or norms that should guide race relations bear noting.

First, there is some variation in the degree of endorsement of the principle of racial equality and integration. In general, the more public and impersonal the arena, the greater the evidence of movement toward endorsing ideals of integration and equality. Thus, support for unconstrained access to housing for Blacks has undergone tremendous positive change, but still lags behind endorsement of access to schools and jobs. More telling, racially mixed marriage still encounters some resistance, with one in five Whites as recently as 1990 supporting laws that would ban such marriages, and an even higher percentage expressing personal disapproval of them (Figure 9-4).

Second, Blacks have long rejected segregation. Although the available data for tracing long-term attitudinal trends among Blacks are much more limited than for Whites, it is clear that Blacks have overwhelmingly favored integrated schools and neighborhoods and desired equal access to employment opportunities. And Blacks have long been less likely than Whites to object to racially mixed marriages, presumably because such strictures were viewed as one element in a system of race-based oppression.

Third, the positive trend among Whites on these principles across the domains of schools, public transportation, jobs, housing, politics, and even intermarriage is steady and unabated. Despite intense discussion of a possible "racial backlash" in the 1960s in response to Black protests, or in the 1970s in response to school busing efforts and the implementation of affirmative action, or even in the 1990s in the wake of events such as the

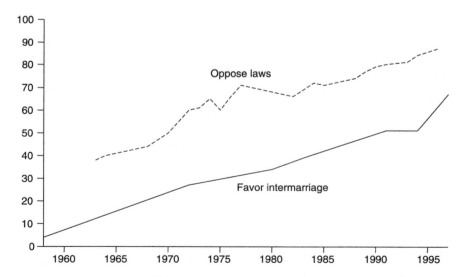

FIGURE 9-4  Trends in Whites' attitudes about racial intermarriage. SOURCE: Adapted from Schuman et al. (1997). *Oppose Laws:* Do you think there should be laws against marriages between Blacks and Whites? *Favor Intermarriage*: Do you approve or disapprove of marriage between Whites and non-Whites?

riots in Los Angeles, support for principles of racial equality and integration has been sweeping and robust. So much so, that it is reasonable to describe it as a change in fundamental norms with regard to race.

## Complexity of Changing How We Live and What We Want Government to Do

Unfortunately, it is not possible to infer from the positive change in attitudes toward principles of equality and integration that either public policy or the texture of day-to-day life for most Americans would quickly come to mirror this apparent consensus on ideals. Consider first the issue of integrating neighborhoods and schools. It is clear that numbers matter (see Figures 9-1 and 9-2). When Whites were asked about living in integrated areas or sending their children to integrated schools, their willingness to do so decreased as the percentage of Blacks rose (compare trends for Few, Half, and Most in Figure 9-1).

Also, the meaning of integration differs for Blacks and Whites. It is clear that most Whites prefer to live in overwhelmingly White neighborhoods even though they are open to living with a small number of Blacks. Blacks prefer to live in integrated neighborhoods, but also prefer to be present in substantial numbers—numbers high enough, however, to generate discomfort for most Whites.

With respect to public policy issues, there have been long-running debates about equal opportunity policies and affirmative action, and the trend data suggest that there is a significant substantive division in opinion. Programs that are compensatory in nature—that aim to equip minorities to be more effective competitors or that engage in special outreach and recruitment efforts—are reasonably popular. Policies that call for explicit racial preferences have long been unpopular, with the use of quotas rejected by Whites and Blacks alike (Lipset and Schneider, 1978; Kluegel and Smith, 1986; Bobo and Kluegel, 1993; Steeh and Krysan, 1996).

There is, however, some divergence of opinion about affirmative-action policies by race. Blacks and Hispanics tend to support affirmative-action type policies, whether aimed at improving training and competitive resources of minority group members or calling for preferences in hiring and promotion. A majority of Whites support the more compensatory policies, but fewer support preferential policies (Figures 9-5 and 9-6).

### Persistent Negative Stereotyping

A major factor influencing limits to integration and social policy with respect to race lies in the problem of antiminority, especially anti-Black, stereotyping. There is evidence that negative racial stereotypes of minor-

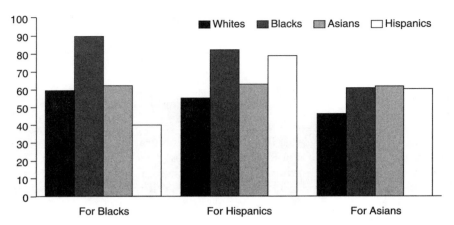

FIGURE 9-5  Support for race-based job training and education assistance programs, by race. SOURCE: Los Angeles Survey of Urban Inequality (1994).

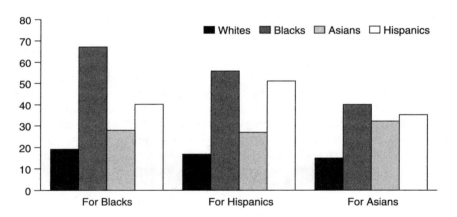

FIGURE 9-6  Support for race-based preferences in hiring and promotion, by race. SOURCE: Los Angeles Survey of Urban Inequality (1994).

ity groups, especially of Blacks and Hispanics, remain common among Whites. As Sniderman and Carmines (1997) put it, "it is simply wrong to suppose that there is a shortage of White Americans willing to say, publicly, something overtly negative about Black Americans" (p. 63). There is evidence that minority groups may also stereotype one another, though the story here is a good deal more complicated.

It is important to clarify what is meant by "stereotype." A stereotype is "a set of beliefs about the personal attributes of members of a particular social category" or "a set of cognitions that specify the personal qualities, especially personality traits, of members of an ethnic group" (Ashmore and Del Boca, 1981:13). As Hamilton and Trolier put it, stereotypes are "cognitive structures that contain the perceiver's knowledge, beliefs, and expectations about human groups" (1986:133). Thus, racial stereotyping involves projecting assumptions or expectations about the likely capacities and behaviors of members of a racial or ethnic group onto members of that group. Thus, stereotyping has a strong potential to influence other perceptions about, behavior toward, and patterns of interaction with members of the stereotyped group.

Historically, racial stereotyping denoted beliefs that were categorical or extreme, negative in valence, rigidly held, and as a consequence of these features, inherently bad (Ashmore and Del Boca, 1981; Jackman, 1994). Modern social scientists, however, limit the meaning of the stereotyping concept to the ideas or perceptions about groups, without assuming these ideas are necessarily categorical, negative, rigid, or even bad (Ashmore and Del Boca, 1981; Stephan, 1985). As a matter of definition, it is better to think of stereotypes much like any other cognition. Whether these assumed characteristics exist is thus a matter for empirical assessment. Indeed, some stereotypes may have a kernel of truth in them, such as disproportionate Black dependence on welfare or involvement in crime. Such perceptions become problematic, and more akin to prejudice, to the extent they resist modification when presented with new information, are applied categorically to individuals, or both.

Social psychologists commonly distinguish between cultural stereotypes and personal stereotypes, or personal beliefs. Cultural stereotypes refer to widely shared ideas about members of particular racial or ethnic groups (Devine, 1989; Devine and Elliot, 1995). Any particular individual, while almost certainly aware of the broad cultural stereotype about a salient racial or ethnic group, need not personally accept or adhere to that stereotype. Hence, it is of both analytical and (as we shall argue) practical importance to recognize the distinction.

The impetus to accept or adhere to prevailing stereotypes has several sources or origins (Pettigrew, 1981; Duckitt, 1992; Brown, 1995). Individuals may come to accept stereotypes through

- *social learning*: socialization into a particular culture or other direct contact with members of particular racial or ethnic groups, or vicarious learning experiences such as through the media;
- *motivation*: rationalization of some externality or instrumental consideration—e.g., it is easier to exploit and deny rights to those one perceives as inferior—or of a personality attribute—e.g., ethnocentric, intol-

erant, authoritarian people require others to feel superior to, and so choose to believe more negative stereotypes of others, often minority group members;

- *cognitive biases*: rare or infrequently occurring phenomena, especially if given a strongly negative evaluation, can assume unwarranted prominence in memory, such as a perception of minority group members as prone to crime and violence. In addition, once categorization has occurred, it is common to exaggerate between-group differences and to underestimate within-group variation

After a long period of inattention, survey researchers began in the 1980s to focus on racial stereotypes, following the work of Mary Jackman. Beginning with Jackman and Senter (1980, 1983) and Jackman (1994), several major social surveys have shown that negative stereotyping of racial and ethnic minorities, especially involving Whites' views of Blacks, remain widespread (Smith, 1990; Sniderman and Piazza, 1993; Sniderman and Carmines, 1997; Bobo and Kluegel, 1993, 1997). In part, this resurgence of interest reflected a move to different ways of measuring stereotypes; bipolar trait rating or other means of expressing relative judgments replaced previous reliance on categorical agree-or-disagree statements. In part, this resurgence of interest reflected a perception that racial stereotypes had, in fact, changed in form of expression to a more qualified nature, which the methodological innovation allowed researchers to tap.

Gauging the exact level of negative stereotyping is not an easy task. One relatively conservative estimate is offered by Sniderman and Piazza (1993) who maintain that:

> Notwithstanding the cliché that Whites will not openly endorse negative racial stereotypes for fear of appearing to be racist, large numbers of them—rarely less than one in every five and sometimes as many as one out of every two—agree with frankly negative characterizations of Blacks, particularly characterizations of Blacks as irresponsible and as failing to work hard and to make a genuine effort to deal with their problems on their own (p. 12).

This accounting is a bit complicated, on two scores. First, many Whites were found also to hold positive-trait perceptions of Blacks, not merely negative ones. Second, only a minority of Whites were found to hold uniformly negative views of Blacks—roughly 22 percent of Sniderman and Carmines' (1997) national sample. In some absolute sense, that almost one quarter of Whites hold consistently negative stereotypical views of Blacks is not a large number; however, given that almost all Whites express some negative stereotypes of Blacks, and nearly one quarter hold firmly negative views, the potential for anti-Black bias in many settings is actually quite large even with these conservative estimates.

It is important to note that the observed spread of negative stereotyping depends on both the exact trait examined and the method of assessment. As regards the method of assessment, absolute ratings of Blacks, for example, tend to reveal less prevalent negative stereotypes than do relative or difference-score ratings comparing images of Whites and of Blacks. For example, Jackman's 1975 survey found that 25 percent of Whites gave absolute negative ratings of Blacks' intelligence, 30 percent gave absolute negative ratings of Blacks' dependability, and 36 percent gave absolute negative ratings of Blacks' industriousness—i.e., believe Blacks are lazy. In contrast to how these White respondents rated Whites as a group, the degree of stereotyping against Blacks was higher; 57 percent gave a more negative relative rating to Blacks concerning intelligence, 56 percent did so concerning dependability, and 37 percent did so concerning laziness.

A similar pattern of nontrivial absolute negative ratings and of even more broadly negative relative ratings of Blacks is obtained from 1990 General Social Survey (GSS) data. Bobo and Kluegel (1997:100-101) show that 31 percent of Whites gave Blacks a low absolute rating in terms of intelligence, 47 percent did so in terms of laziness, 54 percent did so concerning proclivity to violence, and 59 percent did so concerning preference to live off of welfare. The relative ratings are higher in each instance, sometimes substantially so. Thus, the figures are 54 percent rating Blacks as less intelligent compared to the rating for Whites, 62 percent rating Blacks as lazier, 56 percent rating Blacks as more prone to violence, and fully 78 percent rating Blacks as preferring to live off of welfare as compared to Whites.

Jackman and others (Jaynes and Williams, 1989; Bobo, 1997; Bobo and Kluegel, 1997) make the important point that racial stereotypes are now more qualified in character. The perceived differences between Blacks and Whites are expressed, if not also understood, as more a matter of degree than a matter of categorical distinction. But also, the differences appear to be understood or interpreted in more cultural and volitional terms. To the extent there are differences, comparatively few Whites appear to believe they are inherent or biological in origin. These negative stereotypes often also apply in terms of Whites' views of Hispanics (Smith, 1990). Although Whites' views of Asians and Pacific Islanders are seldom as negative as those regarding Blacks and Hispanics, even Asians and Pacific Islanders typically receive unfavorable relative ratings. The 1990 GSS reported that considerably more than 50 percent of Whites rated Blacks and Hispanics as less intelligent. A similar percentage rated Blacks and Hispanics as prone to violence. Considerably more

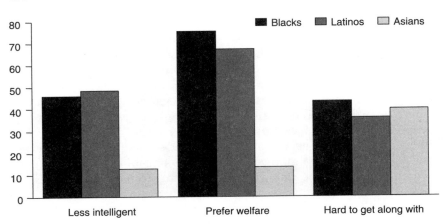

FIGURE 9-7  Percentage of Whites rating racial minorities as inferior to Whites.
SOURCE: Los Angeles Survey of Urban Inequality (1994).

than two-thirds of Whites rated Blacks and Hispanics as actually preferring to live off welfare.

One example of such patterns is shown in Figure 9-7. Substantial
percentages of Whites rated Blacks and Hispanics as less intelligent, preferring to live off welfare, and hard to get along with socially. Research
suggests that these stereotypes differ in several important ways from
stereotypes that were prevalent in the past. First, they are much more
likely to be understood as the product of environmental and group cultural traditions, whereas, in the past, they were unequivocally taken as
the product of natural endowment. Second, there is growing evidence
that many Whites are aware of traditional negative stereotypes of Blacks,
as anyone immersed in American culture would be, but personally reject
the negative stereotype and its implications (Devine and Elliot, 1995). The
problem is that in many face-to-face interactions, the traditional stereotype controls perception and behavior (Devine, 1989). The end result is
bias and discrimination against minorities.

In terms of the social consequences of these stereotypes, research suggests that stereotyping likely influences interpersonal interactions (Anderson, 1990; Feagin and Sikes, 1994), processes of racial residential segregation (Farley et al., 1994; Bobo and Zubrinsky, 1996), and the larger political
environment (Bobo and Kluegel, 1993; Hurwitz and Peffley, 1997; Peffley
et al., 1997). Research indicating Whites' fearfulness of a Black stranger is
indicative. Based on a survey involving the use of sophisticated experimental vignettes, St. John and Heald-Moore (1995) found that Whites
were more fearful of a Black stranger than of a White stranger. This was

true irrespective of other situational factors such as time of day or neighborhood characteristics. The degree of fear was strongly conditioned by only two factors: age and gender of the Black person (young Black males were feared more than others) and age of the White person (feelings of fear and vulnerability were greatest among older Whites). In subsequent work, St. John and Heald-Moore (1996) found a strong interaction between race of the stranger, level of fear, and level of racial prejudice among Whites.

> We found that for Whites, encounters with Black strangers in public settings evoke more fear of victimization than encounters with White strangers. We also found that the effect of the race of strangers encountered is conditioned by racial prejudice. That is, encounters with Black strangers evoke greater levels of fear in Whites who have high levels of prejudice than in Whites who have lower levels. However, even Whites who gave the least prejudiced response to all the items of the prejudice scale were more fearful of encounters with Black than with White strangers (1996:281).

This work implies that the interaction between Blacks and Whites in many public settings is rife with the potential for missteps, misunderstanding, and insult. Precisely this sort of dynamic is suggested by events and experiences recounted in qualitative interviews with middle-class Blacks (Feagin, 1991; Cose, 1993; Feagin and Sikes, 1994).

Negative stereotyping appears to play a role in reproducing larger structural patterns of racial residential segregation (Massey and Denton, 1993). Based on data from the 1992 Detroit Area Study (DAS), Farley and colleagues (1994) found that negative stereotyping of Blacks strongly predicted Whites' willingness to share integrated neighborhood space with Blacks. In subsequent work, involving data from the Los Angeles County Social Survey (LACSS), Bobo and Zubrinsky (1996) found that this effect was not restricted to Whites' reactions to Blacks. The effect of negative stereotyping on openness to residential integration also applied when Whites were reacting to the prospect of Hispanic or Asian neighbors. It is important to note that both of these surveys showed that the effect of negative stereotyping on attitudes on residential integration was independent of perceptions about the average class status of Blacks (for 1992 DAS) and of perceptions of the average class status of Blacks, Hispanics, and Asians (for 1992 LACSS). That is, distinctly racial stereotyping influenced Whites' willingness to live in integrated communities.

Stereotyping also appears to play an important role in modern politics, especially with regard to some types of race-targeted social policies (Bobo and Kluegel, 1993) as well as to some issues with a more implicit racial component such as crime (Hurwitz and Peffley, 1997) and welfare-related policy issues (Gilens, 1995, 1996a; Peffley et al., 1997). Research in this area makes clear the general importance of racial attitudes, but also often highlights the complex and conditional nature of the effects of negative racial stereotyping. For example, using survey-based experimental data from a 1994 survey in Lexington, Kentucky, Hurwitz and Peffley (1997) found that the impact of negative stereotyping of Blacks on Whites' views of crime, criminals, and crime policy issues hinged on other contextual information. Aspects of the nature of the crime, the criminal, and the policy all mattered. To the extent these contextual features were consistent with the broad cultural stereotypes of Blacks—as part of a violent, self-perpetuating, ghetto-inhabiting, poor underclass—the more pronounced the effect of negative stereotyping on the judgments made. For example, stereotypes about Blacks strongly influenced the degree of hostile reactions to a Black car-jacking suspect but not to a Black corporate embezzler. The alleged car-jacker had all the trappings consistent with the cultural-stereotype "street thug" and elicited a powerful resonance with underlying stereotypes about Blacks. The corporate embezzler is a business executive—i.e., did not fit the cultural stereotype of Blacks— and, thus, even though described as Black, did not generate reactions strongly related to underlying stereotypes of Blacks. Hurwitz and Peffley (1997) also found that negative stereotyping encouraged support for punitive responses to crime, but had no impact on views of crime-prevention policies. Thus, stereotyping of Blacks was not uniformly of political relevance, but if other contextual information was stereotype-consistent, a strong reverberation with the underlying stereotype emerged.

### Disagreement About the Prevalence of Racial Discrimination

In many ways, the centerpiece of the modern racial divide comes in the evidence of sharply divergent beliefs about the current level, effect, and nature of discrimination. Blacks and Hispanics, and many Asians as well, feel it and perceive it in most domains of life. Many Whites acknowledge that some discrimination remains, but they tend to downplay its contemporary importance. A comparatively small percentage of Whites, but a comparatively high percentage of Blacks and Hispanics, express the view that there is "a lot" of discrimination against, respectively, Blacks, Hispanics, and Asians seeking "good-paying jobs" (Figure 9-8). It is interesting to note that Blacks and Hispanics have lower, but still substantial, percentages acknowledging belief of such discrimination against the other. Neither Whites, Blacks, Hispanics, nor Asians themselves tend to see "a lot" of discrimination against Asians in obtaining better-paying jobs.

Views of police and the criminal justice system constitute an arena of often-acute racial group differences in opinion. For example, Schuman et

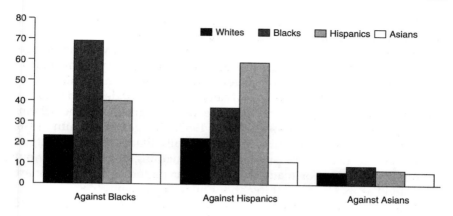

FIGURE 9-8  Percentage of Whites, Blacks, Hispanics, and Asian/Pacific Islanders who believe there is "a lot" of discrimination in getting good-paying jobs, by
race. SOURCE: Los Angeles Survey of Urban Inequality (1994).

al. (1997:265) report that in 1995, approximately 88 percent of Blacks in an
ABC News/*Washington Post* poll felt that the police treat Blacks unfairly
as compared to only 47 percent of Whites. Their analysis showed that the
gap between Blacks' and Whites' views on police treatment actually grew
larger between the late 1980s and mid-1990s. This pattern may reflect a
number of prominent and dramatic incidents of police abuse during the
1990s such as the Rodney King beating, the Abner Louima beating, and,
in 1999, the murder of Amadou Diallo by New York City police. Tuch and
Weitzer's (1997) trend analyses showed that Blacks' views of the police
tend to exhibit more dramatically adverse reactions in the wake of highly
publicized police brutality cases than is true among Whites, and that the
adverse impact on views of the police tends to be longer lasting for Blacks
as well. Nowhere was the magnitude and palpable tension of this divide
more in evidence than along the sharp polarization of views between
Blacks and Whites in the wake of the criminal trial of O.J. Simpson for the
murder of his ex-wife Nicole Brown Simpson and her friend Ronald
Goldman.

Minorities not only perceive more discrimination, they also see it as
more "institutional" in character. Many Whites tend to think of discrimination as either mainly a historical legacy of the past or as the idiosyncratic behavior of the isolated bigot. In short, to Whites, the officers who
tortured Abner Louima constitute a few bad apples. To Blacks, these officers represent only the tip of the iceberg. To Whites, the Texaco tapes are
shocking. To Blacks, the tapes merely reflect that in this one instance the
guilty were caught.

But differences in perception cut deeper than this. For Blacks and Hispanics—and, to a lesser extent, Asians—modern racial bias and discrimination are central factors in the problem of minority disadvantage. Although many Whites recognize that discrimination plays some part in higher rates of unemployment, poverty, and a range of hardships in life that minorities often face, the central cause is usually understood to be the level of effort and cultural patterns of the minority group members themselves (Schuman, 1971; Apostle et al., 1983; Kluegel and Smith, 1986; Schuman et al., 1997). For minorities, especially Blacks, it is understood that the persistence of race problems has something to do with how our institutions operate. For many Whites, larger patterns of inequality are understood as mainly something about minorities themselves.

At issue here is not only how extensive one believes discrimination to be in any particular domain, but also whether one sees individual or social structural factors as key sources of persistent racial economic inequality (Kluegel and Smith, 1982; Kluegel, 1990). Figure 9-9 charts national survey data to show Whites' perceptions and beliefs about, respectively, the individualistic (Figure 9-9a) and the structural (Figure 9-9b) bases of Black-White economic inequality. Two immediate contrasts distinguish the figures. First, endorsement of the various "individualistic" statements is usually higher than that for any "structural" statement. Thus, among the four structural items, only the conceptually ambiguous "no chance for an education" item (Kluegel, 1990) is endorsed by more than 50 percent of Whites, whereas several of the individualistic items exceed 60 percent White agreement. Furthermore, this comparatively weak structural attribution shows a downward trend over time. To be sure, the individualistic account of Black-White inequality with the most immediately racist import—a belief in innate differences in ability—has steadily declined and is now endorsed by only a small percentage of Whites. Yet, the most popular view holds that Blacks should "try harder," should get ahead "without special favors," and fall behind because they "lack motivation." Second, several of the individualistic items show small, but noteworthy, trends toward growing acceptance. Thus, these patterns confirm Kluegel's (1990) speculation that Whites show decreased acceptance of most of the structural bases of racial inequality.

The results of two surveys highlight a crucial distinction between idiosyncratic and episodic, and between institutional and structural, views of discrimination. Local and national surveys showed that high percentages of both Blacks and Whites disapproved of the 1992 Simi Valley jury verdict that exonerated the White Los Angeles police officers who beat Black motorist Rodney King (Bobo et al., 1994). However, in a Los Angeles survey conducted immediately after the verdict and subsequent social upheaval, Blacks and Whites disagreed sharply about whether the courts

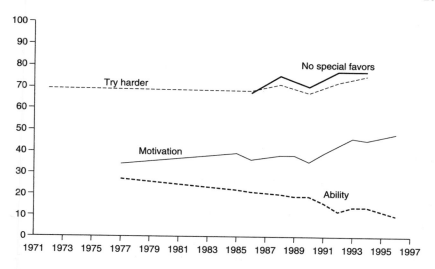

FIGURE 9-9a   Trends in Whites' beliefs about individualistic bases of Black/
White economic inequality. SOURCE: Adapted from Schuman et al. (1997). *Try
Harder*: We asked people why they think White people seem to get more of the
good things in life in America—such as better jobs and more money—than Black
people do. Do you agree or disagree with each reason as to why White people
seem to get more of the good things in life? It's really a matter of some people not
trying hard enough; if Blacks would only try harder they would be just as well off
as Whites. *No Special Favors*: Irish, Italians, Jewish, and many other minorities
overcame prejudice and worked their way up. Blacks should do the same without any special favors. *Motivation*: On the average Blacks have worse jobs,
income, and housing than White people. Do you think these differences are
mainly due to discrimination? Do you think these differences are because most
Blacks just don't have the motivation or will power to pull themselves up out of
poverty? *Ability*: (Same introduction as Motivation above) Do you think these
differences are . . . because most Blacks have less inborn ability to learn?

and criminal justice system were generally unfair to Blacks. Approximately 80 percent of Blacks in Los Angeles agreed that Blacks usually do
not get fair treatment in the courts and criminal justice system, compared
with only 39 percent of Whites (Bobo et al., 1994:111). Similarly, the DAS
survey found that approximately 82 percent of Whites felt that Blacks
"very often" or "sometimes" missed out on good housing because individual White owners would not sell or rent to them; 85 percent of Blacks
expressed such views (Farley et al., 1993:19). When asked about discrimination by such institutional actors as "real estate agents" and "banks and

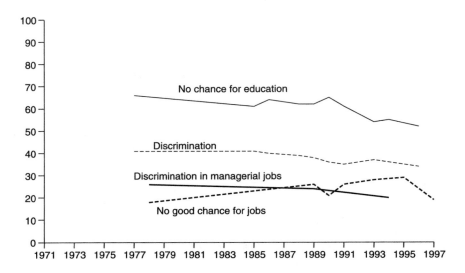

FIGURE 9-9b  Trends in Whites' structural beliefs about Black/White economic inequality.  SOURCE: Adapted from Schuman et al. (1997).  *Discrimination*: On the average Blacks have worse jobs, income, and housing than White people.  Do you think these differences are . . . mainly due to discrimination?  *No Chance for Education*:  (Same introduction as Discrimination above) Do you think these differences are . . . because most Blacks just don't have the chance for education that it takes to rise out of poverty?  *No Chance for Jobs*:  In general, do you think Blacks have as good a chance as White people in your community to get any kind of job for which they are qualified, or don't you think they have as good a chance?  *Discrimination in Managerial Jobs*:  In your area, would you say Blacks generally are discriminated against or not in getting managerial jobs?

lenders," however, the Black-White gap in views increased to 22 percent and 34 percent, respectively. Indeed, Blacks saw discrimination as slightly more prevalent by "banks and lenders" than by individual White homeowners.

It is difficult to overestimate the importance of the sharp divide over the understanding and experience of racial discrimination to the present-day racial impasse in America (Sigelman and Welch, 1989). Sustained and constructive discourse about matters of race will surely remain difficult insofar as Blacks are (1) more likely than Whites to see discrimination in particular domains and situations; (2) more likely to see discrimination as institutional rather than episodic; (3) more likely to see discrimination as a central factor in larger patterns of racial inequality; and (4) more likely to regard racial discrimination as personally important and emotionally involving.

## Deepening Pessimism and Alienation

In many corners, there is a feeling of pessimism about the state of race relations. A 1997 survey conducted by the Joint Center for Political and Economic Research found that only 40 percent of Blacks rated race relations in their community as "excellent" or "good" and more than 20 percent rated community race relations as "poor." In contrast, 59 percent of Whites rated local race relations as "excellent" or "good," though better than 10 percent rated them as "poor." The results of a recent Gallup survey are, in some respects, more pessimistic; roughly 33 percent of Blacks and Whites described race relations as having gotten worse in the past year. What is more, 58 percent of Blacks and 54 percent of Whites expressed the view that "relations between Blacks and Whites will always be a problem for the United States."

This problem takes the form of particularly acute cynicism and alienation among Blacks, though there are signs of frustration among Hispanics and some APIs as well. Among Blacks, University of Chicago political scientist Michael Dawson's National Black Politics Survey, conducted in 1993 (Dawson, 1995), found that 86 percent of Blacks agreed with the statement that "American society just hasn't dealt fairly with Black people." Fifty-seven percent of Blacks rejected the idea that "American society has provided Black people a fair opportunity to get ahead in life," and 81 percent agreed with the idea that "American society owes Black people a better chance in life than we currently have."

A major survey of Los Angeles county residents (the Los Angeles County Social Survey, conducted by this author in 1992) shows that although Blacks expressed the highest and most consistently alienated views, an important percentage of the Hispanic and Asian population did so as well. Thus, for example, 64 percent of Hispanics and 42 percent of Asians agreed with the idea that their groups were owed a better chance in life (Figure 9-10). This places these two groups in between the high sense of deprivation observed among Blacks and the essentially nonexistent feeling of deprivation observed among Whites.

The concern about Black cynicism, however, is acute for two reasons. First, there are signs that the feelings of alienation and deprivation are greatest in an unexpected place: among the Black middle class, especially so among well-educated and high-earning Blacks. Second, there is a concern that these feelings of alienation and deprivation may be contributing to a weakening commitment to the goal of racial integration. Among the potentially discouraging signs in this regard is a recent significant rise in

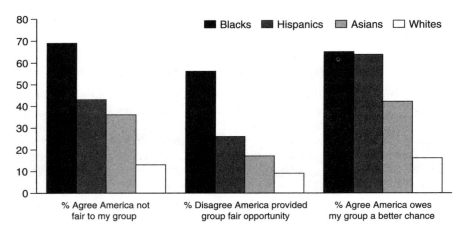

FIGURE 9-10  Percentage of Blacks, Hispanics, Asian/Pacific Islanders, and Whites agreeing or disagreeing with fairness statements regarding ethnic group deprivation. SOURCE: Los Angeles County Social Survey (1992).

the number of Blacks who think it is time to form a separate national political party (Figure 9-11). The 1993 National Black Politics Survey showed that this figure was at 50 percent, up substantially from about 30 percent in 1984. In addition, Blacks continue to feel a strong connection between the fate of the group as a whole and that of the individual Black. Thus, the 1993 National Black Politics Study shows a slow but steady rise in the percentage of Blacks expressing the view that there was a strong connection between their fate as an individual and the fate of the group as a whole. This tendency is especially pronounced among highly educated Blacks.

In her wide-ranging assessment of data on Black public opinion, political scientist Jennifer Hochschild identifies Black disaffection, particularly among the middle class, as one of the most disturbing trends for the future of American democracy. This disaffection, she finds, expresses itself not merely as "Black rage," grievance, and alienation, but it also involves a deep questioning of the American dream and prospects for the future. On one level, this reflects the uncertainties of racial minority status, especially for the middle class, in a society that has not yet overcome racism (Hochschild, 1995):

> . . . middle-class Blacks find their lives much more problematic than do middle-class Whites, so the comfort that a broader education, better job, and more money usually bring to Whites is denied to similarly situated Blacks. Thus the paradox of succeeding more and enjoying it less . . . (p. 93).

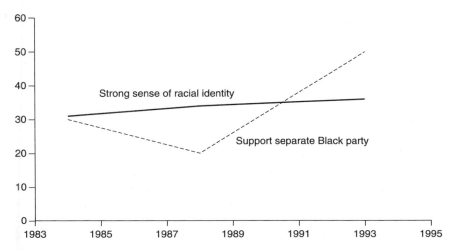

FIGURE 9-11  Importance of race to Blacks. SOURCE: Adapted from Dawson (1994), Tate (1993), and Dawson (1995).

This paradox has quite wide-ranging social implications. Hochschild writes:

> Black and White increasingly diverge in their evaluations of whether the American dream encompasses African Americans . . . middle-class Blacks are increasingly disillusioned with the very ideology of the dream itself, and poor Blacks may not be far behind . . . .

> The ideology of the dream has always relied on previously poor Americans not only achieving upward mobility, but also recognizing that they had done so, feeling gratified, and consequently deepening their commitment to the dream and the nation behind it. That, very roughly speaking, has been the experience of most immigrants. But middle-class Blacks are not following the prescribed pattern. They recognize their own mobility, they are pleased by it, but their commitment to the American dream is declining, not rising. That is an unprecedented risk to an ideology that depends so heavily on faith in its ultimate fairness and benevolence (pp. 86-87).

The sense of alienation among many Blacks then includes a profound critique of American institutions and culture. As Cornell West put it, "The accumulated effect of the Black wounds and scars suffered in a White-dominated society is a deep-seated anger, a boiling sense of rage, and a passionate pessimism regarding America's will to justice" (West, 1993:18).

In an earlier era, these sorts of ideas would have been associated with activist Malcolm X, the "prophet of Black rage," according to Cornell

West. The connection between the insight and rhetoric of Malcolm X and the dilemma of the modern Black middle class is not hard to unearth. As West put it, "One rarely encounters a picture of Malcolm X (as one does of Martin Luther King, Jr.) in the office of a Black professional, but there is no doubt that Malcolm X dangles as the skeleton in the closet lodged in the racial memory of most Black professionals" (1993:97).

The survey data, and summaries of them, however, cannot convey the full depth and range of Black responses, and some Black writers have recently given voice to this sense of discontent. In his recent autobiography, journalist Sam Fulwood describes coming to consciousness as a "blue chip Black"—a Black person slated for success in the mainstream White economy. A teacher explains to him that, unlike his friends, he will be attending the traditionally White junior high school, because, as the teacher expressed it to Fulwood, "I am absolutely certain that you can hold your own with the best" White students. This became a defining moment for the young Fulwood, hopeful that a bright future, free of racial bias, would be his. His adult life experiences proved sharply disillusioning, however (Fulwood, 1996):

> I evolved that day into a race child. I believed I would, in due time, illuminate the magnificent social changes wrought by racial progress. Overt racial barriers were falling and I, son of a minister and a schoolteacher, fully credentialed members of Charlotte's Black middle class, thought my future would be free of racism and free of oppression. I believed I was standing at the entrance to the Promised Land. Now, as the twentieth century exhausts itself, I am awakening from my blind belief in that American dream. I am angrier than I've ever been (p. 2).

The depth of his sense of rage grew when he returned to the United States from a trip in South Africa:

> I returned from South Africa with a new definition of American-style racism and classism, and how they acted like a pair of invisible hands molding the contours of my life. I wasn't in control of my destiny in the United States; I was living in Alice's Wonderland. The rules of life were always defined by someone White who decided whether what I did was acceptable, legal behavior. I knew more of the rules, so I played the game better than poorer Blacks, who didn't know or didn't care to play the game at all. But I was still only a pawn in the White man's match (p. 164).

One acute source of Fulwood's frustration sprang from the inability of Whites to see or even admit the contemporary potency of racism.

> Over the course of my life, I realized, so much had changed in me, but so little had changed in the outside world. Racism surrounded me. I could perceive it, but I was powerless to prove conclusively to anyone

who was not Black how corrosive it could be (p. 208). . . . I have a
boulder of racial attitudes on my back, and at work I must toil among
White people and pretend that the dead weight is not there (p. 213).

In the end, Fulwood decides to live in an affluent Black suburb and, more
important, to assure that his daughter is raised with a more acute sense of
race identity and of the challenge posed by enduring racism than was he.
"My daughter," he declares in the opening pages of the book, "will not be
a second-generation blue-chip Black, laboring under the mistaken belief
that race will one day be coincidental, unimportant or ignored in her life"
(1996:5).

Journalist Jill Nelson writes with a deeper sense of bitterness and
despair. For her, much of the dilemma of Black middle-class success comes
in having to suppress feelings of rage against a society and a world of
work still massively insensitive to the historic and modern weight of
racism, in order to maintain a precarious middle-class livelihood (Nelson,
1993):

> I've also been doing the standard Negro balancing act when it comes to
> dealing with White folks, which involves sufficiently blurring the edges
> of my being so that they don't feel intimidated, while simultaneously
> holding on to my integrity. There is a thin line between Uncle Tomming
> and Mau-Mauing. To fall off that line can mean disaster. On the one side
> lies employment and self-hatred: on the other, the equally dubious hon-
> or of unemployment with integrity. Walking that line as if it were a
> tightrope results in something like employment with honor, although
> I'm not sure exactly how that works (p. 10).

Like Fulwood, the eminent religion scholar C. Eric Lincoln writes of
both the permeating quality of the racial divide and the pain of being
rendered socially invisible by virtue of race (Lincoln, 1996):

> In America, race is the touchstone of all value, the prism through which
> all else of significance must be refracted before relationships can be de-
> fined or relevance ascertained. There is no order of reality large enough
> to transcend its pervasiveness, small enough to escape its intrusiveness,
> or independent enough to avoid its imprimatur (pp. 45-46). . . . Every
> Black American knows firsthand the slander of invisibility. Anonymity.
> It comes in a thousand ways: a word, a gesture, a conversation that
> moves over and around him as though he or she were not present. Invis-
> ibility is most painful when it is preclusive—jobs not offered, invitations
> not issued, opportunities denied. It is a lifelong incubus from which few
> if any African Americans ever escape completely, no matter what their
> achievements. Racial anonymity derives from the presumption of incon-
> sequence—the inconsequence of Black persons and of their achieve-
> ments, actual or potential (p. 94).

Even mainstream political figures such as Kweisi Mfume, while never succumbing completely to a sense of Black alienation, nonetheless share many of these same sentiments. Mfume describes coming to consciousness in explaining when, during his college days, he changed his name from Frizzell Gray to Kweisi Mfume (Mfume, 1996):

> Anyone who spent more than a moment with me knew that I believed that a terrible hoax was being played on Black people in this country. I believed that most of us were going to live and die without ever having experienced anything near what was promised in the Declaration of Independence about life, liberty, and the pursuit of happiness. We weren't at all protected under the laws of the land—Black people were citizens in name only. We were a people chronically and institutionally disenfranchised, feeding off the scraps of the educational system, the job market, and any other channels leading to a life of dignity. . . . Yet, Black people were expected to believe in the American Dream as much as White people did. Why should we? The very notion was obscenely cynical, and any Black man or woman who thought differently was living in a fool's paradise. My disdain for the system was evident as a new wave of militancy engulfed my persona. I didn't just *wear* a bush, I *was* a bush that burned with revolutionary fervor, from the wildfires of racism and prejudice that smoldered around me (p. 189, emphasis in original).

These represent a few of the numerous other memoirs that express similar sentiments—bell hooks, Marcus Mabry, Rosemary Bray, or Nathan McCall, to name a few.

## THEORETICAL INTERPRETATIONS OF RACIAL ATTITUDES

To interpret the set of patterns described above is no simple task. To capture their full complexity, four broad schools of thought have been implemented: symbolic racism theory, political ideology and value commitment theory, aversive racism theory, and notions of group position and laissez-faire racism theory. Each theoretical tradition has identified important features of the dynamics of modern racial attitudes and relations. Three of these accounts point to a change or reconfiguration in the nature of racism; the other suggests that more and more matters—beyond race and racism—are important to the discourse about race.

Aversive racism should be distinguished from dominative racism. Dominative racism involves open/overt derogation and oppression of a racial minority group. Aversive racism has been defined by social psychologists Samuel Gaertner and John Dovidio as involving racism among the well intentioned (1986). Accordingly, in the post-Civil Rights era, most Whites hold many racially egalitarian outlooks (as summarized above). Indeed, it is likely racial egalitarianism is an important aspect of self-conception. At the same time, most Whites are exposed to a history, culture, and current set of social forces that encourage negative feelings toward and beliefs about Blacks. This creates, on a level not necessarily open to conscious awareness or manipulation, a deep ambivalence toward Blacks. The practical result, as Gaertner and Dovidio have shown in a convincing program of field and laboratory experimental research, is that whenever the norm of racial egalitarianism is rendered ambiguous, differential and negative treatment of Blacks by Whites tends to occur.

This research is impressive not merely for its experimental basis, but also for focusing on observable behaviors, not merely attitudinal expression. Furthermore, it resonates powerfully with sociological findings, whether ethnographic (Anderson, 1990), in-depth interview material (Feagin and Sikes, 1994), or survey responses (Sigelman and Welch, 1989; Bobo and Suh, 2000; Forman et al., 1997), which point to the subtlety and complex character of much modern racial discrimination. The lesson for the broader argument is that Whites' attitudes are often ambivalent and that, under certain conditions, that ambivalence can result in substantial and repeated behavioral discrimination against Blacks.

Symbolic racism is a theory of modern prejudice proposed by David Sears and his colleagues (Kinder and Sears, 1981; Sears, 1988). It maintains that a new form of politically potent anti-Black prejudice emerged after the Civil Rights era. The waning of "old-fashioned racism," or more appropriately "Jim Crow racism," which involved overt derogation of Blacks as inferior to Whites and explicit insistence on racial segregation, opened the door to newer, more subtle anti-Black sentiments. These new sentiments fused deeply rooted anti-Black feelings, typically learned early in life, with other long-standing American values such as the Protestant work ethic. Thus, when Blacks demand integration or such policies as affirmative action, according to this theory, many Whites react with opposition based on this attitude. The symbolic racist resents Blacks' demands and views them as unfair impositions on a just and good society. According to Kinder and Sanders (1996) this new type of racial resentment crystallized during the mid- to late 1960s as Whites watched social protest and rising Black militancy pose an increasing challenge to their social order. Although the theory of symbolic racism began as an effort to understand the dynamics of Black-White relations, especially in the political realm, it has been extended to include how Whites respond to Hispanics and to such issues as bilingual education and immigration policies (Huddy and Sears, 1995).

Empirically, research on symbolic racism has sought to establish that narrow, objective self-interest has little bearing on why Black candidates for political office become controversial (Kinder and Sears, 1981; Citrin et al., 1990), or why Whites mobilize against school busing (Sears et al., 1979;

McConahay, 1982), or may oppose affirmative action (Sears, 1988). Thus, for example, having children in the public schools or living in an area where busing is used for desegregation does not affect attitudes on school busing.

In addition, symbolic racism research has set out to establish that measures of traditional, old-fashioned racism do not predict issue positions or candidate preferences as strongly as do measures of symbolic racism. Symbolic racism has been measured in a variety of ways, with some recent consensus that it involves resentment of minority demands, resentment of special treatment or consideration of minorities, and a tendency to deny the potency of racial discrimination (Sears, 1988; Kinder and Sanders, 1996). The theory has been the subject of wide controversy and critical assessment (see, e.g., Bobo, 1983, 1988; Schuman et al., 1985; Weigel and Howes, 1985; Sniderman and Tetlock, 1986; Sidanius et al., 1992; Tetlock, 1994; Wood, 1994). Despite the number and findings of these many critical assessments, symbolic-racism researchers have effectively substantiated an important aspect of the issue: racial attitudes have changed in important ways; yet, negative views of Blacks remain both all too common and all too often of tangible political consequence.

One way to understand this change has recently been theorized as a shift from a dominant ideology of "Jim Crow racism" to a dominant ideology of "laissez-faire racism" (Bobo et al., 1997; Bobo and Smith, 1998). Accordingly, we have witnessed the virtual disappearance of overt bigotry, demands for strict segregation, advocacy of governmentally enforced discrimination, and adherence to the belief that Blacks are categorically the intellectual inferiors of Whites. Yet, overt racism has evidently not been supplanted by an embracing and democratic vision of the common humanity, worth, dignity, and equal membership in the polity for Blacks. Instead, the tenacious institutionalized disadvantages and inequalities created by the long slavery and Jim Crow eras are now popularly accepted and condoned under a modern free-market or laissez-faire racist ideology. This new ideology incorporates negative stereotypes of Blacks; a preference for individualistic, and rejection of structural, accounts of racial inequality; and an unwillingness to see government actively work to dismantle racial inequality. This new pattern of belief is more subtle and covert than its predecessor, making it more difficult to directly confront; it is also more amenable to the more fluid and permeable set of racial divisions in the social order.

Much of the broad empirical basis for the laissez-faire racism argument has been reviewed above. Using data from the 1990 GSS, Bobo and Kluegel (1997) examined four hypotheses derived from the theory of laissez-faire racism and found that (1) contemporary racial stereotyping and negation of social responsibility for Black conditions constitute distinct attitudinal dimensions; (2) traditional, overt racist outlooks were more strongly rooted in region of residence (South versus nonsouth), age, and level of education than were the elements of laissez-faire racism (stereotyping and social responsibility beliefs), which is consistent with Jim Crow-style racism being older and more regionally specific and laissez-faire racism being a more contemporary, nationally shared outlook; and (3) beliefs about reasons for general, socioeconomic (not race-specific) inequality play a larger role in laissez-faire racism than they did in Jim Crow racism. Bobo and Kluegel (1997) suggest that, "If Jim Crow racism is no longer seen to serve the defense of economic privilege, then there is no reason to expect that beliefs that justify the stratification order in general will affect it. If elements of laissez-faire racism are seen as defending White economic privilege, then justifications of economic inequality in general should motivate stereotyping and the denial of social responsibility for Blacks' conditions" (pp. 96-97). Fourth, they found that although both Jim Crow and laissez-faire racism affect Whites' support for race-targeted social policies, the elements of laissez-faire racism were stronger influences.

Of course, it is possible to doubt the need to invoke racism at all as a central element of the modern racial divide. At least at the level of politics and political debate, this precise point has been the message offered by Paul Sniderman and colleagues (Sniderman and Piazza, 1993; Sniderman and Carmines, 1997). They developed a four-part argument. First, they assert that racism is not an important part of the modern politics of race, especially in terms of the debate over affirmative action. Second, they assert that if many Whites object to affirmative action or other race-targeted policies, it has more to do with broad American values about fairness, justice, individualism, and traditional conservatism than with racism or prejudice. In short, there are principled foundations to the politics of race, deriving from political values and ideology. Accordingly, they feel, those advancing the symbolic-racism argument have seriously misunderstood the current political divide over affirmative action. Third, to the extent prejudice now matters in politics, it is generally most pronounced among the least politically sophisticated segments of the public (Sniderman and Piazza, 1993) and poses the greatest political challenge among liberals (Sniderman and Carmines, 1997). Fourth, there are distinct types of issue agendas in political discourse about race: a social-welfare agenda focusing on the economic circumstances of Blacks; an equal-treatment agenda concerned with banning discrimination; and a race-conscious agenda focusing on preferential treatment of Blacks. In each domain, a different mix of attitudes, values, and beliefs is said to influence political thinking.

Spanning nearly a decade now, Sniderman and colleagues' program of research is innovative, vigorously pursued, and has identified a number of intriguing empirical patterns. By drawing on survey-based experiments, as Schuman and Bobo (1988) proposed, Sniderman and colleagues combined the power of controlled experiments with the representativeness of national surveys: the certainty of casual inference and ability to generalize results are thus greater. Two contributions loom large in this work. First, political ideology is an element in how many Whites think about race-related issues such as affirmative action. There is much debate, as yet unresolved, over how large a role pure ideology plays in race politics (Sidanius et al., 1996). But Sniderman and colleagues have rightly cautioned against a monolithic view that prejudice and racism are the whole story. Second, a number of their experimental results suggest that prejudice against Blacks does more to account for views among liberal Whites than it does among conservative Whites (see, especially, Sniderman and Carmines, 1997). If so, it may be the case that prejudice has less of a role in unifying the right than it does in dividing the left.

## CONCLUSIONS AND IMPLICATIONS

The glass is half-full or the glass is half-empty, depending on what one chooses to emphasize. If one compared the racial attitudes prevalent in the 1940s with those commonly observed today, it is easy to be optimistic. A nation once comfortable as a deliberately segregationist and racially discriminatory society has not only abandoned that view, but now overtly, positively endorses the goals of racial integration and equal treatment. There is no sign whatsoever of retreat from this ideal, despite events that many thought would call it into question. The magnitude, steadiness, and breadth of this change should be lost on no one.

The death of Jim Crow racism has left us in an uncomfortable place, however; a state of laissez-faire racism. We have high ideals, but cannot agree on the depth of the remaining problem—we are open to integration, but in very limited terms and only in specific areas. There is political stagnation over some types of affirmative action, and persistent negative stereotyping of racial minorities; and a wide gulf in perceptions regarding the importance of racial discrimination remains. The level of misunderstanding and miscommunication is, thus, easy to comprehend.

The positive patterns in attitude and belief have important parallels in more concrete social trends. Two examples—demographic data showing modest declines in racial residential segregation in most metropolitan areas, and the growing suburbanization of Blacks, Hispanics, and Asians—match the broad shift in attitudes on the principle of residential integration and openness to at least small amounts of real racial mixing in neighborhoods. In addition, the greater tolerance for interracial marriages, including Black-White marriages, is mirrored in the significant rise in the actual number of such unions, although Black-White intermarriages are the least common form of racial intermarriage for Whites.

We should always bear in mind that attitudes are but one important input to behavior. Most centrally, situational constraints—such as those intended to be addressed by equal opportunity mandates and antidiscrimination laws—or the expectations of significant others in our lives, affect whether, and when, there is a correspondence among attitude, beliefs, and behavior.

Is it possible to change attitudes? The record of change I have reviewed makes it plain that attitudes can change and in important ways. Education and information can help. The better educated, especially those who have gone to college, are typically found to express more positive racial attitudes. It is also clear that many Americans hold inaccurate beliefs about the size of racial minority groups and about such social conditions as group differences in the level of welfare dependency. However, education and information campaigns alone are unlikely to do the job that remains ahead of us if we are to genuinely become one society in the twenty-first century. Attitudes are most likely to change when the broad social conditions that create and reinforce certain types of outlooks change and when the push to make such change comes from a united national leadership that speaks with moral conviction of purpose. That is, it is essential to speak to joblessness and poverty in the inner city, to failing schools, and to a myriad of forms of racial bias and discrimination that people of color often experience, which has not yet effectively been communicated to all American citizens.

To pose the question directly: Are we moving toward a color-blind society or toward deepening racial polarization? America is not a color-blind society. We stand uncomfortably at a point of defeating Jim Crow racism, but unsure whether, through benign neglect, to allow the current inequalities and polarization to take deeper root, or to face directly and proactively the challenges of bias, miscommunication, and racism that remain.

As a people, we feel quite powerfully the tug, indeed the exhortation, of Dr. King's dream to become a nation that embodies the ideals of racial equality and integration. It is important to seize on the steady commitment to these ideals of racial equality and integration. The risk of failing to do so, is that a new, free-market ideology of racism—laissez-faire racism—may take hold, potentially worsening an already serious racial divide.

# REFERENCES

Alba, R.
  1992   Ethnicity. Pp. 575-584 in *Encyclopedia of Sociology*, E. Borgatta and M. Borgatta, eds. New York: MacMillan.
Allport, G.
  1954   *The Nature of Prejudice*. Reading, Mass.: Addison-Wesley.
Anderson, E.
  1990   *Streetwise: Race, Class, and Change in an Urban Community*. Chicago: University of Chicago Press.
Apostle, R., C. Glock, T. Piazza, and M. Suelzle
  1983   *The Anatomy of Racial Attitudes*. Berkeley, Calif.: University of California Press.
Ashmore, R., and F. Del Boca
  1981   Conceptual approaches to stereotypes and stereotyping. Pp. 1-35 in *Cognitive Processes in Stereotyping and Intergroup Behavior*, D. Hamilton, ed. Hillsdale, N.J.: Erlbaum.
Bell, D.
  1992   *Faces at the Bottom of the Well: The Permanence of Racism*. New York: Basic Books.
Bobo, L.
  1983   Whites opposition to busing: symbolic racism or realistic group conflict? *Journal of Personality and Social Psychology* 45:1196-1210.
  1988   Group conflict, prejudice, and the paradox of contemporary racial attitudes. Pp. 85-114 in *Eliminating Racism: Profiles in Controversy*, P. Katz and D. Taylor, eds. New York: Plenum.
  1997   The color line, the dilemma, and the dream: Racial attitudes and relations in America at the close of the twentieth century. Pp. 31-55 in *Civil Rights and Social Wrongs: Black-White Relations Since World War II*, J. Higham, ed. University Park: Pennsylvania State University Press.
Bobo, L., and J. Kluegel
  1993   Opposition to race-targeting: Self-interest, stratification ideology, or racial attitudes? *American Sociological Review* 58:443-464.
  1997   Status, ideology, and dimensions of Whites' racial beliefs and attitudes: Progress and stagnation. Pp. 93-120 in *Racial Attitudes in the 1990s: Continuity and Change*, S. Tuch, and J. Martin, eds. Westport, Conn.: Praeger.
Bobo, L., J. Kluegel, and R. Smith
  1997   Laissez-faire racism: The crystallization of a kinder, gentler, anti-Black ideology. Pp. 15-42 in *Racial Attitudes in the 1990s; Continuity and Change*, S. Tuch and J. Martin, eds. Westport, Conn.: Praeger.
Bobo, L., and R. Smith
  1998   From Jim Crow racism to laissez faire racism: The transformation of racial attitudes. Pp. 182-220 in *Beyond Pluralism: Essays on the Conception of Groups and Group Identities in America*, W. Katkin, N. Landsman, and A. Tyree, eds. Urbana, Ill.: University of Illinois Press.
Bobo, L., and S. Suh
  2000   Surveying racial discrimination: Analyses from a multiethnic labor market. Pp. 527-564 in *Prismatic Metropolis: Inequality in Los Angeles*, L. Bobo, M. Oliver, J. Johnson, and A. Valenzuela, Jr., eds. New York: Russell Sage Foundation.
Bobo, L., and C. Zubrinsky
  1996   Attitudes on residential integration: Perceived status differences, mere in-group preference, or racial prejudice? *Social Forces* 74:883-909.

Bobo, L., C. Zubrinsky, J. Johnson, and M. Oliver
    1994    Public opinion before and after a spring of discontent. Pp. 103-133 in *The Los Angeles Riots: Lessons for the Urban Future*, M. Baldassare, ed. Boulder, Colo.: Westview Press.
Bonilla-Silva, E.
    1996    Rethinking racism: Toward a structural interpretation. *American Sociological Review* 62:465-480.
Brown, R.
    1995    *Prejudice: Its Social Psychology*. Cambridge, U.K.: Blackwell.
Citrin, J., D. Green, and D. Sears
    1990    White reactions to Black candidates: When does race matter? *Public Opinion Quarterly* 54:74-96.
Cose, E.
    1993    *The Rage of a Privileged Class*. New York: Harper Collins.
Dawson, M.
    1994    *Behind the Mule: Race and Class in African American Politics*. Princeton: Princeton University Press.
    1995    Structure and ideology: The shaping of Black public opinion. Unpublished manuscript, Department of Political Science, University of Chicago.
Delgado, R.
    1996    *The Coming Race War? And Other Apocalyptic Tales of America After Affirmative Action and Welfare*. New York: New York University Press.
Devine, P.
    1989    Stereotypes and prejudice: Their automatic and controlled components. *Journal of Personality and Social Psychology* 56:5-18.
Devine, P., and A. Elliot
    1995    Are racial stereotypes really fading? The Princeton trilogy revisited. *Personality and Social Psychology Bulletin* 21:1139-1150.
Drake, St. C., and H. Cayton
    1945    *Black Metropolis; A Study of Negro Life in a Northern City*. Chicago: University of Chicago Press.
Duckitt, J.
    1992    *The Social Psychology of Prejudice*. New York: Praeger.
Farley, R., C. Steeh, T. Jackson, M. Krysan, and K. Reeves
    1993    Continued racial residential segregation in Detroit: 'Chocolate city, vanilla suburbs' revisited. *Journal of Housing Research* 4:1-38.
    1994    Stereotypes and segregation: Neighborhoods in the Detroit area. *American Journal of Sociology* 100:750-780.
Feagin, J.
    1991    The continuing significance of race: Anti-Black discrimination in public places. *American Sociological Review* 56:101-116.
    1997    Fighting White racism: The future of equal rights in the United States. Pp. 29-45 in *Civil Rights and Race Relations in the Reagan-Bush Era*, S. Myers, ed. New York: Praeger.
Feagin, J., and M. Sikes
    1994    *Living With Racism: The Black Middle Class Experience*. Boston: Beacon.
Forman, T., D. Williams, and J. Jackson
    1997    Race, place and discrimination. *Perspectives on Social Problems* 9:231-261.
Fulwood, S., III
    1996    *Waking from the Dream: My Life in the Black Middle Class*. New York: Anchor.

Gaertner, S., and J. Dovidio
 1986 The aversive form of racism. Pp. 61-90 in *Prejudice, Discrimination, and Racism*, J. Dovidio and S. Gaertner, eds. New York: Academic Press.
Gilens, M.
 1995 Racial attitudes and opposition to welfare. *Journal of Politics* 57:994-1014.
 1996a Race coding and White opposition to welfare. *American Political Science Review* 90:593-604.
 1996b Race and poverty in America: Public misperceptions and the American news media. *Public Opinion Quarterly* 60:515-541.
Hacker, A.
 1992 *Two Nations: Black and White, Separate, Hostile, Unequal*. New York: Scribners.
Hamilton, D., and T. Trolier
 1986 Stereotypes and stereotyping: An overview of the cognitive approach. Pp. 127-164 in *Prejudice, Discrimination, and Racism*, J. Dovidio and S. Gaertner, eds. New York: Academic Press.
Hochschild, J.
 1995 *Facing up to the American Dream: Race, Class, and the Soul of the Nation*. Princeton: Princeton University Press.
Huddy, L., and D. Sears
 1995 Opposition to bilingual education: Prejudice or the defense of realistic interests? *Social Psychology Quarterly* 58:133-143.
Hurwitz, J., and M. Peffley
 1997 Public perceptions of race and crime: The role of racial stereotypes. *American Journal of Political Science* 41:375-401.
Jackman, M.
 1977 Prejudice, tolerance, and attitudes toward ethnic groups. *Social Science Research* 6:145-169.
 1994 *The Velvet Glove: Paternalism and Conflict in Gender, Class, and Race Relations*. Berkeley: University of California Press.
Jackman, M., and M. Senter
 1980 Images of social groups: Categorical or qualified? *Public Opinion Quarterly* 44:341-361.
 1983 Different, therefore unequal: Beliefs about trait differences between groups of unequal status. *Research in Social Stratification and Mobility* 2:309-335.
Jaynes, G., and R. Williams, Jr.
 1989 *A Common Destiny: Blacks and American Society*. Washington, D.C.: National Academy Press.
Jones, J.
 1972 *Prejudice and Racism*. New York: McGraw Hill.
 1986 Racism: A cultural analysis of the problem. Pp. 279-314 in *Prejudice, Discrimination, and Racism*, J. Dovidio and S. Gaertner, eds. New York: Academic Press.
 1988 Racism in Black and White: A bicultural model of reaction and evolution. Pp. 117-136 in *Eliminating Racism: Profiles in Controversy*, P. Katz and D. Taylor, eds. New York: Plenum.
Kinder, D., and L. Sanders
 1996 *Divided by Color: Racial Politics and Democratic Ideals*. Chicago: University of Chicago Press.
Kinder, D., and D. Sears
 1981 Prejudice and politics: Symbolic racism versus racial threats to the good life. *Journal of Personality and Social Psychology* 40:414-431.

Kleinpenning, G., and L. Hagendoorn
    1993    Forms of racism and the cumulative dimension of ethnic attitudes. *Social Psychology Quarterly* 56:21-36.
Kluegel, J.
    1990    Trends in Whites' explanations of the gap in Black-White socioeconomic status, 1977-1989. *American Sociological Review* 55:512-525.
Kluegel, J., and E. Smith
    1982    Whites' beliefs about Blacks' opportunity. *American Sociological Review* 47:518-532.
    1986    *Beliefs about Inequality: Americans' Views of What is and What Ought to Be.* New York: Aldine de Gruyter.
Lincoln, C.
    1996    *Coming Through the Fire: Surviving Race and Place in America.* Durham, N.C.: Duke University Press.
Lipset, S., and W. Schneider
    1978    The Bakke Case: How would it be decided at the Bar of Public Opinion?" *Public Opinion* 1:38-44.
Massey, D., and N. Denton
    1993    *American Apartheid: Segregation and the Making of the Underclass.* Cambridge, Mass.: Harvard University Press.
McConahay, J.
    1982    Self-interest versus racial attitudes as correlates of anti-busing attitudes in Louisville: Is it the buses or the blacks? *Journal of Politics* 44:692-720.
Mfume, K.
    1996    *No Free Ride: From the Mean Streets to the Mainstream.* New York: Ballantine.
Montagu, A.
    1964    *The Concept of Race.* New York: Collier-Macmillan.
Nelson, J.
    1993    *Volunteer Slavery: My Authentic Negro Experience.* Chicago: Noble Press.
Niemi, R., J. Mueller, and T. Smith
    1989    *Trends in Public Opinion: A Compendium of Survey Data.* New York: Greenwood.
Omi, M., and H. Winant
    1986    *Racial Formation in the United States: From the 1960s to the 1980s.* Routledge & Kegan Paul.
Patterson, O.
    1997    *The Ordeal of Integration: Progress and Resentment in America's "Racial" Crisis.* New York: Civitas.
Peffley, M., J. Hurwitz, and P. Sniderman
    1997    Racial stereotypes and Whites' political views of Blacks in the context of welfare and crime. *American Journal of Political Science* 41:30-60.
Petersen, W.
    1982    Concepts of ethnicity. Pp. 1-26 in *Concepts of Ethnicity: Dimensions of Ethnicity,* S. Thernstrom, A. Orlov, and O. Handlin, eds. Cambridge: Harvard University Press.
Pettigrew, T.
    1981    Extending the stereotype concept. Pp. 303-332 in *Cognitive Processes in Stereotyping and Intergroup Behavior,* D. Hamilton, ed. Hillsdale, N.J.: Earlbaum.
Rowan, C.
    1996    *The Coming Race War in America: A Wake-Up Call.* New York: Little, Brown.
St. John, C., and T. Heald-Moore
    1995    Fear of Black strangers. *Social Science Research* 24:262-280.

1996    Racial prejudice and fear of criminal victimization by strangers in public settings. *Sociological Inquiry* 66:267-284.

Schuman, H.
1971    Free will and determinism in beliefs about race. Pp. 375-380 in *Majority and Minority: The Dynamics of Racial and Ethnic Relations*, N. Yetman and C. Steele, eds. Boston, Mass.: Allyn & Bacon.
1995    Attitudes, beliefs, and behavior. Pp. 68-89 in *Sociological Perspectives on Social Psychology*, K. Cook, G. Fine, and J. House, eds. Boston: Allyn & Bacon.

Schuman, H., and L. Bobo
1988    Survey-based experiments on White racial attitudes toward residential integration. *American Journal of Sociology* 94: 273-299.

Schuman, H., C. Steeh, and L. Bobo
1985    *Racial Attitudes in America: Trends and Interpretations*. Cambridge, Mass.: Harvard University Press.

Schuman, H., C. Steeh, L. Bobo, and M. Krysan
1997    *Racial Attitudes in America: Trends and Interpretations*. Revised edition. Cambridge: Harvard University Press.

Sears, D.
1988    Symbolic racism. Pp. 53-84 in *Eliminating Racism: Profiles in Controversy*, P. Katz and D. Taylor, eds. New York: Plenum.

Sears, D., C. Hensler, and L. Speer
1979    Whites' opposition to busing: Self-interest or symbolic politics? *American Political Science Review* 73:369-384.

Sears, D., C. van Laar, M. Carrillo, and R. Kosterman
1997    Is it really racism? The origins of White Americans' opposition to race-targeted policies. *Public Opinion Quarterly* 61:16-53.

See, K., and W. Wilson
1989    Race and ethnicity. Pp. 223-242 in *Handbook of Sociology*, N.J. Smelser, ed. Beverly Hills, Calif.: Sage.

Shipler, D.
1997    *A Country of Strangers: Blacks and Whites in America*. New York: Knopf.

Sidanius, J., E. Devereux, and F. Pratto
1992    A comparison of symbolic racism theory and social dominance theory as explanations for racial policy attitudes. *Journal of Social Psychology* 132:377-395.

Sidanius, J., F. Pratto, and L. Bobo
1996    Racism, conservatism, affirmative action, and intellectual sophistication: A matter of principled conservatism or group dominance? *Journal of Personality and Social Psychology* 70:476-490.

Sigelman, L., and S. Welch
1989    *Black Americans' Views of Racial Inequality: The Dream Deferred*. New York: Cambridge University Press.

Sleeper, J.
1997    *Liberal Racism*. New York: Viking.

Smith, T.
1990    Ethnic images. General Social Survey Technical Report, No. 19. National Opinion Research Center. University of Chicago.

Sniderman, P., and E. Carmines
1997    *Reaching Beyond Race*. Cambridge: Harvard University Press.

Sniderman, P., and T. Piazza
1993    *The Scar of Race*. Cambridge: Harvard University Press.

Sniderman, P., and P. Tetlock
    1986    Symbolic racism: Problems of political motive attribution. *Journal of Social Issues*
            42:129-150.
Steeh, C., and M. Krysan
    1996    The polls-trends: Affirmative action and the public. *Public Opinion Quarterly*
            60:128-158.
Steinberg, S.
    1998    Social science and the legitimation of racial hierarchy. *Race and Society* 1:5-14.
Stephan, W.
    1985    Intergroup relations. Pp. 599-658 in *Handbook of Social Psychology*, Volume 2, 3rd
            edition, G. Lindzey and E. Aronson, eds. New York: Random House.
Stone, J.
    1985    *Racial Conflict in Contemporary Society*. Cambridge, Mass.: Harvard University
            Press.
Tate, K.
    1993    *From Protest to Politics: The New Black Voters in American Elections*. New York:
            Russell Sage.
Tetlock, P.
    1994    Political psychology or politicized psychology: Is the road to scientific hell paved
            with good moral intentions? *Political Psychology* 15:509-529.
Thernstrom, S., and A. Thernstrom
    1997    *America in Black and White: One Nation Indivisible*. New York: Simon and Schuster.
Tuch, S., and R. Weitzer
    1997    The polls-trends: Racial differences in attitudes toward the police. *Public Opinion
            Quarterly* 61:642-663.
Weigel, R., and P. Howes
    1985    Conceptions of racial prejudice: Symbolic racism reconsidered. *Journal of Social
            Issues* 41:117-138.
West, C.
    1993    *Race Matters*. Boston: Beacon.
Wood, J.
    1994    Is 'symbolic racism' racism? A review informed by intergroup behavior. *Political
            Psychology* 15:673-686.

# 10
# Racial Trends and Scapegoating: Bringing in a Comparative Focus

*Anthony W. Marx*

Racism, according to Webster's dictionary, is a belief that "race" is the primary determinant of human traits and capacities and that racial differences produce an inherent superiority of a particular race. Put into practice, racism refers to relationships in which one group, supposedly distinguished by physical differences, has more power (political, economic, military, etc.) than another, and can and does use that power to act on or against a similarly distinguished oppressed group. Such relations generally build on and reinforce prejudice, but are distinct from prejudice in that prejudice is not necessarily acted on with power and authority. Harms inflicted in accordance with racism range from day-to-day socioeconomic discrimination, or local rules enforcing such discrimination, to national rules of exclusion from all social, civil, or political rights. How many, who, and how those people are so harmed makes a good deal of difference. Also important is whether harm is imposed by an individual, by a local official in a contained area, or by national authority. There is, then, within the arena of racism, a large continuum of tragic outcomes, providing some analytic leverage. If we can account for different outcomes along the continuum—from informal discrimination to national and formal exclusion—we may find clues as to the causes of racism. In other words, explaining the outcomes of racism may suggest its more general root.

Adding historical comparison to an analysis of racial trends in the United States requires looking at different countries' experiences. In so doing, we can more clearly identify distinct forms of racism, and, within each case, we can better assess why that form of racism emerged. Putting together such analyses, we may find a pattern more revealing of the fundamental causes of racism than would be apparent by just looking at one country. The pay-off would be a better understanding of each country's case, including our own, which better equips us to redress or to undermine racism more generally. That aim justifies the abuse and simplifications inherent in generalized comparisons—the kind that can so anger specialists, political partisans, or exceptionalists. In the process we should, of course, try to minimize distortions in each case.

Comparing the United States with South Africa and Brazil creates a particularly powerful tool for understanding racism. These three case studies of relations between African and European descendants present well-known examples of outcomes within the continuum of possible forms of racism. South Africa encoded pervasive discrimination and nationwide political and economic exclusion against a Black majority population. The United States encoded such policies of racial domination more unevenly, and amid significant social discrimination, against a minority Black population. Although Brazil legally encoded neither apartheid nor Jim Crow laws,[1] Afro-Brazilians are nevertheless subject to pervasive, if informal, discrimination and prejudice. In all three cases, race relations were significantly contested, provoking consideration of the enactment of rules of relations (or debates thereof) focusing on the treatment of Blacks by Whites.

My focus is on the legal enactment of racism, itself requiring justification, given that race relations are much broader than their legal enforcement. For instance, social discrimination is often as harmful as legal discrimination, whether it is overt or covert, deliberate or inadvertent, and whether it occurs before, during, or after legal repression. But the legal buttress—i.e., whether racism is encoded and in what form—makes a huge difference in the scale and form of harms so inflicted.

Legal racial domination has proven to be an effective, powerful, and hurtful tool of social control, as made most evident by the most extreme case, apartheid. That set of policies effectively contained—socially, politically, economically, and developmentally—the majority of South Africa's population for close to half a century, inflicting great costs and attracting the disgust and eventual disapproval of much of the world. Legal structures of racism, however, also generate conflict by reinforcing the cohe-

---

[1]The original "Jim Crow" was a character in a nineteenth-century minstrel act, a stereotype of a Black man. As encoded in laws sanctioning ethnic discrimination, the phrase refers to both legally enforced and traditionally sanctioned limitations of Blacks' rights, primarily in the U.S. South.

sion and antagonism of its victims. Eventually such laws demarcating and depriving a specified racial group become the target of domestic protest against the state, evidenced by the Antiapartheid Movement in South Africa, particularly in the 1950s and the 1980s, and the Civil Rights Movement in the United States in the 1960s.

In the absence of apartheid or Jim Crow laws, Brazil has had much less, and no comparable, mass-based social movements or conflict over race per se. Thus, in some ways, Afro-Brazilians are better off than Black Americans or Black South Africans, in not having been subjected to nationally or regionally encoded discrimination; on the other hand, it may be that Afro-Brazilians are worse off, not having a legal target to provoke and direct protest toward, which might have produced more effective social policies against discrimination.

So, the legal structures are important and worth explaining. This is not to suggest that legal structures are all that need to be explained or that they are, in themselves, the single cause of conflict. In fact, given the significance of legal racial domination, we are pushed back analytically to accounting for the emergence of such policies in their varying forms.

The first thing to note is that racial prejudice is the bedrock on which legal racial proscriptions were built, and its significance cannot be overestimated in explaining why Blacks were singled out for the more heinous and persistent forms of ill treatment. At the same time, differences in legal racist practices cannot be fully explained by prejudice, which was (and is) evident in all three countries. In social science, a constant cannot alone explain variation. Pervasive prejudice cannot explain the differences between apartheid and Jim Crow and Brazil's racism despite the lack of encoded proscriptions—i.e., cannot explicate nuances of Blacks' legal exclusion throughout South Africa, in the South in the United States, or nowhere comparably in Brazil. Indeed, if racial prejudice is as pervasive as it seems to be, then it is a necessity—though not a sufficient cause by itself—of legal racist practice, which is less pervasive and more varied. Variations of legal outcomes, however, have significant effects.

I have more fully explored, elsewhere, the historical bases for differences in the racist practices of South Africa, the United States, and Brazil (Marx, 1998). Here, for purposes of historical summary, an overview indicates the multicausality of racism, while revising and building on prior efforts at monocausal explanation.

The long-established demographic differences between the three countries have an important effect on the differences in outcomes. Blacks are a minority population in the United States, now representing roughly 13 percent of the total population. South Africa has the reverse demographic—Whites represent roughly 13 percent of the total population. Approximately half of Brazil's population is people who have some measure of African ancestry, though specification is more complex, given Brazil's different categories. These differences are highly relevant; for example, South Africa's indigenous Black majority has long reinforced the White minority's perceptions of insecurity and need for protection. But it is problematic to suggest that the legal racial outcomes ranging along the continuum are based solely on demographics. Notably Brazil, with its half-Black population, is at the opposite extreme in having had no postabolition, encoded racial segregation. Put more positively, the effect of demography may be curvilinear, with Brazil's close-to-even mix contributing to its unique lack of legal racism.

Legal racist practice was shaped, if not strictly preordained, by slavery. Certainly enslavement powerfully reinforced prejudice; White slave owners needed to justify and defend their heinous form of exploitation, so claimed it reflected the natural order of Blacks' inferiority and, therefore, subjugation by Whites (Fredrickson, 1981). Thus rationalized, slavery helped build the bedrock of prejudice, on which legally encoded racism would also be built, and without which neither would have been constructed. No doubt such prejudice in the United States informed postabolition forms of exploitation and the enactment of Jim Crow legislation.

However, we should not be too quick to describe racism as a direct outcome of slavery. Though described as more "humanitarian" than slavery elsewhere, and thereby supposedly prefiguring the later lack of encoded racial segregation (Tannenbaum, 1946), bondage in Brazil was at least as extensive as in the United States—nationwide, deadly, and exploitative. The high mortality rate among Brazilian slaves was the result of tropical diseases, which also devastated the White population. But that fact does not diminish the heinousness of White slave owners forcibly bringing Blacks into a situation in which they knew there were deadly conditions. Certainly Brazilian slavery fed prejudice, but it did not produce apartheid. Apartheid, in fact, emerged in a country with a significant, though relatively limited and contained, history of slavery (Shell, 1994). So, slavery reinforced prejudice in all three countries, but did not in itself determine the enactment or specific forms of postabolition legal racial domination.

An important reason for the different outcomes is cultural. Inasmuch as Brazil is the only Catholic country in this three-country comparison, it is arguable that the universality of the Catholic church, together with a general notion of an intact social hierarchy in which Blacks could be included (albeit at the bottom), fits with the lack of legal racism in Brazil (Tannenbaum, 1946; Freyre, 1945). Such cultural explanations are as hard to disprove as to prove, and social scientists tend to resist them; yet, there is something distinctive about Latin American race relations that may indeed be cultural. However, there are elements of cultural explanations that should give us pause. For example, the Catholic Church in Brazil was not all that inclusive in its own practices or preachings (do Nascimento, 1979:69; Hoetink, 1967:5, 21); and the Protestantisms of South Africans and Americans did not produce unanimity on issues of race among cobelieving English or Afrikaners in South Africa, or Northerners or Southerners in the United States. As powerful as they remain, cultural explanations also remain difficult to pin down. Practices vary within supposed cultural units, and culture itself changes in its symbolic meanings and interpretations over time and place.

Miscegenation also had an effect on the encoding of racism. In Brazil, because there were few women among the Portuguese colonials, there was a good deal of sex between White men and Black women. The not-surprising result was a large mulatto population, which, arguably, made it harder for Brazil to draw a biracial color line. Discrimination in Brazil remained informal and loose rather than legal and bifurcated (Degler, 1971), but it remained nevertheless (do Valle Silva, 1985). In the United States and South Africa there was also a good deal of sexual mixing across color lines, albeit in somewhat smaller proportions than in Brazil. Yet, such mixing did not prevent the United States or South Africa from drawing varying but rigid artificial lines of race and allocating rights accordingly. Indeed, mixing in the United States and South Africa was used to justify the need for stricter racial categories. Biology, then, does not determine racial encoding; the continuum of skin color has been divided into two groups in the United States, into three or four groups in South Africa, and without the legal use and enforcement of categorical racial inequalities in Brazil. The key is how racial categories are socially constructed, which is not fully reducible to physical distinctions.

There remains Karl Marx's formulation for explaining the use of race to differentiate classes. There is no denying that racist practice has been profitable for business owners, who pay Blacks less, and for Whites, who get paid relatively more. But White Brazilians also profited from racial discrimination, absent legal enforcements. Indeed, discrimination against Blacks may be the one thing capitalists and White laborers agreed on in all three of the countries, forging the basis of a class compromise that benefits Whites (Bonacich, 1972). White economic gains from racism were a powerful part of the incentives for Jim Crow laws and apartheid, with racism also shaping industrialization and urbanization. But here again, the commonality of Whites' economic incentives for racism cannot fully explain the variations in legal outcomes.

Where does this leave us? Looking at these three examples of racist practice, we can test or refine arguments accounting for differences of such practice. Not everyone will agree with how to interpret such comparison; and complex historical analyses do not lend themselves to neat social science results. Demography, the legacies of slavery, miscegenation, culture, class interests—all are important but none wholly determines later outcomes, reaffirming the multicausality of racism.

But racial discrimination—resulting from slavery, culture, or economic interests—did not always exist and need not continue to exist. Racist practices differ by place and change over time; and historical legacies and interests are interpreted accordingly. And where there is such indeterminacy—where people can chose the form of harms they inflict on others—there is sure to be politics, in terms of both intra-White conflict over oppression and discrimination, and Black resistance to repression, thus forcing reform.

To explain resolutions to such indeterminacy, we need to back up and look briefly at the history of the three countries, focusing particularly on those moments when postslavery, racist legal practice was relatively uncertain, debated, and in formation. At those moments we can see what determined the outcomes. Building on demography, culture, economic interests, and historical experiences of slavery and mixing, we must examine whether and how racial prejudice, pervasive in all three cases, was or was not used as a basis for varying forms of legal treatment. Put differently, as suggested in this volume by Michael Omi, race is scientifically meaningless but socially meaningful, though how and why it is so meaningful requires analysis, refined through comparison.

Discrimination (and worse) practiced by Afrikaners and British against the majority Black population in South Africa was as long standing as European settlement and colonialism. If there was a moment when future official treatment of Black Africans was relatively uncertain, it was immediately after the Boer War (1899 to 1902). The British colonials had discriminated against Blacks, but had promised enfranchisement and other reforms if they won the war and gained control of all of South Africa. Those promises won them much Black support in the war effort. The Afrikaners had resisted both reforms and British rule, but after a drawn-out conflict, they lost to overwhelming imperial force. After their victory, however, the British agreed to indefinitely postpone reforms to appease the Afrikaners and, thereby, diminish further conflict and unify White support (Denoon, 1973:14, 242). During the next half century, British and Afrikaners competed for political power, with the British reinforcing racial domination to win Afrikaner support, and Afrikaner nationalists pushing for even further enforcement. The result was a repeated agreement to increasingly subordinate Blacks, which was fully entrenched with the Afrikaner National Party's victory in 1948 and the enactment of more complete apartheid.

The story in the United States is more complex, yet follows a similar pattern. Joined a century earlier in a loosely controlled single polity, the

North increasingly resisted slavery and pushed for reforms resisted by the South. The conflict over regional autonomy versus central control came to a head with the Civil War, and slavery became a strategic cause. As in South Africa, the more liberal and industrial reformers won, but unlike in South Africa, the U.S. North proceeded to fulfill its promised reforms with Congressional Reconstruction, also serving Republicans' electoral interests in gaining Black votes at the time. The South resisted, and eventually even the Northern Republicans decided that appeasement of Southern Whites was more important than reforms for the Black minority. Though few Southern Whites would abandon the more explicitly racist Democratic Party, the possibility of gaining White voters in the South (outnumbering newly enfranchised Black voters) gradually altered the direction of the Republican party (Foner, 1988; Du Bois, 1992; DeSantis, 1959). Rather than impose racial domination from the center, as in South Africa, Northern Republicans instead allowed the South to encode its own order. The result was Jim Crow laws. Superimposed regional tensions and party and economic competition continued, but, as in South Africa, both sides were gradually reconciled by the mutual benefit to White society.

Brazil followed a dramatically different historical trajectory. The same Portuguese descendant elite consistently ruled the country and managed relatively peaceful transitions from slavery to abolition, and from colonialism to empire to republic to democracy, to authoritarianism, and back to democracy. There was no internal war on the scale of the United States' or South Africa's. This is not to suggest there were no conflicts or regional competition—just no overriding violent conflict among Whites by ethnicity or region. Whereas such intra-White conflict in South Africa and the United States was gradually contained by unifying Whites against Blacks, no comparable intra-White conflict in Brazil existed to be so managed. Instead Blacks were officially included in the nation projecting itself as a "racial democracy," though the reality remained one of Black impoverishment and ongoing White discrimination (Roett, 1984; Skidmore, 1974).

The pattern that emerges from this overview can be stated schematically, albeit in somewhat simplified form. Where Whites were in major violent conflict with each other—regionally or nationally—their common racial prejudice against Blacks could be and was used as the basis for eventually restoring White unity, leading to greater codification of that prejudice. Prior prejudice provided the historical raw material or bedrock on which White unity could be built, singling out Blacks as victims to be sacrificed toward that end, though that unity was actually built and shaped by ongoing White tensions and problems. Where Whites were not so divided, there was no need for reconciliation via a scapegoat, and racial domination was not legally encoded—i.e., Brazil. The implication is the centrality of the goal—national solidarity, or efforts by elites to unify a core constituency of loyal supporters to diminish internal conflicts threatening the polity or economy and shared White interests therein. Where such threats exploded and threatened to again, racial exclusion was the glue for White nationalism; and where the threat of disunity was less, racial division itself was diluted by rhetorical inclusion. Either way, nationalism was gradually consolidated.

In South Africa and the United States, codification of racial domination served to preserve and gradually solidify the White nation-state, or, more precisely, a racially defined, cross-ethnic or cross-regional allegiance to the polity. Once established, political parties often built platforms on "the race card," in various forms and guises, to win and maintain support and power. Race was a powerful tool toward that end because of the culture of prejudice forged in conquest and slavery. Blacks were singled out as victims sacrificed for White unity because of the salience of past prejudice, and because they fulfilled the criteria of scapegoats: visible and vulnerable for displacing conflict (Ashmore, 1970). In terms of multi-causality, we have the explicit combination of the status issues of prejudice with class interests, and party concerns for power, following a Weberian model.

The first thing to note at this point is the implication that legal racial domination was likely not an artifact of social dysfunction after all. We tend to see such segregation as an unfortunate but inescapable legacy from past prejudice. I suggest, instead, that racist practices were deliberate and ongoing choices designed to address a more pressing problem—White conflict threatening a unified nation-state and functioning economy. Indeed, these racist policies were repeatedly refined and heightened precisely because they worked at resolving the problem of intra-White conflict, thereby serving the interests of those who sought national unity and development, and profited from them. Segregation, later apartheid, helped ease the English-Afrikaner conflict because exclusion of Blacks was the one thing Whites agreed upon. Similarly, in the United States, although tensions between North and South did not disappear, they diminished enough for the Union to be stabilized, and the exclusion of Blacks appeased the South enough to make this possible.

The power of racism was that it proved so effective at meeting the most pressing challenges of the day, at least for a time. In South Africa, peace forged among Whites at the expense of Blacks allowed for the expansion of tremendous centralized state power and economic development initially based on mineral wealth. In the United States, peace forged among Whites at the expense of Blacks allowed for central-state consolidation and more rapid industrial expansion. In both the United States and South Africa, encoding racism delivered stability, control over a unified state, and economic development less hindered by regional or ethnic intra-White conflict.

If the use of race was so successful for Whites, why did its legal codification end? Here, too, the reasons are multicausal. A major part of the answer, however, is the cost of Black protest. The more segregation was reinforced, the more it forced its victims into a common identity, a recognition of joined fate, which became the basis for rising protest provoked by and targeted against legal Black exclusion. At some point—the 1960s in the United States and the 1990s in South Africa—the benefits of racial domination had been sufficiently locked in for Whites and the costs of protest become close to intolerable. No doubt, international pressures and leadership played huge parts in ushering in the end of legal racism, but it was mass protests that played the leading role in eventually forcing these transitions.

But transition to what? The demarcation from a Jim Crow or apartheid regime to not is pretty explicit. Just as we can specify when those legal edifices were built, we can specify when they are ended—with the passing of legislation or signing of executive orders. But not everything changed, of course. The legal edifices of racism were built on foundations of prior prejudice and discrimination. When the legal structure or scaffolding was dismantled, the prejudice, discrimination, and inequality remained freestanding. The most notable arena of such continuity is economics, with racial discrimination continuing to serve the interests of business profiting from paying lower wages to Black workers, and loyalty of White workers who benefit by being paid more because they are White.

In a sense, the removal of legal structures created a convergence of the three cases discussed here—the United States and South Africa have been "Brazilianized." Post Jim Crow and apartheid, the United States and South Africa can, like Brazil, claim to be "racial democracies," where there is no longer a legal basis for racial discrimination or exclusion from rights. Both countries can, and do, proudly claim to have progressed beyond the bad old days, and to hail the legal equality of opportunity. Proclaiming "racial democracy" does not mean equality of outcome or social equality, or the lack of discrimination or prejudice. But it has produced situations in the United States and South Africa that are, in some respects, similar to situations in Brazil, and as troubling in all three cases.

The first thing to notice about increasing "Brazilianization" is the rise of a rhetoric about color-blindness. The argument now common in the United States is that since legal racial discrimination is over, and has been off the books long enough for its prior effects to have been overcome, then so should any positive legal discrimination be ended. Public opinion polls show growing support of Whites for this position (for poll results, see Jaynes and Williams, 1989:148-156; for the conservative position, see D'Souza, 1995; Steele, 1990). Such color-blindness is defended as just, and also, less abstractly, as a way to move toward a society in which race is truly irrelevant. The implication is that race is no longer a barrier to advancement, and therefore should not be used to redress prior constraints. This is a vision that guides much of the debate and policy in the United States today. It is a vision apparently shared by a majority of the Supreme Court justices. It is a vision projected as fundamentally liberal in its aspiration to treat all people as individuals rather than as members of a group.

A more clearly focused vision shows that even if the legal constraints of racism have been removed in the United States, informal constraints remain. The legacies of the past live on in continued discrimination and inequality (well documented by the studies collected here). The state may be legally color-blind; society is not. For the state then to position itself on the supposed high ground of color-blindness may actually mean it is unwilling to act on the grounds of reality. A color-blind social policy in a color-consciousness society is a form of vision impairment, leaving unchallenged or unregulated racially shaped practices and outcomes. And this result is not the abstract choice of some anthropomorphized unit called "the state"; it is, instead, the purposeful aim of those groups and individuals interested in leaving inequality unchallenged and themselves better off.

The appeal of color-blindness is that it projects as moral what is not; by refusing to see and act on the reality of continued discrimination, the color-blind can project themselves as above the fray, unsullied by manipulations of color. This, of course, leaves the problem unsolved, and, even worse, ensures that the problem will be ignored. As with child or spousal abuse, or so many other harms, recognition of a problem is the first and necessary step toward resolution. The color-blind argument removes that step. It also has the effect of bolstering arguments that remaining Black deprivation is the fault of Blacks and an indication of their inferiority (Herrnstein and Murray, 1994). Ignoring ongoing discrimination encourages a blaming of the victim of and for that discrimination.

The convergence with Brazil is evident. There, racial discrimination is illegal, and its existence widely denied. Nevertheless, Afro Brazilians are much more likely to be poor in a country with the second highest recorded overall income inequality (do Valle Silva, 1985). The widespread assumption in Brazil is that Blacks are poorer because they are less well educated or less well equipped to function in society. Whites and even Afro-Brazilians are encouraged to believe that remaining Black deprivation is the fault of Blacks themselves, diminishing any incentive for public policy intervention. And many argue that race-based policies cannot be used to redress this inequality because, they argue, there is no clear racial demarcation on which to base such policy. In fact, they say, such policies would themselves violate the constitutional guarantee against discrimination of any sort.

Another area of convergence is that of multiculturalism. The United States has long maintained some ambivalence between allowing for cultural diversity and encouraging greater uniformity. Immigrants kept much of their cultural practice and language, but also became assimilated (Glazer and Moynihan, 1970). This ambivalence has not disappeared, although the power of American culture to assimilate has grown, now reaching easily across international borders. But within the United States the growing trend is to give greater weight to cultural autonomy. Now in large part this remains rhetorical—to most Americans there may be some bowing toward Hanukkah or Kwanzaa, but Christmas remains the norm. And certainly a rhetoric of cultural tolerance has not diminished discrimination against Blacks, Hispanics, and other ethnic minorities. Still, there is a sense that everyone is free do as they please—observe any holiday or speak any language, at least in the privacy of their home. Many avowed advocates for the rights of minorities hail such permissiveness as a sign of tolerance.

In Brazil, such multiculturalism has long been so hailed as a signal of tolerance, though the reality may be just the reverse. Brazilians point to the inclusion of African religions and cultural practices in the mainstream as an indication of "racial democracy." If Brazilians were racist, the argument goes, they would have crushed all such belief and activity under European hegemony. Instead, Europeans learn and practice condomble, samba, and capuera. But we know that such respect for African traditions has not implied or brought respect for Africans, and such cultural tolerance takes place within a larger context of projected homogeneity and assimilation toward the mean. Perhaps cultural inclusion provides a useful cover for continued exploitation. The semblance of tolerance and inclusion is maintained, but so is the reality of social exclusion. Everyone dances, sometimes even together, but afterward the Whites still go home to their mansions and the Blacks to their shanties.

A similar implication of multiculturalism may be evident in the United States. Here we have few remaining African religions per se, but African and other group contributions to mainstream U.S. culture are clearly evident in music and religion. Acceptance of these contributions is celebrated by many Americans as indications of tolerance and opportunity, but they remain more symbolic than real. That does not necessarily make such symbols any less powerful as a means of giving people a sense of pride and belonging that might offset or contain potential conflict. I am not suggesting a conscious policy or conspiracy; the fact is, cultural diversity and tolerance is always two edged: it allows contributions from outside the mainstream but it also gives the margins a greater sense of being in that mainstream than more objective measures suggest.

Perhaps most provocatively, Black Americans may possibly be "Brazilianized" in terms of the increasingly limited or disparate collective opposition to their ongoing discrimination. Afro-Brazilians have protested their lower status during this century, most notably with the Frente Negra in the 1930s, and the Movimento Negro Unificado from the 1970s on (Hanchard, 1994). But these movements have remained relatively small and elitist. In fact, the majority of Afro-Brazilians deny that there is any racial discrimination or need for protest as Blacks. In general, they often do not even identify themselves racially. Despite their poverty and social ostracism, discrimination and inequality have not been sufficient to engender a mass collective response, at least thus far.

Black Americans' social movements may be described as increasingly suffering from the travails of Brazilianization. With the end of Jim Crow laws, Blacks are no longer forced together by law, face no explicit legal constraints that could be so challenged. Some Blacks have even joined conservatives in turning the blame for continued deprivation on Blacks themselves. For many Blacks in the United States, continued social inequality and discrimination have not served as a comparably strong unifying or mobilizing force as when discrimination was legal. The result has been, since the 1960s, some diminishment in the unity and level of mass protest of Blacks. This is not to suggest that there was ever unanimity of purpose in the Black community, just, arguably, more than now. Nor am I suggesting that the end of Jim Crow should not be celebrated; what I am suggesting is that the end of legal discrimination perhaps contains opportunities to press for ongoing redress of the ongoing effects of discrimination.

Comparative analyses demonstrate the suggestiveness of comparison—i.e., by thinking about the United States in the context of Brazil, similarities emerge, perhaps even some convergence. In the process, we see some of the downsides of trajectories that might otherwise seem fully positive. Color-blindness may sound liberal, but the Brazilian experience of it suggests color-blindness may not be so liberal in effect. The same is true for multiculturalism. The ironic result of the end of legal racist practice has been a partial diminishment in the mobilization to challenge ongoing injustice.

But we should not be too quick to see the United States as akin to Brazil. History ensures that convergence will go only so far so fast. The United States long suffered from a major intra-White conflict gradually diminished by unifying Whites as such through official domination and exclusion of Blacks. That legal scapegoating solidified Black racial identity and protest. Both continue now outside the legal framework: Whites still displace their own tensions onto Blacks, and Black identity remains strong, as evident in such events as the Million Man March or such practices as distinctive voting patterns. The legacies of racial codification and protest are not so quickly wiped away. Racial identity is firmly entrenched and racial interpretations of conflict are most readily grasped. A generation after Jim Crow, race remains central to the U.S. experience, as reaffirmed in this report. Color-blindness does not come easily to Americans, nor does cultural tolerance. Thus, "Brazilianization" will be an uphill process. Assimilation across race has remained much more halting than across ethnicity, with the physical markers of race still strongly observed. The racially defined block of Black interests and protests remains evident, or at least can be invoked, and this protest remains the basis for possible change and progress.

Even less positively, the remaining salience of race in the United States means that the historical pattern of using denigration of Blacks to unify Whites may be, and still is, called upon. This has been apparent in the recent partisan squabbles about the federal deficit, where agreement on how to resolve this issue seemed to be paved by prior agreement to cut programs targeted to or perceived as benefiting Blacks. It is also evident in the maneuverings within and about other growing minority groups, such as Hispanics, who, arguably, may be increasingly invited to join in a coalition with Whites against Blacks in the long-standing tradition of immigrant absorption. This process will require an increasingly elastic definition of "Whiteness" (again as in the past, say with the absorption of Irish), but given the benefits of a coalition with Whites, will be very appealing to those groups that might otherwise align with Blacks in pressing for reform.

A more general example of continued racial scapegoating in the United States might be the reaction to growing class division among Whites. As the economic divide widens, and the potential for intra-White tension or conflict grows (World Bank, 1998), race remains a ready tool for conflict avoidance through scapegoating. Thus, it seems not coincidental that the rising class divide among Whites has come with a backlash against affirmative action for Blacks, as if that policy benefited primarily Blacks or was to blame for White impoverishment. Looked at realistically, the numbers make this argument ridiculous: Blacks remain too few to have such a determinant impact on the larger group of White poor, but the salience of race rhetoric overwhelms obvious facts. White politicians, perhaps, are not conscious that in attacking affirmative action (for Blacks), they unify their White support among embittered White poor and those of the wealthy fearing a backlash directed against them; but some politicians certainly appear conscious of the benefits of race baiting and aware of the long American tradition of scapegoating Blacks. The majority population still harbors strong anti-Black prejudice, which gives even veiled anti-Black rhetoric great salience and torque. There remains a rich vein of hate to tap and powerful incentives to mine that vein.

Unlike South Africa or Brazil, America's Black population is in the minority; deprivation and denigration of Blacks may be perceived by Whites to have little impact on economic markets or general social satisfaction. However, such arguments or assumptions of imposing harm with impunity are unrealistic in the longer term. The most obvious caveat is that racial domination in varying forms has provoked resistance over time. Legal racial repression has provoked such resistance most pointedly, but even in Brazil's legal "racial democracy" there has been and is resistance. Certainly in the United States (and South Africa), given the legacy of racial identity and conflict, it is hard to imagine that continued discrimination and inequality would not still generate stability-shaking protests, challenging interests and forcing continued attention and possible reform efforts. Such pressure has been the most powerful force for change, and is likely to continue to be so. Black Americans in large numbers remain committed to group solidarity and action, as evident in their ongoing preference for the Democratic Party and its greater focus on social reforms.

Beyond the issue of effective protest or electoral pressure, there are other real and direct costs to continued racism in the United States. Deprivation due to discrimination constrains markets for goods, skews labor markets, and fosters alienation and antisocial behavior requiring costly social policies of support and policing. Resulting tensions and conflict make life less pleasant for all, and sometimes considerably worse than that.

Yet there is another, perhaps more fundamental cost to continued racial scapegoating and discrimination. Using race to avoid or contain White tensions, conflicts, or issues, may be effective at just that. The result is, real issues of concern within the majority remain unaddressed. The most pressing example is again the rise of economic disparity among U.S. Whites. The costs of avoiding this issue are potentially huge. With politicians focusing on race and ignoring economic inequality, voters are increasingly becoming apathetic. Eventually, apathy may turn to anger among the less well off. And we are no longer talking about a small alienated group, but a large and potentially explosive social dislocation. If race is so manipulated to keep us from focusing on potential problems and conflicts, the cost will be high indeed.

Since race has long been used to avoid other conflicts and issues, then it arguably contributes to the festering of those conflicts and issues. If avoidance and scapegoating work for a time, as they have, when they stop being so effective, the results can be devastating. Perhaps that is the lesson to be drawn from our comparison, which has revealed the extent to which race has been so used. Getting beyond racism is valuable in its own right, given the released potential of the people directly hurt by such practice. But getting beyond racism is of value to us all, in that it would allow us to focus on the issues otherwise hidden. Only if we see those issues for what they are, rather than hiding behind our fears or prejudice, do we have a hope of solving them.

This brings us back, finally, to the interaction of racism and nationalism. Historical comparison suggests that in the United States (and South Africa), racial exclusion has been reinforced and codified as a tool for building national loyalty and coherence among a core constituency of Whites otherwise divided. And even where nationalism has been officially inclusive of all, as in Brazil, Blacks were effectively excluded from much of the benefits of national development. The cost has been conflict and social dislocation. Only if we imagine and reinvigorate an inclusive image of civic nationalism, will the political units on which modern politics are built actually serve their populations, without excluded groups having to resort to protest as the only way to successfully seek redress. Only then will the economic and other divisions that still tear at our national fabric be addressed. Failing that, internal discord may continue to work away at the nation-state and undermine the prospects for truly just development.

## REFERENCES

Ashmore, R.
    1970   The problem of intergroup prejudice. Pp. 248-296 in Social Psychology, B. Collins, ed. Reading: Addison-Wesley.
Bonacich, E.
    1972   A theory of ethnic antagonism: The split labor market. American Sociological Review 37(October).
Degler, C.
    1971   Neither Black Nor White. New York: Macmillan.
Denoon, D.
    1973   A Grand Illusion. London: Longman.
DeSantis, V.
    1959   Republicans Face the Southern Question. New York: Greenwood.
do Nascimento, A.
    1979   Brazil: Mixture or Massacre? Dover: Majority Press.
do Valle Silva, N.
    1985   Updating the cost of not being White in Brazil. Pp. 42-55 in Race, Class and Power in Brazil, P. Fontaine, ed. Los Angeles: Center for Afro-American Studies, University of California.
D'Souza, D.
    1995   The End of Racism. New York: Free Press.

Du Bois, W.
    1992   *Black Reconstruction in America*. New York: Atheneum.
Foner, E.
    1988   *Reconstruction*. New York: Harper and Row.
Fredrickson, G.
    1981     Chapter 2 in *White Supremacy*. Oxford: Oxford University Press.
Freyre, G.
    1945   *Brazil: An Interpretation*. New York: Knopf.
Glazer, N., and D. Moynihan
    1970   *Beyond the Melting Pot*. Cambridge: MIT Press.
Hanchard, M.
    1994   *Orpheus and Power*. Princeton: Princeton University Press.
Herrnstein, R., and C. Murray
    1994   *The Bell Curve*. New York: Free Press.
Hoetink, H.
    1967   *The Two Variants in Caribbean Race Relations*. London: Oxford University Press.
Jaynes, G., and R. Williams, eds.
    1989   *A Common Destiny: Blacks and American Society*. Washington, D.C.: National Academy Press.
Marx, A.
    1998   *Making Race and Nation: A Comparison of the United States, South Africa and Brazil*. Cambridge: Cambridge University Press.
Roett, R.
    1984   *Brazil: Politics in a Patrimonial Society*. New York: Praeger.
Shell, R.
    1994   *Children of Bondage*. Hanover, N.H.: University Press of New England.
Skidmore, T.
    1974   *Black Into White*. New York: Oxford University Press.
Steele, S.
    1990   *Content of Our Characters*. New York: St. Martin's Press.
Tannenbaum, F.
    1946   *Slave and Citizen*. New York: Knopf.
World Bank
    1998   *World Development Indicators*. Washington, D.C.: World Bank.

# 11
# Affirmative Action: Legislative History, Judicial Interpretations, Public Consensus

*Carol M. Swain*

Affirmative action is often considered to be a public-policy issue on which Whites and Blacks are hopelessly divided (Delgado, 1996; Hacker, 1992; Kinder and Sanders, 1996; Thernstrom and Thernstrom, 1997). Racial division and polarization, however, do not tell the whole story. Once we move beyond the ambiguity surrounding the term "affirmative action"—and the confusion concerning existing affirmative-action programs—a good deal of agreement is revealed among Whites, Blacks, and members of other racial and ethnic groups concerning many affirmative action-related issues. "Agreement" includes a shared unease about programs involving overt racial preferences coupled with a willingness to support outreach programs as well as programs that benefit the disadvantaged, and certain other types of affirmative-action initiatives. Identifying and building on this agreement and consensus is a necessary first step in the development of any successful race-related public policy in a multiracial society, such as our own.

## DEFINING THE CONCEPT

In 1995, President Clinton appointed investigators to review federal policy on affirmative action. An important and telling finding the investigators reported was that affirmative action had no clear and widely understood definition, and that this contributed to an atmosphere of confusion and miscommunication about affirmative action's goals and modes of implementation (Edley, 1996:15-24; see also Smelser, 1999). Nevertheless, the investigators offered a useful definition of affirmative action as "any effort taken to expand opportunity for women or racial, ethnic and national origin minorities by using membership in those groups that have been subject to discrimination as a consideration [in decision making or allocation of resources]" (Edley, 1996:16-17). Swain (1996:1) offers a somewhat broader definition is offered that involves a "range of governmental and private initiatives that offer preferential treatment to members of designated racial or ethnic minority groups (or to other groups thought to be disadvantaged), usually as a means of compensating them for the effects of past and present discrimination." Both of these definitions suggest a compensatory rationale for affirmative-action programs—i.e., members of groups previously disadvantaged are now to receive the just compensation that is their due in order to make it easier for them to get along in the world. Other useful definitions and characterizations of affirmative action would de-emphasize the retrospective, compensatory, and ameliorative nature of such programs and focus, instead, on the current value of such programs in enhancing diversity, particularly in educational institutions and in the workforce (Bergman, 1996; Bok and Bowen, 1998).

The actual programs that come under the general heading of affirmative action are a diverse lot; they include policies affecting college and university admissions, private-sector employment, government contracting, disbursement of scholarships and grants, legislative districting, and jury selection. Numerous affirmative-action programs have been enacted into law at local, state, and federal levels. In addition to programs that have been mandated by law, many private corporations and universities have developed affirmative-action programs voluntarily. Methods of implementing affirmative-action policies are similarly diverse and in the past have ranged from "hard quotas" to softer methods of outreach, recruitment, and scrupulous enforcement of antidiscrimination norms. Clearly, much of the ambiguity and conceptual fuzziness surrounding affirmative action as a theoretical idea occurs because there are differing forms of the policy and even more differing modes of implementation (Swain et al., 2001).

## EVOLUTION OF AFFIRMATIVE-ACTION POLICY

Many scholars have traced the historical evolution of affirmative-action policy (Belz, 1991; Drake and Holsworth, 1996; Graham, 1990; Skrentny, 1996). Presented here is a very cursory overview of the history of the term in U.S. legislation, major court cases that helped shape public opinion, and analyses of recent public opinion surveys documenting current attitudes about affirmative action.

The actual term "affirmative action" emerged first in labor law in the

1935 National Labor Relations Act (Wagner Act), but it did not become firmly associated with Civil Rights legislation enforcement until 1961, the year President Kennedy issued Executive Order 10925. That order directed federal contractors to take "affirmative action" to ensure nondiscrimination in hiring, promotions, and all other areas of private employment. The concept of affirmative action, however, was not formally defined in the Executive Order, and it went largely unnoticed.

Kennedy's executive order, nevertheless, represented considerable progress over the Civil Rights Acts passed in 1957 and 1960. Unlike the latter, Executive Order 10925 had a real effect in reducing discrimination in at least one area—government contracting. Kennedy's order, however, failed to address many of the concerns of the National Association for the Advancement of Colored People (NAACP) and other civil rights organizations regarding discrimination in public accommodations, housing, government employment, and private-sector employment in firms that did not have contracts with the federal government. In the face of increased White-initiated violence in the South, and mounting pressure from civil rights leaders, Kennedy appealed to Congress to pass legislation mandating equal rights and equal access to all in all public accommodations and jobs in what was, at the time, hailed as "the civil rights bill of the century." The Kennedy-proposed Civil Rights legislation, however, was too drastic for a Congress that was still, to a considerable extent, controlled by southern Democrats. It took the combination of the sympathy generated by Kennedy's assassination in November 1963, the formidable legislative skills of President Lyndon B. Johnson, and the pleas and reassurances of Majority Whip Hubert Humphrey (D-Minnesota) to persuade Congress to pass a comprehensive Civil Rights bill.

Even before the concept of affirmative action was widely in use, opponents of the 1964 Civil Rights legislation argued that the lack of a definition of what constituted discrimination would lead to quotas in employment. Senator James Eastland (D-Mississippi) argued forcefully that the bill would discriminate against White people: "I know what will happen if there is a choice between hiring a White man or hiring a Negro, both having equal qualifications. I know who will get the job. It will not be the White man" (Swain, 1996:6). Largely because of such fears and predictions, the Civil Rights bill was amended explicitly to ban quotas in hiring.

When the bill eventually passed as the Civil Rights Act of 1964, it was comprehensive in its scope. In addition to its employment provisions, it banned discrimination in, for example, public accommodations, public conveyances, theaters, and restaurants; and it authorized the government to withhold federal funds from schools that had not desegregated in compliance with the 1954 *Brown* decision. In all, it contained 11 sections or titles. Title VI and Title VII are most important to the evolving connection between Civil Rights enforcement and affirmative action. Title VI covers discrimination in federally assisted programs, and Title VII covers employment discrimination in all large and medium-sized private businesses. Congress created the Equal Employment Opportunity Commission (EEOC) to monitor Title VII violations, but the original legislation gave the EEOC no power to enforce its dictates. A year later the Labor Department established the Office of Federal Contract Compliance (OFCC, subsequently reorganized and renamed the Office of Federal Contract Compliance Programs, OFCCP), which was charged with regulating federal grants, loans, and contracts.

Far from promoting preferential treatment, Title VII, as originally written and interpreted, merely required employers and admissions officers to stop discriminating. If this was done in an acceptable manner, then businesses were considered to be in compliance with the law. Title VII, however, in combination with related executive orders and key administrative and court decisions, set the stage for stronger affirmative-action measures by requiring businesses doing business with the federal government to compile statistical data about the race and sex of their employees and job applicants in order to demonstrate their compliance with the law (Drake and Holsworth, 1996; Glazer, 1975).

Both Presidents Lyndon Johnson and Richard Nixon were instrumental in moving the country away from "soft" affirmative-action programs, that merely required employers and other private parties to make special efforts to recruit members of previously excluded groups, toward stronger policies mandating preferential treatment of women and minorities. Under these presidents, federal goals began to shift from equal opportunity as defined in the Civil Rights legislation to an emphasis on equal (or proportional) results.

On the specific issue of affirmative action for Blacks, Johnson set the stage for more aggressive, results-oriented policies. In a commencement address at Howard University, in June 1965, President Johnson introduced the powerful image of a shackled runner, which later influenced much of the debate concerning affirmative action:

> You do not take a man who, for years, has been hobbled by chains, liberate him, bring him to the starting line of a race saying, "You are free to compete with all the others," and still believe you have been fair. This is the next and more profound stage of the battle for civil rights. We seek not just freedom of opportunity, not just legal equity, but human ability; not just equality as a right and theory, but equality as a right and result (Johnson, 1965).

Also in 1965, Johnson issued Executive Order 11246, which reaffirmed support for Kennedy's 1961 order linking Civil Rights enforcement with "affirmative action" requirements.

In the aftermath of the bloody Newark and Detroit riots in the summer of 1967, Johnson issued Executive Order 11365, which established a National Advisory Commission on Civil Disorders; it came to be known as the Kerner Commission after its chairman, Otto Kerner, then Governor of Illinois. The Commission was composed largely of White and Black moderates and was directed to answer three basic questions about the riots: What happened? Why did it happen? What can be done to prevent it from happening again? The Commission's report would attribute most of the problems of the inner-city ghettos to racism among Whites.

Paradoxically, it was the conservative President Richard Nixon who was initially responsible for the adoption of racial quotas, the strongest affirmative-action enforcement mechanism. Nixon's endorsement of quotas came in the early 1970s when his administration approved the Philadelphia Plan, which involved the direct imposition of hiring goals in the construction trades, to be monitored through OFCC. The U.S. Department of Labor (USDL) subsequently issued Revised Order #4 that, in effect, amended Johnson's Executive Order 11246 by extending the quota-like features of the Philadelphia Plan to all private contractors doing business with the federal government. Contractors were now required to establish target "goals and timetables" for the hiring of "underutilized" minority group members and women, and to show "good faith efforts" to meet these hiring goals and timetables. Although not a rigid quota system, the "goals and timetables" requirement was a results-oriented approach to employment policy that its critics would charge operated, in practice, little differently than a quota system. Labor Department staff supported the new "goals and timetables" approach as a way of ending old-style discrimination and securing positive results for previously excluded groups (Skrentny, 1996). Because Nixon had previously opposed legislative initiatives thought to be beneficial to Blacks and other minorities, there was some speculation as to why he would endorse the use of quotas. One theory is that he'd hoped to sow dissention and division among core Democratic groups (Kahlenberg, 1996:22).

Thus, affirmative action evolved from a vague concept buried in an executive order, to a set of legal regulations and practices. The shift from "weak" to "strong" methods of policy enforcement, it is important to recognize, was largely the result, not of legislative action, but of decisions made in the executive branch of the federal government and in federal regulatory agencies such as the USDL and the U.S. Department of Health, Education and Welfare. Partly as a result of the riots of the late 1960s, many policy makers had come to view stronger measures than race-neutral nondiscrimination as necessary, at least as a transitional step, toward the goal of achieving a color-blind society, and as a necessary means of ensuring that Whites would not discriminate against Blacks (Belz, 1991; Graham, 1990).

## THE ROLE OF THE COURTS IN EXPANDING, AND LATER RESTRICTING, AFFIRMATIVE ACTION

### Employment Discrimination

The U.S. Supreme Court rendered a crucial decision in the case of *Griggs v. Duke Power Co.* (401 U.S. 424, 1971), an early employment discrimination case, in which the Court ruled unanimously that under Title VII of the 1964 Civil Rights Act, any screening device that produced unequal consequences for different races—i.e., what in employment law came to be known as "disparate impact" in the sense of disproportionate group harm—would be held to constitute invidious employment discrimination unless the screening device were shown to be clearly job-related. Four years after *Griggs*, the Court reaffirmed its support for the disparate impact approach in *Albemarle Paper Company v. Moody* (422 U.S. 405, 1975), a case in which employers sought to protect themselves against discrimination charges by hiring enough minorities to counteract any statistical charges of racial imbalance.

Nevertheless, a year later in *Washington v. Davis* (426 U.S. 229, 1976), the Court refused to extend the theory of disparate impact developed in Title VII cases to discrimination cases brought under the equal protection provisions of the U.S. Constitution. The Court held that to establish a *constitutional* claim of unequal treatment (as opposed to a statutory claim of discrimination under Title VII), there had to be a showing of intent to discriminate, not simply a showing of disparate impact. The case in question involved unsuccessful applicants for positions of policemen in the District of Columbia, who charged that the police department's use of a written test was discriminatory because Blacks had a disproportionately high failure rate. At the time the case was brought before the federal courts, Title VII, which would later be extended in scope, did not cover municipal employees.

In 1989, the Court, reflecting the more politically conservative influence of justices appointed by President Ronald Reagan, shifted the burden of proof in disparate impact cases from businesses to plaintiffs, making it more difficult to sustain an employment discrimination claim under Title VII. The switch occurred in the Court's ruling in *Ward's Cove Packing Co. v. Atonio* (490 U.S. 642, 1989), and *Price Waterhouse v. Hopkins* (490 U.S. 228, 1989). The Court in *Ward's Cove* ruled that "a simple statistical comparison of racial percentages between skilled and unskilled jobs was insufficient to make a *prima facie* case" of employment discrimination (Hall, 1992:21). In *Price Waterhouse* the Court shifted the burden even further by requiring the plaintiff to prove that "employment practices substantially depended on illegitimate criteria" (Hall, 1992:351). However, the 1991 Civil Rights Act, which was passed by a Democratic congress and, with some reluctance, signed into law by President Bush, overturned *Ward's Cove* by limiting the ability of employers to use "business necessity" as a defense against discrimination claims under Title VII. It also overruled the Court's decision in *Patterson v. McLean Credit Union* (491 U.S. 164, 1989), where the Court had invalidated a Black woman's attempt to seek relief from racial harassment under the 1866 Civil Rights Act.

Charges of "reverse discrimination" became common during the 1970s, as more and more corporations and private businesses, often under pressure from federal enforcement agencies, began more aggressive hiring of minorities and women. The question of whether Title VII of the Civil Rights Act also protected Whites against discrimination arose in *McDonald v. Sante Fe Transportation Company* (427 U.S. 273, 1976). The case involved a company where two White employees who had been charged with theft were fired, while a Black employee similarly charged had been retained. The Court ruled unanimously that Whites as well as Blacks are protected from racial discrimination under the antidiscrimination provisions of Title VII.

Despite this ruling, a number of subsequent court decisions would hold that Title VII permitted the preferential treatment of minorities and women in hiring and promotion decisions (but not in decisions affecting layoffs) if such treatment were part of an affirmative-action plan designed to increase the employment of previously excluded or underrepresented groups. Perhaps the most important of these decisions came in the case of *United Steelworkers of America v. Weber* (443 U.S. 193, 1979). The *Weber* case involved a White, blue-collar worker (Brian F. Weber) who was refused admission to an on-the-job training program at the Kaiser Aluminum Company plant at which he worked, although he had higher seniority than some of the minority workers who were accepted. In an attempt to increase minority representation in its workforce, Kaiser Aluminum had developed two seniority lists, one for Whites and one for Blacks, and it filled its vacancies by selecting persons from the top of each list. Weber filed suit, claiming that the 1964 Civil Rights Act specifically prohibited this use of racial quotas. Although winning at the district court level, Weber lost in the Supreme Court, which claimed that Title VII, though not *requiring* race-conscious affirmative-action preferences in employment, nevertheless *permitted* them if the purpose was to increase the employment of groups previously discriminated against. "It would be ironic indeed," Justice Brennan wrote in the majority decision, "if a law triggered by a nation's concern over centuries of racial injustice and intended to improve the lot of those who had 'been excluded from the American dream for so long' constituted the first legislative prohibition of all voluntary, private, race-conscious efforts to abolish traditional patterns of racial segregation and hierarchy" (Brennan at 443 U.S.:193).

Quota-like employment practices were also upheld by the Court in *Local 28 Sheet Metal Workers International Association v. Equal Employment Opportunity Commission* (478 U.S. 421, 1986), where in a five-to-four decision a lower court ruling was allowed to stand that imposed a race-based quota requirement on a labor union. Similarly, in *United States v. Paradise* (480 U.S. 149, 1987), the Court, in another five-to-four decision, affirmed the constitutionality of a quota system involving the hiring of state police. Gender-based preferences would also be upheld under Title VII in the important case of *Johnson v. Transportation Agency, Santa Clara County* (480 U.S. 616, 1987). In these cases, Belz argues, the Court acknowledged that affirmative action is a prospective policy based on the idea of group rights that aims at achieving racial and gender balance, under the idea of proportional representation that is inherent in the disparate impact theory (Belz, 1991).

The Court's support for affirmative action, however, was tenuous as shown by the many five-to-four decisions, and restrictions were placed on affirmative-action programs in a number of areas. In *Firefighters Local Union No. 1794 v. Stotts* (467 U.S. 561, 1984), for instance, the Court considered the validity of a district court order modifying the arrangements of a consent decree for hiring and promoting Black firefighters in Memphis. The decree attempted to protect newly hired Black workers from the "last hired, first fired" layoff policy by ruling that the use of the seniority system was illegitimate. The Supreme Court found the district court in violation of Title VII and modified the consent decree. A similar action occurred in *Wygant v. Jackson Board of Education* (476 U.S. 267, 1986), where the Court ruled that an affirmative-action plan that protected Black teachers while White teachers with more seniority were being laid off violated Title VII.

### Set-Asides

One form of affirmative-action preference that became popular among state and municipal governments in the mid-1970s was the minority contracting set-aside. Set-aside programs usually involve the reservation of a fixed proportion of public contracting dollars that by law must be spent on the purchase of goods and services provided by minority-owned businesses. Like preferences in hiring, set-asides have been enormously controversial and cries of "reverse discrimination" abound.

The Supreme Court first took up set-asides in the case of *Fullilove v. Klutznick* (448 U.S. 448, 1980), which challenged a provision of a federal law passed during the Carter administration. That provision required that 10 percent of federal funds allocated to state and local governments for public works projects be used to purchase goods and services from companies owned by members of six specified minority groups. The Court held in this case that the federal set-aside law did not violate the equal protection provisions of the federal Constitution on the grounds that the set-aside provision was a legitimate remedy for present competitive disadvantages resulting from past illegal discrimination.

Nine years later, however, in *Richmond City v. J.A. Croson Co.* (488 U.S. 469, 1989), the Court, again reflecting the influence of the Reagan-era appointees, held that racial classifications within state and local set-aside programs were inherently suspect and were to be subject to the most searching standard of constitutional review ("strict scrutiny") under the equal protection provisions of the Fourteenth Amendment. By a six-to-three vote, the Court invalidated the Richmond City Council's set-aside plan that had required contractors to subcontract at least 30 percent of the dollar value of contracts to minority-owned businesses.

The following year, however, in *Metro Broadcasting Inc. v. Federal Communications Commission* (110 S.Ct. 2997, 1990), the Court ruled constitutional a policy developed by the Federal Communications Commission that granted preferences in the purchase of broadcast licenses to minority-controlled firms. In a five-to-four decision, the Court held that, in this case, the race-based classification was "benign" in intent, and as such should not be subject to the "strict scrutiny" standard of constitutional review. Rather, an intermediate level of scrutiny was held to be appropriate. In this case, the state's objective of enhancing broadcast diversity was important enough, the Court majority declared, to validate the state's use of an otherwise suspect racial classification.

Five years later, however, in *Adarand Contractors Inc. v. Pena* (515 U.S. 200, 1995), the Court ruled that however benign in intent, affirmative-action programs that draw racial classifications, even those at the federal level, *are* subject to strict scrutiny. To critics, at least, it seemed that the Court had abruptly turned its back on settled law, particularly in regard to its earlier decisions affirming racial preferences at the federal level in *Metro Broadcasting* and *Fullilove*. Justice Clarence Thomas, a Bush appointee, the only Black on the Court, and a long-time foe of racial preferences of all kinds, issued his concurring opinion defending the color-blind principle of racial justice:

That these programs may have been motivated, in part, by good intentions, cannot provide refuge from the principle that under our Constitution, the government may not make distinctions on the basis of race. As far as the Constitution is concerned, it is irrelevant whether a government's racial classifications are drawn by those who wish to oppress a race or by those who have a sincere desire to help those thought to be disadvantaged (515 U.S. at 240, Thomas concurring opinion).

## Education

Equally important—and equally controversial—were court cases dealing with affirmative action in higher education. Beginning in the late 1960s, many universities and professional schools began admitting minority students, particularly Blacks and Hispanics, with substantially lower grades and lower scores on standardized tests than White students. Many White students charged "reverse discrimination," and some brought suit in federal court, claiming that affirmative action in higher education was a violation of Title VI of the 1964 Civil Rights Act, as well as of the equal protection provisions of the U.S. Constitution.

The first of these cases to come before the Court was *DeFunis v. Odegaard* (416 U.S. 312, 1974), involving a White applicant, Marco DeFunis, who had applied for admission to the law school of the University of Washington. DeFunis's application for admission had originally been rejected, despite the fact that lower-scoring minority students had been admitted under a special admissions procedure. The procedure sorted applicants into two race-based applicant pools, with a much less rigorous standard applied to the minority group. Although the Supreme Court initially accepted the case and heard oral arguments, it finally decided to declare the case moot because DeFunis had been accepted to the University of Washington law school, by order of a lower court, and was nearing completion of his studies. Thus the decision in the case would have had no effect on him. *DeFunis* was an important case, however, because of a dissenting opinion against the decision to moot by Justice William O. Douglas. Although generally considered the Court's leading liberal theorist, Douglas in his dissent offered a ringing denunciation of race-based admissions policies. Despite their benign intent, Douglas claimed, such policies were stigmatizing to minority groups by suggesting that minorities "cannot make it on their individual merit." That, he said, "is a stamp of inferiority that a state is not permitted to place on any lawyer" (Dworkin, 1977:63-83).

Two years after the decision to moot in *DeFunis*, the Court again took up the issue of special preferences in higher education in the case of *Regents of the University of California v. Bakke* (438 U.S. 265, 1978). Alan P.

Bakke, a 32-year-old White mechanical engineer, had twice sought admission to the University of California at Davis Medical School. Both times he was rejected, despite the fact that his college grade point average and his score on the Medical College Admission Test were substantially higher than those of most of the minority students who were accepted. Because Davis filled 16 of its 100 entering slots through a special admissions program open only to minorities, Bakke claimed that he was a victim of reverse discrimination. Minority applicants, his lawyers pointed out, were permitted to compete for all of the 100 seats in the entering class, while Whites could only compete for the 84 "regular" seats specifically open to them. In a long-awaited decision, written by Justice Lewis Powell, the Court struck down the preferential admissions program at Davis as incompatible with the Fourteenth Amendment's Equal Protection Clause, and ordered Bakke admitted. However, although ruling against Davis's explicit racial-quota system, Powell declared, in his opinion, that admissions officers in institutions such as the Davis medical school could take race into account as one of many "plus" factors designed to enhance the diversity of a school's student body.

The *Bakke* case was, in many ways, the most publicized of all the affirmative-action cases to come before the U.S. Supreme Court, and probably generated more heated commentary than any other case. It dealt with an issue that was even more contentious than affirmative action in employment, and one that drove the deepest wedge between traditionally liberal Jewish groups (most of which supported Bakke's position) and Black groups (most of which supported the position of the University of California at Davis Medical School). Justice Powell's decision was seen in many quarters as a Solomonic compromise, with something good in it for each side. To the disappointment of affirmative-action critics, however, the decision seemed to have little effect in changing the affirmative-action policies at most universities and professional schools, which continued to aggressively recruit and admit minority students who in some cases had lower grades and test scores than White students.

Affirmative action in higher education continued to suffer major setbacks during the 1990s. Borrowing from the activist strategy of civil rights groups, two public interest law firms, the Center for Individual Rights (CIR) and the Institute of Justice, recruited aggrieved White students to file reverse discrimination suits against institutions of higher learning. In 1995, the CIR litigated *Hopwood v. Texas* (78 F.3d 932 Fifth Circuit, 1995), the first high-profile, higher education, affirmative-action case since *Bakke*. Cheryl Hopwood, a White woman from a disadvantaged background, was denied admission to the University of Texas Law School, despite having higher test scores and grades than some of the Blacks and Mexicans admitted that year. Hopwood and three White males who were also denied admission brought a racial discrimination suit against the law school. Although the plaintiffs lost in a lower court decision, they won their case when it reached the U.S. Court of Appeals for the Fifth Circuit, which ruled in Hopwood's favor. *Hopwood* became legally binding in the states located in the Fifth Circuit region (Louisiana, Mississippi, and Texas), after the Supreme Court refused to review the case. The *Hopwood* decision has encouraged similar suits in other states.

Until 1997, the higher education cases involved disappointed applicants to professional schools. But a new twist was introduced in 1997 when two White undergraduates, Jennifer Gratz and Patrick Hamacher, filed racial discrimination suits against the University of Michigan and its administrators alleging discrimination in the university's undergraduate program. At roughly the same time, White applicant Barbara Grutter sued the University of Michigan Law School, also charging reverse discrimination. In 1998, the cases of *Gratz and Hamacher v. University of Michigan* and *Grutter v. Michigan* were combined into a class-action suit that is still pending before Michigan's U.S. District Court. Adverse decisions in the Michigan cases, in conjunction with the direct and indirect impact of California's antiaffirmative-action initiative Proposition 209, could effectively eliminate race-conscious affirmative action in higher education. Already the effects of the ballot initiatives and court cases have been felt in California and Texas, where fewer minority students have applied to state universities, and fewer have been admitted to the flagship universities.

## THE POLITICAL MILIEU OF AFFIRMATIVE ACTION

In the 1980s and 1990s, affirmative action became more politicized than ever as politicians began to view it as an issue that could win them votes. Antiaffirmative action sentiments were perhaps most visible in the 1990 North Carolina senatorial race between the Black Democrat Harvey Gantt and the Republican incumbent Jesse Helms (Applebome, 1990). During the last week of the campaign, while trailing Gantt in the polls, Helms aired a series of antiaffirmative-action television commercials, which were likely responsible for his victory. The commercial that got the most attention nationally featured the hands of a White male crumbling a job application, with the voice-over stating that although the White applicant needed the job, it was given to a lesser qualified minority because of a racial preference. The advertisement accused Harvey Gantt and Massachusetts Senator Ted Kennedy of favoring racial quotas. A second Helms advertisement showed a broadcasting station that Gantt had purchased through a federal set-aside program, then sold some weeks later to a White businessman for a huge profit. The voice-over explained how the minority community was outraged by the sale, but that the deal made Gantt a millionaire. Postelection voter surveys attributed Gantt's defeat to increased turnout among Whites spurred to vote by Helm's anti-affirmative-action advertisements.

The frustration of Whites over affirmative-action programs was also given credit for former Klansman David Duke's ability to win 55 percent of the White vote in Louisiana's 1991 gubernatorial race. Three years earlier, Duke won 44 percent of the vote in his senatorial campaign. According to political analyst Gary Esolen, Duke's message was always the same:

> Why do reporters and politicians pick on me and say hateful things about me when anyone can see I'm a nice guy and reasonable fellow? Besides, even if I did say and do extreme things once or twice that's all over with now.
>
> The real reason they pick on me is that they are afraid of my message on the issues, which is that affirmative action has gone too far and become racism in the reverse, the Black underclass is dragging us down, we can't afford welfare, and it's time White people had some rights again (Esolen, 1992:137-138).

Polling data suggest that Duke's antiaffirmative-action message resonated very well among Whites in Louisiana.

A development of even greater national significance occurred in California in 1995, when two academics, Glynn Custred and Thomas Wood, started the California Civil Rights Initiative (CCRI), a ballot proposal outlawing government-sponsored racial preferences, which became Proposition 209. When it was passed in 1996, the law was immediately challenged by the American Civil Liberties Union, but was upheld by decisions handed down in 1997 by the U.S. Ninth Circuit Court of Appeals and the U.S. Supreme Court.

Control of the political agenda and of the language used in the initiative was an important factor in the passage of Proposition 209—i.e., "the state shall not discriminate against or grant preferential treatment to any individual or group on the basis of race, sex, color, ethnicity, or national origin in the operation of public employment, public education, or public contracting" (California Constitution, Article I, Section 31). In 1998, a similarly worded initiative passed in the state of Washington. Although one could speculate that White Californians' fears about the state's increasingly racially diverse population—a 43 percent minority population in 1990—was a driving force behind the passage of Proposition 209, this would not explain the outcome in Washington where the minority population was only 13 percent; rather, the language of these two ballot initiatives seems to have been a key factor in their passage.

In Houston, Texas, supporters of the city's various affirmative-action programs were able to word the initiative and frame the issue in a manner more favorable to their cause, so that voters voted on whether they wanted to dismantle all affirmative-action programs for women and other minorities, rather than whether they wanted to end all racial or gender discrimination. With the question so-framed, a clear majority of voters voted not to eliminate affirmative action. In the two states where affirmative-action opponents controlled the agenda, voters voted against state supported "discrimination " and "preferential treatment" rather than for affirmative action. The key difference between the measures that passed and the one that failed seems to have been wording.

Politicians, scholars, and the media largely control how affirmative action is presented to the public and debated. Hochschild (1999:619-620) argues that "in the current American racial culture, affirmative action is more important to participants in the policy debate as a weapon with which to attack enemies in order to win some other battle than as an issue in and for itself." Political actors, she argues, "find affirmative action an immensely valuable issue over which to debate, and therefore have little desire to figure out just how it operates" (Hochschild, 1999:629). These political actors often speak and act as if they know what the American people think about affirmative action. Research shows, however, that the actual positions that Americans hold about affirmative action are often more complex and less polarized than one would discern from the rhetoric of public debate.

## MEASURING PUBLIC SUPPORT FOR AFFIRMATIVE ACTION

It is generally believed that White Americans oppose, whereas Blacks enthusiastically embrace, affirmative-action programs. Racial polarization is seen as characterizing the dominant views of both groups, and there are survey data to support this view. After years of focusing on polarization between Whites and Blacks, however, survey researchers have begun to realize that public opinion on the issue is highly sensitive to question wording and question context. Attitudes about affirmative action often depend on how survey questions are framed, the answer choices that respondents are given, and the context of the questions. It is how we define and measure support for affirmative-action policy that determines, to a large extent, what we eventually find (Adkins, 1996; Gamson and Modigliani, 1987; Kinder and Sanders, 1990, 1996; Schuman et al., 1997; Sigelman and Welch, 1991:144; Steeh and Krysan, 1996; Stoker, 1997; Swain et al., 2000). Respondents' answers to direct questions about their support of, or opposition to, affirmative action tell little about the types of public policies that a given individual will endorse. In fact,

Norman (1995) observed that respondents who say they oppose affirmative action may actually support more types of affirmative-action programs than a person who identifies himself as an affirmative-action supporter may.

Greater awareness of the sensitivity of affirmative-action questions to framing and contextual problems has led some researchers to conclude that validity could be greatly improved by abandoning use of the term "affirmative action" and, instead, describing the content of specific policies (Adkins, 1996; Fine 1992; Steeh and Krysan, 1996). Because of the problem of context and question framing, much of the survey data on public attitudes in this area is difficult to interpret.

Stoker (1997), in particular, has argued that survey questions that generalize across, or ignore, the context in which affirmative-action programs are implemented greatly misrepresent public opinion on the issue. The context of a question can include the reason why the program was adopted, the location of the question in the survey, and what preceded it. In describing a series of affirmative-action scenarios for people to respond to, Stoker provided either no context to justify the implementation of racial quotas or two rationales—underrepresentation of minorities and proven discrimination by a given company:

Question 1: No Context
*Do you think that large companies should be required to give a certain number of jobs to Blacks or should the government stay out of this?*

Question 2: Underrepresentation Context
**There are some large companies where Blacks are underrepresented.** *. . . Do you think that these large companies should be required to give a certain number of jobs to Blacks, or should the government stay out of this?*

Question 3: Proven Discrimination Context
**There are some large companies with employment policies that discriminate against Blacks.** *. . . Do you think these large companies should be required to give a certain number of jobs to Blacks, or should the government stay out of this?*

Stoker found considerable support for compensatory measures based on the proven discrimination scenario; she also notes that proven discrimination is the only instance for which the Supreme Court in recent years has endorsed the use of quotas.

White support for racial quotas was weakest on Question 2, where quotas are being used to remedy underrepresentation. Organizational leaders, college presidents, corporate executives, and state and local governments often point to the underrepresentation of minorities as their justification for implementing or expanding affirmative-action measures. But while diversifying the workplace is a value that many corporations, public bodies, and academic institutions share, many White Americans do not believe that this is a sufficient justification for racial quotas. Stoker's data suggest that societal elites must develop a more compelling reason to justify preferential treatment than simply the underrepresentation of minorities if they hope to win greater public support.

Sniderman and Piazza (1993) conclude that dislike of affirmative-action policies is causing some Whites to dislike Blacks. They found that when asked the question below before being asked questions about Black stereotypes, White respondents were more likely to stereotype Blacks negatively than a similar group who encountered the stereotype questions first.

*In a nearby state, an effort is being made to increase dramatically the number of Blacks working in state government. This means that a large number of jobs will be reserved for Blacks, even if their scores on merit exams are lower than those of Whites who are turned down for the jobs. Do you favor or oppose this policy?*

The context and the wording of Sniderman and Piazza's question also show, however, that respondents were asked about two forms of affirmative action that are now illegal: race norming, in which the test scores of Blacks are compared only to the scores of other Blacks, and quotas as a remedy for underrepresentation. White respondents were reacting negatively to clearly unfair public policies and practices that the U.S. Supreme Court declared unconstitutional years ago and that Congress banned with its passage of the 1991 Civil Rights Act. Many White Americans who are incensed by such policies are unaware that they are illegal and, in fact, probably think that quotas are an essential part of affirmative-action programs. Researchers should be aware that widely reported survey responses to questions about aspects of affirmative-action policy that may actually have changed can reinforce false notions about affirmative action and add to the public's confusion and misconceptions about the policy.

Survey questions that elicit the greatest degree of racial polarization are sensitive to framing and contextual issues that go beyond question wording. For instance, responses to the questions below are no doubt influenced by the inclusion of the words "past discrimination" and the differential meanings that these words hold for different Americans depending on their backgrounds, ages, and current events at the time. Racial polarization was particularly evident in responses to questions asked in the late 1970s, in the wake of two 1978 Supreme Court decisions: the

*Bakke* decision and the decision not to review a lower court ruling supporting American Telephone and Telegraph Company's affirmative-action program against charges of reverse discrimination (Johnson, 1983).

> *(1) Some people say that because of past discrimination against Blacks, preference in hiring and promotion should be given to Blacks. Others say that preferential hiring and promotion of Blacks is wrong because it gives Blacks advantages they haven't earned. What about your opinion—are you for or against preferential hiring and promotion of Blacks?*

> *(2) Some people say that because of past discrimination, it is sometimes necessary for colleges and universities to reserve openings for Blacks and other students. Others oppose quotas because they give to Blacks advantages that they haven't earned. What about your opinion—are you for or against quotas to admit Black students?*

> *(3) After years of discrimination, is it only fair to set up special programs to make sure that women and minorities are given every chance to have equal opportunities in employment and education?*

To Question 1, 85 percent of Whites and 32 percent of Blacks opposed preferential treatment. To Question 2, 70 percent of Whites and 20 percent of Blacks opposed quotas. All three questions make reference to past discrimination; but the respondent is left to infer independently whether the question is about slavery or blatant pre-Civil Rights discrimination. Blacks' support is greatest for Question 3; 91 percent agree that after years of discrimination, it's only fair to set up special programs for women and minorities (Johnson, 1983:302). Racial polarization is much less evident, however, on a Gallup poll question (*Gallup Index*, 1977) asked a year earlier.

> *Some people say that to make up for past discrimination, women and members of minority groups should be given preferential treatment in getting jobs and places in college. Others say that ability, as determined by test scores, should be the main consideration. Which point comes closest to how you feel on this matter?*

Eighty-three percent of White respondents and 64 percent of Black respondents said that ability, as determined by test scores, should be the main consideration in employment and college admissions decisions. In a different poll, an interesting pattern appeared in the responses of Black leaders and the general public. In response to a question asking whether preferential treatment or ability should be used in obtaining jobs and college placement, 77 percent of Black leaders endorsed preferential treatment, while only 23 percent of the Black public did (Lichter, 1985).

Examination of a range of survey questions shows that Whites and Blacks are not as polarized as is commonly believed, and in some policy areas they seem to be moving more toward consensus. Blacks are by no means enthusiastic supporters of racial preferences, and in recent years have given affirmative action a less than ringing endorsement. They have strongly endorsed self-help initiatives. As many as 70 percent of Blacks, for instance, agreed with the majority of Whites that Blacks should pull themselves up as other groups have done (Sniderman and Carmines, 1997).

> The Irish, the Italians, and the Jews and many other minorities overcame prejudice and worked their way up. Blacks should do the same without any special favors.

Similarly, 48 percent of Blacks agreed with 53 percent of Whites on a 1997 Joint Center for Political and Economic Studies (JCPS) question that stated, "Blacks who can't get ahead in the U.S. are mostly responsible for their own condition." Fifty-nine percent of Black Republicans and 57 percent of Blacks making more than $60,000 a year agreed with the majority of Whites on this question (Bositis 1997a, 1997b).

The lack of Blacks' enthusiasm for affirmative action reveals itself on a question asked in 1984 by the National Black Election Study (NBES). Only 43 percent of Blacks agreed with the statement:

> Because of past discrimination, minorities should be given special consideration when decisions are made about hiring applicants.

On a related NBES question stating that "job applicants should be judged solely on the basis of test scores and other individual qualities," 54 percent of Blacks agreed. The NBES revealed no groundswell of Black support for affirmative-action policies.

When asked in 1988 whether "Blacks and other minorities should receive preference in hiring to makeup for past inequalities," only 48 percent of Blacks agreed; 44 percent disagreed. White and Hispanic disagreement, however, was greater: 85 percent of Whites disagreed (only 10 percent supported preferences), along with 64 percent of Hispanics (31 percent supported preferences). On another question, a majority of the three groups opposed preferential treatment in college admissions. A 1991 *Newsweek* poll showed 72 percent of Whites opposed to preferential treatment in hiring (only 19 percent favored the idea), while Blacks were again almost evenly split, 48 percent against to 42 percent in favor. Similar patterns of ambivalence among Blacks have been seen in other recent polls (Schneider, 1991).

In a 1997 survey commissioned by JCPS, the following question was asked of a random sample of the U.S. population:

*We should make every possible effort to improve the position of Blacks even if it means giving them preferential treatment.*

Of those responding to the survey, almost a majority of Blacks (49 percent to 45 percent) and an overwhelming percentage of Whites (83 percent to 15 percent) opposed preferential treatment of Blacks as a means of improving the group's societal position. A further demographic breakdown showed that a majority of Black baby boomers, Black men, college-educated Blacks, and Blacks earning more than $15,000 per year opposed preferential treatment (Bositis, 1997a).

All respondents, including Blacks, seem to oppose giving a lesser-qualified minority a job over a better-qualified White applicant (Norman, 1995). We asked the following split ballot, random assignment question on the 1996 Princeton Survey:

*Suppose that a company that has few (female/minority/Black) employees were choosing between two people who applied for a job. If both people were equally qualified for the job and one was (a woman/a minority person/a Black person), and the other (a man/was not a minority person/White) do you think the company should hire the (woman/minority person/ Black person), hire the (man/other person/White person), or should they find some other way to choose?*

When "minorities" were mentioned, 82 percent of Whites and 71 percent of Blacks said the company should find some other way to choose. Only 22 percent of Blacks and 12 percent of Whites said that an under-represented minority should be hired. On a follow-up question, 66 percent of the respondents who had favored hiring a qualified minority applicant over a nonminority applicant said that they would not feel the same way if the minority person "was slightly less qualified" than the other person. Consistent with these findings, Norman (1995:49) reports that there is consensus opposition among all Americans to giving a minority applicant a job instead of a better-qualified White, even if the workplace has few minorities; and only 13 percent of women and 22 percent of Blacks approved of such a policy.

The majority of survey respondents agree on certain types of policies designed to ensure equal opportunity in education and job training, provided those policies are open to all who are qualified (Lipset and

Schneider, 1978; Lipset, 1992; December 6-7, 1997, *New York Times*-CBS Poll; Sniderman and Piazza, 1993; Sniderman and Carmines, 1997). Whites are generally not supportive of programs designed exclusively for Blacks and other racial minorities, though they are somewhat more amenable to programs that help women. Self-interest could obviously be a factor here, though White women are not among affirmative action's strongest supporters.

Although White racism may be a factor in some White opposition to preferential treatment of racial minorities, there are principled reasons that might account for some of their behaviors (Sniderman and Piazza, 1993; Sniderman and Carmines, 1997). Perhaps equal opportunity programs and job-training programs garner more support because they are racially inclusive and available to all who are disadvantaged. Similarly, group preferences in college and university admissions—e.g., for athletes, musicians, and offspring of alumni—garner significant White support because they are not restrictive.

Knowledge of Americans' unease with racial preference programs has led some scholars to call for race-neutral public policies, based on the assumption that a consensus exists for such programs, or can be built where it is absent (Kahlenberg, 1996; Wilson, 1980, 1987, 1996). Race-neutral programs are attractive because they are not as vulnerable as racial preference programs to judicial attacks and can survive the test of "strict scrutiny" under the Fourteenth Amendment's Equal Protection Clause. However, it has been pointed out that race-neutral programs will not necessarily lead to the kind of diversified workforce and university campuses that many people desire (Bok and Bowen, 1998; Appiah and Gutmann, 1996; Glazer, 1995). To remove race differentials purported to be inherent in standardized tests, social scientists such as William Julius Wilson (1999) argue in favor of flexible merit-based criteria in college admissions that would de-emphasize standardized test scores and take into consideration some combination of race and class. In addition, Wilson is in favor of comprehensive policies that would embrace all races. He also favors a shift in national focus by referring to "affirmative opportunity" programs rather than the ambiguous term "affirmative action." Race-neutral programs are part of a set of unresolved issues that must be debated at greater length by those concerned with racial justice and racial harmony in America.

## CONSENSUS ON RACE, CLASS, AND COLLEGE ADMISSIONS

Racial consensus among ordinary Americans—but not among elites—can be found in the highly contentious area of college admissions. Survey data indicate that most Americans reject the use of race as a primary criterion in college and university admissions. Their rejection of racial preferences, however, does not indicate that they believe that admission to colleges and universities should be automatically awarded to the highest-scoring students. Americans seem to want a system flexible enough to allow consideration of the circumstances that a person has had to overcome to achieve, whatever scores are presented to the admissions committee. Under some conditions, Americans will support the admission of a less-prepared student who has had to overcome severe hardship, even if that means that a member of their own racial group loses out.

Using a vignette embedded in a national survey, Swain et al. (2000) randomly assigned the races and genders of two hypothetical students so that 16 possible combinations of race and gender were presented to equal numbers of respondents randomly assigned to answer the question below:[1]

> *Please suppose that a state university is deciding between two high school seniors who have applied for admission. I will read you a brief description of these two students. Then I will ask you to decide, if the college has space for only one more student, which of these do you think they should admit?" The interviewer then explains that "the first student attends a local public high school where [he or she] has maintained a B average. [He or she] is a [Black or White] student from a low-income family and has held a job throughout high school to help support [his or her] family. [He or she] scored slightly below average on [his or her] college admission tests. The second student attends a well-respected private school, where [he or she] has been an A student. [He or she] comes from a prominent [White or Black] family and has spent two summers studying abroad. [He or she] scored well on [his or her] college admission tests." The interviewer next asks, "Based on what I have told you about these two students, which one do you think the college should admit?" After respondents have given their answer, they are asked "Regardless of who you think should be admitted, which student do you think the college would probably admit?*

Swain, Rodgers, and Silverman found that a majority of respondents favored admission of the B student whenever the two students were from

---

[1]The data for this vignette come from a national survey of English-speaking adults administered during the summer and fall of 1996 by Response Analysis of Princeton, New Jersey, that the lead author commissioned. A total of 1,875 respondents were interviewed as part of a random-digit telephone survey, consisting of 1,070 adults, plus a targeted second sample of 805 African Americans. For additional information about this vignette and the statistical tests performed, see Swain et al. (2000).

the same racial group. The strongest support for the B student occurred when both students were White. If both students were Black a majority of respondents favored the B student, but by a smaller margin. In a mixed-race condition, support for the B student dropped; indeed, a majority of White respondents then favored a Black A student over a White B student, with this preference being strongest among highly educated Whites. Blacks favored the B student, even in the mixed-race situation in which the A student was Black, and the B student was White; and their support increased with education. Whites with a high school education or less preferred the B student by a margin of 21 to 16 (57 percent). On the other hand, 81 percent of White college graduates favored the Black A student over the White B student.

Despite their own preferences, the majority of respondents (around 90 percent in the same-race conditions and 80 percent in the mixed-race conditions) believed that the institution would select the A student. In the mixed-race condition, however, about 20 percent of respondents of each race believed that a B student of the opposite race would be admitted over an A student of their racial group. The belief that the A student would be admitted over the B student was even stronger among the B student's supporters—i.e., the majority of respondents did not expect the institution to operate in a manner that they considered just. Whites and Blacks agreed on this matter.

The college admissions vignette suggests that people want university officials to exercise some flexibility in defining merit criteria, and they want a system that creates opportunities for the disadvantaged. The majority do not believe that diversity enhancement is a compelling reason for racial preferences in college admissions, or that being Black is equivalent to being disadvantaged. A December 1997 *New York Times*-CBS poll of a random sample of the U.S. population found consensus on the items below:

> *Suppose a White student and a Black student are equally qualified, but a college can admit only one of them. Do you think the college should admit the Black student in order to achieve more racial balance in the college, or do you think racial balance should not be a factor?"*

Of those expressing a view, 77 percent of Whites and 72 percent of Blacks said that the race of the student should not be a factor. Clearly, these people felt that the institution should find some other way to choose. For them, perhaps, flipping a coin would be better than choosing students based on race.

A second question, about students with similar backgrounds and unequal qualifications, met with a similar response:

> *Suppose there is a White student who has an A average and a Black student who has a B average, and the students are equal in every other way, but a college can admit only one of them. Do you think the college should admit the Black student in order to achieve more racial balance, or do you think that racial balance should not be a factor?*

Among those expressing an opinion, a decisive majority of both races (more than 75 percent of Blacks and more than 90 percent of Whites) said that the A student should be admitted over the B student.

For a related question, opinions changed when evidence was brought to bear that showed achievement despite unequal starting points:

> *In general, in hiring, promoting, and college admissions, do you think that it is a good idea or a poor idea to select a person from a poor family over a person from a middle-class or rich family if the person from the poor family and the person from the rich family are equally qualified?*

Fifty-three percent of Whites and 65 percent of Blacks said that it was a good idea. Clearly, Whites and Blacks can agree on helping the disadvantaged in many important situations; this has obvious implications for public policies.

Fifty-nine percent of White respondents in the NYT-CBS Poll favored special educational programs to help minorities compete more effectively for college admissions, 64 percent favored job-training programs for minorities in industries where they were underrepresented, and 65 percent endorsed laws to protect minorities against racial discrimination. However, Whites disagreed with Blacks about the continued need for affirmative-action programs. When the term, "affirmative action" was used in the question, a majority of Whites wanted affirmative action ended (13 percent) or phased out over the next few years (45 percent). The majority of Blacks (80 percent, compared to 35 percent of Whites) felt that affirmative-action programs and racial preferences are needed to ensure diversity and to make up for past discrimination. Still, 67 percent of Blacks agreed with 81 percent of Whites that as a result of affirmative-action policies, less qualified individuals are sometimes hired and admitted to colleges.

The responses to the Swain, Rodgers, and Silverman college admissions vignette suggests that many Americans are committed to principles that allow for a substantially broader definition of merit than that used by the leading protagonists in the affirmative-action debate. That broader definition of merit includes consideration of the obstacles and hurdles that a given person has had to overcome to achieve the scores presented to the admissions committee. Although a majority of Americans seem to agree that a hardworking underdog deserves a break, they clearly oppose the use of race even as a tiebreaker between two similarly advantaged persons. This agreement between the races might have been overlooked had the researchers simply asked respondents their views of affirmative action. Given such agreement, college and university admissions officials may have more latitude than many now assume. Americans seem to be asking them to take into consideration more factors than academic preparation alone. At the same time, neither Whites nor Blacks believe that racial preferences should play a significant role in college admissions decisions. This agreement might also have been overlooked if the authors had used code words in the vignette or asked about preferential treatment of the B student; most likely, a majority of Whites and a plurality of Blacks would have said no.

Consistent with other studies, the above data suggest that Americans care about helping those disadvantaged who try to help themselves. Americans seem to want to live in a country where hardworking, disciplined, and self-reliant people can rise above their initial station in life. Despite evidence that some middle-class Blacks have become cynical about the ideal of the American Dream (Hochschild, 1995), the more highly educated Black respondents in the Swain, Rodgers, and Silverman study seemed eager to help make the dream a reality for the disadvantaged, and supported the B student regardless of the B student's race.

Americans can agree on the types of policies that they want for their children. In a national poll geared exclusively to children's issues, Bositis (1997b) found Whites, Blacks, and Hispanics in agreement on several important issues. Clear majorities of each group supported universal healthcare for children, opposed "gangsta rap," and even endorsed then-House Speaker Newt Gingrich's controversial proposal for the government to build orphanages for children from dangerous or unhealthy homes. The poll, however, found a significant generational gap between old and young for both Whites and Blacks; younger people were more supportive of the proposals than older people. Likewise, younger people endorsed school vouchers and governmental spending on education to a greater degree than older people. Interestingly, Blacks and Hispanics were more supportive than Whites of government vouchers for parents to send their children to "the public, private, or parochial school of choice."

Although survey data reveal considerable agreement between Whites and Blacks, and seem to support a convergence hypothesis, race-of-interviewer effects might arguably account for some of the changes reported in the attitudes of Blacks. Since 1964, for example, the percentage of Blacks interviewing Blacks in the NBES has dropped significantly. Anderson et al. (1988a, 1988b) have shown that some questions are susceptible to race-of-interviewer effects, especially questions on government assistance to minorities. Race-of-interviewer effects do not, however, account for all of it; agreement and convergence has been seen even in polls where the race of interviewer was matched to the respondent (Bositis, 1997a, 1997b; 1996 Princeton National Survey). The preponderance of data indicates a non-trivial amount of agreement among Black and White respondents on a host of important issues that go beyond those mentioned in this paper. This agreement can and should be used to help shape public policies in ways that ensure maximum support among all Americans.

## WHY RACIAL DISAGREEMENT OCCURS

When Whites and Blacks disagree about affirmative-action issues, some of their differences can be explained by the differing conceptual schemas that they use, as well as divergent framing effects that cause groups to see the world through different lenses. In psychology, a schema is a cognitive structure of prior learning and knowledge that draws on past experience to guide the processing of new information and the retrieval of stored memories (Conover and Feldman, 1984:96). Such schemas can be content-specific and based on categories such as race, sex, and social class. Cognitive schemas of this type color how a person views the world. For a White person, the schema used to interpret affirmative action might include direct experience with reverse discrimination, as well as prejudicial observations about minorities based on stereotypes. Awareness of racial discrimination against Blacks may not be on the radar screen of the average White American. A Black person's schema, on the other hand, may be constructed around individual and group experiences with overt discrimination.

Blacks in focus groups commissioned in 1995 never defined affirmative action in terms of preferential treatment; and when they discussed quotas, they used the term differently than Whites and members of most other groups. For them, quotas were restrictions used to limit the number of minorities in a given setting. A Black male in Edison, New Jersey, commented that employment quotas make sure that "only a certain number of Blacks can succeed, or benefit from affirmative action, when maybe there's a whole cluster of people that are qualified. Maybe affirmative action says . . . you have to have three . . . [Blacks]. What about the rest of those people?" To them, the possibility remained strong that qualified Blacks will be overlooked once a certain threshold has been reached by a given institution (Swain et al., 2001).

Discussions of discrimination dominated the affirmative-action discourse in these focus groups, with several Blacks viewing affirmative action as the only, albeit flawed, way to combat the continuing problem of racial bias. Whites, not seeing the extent of the continuing discrimination against Blacks, or not really understanding the links that Blacks make between affirmative action and protection against bias, see affirmative action as reverse discrimination (Gamson and Modigliani, 1987; Gamson, 1991). Different cognitive schemas and the internalization of different ways of framing the problem to be addressed may thus help to explain continued racial polarization in this area.

Perhaps an even greater consensus among Americans could be forged if Whites were made aware of the nature and extent of racial discrimination that Blacks experience. Highly publicized racist incidents and blatantly discriminatory practices show that overt racial discrimination has not been eliminated from the American scene and that it crops up in the unlikeliest places. Most Whites do not observe overt discrimination as a matter of course, unless they have been sensitized to something made highly visible, such as the frequency with which Black motorists are interrogated by the police, something they have witnessed or had their attention drawn to. Blacks and other racially identifiable minorities are exposed to and see more racial discrimination than White Americans do. It is the differential experiences with discrimination that cause some disagreement among Whites and Blacks about the need for certain types of public policies. Thus, their vastly different perceptions make it difficult for the two groups to communicate.

One thing that might help close the gap in perception is studies that can identify and expose hidden racism and discrimination in housing, employment, police actions, and college admissions. Such studies can heighten public awareness of the pervasiveness of discrimination and remove one of the sources of disagreement between Whites and Blacks— their assessments of the amount of discrimination minorities face in everyday life. The implementation of more audit studies, in which similarly matched Whites and minorities test the fairness of the system by applying for housing, jobs, apartments, etc., is one possible solution. If more Whites are sensitized to the discrimination that Blacks and other minorities confront, their sense of fairness may lead them to support increased enforcement of antidiscrimination laws. Given existing congressional attitudes toward funding government audits, it may be necessary for private foundations to step in to fund these studies. More evidence of documented discrimination collected from government- and privately financed audit studies could be used to pressure Congress to adequately fund the agencies charged with monitoring discrimination. Moreover, greater punitive damages against companies and institutions that engage in discriminatory actions would be helpful as a deterrent. Of course, this will not totally alleviate the problem, but increased public awareness and pressure could lead to increased funding for agencies like EEOC. Increased awareness and pressure could also lead to changes in individual behavior, which might be cumulative over time.

## SUMMARY AND CONCLUSION

Affirmative action is a complicated national issue, and there are no easy answers. The issue has historically been, and continues to be, plagued by ambiguity surrounding the concept and by the ways in which the various policies have been implemented. Confusion also stems from factors including the self-serving interpretations of politicians and inaccurate media portrayals. Government officials who rely on public-opinion polls to guide them in their decisions about affirmative-action programs need to exercise caution in how they interpret survey results. It is grossly inaccurate to conclude that racial polarization characterizes the opinions of most Americans on affirmative-action and related issues. How Americans feel about affirmative-action programs depends on a number of factors, including who the beneficiaries of the program are and whether the program was adopted to address proven discrimination. Neither Whites nor Blacks are enthusiastic supporters of racial preference programs; however, both groups favor creating opportunities and helping disadvantaged people. Agreement and consensus among Americans on affirmative action-related issues are detected most readily when respondents to national surveys are presented with clear-cut questions and concrete examples that allow them to decide among choices that they understand. Government officials and public-policy makers should consider the identification and expansion of areas of consensus and agreement among racial groups as part of their official mandates. Racial harmony is a goal worth striving for. Our society is becoming increasingly racially diverse. To achieve any measurable success in race relations, compromise, consensus building, and open discussion are essential as we enter the twenty-first century.

## ACKNOWLEDGMENTS

The Mellon Foundation, the Smith-Richardson Foundation, the Sloan Foundation, and the National Science Foundation SBR-9357951 supported the 1996 Princeton Survey and 1995 focus groups. I am also indebted to the Center for Advanced Study in the Behavioral Sciences and many of its 1997-1998 visiting scholars. In addition, I wish to thank Jennifer Hochschild and Neil Smelser for commenting on an earlier draft of this paper.

# REFERENCES

Adkins, R.
  1996  Affirmative action and public opinion polls, in *Race Versus Class: The New Affirmative Action Debate*, C. Swain, ed. Baltimore: University Press of America.
Anderson, B., B. Silver, and P. Abramson
  1988a  The effects of race of interviewer on measures of electoral participation by Blacks in SRC national election studies. *Public Opinion Quarterly* 52:53-83.
  1988b  The effects of race of interviewer on race-related attitudes of Black respondents in SRC/CPS national election studies. *Public Opinion Quarterly* 52:289-324.
Appiah, A., and A. Gutmann
  1996  *Color Consciousness: The Political Morality of Race.* Princeton: Princeton University Press.
Applebome, P.
  1990  Helms kindled anger in the campaign, and may have set the tone for others. *New York Times* (November 8).
Belz, H.
  1991  *Equality Transformed: A Quarter Century of Affirmative Action.* New Brunswick, N.J.: Transition Books.
Bergman, B.
  1996  *In Defense of Affirmative Action.* New York: Basic Books.
Bok, D., and W. Bowen
  1998  *The Shape of the River.* Princeton: Princeton University Press.
Bositis, D.
  1997a  Joint Center for Political and Economic Studies 1997 National Opinion Poll on Race Relations (June). Washington, D.C.: Joint Center for Political and Economic Studies.
  1997b  Joint Center for Political and Economic Studies 1997 National Poll on Children's Issues (June). Washington, D.C.: Joint Center for Political and Economic Studies.
Conover, P., and S. Feldman
  1984  How people organize the political world: A schematic model. *American Journal of Political Science* 25:617-645.
Delgado, R.
  1996  *The Coming Race War? And Other Apocalyptic Tales of America after Affirmative Action and Welfare.* New York: New York University Press.
Drake, A., and R. Holsworth
  1996  *Affirmative Action and the Stalled Quest for Black Progress.* Urbana, Ill.: University of Illinois Press.
Dworkin, R.
  1977  *DeFunis v. Sweatt.* In *Equality and Preferential Treatment*, M. Cohen, T. Nagel, and T. Scanlon, eds. Princeton: Princeton University Press.
Edley, C., Jr.
  1996  *Not All Black and White: Affirmative Action and American Values.* New York: Hill and Wang.
Esolen, G.
  1992  David Duke's use of television. in *The Emergence of David Duke and the Politics of Race*, D. Rose, ed. Chapel Hill: University of North Carolina Press.
Fine, T.
  1992  The impact of issue framing on public opinion toward affirmative-action programs. *Social Science Journal* 29(3):323-334.
*Gallup Index*
  1977  Report no. 143 (June). Princeton, N.J.: Gallup Organization.

Gamson, W.
1991   *Talking Politics.* New York: Cambridge University Press.
Gamson W., and A. Modigliani
1987   The changing culture of affirmative action. *Research in Political Sociology* 3:137-177.
Glazer, N.
1975   *Affirmative Discrimination.* New York: Basic Books.
1995   Race, not class. *The Wall Street Journal* (April 5):A12.
Graham, H.
1990   *The Civil Rights Era: Origins and Development of National Policy.* New York: Oxford University Press.
Hacker, A.
1992   *Two Nations: Separate, Hostile, Unequal.* New York: Ballantine Books.
Hall, K., ed.
1992   *The Oxford Companion to the Supreme Court of the United States.* New York: Oxford University Press.
Hochschild, J.
1995   *Facing up to the American Dream.* Princeton: Princeton University Press.
1999   Affirmative action as culture warfare. In *The Cultural Territories of Race: White and Black Boundaries*, M. Lamont, ed. Chicago: University of Chicago Press.
Johnson, C.
1983   Black support for affirmative-action programs. *Phylon* XLIV(4).
Johnson, L.
1965   Howard University commencement address. Washington, D.C., June 4.
Kahlenberg, R.
1996   *The Remedy: Class, Race, and Affirmative Action.* New York: Basic Books.
Kinder, D., and L. Sanders
1990   Mimicking political debate with survey questions: The case of affirmative action for Blacks. *Social Cognition* 8(Spring):73-103.
1996   *Divided by Color.* Chicago: University of Chicago Press.
Lichter, L.
1985   Who speaks for Black America? *Public Opinion Quarterly* (August/September):43.
Lipset, S.
1992   Affirmative action and the American creed. *The Wilson Quarterly* 16(Winter):52-62.
Lipset, S., and W. Schneider
1978   The Bakke case: How would it be decided in the court of public opinion. *Public Opinion* (March/April):38-44.
Norman, J.
1995   America's verdict on affirmative action is decidedly mixed. *Public Perspective* 6(June/July):49-52.
Schneider, W.
1991   In job quota debate, advantage GOP. *National Journal* (June 8):1374.
Schuman, H., C. Steeh, L. Bobo, and M. Krysan
1997   *Racial Attitudes in America.* Cambridge, Mass.: Harvard University Press.
Sigelman, L., and S. Welch
1991   *Black American Views of Inequality: The Dream Deferred.* New York: Cambridge Press.
Skrentny, J.
1996   *The Ironies of Affirmative Action: Politics, Culture, and Justice in America.* Chicago: University of Chicago Press.

Smelser, N.
  1999    Problematics of affirmative action: A view from California. In *Dilemma and Promise: Perspectives on Racial Diversity in Higher Education*, E. Lowe, Jr., ed. Princeton: Princeton University Press.
Sniderman, P., and E. Carmines
  1997    *Reaching Beyond Race*. Cambridge, Mass.: Harvard University Press.
Sniderman, P., and T. Piazza
  1993    *The Scar of Race*. Cambridge, Mass.: Harvard University Press.
Steeh, C., and M. Krysan
  1996    Poll trends: Affirmative action and the public, 1971-1995. *Public Opinion Quarterly* 60:128-158.
Stoker, L.
  1997    Understanding Whites' resistance to affirmative action: The role of principled commitments and racial prejudice. In *Perception and Prejudice: Race and Politics in the United States*, J. Hurwitz and M. Peffley, eds. Chicago: University of Chicago Press.
Swain, C., ed.
  1996    *Race Versus Class: The New Affirmative Action Debate*. Baltimore: University Press of America.
Swain, C., K. Greene, and C. Wotipka
  2001    Understanding racial polarization on affirmative action issues: The view from
  forth-   focus groups. In *Color Lines: Affirmative Action, Immigration, and Civil Rights Op-*
  coming   *tions for America*, J. Skrentny, ed. Chicago: University of Chicago Press.
Swain, C., R. Rodgers, and B. Silverman
  2000    Life after Bakke where Whites and Blacks agree: Public support for fairness in educational opportunities. *Harvard BlackLetter Law Journal* 16(Spring).
Thernstrom, S., and A. Thernstrom
  1997    *America in Black and White*. New York: Simon and Schuster.
Wilson, W.
  1980    *The Declining Significance of Race*, 2nd ed. Chicago: University of Chicago Press.
  1987    *The Truly Disadvantaged*. Chicago: University of Chicago Press.
  1996    *When Work Disappears: The World of the New Urban Poor*. New York: Knopf.
  1999    *The Bridge Over the Racial Divide: Rising Inequality and Coalition Politics*. Berkeley, Calif.: University of California Press.

# 12
# Test-Score Trends Along Racial Lines, 1971 to 1996: Popular Culture and Community Academic Standards

*Ronald F. Ferguson*

> Between me and the other world, there is ever an unasked question: unasked by some through feelings of delicacy; by others through the difficulty of rightly framing it. All, nevertheless, flutter round it. They approach me in a half-hesitant sort of way, eye me curiously or compassionately, and then, instead of saying directly, How does it feel to be a problem? they say, I know an excellent colored man in my town; or, I fought at Mechanicsville; or, Do not the Southern outrages make your blood boil? At these, I smile . . . . To the real question, How does it feel to be a problem? I answer seldom a word.

So ends the first paragraph of W.E.B. Du Bois's classic masterpiece, *The Souls of Black Folk* (1903:3). Today, more than 90 years later, Black folk are still considered by some to be a problem. People approach furtively, with the same unasked question. A major reason is that Blacks, Hispanics, American Indians, and some sub-groups among Asians have lower test scores than Whites. This complicates efforts to achieve racial and ethnic balance in selective institutions. If test scores were equal, on average, among the races, there would be little need for current debates about affirmative action in college admissions. There would be no need for race norming on entry examinations for professions such as police and firefighters. Certification testing for new teachers would not so dramatically affect the racial composition of the nation's teacher work-force. The hourly earnings gap among racial groups would be only a fraction of what it is currently. Whether we like it or not, test scores, and the skills they measure, matter.

In an act of substantial wisdom, the U.S. Congress in the late 1960s directed the U.S. Department of Education to create a nationally representative data series with which to make academic proficiency comparisons across age, gender, race/ethnicity, and time. The result was the National Assessment of Educational Progress (NAEP), administered by the Educational Testing Service (ETS) under contract with the National Center for Education Statistics (NCES). Before NAEP, no nationally representative data existed for making test-score comparisons across time for school-aged children. Relying heavily on data from NAEP, this chapter summarizes and offers tentative explanations for trends in reading and math scores among Black, Hispanic, and White children from the early 1970s through 1996. Neither American Indians and Alaska Natives nor Asians and Pacific Islanders was separately identified in NAEP during the period examined here and, therefore, neither of these groups is addressed.

Black-White and Hispanic-White achievement test-score gaps of 30 years ago were neither genetically preordained nor otherwise immutable. The headline is that progress has occurred. Average scores for all groups are higher. Racial disparity is lower. NAEP data show that the Black-White reading-score gap for 17-year-olds narrowed 45 percent since 1971. The Hispanic-White gap narrowed 27 percent since 1975—the first year Hispanics were distinguished separately. The mean gap in math scores has fallen by 33 percent for Blacks and 35 percent for Hispanics, compared with Whites. These and other numbers show that Black and Hispanic children have made important progress since the early 1970s, both absolutely and relative to Whites.[1] For Blacks especially, however, progress has been variable—at times rapid, but at other times halted or even reversed. The reasons for this variability are not clear. Changes in such areas as parenting, curriculum, teacher skill, and class size occur unevenly over time and might well be part of the story. Popular culture might be important as well

The chapter begins with a review of test-score trends for Blacks, Hispanics, and Whites. The middle of the chapter tries to explain the pattern of stops and starts in progress for teenagers, especially Black teenagers. The last third of the chapter reviews some ideas and evidence about how communities of student's peers, parents, and teachers affect education incentives and standards differently for Black youth.

## WHAT ARE THE TRENDS?

To determine trends, the content of the NAEP trend assessments has remained virtually constant since they began for reading in 1971 and for

---

[1]As a check on the accuracy of NAEP trends reviewed, Hedges and Nowell (1998) assembled all other nationally representative data sets since 1965 that have race-specific test scores for Black and White children. Most of these data sets are cross-sectional, not longitudinal. Hedges and Nowell focus on the difference between Blacks' and Whites' scores, measured in standard deviations (SD). Examining the gap across exams administered in different years, they found a narrowing of the gap, just as NAEP does.

math in 1973. The other type of NAEP exam, called the "main assessment," changes to reflect current ideas and priorities. Each trend assessment was repeated every four years through 1990; then the schedule shifted to every two years, with smaller samples. NAEP scores range from 0 to 500. Scores for 9-, 13-, and 17-year-olds are all expressed on the same scale. Tables 12-1 and 12-2 show scores for reading and math. Both tables cover mean scores for Blacks, Hispanics, and Whites through 1996. In any given year, the standard deviation (SD) of scores within an age group is about 30 points for math and 40 points for reading. The standard errors (SE) of the mean scores are shown in parentheses on the tables.

### Trends for Nine-Year-Olds

Reading scores for nine-year-olds rose mostly during the 1970s, but the increase in math scores occurred mostly in the mid-to-late 1980s. It seems almost certain that effective curricular and instructional changes focused more on reading in the 1970s and more on math in the 1980s. In support of this proposition—that instruction in different subjects was improved at different times—is the fact that reading scores declined slightly for Black and Hispanic nine-year-olds in the late 1980s at the same time that math scores improved the most.

O'Day and Smith (1993) conjecture that the increased emphasis on basic skills between the late 1960s and the early 1980s contributed importantly to improvement in reading scores for all students, but especially for racial-minority students. Measures to strengthen math instruction helped all three groups of nine-year-olds to achieve roughly equal progress in the late 1980s.

Changes in disparity do not follow the same general timing as changes in overall performance. All of the catching up with Whites that Black nine-year-olds achieved was done by 1986 for math and 1988 for reading (Table 12-2). After that, Blacks lost a little ground but regained it by 1996. For reading, Hispanic-White disparity follows a pattern similar to the Black-White disparity, but there is a strangely unstable pattern for math. It seems likely that the composition of the Hispanic student sample was changing in ways that, for the broad group, make these comparisons over time less dependable. For Blacks, however, it is noteworthy that reductions in Black-White disparity follow a similar time pattern for both reading and math. This suggests that the factors helping Blacks narrow the gap on one subject, also helped in the other.

I have shown elsewhere (Ferguson, 1998b) that Black-White disparity in reading and math scores for nine-year-olds follows the same nonlinear trajectory as national reductions in pupil-to-teacher ratios for elementary schools. Not only do inflection points match closely when class-size and

Black-White disparity are graphed, but multiple regression lines fit well even after including a separate control for a linear trend (see Ferguson, 1998b, Figure 9-4). One might expect this association between test-score disparity and class size if (1) reducing class size helps Black students more than White students or (2) class sizes fell more in schools where Blacks attend. It appears that both are true for the period since 1970.

First, the proposition that smaller classes help students learn was tested in the Tennessee Star Experiment conducted in the 1980s, the largest random-assignment study ever done to test that theory. Roughly 6,500 students in 80 schools were assigned randomly to either small (13 to 17 students) or large (22 to 25 students) classes. Estimated benefits of small classes were larger for Black than for White students and larger in inner-city schools. Second, elementary pupil-to-teacher ratios fell nationally by roughly 25 percent between 1970 and 1990 (National Center for Education Statistics, 1996b). Moreover, class sizes appear to have been reduced more for Blacks than for Whites. When Coleman (1966) conducted the classic study *Equality of Educational Opportunity*, class sizes were still somewhat larger for Blacks than for Whites. By 1990, national data show no overall differences in pupil-to-teacher ratios by race (Black/White) or by socioeconomic status, as measured by the percentage of students eligible for free-and-reduced lunch subsidies.[2] Certainly, more than class size was changing over this period in the schooling of nine-year-olds. Civil rights gains and positive changes in family educational background might be important as well (Grissmer et al., 1998). Nonetheless, it appears quite likely that class-size reductions that affected Blacks (and perhaps Hispanics) more than Whites are part of the explanation for reductions in Black-White test-score disparity from 1970 through the late 1980s.

Despite this evidence, there is an active debate among researchers about whether class size matters at all. My reading of the evidence (Ferguson, 1998b) is that it does, at least for elementary schools. However, Hanushek (1998), Krueger (1997), and Greenwald et al. (1996) argue on various sides of the debate.

---

[2]See Ferguson (1998b, Table 9-11) for the author's calculations for 1987-1992 using the U.S. Department of Education's Common Core of Data Surveys, School-Level file. Nationally, the pupil-to-teacher ratio was between 17 and 18, independent of the percentage of Black students or the percentage qualifying for free-and-reduced lunch subsidies. (Note that actual class sizes tend to be about 25 percent larger than pupil-to-teacher ratios because teachers have periods off during the day for planning and lunch.) Some authors (e.g., Boozer and Rouse, 1995) suggest that this apparent parity masks differences in class size among students with similar needs. Though a distinct and important possibility, this remains to be established in nationally representative samples.

TABLE 12-1 NAEP Scores for Black, Hispanic, and White 9-, 13-, and 17-Year-Olds

A. Reading Scores, 1971 Through 1996

| | Age | 1971 | 1975 | 1980 | 1984 | 1988 | 1990 | 1992 | 1994 | 1996 |
|---|---|---|---|---|---|---|---|---|---|---|
| Black | 17 | 238.7 (1.7) | 240.6 (2.0) | 243.1 (1.8) | 264.3 (1.0) | 274.4 (2.4) | 267.3 (2.3) | 260.6 (2.1) | 266.2 (3.9) | 265.4 (2.7) |
| | 13 | 224.4 (1.2) | 225.7 (1.3) | 232.8 (1.5) | 236.3 (1.2) | 242.9 (2.4) | 241.5 (2.2) | 237.6 (2.3) | 234.3 (2.4) | 235.6 (2.6) |
| | 9 | 170.1 (1.7) | 181.2 (1.2) | 189.3 (1.8) | 185.7 (1.4) | 188.5 (2.4) | 181.8 (2.9) | 184.5 (2.2) | 185.4 (2.3) | 190.0 (2.7) |
| Hispanic | 17 | n.a. | 252.4 (3.6) | 261.4 (2.7) | 268.1 (4.3) | 270.8 (4.3) | 274.8 (3.6) | 271.2 (3.7) | 263.2 (4.9) | 264.7 (4.1) |
| | 13 | n.a. | 232.5 (3.0) | 237.2 (2.0) | 239.6 (2.0) | 240.1 (3.5) | 237.8 (2.3) | 239.2 (3.5) | 235.1 (1.9) | 239.9 (2.9) |
| | 9 | n.a | 182.7 (2.2) | 190.2 (2.3) | 187.1 (3.1) | 193.7 (3.5) | 189.4 (2.3) | 191.7 (3.1) | 185.9 (3.9) | 194.1 (3.5) |
| White | 17 | 291.4 (1.0) | 293.0 (0.6) | 292.8 (0.9) | 295.2 (0.7) | 294.7 (1.2) | 296.6 (1.2) | 297.4 (1.4) | 295.7 (1.5) | 294.4 (1.2) |
| | 13 | 260.9 (0.7) | 262.1 (0.7) | 264.4 (0.7) | 262.5 (0.6) | 261.3 (1.1) | 262.3 (0.9) | 266.4 (1.2) | 265.1 (1.1) | 267.0 (1.0) |
| | 9 | 214.0 (0.9) | 216.6 (0.7) | 221.3 (0.8) | 218.2 (0.9) | 217.7 (1.4) | 217.0 (1.3) | 217.9 (1.0) | 218.0 (1.3) | 219.9 (1.2) |

B. Math Scores, 1973 Through 1996

| | Age | 1973 | 1978 | 1982 | 1986 | 1990 | 1992 | 1994 | 1996 |
|---|---|---|---|---|---|---|---|---|---|
| Black | 17 | 270.0 (1.3) | 268.4 (1.3) | 271.8 (1.2) | 278.6 (2.1) | 288.5 (2.8) | 285.8 (2.2) | 285.5 (1.8) | 286.4 (1.7) |
| | 13 | 228.0 (1.9) | 229.6 (1.9) | 240.4 (1.6) | 249.2 (2.3) | 249.1 (2.3) | 250.2 (1.9) | 251.5 (3.5) | 252.1 (1.3) |
| | 9 | 190.0 (1.8) | 192.4 (1.1) | 194.9 (1.6) | 201.6 (1.6) | 208.4 (2.2) | 208.0 (2.0) | 212.1 (1.6) | 211.6 (1.4) |
| Hispanic | 17 | 277.0 (2.2) | 276.3 (2.3) | 276.7 (1.8) | 283.1 (2.9) | 283.5 (2.9) | 292.2 (2.6) | 290.8 (3.7) | 292.0 (2.1) |
| | 13 | 239.0 (2.2) | 238.0 (2.0) | 252.4 (1.7) | 254.3 (2.9) | 254.6 (1.8) | 259.3 (1.8) | 256.0 (1.9) | 255.7 (1.6) |
| | 9 | 202.0 (2.4) | 202.9 (2.2) | 204.0 (1.3) | 205.4 (2.1) | 213.8 (2.1) | 211.9 (2.3) | 209.9 (2.3) | 214.7 (1.7) |
| White | 17 | 310.0 (1.1) | 305.9 (0.9) | 303.7 (0.9) | 307.5 (1.0) | 309.5 (1.0) | 311.9 (0.8) | 312.3 (1.1) | 313.4 (1.4) |
| | 13 | 274.0 (0.9) | 271.6 (0.8) | 272.4 (1.0) | 273.6 (1.3) | 276.3 (1.1) | 278.9 (0.9) | 280.8 (0.9) | 281.2 (0.9) |
| | 9 | 225.0 (1.0) | 224.1 (0.9) | 224.0 (1.1) | 226.9 (1.1) | 235.2 (0.8) | 235.1 (0.8) | 236.8 (1.0) | 236.9 (1.0) |

Note: Standard errors (SE) of mean scores are shown in parentheses.

SOURCE: National Assessment of Educational Progress (1996).

TABLE 12-2 NAEP Score Gaps and Percentage of Gap Remaining

A. Gaps in Reading Scores

|  | White-Black Gap | | | White-Hispanic Gap | | |
|---|---|---|---|---|---|---|
|  | 17-year-olds | 13-year-olds | 9-year-olds | 17-year-olds | 13-year-olds | 9-year-olds |
| 1971 | 52.7 | 36.5 | 43.9 | n.a. | n.a. | n.a. |
| 1975 | 52.4 | 36.4 | 35.4 | 40.6 | 29.6 | 33.9 |
| 1980 | 49.7 | 31.6 | 32.0 | 31.4 | 27.2 | 31.1 |
| 1984 | 30.9 | 26.2 | 32.5 | 27.1 | 22.9 | 31.1 |
| 1888 | 20.3 | 18.4 | 29.2 | 23.9 | 21.2 | 24.0 |
| 1990 | 29.3 | 20.8 | 35.2 | 21.8 | 24.5 | 27.6 |
| 1992 | 36.8 | 28.8 | 33.4 | 26.2 | 27.2 | 26.2 |
| 1994 | 29.5 | 30.8 | 32.6 | 32.5 | 30.0 | 32.1 |
| 1996 | 29.0 | 31.4 | 29.9 | 29.7 | 27.1 | 25.8 |
|  | Percentage of the 1971 Gap Remaining | | | Percentage of the 1975 Gap Remaining | | |
| 1971 | 100.0 | 100.0 | 100.0 | n.a. | n.a. | n.a. |
| 1975 | 99.4 | 99.7 | 80.6 | 100.0 | 100.0 | 100.0 |
| 1980 | 94.3 | 86.6 | 72.9 | 77.3 | 91.9 | 91.7 |
| 1984 | 58.6 | 71.8 | 74.0 | 66.7 | 77.4 | 91.7 |
| 1888 | 38.5 | 50.4 | 66.5 | 58.9 | 71.6 | 70.8 |
| 1990 | 55.6 | 57.0 | 80.2 | 53.7 | 82.8 | 81.4 |
| 1992 | 69.8 | 78.9 | 76.1 | 64.5 | 91.9 | 77.3 |
| 1994 | 56.0 | 84.4 | 74.3 | 80.0 | 101.4 | 94.7 |
| 1996 | 55.0 | 86.0 | 68.1 | 73.2 | 91.6 | 76.1 |

## Trends in Learning After Age Nine

The fact that Black and Hispanic children reach the age of nine with fewer math and reading skills on average than Whites is mostly because Black and Hispanic children begin school with fewer skills. Once enrolled in school there is the chance that Black and Hispanic children could learn more than Whites but still have lower levels of skill because they start so far behind. We know that, on average, Black and Hispanic four- and five-year-olds score lower on tests of school readiness than Whites and lower on exams in early school years (Phillips et al., 1998a, 1998b). Phillips et al. (1998b) use a congressionally mandated, nationally representative, longitudinal data set called Prospects. Data collection began in 1991 for three birth cohorts—one in the first grade, one in the third grade, and one in the seventh grade. Phillips et al. conclude from their analysis of the Prospects data that Blacks appear to have learned less than Whites during the 1990s. Indeed, data from NAEP suggest the same; however,

TABLE 12-2 *Continued*

B. Gaps in Math Scores

| | White-Black Gap | | | White-Hispanic Gap | | |
|---|---|---|---|---|---|---|
| | 17-<br>year-olds | 13-<br>year-olds | 9-<br>year-olds | 17-<br>year-olds | 13-<br>year-olds | 9-<br>year-olds |
| 1973 | 40.0 | 46.0 | 35.0 | 33.0 | 35.0 | 23.0 |
| 1978 | 37.5 | 42.0 | 31.7 | 29.6 | 33.6 | 21.2 |
| 1982 | 31.9 | 32.0 | 29.1 | 27.0 | 20.0 | 20.0 |
| 1986 | 28.9 | 24.4 | 25.3 | 24.4 | 19.3 | 21.5 |
| 1990 | 21.0 | 27.2 | 26.8 | 26.0 | 21.7 | 21.4 |
| 1992 | 26.1 | 28.7 | 27.1 | 19.7 | 19.6 | 23.2 |
| 1994 | 26.8 | 29.3 | 24.7 | 21.5 | 24.8 | 26.9 |
| 1996 | 27.0 | 29.1 | 25.3 | 21.4 | 25.5 | 22.2 |
| | Percentage of<br>1973 Gap Remaining | | | Percentage of<br>1973 Gap Remaining | | |
| 1973 | 100.0 | 100.0 | 100.0 | 100.0 | 100.0 | 100.0 |
| 1978 | 93.8 | 91.3 | 90.6 | 89.7 | 96.0 | 92.2 |
| 1982 | 79.7 | 69.6 | 83.1 | 81.8 | 57.1 | 87.0 |
| 1986 | 72.2 | 53.0 | 72.3 | 73.9 | 55.1 | 93.5 |
| 1990 | 52.5 | 59.1 | 76.6 | 78.8 | 62.0 | 93.0 |
| 1992 | 65.2 | 62.4 | 77.4 | 59.7 | 56.0 | 100.9 |
| 1994 | 67.0 | 63.7 | 70.6 | 65.2 | 70.9 | 117.0 |
| 1996 | 67.5 | 63.3 | 72.3 | 64.8 | 72.9 | 96.5 |

SOURCE: National Assessment of Educational Progress (1996).

NAEP data for the 1970s and 1980s tell a different story. For the 1970s and 1980s, both Black and Hispanic gains appear much of the time to be greater than those for Whites. Hence, the answer to whether Blacks or Hispanics learn more or less than Whites during the school years may differ across time.

ETS selects a new NAEP sample each year, so children tested at one age from a particular birth cohort are not the same as those tested from the same birth cohort four years later. Nonetheless, data showing differences between 9- (or 13-) year-olds' scores one year and 13- (or 17-) year-olds' scores four years later provide the best nationally representative approximations available for measuring learning gains from ages 9 to 13 and 13 to 17, and measuring changes over time (see Figure 12-1).

Of course, using NAEP in this way only makes sense if we assume that children tested at, for example, age 13, had roughly the same distribution of scores at age 9 as the members of their cohort that NAEP actually tested at age 9. This seems likely, since NAEP samples are constructed to be nationally representative. Still, using NAEP for this type of approximation is necessarily imperfect for three reasons: (1) the 17-year-old sample does not cover dropouts; (2) the 13- and 17-year-old samples include recent immigrants who, of course, were not tested four years earlier; and (3) NAEP does not test children labeled as having learning disorders. The first two of these three reasons are probably greater problems for data for Hispanic students than for Blacks or Whites because the Hispanic dropout rate is higher, as is the Hispanic immigration rate. (The interval properties I assume below for comparing test score gains are probably only appropriate for comparing intervals where the average scores are very similar. I do not assume, for example, that a gain of say 20 points, from 170 to 190 for 9-year-olds, represents the same amount of learning or degree of difficulty as a 20-point gain, from say 250 to 270, for 17-year-olds. No such comparisons across disparate ranges are necessary for the way that I use the scores.)

Tables 12-1 and 12-2, along with Figure 12-1, represent a fairly complete summary of trends for reading and math scores over the past few decades. There is too much here to discuss it all in detail. However, there is one pattern that deserves special attention. Specifically, the test-score pattern for Black students who were age 9 in 1984 is a fascinating anomaly. As 13-year-olds in 1988, this cohort had scores that were closer to White children's than for any other cohort of 13-year-old Blacks. Indeed, the difference between Black and White 13-year-olds in 1988 was less than half the difference that existed for the same age group in 1971. After 1988, however, by the time that they were 17 years old, the gap between Blacks and Whites in the cohort more than doubled. This represents a marked deceleration in academic progress both absolutely and relative to Whites and Hispanics. It is typical in statistical time series for rapid advancements to be followed by "corrective" periods of slower growth (i.e., regression to the mean). I cannot rule out that this accounts for some of the pattern; however, I suspect something more fundamental was happening.

To investigate further, I examined unpublished NAEP data that give breakouts by region, type of community, type of school, and parents' education. For this cohort of Black children, the pattern of rapid progress from ages 9 to 13, followed by very slow progress from ages 13 to 17, shows up for all four census regions, all four types of communities, public and nonpublic schools, and all three levels of parents' education! The fact that it shows up for both public and nonpublic schools suggests that the explanation is not some fundamental change in public school policies or practices. Further, this period shows the biggest ever gain for Whites from ages 13 to 17, which also suggests that something other than school

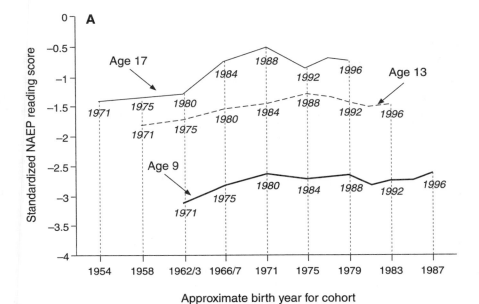

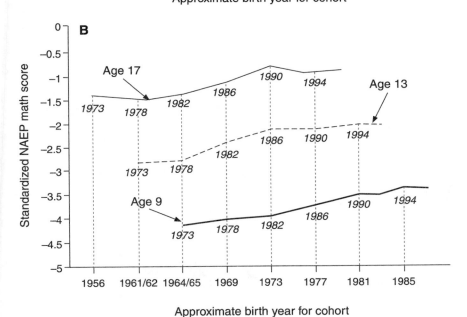

FIGURE 12-1  Standardized NAEP (A) reading and (B) math scores for Black 9-, 13-, and 17-year-olds (Metric = S.D.'s below 17-year-old Whites' 1996 mean).  Labels on lines give the year that the tests were taken.

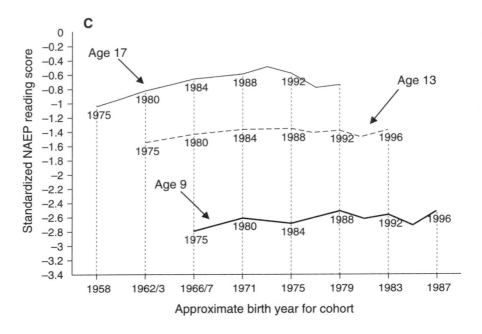

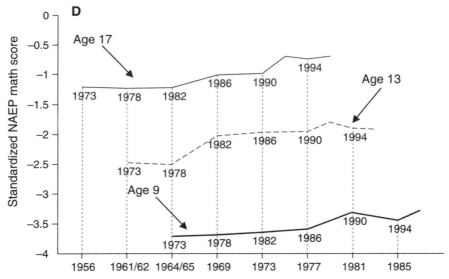

FIGURE 12-1  Standardized NAEP (C) reading and (D) math scores for Hispanic 9-, 13-, and 17-year-olds (Metric = S.D.'s below 17-year-old Whites' 1996 mean). Labels on lines give the year that the tests were taken.

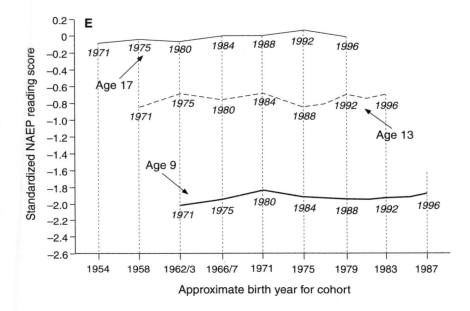

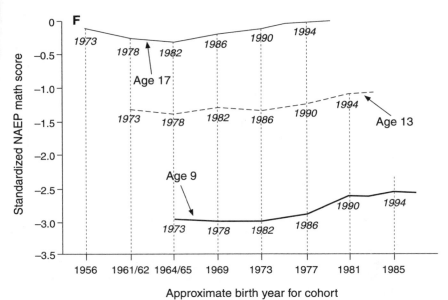

FIGURE 12-1 Standardized NAEP (E) reading and (F) math scores for White 9-, 13-, and 17-year-olds (Metric = S.D.'s below 17-year-old Whites' 1996 mean). Labels on lines give the year that the tests were taken.

policy is at work. Again, there is a possibility that the pattern is an artifact of the way the data were collected and processed. This possibility deserves investigation. For the time being, however, it seems reasonable to assume that the pattern is not an artifact.

This pattern of poor performance in high school is not unprecedented. The paltry 0.44 SD (16.2 points) that the 1975 birth cohort of Black youth gained as 13- and 17-year-olds, in 1988 and 1992, is essentially the same as the 0.45 SD (17.7 points) that another cohort achieved in 1971 and 1975. In addition, it is highly suggestive to compare 13-year-olds in 1975 with 17-year-olds in 1980. The mean score for Black 13-year-olds in 1975 is only 0.44 SD below the mean for 17-year-olds in 1980. Hence, it appears that Black teenagers were not developing their reading skills in the 1970s. For 13- to 17-year-olds, both Blacks and Whites (NAEP did not distinguish Hispanics in 1971), similarities between 1971-1975 and 1988-1982 are striking. In both periods, the score at the 5th percentile for Black 17-year-olds was actually lower than the score at the 5th percentile for 13-year-olds in the same cohort four years earlier (Table 12-3). With this negative change in scores, it is not surprising that disparity in scores—even among Blacks—became much greater by age 17 than it was at age 13. However, gains near the top of the distribution were comparatively low as well: growth in scores in the top 10 percent of these cohorts that were 13 in 1971 and 1988 was only two-thirds as great as for the cohort that was 13 in 1984. The latter cohort appears to have been more academically engaged after age 13. The 13-year-old cohort of Blacks in 1988 scored higher at every point in the distribution than Blacks who were 13 in 1984; yet, by age 17, the rank ordering of the two cohorts had reversed, with the younger cohort doing worse at every point in the distribution. This is not true for Whites. The younger cohort of 17-year-old Whites outscored its older siblings at every point in the distribution except the very bottom.

Progress over the next few decades similar to the rates that 17-year-olds attained from 1980 to 1988 could produce a dramatic narrowing of Black-White gaps in reading and math, and Hispanic-White gaps in reading. On the other hand, if the lack of relative progress achieved after 1988 continues, disparities will remain or widen. Whether one chooses to be hopeful or pessimistic depends on what one believes about the underlying causes for the leveling off that occurred after the late 1980s. [See the Appendix for a discussion of Scholastic Aptitude Test (SAT) score trends. Similar to NAEP, for both reading and math, racial gaps narrowed rapidly during the 1980s, but this stopped by 1990.]

TABLE 12-3 Percentiles of NAEP Reading Scores for 13- and 17-Year-Olds by Race, for Four Cohorts

| | Whites | | | Blacks | | | |
|---|---|---|---|---|---|---|---|
| Column | Score Age 13 | Score Age 17 | Diff. Col 2 Minus 1 | Score Age 13 | Score Age 17 | Diff. Col 5 Minus 4 | Diff. Col 3 Minus 6 |
| | 1 | 2 | 3 | 4 | 5 | 6 | 7 |
| Year | 1988 | 1992 | 1992-1988 | 1988 | 1992 | 1992-1988 | |
| Percentile | | | | | | | |
| | | | | | | | |
| | | | | **1984 Cohort** | | | |
| 5 | 204.0 | 228.1 | 24.1 | 190.6 | 187.9 | -2.7 | 26.8 |
| 10 | 217.1 | 244.9 | 27.8 | 202.2 | 206.2 | 4.0 | 23.8 |
| 25 | 238.3 | 272.3 | 34.0 | 222.0 | 235.1 | 13.1 | 20.9 |
| 50 | 262.2 | 300.1 | 37.9 | 242.4 | 262.5 | 20.1 | 17.8 |
| 75 | 285.1 | 324.5 | 39.4 | 263.6 | 288.3 | 24.7 | 14.7 |
| 90 | 304.2 | 346.6 | 42.4 | 283.6 | 312.0 | 28.4 | 14.0 |
| 95 | 315.8 | 359.0 | 43.2 | 298.9 | 327.0 | 28.1 | 15.1 |
| 95th-5th | 111.8 | 130.9 | 19.1 | 108.3 | 139.1 | 30.8 | -11.7 |
| 90th-10th | 87.1 | 101.7 | 14.6 | 81.4 | 105.8 | 24.4 | -9.8 |

*Table continued on next page*

TABLE 12-3 Continued

| | Whites | | | Blacks | | | |
|---|---|---|---|---|---|---|---|
| | Score Age 13 | Score Age 17 | Diff. Col 2 Minus 1 | Score Age 13 | Score Age 17 | Diff. Col 5 Minus 4 | Diff. Col 3 Minus 6 |
| Column | 1 | 2 | 3 | 4 | 5 | 6 | 7 |
| | 1980 Cohort | | | | | | |
| Year | 1984 | 1988 | 1988-1984 | 1984 | 1988 | 1988-1984 | |
| Percentile | | | | | | | |
| 5 | 204.9 | 232.6 | 27.7 | 180.1 | 214.4 | 34.3 | -6.6 |
| 10 | 218.3 | 247.3 | 29.0 | 192.4 | 227.8 | 35.4 | -6.4 |
| 25 | 240.6 | 271.4 | 30.8 | 213.3 | 250.5 | 37.2 | -6.4 |
| 50 | 263.4 | 295.4 | 32.0 | 236.4 | 274.3 | 37.9 | -5.9 |
| 75 | 285.6 | 319.9 | 34.3 | 259.3 | 299.6 | 40.3 | -6.0 |
| 90 | 305.0 | 339.7 | 34.7 | 280.3 | 321.0 | 40.7 | -6.0 |
| 95 | 316.8 | 351.6 | 34.8 | 292.7 | 333.1 | 40.4 | -5.6 |
| 95th-5th | 111.9 | 119.0 | 7.1 | 112.6 | 118.7 | 6.1 | 1.0 |
| 90th-10th | 86.7 | 92.4 | 5.7 | 87.9 | 93.2 | 5.3 | 0.4 |

**1976 Cohort**

| Year Percentile | 1980 | 1984 | 1984-1980 | 1980 | 1984 | 1984-1980 | |
|---|---|---|---|---|---|---|---|
| 5 | 209.0 | 228.5 | 19.5 | 178.6 | 201.9 | 23.3 | -3.8 |
| 10 | 221.8 | 243.5 | 21.7 | 190.6 | 216.0 | 25.4 | -3.7 |
| 25 | 242.8 | 267.7 | 24.9 | 210.9 | 239.0 | 28.1 | -3.2 |
| 50 | 265.1 | 293.6 | 28.5 | 232.6 | 264.0 | 31.4 | -2.9 |
| 75 | 286.9 | 318.8 | 31.9 | 254.8 | 288.3 | 33.5 | -1.6 |
| 90 | 305.7 | 340.6 | 34.9 | 275.0 | 310.5 | 35.5 | -0.6 |
| 95 | 316.9 | 353.5 | 36.6 | 286.2 | 323.6 | 37.4 | -0.8 |
| 95th-5th | 107.9 | 125.0 | 17.1 | 107.6 | 121.7 | 14.1 | 3.0 |
| 90th-10th | 83.9 | 97.1 | 13.2 | 84.4 | 94.5 | 10.1 | 3.1 |

**1967 Cohort**

| Year Percentile | 1971 | 1975 | 1975-1971 | 1971 | 1975 | 1975-1971 | |
|---|---|---|---|---|---|---|---|
| 5 | 204.6 | 225.9 | 21.3 | 166.3 | 164.7 | -1.6 | 22.9 |
| 10 | 217.9 | 241.7 | 23.8 | 178.0 | 182.1 | 4.1 | 19.7 |
| 25 | 239.4 | 267.0 | 27.6 | 199.1 | 210.4 | 11.3 | 16.3 |
| 50 | 262.0 | 294.0 | 32.0 | 223.3 | 239.3 | 16.0 | 16.0 |
| 75 | 283.5 | 319.9 | 36.4 | 245.5 | 268.1 | 22.6 | 13.8 |
| 90 | 302.2 | 343.2 | 41.0 | 264.8 | 294.1 | 29.3 | 11.7 |
| 95 | 313.1 | 357.0 | 43.9 | 276.8 | 309.7 | 32.9 | 11.0 |
| 95th-5th | 108.5 | 131.1 | 22.6 | 110.5 | 145.0 | 34.5 | -11.9 |
| 90th-10th | 84.3 | 101.5 | 17.2 | 86.8 | 112.0 | 25.2 | -8.0 |

SOURCE: Adapted from National Assessment of Educational Progress (1992: A-153 to A-156), and author's calculations.

## WHAT DISTINGUISHED THE 1980s?

After teenagers gained so little in the 1970s, what explains such extraordinary progress during the 1980s, especially for Blacks? Grissmer et al. (1998) tested a number of hypotheses and found that "Positive changes in family characteristics can explain nearly all the White gains but only a small part of the Black gains" (p. 221). The evidence they reviewed suggests that gains for Black students who were in elementary school during the 1970s and in high school during the early-to-mid 1980s are at least partly explained by reduced class sizes, racial desegregation, and more-demanding coursework. I agree; more-demanding coursework was part of a broad-based movement for accountability in the 1980s.

### Heightened Accountability

The 1980s were a period of heightened accountability for teachers and administrators in public education, and perhaps private education as well. Publication of *A Nation at Risk* (Gardner et al., 1983) was a major event, but only one among many events that symbolized a concern that failure to produce a well-educated citizenry would seriously threaten the nation's future stability and prosperity. Hence, the decade produced statements of concern about disparities in educational performance. The Commission on Minority Participation in Education and American Life (1988) wrote:

> If these disparities are allowed to continue, the United States inevitably will suffer a compromised quality of life and a lower standard of living. Social conflict will intensify. Our ability to compete in world markets will decline, our domestic economy will falter, our national security will be endangered. In brief, we will find ourselves unable to fulfill the promise of the American dream.

Whatever the degree of overstatement, this was not a plea for altruism. It was a declaration of national self-interest that many people believed then as they do now.

The appointment of this commission and others reflected forces that had been building since the late 1970s. Among the most visible changes in primary and secondary education during the 1980s was the proliferation of initial state-certification testing for new teachers: 3 states in 1980, 20 in 1984, 40 in 1988, and 42 in 1990 (National Center for Education Statistics, 1991, Table 148). Over time, certification testing has the greatest effect on schools where the teachers who fail the tests would otherwise have taught. In many cases, these are schools that serve disproportionate numbers of Black children. Most studies that consider the question find that teachers' test scores are statistically significant predictors of their students' scores [see Greenwald et al. (1996) for a meta-analysis that includes teacher test scores; see also Ferguson (1998b) for discussion and evidence on teacher testing].

I am not suggesting that certification testing, per se, is a major reason that Black students made such remarkable gains during the 1980s. It seems unlikely that new teachers would have such a sudden impact. The introduction of certification testing was part of a movement in American education to improve the quality of schools, especially the weakest. A clear possibility is that Black students benefited disproportionately from that movement. The rise in math scores that virtually all groups achieved during the decade seems to be further evidence of the movement's impact.

## Higher-Level, More Demanding Courses

Figure 12-2 shows annual changes in the number of students taking math (algebra and higher) and English courses among those students graduating from high school during the 1980s and the early 1990s. There was not much change in the number of students taking English, possibly because most students are automatically enrolled in an English course most semesters. The only way to increase the number would have been for students to take more than one English course per semester. For math, however, increases were substantial.

From 1982 through 1990, the average number of math courses that students took (algebra or higher) rose by almost a full course for Blacks and Hispanics and by almost half a course for Whites. From 1990 through 1994, however, the propensity to take more advanced courses in math slowed for Blacks but accelerated for Whites and Hispanics. This timing coincides with trends in NAEP math scores. From 1982 through 1990, NAEP math scores for 17-year-olds rose about 4 points for Whites, about 9 points for Hispanics, and about 17 points for Blacks. Conversely, from 1990 through 1994, NAEP math scores fell by 3 points for Blacks, but rose by 3 points for Whites and 7 points for Hispanics. Using the SE of the average NAEP scores (shown in parentheses in Table 12-1B), we see that the changes in average math scores during the early 1990s was of the same order of magnitude as their SEs. Hence, they are not statistically distinguishable from zero; nonetheless, their directions seem consistent with changes in course taking. This general similarity in timing does not prove causation, but it tends to support the conjecture that course taking is part of the explanation for the NAEP trends in math, especially for the 1980s.

Blacks were taking higher-level courses as the 1990s approached. As shown in Figure 12-2, their scores were rising, compared to Blacks who took the same courses (or at least courses with the same titles) in 1978 (Table 12-4). The same is true for Whites and Hispanics, but to a lesser extent. In addition, Figure 12-1 (B, D, and F) indicates that math-score

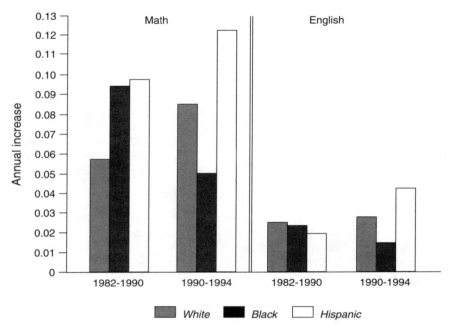

FIGURE 12-2 Annual growth in average number of math (algebra and higher) and English courses, for students graduating from high school, by race/ethnicity. SOURCE: Adapted from National Center for Education Statistics (1998:Table 136).

gains for 17-year-olds during the 1980s were building on the positive trends of the same cohorts at ages 9 to 13. Hence, improvements in the quality of math instruction at all levels—elementary, middle, and high school—probably helped to account for rising scores.

Trends in reading scores are not as similar among Blacks, Whites, and Hispanics, as are trends for math scores. Trends for Black 17-year-olds in particular, present a real puzzle. Their mean reading score in 1988 was 274 with an SE of 2.4 points. By 1992, the mean score had fallen by almost 14 points—6 times the SE. Indeed, the mean reading score for Black 17-year-olds was lower in 1992 than in 1984. Changes in such things as parenting, school resources, curriculum, instruction, and even school violence " . . . do not appear to be large enough to explain the drop in Black seventeen-year-olds' reading scores. This important question remains unresolved" (Grissmer et al., 1998:223).

The distributions of NAEP reading-score gains from ages 13 to 17 are remarkably similar for the 17-year-old Black cohorts in 1975 and 1992. That both groups achieved small gains from ages 13 to 17 is also apparent in Figure 12-1.

TABLE 12-4 Mathematics Proficiency of 17-Year-Olds, by Highest Math Course Taken and Race/Ethnicity, 1978 and 1990

| | All Areas | General Math or Pre-Algebra | Algebra I | Geometry | Algebra II | Calculus or Pre-Calculus |
|---|---|---|---|---|---|---|
| 1978 | | | | | | |
| White | 306 | 272 | 291 | 310 | 325 | 338 |
| Black | 269 | 247 | 264 | 281 | 292 | 297 |
| Hispanic | 277 | 256 | 273 | 294 | 303 | 306 |
| 1990 | | | | | | |
| White | 310 | 277 | 292 | 304 | 323 | 347 |
| Black | 289 | 264 | 278 | 285 | 302 | 329 |
| Hispanic | 284 | 259 | 278 | 286 | 306 | 323 |
| Change 1978-1990 | | | | | | |
| White | 4 | 5 | 1 | -6 | -2 | 9 |
| Black | 20 | 17 | 14 | 4 | 10 | 31 |
| Hispanic | 7 | 3 | 5 | -8 | 3 | 17 |

SOURCE: National Center for Education Statistics (1996a, Table 121).

## WHAT ROLE MIGHT POPULAR CULTURE HAVE PLAYED?

Rhythm and blues artist James Brown is not known for enunciation, but his words were as clear as could be in 1969 when he shouted "I'm Black and I'm proud!" on his hit record that remains an anthem for the period. In an act of collective self-determination, young Black leaders in the late 1960s and early 1970s no longer accepted the labels "Negro" or "colored." Their political message rejected the hegemony of White society, asserted a need to mobilize "Black power," and spurned integration as a legitimate goal for Blacks in a racist society. The Civil Rights Movement of the 1950s and 1960s had pushed for integration and assimilation. It had raised hopes that equal opportunity was possible and could make the American dream real for Blacks. But impatience grew. Riots rocked the cities and Black leadership evolved.

In the early 1970s, court-ordered busing for school integration disrupted the lives of middle and high school students. Simultaneously, any focus on academic excellence was being blurred by oppositional messages decrying assimilation—muddying what, before, had been a clear consensus that it was okay to aspire to the White American dream. Allegations proliferated that schools were not teaching the whole truth about history; and with their legitimacy thus questioned, some schools, especially those serving Blacks, tried to make their curriculums more multicultural. Students agitated for Black history courses, not advanced algebra. Academic excellence was not categorically rejected by Black youth culture, but neither was it effectively promoted as a worthy and legitimate pursuit by many adults. Gradually, tensions seemed to fade. In music, R&B lost its political edge and disco reigned supreme (George, 1998). Still, neither the early nor the late 1970s delivered a clear message to Black teenagers that they should focus on schooling and learning. It seems entirely plausible to me that forced busing, mixed messages from Black leaders, and a youth culture searching for ways to be authentically Black are key parts of the explanation for why Black 13- to 17-year-olds achieved such meager reading-score gains during the 1970s.

The unusually small gains Black teenagers achieved in reading during the 1970s are matched only by what they achieved from 1988 to 1992. It appears that Black (and perhaps also Hispanic) youth were relatively disengaged from activities that could otherwise have enhanced their reading skills. Clearly, their disengagement from academic endeavors was not total; gains in math scores seem less affected, and there were minimal gains in reading. Still, it seems that something important was different; popular culture is a prime suspect.

## Less Leisure Reading

A natural place to look for changes in youth culture is in the ways that youth spend their time. Fortunately, ETS collects data on such things when it administers the NAEP reading exams. Table 12-5 includes data for leisure reading, telling friends about good books, and watching television; Table 12-6 addresses time spent doing homework. Table 12-5 shows that Blacks spend more time watching television than Whites and Hispanics, and Hispanics watch more than Whites. There is not, however, much of a trend in hours watched that might help explain why test scores peaked for minority youth at the end of the 1980s. Hence, if a change in television habits is part of the story for test scores, it has to be a change in what youth watched, not how long they sat in front of the television.

Table 12-6 shows that Black 17-year-olds devoted somewhat more time to homework in 1988, when their reading scores peaked, than in 1992, when their scores were lowest. Generally, however, reports of time on homework are remarkably similar for the three racial groups, and there appear to be no major racial differences in trends. Lacking a much more elaborate multivariate analysis, trends for time spent doing homework and watching television appear to have no clear implications for trends in reading scores.

Conversely, there appears to be a strong (one might even say striking) correlation between reading scores and leisure reading. Jencks and Phillips (1999) found that leisure reading is a statistically significant predictor of reading, but not math, scores for high school students. Reading scores for Black youth follow both ups and downs in leisure reading from 1988 through 1996 (see Table 12-5 and Figure 12-3). For Whites, leisure reading held steady from 1984 through 1994, then dipped in 1996. For Blacks and Hispanics, the percentage of 17-year-olds reporting that they read almost daily for pleasure dropped by half from 1984 to 1994. The drop for Black youth who were 13 years old in 1988 is especially dramatic. In 1988, 35.5 percent of 17-year-old Blacks read almost daily for pleasure, but by 1992 the number for 17-year-old Blacks was only 14.7 percent. This 14.7 percent represents a cohort of which 36.6 percent answered affirmatively that they read almost daily for pleasure as 13-year-olds in 1988. This essentially matches the 37.2 percent who answered affirmatively among Whites.

## Hip Hop's Explosive Growth

The year 1988 was the watershed year for "hip hop." After only 3 gold records before 1988, there were 17 in 1988 alone. It was the year that mainstream music video outlets forcefully embraced this movement in

TABLE 12-5 Trends in NAEP Reading Scores, Leisure Reading, Telling Friends About Good Books, and Watching Television Among 17-Year-Olds

| | 1984 | 1988 | 1990 | 1992 | 1994 | 1996 |
|---|---|---|---|---|---|---|
| NAEP reading scores | | | | | | |
| Black | 264.3 (1.0) | 274.4 (2.4) | 267.3 (2.3) | 260.6 (2.1) | 266.2 (3.9) | 265.4 (2.7) |
| Hispanic | 268.1 (2.2) | 270.8 (4.3) | 274.8 (3.6) | 271.2 (3.7) | 263.2 (4.9) | 264.7 (4.1) |
| White | 295.2 (0.7) | 294.7 (1.2) | 296.6 (1.2) | 297.4 (1.4) | 295.7 (1.5) | 294.4 (1.2) |
| Percent who read almost daily for fun | | | | | | |
| Black | 30.5 (1.9) | 35.3 (6.0) | 20.0 (5.7) | 14.7 (3.3) | 16.4 (4.5) | 21.0 (4.6) |
| Hispanic | 26.1 (2.2) | n.a. | n.a. | n.a. | 13.4 (3.7) | 19.6 (7.5) |
| White | 31.3 (0.9) | 27.6 (2.3) | 35.4 (2.2) | 29.2 (1.8) | 32.6 (3.3) | 23.6 (2.5) |
| Percent who at least occasionally tell friends about good books | | | | | | |
| Black | 74.8 (1.9) | 78.1 (3.8) | 71.3 (5.0) | 65.1 (5.4) | 61.9 (5.0) | 67.3 (8.0) |
| Hispanic | 78.2 (2.4) | n.a. | n.a. | n.a. | 72.2 (5.1) | 66.5 (8.2) |
| White | 77.1 (1.0) | 73.7 (2.2) | 69.0 (2.5) | 70.6 (1.9) | 70.8 (2.5) | 69.6 (3.4) |
| Percent who spend more than 2 hours daily watching television | | | | | | |
| Black | 62.9 (1.0) | 63.1 (2.0) | 65.0 (1.9) | 66.4 (1.5) | 66.2 (2.5) | 64.8 (2.3) |
| Hispanic | 48.2 (1.5) | 44.4 (3.0) | 37.8 (5.2) | 45.5 (2.8) | 50.7 (2.2) | 49.9 (3.0) |
| White | 40.2 (0.9) | 35.2 (1.1) | 32.9 (0.9) | 30.3 (0.9) | 29.7 (1.4) | 28.4 (1.2) |

Note: Standard errors of mean scores are in parentheses.

TABLE 12-6 Trends in Time Spent on Homework for Black, Hispanic, and White 17-Year-Olds, 1980 to 1996

|  | 1980 | 1984 | 1988 | 1990 | 1992 | 1994 | 1996 |
|---|---|---|---|---|---|---|---|
| **Hispanics** | | | | | | | |
| None | 38.1 | 30.5 | 13.5 | 26.7 | 26.4 | 23.2 | 25.8 |
|  | (2.7) | (1.4) | (2.8) | (3.5) | (3.0) | (2.4) | (2.6) |
| Didn't do it | 11.5 | 11.0 | 15.3 | 10.2 | 10.1 | 11.2 | 13.7 |
|  | (1.5) | (1.0) | (2.8) | (2.1) | (1.8) | (2.0) | (1.8) |
| Less than 1 hour | 23.1 | 23.4 | 27.5 | 26.0 | 30.4 | 31.5 | 28.6 |
|  | (1.8) | (1.8) | (3.9) | (2.9) | (3.3) | (4.0) | (2.4) |
| 1-2 hours | 20.2 | 22.6 | 26.3 | 23.1 | 23.6 | 24.6 | 24.9 |
|  | (2.0) | (1.2) | (4.1) | (2.0) | (2.4) | (2.4) | (2.6) |
| More than 2 hours | 7.0 | 12.5 | 17.4 | 14.0 | 9.6 | 9.5 | 7.1 |
|  | (0.7) | (0.8) | (2.5) | (2.1) | (1.3) | (1.8) | (1.3) |
| Total 1 hour or more | 27.2 | 35.1 | 43.7 | 37.1 | 33.2 | 34.1 | 32.0 |
| **Blacks** | | | | | | | |
| None | 39.0 | 24.6 | 24.2 | 27.6 | 32.2 | 27.3 | 25.2 |
|  | (2.6) | (1.4) | (2.4) | (1.9) | (3.8) | (3.1) | (3.5) |
| Didn't do it | 8.4 | 7.2 | 9.8 | 8.6 | 7.3 | 9.1 | 11.2 |
|  | (0.5) | (0.6) | (1.0) | (1.3) | (1.1) | (1.5) | (1.6) |
| Less than 1 hour | 19.7 | 25.8 | 27.9 | 25.7 | 28.4 | 23.3 | 25.3 |
|  | (1.0) | (1.2) | (2.3) | (2.2) | (2.2) | (1.8) | (2.3) |
| 1-2 hours | 23.0 | 30.0 | 27.0 | 26.5 | 24.3 | 29.5 | 26.8 |
|  | (1.7) | (1.1) | (2.1) | (2.2) | (2.2) | (1.9) | (3.1) |
| More than 2 hours | 9.9 | 12.4 | 11.1 | 11.5 | 7.8 | 10.9 | 11.5 |
|  | (0.9) | (0.6) | (2.0) | (1.5) | (1.3) | (1.8) | (2.0) |
| Total 1 hour or more | 32.9 | 42.4 | 38.1 | 38.0 | 32.1 | 40.4 | 38.3 |
| **Whites** | | | | | | | |
| None | 30.3 | 21.7 | 21.1 | 21.8 | 20.5 | 22.7 | 22.6 |
|  | (1.3) | (0.9) | (1.6) | (1.1) | (1.0) | (1.6) | (1.6) |
| Didn't do it | 13.1 | 12.2 | 14.1 | 13.4 | 13.1 | 11.8 | 14.0 |
|  | (0.5) | (0.5) | (0.8) | (0.7) | (0.6) | (0.7) | (0.7) |
| Less than 1 hour | 24.3 | 26.6 | 28.0 | 28.6 | 29.2 | 27.8 | 28.6 |
|  | (0.6) | (0.5) | (1.1) | (1.0) | (1.0) | (1.0) | (1.1) |
| 1-2 hours | 22.6 | 26.6 | 25.8 | 24.5 | 25.7 | 25.2 | 23.6 |
|  | (0.6) | (0.6) | (1.6) | (0.8) | (0.9) | (1.3) | (1.1) |
| More than 2 hours | 9.6 | 12.9 | 10.9 | 11.7 | 11.5 | 12.5 | 11.2 |
|  | (0.5) | (0.7) | (1.1) | (0.8) | (0.9) | (1.1) | (0.8) |
| Total 1 hour or more | 32.2 | 39.5 | 36.7 | 36.2 | 37.2 | 37.7 | 34.8 |

Note: Standard errors of mean scores are in parentheses.

SOURCE: Unpublished NAEP data provided to the author by the Educational Testing Service.

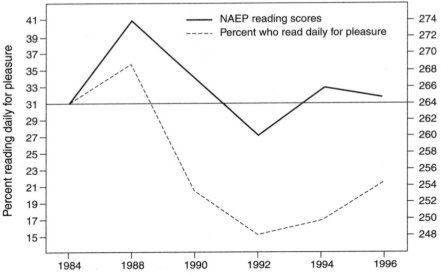

FIGURE 12-3  Trends in NAEP reading scores and reading for pleasure among Black 17-year-olds, 1984 to 1996. SOURCE: Educational Testing Service, unpublished data.

Black and Hispanic youth culture that had been developing on urban streets since the mid-to-late 1970s. George's book *Hip Hop America* (1998) is regarded by many as the definitive text on hip hop's origins and evolution (also see Rose, 1994; Southern, 1997). Hip hop is a multifaceted blend of the new and the old in Black and Hispanic culture. The nation first glimpsed it in the late 1970s when national media exposed wide audiences to the artistic graffiti on New York City subway trains and the acrobatic "break dancing" on New York City's streets. Elements of it spread quickly across the country. George (1998) describes hip hop as "a product of post-civil rights America" (p. viii).

For Black and Hispanic youth, more than for Whites, hip hop probably transcends the realm of entertainment to become an integral aspect of identity and a lens through which to understand the world. Many of the messages in hip hop mix social-class perspectives with racial commentary from an explicitly Black and Hispanic point of view, especially in "gangsta" rap, which became popular rapidly during precisely the period under focus here; messages were oppositional and challenging to mainstream culture in an "in-your-face" confrontational style (see, for discussion, Rose, 1991; Dyson, 1996; Martinez, 1997; McLaurin, 1995).

Gangsta rap and associated forms of dress and personal expression began as legitimate cultural insignia among a minority of Black youth. Indeed, it has been noted that "hip hop culture is one of the few cultural movements that has been shaped and, to a large extent, controlled by young Black males" (Nelson, 1991, cited in McLaurin, 1995). Drugs, gangs, and activities associated with the marketing and consumption of crack cocaine, admittedly relevant to a minority of Black youth, are a factor in the effect of this popularized form of expression. The music that emanated from such lifestyles was highly original, entertaining, and marketable. Although the experiences that it reflected may have been authentic for only some youth, others embraced the expressions and began to mimic the styles and behaviors of gangsta rap and other hip-hop personalities. Did this affect learning and school engagement more for Black and Hispanic youth than for Whites? I think the answer is almost surely yes. The drop in leisure reading after 1988 may well have been the result of a shift toward listening to this popular new music.

Of course, rap is not unique in affecting identity. Various forms of music are integral to most human cultures and identities. For Blacks, "Negro spirituals" emanated from the time of slavery, jazz and blues from early in the twentieth century, rhythm and blues from after World War II, and so on through funk and disco to rap. Rap is simply the latest addition, and it combines elements of all the others. Concerning the effect of rap in Black identity, one pair of music historians go so far as to write "After a number of years of being lulled into complacency by popular music and disco, rap music has reintroduced Black identity and consciousness" (Berry and Looney, 1996:266).

### Rap Music and Achievement-Related Judgments

Students derive their aspirations and standards for academic performance from parents, teachers, peers, carriers of popular culture, and their own sense of what is achievable and appropriate. Generally, an adolescent's sense of what is appropriate for him or her feels more autonomously determined than it actually is (Muuss, 1988). Different literatures have different emphases, but, generally, identity involves the internalized self (what youth think about themselves), the persona (how youth behave), and the reputation (what others think about the youth). Social forces and the demands they place on youth—for styles of dress, speech, time use, and behavior—affect all three aspects of identity. A few recent studies have sought to examine whether rap music can affect the identities and achievement orientations of Black youth (Johnson et al., 1995, Zillmann et al., 1995; Hanson, 1995; Orange, 1996).

Johnson et al. (1995) sought mainly to assess the effects of exposure to violent rap videos on attitudes toward the use of violence. However, their other purpose was to study the effect of exposure to rap music on perceptions of the usefulness of education. Their study involved 46 Black males, ages 11 to 16, in Wilmington, North Carolina. All were enrolled in school (grades 6 through 10) and were participants at an inner-city boys club. They were randomly assigned to three groups. One group watched a series of eight rap music videos containing violent lyrics or imagery. The second group watched the same number of videos, but not containing any violence. The third group, the controls, watched no videos at all.

Following the videos, the boys were invited to participate in an exercise to assess their decision-making skills. The study found that those youth who had watched the violent videos were more likely, by a statistically significant margin, to condone the use of violence in the decisions they were asked to consider. More important for our purposes here, the study also found statistically significant effects on perceptions related to achievement. Specifically, the subjects were asked to read a passage "involving two young friends who chose different paths in life. Bobby chose to go to college and pursue a law degree and Keion chose not to go to college. Bobby came home for a break and Keion came to pick him up in his new BMW and he was wearing nice clothes and nice jewelry. When Bobby asked Keion how he could afford all those nice things without a job, Keion told Bobby to go for a ride with him and not worry about how he could afford the things. Keion picked up four girls and they all commented on how nice his clothes and car were. Bobby told Keion that he would have nice cars, and so on, when he finished school and Keion replied that he 'did not need college' to get nice things" (Johnson et al., 1995:33).

When asked whether they wanted to be like Bobby or Keion, youth in the control group, who had not watched either set of rap videos, wanted to be more like Bobby, the aspiring lawyer, by a statistically significant margin. There was no difference between the youth who had watched the violent and nonviolent videos, in who they wanted to emulate—Keion. When asked about the likelihood that Bobby would successfully complete law school, youth in the control group were more optimistic about Bobby's chances, again by a statistically significant margin.

If watching rap videos and listening to rap music promote cynicism about societal fairness, and about the prospects of people who work hard experiencing success, then it might also detract from academic engagement and performance. Mickelson (1990) found that those students earn lower grades who agree more with statements such as ". . . my parents tell me to get a good education to get a good job," but "[b]ased on their experiences, people like us are not always paid or promoted according to our education." Mickelson calls these "concrete beliefs," as opposed to "abstract beliefs"—i.e., that success requires education and effort.

Mickelson also noted that Black students agreed as much as, or more than, White students, that success requires effort; but the Black students did not believe as much as White students that life is fair and that people always get what they deserve.

Hanson (1995) conducted a number of studies using "schema theory." Schema theory, in this context, suggests that popular music and music videos are structured around themes that are "schematically represented in memory" (p. 46). Subjects tend rather automatically to use these schema as the basis for interpretations, social judgments, and decisions soon after the video has been viewed, or soon after memories of the video are brought to mind. Hanson reports that violent hard-rock videos often affect attitudes about violence in a manner similar to what Johnson et al. (1995) found using violent rap videos; she concludes that both her and Johnson and colleagues' studies "clearly indicate the power of the themes contained in music videos to alter, at least temporarily, the kinds of social judgements people make" (Hanson, 1995:50). She goes on to suggest that, at least theoretically, cognitive priming of the type contained in rap videos "has the capacity to make frequently primed schemas become chronically highly accessible" (Hanson, 1995).

Hence, youth who devote a lot of time to listening to any type of music, including rap, may be more likely to interpret the world in ways consistent with the messages in that music. This might be especially so for those who come to use rap music consciously as a source of information about the world. One well-known performer, Chuck D of the group Public Enemy, has asserted that "Rap music is Black folks' CNN" (McLaurin, 1995:306).

The degree to which Black youth use rap music as a source of information or insight is unclear. Similarly, my suggestion here that the rise of rap music may help account for the drop in leisure reading and reading scores for Black and Hispanic students should be regarded as tentative until more evidence is found to support it.

## PEER PRESSURE TO NOT "ACT WHITE"

One often hears that fear of "acting White" prevents Black and Hispanic students from striving to meet higher standards.[3] To illustrate the

---

[3]The phrase "acting White" in the academic literature is most associated with the work of Signithia Fordham and John Ogbu (see, for example, Ogbu, 1978; Fordham and Ogbu, 1986; Fordham, 1988; and Belluck, 1999). In two highly influential papers, Philip Cook and Jens Ludwig (1997, 1998) present evidence they believe is inconsistent with the "acting White" hypothesis as an explanation for the Black-White achievement gap. Using nationally representative data for high school students, they find few Black-White differences across several

subtle influence of the acting-White challenge, provided below are three examples from an inner-ring suburb of a Midwestern city, from unpublished transcripts of interviews and focus groups conducted by anthropologist John Ogbu in May 1997. The racial composition in the district is roughly 50:50 Black/White, but there is a wide difference in academic performance. The vast majority of the children in top academic sections are White and most of those in the lower sections are Black. Many of the Black and White parents are professionals; and most people agree that the Black students underperform.

For each example, consider whether the fear of acting White might be an impediment to closing the Black-White achievement gap, and whether it might be affected by elements of the hip-hop culture, as discussed above.

- First Example: A Middle-School Principal Seeks Answers
[The principal is speaking.]

We had a youngster working in our office during his study halls. He was very bright. And I go and evaluate classes all the time. He sat in front of me in one of our science classes. The teacher asked a question. He didn't put his hand up. I heard him mutter under his breath—the right answer. I poked him, and said, "Hey, what's going on here?" He said, "You don't have to ride home on the bus like I do." I said, "You're right; I don't." "You don't have to play in the neighborhood with all the other kids." I said, "You're right. I don't understand." He said, "I don't want 'em to know I'm smart. They'll make fun of me. I won't have any friends." I said, "So you'd rather sit there and pretend that you don't know than face kids who might say you're smart?" And he even said, "Worse than smart." I said, "Well, what's worse than that in your world?" He said, "Where I live, they're gonna say I'm White." I said, "Oh." I said, "Now I, I think I understand. I don't agree with you, but I hear what you're saying."

We lack good quantitative evidence of whether the pattern in this passage—i.e., holding back for fear of ostracism—happens more often for

---

measures of school effort. Further, they find that high-achieving Black students seem to feel just as popular, perhaps even more popular, than do low achievers. Hence, they conclude, the focus of efforts to improve the performance of Black students should be on equalizing educational opportunities, not on trying to overcome the fear of acting White. I agree. At the same time, Cook and Ludwig agree that their work has no bearing on the question of whether fear of acting White prevents Black students from working harder than Whites, which might be required to narrow the Black-White achievement gap. For a much more detailed and subtle discussion of these and related issues, see Ferguson (forthcoming).

Black students than for Whites, and how much it affects academic performance, but this is not an unusual report.

• Second Example: Ambivalence of a Black Student Leader
The following speaker is a male student selected for interviewing from among a small group of Black student leaders. First, he addresses the challenge of being smart without acting White and his own feeling that people who sound White are selling out:

> I just love to hear Michael Jordan because he sounds very intelligent without, you know, sounding White, like, what other people call, like, a [sic] "oreo sound." He sounds actually like a strong, Black male who can actually talk to the people intelligently, which is actually hard to do. I mean, hard to sound like, "Oh, I'm not selling out," or things like that. . . . I've seen some people who, like (I wouldn't want to say, I don't know), but, you know, that's good for them if that's the path they chose to lead.

Second, he struggles with the trade-off between staying with other Black students in college preparatory (CP) courses, versus getting a better education in the honors courses. He begins by saying that it is not important to take honors courses, but then explains that honors courses provide a better atmosphere for learning.

> I don't really find it very important to take honors. I've taken all kinds of, like, honors, CP, and everything. I just feel you that you should take whatever you can do well in. I mean, being in some CP classes it's, like it's a different atmosphere. It's, like, it's harder for the teacher to teach in some of those classes; she has to, like, deal with people causing problems and laughing and throwing people out of class. And I feel it hurts the people who want to learn . . . . And then honors classes, it's, like, everybody just sits there nice and soft and everybody listens in those classes. Everybody's more, everybody puts their education at the top of their priorities. Within the CP classes, everybody is just, like, chillin', laughin', jokin' at the teacher. And you see, like, everybody coming out of these Saturday schools . . . . I mean, not all of 'em are troublemakers, but I mean you hardly see White people wantin' a Saturday school.

Should he stay mostly in the honors classes, where he's one of only a few Blacks, or should he take the CP courses where the majority of the students are Black? Does his apparent ambivalence reflect a concern about being able to do well in the honors courses, a concern about acting White and selling out, or both? Do White students face such pressures equally? Would the Black-White achievement gap be affected if Black students received help in coping with such issues?

• Third Example: Acting Ghetto

One way to not act White is to act ghetto. Here, the same Black male student as above reflects on, and clearly rejects, the polar opposite of acting White:

> It seems to me, almost, like Black students act as ghetto as possible, like, as much of the time as they can. And I think that that's a lot of the problem. Because you'll be sitting in class, and people will just leave, or, like, we're in class, and the teacher handed a test to somebody, and they just, like, here you can have it back. That's just ridiculous.

Similarly, Ainsworth-Darnell and Downey (1998), found, using national data, that teachers rate Black students as more frequently disruptive and as putting forth less effort. The Black-White differences that they found were not very large, but remained statistically significant after accounting for family income, parental occupations, and parental education.

These issues need to be handled at the community level, in alliances among teachers, students, parents, and administrators. As I describe in Ferguson (1998a), evidence tends to support the conclusion that teachers' perceptions and expectations have an important effect on the performance of Black students, more than Whites (Casteel, 1997; Kleinfeld, 1972; Jussim et al., 1996). If we can equip teachers with the skills to encourage and motivate students, the fear of acting White and the peer norms that sometimes reward "acting ghetto" need not carry the day. Professional development opportunities that help teachers in this regard could be quite important next steps.

## PARENTAL AND TEACHER STANDARDS

Teachers hold to higher standards those students they expect can perform at higher levels. One student who earns a grade of C may receive a reprimand for slacking off, while another with the same grade receives praise because it seems to reflect his best effort. The literature is clear on finding that teachers expect less, on average, from Black students than Whites (Ferguson, 1998a; Brophy, 1985; Good, 1987; Howard and Hammond, 1985; Jussim et al., 1996; Taylor, 1979). The few studies that take students' past grades and test scores into account find that teachers have the same expectations on average for Black and White students who have performed equally in the past. Hence, by this notion of expectations conditional on past performance, teachers are not racially biased, even though they expect less of Blacks, because Blacks' past performance predicts their lower future performance. Using a notion of expectations based on students' latent potentials, teachers may or may not underestimate

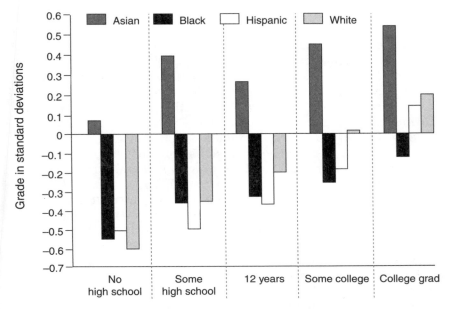

FIGURE 12-4 "What is the lowest grade you can get without your parents getting upset?" Answers by student's race/ethnicity and mother's education. Y-axis is in standard deviations (1 letter grade per s.d.) around a mean of C+. Sample sizes for bars, from left to right on the diagram: 56, 15, 128, 31; 46, 47, 99, 115; 150, 126, 167, 866; 128, 137, 111, 882; 328, 138, 78, 1525. Source: Author's calculations, using data supplied by Laurence Steinberg for high schools in Wisconsin and San Francisco during the 1980s.

Black or Hispanic students' latent potentials by more than they underestimate Whites'. Because potential is not apparent until it shows itself, there is no way of proving or calibrating whether bias has a role here. Nonetheless, teachers who underestimate their students' potentials probably underinvest in the search for ways of unlocking it. Reverend Robert Schuller says, "Any fool can count the seeds in an apple, but only God can count the apples in a seed." If we believed more in children's potential, we might invest more effort in cultivation and aim for larger harvests.

These statements about expectations and standards apply as much to parents as to teachers. Figure 12-4 is based on a survey of students in nine high schools in Wisconsin and San Francisco during the 1980s.[4] It provides a striking illustration of the fact that parental standards can differ by race and parents' education. Students were asked, "What is the lowest grade you can get without your parents getting upset?" The mean answer was between C and C+, with a standard deviation of about one marking level (e.g., the difference between C+ and B–).

The most outstanding feature of Figure 12-4 is the performance Asian students perceive that their parents hold them accountable for; it is a higher level of performance than the other student groups perceive is expected of them. Asians whose parents are high school dropouts report higher grade-level thresholds for provoking parental anger than do White, Black, or Hispanic students whose parents have four-year college degrees. Conversely, Black students whose parents are college graduates report, on average, almost the same parental standards as Whites whose parents are high school graduates and have not attended college at all. If teachers, parents, and peers hold Black and sometimes Hispanic students to lower standards than Whites and Asians, part of the reason is that Black and Hispanic students have historically performed at lower levels. But this can change. Especially when help is available, students tend to strive at least for the minimum standards that people around them set. National surveys show that students of all racial groups think the standards are too low.

## WHAT STUDENTS THINK ABOUT THEIR SCHOOLS

Trends in NAEP indicate that achievement scores have risen over the past three decades. Presumably, minimum standards have risen as well. A nationally representative survey of high school students conducted in 1996, however, indicates that neither Black, Hispanic, nor White students feel that standards are high enough (Public Agenda, 1997). The survey covered 1,000 randomly selected high school students, plus another 1,120 over-sample interviews for Blacks, Hispanics, private high school students, middle school students, and students from two metropolitan areas. Tables 12-7 through 12-9 present selected items from the report. For the most part, I have selected items that show racial differences or items that have direct bearing on the question of standards.

Fifty-six percent of Black students, 45 percent of Hispanic students,

---

[4]The numbers in Figure 12-3 come from a multiyear project by Laurence Steinberg, B. Bradford Brown, and Sanford Dornbusch. The project produced a number of papers, but many of their findings are summarized in a book by Steinberg (1996). The tabulations in Figure 12-3 are my own, using the raw data graciously provided by Steinberg.

TABLE 12-7 Percent Responding That the Problem Is "Very Serious" or "Somewhat Serious" in Their School

(Question: Here are some problems different schools could have. Please tell me how serious a problem this is in your school.)

| | High School Students | | | |
| | Whites | Blacks | Hispanics | Private School |
|---|---|---|---|---|
| Too many teachers are doing a bad job | 36 | 56 | 45 | 22 |
| Not enough emphasis on the basics such as reading, writing and math | 30 | 49 | 41 | 16 |
| Too many kids get passed to the next grade when they should be held back | 41 | 58 | 49 | 16 |
| Too many students get away with being late to class and not doing their work | 49 | 58 | 50 | 35 |
| Students pay too much attention to what they're wearing and not what they look like | 73 | 81 | 79 | 42 |
| Classes are too crowded | 42 | 52 | 45 | 14 |

SOURCE: Public Agenda (1997, Table 4). Reprinted with permission from Public Agenda, New York.

and 36 percent of White students reported "Too many teachers are doing a bad job" is a "very serious" or "somewhat serious" problem in their school (Table 12-7). Items related to "doing a bad job" included not emphasizing basics such as reading, writing, and math; passing students to the next grade when they should be held back; and allowing students to get away with being late to class and not doing their work. More Black than Hispanic students and more Hispanic than White students report these to be problems. It appears either that Black students have higher standards for their schools (which seems unlikely) or that Black students receive a lower standard of instruction. Students in the private school sample, which is not differentiated by race, report far fewer of these problems than do students in public schools.

TABLE 12-8 Percent Responding That the Proposed Change Would Get Them to Learn "a Lot More"

(Question: Now I'm going to read a list of things that might get you to learn more and ask if you think they'll really work. Remember, I'm not asking if you like these ideas, only if you think they will actually get you to learn more.)

| | High School Students | | | |
| | Whites | Blacks | Hispanics | Private School |
| --- | --- | --- | --- | --- |
| Having more good teachers | 60 | 75 | 69 | 74 |
| Getting your class work checked and redoing it until it's right | 58 | 74 | 69 | 61 |
| Kicking constant troublemakers out of class so teachers can concentrate on the kids who want to learn | 50 | 66 | 58 | 50 |
| Knowing that more companies in your area are using high school transcripts to decide who to hire | 48 | 62 | 49 | 46 |
| Knowing you'll get something you want from your parents if you do well | 27 | 43 | 44 | 27 |

SOURCE: Public Agenda (1997, Table 5). Reprinted with permission from Public Agenda, New York.

Sixty-two percent of Blacks, 49 percent of Hispanics, and 48 percent of Whites say they would learn "a lot more" if they knew that companies in the area were using high school transcripts to decide whom to hire (Table 12-8). Other measures that might get them to learn "a lot more" include having more good teachers, having work checked and then redoing it, removing chronic troublemakers from class, and receiving material incentives from parents. Answers on each of these questions indicate that children of all three racial groups believe they could learn a lot more than they currently do.

Table 12-9 lists 10 characteristics of effective teachers, and whether students believe that "most" of their current teachers have these characteristics. A majority of students respond that teachers with any of 9

TABLE 12-9 Percent Responding That Certain Kinds of Teachers Would Lead Them to Learn "a Lot More"/Percent Responding "Most" of Their Teachers Are Like That Item Now

(Question: Now I'm going to talk about different kinds of teachers and ask you if you think they lead you to learn more or not.)

| | High School Students | | | |
| | Whites | Blacks | Hispanics | Private School |
|---|---|---|---|---|
| A teacher who tries to make lessons fun and interesting | 79/25 | 76/25 | 78/23 | 84/39 |
| A teacher who is enthusiastic and exited about the subject they teach | 71/29 | 71/28 | 72/32 | 71/32 |
| A teacher who knows a lot about the subject they teach | 70/47 | 74/49 | 72/47 | 77/63 |
| A teacher who treats students with respect | 68/42 | 75/37 | 68/50 | 73/63 |
| A teacher who gives students a lot of individual help with their work | 67/33 | 76/31 | 69/31 | 78/51 |
| A teacher who uses hands-on projects and class discussion | 68/23 | 67/31 | 68/19 | 70/33 |
| A teacher who explains lessons very carefully | 64/33 | 72/38 | 72/35 | 71/48 |
| A teacher who challenges students to constantly do better and learn more | 63/33 | 79/42 | 69/36 | 74/51 |
| A teacher who personally cares about his students as people | 62/30 | 68/31 | 66/31 | 71/58 |
| A teacher who knows how to handle disruptive students | 45/28 | 52/35 | 44/35 | 52/44 |

SOURCE: Public Agenda (1997, Table 11). Reprinted with permission from Public Agenda, New York.

characteristics (the exception is "knows how to handle disruptive students") could inspire them to learn "a lot more." For all characteristics, no public-school students reported that most of their teachers had the characteristics listed. On the other hand, for 5 of the 10 characteristics, a majority of private-school students say that most of their teachers fit the description. For most of the items in Table 12-9, Black and Hispanic students rate their teachers higher on average than White students rate theirs. How do we reconcile this with Table 12-7, where larger percentages of Black and Hispanic than White students report that too many teachers are doing a bad job? One possibility is that schools serving Black and Hispanic students have a larger percentage of dedicated teachers *and* a larger percentage of teachers doing a bad job. Another possibility is that Black and Hispanic students have lower threshold standards than Whites do for judging teachers, so that Blacks would rate any given teacher performance higher than Whites would. If this latter interpretation is closer to correct, then it is even more a problem that a larger percentage of Black and Hispanic than White students agree that "too many teachers are doing a bad job." The correct interpretation is impossible to glean from these data, but the issues are important, and the Public Agenda survey has at least begun to inform the discussion.

The Public Agenda survey results as well as the more extended discussion of standards-related issues above, suggest that children can do more than we are asking of them. Moreover, they know it. It appears that standards of effort and performance for Black and Hispanic students, and perhaps for teachers and parents as well, are lower than what will be required to avoid a future of continued racial disparity in academic achievement. We have underestimated children's potentials. We can and should produce a larger harvest.

## CONCLUSION

Children's knowledge includes what they already know before arriving at school and what they learn once there. The average Black or Hispanic child in the United States has fewer school-related skills than the average White child at the beginning of kindergarten. This is true even among households that appear equal in parental schooling and socioeconomic status [see Chapters 4 and 7 in Jencks and Phillips (1998)]. Once a child enters school already less proficient than his peers, catching up requires more than keeping up; equal progress merely maintains initial disparities.

Basic skill gaps among White, Black, and Hispanic children, as measured by standardized test scores, have narrowed substantially over the past 30 years. Large gaps remain, but more progress is possible if we set high standards and do what it takes to achieve them. If we care about equality of results, then we must face the fact that catching up requires running faster than the competition: the only way for Black and Hispanic students in a given birth cohort to narrow the gap with Whites during the school years is for them to learn more than Whites do. Although NAEP cannot measure changes in proficiency between school entry and age nine, data from NAEP suggest that Black and Hispanic children often have learned more than Whites after age nine, but not for all time periods, and not enough to come even close to closing the test-score gap. Accelerating progress on closing these gaps can be facilitated by a more supportive popular culture, by teachers and parents who set high standards, and by a society that provides the necessary resources and incentives to keep it all on track. Responsive teaching can weaken the link between past and future performance for an individual child. Similarly, a responsive and determined society can change prospects for large numbers of children— of all races and ethnicities—whose potential otherwise might be wasted.

## ACKNOWLEDGMENTS

This paper was initially prepared for the National Research Council Conference on Racial Trends in the United States, held October 15 and 16, 1998, at the National Academy of Sciences in Washington, D.C. Work on the paper has benefited from the financial support of the Annie E. Casey Foundation, the John D. and Catherine T. MacArthur Foundation, and the Rockefeller Foundation, through their support for the National Community Development Policy Analysis Network Project on Education and Youth in Community Development. Jordana Brown helped to collect the materials on which this paper is based and has provided helpful comments that improved the paper. William T. Dickens, Christopher Jencks, and Meredith Phillips also provided helpful comments.

## APPENDIX
## TRENDS IN SCHOLASTIC APTITUDE TEST SCORES

Scholastic Aptitude Test (SAT) scores represent that segment of the high school population planning to apply to colleges where the SAT is required in the application. Hence, SAT scores and trends are not based on a random sample of all students. Further, characteristics of the sample, such as what percentage of students it represents, change over time. Still, SAT does provide a national time series of scores with which to compare the NAEP scores. Figure 12-A shows changes since 1976 in SAT scores for Blacks, Mexicans, and Whites. (Note that Mexicans' scores for the SAT

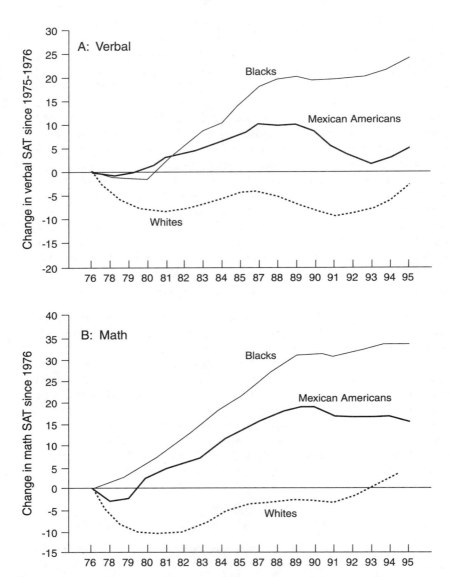

FIGURE 12-A Changes since 1976 in SAT (A) verbal and (B) math scores by racial/ethnic background (three-year moving averages). SOURCE: National Center for Education Statistics (1996a, Table 128).

are for a smaller segment of the Hispanic population than NAEP because NAEP includes additional Hispanic nationalities. Do not assume close comparability.) All three groups achieved higher scores in math during the 1980s. (College enrollment rates for new high school graduates during the mid-to-late 1980s were rising.) This is consistent with trends in the NAEP. The similarity of math trends for different racial groups and across both NAEP and SAT indicates that there was probably a narrow range of forces causing the changes across the board. These probably included changes in course-taking, curriculum, and instruction. For both NAEP and SAT, verbal scores are more variable than math, with less of a common pattern across groups. However, just as with NAEP, the most salient thing to notice about Blacks in these two figures is that both verbal and math progress stops abruptly at the end of the 1980s, after a decade of rapid improvement.

## REFERENCES

Ainsworth-Darnell, J., and D. Downey
    1998    Assessing the oppositional-culture explanation for racial/ethnic differences in school performance. *American Sociological Review* 60(4):536-553.
Belluck, P.
    1999    Reason is sought for lag by blacks in school effort. *New York Times* (July 4):1.
Berry, V., and H. Looney, Jr.
    1996    Rap music, black men, and the police. In *Mediated Messages and African American Culture: Contemporary Issues*, V. Berry and C. Manning-Miller, eds. Thousand Oaks, Calif.: Sage Publications.
Boozer, M., and C. Rouse
    1995    Intraschool variation in class size: Patterns and implications. Working paper No. 5144. National Bureau of Economic Research.
Brophy, J.
    1985    Teacher-student interaction. In *Teacher Expectancies*, J. Dusek, ed. Hillsdale, N.J.: Lawrence Erlbaum Associates.
Casteel, C.
    1997    Attitudes of African American and Caucasian eighth grade students about praises, rewards, and punishments. *Elementary School Guidance and Counseling* 31(April):262-272.
Coleman, J., and E. Campbell, et al.
    1966    *Equality of Educational Opportunity*. Washington, D.C.: U.S. Government Printing Office.
Commission on Minority Participation in Education and American Life
    1988    *One-Third of a Nation*. Washington, D.C.: American Council on Education/Education Commission of the States.
Cook, P., and J. Ludwig
    1997    Weighing the burden of "acting white": Are there race differences in attitudes toward education? *Journal of Policy Analysis and Management* 16(2):656-678.
    1998    The burden of "acting white": Do black adolescents disparage academic achievement? In *The Black-White Test Score Gap*, C. Jencks and M. Phillips, eds. Washington, D.C.: Brookings Institution Press.

Du Bois, W.E.B.
  1903    *The Souls of Black Folk.*  Chicago: McClurg.
Dyson, M.
  1996    *Between God and Gangsta Rap: Bearing Witness to Black Culture.*  New York: Oxford University Press.
Ferguson, R.
  1998a   Teachers' perceptions and expectations and the black-white test score gap. In *The Black-White Test Score Gap,* C. Jencks and M. Phillips, eds. Washington, D.C.: Brookings Institution Press.
  1998b   Can schools narrow the black-white test score gap? In *The Black-White Test Score Gap,* C. Jencks and M. Phillips, eds. Washington, D.C.: Brookings Institution Press.
Forth-    Race and the social determinants of high-school achievement. In *Brookings Papers*
coming    *on Education Policy, 2001,* D. Ravitch, ed. Washington, D.C.: Brookings Institution Press.
Fordham, S.
  1988    Racelessness as a factor in black students' success: Coping with the burden of "acting white." *Harvard Education Review* 58(1):54-84.
Fordham, S., and J. Ogbu
  1986    Black students' school success: Coping with the burden of "acting white." *The Urban Review* 18(3):176-206.
Gardner, D., et al.
  1983    *A Nation At Risk: The Imperative for Educational Reform.*  Washington, D.C.: U.S. Government Printing Office.
George, N.
  1998    *Hip Hop America.*  New York: Viking Press.
Good, T.
  1987    Two decades of research on teacher expectations: Findings and future directions. *Journal of Teacher Education* (July-August):32-47.
Greenwald, R., L. Hedges, and R. Laine
  1996    The effect of school resources on student achievement. *Review of Educational Research* 66:361-396.
Grissmer, D., A. Flanagan, and S. Williamson
  1998    Why did the black-white test score gap narrow in the 1970s and 1980s? In *The Black-White Test Score Gap,* C. Jencks and M. Phillips, eds. Washington, D.C.: Brookings Institution Press.
Hanson, C.
  1995    Predicting cognitive and behavioral effects of gangsta rap. *Basic and Applied Social Psychology* 16(1,2):43-52.
Hanushek, E.
  1998    The evidence on class size. Occasional paper 98-1. University of Rochester, W. Allen Wallis Institute of Political Economy.
Hedges, L., and A. Nowell
  1998    Black-white test score convergence since 1965. In *The Black-White Test Score Gap,* C. Jencks and M. Phillips, eds. Washington, D.C.: Brookings Institution Press.
Howard, J., and R. Hammond
  1985    Rumors of inferiority. *New Republic* 72(9).
Jencks, C., and M. Phillips
  1998    *The Black-White Test Score Gap.*  Washington, D.C.: Brookings Institution Press.

1999    Aptitude or achievement: Why do test scores predict educational attainment and earnings? In *Learning and Earning: How Schools Matter,* S. Mayer and P. Peterson, eds. Washington, D.C.: Brookings Institution Press.

Johnson, J., L. Jackson, and L. Gatto
1995    Violent attitudes and deferred academic aspirations: Deleterious effects of exposure to rap music. *Basic and Applied Social Psychology* 16(1,2):27-41.

Jussim, L., J. Eccles, and S. Madon
1996    Social perception, social stereotypes, and teacher expectations: Accuracy and the quest for the powerful self-fulfilling prophesy. *Advances in Experimental Social Psychology* 28:281-387.

Kleinfeld, J.
1972    The relative importance of teachers and parents in the formation of Negro and white students' academic self-concepts. *Journal of Educational Research* 65:211-212.

Krueger, A.
1997    Experimental estimates of education production functions. Draft. Princeton University and National Bureau of Economic Research.

Martinez, T.
1997    Popular culture as oppositional culture: Rap as resistance. *Sociological Perspectives* 40(2):265-286.

McLaurin, P.
1995    An examination of the effect of culture on pro-social messages directed at African-American at-risk youth. *Communication Monographs* 62(December):321-325.

Mickelson, R.
1990    The attitude-achievement paradox among black adolescents. *Sociology of Education* 63:44-61.

Muuss, R.
1988    Friendship patterns and peer-group influences: An ecological perspective based on Bronfenbrenner, Kandel and Dunphy. Chapter 14 in *Theories of Adolescence.* New York: McGraw-Hill.

National Center for Education Statistics
1991    *Digest of Education Statistics 1991.* Washington, D.C.: Government Printing Office.
1992    *NAEP Trends in Academic Progress.* Washington, D.C.: U.S. Department of Education.
1996a   *Digest of Education Statistics 1996.* Washington, D.C.: Government Printing Office.
1996b   *NAEP Trends in Academic Progress.* Washington, D.C.: U.S. Department of Education.
1998    *Digest of Education Statistics 1998.* Washington, D.C.: Government Printing Office.

Nelson, H.
1991    *Bring the Noise: A Guide to Rap Music and Hip-Hop Culture.* New York: Harmony Books.

O'Day, J., and M. Smith
1993    Systemic reform and educational opportunity. In *Designing Coherent Education Policy: Improving the System* , S. Fuhrman, ed. San Francisco: Jossey-Bass Publishers.

Ogbu, J.
1978    *Minority Education and Caste: The American System in Cross-Cultural Comparison.* New York: Academic Press.

Orange, C.
1996    Rap videos: A source of undesirable vicarious empowerment for African-American males. *High School Journal* (April/May).

Phillips, M., J. Crouse, and J. Ralph
    1998a Does the black-white test-score gap widen after children enter school?  In *The Black-White Test Score Gap*, C. Jencks and M. Phillips, eds.  Washington, D.C.: Brookings Institution Press.
Phillips, M., J. Brooks-Gunn, G. Duncan, P. Klebanow, and J. Crane
    1998b Family background, parenting practices, and the black-white test score gap.  In *The Black-White Test Score Gap*, C. Jencks and M. Phillips, eds.  Washington, D.C.: Brookings Institution Press.
Public Agenda
    1997 *Getting By: What American Youth Really Think About Their Schools.  Summary Report of Survey and Focus Group Results.*  Washington, D.C.:  Public Agenda.
Rose, T.
    1991 'Fear of a black planet': Rap music and Black cultural politics in the 1990s. *Journal of Negro Education* 60(3):276-290.
    1994 *Black Noise:  Rap Music and Black Culture in Contemporary America.*  Middletown, Conn.: Wesleyan University Press.
Southern, E.
    1997 *The Music of Black Americans: A History.*  Third Edition.  New York: W.W. Norton and Company.
Steinberg, L.
    1996 *Beyond the Classroom.*  New York: Simon and Schuster.
Taylor, M.
    1979 Race, sex, and the expression of self-fulfilling prophecies in a laboratory teaching situation. *Personality and Social Psychology* 6:897-912.
Zillmann, D., C. Aust, K. Hoffman, C. Love, V. Ordman, J. Pope, and P. Seigler
    1995 Radical rap: Does if further ethnic division? *Basic and Applied Social Psychology* 16(1,2):1-25.

# 13
# Residential Segregation and Neighborhood Conditions in U.S. Metropolitan Areas

*Douglas S. Massey*

Social scientists have long studied patterns of racial and ethnic segregation because of the close connection between a group's spatial position in society and its socioeconomic well-being. Opportunities and resources are unevenly distributed in space; some neighborhoods have safer streets, higher home values, better services, more effective schools, and more supportive peer environments than others. As people and families improve their socioeconomic circumstances, they generally move to gain access to these benefits. In doing so, they seek to convert past socioeconomic achievements into improved residential circumstances, yielding tangible immediate benefits and enhancing future prospects for social mobility by providing greater access to residentially determined resources.

Throughout U.S. history, racial and ethnic groups arriving in the United States for the first time have settled in enclaves located close to an urban core, in areas of mixed land use, old housing, poor services, and low or decreasing socioeconomic status. As group members build up time in the city, however, and as their socioeconomic status rises, they have tended to move out of these enclaves into areas that offer more amenities and improved conditions—areas in which majority members are more prevalent—leading to their progressive spatial assimilation into society.

The twin processes of immigrant settlement, on the one hand, and spatial assimilation, on the other, combine to yield a diversity of segregation patterns across groups and times, depending on the particular histories of in-migration and socioeconomic mobility involved (Massey, 1985). Groups experiencing recent rapid in-migration and slow socioeconomic mobility tend to display relatively high levels of segregation, whereas those with rapid rates of economic mobility and slow rates of in-migration tend to be more integrated.

When avenues of spatial assimilation are systematically blocked by prejudice and discrimination, however, residential segregation increases and persists over time. New minorities arrive in the city and settle within enclaves, but their subsequent spatial mobility is stymied, and ethnic concentrations increase until the enclaves are filled, whereupon group members are forced into adjacent areas, thus expanding the boundaries of the enclave (Duncan and Duncan, 1957). In the United States, most immigrant groups experienced relatively few residential barriers, so levels of ethnic segregation historically were not very high. Using a standard segregation index (the index of dissimilarity), which varies from 0 to 100, European ethnic groups rarely had indexes of more than 60 (Massey, 1985; Massey and Denton, 1992).

Blacks, in contrast, traditionally experienced severe prejudice and discrimination in urban housing markets. As they moved into urban areas from 1900 to 1960, therefore, their segregation indices rose to unprecedented heights, compared with earlier times and groups. By mid-century, segregation indices exceeded 60 virtually everywhere; and in the largest Black communities they often reached 80 or more (Massey and Denton, 1989b, 1993).

Such high indices of residential segregation imply a restriction of opportunity for Blacks compared with other groups. Discriminatory barriers in urban housing markets mean individual Black citizens are less able to capitalize on their hard-won attainments and achieve desirable residential locations. Compared with Whites of similar social status, Blacks tend to live in systematically disadvantaged neighborhoods, even within suburbs (Schneider and Logan, 1982; Massey et al., 1987; Massey and Fong, 1990; Massey and Denton, 1992).

In a very real way, barriers to spatial mobility are barriers to social mobility; and a racially segregated society cannot logically claim to be "color blind." The way a group is spatially incorporated into society is as important to its socioeconomic well-being as the manner in which it is incorporated into the labor force. It is important, therefore, that levels and trends in residential segregation be documented so that this variable can be incorporated fully into research and theorizing about the causes of urban poverty. To accomplish this, presented here is an overview and interpretation of historical trends in the residential segregation of Blacks, Hispanics, and Asians.

## LONG-TERM TRENDS IN BLACK SEGREGATION

Massey and Hajnal (1995) examined historical trends in Black segregation at the state, county, municipal, and neighborhood levels. Their interpretation focused on two specific time periods—pre-World War II; 1900 to 1940; and postwar, from 1950 to 1990. Table 13-1 presents their data[1] on the geographic structure of Black segregation and racial isolation during the earlier period. Because of data limitations, segregation or isolation at the municipal level during this early period could not be measured.

As Table 13-1 shows, Blacks and Whites were distinctly segregated from one another across state boundaries early in the twentieth century. In 1900, for example, 64 percent of all Blacks would have had to move to a different state to achieve an even distribution across state lines, and most Blacks lived in a state that was 36 percent Black. These figures simply state the obvious, that in 1900, some 90 percent of Blacks lived in a handful of southern states, which contained only 25 percent of all Whites (U.S. Bureau of the Census, 1979).

The isolation index shows that in the South, most Blacks lived in rural counties that were approximately 45 percent Black, yielding a high degree of segregation and racial isolation at the county level as well. The dissimilarity index for 1900 reveals that nearly 70 percent of all Blacks would have had to shift their county of residence to achieve an even racial distribution across county lines.

At the beginning of this century, for Blacks, the typical residential setting was southern and rural; for Whites it was northern and urban. Under conditions of high state- and county-level segregation, race relations remained largely a regional problem centered in the South. Successive waves of Black migration out of the rural South into the urban North transformed the geographic structure of Black segregation during the twentieth century, however, ending the regional isolation and rural confinement of Blacks. From 1900 to 1940, the index of Black-White dissimilarity fell from 64 to 52 at the state level and from 69 to 59 at the county level. Black isolation likewise dropped from 36 to 24 within states, and from 45 to 32 within counties.

The movement of Blacks out of rural areas, however, was accompa-

---

[1]Residential segregation was measured using the index of dissimilarity, and racial isolation was measured using the P* index (Massey and Denton, 1988). The index of dissimilarity is the relative number of Blacks who would have to change geographic units so that an even Black-White spatial distribution could be achieved. The P* index is the percentage of Blacks residing in the geographic unit of the average Black person.

TABLE 13-1 Indices of Black-White Segregation Computed at Three
Geographic Levels, 1900 to 1940

| | Years | | | | |
|---|---|---|---|---|---|
| | 1900 | 1910 | 1920 | 1930 | 1940 |
| **Between states** | | | | | |
| Dissimilarity | 64 | 65 | 61 | 54 | 52 |
| Isolation | 36 | 34 | 30 | 25 | 24 |
| **Between counties** | | | | | |
| Dissimilarity | 69 | 70 | 66 | 60 | 59 |
| Isolation | 45 | 43 | 38 | 33 | 32 |
| **Between wards** | | | | | |
| Dissimilarity | | | | | |
| Boston | — | 64 | 65 | 78 | 79 |
| Buffalo | — | 63 | 72 | 81 | 82 |
| Chicago | — | 67 | 76 | 85 | 83 |
| Cincinnati | — | 47 | 57 | 73 | 77 |
| Cleveland | — | 61 | 70 | 85 | 86 |
| Philadelphia | — | 46 | 48 | 63 | 68 |
| Pittsburgh | — | 44 | 43 | 61 | 65 |
| St. Louis | — | 54 | 62 | 82 | 84 |
| Average | — | 56 | 62 | 76 | 78 |
| Isolation | | | | | |
| Boston | 06 | 11 | 15 | 19 | — |
| Buffalo | 04 | 06 | 10 | 24 | — |
| Chicago | 10 | 15 | 38 | 70 | — |
| Cincinnati | 10 | 13 | 27 | 45 | — |
| Cleveland | 08 | 08 | 24 | 51 | — |
| Philadelphia | 16 | 16 | 21 | 27 | — |
| Pittsburgh | 12 | 12 | 17 | 27 | — |
| St. Louis | 13 | 17 | 30 | 47 | — |
| Average | 10 | 13 | 23 | 39 | — |

SOURCE: Massey and Hajnal (1995).

nied by their progressive segregation within cities. Although we lack
indices of Black-White dissimilarity for 1900, research has demonstrated
that Blacks were not particularly segregated in northern cities during the
nineteenth century. Ward-level dissimilarity for Blacks in 11 northern
cities circa 1860 had average indices of approximately 46 (Massey and
Denton, 1993).

By 1910, however, the eight cities listed in Table 13-1 had an average
index of 56, and the level of Black-White dissimilarity increased sharply

during each decade after 1910, suggesting the progressive formation of Black ghettos in cities throughout the nation. As Lieberson (1980) has shown, the growth of Black populations in urban areas triggered the imposition of higher levels of racial segregation within cities. Before the U.S. Supreme Court declared them unconstitutional in 1916, many U.S. cities actually passed apartheid laws establishing separate Black and White districts. Thereafter, however, segregation was achieved by less formal means (see Massey and Denton, 1993:26-42). Whatever the mechanism, the end result was a rapid increase in Black residential segregation, with the neighborhood segregation index rising from 56 to 78 between 1910 and 1940, a remarkable increase of 39 percent in just three decades.

The combination of growing urban Black populations and higher levels of segregation could only produce one possible outcome—higher levels of Black isolation. In 1900, the relatively small number of urban Blacks and the rather low level of Black-White segregation resulted in a low degree of racial isolation within neighborhoods. Among the eight cities shown in Table 13-1, the average isolation index was just 10; the typical urban Black resident lived in a ward that was 90 percent non-Black. Moreover, the index of isolation did not vary substantially from city to city. Urban Blacks early in the century were quite likely to know and interact socially with Whites (Massey and Denton, 1993:19-26). Indeed, on average they were more likely to share a neighborhood with a White person than with a Black person.

By 1930, however, the geographic structure of segregation had changed dramatically, shifting from state and county levels to the neighborhood level. The average isolation index was now 39 in neighborhoods, indicating that most Black residents in the cities under study lived in a ward that was almost 40 percent Black. In some cities, the degree of racial isolation reached truly extreme levels. The transformation was most dramatic in Chicago, where the isolation index went from 10 in 1900 to 70 in 1930, by which time, moreover, the dissimilarity index had reached 85. Similar conditions of intense Black segregation occurred in Cleveland, which by 1930 displayed a dissimilarity index of 85 and an isolation index of 51.

During the first half of the twentieth century, therefore, Black segregation was characterized by countervailing trends at opposite ends of the American geographic hierarchy. As Blacks and Whites became more integrated across states and counties, and as the regional isolation of Blacks declined, progressively higher levels of segregation were imposed on Blacks within cities. The regional integration of Blacks was accompanied by neighborhood segregation in the creation of urban ghettos that caused higher indices of segregation at the neighborhood level. In the course of this shift, however, one outcome remained constant: White exposure to Blacks was minimized. The only thing that changed was the geographic level at which the most extreme indices of segregation occurred.

Table 13-2 shows trends in Black segregation and racial isolation during the decades following World War II. In addition to indices computed at the state, county, and neighborhood levels, data permit a series of measures to be computed at the city level. These computations are based on cities with more than 25,000 inhabitants and measure the degree to which Blacks and Whites reside in separate municipalities.

From 1950 to 1970, the move toward integration at the state and county levels continued as Black out-migration from the South accelerated after World War II. At the state level, the Black-White segregation index dropped from 42 in 1950 to 28 in 1970, and at the county level from 52 to 47. Over the same period, the degree of Black isolation decreased from 20 to 16 at the state level, and from 27 to 23 in counties. As a result, from 1900 to 1970, macro-level segregation largely disappeared from the United States. Indices of Black segregation and racial isolation at the state level were cut in half, with segregation going from 64 to 28 and isolation from 36 to 16. Through a process of out-migration and regional redistribution, Blacks and Whites came to live together in states and counties throughout the nation. By 1970, race relations were no longer a regional problem peculiar to the South; race relations became a salient issue of national scope and importance.

The integration of Blacks at the state and county levels culminated around 1970, when Black migration from the South waned and then reversed, causing state-level indices to stabilize. After 1970, the index of Black-White dissimilarity at state levels remained fixed at 28, while Black isolation held virtually constant at 16 or 17. At the county level, indices of Black-White dissimilarity varied narrowly from 46 to 48, while the degree of Black isolation increased slightly from 23 to 26.

At the neighborhood level, however, Black segregation continued to increase from 1950 to 1970, although at a decelerating pace that reflected the high level of racial segregation already achieved. The average dissimilarity index for the 12 metropolitan areas shown in Table 13-2 stood at 77 in 1950, rising to 81 in 1960, and 83 in 1970. Throughout this period, the average index of Black isolation stood at 67, indicating that most Black urban dwellers lived in a census tract[2] that was two-thirds Black. Thus the

---

[2]Tracts are relatively small, homogenous spatial units of 3,000 to 6,000 people defined by the U.S. Bureau of the Census to approximate urban "neighborhoods" (White, 1987). Although the Census Bureau endeavors to maintain constant boundaries between censuses, population shifts and physical changes invariably require reclassifications that yield small inconsistencies over time. These changes, however, are unlikely to affect broad trends and patterns.

TABLE 13-2 Indices of Black-White Segregation Computed at Four Geographic Levels, 1950 to 1990

| | Years | | | | |
|---|---|---|---|---|---|
| | 1950 | 1960 | 1970 | 1980 | 1990 |
| **Between states** | | | | | |
| Dissimilarity | 42 | 34 | 28 | 28 | 28 |
| Isolation | 20 | 18 | 16 | 17 | 17 |
| **Between counties** | | | | | |
| Dissimilarity | 52 | 49 | 47 | 48 | 46 |
| Isolation | 27 | 24 | 23 | 26 | 26 |
| **Between cities (>25,000)** | | | | | |
| Dissimilarity | 35 | 35 | 40 | 49 | 49 |
| Isolation | 19 | 24 | 29 | 35 | 35 |
| **Between tracts** | | | | | |
| Dissimilarity | | | | | |
| Chicago | 88 | 90 | 92 | 88 | 86 |
| Cleveland | 87 | 90 | 91 | 88 | 85 |
| Dayton | 87 | 90 | 87 | 78 | 75 |
| Detroit | 83 | 87 | 88 | 87 | 88 |
| Greensboro | 59 | 67 | 65 | 56 | 60 |
| Houston | 71 | 79 | 78 | 70 | 67 |
| Indianapolis | 77 | 80 | 82 | 76 | 74 |
| Milwaukee | 86 | 86 | 91 | 84 | 83 |
| Philadelphia | 71 | 76 | 80 | 79 | 77 |
| Pittsburgh | 69 | 75 | 75 | 73 | 71 |
| San Diego | 65 | 69 | 83 | 64 | 58 |
| Average | 77 | 81 | 83 | 77 | 75 |
| Isolation | | | | | |
| Chicago | — | 84 | 86 | 83 | 84 |
| Cleveland | — | 80 | 82 | 80 | 81 |
| Dayton | — | 78 | 73 | 65 | 62 |
| Detroit | — | — | 76 | 77 | 82 |
| Greensboro | — | 64 | 56 | 50 | 56 |
| Houston | — | 73 | 66 | 59 | 64 |
| Indianapolis | — | — | 65 | 62 | 61 |
| Milwaukee | — | — | 74 | 70 | 72 |
| Philadelphia | — | — | 68 | 70 | 72 |
| Pittsburgh | — | 47 | 54 | 54 | 53 |
| San Diego | — | 42 | 42 | 26 | 36 |
| Average | — | 67 | 67 | 63 | 66 |

SOURCE: Massey and Hajnal (1995).

geographic structure of segregation that emerged early in the century was fully formed and stable by 1970. Whites and Blacks were integrated at the state and county levels, but segregated at the neighborhood level. Of the 12 metropolitan areas shown in the table, 9 had tract-level dissimilarity indices in excess of 80 in 1970, and 8 had isolation indices of 66 or more. By the end of the Civil Rights era, the geographic isolation of urban Blacks, on the neighborhood level, was nearly complete. Although the number of cases examined here is small, the trends are consistent with those established by Massey and Denton (1987), based on a larger sample of metropolitan areas.

The Fair Housing Act of 1968 theoretically put an end to housing discrimination; however, residential segregation proved to be remarkably persistent (Massey and Denton, 1993:186-216). Among the 12 cities shown in Table 13-2, the average segregation index fell slightly from 1970 to 1990, going from 83 to 75, but Black isolation indices hardly changed. Scanning trends among individual metropolitan areas, it is difficult to detect a consistent pattern toward residential integration between 1970 and 1990, although Frey and Farley (1994) report some movement toward integration in smaller metropolitan areas, particularly those containing small Black populations, military bases, universities, or large stocks of post-1970 housing.

Despite the relative stability of segregation achieved by 1970 at the state, county, and neighborhood levels, a remarkable change was occurring at the city level. From 1950 onward, Blacks and Whites were becoming more and more segregated across *municipal* boundaries. After 1950, Blacks and Whites not only tended to live in different neighborhoods; increasingly they lived in different municipalities as well. After 1950, in other words, Blacks and Whites came to reside in wholly different towns and cities. From 1950 to 1980, the index of Black-White dissimilarity increased from 35 to 49 at the municipal level, a change of 40 percent in just 30 years, a shift that was remarkably similar to the rapid change observed in neighborhood-level segregation during the early period of ghetto formation. Black isolation went from an index of 19 to 35 at the municipal level, an increase of 84 percent. By the end of the 1970s, the average Black urban dweller lived in a municipality that was 35 percent Black; and one-half of all urban Blacks would have had to exchange places with Whites to achieve an even municipal distribution.

The emergence of significant municipal-level segregation in the United States reflects demographic trends that occurred in all parts of the urban hierarchy—in nonmetropolitan areas as well as central cities and suburbs. In 1950, there were no predominantly Black central cities in the United States. Among cities with more than 100,000 inhabitants, none had a Black percentage in excess of 50 percent. By 1990, however, 14 cities were at least 50 percent Black, including Atlanta, Baltimore, Detroit, Gary, Newark, New Orleans, and Washington; together they were home to 11 percent of all Blacks in the United States. In addition, another 11 cities were approaching Black majorities by 1990, with percentages ranging from 40 percent to 50 percent, including Cleveland, St. Louis, and Oakland. Among cities with populations of 25,000 or more, only two municipalities in the entire United States were more than 50 percent Black in 1950, both in the South; but by 1990 the number had increased to 40. Some of these cities—such as Prichard, Alabama; Kinston, North Carolina; and Vicksburg, Mississippi—were located in nonmetropolitan areas of the South. Others—such as Maywood, Illinois; Highland Park, Michigan; and Inglewood, California—were suburbs of large central cities in the North and West.

## RECENT TRENDS IN BLACK SEGREGATION

Table 13-3 shows indicators of Black residential segregation for the 30 U.S. metropolitan areas with the largest Black populations. As in Tables 13-1 and 13-2, these data are used to evaluate racial segregation from two vantage points. The first three columns show trends in the indices of spatial separation between Blacks and Whites using the index of dissimilarity, and the next three columns show trends in indices of Black residential isolation. The indices for 1970 and 1980, from Massey and Denton (1987), are metropolitan areas based on 1970 boundaries. Indices for 1990, from Harrison and Weinberg (1992), are based on 1990 geographic definitions. White and Black Hispanics were excluded, by both sets of researchers, from their subject sets of Whites and Blacks, and both sets of researchers computed indices using tracts as units of analysis.

Among the northern metropolitan areas shown, there is little evidence of any trend toward Black residential integration. Black segregation indices averaged about 85 in 1970, 80 in 1980, and 78 in 1990, a decline of only 8 percent in 20 years. Dissimilarity indices more than 60 are generally considered high, whereas those between 30 and 60 are considered moderate (Kantrowitz, 1973). At the rate of change observed between 1970 and 1990, the average level of Black-White segregation in northern areas would not reach the lower limits of the high range until the year 2043. At the slower rate of change prevailing from 1970 to 1980, it would take until 2067. As of 1990, no large northern Black community approached even a moderate level of residential segregation.

Indeed, in most metropolitan areas, racial segregation remained very high throughout the 20-year period. Dissimilarity indices were essentially constant in seven metropolitan areas—Cincinnati, Detroit, Gary, New York, Newark, and Philadelphia; in seven others—Buffalo, Chicago,

TABLE 13-3 Trends in Black Segregation and Isolation in the 30
Metropolitan Areas with the Largest Black Populations, 1970 to 1990

| Metropolitan | Dissimilarity Indices | | | Isolation Indices | | |
|---|---|---|---|---|---|---|
| | 1970[a] | 1980[a] | 1990[b] | 1970[a] | 1980[a] | 1990[b] |
| Northern | | | | | | |
| Boston, MA | 81.2 | 77.6 | 68.2 | 56.7 | 55.1 | 51.2 |
| Buffalo, NY | 87.0 | 79.4 | 81.8 | 71.2 | 63.5 | 68.1 |
| Chicago, IL | 91.9 | 87.8 | 85.8 | 85.5 | 82.8 | 83.9 |
| Cincinnati, OH | 76.8 | 72.3 | 75.8 | 59.1 | 54.3 | 61.0 |
| Cleveland, OH | 90.8 | 87.5 | 85.1 | 81.9 | 90.4 | 80.8 |
| Columbus, OH | 81.8 | 71.4 | 67.3 | 63.5 | 57.5 | 52.5 |
| Detroit, MI | 88.4 | 86.7 | 87.6 | 75.9 | 77.3 | 82.3 |
| Gary-Hammond-  E. Chicago, IL | 91.4 | 90.6 | 89.9 | 80.4 | 77.3 | 84.2 |
| Indianapolis, IN | 81.7 | 76.2 | 74.3 | 64.5 | 62.3 | 61.0 |
| Kansas City, MO | 87.4 | 78.9 | 72.6 | 74.2 | 69.0 | 61.6 |
| Los Angeles-Long  Beach, CA | 91.0 | 81.1 | 73.1 | 70.3 | 60.4 | 69.3 |
| Milwaukee, WI | 90.5 | 83.9 | 82.8 | 73.9 | 69.5 | 72.4 |
| New York, NY | 81.0 | 82.0 | 82.2 | 58.8 | 62.7 | 81.9 |
| Newark, NJ | 81.4 | 81.6 | 82.5 | 67.0 | 69.2 | 78.6 |
| Philadelphia, PA | 79.5 | 78.8 | 77.2 | 68.2 | 69.6 | 72.2 |
| Pittsburgh, PA | 75.0 | 72.7 | 71.0 | 53.5 | 54.1 | 53.1 |
| St. Louis, MO | 84.7 | 81.3 | 77.0 | 76.5 | 72.9 | 69.5 |
| San Francisco-  Oakland, CA | 80.1 | 71.7 | 66.8 | 56.0 | 51.1 | 56.1 |
| Average | 84.5 | 80.1 | 77.8 | 68.7 | 66.1 | 68.9 |
| Southern | | | | | | |
| Atlanta, GA | 82.1 | 78.5 | 67.8 | 78.0 | 74.8 | 66.5 |
| Baltimore, MD | 81.9 | 74.7 | 71.4 | 77.2 | 72.3 | 70.6 |
| Birmingham, AL | 37.8 | 40.8 | 71.7 | 45.1 | 50.2 | 69.6 |
| Dallas-Ft. Worth, TX | 86.9 | 77.1 | 63.1 | 76.0 | 64.0 | 58.0 |
| Greensboro-  Winston Salem, NC | 65.4 | 56.0 | 60.9 | 56.1 | 50.1 | 55.5 |
| Houston, TX | 78.1 | 69.5 | 66.8 | 66.4 | 59.3 | 63.6 |
| Memphis, TN | 75.9 | 71.6 | 69.3 | 78.0 | 75.9 | 75.0 |
| Miami, FL | 85.1 | 77.8 | 71.8 | 75.2 | 64.2 | 74.1 |
| New Orleans, LA | 73.1 | 68.3 | 68.8 | 71.3 | 68.8 | 71.9 |
| Norfolk-  Virginia Beach, VA | 75.7 | 63.1 | 50.3 | 73.5 | 62.8 | 55.9 |
| Tampa-St. Petersburg, FL | 79.9 | 72.6 | 69.7 | 58.0 | 51.5 | 51.0 |
| Washington, DC | 81.1 | 70.1 | 66.1 | 77.2 | 68.0 | 66.7 |
| Average | 75.3 | 68.3 | 66.5 | 69.3 | 63.5 | 64.9 |

[a]Indices are from Massey and Denton (1987).
[b]Indices are from Harrison and Weinberg (1992).

Cleveland, Indianapolis, Milwaukee, Pittsburgh, and St. Louis—small declines still left Blacks extremely segregated. All the latter metropolitan areas had dissimilarity indices exceeding 70 in 1990, and in four cases, the index was more than 80. No other ethnic or racial group in the history of the United States has ever, even briefly, experienced such high levels of residential segregation (Massey and Denton, 1993).

A few metropolitan areas experienced significant declines in the level of Black-White segregation between 1970 and 1990, although the pace of change slowed considerably during the 1980s, compared with the 1970s. In Columbus, Ohio, for example, Black-White dissimilarity fell by more than 10 index points from 1970 to 1980 (from 82 to 71), but then dropped by only 4 points through 1990. Likewise, San Francisco dropped from 80 to 72 during the 1970s, but went to just 68 by 1990.

The only areas that experienced a sustained decline in Black-White segregation across both decades were Los Angeles and Boston; but in each case, the overall index of segregation remained well within the high range. The drop in Los Angeles probably reflects the displacement of Blacks by the arrival of large numbers of Asian and, particularly, Hispanic immigrants (Massey and Denton, 1987). By 1990, for example, Watts, the core of the 1960s Black ghetto, had become predominantly Hispanic (Turner and Allen, 1991). The arrival of more than a million new immigrants in Los Angeles County between 1970 and 1980 put substantial pressure on the housing stock, and increased intergroup competition for residential units, especially at the low end of the market, leading to considerable neighborhood flux and residential mixing (Frey and Farley, 1996).

When large Black communities are subject to high levels of segregation, intense racial isolation is inevitable. In 1990, six metropolitan areas—Chicago, Cleveland, Detroit, Gary, New York, and Newark—had isolation indices of 80 or more, meaning that most Black people lived in neighborhoods that were more than 80 percent Black. Detailed analyses of neighborhoods show, however, that this overall average is misleading, because it represents a balance between a small minority of Blacks who reside in highly integrated neighborhoods and a large majority of Blacks who live in all-Black neighborhoods (Denton and Massey, 1991). Moreover, in four of the six metropolitan areas, the level of Black isolation actually increased between 1970 and 1990.

In other northern areas, the prevailing pattern of change in racial isolation was one of stability, with shifts of less than 5 percent from 1970 to 1990. The average isolation index of 68.9 in 1990 was virtually identical to the index of 68.7 observed two decades earlier; in other words, 20 years after the Fair Housing Act, Blacks were still unlikely to come into residential contact with members of other groups. The large ghettos of the North have remained substantially intact and were largely unaffected by Civil Rights legislation of the 1960s.

Trends in Black segregation and isolation are somewhat different in the South, where segregation levels traditionally have been lower because of the distinctive history and character of southern cities. With social segregation enforced by Jim Crow legislation, Blacks and Whites before 1960 often lived in close physical proximity, with Black-inhabited alleys being interspersed between larger, White-occupied avenues (Demerath and Gilmore, 1954). During the postwar housing boom, moreover, rural Black settlements were often overtaken by expanding White suburbs, thereby creating the appearance of racial integration. For these and other reasons, Black-White segregation scores in the South traditionally have averaged about 10 points lower than in the North (Massey and Denton, 1993).

This regional differential is roughly maintained, as shown in Table 13-1, but southern areas display considerably greater diversity, despite the regional averages, than in the North. In some metropolitan areas, such as Baltimore, Houston, and Tampa, significant declines in segregation occurred during the 1970s, but declines slowed during the 1980s. In others, such as Dallas, Miami, and Norfolk, steady declines occurred throughout both decades. In Memphis and New Orleans, relatively small changes occurred, no matter which decade one considers. Two southern areas displayed increasing levels of Black-White segregation—Birmingham, where the increase was very sharp after 1970, and Greensboro, where an initial decline during the 1970s was reversed during the 1980s.

In general, then, Black-White segregation scores in the South appear to be converging on indices from 60 to 70, yielding an average of 67 and maintaining the traditional differential compared with the North. Metropolitan areas with segregation indices higher than the 60 to 70 range in 1970 experienced decreasing segregation, whereas those with indices less than 60 to 70 displayed increasing segregation; and those with indices within that range did not change much.

Only Norfolk differed from this pattern, with a significant and sustained decline in segregation during both decades, producing by 1990 a level of Black-White dissimilarity well within the moderate range. Many Norfolk residents are in the military, which has been more successfully integrated than other institutions in American life (Moskos and Butler, 1996; see also Volume II, Chapter 8). Frey and Farley (1994) demonstrated that areas dominated, economically, by military bases have significantly lower levels of Black-White segregation than others, controlling for a variety of other factors.

Although indices of Black-White dissimilarity may be lower in the South, the relative number of Blacks in urban areas is greater; so the average level of racial isolation within neighborhoods is not much different than in the North. From 1970 to 1990, there was relatively little change in the overall degree of Black isolation, with the average index decreasing from 69 in 1970 to 65 in 1990. In four southern areas—Baltimore, Memphis, Miami, and New Orleans—the Black isolation index was more than 70 in both decades; and in Birmingham, the index of Black isolation rose from 45 to 70 between 1970 and 1990. Only in Norfolk, which was rapidly desegregating, and in Tampa, which had relatively few Blacks, did isolation scores fall below 60. In most cities in the South, as in the North, Blacks were relatively unlikely to share neighborhoods with members of other racial or ethnic groups.

Thus, despite evidence of change in the South, Blacks living within the nation's largest urban Black communities are still highly segregated and spatially isolated from the rest of American society. Of the 30 northern and southern areas examined here, 19 still had Black-White dissimilarity indices in excess of 70 in 1990, and 12 had isolation indices in excess of 70. Either in absolute terms or in comparison to other groups, Blacks remain a very residentially segregated and spatially isolated people.

## RECENT TRENDS IN HISPANIC SEGREGATION

Based on the historical experience of Blacks, recent demographic trends for Hispanics would be expected to have produced increasing levels of segregation during the 1970s and 1980s. In this period, there has been a remarkable resurgence of Hispanic immigration, yielding rapidly growing Hispanic populations in many metropolitan areas. In the Los Angeles metropolitan area, for example, the Hispanic population increased by 1.3 million between 1970 and 1990; Hispanics went from being 28 percent of the population to 38 percent. Because migrant networks channel new arrivals to neighborhoods where immigrants have already settled, such rapid in-migration could be expected to increase the concentration of Hispanics within enclaves and raise overall levels of isolation and segregation (Massey, 1985).

Although spatial assimilation may occur as income rises and the generations succeed one another, these socioeconomic mechanisms occur at a much slower pace than immigration and settlement. During periods of rapid immigration, therefore, segregation levels tend to rise; and the greater and more rapid the immigration, the more pronounced the increase in segregation.

Table 13-4 presents indicators of Hispanic-White dissimilarity and Hispanic residential isolation for the 30 metropolitan areas containing the largest Hispanic communities in the United States. In a significant subset of these metropolitan areas, Hispanics constitute an absolute majority of

TABLE 13-4 Trends in Hispanic Segregation and Isolation in the 30
Metropolitan Areas with the Largest Hispanic Populations, 1970 to 1990

| Metropolitan Area | Dissimilarity Indices | | | Isolation Indices | | |
|---|---|---|---|---|---|---|
| | 1970[a] | 1980[a] | 1990[b] | 1970[a] | 1980[a] | 1990[b] |
| Hispanic majority | | | | | | |
| Brownsville-Harlingen, TX | 54.0[c] | 42.0[d] | 39.8 | NA | NA | 85.2 |
| Corpus Christi, TX | 55.9 | 51.6 | 47.5 | 63.5 | 63.6 | 67.8 |
| El Paso, TX | 49.6 | 51.2 | 49.7 | 71.5 | 74.1 | 80.0 |
| McAllen-Pharr, TX | 62.0[c] | 48.0[d] | 37.9 | NA | NA | 87.4 |
| Miami, FL | 50.4 | 51.9 | 50.3 | 46.5 | 58.3 | 73.4 |
| San Antonio, TX | 59.1 | 57.2 | 53.7 | 67.5 | 67.5 | 69.1 |
| Average | 55.2 | 50.3 | 46.5 | 62.3 | 65.9 | 77.2 |
| Other metropolitan | | | | | | |
| Albuquerque, NM | 45.7 | 42.5 | 41.9 | 54.4 | 50.6 | 53.4 |
| Anaheim-Santa Ana, CA | 32.0 | 41.6 | 49.9 | 19.4 | 31.0 | 50.1 |
| Bakersfield, CA | 50.8 | 54.5 | 55.4 | 34.9 | 42.1 | 55.7 |
| Chicago, IL | 58.4 | 63.5 | 63.2 | 25.1 | 38.0 | 51.3 |
| Dallas-Ft. Worth, TX | 42.5 | 47.8 | 49.5 | 18.6 | 24.0 | 41.1 |
| Denver-Boulder, CO | 47.4 | 47.4 | 46.5 | 27.4 | 27.5 | 33.8 |
| Fresno, CA | 40.8 | 45.4 | 47.8 | 37.6 | 44.6 | 58.7 |
| Houston, TX | 45.3 | 46.4 | 49.3 | 26.9 | 32.8 | 49.3 |
| Jersey City, NJ | 54.8 | 48.8 | 42.9 | 34.5 | 46.5 | 56.0 |
| Los Angeles, CA | 46.8 | 57.0 | 61.1 | 37.8 | 50.1 | 71.5 |
| Nassau-Suffolk, NY | 29.1 | 36.2 | 42.3 | 6.0 | 9.6 | 22.1 |
| New York, NY | 64.9 | 65.6 | 65.8 | 36.1 | 40.0 | 66.6 |
| Newark, NJ | 60.4 | 65.6 | 66.7 | 16.7 | 26.3 | 48.5 |
| Oxnard-Simi Valley, CA | NA | NA | 52.3 | NA | NA | 51.2 |

the total population, a condition that does not hold for any of the Black communities listed in Table 13-3. Because large minority populations increase the demographic potential for isolation, and because theorists hypothesize that high minority percentages foment greater discrimination on the part of majority members (Allport, 1958; Blalock, 1967), indices are tabulated separately for areas where Hispanics comprise a majority or near-majority (48 to 49 percent) of the population.

Despite the fact that demographic conditions in these metropolitan areas operate to maximize the potential for segregation, the degree of Hispanic-White residential dissimilarity proved to be quite moderate, and actually decreases over the two decades, going from an average of 55 in 1970 to 47 in 1990. Indices of Hispanic-White segregation were essentially constant in El Paso and Miami, and changed little in San Antonio and

TABLE 13-4 *Continued*

| Metropolitan Area | Dissimilarity Indices | | | Isolation Indices | | |
|---|---|---|---|---|---|---|
| | 1970[a] | 1980[a] | 1990[b] | 1970[a] | 1980[a] | 1990[b] |
| Philadelphia, PA | 54.0 | 62.9 | 62.6 | 10.6 | 21.6 | 42.9 |
| Phoenix, AZ | 48.4 | 49.4 | 48.1 | 32.1 | 32.1 | 39.8 |
| Riverside-San Bernadino, CA | 37.3 | 36.4 | 35.8 | 30.2 | 31.6 | 42.7 |
| Sacramento, CA | 34.7 | 36.4 | 37.0 | 16.3 | 16.5 | 23.9 |
| San Diego, CA | 33.1 | 42.1 | 45.3 | 19.8 | 26.9 | 43.6 |
| San Francisco-Oakland, CA | 34.7 | 40.2 | 43.9 | 19.2 | 19.3 | 41.1 |
| San Jose, CA | 40.2 | 44.5 | 47.8 | 29.6 | 31.7 | 47.1 |
| Tampa, FL | 56.0 | 48.4 | 45.3 | 25.0 | 18.2 | 21.5 |
| Tucson, AZ | 52.6 | 51.9 | 49.7 | 46.7 | 43.1 | 48.8 |
| Washington, DC | 31.8 | 30.5 | 40.9 | 4.3 | 5.4 | 22.5 |
| Average | 45.3 | 48.0 | 49.6 | 26.5 | 30.8 | 45.1 |

Note: The Massey-Denton computations did not include several metropolitan areas that housed large Hispanic populations in 1990; therefore, additional indices have been taken from Lopez (1981) and Hwang and Murdock (1982). These figures, however, were computed for central cities rather than metropolitan areas and are therefore somewhat higher thus underestimating increases and overestimating declines in the level of Hispanic-White segregation.

[a]Indices are from Massey and Denton (1987).
[b]Indices are from Harrison and Weinberg (1992).
[c]Indices are from Lopez (1981).
[d]Indices are from Hwang and Murdock (1982).

Corpus Christi. In Brownsville and McAllen, there were pronounced declines in segregation; but in no case was there an increase in Hispanic segregation from Whites within Hispanic-majority areas.

Indices of isolation, in contrast, were high and rose somewhat from 1970 to 1990. The increases did not stem from an increasing tendency for Whites and Hispanics to live apart, however, but from the large size and rapid growth of the Hispanic population. Isolation indices of 85 and 87 in Brownsville and McAllen mainly reflect the fact that Hispanics represent 82 and 85 percent of the metropolitan populations, respectively. Even if Hispanics were evenly distributed, high levels of Hispanic-White contact are impossible to achieve in areas that are so predominantly Hispanic.

Among Blacks, however, isolation indices in the 80s, as in Chicago and Detroit, generally reflect the intense segregation of Blacks, rather than high Black population percentages; in both these metropolitan areas, Blacks constitute about 22 percent of the population. The contrast in the indices between Hispanics and Blacks is put into perspective by comparing indices for Hispanics in San Antonio with indices for Blacks in northern areas (see Table 13-1). Although Hispanics constitute 48 percent of San Antonio's population, its Hispanic-White dissimilarity index of 54 is less than that for Black-White indices in any northern area; and San Antonio's Hispanic isolation index of 69 is less than it is for 7 of the 18 Black isolation indices.

A better indication of what happens to Hispanics in U.S. cities can be seen by examining segregation measures computed for metropolitan areas where Hispanics do not constitute such a large percentage of the population. On average, indices of Hispanic-White dissimilarity changed little in these areas, moving upward slightly from 45 in 1970 to 50 in 1990. In about one-third of these metropolitan areas—Chicago, Denver, Houston, New York, Phoenix, Riverside, Sacramento, and Tucson—Hispanic segregation remained nearly constant from 1970 to 1990; and in three cases—Albuquerque, Jersey City, and Tampa—indices of Hispanic-White dissimilarity decreased somewhat over the decades. In the remainder of the areas, indices of Hispanic segregation increased. In most cases, the increases were modest; but in several instances, segregation increased substantially over the two decades. In Los Angeles, for example, indices of Hispanic-White segregation increased from 47 to 61; in Anaheim the increase was from 32 to 50. Large increases were also recorded in Nassau-Suffolk, San Diego, San Francisco, and Washington, D.C. In all these metropolitan areas there were rapid rates of Hispanic population growth and immigration from 1970 to 1990.

Despite these increases, indices of Hispanic-White segregation still remained moderate in 1990. Only 5 of the 24 metropolitan areas displayed indices in excess of 60. In 3 of these—New York, Newark, and Philadelphia—Puerto Ricans predominated; and since 1970, this group has stood apart from other Hispanic populations in displaying uniquely high levels of segregation (Jackson, 1981; Massey, 1981), a pattern largely attributable to the fact that many Puerto Ricans are of African ancestry (Massey and Bitterman, 1985; Massey and Denton, 1989a). The two remaining areas are Los Angeles, which experienced more Hispanic immigration than any other metropolitan area in the country, and Chicago, which contained a large population of Puerto Ricans in addition to a rapidly growing Mexican immigrant community.

Reflecting the increase in the proportion of Hispanics in most metropolitan areas, Hispanic isolation indices rose markedly throughout the nation. In those few areas where rates of Hispanic population increase were relatively slow—Albuquerque, Denver, Phoenix, and Tucson—the level of Hispanic isolation hardly changed; but as the rate of Hispanic immigration increased, so did the extent of spatial isolation. Given its popularity as a destination for Hispanic immigration, Hispanic isolation rose most strongly in Southern California cities, going from 19 to 50 in Anaheim, 38 to 72 in Los Angeles, and 20 to 40 in San Diego.

By 1990, isolation indices equaled or exceeded 50 in about half of the metropolitan areas under consideration, but in only two cases—New York and Los Angeles, the two metropolitan areas with the largest Hispanic communities—did the index exceed 60. By way of contrast, only eight of the 30 Black communities examined earlier had Black isolation indices less than 60. Although contemporary demographic conditions suggest trends toward high segregation and rising isolation among Hispanics, they still do not display the high index ratings characteristic for Blacks in large urban areas.

## RECENT TRENDS IN ASIAN SEGREGATION

Although Asian immigration into U.S. urban areas accelerated rapidly after 1970, Asian populations are still quite small compared with either Black or Hispanic populations. Moreover, Asians are more highly concentrated regionally and found in a relatively small number of metropolitan areas. Table 13-5, therefore, presents indices of Asian segregation and isolation only for the 20 largest Asian communities, rather than the 30 largest.

Again demographic conditions for Asians favor substantial increases in segregation and isolation. In most metropolitan areas, immigration led to the rapid expansion of a rather small 1970 population base. In some areas, the number of post-1970 migrants actually exceeds the size of the original Asian community severalfold. Only 25,000 Asians lived in the Anaheim-Santa Ana metropolitan area in 1970, for example, but by 1990, their number had multiplied ten times, to 249,000. Over the same period, the Asian community of Los Angeles quadrupled, going from 243,000 to 954,000; and Chicago's Asian population grew from 62,000 to 230,000. In such cases, where a sudden massive in-migration overwhelms a small, established community, indices of segregation often decrease initially as new arrivals distribute themselves widely, and then increase as these pioneers attract subsequent settlers to the same residential areas.

Such a pattern of decreasing and then increasing Asian segregation is the most common pattern of change among the metropolitan areas shown in Table 13-5. The Asian-White dissimilarity index averaged 44 in 1970, decreased to 36 in 1980, and then increased to 41 in 1990. This basic trend occurred in 12 of the 20 metropolitan areas. In three more areas, an initial decline was followed by no change from 1980 to 1990. Only one area—

TABLE 13-5 Trends in Asian Segregation and Isolation in the 20 Metropolitan Areas with the Largest Asian Populations, 1970 to 1990

| Metropolitan Area | Dissimilarity Indices | | | Isolation Indices | | |
|---|---|---|---|---|---|---|
| | 1970[a] | 1980[a] | 1990[b] | 1970[a] | 1980[a] | 1990[b] |
| Anaheim, CA | 27.4 | 24.9 | 33.3 | 2.6 | 7.7 | 22.4 |
| Boston, MA | 49.9 | 47.4 | 44.8 | 8.0 | 10.5 | 12.9 |
| Chicago, IL | 55.8 | 43.9 | 43.2 | 7.6 | 8.7 | 15.9 |
| Dallas, TX | 43.9 | 29.1 | 40.5 | 1.7 | 2.6 | 9.6 |
| Fresno, CA | 35.1 | 22.9 | 43.4 | 5.7 | 5.3 | 33.1 |
| Houston, TX | 42.7 | 34.6 | 45.7 | 1.5 | 4.5 | 15.7 |
| Los Angeles, CA | 53.1 | 43.1 | 46.3 | 12.3 | 15.2 | 40.5 |
| Minneapolis, MN | 45.2 | 36.9 | 41.2 | 3.0 | 6.2 | 15.1 |
| Nassau-Suffolk, NY | 42.2 | 34.5 | 32.4 | 1.0 | 2.2 | 5.9 |
| New York, NY | 56.1 | 48.1 | 48.4 | 11.6 | 14.3 | 32.8 |
| Newark, NJ | 50.2 | 34.4 | 29.6 | 1.5 | 2.9 | 7.5 |
| Paterson-Clifton-Passaic, NJ | 46.6 | 40.4 | 34.4 | 1.3 | 3.1 | 12.1 |
| Philadelphia, PA | 49.1 | 43.7 | 43.2 | 2.4 | 4.0 | 11.0 |
| Riverside-San Bernadino, CA | 31.9 | 21.5 | 32.8 | 2.5 | 4.1 | 10.2 |
| Sacramento, CA | 47.6 | 35.5 | 47.7 | 11.8 | 11.6 | 23.6 |
| San Diego, CA | 41.3 | 40.5 | 48.1 | 5.9 | 11.1 | 29.1 |
| San Francisco-Oakland, CA | 48.6 | 44.4 | 50.1 | 21.0 | 23.2 | 46.0 |
| San Jose, CA | 25.4 | 29.5 | 38.5 | 5.3 | 11.6 | 36.6 |
| Seattle, WA | 46.6 | 33.3 | 36.5 | 11.7 | 12.4 | 20.0 |
| Washington, DC | 36.5 | 26.8 | 32.3 | 2.2 | 5.7 | 12.6 |
| Average | 43.8 | 35.8 | 40.6 | 6.0 | 8.3 | 20.6 |

[a]Indices are from Massey and Denton (1987).
[b]Indices are from Harrison and Weinberg (1992).

San Jose—experienced a sustained increase in Asian segregation; but it began from a very low level of segregation in 1970. Four areas displayed uninterrupted declines in segregation across both decades—Boston, Nassau-Suffolk, Newark, and Paterson.

Despite rapid immigration and population growth, Asian segregation indices remained quite moderate in 1990. Increases observed between 1980 and 1990 simply restored the indices to their 1970 levels, yielding little net change over the two decades. Thus, Asian-White dissimilarity indices ranged from the low 30s in Anaheim, Nassau-Suffolk, Newark, Riverside, and Washington to 50 in San Francisco-Oakland. In no metropolitan area did the index of Asian segregation approach the high levels characteristic of Blacks in the nation's largest metropolitan areas.

Rapid Asian immigration into moderately segregated communities did produce rather sharp increases in the extent of Asian isolation, however, consistent with a process of enclave consolidation. The most pronounced increases occurred in areas where southeast-Asian refugees settled in large numbers—Anaheim, where the isolation index rose from 3 in 1970 to 22 in 1990; Fresno, where the increase was from 6 to 33; and San Diego, where the increase was from 6 to 29. Despite these increases, however, Asians still are not very isolated anywhere, including San Francisco-Oakland, where they constitute a higher percentage of the population (21 percent) than in any other metropolitan area. The isolation index of 46 means that Asians in the Bay Area are more likely to share a neighborhood with non-Asians than with each other; and in Los Angeles, which received the highest number of Asian immigrants between 1970 and 1990, the isolation index rose to just under 41. Thus, the largest and most segregated Asian communities in the United States are much less isolated than the most integrated Black communities.

## BLACK HYPERSEGREGATION

Despite their apparent clarity, the above data actually understate the extent of Black isolation in U.S. society, because the data only incorporate two dimensions of segregation: evenness, as measured by the dissimilarity index, and isolation, as measured by the $P^*$ index. Massey and Denton (1988, 1989b), however, conceptualize segregation as a multidimensional construct. They contend there are five dimensions of spatial variation; in addition to evenness and isolation, residential segregation should be conceptualized in terms of clustering, concentration, and centralization. This five-dimensional conceptualization of segregation recently has been updated and revalidated with 1990 data (Massey et al.,1996).

*Clustering* is the extent to which minority areas adjoin one another spatially. It is maximized when Black neighborhoods form one large, contiguous ghetto; and it is minimized when they are scattered, as in a checkerboard pattern. *Centralization* is the degree to which Blacks are distributed in and around the center of an urban area, usually defined as the central-business district. *Concentration* is the relative amount of physical space occupied by Blacks; as segregation increases, Blacks are increasingly confined to smaller, geographically compacted areas.

A high level of segregation on any single dimension is problematic because it isolates a minority group from amenities, opportunities, and resources that affect socioeconomic well-being. As high levels of segregation accumulate across dimensions, however, the deleterious effects of segregation multiply.  Indices of evenness and isolation (i.e., dissimilarity and P*), by themselves, cannot capture this multidimensional layering of segregation; therefore, there is a misrepresentation of the nature of Black segregation and an understatement of its severity.  Blacks are not only more segregated than other groups on any single dimension of segregation; they are more segregated across all dimensions simultaneously.

Massey and Denton (1993) identified a set of 16 metropolitan areas that were highly segregated—i.e., had an index higher than 60—on at least four of the five dimensions of segregation, a pattern they called "hypersegregation."  These metropolitan areas included Atlanta, Baltimore, Buffalo, Chicago, Cleveland, Dallas, Detroit, Gary, Indianapolis, Kansas City, Los Angeles, Milwaukee, New York, Newark, and St. Louis.  Within this set of areas, the Black-White dissimilarity index averaged 82, the average isolation index was 71, the mean clustering index was 58, the mean centralization index was 88, and the average concentration index was 83.  By way of contrast, neither Hispanics nor Asians were hypersegregated within *any* metropolitan area.

These 16 metropolitan areas are among the most important in the country, incorporating 6 of the 10 largest urban areas in the United States.  Blacks in these areas live within large, contiguous settlements of densely inhabited neighborhoods packed tightly around the urban core.  Inhabitants typically would be unlikely to come into contact with non-Blacks in the neighborhood where they live.  If they were to travel to an adjacent neighborhood, they would still be unlikely to see a White face.  If they went to the next neighborhood beyond that, no Whites would be there either.  People growing up in such an environment would have little direct experience with the culture, norms, and behaviors of the rest of American society, and have few social contacts with members of other racial groups.

Denton (1994) reexamined the issue of hypersegregation using data from the 1990 Census.  According to her analysis, not only has Black hypersegregation continued, in many ways it has grown worse.  Of the 16 metropolitan areas defined as hypersegregated in 1980, 14 remained so in 1990.  In Atlanta the index of spatial concentration decreased to 59, just missing the criteria for hypersegregation, and in Dallas the isolation index decreased to 58.  But both these figures are *just* below the threshold index of 60.  All other metropolitan areas that were hypersegregated in 1980 showed an increase on at least one dimension by 1990.  In 10 areas, isolation increased; concentration grew more acute in 9 areas; and clustering increased in 8.  In Newark and Buffalo, segregation increased in all five dimensions simultaneously; and in Detroit, segregation increased on all dimensions but one.

In short, areas that were hypersegregated in 1980 generally remained so in 1990, and there was little evidence of movement away from this extreme pattern. On the contrary, hypersegregation appears to have spread to several new urban areas during the 1980s. Of the 44 nonhypersegregated metropolitan areas studied by Massey and Denton in 1980, Denton (1994) found that 6 had come to satisfy the criteria by 1990—Birmingham, Cincinnati, Miami, New Orleans, Oakland, and Washington, D.C.—bringing the total number of hypersegregated metropolitan areas to 20. Taken together, these 20 contain roughly 11 million Blacks and constitute 36 percent of the entire U.S. Black population. As already pointed out, the percentage of Hispanics and Asians who are hypersegregated is zero.

## EXPLAINING THE PERSISTENCE OF RACIAL SEGREGATION

A variety of explanations have been posited to account for the unusual depth and persistence of Black segregation in American cities. One hypothesis is that racial segregation reflects class differences between Blacks and Whites—i.e., because Blacks, on average, have lower incomes and fewer socioeconomic resources than Whites, they cannot afford to move into White neighborhoods in significant numbers. According to this hypothesis, Black-White segregation, to some extent, reflects segregation on the basis of income, with poor households, which happen to be predominantly Black, living in different neighborhoods than affluent households, which happen to be disproportionately White.

This explanation has not been sustained empirically, however. When indices of racial segregation are computed within categories of income, occupation, or education, researchers have found that levels of Black-White segregation do not vary by social class (Farley, 1977; Simkus, 1978; Massey, 1979, 1981; Massey and Fischer, 1999). According to Denton and Massey (1988), Black families annually earning at least $50,000 were just as segregated as those earning less than $2,500. Indeed, Black families annually earning more than $50,000 were more segregated than Hispanic or Asian families earning less than $2,500. In other words, the most affluent Blacks appear to be more segregated than the poorest Hispanics or Asians; and in contrast to the case of Blacks, Hispanic and Asian segregation levels fall steadily as income rises, reaching low or moderate levels at incomes of $50,000 or more (Denton and Massey, 1988).

Another explanation for racial segregation is that Blacks prefer to live in predominantly Black neighborhoods, and that segregated housing simply reflects these preferences. This line of reasoning does not square well with survey evidence on Black attitudes, however. Most Blacks continue to express strong support for the ideal of integration. When asked on opinion polls whether they favor "desegregation, strict segregation, or something in-between," Blacks answer "desegregation" in large numbers (Schuman et al., 1985). Blacks are virtually unanimous in agreeing that "Black people have a right to live wherever they can afford to," and 71 percent would vote for a community-wide law to enforce this right (Bobo et al., 1986).

Black respondents are not only committed to integration as an ideal, survey results suggest they also strongly prefer it in practice. When asked about specific neighborhood racial compositions, Blacks consistently select racially mixed areas as most desirable (Farley et al., 1978, 1979, 1994; Clark, 1991). Although the most popular choice is a neighborhood that is half-Black and half-White, as late as 1992, nearly 90 percent of Blacks in Detroit would be willing to live in virtually any racially mixed area (Farley et al., 1994).

Although Blacks express a reluctance about moving into all-White neighborhoods, this apprehension does not indicate a rejection of White neighbors per se, but stems from well-founded fears of hostility and rejection. Among Black respondents to a 1976 Detroit survey who expressed a reluctance to moving into all-White areas, 34 percent thought that White neighbors would be unfriendly and make them feel unwelcome, 37 percent felt they would be made to feel uncomfortable, and 17 percent expressed a fear of outright violence (Farley et al., 1979). Moreover, 80 percent of all Black respondents rejected the view that moving into a White neighborhood constituted a desertion of the Black community. More recently, Jackson (1994) linked the reluctance of Blacks to "pioneer" White areas not only to fears of rejection by White neighbors, but also to an *expectation* of discrimination by real estate agents and lenders.

Thus evidence suggests that racial segregation in urban America is not a voluntary reflection of Black preferences. If it were up to them, Blacks would live in racially mixed neighborhoods. But it is not up to them only, of course; their preferences interact with those of Whites and, thus, produce the residential configurations actually observed. Even though Blacks may prefer neighborhoods with an even racial balance, integration will not occur if most Whites find this level of racial mixing unacceptable.

On the surface, Whites seem to share Blacks' ideological commitment to open housing. The percentage of Whites on national surveys who agree that "Black people have a right to live wherever they can afford to" approached 90 percent in the late 1970s; and the percentage who disagreed with the view that "White people have a right to keep Blacks out of their [Whites'] neighborhoods," reached 67 percent in 1980. At present, few Whites openly call for the strict segregation of American society (Schuman et al., 1985, 1998; Sniderman and Piazza, 1993; Hochschild, 1995).

However, Whites remain quite uncomfortable with the implications of open housing in practice; only 40 percent, in 1980, said they would be willing to vote for a community-wide law stating that "a homeowner cannot refuse to sell to someone because of their race or skin color" (Schuman and Bobo, 1988). In other words, 60 percent of Whites would vote *against* an open housing law, which, in fact, has been federal law for 25 years.

White support for open housing generally declines as the hypothetical number of Blacks in their neighborhood increases. Whereas 86 percent of Whites in 1978 said they would not move if "a Black person came to live next door," only 46 percent stated they would not move if "Black people came to live in large numbers," and only 28 percent of Whites would be willing to live in a neighborhood that was half-Black and half-White (Schuman et al., 1985). Likewise, the severity of White prejudice toward Blacks increases as the percentage of Blacks in the area increases, a relationship that is *not* observed for Hispanics or Asians (Taylor, 1998).

When questions are posed about specific neighborhood compositions, moreover, it becomes clear that White tolerance for racial mixing is quite limited. According to Farley et al. (1994), 16 percent of Whites responding to a 1992 Detroit survey said they would feel uncomfortable in a neighborhood where only 7 percent of the residents were Black; 13 percent would be unwilling to enter such an area. When the Black percentage reaches 20 percent, one-third of all Whites say they would be unwilling to enter, 30 percent would feel uncomfortable, and 15 percent would seek to leave. A neighborhood about 30 percent Black exceeds the limits of racial tolerance for most Whites; 59 percent would be unwilling to move in, 44 percent would feel uncomfortable, and 29 percent would try to leave. Beyond a 50:50 balance, a neighborhood becomes unacceptable to all except a small minority of Whites; 73 percent said they would not wish to move into such a neighborhood, 53 percent would try to leave, and 65 percent would feel uncomfortable. As was stated, most Blacks feel a 50:50 racial mixture is desirable. This fundamental disparity between the two races has been confirmed by surveys conducted in Milwaukee, Omaha, Cincinnati, Kansas City, and Los Angeles (Clark, 1991).

The discrepancy between Whites' acceptance of open housing in principal and their reluctance to live among Blacks in practice yields a rather specific hypothesis about the nature of trends in Black-White segregation over the past 20 years. Hypothetically, declines in Black-White segregation should be confined primarily to metropolitan areas with relatively small Black populations, because in these places, desegregation can occur without Whites having to share their neighborhoods with too many Black people (Massey and Gross, 1991). If Black people make up 3 percent of the metropolitan population, for example, then complete desegregation yields an average of 3 percent Black within every neighborhood, which is well within most Whites' tolerance limits. If, however, Black people make up 20 percent of the metropolitan population, desegregation would produce neighborhoods that are 20 percent Black, on average, which exceeds the tolerance limits of many Whites, creates instability, and fuels a process of neighborhood turnover. In keeping with this hypothesis, Krivo and Kaufman (1999) show that desegregation between 1980 and 1990 was quite likely where the Black population was small but very unlikely where it was large. As a result, observed declines in segregation during the 1980s were confined largely to metropolitan areas that contained very few Blacks.

Over the last three decades, U.S. metropolitan areas have been transformed by immigration and many have moved well beyond the simple Black-White dichotomy of earlier years, necessitating new approaches to the measurement of racial attitudes. A recent survey in Los Angeles sought to replicate the Detroit survey within an ethnically diverse metropolis. Analysis of these data by Zubrinsky and Bobo (1996) showed that all non-Black groups—Whites, Asians, and Hispanics—attribute a variety of negative traits to Blacks and consider Blacks to be the least desirable neighbors (see, also, Bobo and Zubrinsky, 1996). Blacks experience by far the greatest likelihood of hostility from other groups, and are universally acknowledged to face the most severe housing discrimination. The end result is a clear hierarchy of neighborhood racial preferences in Los Angeles, with Whites at the top, followed by Asians and Hispanics, and Blacks at the bottom. Segregation does not result from Black ethnocentrism so much as from avoidance behavior by other groups, all of whom seek to circumvent potential coresidence with Blacks.

These contrasting racial attitudes create large intergroup disparities in the demand for housing in racially mixed neighborhoods. Given the violence, intimidation, and harassment that historically have followed their entry into White areas, Blacks express reluctance at being first across the color line. After one or two Black families have moved into a neighborhood, however, Black demand grows rapidly, given the high value placed on integrated housing. This demand escalates as the Black percentage rises toward 50 percent, the most preferred neighborhood configuration; beyond this point, Black demand stabilizes and then falls off as the Black percentage rises toward 100 percent.

The pattern of White, Asian, and Hispanic demand for housing in racially mixed areas follows precisely the opposite trajectory. Demand is strong for homes in all-White areas, but once one or two Black families enter a neighborhood, demand begins to falter as some non-Black families leave and others refuse to move in. The acceleration in residential turnover coincides with the expansion of Black demand, making it likely that outgoing White, Hispanic, or Asian households are replaced by Black families. As the Black percentage rises, overall demand drops ever more steeply, and Black demand rises at an increasing rate. By the time Black demand peaks at the 50 percent mark, practically no other groups are willing to enter and most are trying to leave. Thus, racial segregation appears to be created by a process of racial turnover fueled by the persistence of significant anti-Black prejudice on the part of virtually every other group.

This model of racial change was proposed two decades ago by Schelling (1971), who argued that integration is an unstable outcome because Whites prefer lower minority proportions than Blacks—even though Whites might accept some Black neighbors. Yet by itself, Schelling's explanation is incomplete. Whites can only avoid coresidence with Blacks if mechanisms exist to keep Blacks out of neighborhoods to which they might otherwise be attracted. Whites can only flee a neighborhood where Blacks have entered if there are other all-White neighborhoods to go to, and this escape will only be successful if Blacks are unlikely or unable to follow.

Racial discrimination was institutionalized in the real estate industry during the 1920s and well established in private practice by the 1940s (Massey and Denton, 1993). Evidence shows that discriminatory behavior was widespread among realtors at least until 1968, when the Fair Housing Act was passed (Helper, 1969; Saltman, 1979). After that, outright refusals to rent or sell to Blacks became rare, given that overt discrimination could lead to prosecution under the law.

Black home seekers now face a more subtle process of exclusion. Rather than encountering "White only" signs, they encounter a covert series of barriers. Blacks who inquire about an advertised unit may be told that it has just been sold or rented; they may be shown only the advertised unit and told that no others are available; they may only be shown houses in Black or racially mixed areas and led away from White neighborhoods; they may be quoted a higher rent or selling price than Whites; they may be told that the selling agents are too busy and to come back later; their phone number may be taken but a return call never made; they may be shown units but offered no assistance in arranging financing; or they simply may be treated brusquely and discourteously in hopes that they will leave.

Although individual acts of discrimination are small and subtle, they have a powerful cumulative effect in lowering the probability of Black entry into White neighborhoods. Because the discrimination is latent, however, it is not easily observable, and the only way to confirm whether or not it has occurred is to compare the treatment of both Black and White clients that have similar social and economic characteristics. If White clients receive systematically more favorable treatment, then one can safely conclude that discrimination has taken place (Fix et al., 1993).

Differences in the treatment of White and Black home seekers are measured by means of a housing audit. Teams of White and Black auditors are paired and sent to randomly selected realtors to pose as clients seeking a home or apartment. The auditors are trained to present comparable housing needs and family characteristics, and to express similar tastes; they are assigned equivalent social and economic traits by the investigator. After each encounter, the auditors fill out a detailed report of their experiences and the results are tabulated and compared to determine the nature and level of discrimination (Yinger, 1986, 1989).

Local fair-housing organizations began to conduct such studies at the end of the 1960s. These efforts revealed that discrimination was continuing despite the Fair Housing Act. A 1969 audit of realtors in St. Louis, for example, documented a pattern and practice of discrimination sufficient to force four realty firms to sign a consent decree with the U.S. Department of Justice wherein they agreed to desist from certain biased practices (Saltman, 1979). Likewise, a 1971 audit study carried out in Palo Alto, California, found that Blacks were treated in a discriminatory fashion by 50 percent of the area's apartment complexes; and a 1972 audit of apartments in suburban Baltimore uncovered discrimination in more than 45 percent of the cases (Saltman, 1979).

Racial discrimination clearly persisted through the 1980s. In one 1983 Chicago study, suburban realtors showed homes to 67 percent of White auditors but only 47 percent of Black auditors (Hintzen, 1983). Another Chicago study done in 1985 revealed that Whites were offered financial information at nearly twice the rate it was offered to Blacks (Schroeder, 1985). One developer working in Chicago's south suburbs refused to deal with Blacks at all; Blacks were always told that no properties were available, even though 80 percent of Whites were shown real estate (Bertram, 1988). In the same study, realtors told 92 percent of Whites that apartments were available but gave this information to only 46 percent of Blacks.

Audit studies of other metropolitan areas reveal similar levels of racial discrimination. According to Yinger's (1986) review of studies conducted in metropolitan Boston and Denver during the early 1980s, Black home seekers had between a 38 and a 59 percent chance of receiving unfavorable treatment, compared to Whites, on any given real estate transaction. Through various lies and deceptions, Blacks were informed of only 65 of every 100 units presented to Whites, and they inspected fewer than 54 of every 100 shown to Whites.

In 1987, Galster (1990a) wrote to more than 200 local fair-housing organizations and obtained written reports of 71 different audit studies carried out during the 1980s—21 in the home sales market and 50 in the rental market. Despite differences in measures and methods, he concluded that "racial discrimination continues to be a dominant feature of metropolitan housing markets in the 1980s" (p. 172). Using a conservative measure of racial bias, he found that Blacks averaged a 20 percent chance of experiencing discrimination in the sales market and a 50 percent chance in the rental market.

Studies have also examined the prevalence of "steering" by real estate agents. Steering occurs when White and Black clients are guided to neighborhoods that differ systematically with respect to social and economic characteristics, especially racial composition. A study carried out in Cleveland during the early 1970s found that 70 percent of companies engaged in some form of steering (Saltman, 1979); and an examination of realtors in metropolitan Detroit during the mid-1970s revealed that, compared to Whites, Blacks were shown homes in less-expensive areas that were located closer to Black population centers (Pearce, 1979).

Galster (1990b) studied six real estate firms located in Cincinnati and Memphis and found that racial steering occurred in roughly 50 percent of the transactions sampled during the mid-1980s. As in the Detroit study, homes shown to Blacks tended to be in racially mixed areas and were more likely to be adjacent to neighborhoods with a high percentage of Black residents. White auditors were rarely shown homes in integrated neighborhoods, unless they specifically requested them, and even after the request was honored, they continued to be guided primarily to homes in White areas. Sales agents also made numerous positive comments about White neighborhoods to White clients but said little to Black home buyers. In a broader review of 36 different audit studies, Galster (1990c) discovered that such selective commentary by agents is probably more common than overt steering.

These local studies, however suggestive, do not provide a comprehensive national assessment of housing discrimination in contemporary American cities. The first such effort was mounted by the U.S. Department of Housing and Urban Development (HUD) in 1977. The study covered 40 metropolitan areas with significant Black populations and confirmed the results of earlier local audits. Discrimination clearly was not confined to a few isolated cases. Nationwide, Whites were favored on 48 percent of transactions in the sales market and on 39 percent of those in the rental market (Wienk et al., 1979).

The 1977 HUD audit survey was replicated in 1988; the Housing Discrimination Study (HDS) covered both the rental and sales markets, and the auditors were given incomes and family characteristics appropriate to the housing unit advertised (Yinger, 1995). Twenty audit sites were randomly selected from among metropolitan areas having a central city population exceeding 100,000 with Blacks constituting more than 12 percent of the population. Real estate ads in major metropolitan newspapers were randomly sampled.

The typical advertised unit was located in a White, middle-to-upper-class area, as were most of the real estate offices; remarkably few homes were in Black or racially mixed neighborhoods. Even after controlling for the social and economic composition of its neighborhood, the percentage of Black residents was a strong predictor of whether a unit was advertised at all (Turner et al., 1991). Galster and his colleagues found a similar bias in real estate advertising in Milwaukee from 1981 to 1984 (Galster et al., 1987). Compared to homes in White areas, those in racially mixed or Black areas were much less likely to be advertised, much more likely to be represented by one-line ads when they were advertised, and much less likely to be favorably described. Real estate companies apparently do a poor job of marketing homes in racially mixed neighborhoods, thereby restricting White demand for integrated housing and promoting segregation.

Realtors were approached by auditors who inquired about the availability of the advertised unit; they also asked about other units that might be on the market. Based on the results, HDS provided evidence that discrimination against Blacks had declined little since 1977. Indeed, it appears the 1977 HUD study may have understated both the incidence and severity of housing discrimination in American cities (Yinger, 1995). According to HDS data, housing was made more available to Whites in 45 percent of the transactions in the rental market and in 34 percent of those in the sales market. Whites received more favorable credit assistance in 46 percent of sales encounters, and were offered more favorable terms in 17 percent of rental transactions. When housing availability and financial assistance were considered together, the likelihood of experiencing racial discrimination was 53 percent in both the rental and sales markets.

The sales audits also assessed the frequency of racial steering; when this form of discrimination was also considered, the likelihood of discrimination rose to 60 percent (Yinger, 1995). Because these figures refer to the odds on any single visit to a realtor, over a series of visits, they accumulate to extremely high probabilities—well over 90 percent in three visits. In the course of even the briefest search for housing, therefore, Blacks are almost certain to encounter discrimination.

In addition to measuring the incidence of discrimination—i.e., the percentage of encounters during which discrimination occurs—HDS also measured its severity—i.e., the number of units made available to Whites but not to Blacks. In stark terms, Blacks were systematically shown, offered, and invited to inspect far fewer homes than comparably qualified Whites. As a result, Blacks' access to urban housing is substantially reduced.

The likelihood that an additional unit was shown to Whites but not Blacks was 65 percent, and the probability that an additional unit was recommended to Whites but not Blacks was 91 percent. The HDS auditors encountered equally severe bias in the marketing of nonadvertised units; the likelihood that an additional unit was inspected by Whites only was 62 percent, and the probability that Whites only were invited to see another unit was 90 percent. Comparable results were found in urban sales markets, where the severity of discrimination varied from 66 percent to 89 percent. Thus, no matter what index one considers, between 60 percent and 90 percent of the housing units made available to Whites were not brought to the attention of Blacks (Yinger, 1995).

The 1988 HDS audit found equally severe discrimination in the provision of credit assistance to home buyers. Of every 100 times that agents discussed a fixed-rate mortgage, 89 of the discussions were with Whites only, and of 100 times that adjustable-rate loans were brought up, 91 percent of the discussions excluded Blacks (Yinger, 1995).

Although these audit results are compelling, they do not directly link discrimination to segregation. They show only that discrimination and segregation exist and persist simultaneously across time. Fortunately, several studies have been conducted to document and quantify the links among discrimination, prejudice, and segregation.

Using data from the 1977 HUD audit study, Galster (1986) related cross-metropolitan variation in housing discrimination to the degree of racial segregation in different urban areas. He not only confirmed the empirical linkage, he also discovered that segregation itself has important feedback effects on socioeconomic status (see also Galster and Keeney, 1988). Discrimination not only leads to segregation; segregation, by restricting economic opportunities for Blacks, produces interracial economic disparities that incite further discrimination and more segregation.

In a detailed study of census tracts in the Cleveland area, Galster found that neighborhoods that were all-White or racially changing evinced much higher rates of discrimination than areas that were stably integrated or predominantly Black (Galster, 1987, 1990d). Moreover, the pace of racial change was strongly predicted by the percentage of Whites who agreed that "White people have a right to keep Blacks out of their neighborhoods." Areas where such sentiment was documented experienced systematic White population loss after only a few Blacks had moved in, and the speed of transition accelerated rapidly beyond a point of 3 percent Black. Tracts where Whites expressed a low degree of racist sentiment, however, showed little tendency for White flight up to a composition of around 40 percent Black. Rather than declining in significance, race remains the dominant organizing principle of U.S. urban housing markets. When it comes to determining where, and with whom, Americans live, race appears to overwhelm other considerations.

Compared with Blacks, relatively few studies of prejudice and discrimination against Hispanics have been conducted, and there are no national studies that examine attitudes and behaviors concerning Asians. Hakken (1979) found that discrimination against Hispanics in the rental housing market of Dallas was as likely as that against Blacks, and similar results were reported by Feins and colleagues for Boston (Feins et al., 1981). James and Tynan (1986) replicated these results in a study of Denver's sales market, but they found a substantially lower probability of discrimination against Hispanics in the rental market; and despite the relatively high likelihood of discrimination in home sales, in reality, severity of discrimination against Hispanics was not great; the average number of housing units offered to Hispanics was not significantly different than the number offered to non-Hispanic Whites (James and Tynan, 1986).

As with Blacks, however, discrimination against Hispanics appears to have a racial basis. Hakken (1979) found that dark-skinned Chicanos were more likely to experience discriminatory treatment than Blacks, whereas light-skinned Hispanics were less likely to experience such treatment. Consistent with this finding, Massey and Denton (1992) found that Mexicans who identified themselves as mestizos (people of mixed European and Indian origin) were less likely to achieve suburban residence than those who identified themselves as White.

The extent of the racial effect is greater among Caribbean Hispanics, particularly Puerto Ricans, among whom the racial continuum runs from European to African. Denton and Massey (1989) showed that for Puerto Ricans who identified themselves as Black, housing was as segregated as for U.S. Blacks, whereas those who identified themselves as White experienced low-to-moderate levels of separation. Discrimination was mixed for Caribbean Hispanics who said they were of mixed Black-White origins, but were much closer to the high level of Black segregation. The degree of segregation experienced by racially mixed Caribbean Hispanics was generally greater than that experienced by racially mixed Mexicans, suggesting greater White antipathy toward Africans than Amerindians.

The most complete and systematic data on the treatment of Hispanics in urban real estate markets comes from HUD's 1988 HDS (Yinger, 1995). Results from this study indicate that the overall incidence of housing discrimination was greater for Hispanics than Blacks in the sales market (42 versus 34 percent), but less for Hispanics than Blacks in the rental market (32 versus 45 percent), replicating the earlier results of James and Tynan (1986) in Denver. Also in keeping with the findings of James and Tynan was the fact that the severity of discrimination in the sales market was considerably lower for Hispanics than for Blacks; whereas the marginal probability that an additional housing unit was denied to Blacks was 88 percent, it was only 66 percent for Hispanics. As in earlier research, in the 1988 HDS, race figured prominently in the treatment of Hispanics—dark-skinned Hispanics were much more likely to experience discrimination in the sales market than light-skinned Hispanics (Yinger, 1995). Paradoxically, therefore, recent research on discrimination involving Hispanics reaffirms the conclusion that race remains the dominant organizing principle in U.S. urban housing markets.

## SEGREGATION AND THE CONCENTRATION OF POVERTY

The past two decades have been hard on the socioeconomic well-being of many Americans. The structural transformation of the U.S. economy from goods production to service provision generated a strong demand for workers with high and low levels of schooling, but offered few opportunities for those with modest education and training. In the postindustrial economy that emerged after 1973, labor unions withered, the middle class bifurcated, income inequality grew, and poverty spread; and this new stratification between people was accompanied by a growing spatial separation between them. The stagnation of income proved to be remarkably widespread, and inequality rose not only for minorities—Blacks, Hispanics, and Asians—but also for non-Hispanic Whites (Danziger and Gottschalk, 1995; Levy, 1995; Morris et al., 1994). As a result of their continued racial segregation, however, the spatial concentration of poverty was especially severe for Blacks (Massey and Eggers, 1990; Massey et al., 1991; Krivo et al., 1998). High levels of income inequality paired with high levels of racial or ethnic segregation result in geographically concentrated poverty, because the poverty is localized in a small number of densely settled, racially homogenous, tightly clustered areas, often in an older, urban core abandoned by industry. Had segregation not been in place, the heightened poverty would be distributed widely throughout the metropolitan area (Massey, 1990; Massey and Denton, 1993). By 1990, 83 percent of poor inner-city Blacks lived in neighborhoods that were at least 20 percent poor (Kasarda, 1993).

In a recent paper, Massey and Fischer (2000) broadened this theoretical perspective by arguing that racial segregation interacts with any structural shift that affects the distribution of income, or the spatial configuration of the classes, to concentrate poverty spatially. Specifically, they hypothesize that as racial segregation increases, decreasing incomes, increasing inequality, increasing class segregation, and increasing immigration are more strongly translated into geographic isolation of the poor. Thus, these structural trends produce high and increasing concentrations of poverty for highly segregated groups, but low and falling concentrations of poverty among nonsegregated groups.

Because more than 70 percent of urban Blacks are highly segregated, but 90 percent of all other groups are not, the population of poor experiencing high concentrations of poverty is overwhelmingly Black (Massey and Fischer, 2000). Given the interaction between racial segregation and the changing socioeconomic structure of American society, the issue of race cannot be set aside to focus on the politics of race versus class. Although the implementation of policies that raise average incomes, lower income inequality, and reduce class segregation would lower the spatial isolation of the urban poor, policies to promote the desegregation of urban society would probably have an even greater effect, given segregation's critical role in determining how these factors generate concentrated poverty.

## THE CONSEQUENCES OF CONCENTRATED POVERTY

The argument that the prevalence of concentrated poverty among Blacks decisively undermines the life chances of the Black poor was first made forcefully by Wilson (1987). He argued that class isolation, through a variety of mechanisms, reduced employment, lowered incomes, depressed marriage, and increased unwed childbearing *over and above any effects of individual or family deprivation*. At the time Wilson made this argument, relatively little evidence existed to support it (Jencks and Mayer, 1990), but over the past decade a growing number of studies have accumulated to sustain the basic thrust of Wilson's hypothesis.

In 1988, the Rockefeller and Russell Sage Foundations funded the Social Science Research Council (SSRC) to establish a program of research into the causes and consequences of persistent urban poverty. One SSRC subcommittee—the Working Group on Communities and Neighborhoods, Family Processes, and Individual Development—met regularly over the next eight years to conceptualize and then implement a program of research to determine how concentrated poverty affected social and cognitive development. The ultimate product was a recently published series of studies (Brooks-Gunn et al., 1997) examining the effect of neighborhood conditions on cognitive and social development at three points in the life cycle—early childhood (ages 3-7), late childhood/early adolescence (ages 11-15), and late adolescence (ages 16-19).

These empirical analyses clearly show that socioeconomic inequality is perpetuated by mechanisms operating at the neighborhood level, although the specific pathways are perhaps more complex than Wilson or others imagined. Not only do neighborhood effects vary in their nature and intensity at different stages of the life cycle, they are often conditioned by gender, mediated by family processes, and possibly interactive in how they combine with individual factors to determine social outcomes. Despite these complexities, however, research permits three broad generalizations.

- First, neighborhoods seem to influence individual development most powerfully in early childhood and late adolescence.
- Second, the spatial concentration of affluence appears to be more important in determining cognitive development and academic achievement than the concentration of poverty.
- Third, the concentration of male joblessness affects social behavior more than cognitive development, particularly among Blacks.

These effects persist even after controlling for unobserved heterogeneity. Thus, Wilson's (1987) theory is basically correct—there is something to the hypothesis of neighborhood effects.

One of the most important disadvantages transmitted through prolonged exposure to the ghetto is educational failure. Datcher (1982) estimates that moving a poor Black male from his typical neighborhood (66 percent Black with an average annual income of $8,500) to a typical White neighborhood (86 percent White with a mean income of $11,500) would raise his educational attainment by nearly a year. Corcoran and colleagues (1989) found similar results. Crane (1991) likewise shows that the dropout probability for Black teenage males increases dramatically as the percentage of low-status workers in the neighborhood increases. Residence in a poor neighborhood also decreases the odds of success in the labor market. Datcher (1982) found that growing up in a poor Black area lowered male earnings by at least 27 percent, although Corcoran and colleagues (1989) put the percentage at about 18 percent.

Exposure to conditions typical of the ghetto also dramatically increase the odds of pregnancy and childbirth among teenage girls. According to estimates by Crane (1991), the probability of a teenage birth increases dramatically as the percentage of low-status workers in the neighborhood increases. Similarly, Hogan and Kitagawa (1985) found that living in a very poor neighborhood raised the monthly pregnancy rate among Black adolescents by 20 percent and lowered the age at which they became sexually active. Furstenburg et al. (1987) have shown that attending school in integrated, rather than segregated, classrooms substantially lowers the odds that 15-to-16-year-old Black girls will experience sexual intercourse. Brooks-Gunn et al. (1993) found that the probability of giving birth before age 29 rose markedly as the percentage of high-income families fell.

In a dynamic longitudinal analysis that followed young Black men and women from ages 15 to 30, Massey and Shibuya (1995) found that young men who live in neighborhoods of concentrated male joblessness are more likely to be jobless themselves, controlling for individual and family characteristics, and that Black women in such neighborhoods were significantly less likely to get married.

Massey and Shibuya (1995) also linked concentrated disadvantage to higher probabilities of criminality, a link well-documented by Krivo and Peterson (1996) using aggregate data. The concentration of criminal activity that accompanies the concentration of deprivation accelerates the process of neighborhood transition and, for Blacks, resegregation (Morenoff and Sampson, 1997); it also helps drive up rates of Black-on-Black mortality, which have reached heights unparalleled for any other group (Almgren et al., 1998; Guest et al., 1998). The spatial concentration of crime presents special problems for the Black middle class, who must adopt extreme strategies to insulate their children from the temptations and risks of the street (Anderson, 1990; Patillo, 1998).

The quantitative evidence thus suggests that any process that concentrates poverty within racially isolated neighborhoods will simultaneously increase the odds of socioeconomic failure within the segregated group. People who grow up and live in environments of concentrated poverty and social isolation are more likely to become teenage parents, drop out of school, achieve low educations, earn lower adult incomes, and become involved with crime—either as perpetrator or victim.

One study has directly linked the socioeconomic disadvantages suffered by individual minority members to the degree of segregation they experience in society. Using individual, community, and metropolitan data from the 50 largest U.S. metropolitan areas in 1980, Massey et al. (1991) showed that group segregation and poverty rates interacted to concentrate poverty geographically within neighborhoods, and that exposure to neighborhood poverty subsequently increased the probability of male joblessness and single motherhood among group members. In this fashion, they linked the structural condition of segregation to individual behaviors widely associated with the underclass through the intervening factor of neighborhood poverty, holding individual and family characteristics constant. As the structural factor controlling poverty concentration, segregation is directly responsible for the perpetuation of socioeconomic disadvantage among Blacks.

## THE ROAD AHEAD

This review yields several well-supported conclusions about residential segregation in the United States at the end of the twentieth century.

- First, the extreme segregation of Blacks continues unabated in the nation's largest metropolitan areas, and is far more severe than anything experienced by Hispanics or Asians.
- Second, this unique segregation can in no way be attributed to class.
- Third, although Whites now accept open housing in principle, they have yet to come to terms with its implications in practice. Whites still harbor strong anti-Black sentiments and are unwilling to live with more than a small percentage of Blacks in the neighborhood. As a result, declines in Black-White segregation have been confined almost entirely to metropolitan areas where few Blacks live.
- Fourth, color prejudice apparently extends to dark-skinned Hispanics, and discrimination against both Blacks and Afro-Hispanics is remarkably widespread in U.S. housing markets. Through a variety of deceptions and exclusionary actions, Black access to housing in White neighborhoods is systematically reduced.
- Fifth, White biases and discrimination apparently do not extend to Asians or light-skinned Hispanics, at least to the same degree. In no metropolitan area are Asians or Hispanics hypersegregated; and despite the recent arrival of large numbers of immigrants and rapid rates of population growth, they display levels of segregation and isolation that are far below those of Blacks.
- Sixth, as a result of segregation, poor Blacks are forced to live in conditions of intensely concentrated poverty. Recent shifts in U.S. socioeconomic structure and patterns of class segregation have interacted with Black segregation to produce unusual concentrations of poverty among Blacks. Poor Blacks are far more likely to grow up and live in neighborhoods surrounded by other poor people than poor Whites, Hispanics, or Asians.
- Finally, as a result of their prolonged exposure to high rates of neighborhood poverty, Blacks experience much higher risks of educational failure, joblessness, unwed childbearing, crime, and premature death compared with other groups.

Given the central role that residence plays in determining one's life chances, these results suggest the need to incorporate the effects of racial segregation more fully into theories about the perpetuation of poverty and the origins of the urban underclass. These results also suggest the need to incorporate desegregation efforts more directly into public policies developed to ameliorate urban poverty. All too often, U.S. policy debates have devolved into arguments about the relative importance of race versus class. The issue, however, is not whether race *or* class perpetuates the urban underclass, but how race *and* class *interact* to undermine the social and economic well-being of Black Americans.

Public policies must address both race and class issues if they are to be successful. Race-conscious steps need to be taken to dismantle the institutional apparatus of segregation, and class-specific policies must be implemented to improve the socioeconomic status of Blacks. By themselves, programs targeting low-income Blacks will fail because they will be swamped by powerful environmental influences arising from the disastrous neighborhood conditions that Blacks experience because of segregation. Likewise, efforts to reduce segregation will falter unless Blacks acquire the socioeconomic resources that enable them to take full advantage of urban housing markets and the benefits they provide.

Eliminating residential segregation will require the direct involvement of the federal government to an unprecedented degree, and two departments—Housing and Urban Development, and Justice—must throw their institutional weight behind fair-housing enforcement if residential desegregation is to occur. If the ghetto is to be dismantled, HUD, in particular must intervene forcefully in eight ways.

1. HUD must increase its financial assistance to local fair-housing organizations to enhance their ability to investigate and prosecute individual complaints of housing discrimination. Grants made to local agencies dedicated to fair-housing enforcement will enable them to expand their efforts by hiring more legal staff, implementing more extensive testing programs, and making their services more widely available.

2. HUD should establish a permanent testing program capable of identifying realtors who engage in a pattern and practice of discrimination. A special unit dedicated to the regular administration of housing audits should be created in HUD under the Assistant Secretary for Fair Housing and Equal Opportunity. Audits of randomly selected realtors should be conducted annually within metropolitan areas that have large Black communities, and when evidence of systematic discrimination is uncovered, the department should compile additional evidence and turn it over to the Attorney General for vigorous prosecution. Initially these audits should be targeted to hypersegregated cities.

3. A staff should be created at HUD under the Assistant Secretary for Fair Housing and Equal Opportunity to scrutinize lending data for unusually high rates of rejection among minority applicants and Black neighborhoods. When the rejection rates cannot be explained statistically by social, demographic, economic, credit histories, or other background factors, a systematic case study of the lending institution's practices should be initiated. If clear evidence of discrimination is uncovered, the case should be referred to the Attorney General for prosecution, and/or an

equal-opportunity lending plan should be conciliated, implemented, and monitored.

4. Funding for housing-certificate programs, authorized under Section 8 of the 1974 Housing and Community Development Act, should be expanded, and programs modeled on the Gautreaux Demonstration Project or the Move to Opportunity Program should be more widely implemented. Black public-housing residents in Chicago who moved into integrated settings through this demonstration project have been shown to have had greater success in education and employment than a comparable group who remained behind in the ghetto (see Rosenbaum et al., 1988; Rosenbaum and Popkin, 1991; Rosenbaum, 1991).

5. Given the overriding importance of residential mobility to individual well-being, hate crimes directed against Blacks moving into White neighborhoods must be considered more severe than ordinary acts of vandalism or assault. Rather than being left only to local authorities, they should be prosecuted at the federal level as violations of the victim's civil rights. Stiff financial penalties and jail terms should be imposed, not in recognition of the severity of the vandalism or violence itself, but to acknowledge the serious damage that segregation does to our national well-being.

6. HUD should work to strengthen the Voluntary Affirmative Marketing Agreement, a pact between HUD and the National Association of Realtors, instituted during the Ford Administration. The agreement originally established a network of housing resource boards to enforce the Fair Housing Act with support from HUD; during the Reagan Administration, funds were cut and the agreement was modified to relieve realtors of responsibility for fair-housing enforcement. New regulations also prohibited the use of testers by local resource boards and made secret the list of real estate boards that had signed the agreement. In strengthening this agreement, this list should once again be made public, the use of testers should be encouraged, and the responsibilities of realtors to enforce the Fair Housing Act should be spelled out explicitly.

7. HUD should establish new programs and expand existing programs to train realtors in fair-housing marketing procedures, especially those serving Black neighborhoods. Agents serving primarily White clients should be instructed about advertising and marketing methods to ensure that Blacks in segregated communities gain access to information about housing opportunities outside the ghetto, whereas agents serving primarily Black clients should be trained to market homes throughout the metropolitan area, and instructed especially in how to use multiple-listing services. HUD officials and local fair-housing groups should carefully monitor whether realtors serving Blacks are given access to multiple-listing services.

8. The Assistant Secretary for Fair Housing and Equal Opportunity at HUD must take a more active role in overseeing real estate advertising and marketing practices, two areas that have received insufficient federal attention in the past. Realtors in selected metropolitan areas should be sampled and their advertising and marketing practices regularly examined for conformity with federal fair-housing regulations. HUD should play a larger role in ensuring that Black home seekers are not systematically and deliberately overlooked by prevailing marketing practices.

For the most part, these policies do not require major changes in legislation. What they require is political will. Given the will to end segregation, the necessary funds and legislative measures will follow. For America, failure to end segregation will perpetuate a bitter dilemma that has long divided the nation. If segregation is permitted to continue, poverty inevitably will deepen and become more persistent within a large share of the Black community, crime and drugs will become more firmly rooted, and social institutions will fragment further under the weight of deteriorating conditions. As racial inequality sharpens, White fears will grow, racial prejudices will be reinforced, and hostility toward Blacks will increase, making the problems of racial justice and equal opportunity even more insoluble. Until we decide to end the long reign of American apartheid, we cannot hope to move forward as a people and a nation.

## REFERENCES

Allport, G.
    1958    *The Nature of Prejudice*. Garden City, N.Y.: Doubleday Anchor.
Almgren, G., A. Guest, G. Imerwahr, and M. Spittel
    1998    Joblessness, family disruption, and violent death in Chicago: 1970-1990. *Social Forces* 76:1465-1494.
Anderson, E.
    1990    *Streetwise: Race, Class, and Change in an Urban Community*. Chicago: University of Chicago Press.
Bertram, S.
    1988    *An Audit of the Real Estate Sales and Rental Markets of Selected Southern Suburbs*. Homewood, Ill.: South Suburban Housing Center.
Blalock, H.M., Jr.
    1967    *Toward a Theory of Minority-Group Relations*. New York: Wiley.
Bobo, L., H. Schuman, and C. Steeh
    1986    Changing racial attitudes toward residential integration. Pp. 152-169 in *Housing Desegregation and Federal Policy*, J. Goering, ed. Chapel Hill: University of North Carolina Press.
Bobo, L., and C. Zubrinsky
    1996    Attitudes on residential integration: Perceived status differences, mere in-group preference, or racial prejudice? *Social Forces* 74:883-909.

Brooks-Gunn, J., G. Duncan, and J. Aber, eds.
    1997  *Neighborhood Poverty: Context and Consequences for Children.* New York: Russell
          Sage
Brooks-Gunn, J., G. Duncan, P. Klebanov, and N. Sealand
    1993  Do neighborhoods influence child and adolescent development? *American Journal
          of Sociology* 99:353-395.
Clark, W.
    1991  Residential preferences and neighborhood racial segregation: A test of the
          Schelling segregation model. *Demography* 28:1-19.
Corcoran, M., R. Gordon, D. Laren, and G. Solon
    1989  Effects of family and community background on men's economic status. Work-
          ing Paper 2896, National Bureau of Economic Research, Cambridge, Mass.
Crane, J.
    1991  The epidemic theory of ghettos and neighborhood effects on dropping out and
          teenage childbearing. *American Journal of Sociology* 96:1226-1259.
Danziger, S., and P. Gottschalk
    1995  *America Unequal.* Cambridge:  Harvard University Press and the Russell Sage
          Foundation.
Datcher, L.
    1982  Effects of community and family background on achievement. *The Review of
          Economics and Statistics* 64:32-41.
Demerath, N., and H. Gilmore
    1954  The ecology of southern cities. Pp. 120-125 in *The Urban South*, R. Vance and N.
          Demerath, eds. Chapel Hill: University of North Carolina Press.
Denton, N.
    1994  Are African Americans still hypersegregated? Pp. 49-81 in *Residential Apartheid:
          The American Legacy*, R. Bullard, J. Grigsby III, and C. Lee, eds.  Los Angeles:
          CAAS Publications, University of California.
Denton, N., and D. Massey
    1988  Residential segregation of Blacks, Hispanics, and Asians by socioeconomic status
          and generation. *Social Science Quarterly* 69:797-817.
    1989  Racial identity among Caribbean Hispanics: The effect of double minority status
          on residential segregation. *American Sociological Review* 54:790-808.
    1991  Patterns of neighborhood transition in a multiethnic world. *Demography* 28:41-64.
Duncan, O., and B. Duncan
    1957  *The Negro Population of Chicago: A Study of Residential Succession.* Chicago: Univer-
          sity of Chicago Press.
Farley, R.
    1977  Residential segregation in urbanized areas of the United States in 1970: An analy-
          sis of social class and racial differences. *Demography* 14:497-518.
Farley, R., S. Bianchi, and D. Colasanto
    1979  Barriers to the racial integration of neighborhoods: The Detroit case. *Annals of the
          American Academy of Political and Social Science* 441:97-113.
Farley, R., H. Schuman, S. Bianchi, D. Colasanto, and S. Hatchett.
    1978  "Chocolate city, vanilla suburbs": Will the trend toward racially separate com-
          munities continue? *Social Science Research* 7:319-344.
Farley, R., C. Steeh, M. Krysan, T. Jackson, and K. Reeves
    1994  Stereotypes and segregation: Neighborhoods in the Detroit area. *American Jour-
          nal of Sociology* 100:750-780.

Feins, J., R. Bratt, and R. Hollister
  1981   *Final Report of a Study of Racial Discrimination in the Boston Housing Market*. Cambridge: Abt Associates.
Fix, M., G. Galster, and R. Struyk
  1993   An overview of auditing for discrimination. Pp. 1-68 in *Clear and Convincing Evidence: Measurement of Discrimination in America*, M. Fix and R. Struyk, eds. Washington, D.C.: The Urban Institute Press.
Frey, W., and R. Farley
  1994   Changes in the segregation of Whites from Blacks during the 1980s: Small steps toward a more integrated society. *American Sociological Review* 59:23-45.
  1996   Latino, Asian, and Black segregation in U.S. metropolitan areas: Are multiethnic metros different? *Demography* 33:35-50.
Furstenburg, F. Jr., S. Morgan, K. Moore, and J. Peterson
  1987   Race differences in the timing of adolescent intercourse. *American Sociological Review* 52:511-518.
Galster, G.
  1986   More than skin deep: The effect of housing discrimination on the extent and pattern of racial residential segregation in the United States. Pp. 119-138 in *Housing Discrimination and Federal Policy*, J. Goering, ed. Chapel Hill: University of North Carolina Press.
  1987   The ecology of racial discrimination in housing: An exploratory model. *Urban Affairs Quarterly* 23:84-107.
  1990a  Racial discrimination in housing markets during the 1980s: A review of the audit evidence. *Journal of Planning Education and Research* 9:165-175.
  1990b  Racial steering by real estate agents: Mechanisms and motives. *The Review of Black Political Economy* 19:39-63.
  1990c  White flight from racially integrated neighbourhoods in the 1970s: The Cleveland experience. *Urban Studies* 27:385-399.
  1990d  Neighborhood racial change, segregationist sentiments, and affirmative marketing policies. *Journal of Urban Economics* 27:344-361.
Galster, G., F. Freiberg, and D. Houk
  1987   Racial differentials in real estate advertising practices: An exploratory case study. *Journal of Urban Affairs* 9:199-215.
Galster, G., and W. Keeney
  1988   Race, residence, discrimination, and economic opportunity: Modeling the nexus of urban racial phenomena. *Urban Affairs Quarterly* 24:87-117.
Guest, A., G. Almgren, and J. Hussey
  1998   The ecology of race and socioeconomic distress: Infant and working age mortality in Chicago. *Demography* 35:23-34.
Hakken, J.
  1979   *Discrimination Against Chicanos in the Dallas Rental Housing Market: An Experimental Extension of the Housing Market Practices Survey*. Washington, D.C.: Office of Policy Development and Research, U.S. Department of Housing and Urban Development.
Harrison, R., and D. Weinberg
  1992   Racial and ethnic residential segregation in 1990. Paper presented at the annual meetings of the Population Association of America, Denver, April 13.
Helper, R.
  1969   *Racial Policies and Practices of Real Estate Brokers*. Minneapolis: University of Minnesota Press.

Hintzen, H.
  1983   *Report of an Audit of Real Estate Sales Practices of 15 Northwest Chicago Real Estate Sales Offices.* Chicago: Leadership Council for Metropolitan Open Communities.
Hochschild, J.
  1995   *Facing up to the American Dream: Race, Class, and the Soul of the Nation.* Princeton: Princeton University Press.
Hogan, D., and E. Kitagawa
  1985   The impact of social status, family structure, and neighborhood on the fertility of Black adolescents. *American Journal of Sociology* 90:825-855.
Hwang, S., and S. Murdock
  1982   Residential segregation in Texas in 1980. *Social Science Quarterly* 63(1982):737-748.
Jackson, P.
  1981   Paradoxes of Puerto Rican segregation in New York. Pp. 109-126 in *Ethnic Segregation in Cities*, C. Peach, V. Robinson, and S. Smith, eds. London: Croom Helm.
Jackson, T.
  1994   The other side of the residential segregation equation: Why Detroit area Blacks are reluctant to pioneer integration. Paper presented at the Russell Sage Foundation Multi-City conference.
James, F., and E. Tynan
  1986   Segregation and discrimination against Hispanic Americans. Pp. 83-98 in *Housing Discrimination and Federal Policy*, J. Goering, ed. Chapel Hill: University of North Carolina Press.
Jencks, C., and S. Mayer
  1990   The social consequences of growing up in a poor neighborhood. Pp. 111-186 in *Inner City Poverty in the United States*, L. Lynn, Jr., and M. McGeary, eds. Washington, D.C.: National Academy of Sciences.
Kantrowitz, N.
  1973   *Ethnic and Racial Segregation in the New York Metropolis.* New York: Praeger.
Kasarda, J.
  1993   Inner city concentrated poverty and neighborhood distress: 1970-1990. *Housing Policy Debate* 4(3):253-302.
Krivo, L., and R. Kaufman
  1999   How low can it go? Declining Black-White segregation in a multi-ethnic context. *Demography* 36:93-110.
Krivo, L., and R. Peterson
  1996   Extremely disadvantaged neighborhoods and urban crime. *Social Forces* 75:619-648.
Krivo, L., R. Peterson, H. Rizzo, and J. Reynolds
  1998   Race segregation, and the concentration of disadvantage: 1980-1990. *Social Problems* 45:61-80.
Levy, F.
  1995   Incomes and income inequality. Pp. 1-58 in *State of the Union: America in the 1990s*, R. Farley, ed. New York: Russell Sage.
Lieberson, S.
  1980   *A Piece of the Pie: Blacks and White Immigrants Since 1880.* Berkeley: University of California Press.
Lopez, M.
  1981   Patterns of interethnic residential segregation in the urban Southwest, 1960 and 1970. *Social Science Quarterly* 62:50-63.

Massey, D.
  1979 Effects of socioeconomic factors on the residential segregation of Blacks and Spanish Americans in United States urbanized areas. *American Sociological Review* 44:1015-1022.
  1981 Hispanic residential segregation: A comparison of Mexicans, Cubans, and Puerto Ricans. *Sociology and Social Research* 65:311-322.
  1985 Ethnic residential segregation: A theoretical synthesis and empirical review. *Sociology and Social Research* 69:315-350.
  1990 American apartheid: Segregation and the making of the underclass. *American Journal of Sociology* 96:329-358.
Massey, D., and B. Bitterman
  1985 Explaining the paradox of Puerto Rican segregation. *Social Forces* 64:306-331.
Massey, D., G. Condran, and N. Denton
  1987 The effect of residential segregation on Black social and economic well-being. *Social Forces* 66:29-57.
Massey, D., and N. Denton
  1987 Trends in the residential segregation of Blacks, Hispanics, and Asians. *American Sociological Review* 52:802-825.
  1988 The dimensions of residential segregation. *Social Forces* 67:281-315.
  1989a Residential segregation of Mexicans, Puerto Ricans, and Cubans in U.S. metropolitan areas. *Sociology and Social Research* 73:73-83.
  1989b Hypersegregation in U.S. metropolitan areas: Black and Hispanic segregation along five dimensions. *Demography* 26:373-393.
  1992 Racial identity and the spatial assimilation of Mexicans in the United States. *Social Science Research* 21:235-260.
  1993 *American Apartheid: Segregation and the Making of the Underclass.* Cambridge: Harvard University Press.
Massey, D., and M. Eggers
  1990 The ecology of inequality: Minorities and the concentration of poverty, 1970-1980. *American Journal of Sociology* 95:1153-1189.
Massey, D., and M. Fischer
  1999 Does rising income bring integration? New results for Blacks, Hispanics, and Asians in 1990. *Social Science Research* 28:316-326.
  2000 How segregation concentrates poverty. *Ethnic and Racial Studies* 23:670-691.
Massey, D., and E. Fong
  1990 Segregation and neighborhood quality: Blacks, Hispanics, and Asians in the San Francisco metropolitan area. *Social Forces* 69:15-32.
Massey, D., and A. Gross
  1991 Explaining trends in residential segregation 1970-1980. *Urban Affairs Quarterly* 27:13-35.
Massey, D., A. Gross, and M. Eggers
  1991 Segregation, the concentration of poverty, and the life chances of individuals. *Social Science Research* 20:397-420.
Massey, D., and Z. Hajnal
  1995 The changing geographic structure of Black-White segregation in the United States. *Social Science Quarterly* 76:527-542.
Massey, D., and K. Shibuya
  1995 Unraveling the tangle of pathology: The effect of spatially concentrated joblessness on the well-being of African Americans. *Social Science Research* 24:352-366.

Massey, D., M. White, and V. Phua
  1996   The dimensions of segregation revisited. *Sociological Methods and Research* 25:172-206.
Morenoff, J., and R. Sampson
  1997   Violent crime and the spatial dynamics of neighborhood transition: Chicago, 1970-1990. *Social Forces* 76:31-64.
Morris, M., A. Bernhardt, and M. Handcock
  1994   Economic inequality: New methods for new trends. *American Sociological Review* 59:205-219.
Moskos, C., and J. Butler
  1996   *All That We Can Be: Black Leadership and Racial Integration the Army Way.* New York: Basic Books.
Patillo, M.
  1998   Sweet mothers and gangbangers: Managing crime in a Black middle-class neighborhood. *Social Forces* 76:747-774.
Pearce, D.
  1979   Gatekeepers and homeseekers: Institutional patterns in racial steering. *Social Problems* 26:325-342.
Rosenbaum, J.
  1991   Black pioneers: Do their moves to suburbs increase economic opportunity for mothers and children? *Housing Policy Debate* 2:1179-1214.
Rosenbaum, J., M. Kulieke, and L. Rubinowitz
  1988   White suburban schools' responses to low-income Black children: Sources of success and problems. *The Urban Review* 20:28-41.
Rosenbaum, J., and S. Popkin
  1991   Employment and earnings of low-income Blacks who move to middle class suburbs. Pp. 342-56 in *The Urban Underclass*, C. Jencks and P. Peterson, eds. Washington, D.C.: The Brookings Institution.
Saltman, J.
  1979   Housing discrimination: Policy research, methods, and results. *Annals of the American Academy of Political and Social Science* 441:186-196.
Schelling, T.
  1971   Dynamic models of segregation. *Journal of Mathematical Sociology* 1:143-186.
Schneider, M., and J. Logan
  1982   Suburban racial segregation and Black access to local public resources. *Social Science Quarterly* 63:762-770.
Schroeder, A.
  1985   *Report on an Audit of Real Estate Sales Practices of Eight Northwest Suburban Offices.* Chicago: Leadership Council for Metropolitan Open Communities.
Schuman, H., and L. Bobo
  1988   Survey-based experiments on White racial attitudes toward residential integration. *American Journal of Sociology* 2:273-299.
Schuman, H., C. Steeh, and L. Bobo
  1985   *Racial Attitudes in America: Trends and Interpretations.* Cambridge: Harvard University Press.
Schuman, H., C. Steeh, L. Bobo, and M. Krysan
  1998   *Racial Attitudes in America: Trends and Interpretations.* Cambridge: Harvard University Press.
Simkus, A.
  1978   Residential segregation by occupation and race in ten urbanized areas, 1950-1970. *American Sociological Review* 43:81-93.

Sniderman, P., and T. Piazza
    1993    *The Scar of Race.* Cambridge: Harvard University Press.
Taylor, M.
    1998    The effect of racial composition on racial attitudes of Whites. *American Sociological Review* 63:512-535.
Turner, E., and J. Allen
    1991    *An Atlas of Population Patterns in Metropolitan Los Angeles and Orange Counties.* Occasional Publications in Geography No. 8. Northridge, Calif.: Center for Geographical Studies, California State University at Northridge.
Turner, M., J. Edwards, and M. Mikelsons
    1991    *Housing Discrimination Study: Analyzing Racial and Ethnic Steering.* Washington, D.C.: U.S. Department of Housing and Urban Development, Office of Policy Development and Research.
U.S. Bureau of the Census
    1979    The Social and Economic Status of the Black Population in the United States: An Historical View, 1790-1978. Current Population Reports, Special Studies Series P-23, No. 80. Washington, D.C.: U.S. Government Printing Office.
White, M.
    1987    *American Neighborhoods and Residential Differentiation.* New York: Russell Sage Foundation.
Wienk, R., C. Reid, J. Simonson, and F. Eggers
    1979    *Measuring Racial Discrimination in American Housing Markets: The Housing Market Practices Survey.* Washington, D.C.: U.S. Department of Housing and Urban Development.
Wilson, W.
    1987    *The Truly Disadvantaged: The Inner City, the Underclass, and Public Policy.* Chicago: University of Chicago Press.
Yinger, J.
    1986    Measuring racial discrimination with fair housing audits: Caught in the act. *American Economic Review* 76:991-993.
    1985    The racial dimension of urban housing markets in the 1980s. Pp. 43-67 in *Divided Neighborhoods: Changing Patterns of Racial Segregation*, G.A. Tobin, ed. Newbury Park, Calif.: Sage Publications.
    1989    Measuring discrimination in housing availability. Final Research Report No. 2 to the U.S. Department of Housing and Urban Development. Washington, D.C.: The Urban Institute.
    1995    *Closed Doors, Opportunities Lost: The Continuing Costs of Housing Discrimination.* New York: Russell Sage.
Zubrinsky, C., and L. Bobo
    1996    Prismatic metropolis: Race and residential segregation in the City of Angels. *Social Science Research* 25:335-374.

# 14

# Geography and Opportunity

*Manuel Pastor, Jr.*

P lace matters. Throughout the last several decades, this simple statement has driven much of the research and policy regarding race in America. Investigations of minority unemployment, for example, have often focused on issues of spatial mismatch; research on community social capital has queried about the health of such capital in areas of concentrated poverty; policy on environmental clean-up has recognized that hazards are disproportionately located in minority neighborhoods.

This paper looks at these concerns in terms of geographic distribution of economic and environmental opportunity in major urban areas. The central argument is that historic patterns of suburbanization have contributed to both racial and income inequality. Resources and economic dynamism have abandoned central cities, where most racial minorities live, leaving diminished community structures and hazardous waste in their wake. The resulting racially and socially disparate character of cities and suburbs, and the increasing importance of the suburbs in national voting, has led to a declining political will to deal with poverty, race, and urban decline.

Several recent trends, however, may offer a way out of this pessimistic policy box. First, suburbs themselves are changing. There is an increasing minority presence in suburbs, and many of the older, "inner-ring" suburbs are experiencing economic stresses and, hence, have interests similar to those of their adjacent central cities. Second, the emergent "new regionalism" or "smart growth" framework emphasizes the economic complementarity of cities and suburbs within regions, and gives suburbanites strong reasons to support relinking geographic spaces and diminishing inequalities in opportunities and outcomes. Third, inner-city advocates themselves have begun to realize that the best ticket out of poverty and environmental degradation is to relink their neighborhoods and their residents to regional economic dynamics and environmental decision-making processes.

Whether all this will come together to offer a brighter future for low-income communities of color will depend on federal and local policy. Historically, federal policy has, on balance, encouraged regional frag-mentation and urban sprawl. New strategies should be more supportive of regional collaboration on economic policy, regional connection through public transportation, and regional fairness in the distribution of environ-mental negatives. Locally, fiscal and other factors have led to increasing division and separation of municipalities. New modes of collaboration and dialogue should be developed that also can have positive impacts on racial inequities/reconciliation by building a regional sense of common purpose and common ground.

This brief paper develops these points with reference to general trends in urban America. Because such broad-stroke analysis can obscure the specificities illuminated by the analysis of particular locations, I draw on a number of examples from Los Angeles, a region where urban sprawl, social inequity, environmental degradation, and explosive unrest have often been particularly dramatic.

## HISTORICAL TRENDS

Beginning with Kain (1968), various researchers have stressed that the poor economic outcomes of racial minorities, particularly Blacks, are partly the result of patterns of housing segregation that have prevented minorities from moving in pace with the suburbanization of employment (see Massey and Denton, 1993). This "spatial mismatch" hypothesis has been particularly important in the work of Wilson (1987)—living where the jobs aren't, it is argued, has a negative effect on employment, particu-larly when fixed rail and bus lines are not conducive to "reverse" com-muting.

To examine the general historical pattern, I have drawn data from The State of the Nation's Cities (SNC), a database developed by Rutgers University under a U.S. Department of Housing and Urban Development (HUD) contract, which incorporates information for 74 of the country's largest cities and metropolitan areas, with most variables drawn from the 1970, 1980, and 1990 censuses.[1] As can be seen in Figure 14-1, both popu-

---

[1]SNC was compiled by Norman J. Glickman, Michael Lahr, and Elvin Wyly. It was initially assembled under a U.S. Department of Housing and Urban Development contract

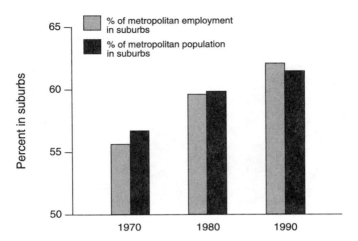

FIGURE 14-1 Suburbanization of employment and population in 74 metropolitan areas, 1970 to 1990. The percent of employment and population in suburbs
has been rising, with employment rising faster.

lation and employment have been shifting to suburban areas, with the
change slightly more pronounced for employment. Of course, minorities
have also participated in this movement to the suburbs; in fact, their
outward movement has been slightly more pronounced than for Whites.
Still, as Figure 14-2 indicates, in 1990, only about 40 percent of Blacks and
Hispanics lived outside of central cities in these 74 metropolitan areas, as
compared to 67 percent of Whites and Asians. Looked at another, and a
perhaps more politically relevant, way, in 1990, about 44 percent of those
living in the 74 central cities were Black or Hispanic; but these groups
constituted only approximately 16 percent of the suburban population in
these 74 metropolitan areas.

   Given the documented job shift away from, and the concentration of
minorities within, central cities, it is not surprising that joblessness, low
wages, and a lack of opportunity disproportionately affect racial minorities, even though formal discrimination has declined in the wake of Civil
Rights legislation. Figures 14-3 and 14-4 indicate that the ratio of suburban to central-city population has risen over time, and that the ratio of

to the Center for Urban Policy Research to meet the data needs of the United Nations'
Habitat II Conference held in Istanbul, Turkey, in June 1996, and has been expanded in
variable coverage since. I specifically used version 2.11A (September 22, 1997).

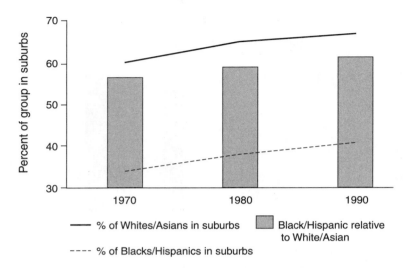

FIGURE 14-2  Suburbanization of the population in 74 metropolitan areas, 1970 to 1990. The percent of Blacks and Hispanics residing in suburbs is rising faster than for other groups, but the suburbanization ratio (percent of group residing in suburbs) is still only about 60 percent of that for Whites and Asians.

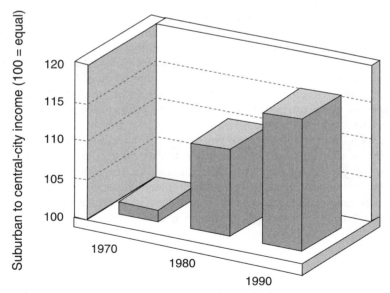

FIGURE 14-3  Ratio of suburban to central-city income, from 1970 to 1990. Suburban income is higher than central-city income, and the imbalance has been rising over time.

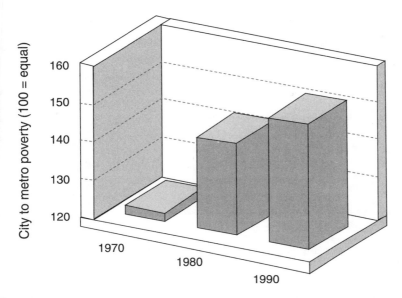

FIGURE 14-4 Ratio of central-city to metropolitan poverty, from 1970 to 1990. Poverty is relatively higher in the central city, and the differential with respect to suburbs is rising over time.

central-city to metropolitan-level poverty has also been on the rise. Given the demographics, the implications for racial equality are clear. There has also been a rise in income inequality within regions (see Figure 14-5), as well as a rise in the variability in income growth between regions (see Figure 14-6). The variability in income growth between regions, however, is not a good candidate for explaining racial inequality. Breaking the 74 metropolitan regions into slow, medium, and fast growers, the proportion of the population that is minority is roughly the same across groups. A more likely explanation is that there are increasing differentials between city and suburb within nearly every region.

To see how this plays out in one specific case, and to get a more detailed analysis that goes beyond broad categories of city and suburb, I combined data on residents from the Public Use Microdata Sample for Los Angeles (L.A.) County with data from the local Association of Governments on the employment base—i.e., where the jobs are actually located—by census tracts for 1980 and 1990. To link the two, I aggregated the tract-level employment data for L.A.'s 58 Public Use Microdata Areas (PUMAs). L.A. County PUMAs have a median population of less than 150,000 and are generally recognizable neighborhoods whose size, scale,

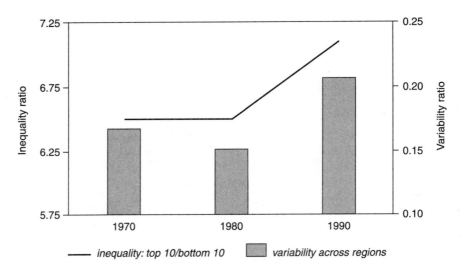

FIGURE 14-5  Metropolitan-level inequality in 74 metropolitan areas, 1970 to 1990.  Income inequality within regions increased during the 1980s, and the variation between regional patterns of inequality increased as well.

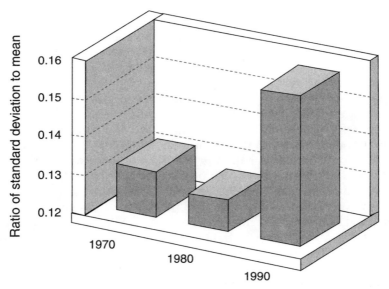

FIGURE 14-6  Variability of income growth by metropolitan area, 1970 to 1990. The variability of per capita income by region has risen, suggesting increasingly different economic performance by region.

and borders seem to approximate localized labor markets (see Pastor and Marcelli, 2001). Using PUMAs allows us to go beyond the usual city/ suburb distinction, which is especially important in the case of L.A., where the central city contains many of its own suburbs, and inner-ring suburbs in the County often exhibit economic conditions worse than the city of Los Angeles.

The 58 PUMAs were arranged in order of job growth during the 1980s; Raphael (1998), Stoll (1997), and others have suggested that this sort of job-growth measure is better than the usual job-density variable, especially for first-time labor-market entrants, like minority youth, because it captures the rate at which job possibilities appear and therefore proxies labor-market tautness. After arranging the sample, I took the fastest growing one-third and slowest growing one-third of the PUMAs and calculated the demographics. The results (Figure 14-7) are striking—the low job-growth areas are 67 percent Black and Hispanic; the fast job-

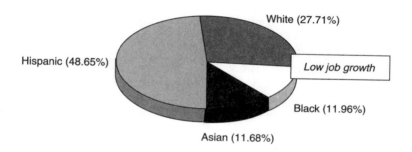

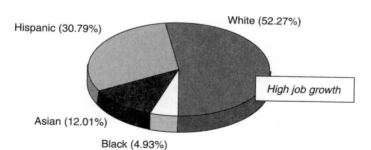

FIGURE 14-7 Ethnic composition of low and high job growth areas in Los Angeles County, 1990. Throughout the 1980s, the percentage of Blacks and Hispanics increased by 8.0 percent in low job growth areas and 6.1 percentage points in high job growth areas, suggesting increasing concentration of minorities in low job growth areas.

growth areas are only 41 percent Black and Hispanic. As noted in Figure 14-7, the minority percentage actually rose more in the low-growth areas, suggesting that Whites may have been more likely to (or able to) follow the jobs, while minority residents were more likely to stay put.

Of course, the problem is not simply one of slow employment growth or job scarcity, per se, in the central city. Many authors have stressed that living in areas of concentrated poverty tends to diminish the relative strength of social networks critical to obtaining jobs (O'Regan, 1993; Pastor and Adams, 1996; Oliver and Lichter, 1996; Ellen and Turner, 1997). O'Regan (1993:331) makes the argument most eloquently; she notes that "networks are largely determined by location" and that "there is a negative externality associated with increased concentration of the poor." Galster and Killen (1995) note that the evidence on space and networks is somewhat tentative (and generally under-modeled), but it does indicate the direction of a spatial effect on network "quality."

Wilson (1996) and others have also stressed what might be called "social-ecologic factors." In neighborhoods where work and wages are scarce, individual survival strategies tend to incorporate skills and behavior patterns that are not conducive to obtaining and retaining employment. For example, developing a tough demeanor or avoiding eye contact may enhance self-protection in a high-poverty, high-crime neighborhood, but these techniques are less successful in a job interview (Wilson, 1996:63-64). Wilson stresses that fundamental values regarding the importance of work and family are quite similar between ghetto residents and others; what differs is the "structure of opportunity" within which to act on those values (see also, Acs and Wissoker, 1991; Galster and Killen, 1995).

If these hypotheses carry weight, then the problems of poor social networks and inadequate incentives are especially important for U.S. minorities. After all, Jargowsky's analysis of the 1990 Census data suggests that poor Blacks were more than five times more likely, and poor Hispanics nearly four times more likely, than poor Whites to live in neighborhoods of concentrated poverty (Jargowsky, 1997:41). Wilson (1996) has argued that the problem of joblessness and limited social networks has become more pronounced as joblessness has grown in ghetto, or high poverty, communities. As Briggs (1997:209) points out, however, there are "dangers of confusing spatial proximity with social interaction" (see also Tienda, 1991).

To check the impact of spatial and "social" (or network) factors on individual level outcomes, L.A.'s Survey of Urban Inequality was used. I regressed (the log of) wages for male workers on a series of typical human-capital and demographic factors (education, work experience, English language proficiency, recentness of immigration, marital status, race/ethnicity) and three other "social ecological" variables (network quality, local job growth, and local/skill mismatch). Network quality is an overall measure of the strength and "quality" of networks, with strength representing the number of ties and the extent of favors that one expects would be extended by network contacts, and quality represented by the labor-market position of those in one's networks.[2] Local job growth is simply the 1980-to-1990 employment increase in the PUMA in which an individual resides. Local/skill mismatch measures the difference between the PUMA-level demand for skills—i.e., the educational levels associated with local jobs—and the supply of skills—i.e., the educational level of the residents in that PUMA. Note that local/skill mismatch doesn't address the individual skill level; it simply suggests whether there is a skill-based spatial mismatch in one's neighborhood that could lead higher-wage employers to look somewhere else for employees (see Holzer and Danziger, 1997). The results, fully presented in Pastor and Marcelli (2001), suggest that location does matter to individual level outcomes and that the quality of one's network—or stock of social capital—is important.[3]

An additional dimension of spatial inequality has to do with the unequal distribution of environmental hazards that are often the byproducts left in central cities by older industrial processes as newer and cleaner employment has radiated outward. Although there have been doubters,[4] a wide array of research indicates that there is a pattern, nationwide, of toxic storage and disposal facilities (TSDFs), toxic air releases, and other locally undesirable land uses (LULUs) being concentrated in minority neighborhoods. Because much of the pattern of industry, and hence waste, is regional, I turn once again to metropolitan Los Angeles.

The entire Southern California area (five counties excluding San Diego) is linked together in a regional association of governments. Figure 14-8 indicates the percentage of Southern California Whites, Blacks, and

---

[2]Although the network quality variable is individually based, many analysts have argued that the quality of one's contacts, at least in terms of their access to employment opportunities, may be profoundly affected by location, in that those living in areas of concentrated poverty are more likely to have poor and poorly connected individuals as their cohorts.

[3]It is interesting that one of the traditional measures of spatial mismatch—average neighborhood commute time—is not a significant predictor if substituted for the better measures described here; this suggests the need to go beyond that usual variable in regression analyses, at least in the case of Los Angeles. For more on spatial mismatch in L.A., and how it might differ from other metro areas, see Pugh (1998:36-38).

[4]Anderton et al. (1994) best represent the doubters. Been (1995) is one of the more careful national-level studies indicating that disproportionate environmental exposure exists, confirming the less rigorous cross-sectional work of United Church of Christ (1987) and the U.S. General Accounting Office (1983). For a recent comprehensive review of the literature, see Szasz and Meuser (1997).

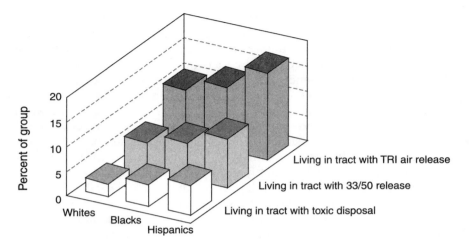

FIGURE 14-8  Exposure by group to environmental negatives in Southern California.  The figure charts the percentage of each group living in a tract with the specified release.  For example, 5.4 percent of Whites live in a tract with a 33/50 release, but 10 percent of Hispanics live in such a tract.

Hispanics who live in a census tract in which one of three types of hazards occurs—TSDFs, a toxic or (TRI) air release, or a 33/50 air release (classified as higher priority for reduction by the Environmental Protection Agency).  As it turns out, Hispanics are particularly likely to live in such areas.  Moreover, population ethnicity (especially percentage Hispanic) seems to factor into the location of these hazards, even in a multivariate regression, which controls for land use, population density, income levels, residents employed in manufacturing, and other relevant variables (Boer et al., 1997; Sadd et al., 1999).

With jobs leaving, social capital slipping, and environmental negatives accumulating, ethnic minorities living in the areas where hazardous waste accumulation is occurring are experiencing distress.[5]  Of course, both everyday experience and the wage and employment "penalties" evidenced in most multivariate regression analyses suggest that race still

---

[5]One issue not covered here is education, another realm where place and race have often intertwined to produce negative and self-reinforcing cycles.  Indeed, the spatial difference in educational quality is, along with the racial composition of schools, one factor that has likely driven trends toward suburbanization; and the resulting shifts in test scores and population simply induce more shifts.  This important topic deserves a full and separate treatment, precluded by the brevity of this paper; as a result, I focus on the direct employment and environmental dimensions of space.

matters significantly and independently for economic success (or lack thereof). But in a world in which legal discrimination has eroded, place and race have become intertwined and geography has become a predictor of both opportunity and outcome.

## UNDERSTANDING THE TRENDS

The 1970-1990 patterns of suburbanization are a continuation of a longer pattern in post-World War II America (Jackson, 1985; Mollenkopf, 1983). Suburbanization was not simply a response to individual preferences for low-density living and proximity to nature (which, in any case, was often eliminated for earlier suburbanites by the later development of yet another out-lying suburb). Certain federal policies, such as the 1956 Interstate Highway Act and the Federal Housing Authority and Veterans Administration home mortgage loan program, were key contributors to metropolitan decentralization, or what by the 1970s was being called urban sprawl. School desegregation and episodic social unrest in inner cities (again, one of the most dramatic examples being offered by Los Angeles with its 1965 Watts riots) pushed the process along by stimulating widespread White exodus from more established central-city neighborhoods and inner-ring suburbs. Continuing practices of housing market discrimination ensured that Blacks got left behind in the outward movement. As a result, inner cities increasingly became repositories for low-income individuals, as the suburbs enjoyed higher tax bases and fewer social program costs—a process that has deepened fiscal divisions between central cities and their suburbs (Massey and Eggers, 1993; Abramson et al., 1995).

As Dreier (1998:10) notes, "since federal policy is typically associated with minority urban dwellers, the assertion that federal policy has tilted the metropolitan playing field toward better off suburbs may seem counter-intuitive." Yet, Dreier calculates that tax "expenditures" (foregone taxes) for the home mortgage interest deduction, a benefit that can only be taken by home-owning, mostly higher-income suburbanites, totaled approximately four times more than HUD directly spent on housing subsidies in 1997. Furthermore, real expenditures on homeowner subsidies (including the interest rate deduction as well as the deductibility of property tax and deferral of capital gains) rose nearly fourfold between 1978 and 1997, while HUD subsidies declined by more than 80 percent during the same period (Dreier, 2001).[6] Meanwhile, federal funds tar-

---

[6]As for the distribution, the top 12 percent of taxpayers received 71 percent of the mortgage-interest benefits in 1995 (also taken from Dreier (2001) with the calculations based on data provided in *Estimates of Federal Tax Expenditures for Fiscal Years 1996-2000*, Washington, D.C.: Joint Committee on Taxation, U.S. Congress, September 1, 1995).

geted to already fiscally starved cities declined by 66 percent in real terms between 1981 and 1993 (Eisinger, 1998). Shorting the central city on development funds, and expanding a system in which housing subsidies rise with home ownership and home values, has provided incentives for further suburbanization.

The impacts of federal policy have often been made worse by state and local measures. In California, for example, tax limitation statutes have constrained government investment in infrastructure and social support. One local-level response has been an increasing reliance on sales tax revenue. This strategy induces municipalities to pursue "big-box" retail (i.e., warehouse retailers), which tends to favor outlying suburban areas, where land is abundant and consumer incomes are higher. Poorer areas, including the older inner-ring suburbs, are unable to assemble large parcels of vacant land and instead rely on redevelopment strategies; however, even wealthier suburbs have caught on to the strategy of declaring "blight" and passing on tax benefits, which gives yet another push to the suburbanization of employment and fiscal resources (Fulton, 1997; Schrag, 1998).

What about the changing distribution of environmental hazards? As noted earlier, several studies have suggested that LULUs are disproportionately located in minority communities; however, there is no standard database that looks at changes in hazard exposure over a long period. The lack of a national database makes a general analysis problematic. To get at this, at least in part, Jim Sadd and I have constructed a database of the high-capacity (over 50 tons per year) TSDFs in Los Angeles County. The database includes both the TSDF locations and date of siting.[7] Coupling this with a database that arranges the 1970 and 1980 Census data into the 1990 tracts, we were able to calculate the changing demographics of toxic areas. To get beyond the fact that the percentages for the minority populations were increasing in both toxic and nontoxic areas, we instead calculated exposure rates—i.e., the percent of the total population living in the County who also live in a tract within one-quarter mile of a high-capacity TSDF—for Blacks and Hispanics versus all others for 1970, 1980, and 1990.

The results are pictured in Figure 14-9. As can be seen, the exposure has been rising over time. Part of this increase is simply that new TSDFs are sited and begin operation in each decade, so all groups are likely to see exposures rise. The increase in the percent of Blacks and Hispanics who are living in tracts within one-quarter mile of a TSDF, however, is

---

[7]Obtaining the date sited involved significant archival work; in the case where a tract has two or more sites, we choose the earliest date.

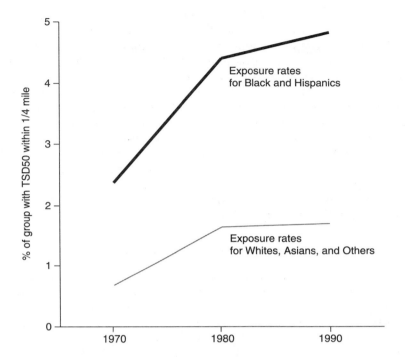

FIGURE 14-9 Exposure to high-capacity toxic facilities over time in Los Angeles County. The exposure to high-capacity toxic storage and disposal facilities (TSD50s) has generally risen over time for both Whites and minorities. The increase has been greatest for Blacks and Hispanics, leading to an even greater exposure differential.

consistently higher, and the differential has been rising over time. One usual response is that minorities are choosing to move into toxic areas, perhaps because of lower property values. Our preliminary examination of this TSDF-dated database, however, suggests that neighborhoods that received new TSDFs in any particular decade had a larger percent of minority residents prior to the siting, suggesting at least some disproportionality in the actual location decision process. Moreover, our logistic analysis of the 1990 data suggests that a higher percent of minorities also live near toxic facilities. Because we have controlled for income, the independent role of race suggests that there is something more occurring here than low-income individuals moving into low-value areas.

The central point is that these patterns in economic and environmental trends are not simply market-driven; they are the result of policy actions at many levels. Sometimes the impacts of policy are indirect and unintended. Those who sought to make the dream of home ownership accessible via federal loan programs and interest rate tax deductions were not consciously out to raid the central cities of America; tax cutters in California may not have had the irrational fiscalization of land use as their main goal; owners of TSDFs may have been more worried about minimizing political resistance than about poisoning people of color. Still, the impacts have been real—and they both reflect a politics of division and isolation by race and place, and reinforce such politics as social distance that result in economic gaps that widen over time. Indeed, it is the resulting political calculus—as suburban votes increase, central cities decline—that makes it difficult to launch and sustain national-level programs for tackling poverty and racial/economic inequality.

## POSSIBLE FUTURE TRENDS

The patterns discussed above, and the fact that they have been partly the result of policy, may lead one to despair. If geography is important to opportunity, the current economic and political configuration situation is sure to exacerbate existing divisions by space and race. Yet, although it is certainly possible that this pattern of disparity will simply continue to worsen, we may actually stand at a unique and positive turning point, in part because of the changing geography of the economy and the shifting demographic and economic nature of suburbs.

The increasing divergence of economic performance by metropolitan area, discussed above, has led Barnes and Ledebur (1998) to characterize the contemporary United States as a sort of common market of economic regions, each with distinctive business clusters and growth patterns. Although the theoretical explanations for this "emergence of the region" remain a bit underdeveloped, one common story suggests that because internationalization has rendered national policies less effective, economic action has descended to the regional or metropolitan level. Why? The region, it seems, is an economic level large enough for economies of scale but small enough for lasting ties between firms and their suppliers as well as between the business, government, and social actors needed to achieve consensus on growth. These ties, i.e., this social capital, is the glue that holds regions together and allows them to become successful (Putnam, 1993; Peirce, 1993).

Recognizing this, a new body of research has suggested that regions plagued by rising inequalities—hence, eroding social capital and lowered "trust"—may experience lower growth. Figure 14-10 illustrates this point by plotting per-capita income growth during the 1980s against the per-

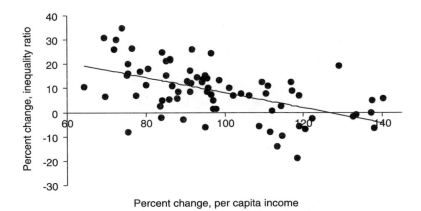

FIGURE 14-10 Per capita income growth and change in inequality in 74 metropolitan areas, 1980 to 1990.

cent change in our inequality measure over the same period. Of course,
the pictured correlation is not causation; relatively rapid growth should
also help diminish inequalities (Jargowsky, 1997:162), and much of the
past research, which has looked at the relationship between employment,
income, city/suburb differentials, and other measures has been plagued
by methodological problems.[8] Two newer studies try to control for simultaneity, and still find that dealing with inequality, poverty, and city-
suburb differentials may indeed help growth (Voith, 1997; Pastor et al.,
2000). As noted below, however, much more work needs to be done.

Despite the unfinished state of this research, some proponents of this
"new regionalism"—i.e., the notion that regions are now the fundamental
economic unit—have stressed the importance of linking city and suburb
in the new metropolitan economies (U.S. Department of Housing and
Urban Development, 1996). A reconfiguration of political space to reflect
the new reality—i.e., the resurrection of the concept of regional government—seems unlikely in most areas if only because few citizens desire
yet another level of government. Still, Swanstrom (1996) argues that the
new thinking about collective regional destinies opens up the opportu-

---

[8]Barnes and Ledebur have conducted a number of studies on city-suburban links, most of
which are summarized in their 1998 volume; see also Savitch et al. (1993). For careful
reviews of the evidence and its limits, see Gottlieb (1998), Harrison (1998), Hill et al. (1994),
and Ihlanfeldt (1995).

nity for a political alliance between cities and their suburbs and informal, multisectoral collaborations on regional development (Downs, 1994).

Another approach to new regionalism, best typified by Orfield (1997), is more confrontational than collaborative. This view suggests that the data used above, which showed only a slow diversification of the suburban population and rising city-suburb differentials, mask an important part of the picture. In fact, suburbs may be distinguished by their proximity to the central city, with many older inner-ring suburbs experiencing changing demographics and economic pressures similar to those experienced by inner-city minorities, and many outer-ring suburbs enjoying high tax bases and few social problems.

As a result, Orfield argues, the central city and its immediate ring— and some low-tax-base cities on the fringe—have a common interest in both reducing urban sprawl and shifting fiscal burdens. In his view, the best solution is regional tax-base sharing because this would eliminate certain incentives for fringe development and allow low-tax areas to improve their social spending. This is a classic coalition strategy—rather than take the "we're all in it together" approach, this new approach stresses that most of us will win if we distribute from those who have gained the most from the United States' contemporary metropolitan configuration.

Although both the collaborative and coalitional approaches differ in their politics, each stresses the changing character of metropolitan areas and the increasing importance of regional economies. Both raise the possibility of a new political calculus supportive of inner city residents—but only if inner-city advocates themselves "think and link" to the region.

This may be quite a stretch from the traditional models of place-based development.[9] Given the pattern of concentrated poverty, many federal and state efforts have targeted particular communities; such is the logic of enterprise and empowerment zones. This has intersected well with the growing importance of community development corporations (CDCs), who themselves have a geographically determined political base and seek to serve and maintain their local constituencies. Such place-based strategies, which often focus on neighborhood revitalization and housing development, also have a racial dimension inasmuch as they can be part and parcel of a minority community's attempt to ensure some control over their environment (Gottlieb, 1997).[10] But as Nowak (1997) warns, CDCs

---

[9]For an excellent review of urban development strategies and a categorization of place-based approaches, see Gottlieb (1997).

[10]Fernandez (1997:93) makes a related point with regard to how minority politicians might resist housing mobility, or "dispersal," strategies because this could dilute a hard-won political base.

risk becoming "managers of decline" unless they reach out and affect regional decision making. In short, overcoming the geography of hardship, in which large-scale forces of deindustrialization and declining wages disproportionately affect particular neighborhoods, requires connecting to the emerging economic dynamism evident in the geography of the region.

Fortunately, inner-city advocates have begun to rethink old models of community development in a way that is potentially conducive to such regional linkages. The new community-building movement, for example, insists on the importance of restoring community fabric (the "bonding ties" of social capital) to encourage development (Walsh, 1997). Some of these community builders have also stressed regional networking as a way to connect individuals and community organizations to external opportunities and resources. They argue that although bonding (within-group) social capital does tie together individuals with immediate common interests, ethnic identities, neighborhood allegiance, or other salient features, what the poor need is bridging (across-group) social capital— the kind that can tie inner-city communities together with individuals and opportunities outside their usual immediate reach.

The notion that linking outside the neighborhood can be beneficial is gaining ground for several reasons. First, a variety of studies of the famous Gautreaux experiment and HUD's evolving Moving to Opportunity program have suggested that actually moving out of a neighborhood expands networks and enhances opportunity (Popkin et al., 1993). Because few community developers really want to encourage exodus, replicating the benefits through links to jobs and other assets seems to be a positive idea. Second, recent research has found that CDCs with better access to regional actors and opportunities tend to have better luck at placing low-income residents in jobs and wielding political and policy influence than do those that remain disconnected (Harrison and Weiss, 1998). Recent research on 10 higher-poverty neighborhoods in Los Angeles County likewise confirms that those better connected to the region exhibit stronger performance in terms of income and employment (Pastor et al., 1997).

Regional approaches may also have something to offer to those worried about issues of environmental justice. Disproportionate exposure is clearly neighborhood-based, but political resistance to such demographic dumping is weak when it occurs at the level and rate of one community at a time. In this context, linkages between communities can be critical. Concerned Citizens of South Central, a mostly Black environmentalist group in inner-city Los Angeles, was able to resist the siting of a waste incinerator in their neighborhood, partly because the group formed powerful alliances with White working class and suburban residents afraid that allowing a waste incinerator area in South L.A. would lead to a series of incinerators placed in their own neighborhoods (Blumberg and Gottlieb, 1989:168).

More broadly, there is one explicitly environmentalist variant of regionalism that focuses on the benefits of compact living and reduced auto dependence, all of which require a more tightly integrated region.[11] Although proponents of this approach are sometimes more concerned with preservation of rural land than the preservation of low-income people, the resulting strategies—which tend to constrain sprawl and force more concentrated development—may be conducive for inner-city revitalization. Portland's experience is that urban growth boundaries have benefited older and poorer suburbs (Rusk, 1998). The "Smart Growth" initiatives gaining ground in Maryland, Florida, and elsewhere may open up possibilities for integrating central-city concerns even as growth is channeled inward by limiting fringe development. Finally, a coalition of St. Louis congregations, led by Black churches, has taken on urban sprawl as a central issue, using this to form alliances with suburban neighbors and redirect resources to urban revitalization (Rusk, 1998). Clearly, equity can be served under the banner of regional environmental sustainability.

Of course, regional thinking on economic and environmental issues is still nascent, and those explicitly calling for links between regionalists, community developers, and minority residents have been few and far between (for emerging voices, see Bollens, 1997; Nowak, 1997). Resistance has come both from inner-city leaders, worried that their concerns will be submerged in a broader regional agenda (Gottlieb, 1997), and from suburbanites still hesitant to hitch their wagons to the rebirth of the central city. The new regionalist approach is also open to the criticism that it represents a rather indirect way of getting at the deeper problems of race in America. Like Wilson's focus on broad- or class-based remedies, it targets the geography of opportunity and networks in a race-neutral policy framework, which may evade some of the harder questions about persistent discrimination and segregation.

This critique may be particularly appropriate inasmuch as one of the reasons for our contemporary urban geography is exactly the racial dynamics of residential settlement in which Whites avoid settling in traditionally Black areas and tend to move when the number of nearby Blacks increases (Massey and Denton, 1993). Still, in an era in which the political will to tackle issues of race and poverty seems minimal, the regional approach at least has the chance for addressing concerns about poverty, even if out of the pure self-interest of threatened suburbs. Moreover, the

---

[11]See Summers (1997) for a characterization of the variants of regionalism.

dynamics of forging regional consensus can bring sectors together for discussions with their neighbors—even those who may live at some distance—and replace the abstract discussions of policy in Washington with the face-to-face (and race-to-race) interactions that can begin building bridging social capital.

## RESEARCH AND POLICY IMPLICATIONS

The argument here is simple—economic opportunity, social capital, and environmental exposure are often spatially based. Given differential patterns of residential settlement, this has had disproportionately negative consequences for racial minorities. The new focus on regions, which tends to stress city-suburb ties and environmental sustainability within a metropolitan area—may offer one way out for both new politics and new policies.

For the argument to really stand up, however, much remains to be done on the research side. First, one of the central premises above is that the federal and state playing fields have been tilted against inner-city residents. Unfortunately, the general writing on this issue tends to be suggestive or interpretive.[12] While it is quite likely that federal highway spending, housing policies, and tax breaks did push along the process of suburbanization, reliable estimates of the size and effect of the subsidies remain elusive. Recovering the past may be difficult; understanding the future might be easier, and profit us better. We could use better mechanisms for geographically disaggregating the impacts of federal spending and policy, hopefully down to the tract or neighborhood level. A recent report by the National Academy of Public Administration (1998) offers some general guidelines for such work, and the Brookings Institution's Center for Urban and Metropolitan Policy has launched a study of this topic for selected metropolitan regions.

Second, we could use much more information about the dynamics of regional economies, with a critical first step being the consolidation of a

---

[12]For an exception, see Parker (1995). Parker concurs with the notion presented here, that researchers would benefit from further disaggregation of federal spending. However, although Parker's evidence suggests that federal expenditures favor central cities (although suburbs have been gaining ground), his analysis is confined to spending from 1983 to 1992, his city-suburb definitions are overly broad, and he includes transfers like Aid to Families with Dependent Children (AFDC) but ignores transfers due to tax expenditures on housing. This is a useful contribution, but it is only a partial answer to the question of whether federal policy has promoted suburbanization—and it explicitly ignores the fact that welfare spending only partially covers the costs of poverty, and so cities receiving significant AFDC payments actually experience fiscal strain (see Gyourko and Summers, 1997).

complete and uniform database on major metropolitan regions. Currently, researchers studying regional dynamics draw on widely varying databases; the consequent variations in variable and geographic definitions, including which U.S. metropolitan areas should and shouldn't be included, mean that discussions that should be about perspectives and hypotheses instead become debates about sample bias and statistical proxies. The SNC database helped advance the discussion, with its attempt at uniformity, but its coverage of both variables and areas should be expanded; especially important would be linkages with data on industrial clusters, employment location, journey-to-work, and environmental hazards.

With a database in place, more could and should be done on the growth-equity linkage. As noted above, the current work has a hopeful message, but there are problems of simultaneity and inadequate model specification. Gottlieb's (1998) excellent review and Harrison's (1998) recent comments indicate just how far behind the methodology really is. As Harrison (1998) points out, documenting more fully whether cities and suburbs are linked—and understanding how—is absolutely necessary to establishing the material base for metropolitanism.

Third, we need more work by political scientists and others on the political dynamics of regions. Traditional studies have tended to look at the presence or absence of metropolitan governments. Yet, in Los Angeles, for example, regional planning is "not controlled by SCAG (the local association of governments) or any other single agency. Rather it is centered—if that is the word—in scattered meetings and negotiations and skirmishes that occur over this 100 square mile region" (Fulton and Newman, 1992). Overall, dynamic regions seem to be characterized by informal public-private alliances that may bridge political jurisdictions (U.S. Department of Housing and Urban Development, 1996). In especially successful regions, like the Silicon Valley, leadership has come from the business sector as well as from other civic entrepreneurs from all walks of life (Henton et al., 1997).

What are the conditions that lead to regional collaboration? Saxenian's (1996) exemplary volume comparing the Boston electronics complex and the Silicon Valley notes that certain industrial clusters and interfirm linkages can create fertile ground for collaboration on growth policies, but many more case studies need to be done (see also Foster, 1997; Savitch and Vogel, 1996). Especially important would be studies of how and when community organizations and inner-city leaders become part of regional efforts. Indergaard's (1997) study is useful in this regard as is Nowak's (1998) review of the Delaware Valley Community Reinvestment Fund's efforts at job placement, venture capital, and regional-jobs policy. More tracking of the evolution of these bridging networks and their impacts would be helpful to policy makers figuring out how targeted regional collaborations can acquire a forward momentum that will lead to more regional efforts in the future (Peirce and Johnson, 1997).

Fourth, we need more work on the changing demographics of the suburbs. To determine whether the inner-ring suburbs share economic and demographic similarities with parts of the central city, we need to go beyond the usual simplified city-suburb typology (Frey and Geverdt, 1998). For example, the City of Los Angeles shows roughly similar demographics and occupational structure as the rest of the County; economic conditions are worse in the City but the differences are less than might be supposed and housing values were actually higher in the central city (Table 14-1). But the City of Los Angeles includes its own suburbs—e.g., the San Fernando Valley—and excludes parts of what is known to residents as South L.A.; these are listed as either unincorporated County territory or separate poor cities. Reconfiguring the geography to include the inner city and adding its inner-ring neighbors shows sharp differences in demographics, economic outcomes, and housing values. Trying another cut—breaking the county into PUMAs, based on demographic changes during 1970 to 1990—offers yet another view that gives a better idea of the stresses minority residents face whether they reside in the center or in the shifting suburbs (Table 14-1). Obviously, much may be gained by finer urban breakdowns than those used thus far.

Fifth, we could use more research on the impacts of the efforts of networks and labor-market intermediaries to connect individuals to employment, particularly at the regional level. The Survey of Urban Inequality, referred to above, asked some important questions about networks. More such survey efforts need to be undertaken,[13] particularly to understand how networks work for different groups. For example, preliminary econometric and anthropological evidence seems to suggest that networks are important for Hispanics in obtaining employment, but reliance on these networks actually leads to lower wages because of the labor-market position of the network members (Falcón, 1995; Pastor and Marcelli, 2001). In short, more attention needs to be paid to the differences between bonding (within-group) and bridging (across-group) social capital and networks.

There is a similar need for more attention to labor-market intermediaries. Such intermediaries arise, in part, because employers want to screen possible workers, and job seekers need resources when social networks

---

[13]For one interesting micro-survey, see Fernandez and Weinberg's 1998 study on how networks affect hiring in one retail bank. The results square well with views that networks matter for both employer and (potential) employee.

TABLE 14-1 Comparative Views on Los Angeles County, 1990

| | Demographics, % of Population | | | | Population Growth since 1970 |
|---|---|---|---|---|---|
| | Anglo | African-American | Latino | Asian | |
| City of L.A./other | | | | | |
| L.A. City | 37.3 | 13.0 | 39.9 | 9.8 | 24.3 |
| Rest of county | 43.1 | 8.9 | 36.5 | 11.5 | 27.5 |
| City-suburb | | | | | |
| Inner city | 15.8 | 19.8 | 55.0 | 9.4 | 27.5 |
| Rest of county | 50.9 | 6.8 | 30.9 | 11.4 | 25.7 |
| Neighborhoods by demography | | | | | |
| Anglo-stayed Anglo | 72.8 | 4.6 | 14.1 | 8.6 | 25.3 |
| Ethnic-stayed ethnic | 3.4 | 38.1 | 55.1 | 3.4 | 18.9 |
| Anglo-large ethnic transition | 18.8 | 12.5 | 59.1 | 9.6 | 37.0 |
| Average transition-now ethnic | 23.0 | 8.1 | 53.0 | 15.9 | 32.7 |
| Average transition-now Anglo | 51.2 | 5.7 | 31.3 | 11.9 | 21.9 |

Economics

| | Blue-collar, % | Job Growth Since 1980, % | Poor, % | Income to Mean | House Value to Mean |
|---|---|---|---|---|---|
| City of L.A./other | | | | | |
| L.A. City | 42.6 | 15.0 | 17.5 | 95.6 | 106.4 |
| Rest of county | 41.4 | 37.0 | 12.7 | 102.5 | 96.4 |
| City-suburb | | | | | |
| Inner city | 55.9 | 7.7 | 24.3 | 67.1 | 74.8 |
| Rest of county | 37.4 | 35.8 | 11.3 | 110.5 | 107.4 |
| Neighborhoods by demography | | | | | |
| Anglo-stayed Anglo | 25.9 | 50.3 | 7.5 | 135.0 | 140.9 |
| Ethnic-stayed ethnic | 60.7 | 22.7 | 28.9 | 55.2 | 58.0 |
| Anglo-large ethnic transition | 52.8 | 4.8 | 18.1 | 81.5 | 79.8 |
| Average transition-now ethnic | 49.4 | 21.6 | 16.4 | 87.8 | 82.1 |
| Average transition-now Anglo | 37.0 | 30.3 | 11.5 | 105.7 | 105.6 |

Note: Economic figures are simple averages across L.A.'s 58 Public Use Microdata Areas. Demographic figures are weighted by population in Public Use Microdata Areas.

are too weak or tend to connect one to lower rungs of the job hierarchy. Unfortunately, those workers who most need intermediaries are those who lack social capital and encounter spatial mismatch, so they are often constrained in their ability to access services or have limited knowledge of their availability. As temporary and contingent work have risen in importance, the intermediary role has also become more important. Understanding which of these intermediaries works best for low-income, spatially isolated residents, and why, will be important for policy (Kazis, 1998).

Sixth, more research on transportation connections to employment would be useful. Gottlieb (1997) bemoans the relative lack of studies using journey-to-work data. The Public Use Microdata Sample contains detailed information about commuting, but even though the place of residence is quite specific—i.e., at the PUMA level—the place of work is simply "the city," implying a loss of specificity for larger areas like Los Angeles. As a result, Pastor and Adams (1996) were forced to drop any subject who worked in the City of Los Angeles or other multi-PUMA jurisdiction in order to look at whether living in a poor neighborhood but working in a wealthier one raised one's income. It did, with interesting implications for reverse commuting programs; but this is based on a selective sample that could be broadened if the Census Bureau collected and geocoded more complete work-address information in 2000.

Seventh, we need more regional-level case studies of the patterns of environmental exposure by race and other variables. Recent research has gone beyond anecdotes and case studies; but in the search for empiricism, there has been a tendency to reach to national levels and large aggregate datasets. This has the advantage of broad coverage; however, industrial structures are often regional in nature, and so is the nature of pollution. Moreover, at a regional level, researchers can generally access such variables as land use and employment as well as the traditional demographic measures available from the U.S. Census. This allows for a fuller picture; and the local-level data will often allow for more serious investigations of, for example, whether the pattern of toxic location is a phenomenon that occurs before a demographic transition or whether there is a minority move-in effect which occurs after. Of course, either outcome results in a worrisome pattern of disproportionate exposure, but the policy implications diverge—when toxics are placed in neighborhoods by race, attention should be paid to cleaning up the politics of the siting process; if minorities aggregate around toxics, perhaps because of lower land values, information campaigns should be used to make everyone aware of the risks that are silently (and perhaps incompletely) signaled via market prices.

Much remains to be done in the research of space and race. We need not wait for the analytical dust to settle completely before we move ahead with some immediate policy measures to address the geography of opportunity. Indeed, there are a variety of exciting experiments and initiatives that point in the right direction and should be continued.

A new policy approach might have three central elements: (1) reversing the federal and state incentives for sprawl with incentives for regional reconnection, (2) facilitating the connection of poorer (usually minority) individuals to the regional economy, and (3) encouraging the fair distribution of environmental hazards produced in the regional economy. These might be broadly called *regional collaboration, regional mobility,* and *regional environmentalism.*

On the collaboration side, one critical element will be increased incentives for regional approaches. The single most effective lever for regional collaboration in recent years has been provided by the Intermodal Surface Transportation Efficiency Act (ISTEA), which was recently reworked as the Transportation Equity Act for the Twenty-first Century (TEA-21).[14] The framework ISTEA presented for multijurisdictional cooperation should be a model for other federal policies, including Section 8 administration and workforce development. A bonus pool of federal funding, regardless of the specific program, could be set aside for local jurisdictions that have demonstrated progress on intraregional collaboration and multisectoral participation. Help could be provided for auditing of the regional economy and its business clusters in order to get a sense of how best to train individuals for upward advancement. Clusters could be graded not only by their contribution to aggregate growth, but also by their accessibility to low-income residents and their mechanisms for upward wage progress.

Hopeful signs abound. HUD is moving to develop a regionalist agenda, Vice President Gore has become a strong proponent of "Smart Growth," and there is rising interest among foundations in how new regional approaches might address central-city poverty and urban development. One interesting experiment under way involves the creation of "location-efficient" mortgages, which reward borrowers who live near public transit (on the grounds that they will spend less money on auto transport and, hence, should qualify for more credit). This will help inner-city residents and constitutes one incentive that leans away from suburbanization. Overcoming the larger incentives, including the mortgage interest rate deduction, will be politically challenging. At the least,

---

[14]For more on TEA-21 and how it might be conducive to placing low-income minority residents in new jobs, see Center for Community Change (1998).

this deduction could be restructured to be more distributionally progressive.

Federal incentives for mobility should come in three areas—housing, transportation, and employment. Allocating low-income housing across the region (via scattered-site approaches and inclusionary zoning) and generating individual housing mobility are necessary to decentralize poverty and allow poorer individuals to connect to acquire new residential networks.

Generating transportation mobility is necessary to allow poorer job-seekers ways to connect to suburbanized employment. HUD's Bridges to Work program, for example, facilitates reverse commuting and is a flexible response to the problems of fixed-rail lines and bus patterns.[15] More generally, the distributional impacts of transportation should be more explicitly taken into account, particularly because they may vary by region. In the Los Angeles area, for example, the continued development of light- and heavy-rail commuter systems (in which riders cover only 7 to 9 percent of service costs) has strained the ability to mount adequate bus service (even though riders here cover 30 to 35 percent of costs). As a result, the bus system, with a more than 80 percent minority ridership, is considered to be the most overcrowded in the United States, and the local metropolitan transit authority was sued by a series of community groups and the NAACP Legal Defense Fund when it attempted to raise bus fares to cover overruns on rail construction (Mann, 1996). Given the crucial role of public transportation for lower-income minority workers (Hodge, 1995), much more attention needs to be paid to equity in transport development and accessibility.

Generating employment mobility should involve more than first-time placement. Although much attention has been focused on the jobless, an equally severe problem is that of the working poor—and it is one that is likely to worsen as ex-welfare recipients flood low-wage labor markets. New directions could involve public provision of continued training as well as efforts to increase firm-sponsored training. These could help those in low-wage, currently dead-end jobs to move up a career ladder. Part of this will also involve CDC-based job training and placement programs, the best of which seem to be deeply connected to their regional labor market (Zdenek, 1998; Melendez, 1996).

---

[15]Fernandez (1997) notes that if firms locate in suburbs to avoid minorities, transportation will not be much help. If such location is driven by land use availability and technological imperatives, then reverse commuting, improved networks, and other measures might help. Despite acknowledging that minority avoidance might be a factor, Fernandez still concurs that transportation strategies can work if these are coupled with information efforts—i.e., labor market intermediaries—and transport subsidies for minority workers.

Finally, one of the most exciting developments in the area of the environment and disproportionate exposure is the Environmental Protection Agency's various Brownfields Initiatives. Given the historic pattern of toxics, low-income minority communities are saddled with industrial sites from which developers, worried about legal entanglements and clean-up costs, may shy. Initiatives to clean up these sites tend to be "win-win" situations—the aggregate level of minority exposure will decline, economic development will result in the inner city, and the public, private, and community sectors will gain experience working together. There are numerous pilot projects under way; most involve a regional approach to the identification of sites and the building of coalitions for implementation. These efforts should be expanded as soon as the preliminary data are in and some lessons learned on how to proceed. The harder task will be determining new rules for future toxic facilities that explicitly take into account racial justice issues.

## CONCLUSION: PLACE, RACE, AND FACE

In explaining the continuing economic difficulties of minorities in the United States, three factors seem critical: place, race, and "face." Place has been the subject of much of the analysis here—racial disparities have been both driven by, and reflected in, geographic differences with regard to access to employment, schools, and opportunity. Race likewise remains an independent factor—careful research by Kirschenman and Neckerman (1991) and Kirschenman et al. (1996) indicates that employers still exhibit preferences to hire nonminorities, with special discrimination faced by Blacks. Finally, "face" refers to the networks or personal connections that can help people move out of poverty, but that are often lacking for those living in areas of concentrated poverty.

It has been difficult for U.S. policy makers and the American public to face up to the second of these barriers—the question of racism and its persistence. The end of de jure segregation led some to believe the civil rights battle had been won, and the new political sentiment against affirmative action reflects a sense that a helping hand is no longer needed. But racism continues, and differential outcomes with regard to the economy and the environment continue to be played out through the social structures and limits imposed by urban geography.

There is, however, hope. Suburbs are changing, creating the opportunity for new political alliances. The idea of regional collaboration across municipalities is gaining ground. Minority community residents and leaders are realizing that they need to "think and link" to the region.

Can this new regionalism framework offer a way out of this downward spiral of increasing geographic isolation, widening racial differentials, and diminishing social capital? Maybe. Clearly, education levels, racial attitudes, and political power will all continue to matter. More research on the geography of opportunity is needed, and the emerging policy experiments must run their course. Still, the hopeful message from the new regionalists is that linking places and people, combining regional strategies, and community development, can be part of a strategy to ameliorate the gaps of race in America.

## REFERENCES

Abramson, A., M. Tobin, and M. VanderGoot
  1995    The changing geography of metropolitan opportunity: The segregation of the poor in U.S. metropolitan areas, 1970 to 1990. *Housing Policy Debate* 6(1):45-72.
Acs, G., and D. Wissoker
  1991    *The Impact of Local Labor Markets on the Employment Patterns of Young Inner-City Males.* Washington, D.C.: The Urban Institute.
Anderton, D., A. Anderson, P. Rossi, J. Oakes, M. Fraser, E. Weber, and E. Calabrese
  1994    Hazardous waste facilities: "Environmental equity" issues in metropolitan areas *Evaluation Review* 18(April):123-140.
Barnes, W., and L. Ledebur
  1998    *The New Regional Economies: The U.S. Common Market and the Global Economy.* Thousand Oaks, Calif.: Sage Publications.
Been, V.
  1995    Analyzing evidence of environmental justice. *Journal of Land Use and Environmental Law* 11(Fall):1-37.
Blumberg, L., and R. Gottlieb
  1989    *War on Waster: Can America Win Its Battle with Garbage?* Washington, D.C.: Island Press.
Boer, J., M. Pastor, Jr., J. Sadd, and L. Snyder
  1997    Is there environmental racism? The demographics of hazardous waste in Los Angeles County. *Social Science Quarterly* 78(4):793-810.
Bollens, S.
  1997    Concentrated poverty and metropolitan equity strategies. *Stanford Law and Policy Review* 8(2):11-23
Briggs, X. de Souza
  1997    Moving up versus moving out: Neighborhood effects in housing mobility programs. *Housing Policy Debate* 8(1):195-234.
Center for Community Change (CCC)
  1998    *Getting to Work: An Organizer's Guide to Transportation Equity.* Washington, D.C.: Center for Community Change.
Downs, A.
  1994    *New Visions for Metropolitan America.* Washington, D.C.: The Brookings Institution.
Dreier, P.
  1998    Trends, characteristics, and patterns in urban America. Paper presented to the Transportation Research Board, Conference on Transportation Issues in Large U.S. Cities, Detroit, June 28.
  2001    *Housing Policy and Devolution—A Delicate Balancing Act.* New York: Century Foundation.

Eisinger, P.
  1998   City politics in an era of federal devolution. *Urban Affairs Review* 33(3):308-325.
Ellen, I., and M. Turner
  1997   Does neighborhood matter? Assessing recent evidence. *Housing Policy Debate* 8(4):833-866.
Falcón, L.
  1995   Social networks and employment for Latinos, Blacks, and Whites. *New England Journal of Public Policy* 11(1):17-28.
Fernandez, R.
  1997   Spatial mismatch: Housing, transportation, and employment in regional perspective. In *The Urban Crisis: Linking Research to Action*, B. Weisbrod and J. Worthy, eds. Evanston, Ill.: Northwestern University Press.
Fernandez, R., and N. Weinberg
  1998   Sifting and sorting: Personal contacts and hiring in a retail bank. *American Sociological Review* 62:883-902.
Foster, K.
  1997   Regional impulses. *Journal of Urban Affairs* 19(4):375-403.
Frey, W., and D. Geverdt
  1998   Changing suburban demographics: Beyond the "Black-White, city-suburb" typology. Paper prepared for Suburban Racial Change, a conference sponsored by the Harvard Civil Rights Project and the Taubman Center on State and Local Government, March 28.
Fulton, W.
  1997   *The Reluctant Metropolis: The Politics of Urban Growth in Los Angeles.* Point Arena, Calif.: Solano Press Books.
Fulton, W., and M. Newman
  1992   When COGS collide. *Planning* 58(1):9-15.
Galster, G., and S. Killen
  1995   The geography of metropolitan opportunity: A reconnaissance and conceptual framework. *Housing Policy Debate* 6(1):10-47.
Gottlieb, P.
  1997   Neighborhood development in the metropolitan economy: A policy review. *Journal of Urban Affairs* 19(2):163-182.
  1998   *The Effects of Poverty on Metropolitan Area Economic Performance: A Policy-Oriented Research Review.* Washington, D.C.: National League of Cities.
Gyourko J., and A. Summers
  1997   *A New Strategy for Helping Cities Pay for the Poor.* Brookings Policy Brief 18. Washington, D.C.: The Brookings Institution.
Harrison, B.
  1998   It takes a region (or does it?): The material basis for metropolitanism and metropolitics. Paper prepared for the Twentieth Annual Research Conference, Association for Public Policy and Management, New York, October.
Harrison, B., and M. Weiss
  1998   *Workforce Development Networks: Community-Based Organizations and Regional Alliances.* Thousand Oaks, Calif.: Sage Publications.
Henton, D., J. Melville, and K. Walesh
  1997   *Grassroots Leaders for a New Economy: How Civic Entrepreneurs are Building Prosperous Communities.* San Francisco: Jossey-Bass Publishers.

Hill, E., H. Wolman, and C. Ford, III
    1994   Do cities lead and suburbs follow? Examining their economic interdependence.
           Paper prepared for the conference Rethinking the Urban Agenda, sponsored by
           the Sydney C. Spivack Program, American Sociological Association, Belmont Con-
           ference Center, Md., May 20-22.
Hodge, D.
    1995   My fair share: Equity issues in urban transportation. In *The Geography of Urban
           Transportation*, S. Hanson, ed. New York: The Guilford Press.
Holzer, H., and S. Danziger
    1997   Are jobs available for disadvantaged groups in urban areas? Paper prepared for
           Michigan State University and University of Michigan, March.
Ihlanfeldt, K.
    1995   The importance of the central city to the regional and national economy: A re-
           view of the arguments and empirical evidence. *Cityscape* 1(2):125-150.
Indergaard, M.
    1997   Community-based restructuring? Institution building in the industrial Midwest.
           *Urban Affairs Review* 32(5):662-682.
Jackson, J.
    1985   *Crabgrass Frontier: The Suburbanization of the United States.* New York: Oxford
           University Press.
Jargowsky, P.
    1997   *Poverty and Place: Ghettos, Barrios, and the American City.* New York: Russell Sage
           Foundation.
Kain, J.
    1968   Housing segregation, Negro employment and metropolitan decentralization.
           *Quarterly Journal of Economics* 25:110-130.
Kazis, R.
    1998   New labor market intermediaries: What's driving them? Where are they headed?
           Paper prepared for the Task Force on Reconstructing America's Labor Market
           Institutions, Sloan School of Management, MIT, June.
Kirschenman, J., P. Moss, and C. Tilly
    1996   Space as a signal, space as a barrier: How employers map and use space in four
           metropolitan labor markets. Working Paper No. 89. New York: Russell Sage
           Foundation.
Kirschenman, J., and K. Neckerman
    1991   "We'd love to hire them, but . . . ": The meaning of race for employers. In
           *The Urban Underclass*, C. Jencks and P. Peterson, eds. Washington, D.C.: The
           Brookings Institution.
Mann, E.
    1996   *A New Vision for Urban Transportation: The Bus Riders Union Makes History at the
           Intersection of Mass Transit, Civil Rights, and the Environment.* Los Angeles: Labor/
           Community Strategies Center.
Massey, D., and N. Denton
    1993   *American Apartheid: Segregation and the Making of the Underclass.* Cambridge, Mass.:
           Harvard University Press.
Massey, D., and M. Eggers
    1993   The spatial concentration of affluence and poverty during the 1970s. *Urban Affairs
           Quarterly* 29(2):299-315.
Melendez, E.
    1996   *Working on Jobs: The Center for Employment Training.* Boston: Mauricio Gaston
           Institute, University of Massachusetts.

Mollenkopf, J.
1983 *The Contested City*. Princeton: Princeton University Press.
National Academy of Public Administration
1998 *Building Stronger Communities and Regions: Can the Federal Government Help?* Washington, D.C.: National Academy of Public Administration.
Nowak, J.
1997 Neighborhood initiative and the regional economy. *Economic Development Quarterly* 11(1):3-10.
1998 Expanding the scope of community development. *Shelterforce* 97(January/February):10-12.
O'Regan, K.
1993 The effect of social networks and concentrated poverty on Black and Hispanic youth unemployment. *The Annals of Regional Science* 27(December):327-342.
Oliver, M., and M. Lichter
1996 Social isolation, network segregation, and job search among African Americans. Paper prepared for University of California, Los Angeles, January.
Orfield, M.
1997 *Metropolitics: A Regional Agenda for Community and Stability*. Washington, D.C.: The Brooking Institution.
Parker, R.
1995 Patterns of federal urban spending: Cities and their suburbs, 1983-92. *Urban Affairs Review* 31(2):184-205.
Pastor, M., Jr., and Adams, A.
1996 Keeping down with the Joneses: Neighbors, networks, and wages. *Review of Regional Economics* 26(2):115-145.
Pastor, M., P. Dreier, E. Grigsby, and M. Lopez-Garza
1997 *Growing Together: Linking Regional and Community Development in a Changing Economy*. Report for the John Randolph Haynes and Dora Haynes Foundation, Occidental College, Los Angeles.
2000 *Regions That Work: How Cities and Suburbs Can Grow Together*. Minneapolis: University of Minnesota Press.
Pastor, M., and E. Marcelli
2001 Men n the hood: Spatial, skill, and social mismatch for male workers in Los Angeles. *Urban Geography*, forthcoming.
Peirce, N., C. Johnson, and J. Hall
1993 *Citistates: How Urban America Can Prosper in a Competitive World*. Washington, D.C.: Seven Locks Press.
Peirce, N., and C. Johnson
1997 *Boundary Crossers: Community Leadership for a Global Age*. College Park, Md.: The Academy of Leadership.
Popkin, S., J. Rosenbaum, and P. Meaden
1993 Labor market experiences of low-income Black women in middle-class suburbs: Evidence from a survey of Gautreaux program participants. *Journal of Policy Analysis and Management* 12(3):556-573.
Pugh, M.
1998 Barriers to work: The spatial divide between jobs and welfare recipients in metropolitan areas. A discussion paper prepared for the Brookings Institution, Center on Urban and Metropolitan Policy, September.
Putnam, R.
1993 *Making Democracy Work: Civic Traditions in Modern Italy*. Princeton: Princeton University Press.

Raphael, S.
   1998    The spatial mismatch hypothesis and Black youth joblessness: Evidence from the
           San Francisco Bay area. *Journal of Urban Economics* 43(1):79-111.
Rusk, D.
   1998    St. Louis congregations challenge urban sprawl. *Shelterforce* 97(January/Febru-
           ary):21-26.
Sadd, J., M. Pastor, T. Boer, and L. Snyder
   1999    "Every breath you take": The demographics of toxic air releases in Southern Cali-
           fornia. *Economic Development Quarterly* 13(2):107-123.
Savitch, H., D. Collins, D. Sanders, and J. Markham
   1993    Ties that bind: Central cities, suburbs, and the new metropolitan region. *Eco-
           nomic Development Quarterly* 7(4):341-357.
Savitch, H., and R. Vogel, eds.
   1996    *Regional Politics: America in a Post-City Age.* Thousand Oaks, Calif.: Sage Publica-
           tions.
Saxenian, A.
   1996    *The Regional Advantage, Culture and Competition in Silicon Valley and Route 128.*
           Cambridge, Mass.: Harvard University Press.
Schrag, P.
   1998    *Paradise Lost: California's Experience, America's Future.* New York: The New Press.
Stoll, M.
   1997    The extent and effect of spatial job search on the and wages of racial/ethnic
           groups in Los Angeles. Paper prepared for University of California, Los Angeles,
           August.
Summers, A.
   1997    *Major Regionalization Efforts Between Cities and Suburbs in the United States.* Phila-
           delphia: University of Pennsylvania, Wharton School, Real Estate Center, Work-
           ing Paper No. 246, March.
Swanstrom, T.
   1996    Ideas matter: Reflections on the new regionalism. *Cityscape: A Journal of Policy
           Development and Research* 2(2)5-21.
Szasz, A., and M. Meuser
   1997    Environmental inequalities: Literature review and proposals for new directions
           in research and theory. *Current Sociology* 45(3):99-120.
Tienda, M.
   1991    Poor people and poor places: Deciphering neighborhood effects on poverty out-
           comes. Pp. 244-262 in *Macro-Micro Linkages in Sociology*, J. Huber, ed. Newbury
           Park, Calif.: Sage Publications.
United Church of Christ, Commission for Racial Justice
   1987    *Toxic Wastes and Race in the United States: A National Report on the Racial and Socio-
           Economic Characteristics of Communities with Hazardous Waste Sites.* New York:
           Public Data Access.
U.S. Department of Housing and Urban Development
   1996    *America's New Economy and the Challenge of the Cities: A HUD Report on Metropoli-
           tan Economic Strategy.* Washington, D.C.: U.S. Department of Housing and Urban
           Development.
U.S. General Accounting Office
   1983    *Siting of Hazardous Waste Landfills and Their Correlation with Racial and Economic
           Status of Surrounding Communities.* Washington, D.C.: U.S. Government Printing
           Office.
Voith, R.
   1997    Do suburbs need cities? *Journal of Regional Science* 38(3):445-464.

Walsh, J.
   1997   *Stories of Renewal: Community Building and the Future of Urban America.* New York: The Rockefeller Foundation.
Wilson, W.
   1996   *When Work Disappears: The World of the New Urban Poor.* New York: Alfred A. Knopf.
   1987   *The Truly Disadvantaged: The Inner City, the Underclass, and Public Policy.* Chicago: The University of Chicago Press.
Zdenek, R.
   1998   Connecting people to jobs: Capitalizing on regional economic development opportunities. *Shelterforce* 97(January/February):13-15.

# APPENDIX
# A

# Acronyms

| | |
|---|---|
| AAP | American Academy of Pediatrics (McLoyd) |
| AFDC | Aid to Families with Dependent Children (Moffitt) |
| AFQT | Armed Forces Qualification Test (Conrad) |
| | |
| BRFSS | Behavioral Risk Factor Surveillance System (Kington) |
| | |
| CBO | Characteristics of Business Owners (Boston) |
| CPS | Current Population Survey (Zhou, Conrad, Smith) |
| | |
| ECA | Epidemiologic Catchment Area Study (Williams) |
| EEO | Equal Employment Opportunity (Holzer) |
| EPESE | Established Populations for Epidemiologic Studies of the Elderly (Kington) |
| ETS | Educational Testing Service (Ferguson) |
| | |
| FAS | fetal alcohol syndrome (McLoyd) |
| | |
| HDS | Housing Discrimination Study (Massey) |
| HHNES | Hispanic Health and Nutrition Examination Survey (Kington) |
| HRS | Health and Retirement Study (Oliver/Shapiro) |
| HUD | U.S. Department of Housing and Urban Development (Pastor) |
| | |
| IHS | Indian Health Service (USDHHS) (Kington, Williams) |

JTPA            Job Taining Partnership Act (Moffitt)

LBW             low birth weight (Kington, Jenkins)
LFPR            labor-force participation rate (Conrad)
LULUs           locally undesirable land uses (Pastor)

NAEP            National Assessment of Educational Progress
                (Ferguson)
NCES            National Center for Education Statistics (Ferguson)
NCHS            National Center for Health Statistics (Kington,
                Williams)
NCS             National Comorbidity Survey (Williams)
NHANES III      Third National Health and Nutrition Examination
                Survey (McLoyd)
NHIS            National Health Interview Survey (Kington)
NICHHD          National Institute of Child Health and Human
                Development (Smith)
NLMS            National Longitudinal Mortality Survey (Kington)
NLSAH           National Longitudinal Study of Adolescent Health
                (McLoyd)
NLSY            National Longitudinal Survey of Youth (Holzer,
                Conrad)
NMES            National Medical Expenditures Survey (Kington)

OMB             U.S. Office of Management and Budget (Kington,
                Williams)

PRWORA          Personal Responsibility and Work Reconciliation Act
                (Moffitt)
PSID            Panel Study of Income Dynamics (Smith, Oliver/
                Shapiro)
PUMAs           Public Use Microdata Areas (in Los Angeles) (Pastor)
PUMS            Public Use Micro Samples  (Conrad)

SCF             Survey of Consumer Finances, Federal Reserve Board
                (Oliver/Shapiro)
SEP             socioeconomic position (Kington)
SES             socioeconomic status (Williams, McLoyd)
SIE             Survey of Income and Education (Conrad)
SIPP            Survey of Income and Program Participation (Oliver/
                Shapiro)
SMOBE           Survey of Minority-Owned Business Enterprises
                (Boston)

| SMSAs | Standard Metropolitan Statistical Areas (Sandefur) |
| SNC | The State of the Nation's Cities (Pastor) |
| SSI | Supplemental Security Income (Moffitt) |
| SSRC | Social Science Research Council (Massey) |

| TANF | Temporary Assistance to Needy Families, was AFDC until 1996 (Moffitt) |
| TSDFs | toxic storage and disposal facilities (Pastor) |

| UCLA | University of California, Los Angeles (Kington) |
| USBC | U.S. Bureau of the Census (Kington, Williams, Boston) |
| USDHHS | U.S. Department of Health and Human Services (Kington, Williams) |

| WIC | Women, Infants, and Children (McLoyd) |

# APPENDIX
# B
# Agenda:
# Research Conference on Racial Trends in the United States

National Academy of Sciences Auditorium
October 15-16, 1998

**October 15**

8:30    *Opening Remarks*
        Bruce Alberts, Chairman, National Research Council
        *and Conference Chairs*
        Neil Smelser (CASBS), William Julius Wilson (Harvard)

9:00    *History and Future*
        Christopher Edley (Harvard)
        *Changing America: Indicators of Well-Being by Race*
        Rebecca Blank (Council of Economic Advisers)

9:45    *Group Discussion of Demographic and Immigration Trends*

        *Discussion Leaders:*
        Reynolds Farley (Russell Sage)
        Mary Waters (Harvard)

        *Paper Authors:*
        Gary Sandefur (Wisconsin): "An Overview of Racial and
            Ethnic Demographic Trends"
        Min Zhou (UCLA): "America Becoming: Contemporary
            Immigration and the Dynamics of Race and Ethnicity"

**10:45** *Selected Questions and Comments from the Audience*

**11:00** *Group Discussion of Income, Wealth, and Welfare Trends*

> *Discussion Leaders:*
> Gerald Jaynes (Yale)
> Sanders Korenman (Baruch College)
> *Paper Authors:*
> James Smith (RAND): "Race and Ethnicity in the Labor Market: Trends Over the Short and Long Run "
> Thomas Shapiro (Northeastern) & Melvin Oliver (Ford): "Wealth and Racial Stratification"
> Robert Moffitt (Johns Hopkins) & Peter Gottschalk (Boston College): "Ethnic and Racial Differences in Welfare Receipt in the United States"

**12:00** *Selected Questions and Comments from the Audience*

**1:15** *Group Discussion of Education Trends*

> *Discussion Leader:*
> Thomas Kane (Harvard)
> *Paper Authors:*
> Ronald Ferguson (Harvard): "Racial Test-Score Trends 1971-1996, Popular Culture and Community Academic Standards"
> Daryl Smith (Claremont): "Racial Trends in Higher Education Policy and Research Implications"
> Sharon Robinson (ETS): "Assessment and Learning Trends in Group Test Score Differences"

**2:00** *Selected Questions and Comments from the Audience*

**2:15** *Group Discussion of Labor Force Trends*

> *Discussion Leaders:*
> Kenneth Chay (Berkeley)
> Marcus Alexis (Northwestern)
> *Paper Authors:*
> Harry Holzer (MSU): "Racial Differences in Labor Market Outcomes Among Men"
> Cecilia Conrad (Pomona): "Racial Trends in Labor Market Access and Wages: Women"

John Sibley Butler (Texas) & Charles Moskos (Northwestern): "Labor Force Trends: The Military as Data"
Thomas Boston (Georgia Tech): "Trends in Minority-Owned Businesses"

3:30   *Selected Questions and Comments from the Audience*

3:45   *Group Discussion of Neighborhood and Geographic Trends*

*Discussion Leaders:*
   Roberto Fernandez (Stanford)
   Paul Jargowsky (Texas)
*Paper Authors:*
   Douglas Massey (Penn): "Residential Segregation and Neighborhood Conditions in U.S. Metropolitan Areas"
   Manuel Pastor (UC Santa Cruz): "Geography and Opportunity"

4:45   *Selected Questions and Comments from the Audience*

5:00   *Adjourn*


## October 16

8:30   *Group Discussion of the Meaning of Race and International Comparisons*

*Discussion Leaders:*
   Anthony Marx (Columbia)
   Richard Alba (SUNY Albany)
*Paper Authors:*
   Michael Omi (Berkeley): "The Changing Meaning of Race"

9:30   *Selected Questions and Comments from the Audience*

9:45   *Group Discussion of Trends Among Asians, Latinos, and Native Americans*

*Discussion Leaders:*
   Rodolfo de la Garza (Texas)
   Matthew Snipp (Stanford)

*Paper Authors:*
Albert Camarillo (Stanford) & Frank Bonilla (Hunter): "Latinos in a Multiracial Society: A New American Dilemma?"
Don Nakanishi (UCLA): "Beyond the Campaign Finance Controversy: Trends and Issues of the New Asian Pacific American Population"
Russell Thornton (Stanford): "Recent Trends Among Native Americans in the United States"

10:45    *Selected Questions and Comments from the Audience*

11:00    *Group Discussion of Racial Attitudes, Affirmative Action, and Political Participation*

*Discussion Leaders:*
James Jones (Delaware)
Jennifer Hochschild (Princeton)
*Paper Authors:*
Lawrence Bobo (Harvard): "Overview of Racial Attitudes and Beliefs"
Carol Swain (Stanford):"Affirmative Action: A Search for Consensus"

12:00    *Selected Questions and Comments from the Audience*

1:15    *Group Discussion of Justice Trends*

*Discussion Leaders:*
Alfred Blumstein (Carnegie-Mellon)
Darnell Hawkins (Illinois)
*Paper Authors:*
Randall Kennedy (Harvard): "Overview of Racial Trends in the Administration of Criminal Justice"

2:00    *Selected Questions and Comments from the Audience*

2:15    *Group Discussion of Health Trends*

*Discussion Leaders:*
James S. Jackson (Michigan)
Beverly Coleman-Miller (HSPH)

*Paper Authors:*
　　Raynard Kington (NCHS) & Herbert Nickens (AAMC):
　　　"Racial and Ethnic Differences in Health: Recent Trends,
　　　Current Patterns, Future Directions"
　　Vonnie McLoyd (Michigan) & Betsy Lozoff (Michigan):
　　　"Behavior and Development in Children and Adolescents"
　　Renee Jenkins (Howard): "Physical Health Issues in Children
　　　and Adolescents"
　　David Williams (Michigan): "Racial Variations in Adult
　　　Health Status: Patterns, Paradoxes, and Prospects"
　　Eugene Oddone (VA), Laura Petersen (VA), Morris
　　　Weinberger: "Health Care Use in the Veterans Health
　　　Administration: Racial Trends and the Spirit of Inquiry"

3:45　　*Selected Questions and Comments from the Audience*

4:00　　*Concluding Discussion of Racial Trends and Research Needs*
　　　　William Julius Wilson, Neil Smelser

4:30　　*Selected Questions and Comments from the Audience*

5:00　　*Adjourn*

# APPENDIX
# C

# Biographical Sketches

**REBECCA M. BLANK** is Dean of the Gerald R. Ford School of Public Policy, Henry Carter Adams Collegiate Professor of Public Policy, and Professor of Economics at the University of Michigan. Prior to going to Michigan, she served as a Member of the President's Council of Economic Advisers from 1997-1999. Professor Blank's research has focused on the interaction between the macroeconomy, government anti-poverty programs, and the behavior and well-being of low-income families.

**ALFRED BLUMSTEIN** is a University Professor and the J. Erik Jonsson Professor of Operations Research, and former Dean of the H. John Heinz III School of Public Policy and Management, of Carnegie Mellon University. His research related to crime and punishment has covered issues of criminal careers, deterrence and incapacitation, sentencing, incarceration practice and policy, racial disproportionality, youth violence, and demographic trends. He was elected to the National Academy of Engineering in 1998.

**LAWRENCE D. BOBO** is Professor of Sociology and Afro-American Studies at Harvard University. Prior to joining the faculty at Harvard he was Professor of Sociology at the University of California, Los Angeles, where he directed the Center for Research on Race, Politics & Society. He is coauthor of *Racial Attitudes in America: Trends and Interpretations*, which won the 1986 Scholarly Achievement Award of the North Central Sociological Association. His research interests include racial attitudes and relations, social psychology, public opinion, and political behavior.

**FRANK BONILLA** is Thomas Hunter Professor of Sociology, Emeritus, at Hunter College of the City University of New York. From 1973 to 1993 Dr. Bonilla was the director of C.U.N.Y.'s Centro de Estudios Puertorriquenos and Professor in C.U.N.Y.'s Ph.D. Programs in Sociology and Political Science. Professor Bonilla's current research, writing, and advocacy efforts are focused on promoting a vitalization of Latino academic and policy research capabilities.

**THOMAS D. BOSTON** is a Professor of Economics in the School of Economics at Georgia Institute of Technology in Atlanta and the owner of Boston Research Group, an Atlanta-based consulting company. Dr. Boston has consulted for dozens of public agencies and private companies and is recognized as one of the country's most knowledgeable experts on minority business issues.

**JOHN SIBLEY BUTLER** holds The Gale Chair in Entrepreneurship and Small Business in the Graduate School of Business (Department of Management) at the University of Texas. He is Chair of the Management Department and holds a joint appointment in Organizational Behavior in the College of Liberal Arts (Sociology). His research is in the areas of organizational behavior, entrepreneurship/new ventures, and general race relations.

**ALBERT CAMARILLO** is a Professor of American History and Director of the Center for Comparative Studies in Race and Ethnicity at Stanford University. He is a past director of the Inter-University Program for Latino Research and the Stanford Center for Chicano Research. In his research, Professor Camarillo has examined the origins of the Chicano civil rights movement, as well as settlement, labor, and immigration patterns in urbanized populations.

**CECILIA A. CONRAD** is an Associate Professor of Economics at Pomona College in Claremont, California. Prior to joining the faculty at Pomona, Professor Conrad taught at Duke University in Durham, North Carolina, and at Barnard College, Columbia University, New York. Her research focuses on the economics of inequality and of the family.

**CHRISTOPHER EDLEY, JR,** is a Professor at Harvard Law School and the Co-Diretor of the Harvard Civil Rights Project. He served as Senior Advisor to President Clinton for the Race Initiative. His acaemic work is primarily in administrative law, but has also included civil rights, federalism, budget policy, and national security law.

**RONALD F. FERGUSON** is Lecturer in Public Policy at the John F. Kennedy School of Government, Harvard University, and Senior Research Associate at the Wiener Center for Social Policy, Harvard University. He is also currently a Visiting Scholar at the College Board.. His research and publications include the effects of teacher quality and other school resources on test scores in public primary and secondary schools; the effects of school quality, parenting practices, and youth culture on the Black-White achievement gap; the influence of technology and other factors on changes in the demand for low-skilled workers; and various other issues related to the quality of life in cities.

**PETER T. GOTTSCHALK** is Professor of Economics at Boston College. He is currently a Research Affiliate at the Institute for Research on Poverty at the University of Wisconsin, Madison, and was previously a Russell Sage Foundation Visiting Scholar and a Brookings Economic Policy Fellow. Professor Gottschalk's main area of research is labor economics, with a special emphasis on income distribution and poverty issues.

**DARNELL F. HAWKINS** is Professor of African-American Studies, Sociology, and Criminal Justice at the University of Illinois in Chicago. He has conducted research on racial disproportionality in the American prison system, homicide patterns and violence as a public-health problem, and public perceptions of crime and punishment.

**HARRY J. HOLZER** is Professor of Public Policy at Georgetown University. He is also a Senior Affiliate of the Joint Center for Poverty Research (University of Chicago and Northwestern University), Research Affiliate of the Institute for Research on Poverty (University of Wisconsin), and a former Chief Economist at the U.S. Department of Labor. Dr. Holzer has written extensively on the labor market problems of minorities and the urban poor.

**RENÉE R. JENKINS** is a Professor and the Chairman of the Department of Pediatrics and Child Health at Howard University. Dr. Jenkins was the first director of Adolescent Medicine in the Department of Pediatrics and Child Health at Howard University and is a past President of the Society for Adolescent Medicine. Her publications and presentations range from adolescent health and sexuality to violence prevention and health issues of minority children.

**RANDALL KENNEDY** is a Professor at Harvard Law School, where he teaches courses on contracts, freedom of expression, and the regulation of race relations.  His recent book, *Race, Crime and the Law*, won the 1998 Robert F. Kennedy Book Prize.

**RAYNARD S. KINGTON** is a Research Medical Officer at the National Center for Health Statistics (N.C.H.S.), where he works primarily on the National Health and Nutrition Examination Survey.  Prior to joining N.C.H.S. in 1997, he was a Senior Scientist in the Social Policy Department at RAND.  Dr. Kington's research has focused on the relationships between race, socioeconomic position, and health status, especially in older populations.

**BETSY LOZOFF,** a behavioral pediatrician, is Director of the Center for Human Growth and Development and Professor of Pediatrics and Communicable Diseases at the University of Michigan.  Her research, teaching, and patient care use a cross-cultural perspective to understand common pediatric issues related to behavior and development.  Her major research focus is on iron deficiency and infant development.

**ANTHONY MARX** is Associate Professor of Political Science at Columbia University.  His research focuses on comparative race relations and includes extensive work in South Africa, Brazil, and the U.S. South.  Professor Marx's book, *Making Race and Nation*, won the 1999 Ralph Bunche Award of the American Political Science Association and the 2000 Barrington Moore Prize of the American Sociological Association.

**DOUGLAS S. MASSEY** is the Dorothy Swaine Thomas Professor of Sociology at the University of Pennsylvania and Chair of its Sociology Department.  He is co-author of the book *American Apartheid: Segregation and the Making of the Underclass,* which won the Distinguished Publication Award of the American Sociological Association, the Otis Dudley Duncan Award of the Section on the Sociology of Population, and the Critics' Choice Award of the American Educational Studies Association.  Professor Massey has also published extensively on U.S.-Mexico migration.  He is a member of the National Academy of Sciences and the American Academy of Arts and Sciences.

**VONNIE C. McLOYD** is a Professor in the Department of Psychology at the University of Michigan in addition to holding a research scientist appointment in the Center for Human Growth and Development.  Dr. McLoyd is a developmental psychologist whose primary research objective is to develop and test models of the processes by which economic hardship (i.e., poverty, parental job loss, parental income loss) affects children's development, with a special focus on development in African

American children.  She received a MacArthur "Genius" Fellowship in 1996.

**FAITH MITCHELL** is Director of the Division on Social and Economic Studies of the Commission on Behavioral and Social Sciences and Education.  She is co-editor of *Premature Death in the New Independent States* (National Academy Press, 1997) and *Governance and Opportunity in Metropolitan America* (National Academy Press, 1999).

**ROBERT A. MOFFITT** is Professor of Economics at Johns Hopkins University.  He is affiliated with the Institute for Research on Poverty, the Joint Center on Poverty Research, and the Harvard Program on Inequality and Social Policy.  He currently chairs the NRC Panel on Data and Methods for the Evaluation of Welfare Reform and is a member of CBASSE.  He is a co-Principal Investigator of the Three-City Study, a major interdisciplinary study of welfare reform.  His research focuses on the effects of the U.S. welfare system on employment, income, family structure, and other behaviors, and on the economics of the low-income population in general

**CHARLES MOSKOS** is a Professor of Sociology at Northwestern University.  His current research deals with race relations in the Army and what lessons that experience may have for civilian society.

**DON T. NAKANISHI** is a Professor and the Director of the U.C.L.A. Asian American Studies Center.  He is the author of numerous books, articles, and policy reports that have focused on topics of access, representation, and influence of Asian Pacific Americans and other ethnic and racial groups in American political, educational, and social institutions. He was appointed by President Clinton to the Civil Liberties Public Education Board.

**HERBERT W. NICKENS** was Vice-President and Director of the Division of Community and Minority Programs at the Association of American Medical Colleges when he died in 1999.

**EUGENE Z. ODDONE** is Director of the Center for Health Services Research in Primary Care at the Veterans Affairs Medical Center in Durham, North Carolina; Chief of the Division of General Internal Medicine at Duke University Medical Center; and Associate Director of Epidemiology Research and the Information Center at V.A.M.C.  His research interests include evaluation of the effectiveness and delivery of ambulatory care with emphasis on hospital readmission and health care cost, assessing the reason for racial disparities in the use and outcomes of health care, evaluation of house staff training, and primary care for H.I.V.-infected patients.

**MELVIN L. OLIVER** is Vice President of the Asset Building and Community Development Program at the Ford Foundation. From 1978 to 1996 he was a member of the faculty at U.C.L.A., teaching at both the graduate and undergraduate levels. An expert on racial and urban inequality and poverty, Dr. Oliver is the author (with Thomas M. Shapiro) of *Black Wealth/White Wealth: A New Perspective on Racial Inequality*, which has received the Distinguished Scholarly Publication Award from the American Sociological Association, the C. Wright Mills Award from the Society for the Study of Social Problems, and the award for the Outstanding Book on the subject of human rights from the Gustavus Myers Center for the Study of Human Rights in North America.

**MICHAEL A. OMI** is Professor of Comparative Ethnic Studies at the University of California, Berkeley. He has written about racial theory and politics, Asian Americans and race relations, right-wing political movements, and race and popular culture.

**MANUEL PASTOR** is Professor of Latin American and Latino Studies and Director of the Center for Justice, Tolerance, and Community at UC Santa Cruz. He has conducted research on Latin American economic issues and U.S. urban issues, and is currently involved in a multi-year project on community-based environmental justice movements.

**LAURA A. PETERSEN** is a health care researcher at the Houston Center for Quality of Care and Utilization Studies and the Center to Study Racial and Ethnic Variations in Medical Interactions at the Houston Veterans Affairs Medical Center (funded by the Agency for Health Care Research and Quality and the National Institutes of Health Office of Minority Health). Her research interests include racial disparities in the use and outcomes of cardiovascular care, as well as the relationship between health care financing mechanisms and acess to health care.

**GARY D. SANDEFUR** is Professor of Sociology and member of the Center for Demography and Ecology at the University of Wisconsin, Madison. Most of his publications deal with issues at the intersection of race and ethnicity, social demography, and public policy. His co-authors, Molly Martin, Jennifer Eggerling, Susan Mannon, and Ann Meier are graduate students in sociology at the University of Wisconsin, Madison. Martin has interests in social demography, poverty, and welfare policy; Eggerling specializes in race and ethnicity and social psychology; Mannon studies agricultural development and change in Central America; and Meier studies social capital and family and education outcomes.

**THOMAS M. SHAPIRO** is Professor of Sociology and Anthropology at Northeastern University. His primary interest is in racial inequality. With Dr. Melvin Oliver, he wrote *Black Wealth/White Wealth*, which was awarded the 1995 C. Wright Mills Award by the Society for the Study of Social Problems, named an Outstanding Book of 1996 by the Gustavus Myers Center for the Study of Human Rights in North America, and received the 1997 Distinguished Scholarly Publication Award from the American Sociological Association.

**NEIL J. SMELSER** is Director of the Center for Advanced Study in the Behavioral Sciences, Stanford, California. From 1958 to 1994 he was on the faculty of Sociology of the University of California, Berkeley, serving as University Professor since 1971. He is a member of the American Academy of Arts and Sciences, the American Philosophical Society, and the National Academy of Sciences.

**JAMES P. SMITH** holds the RAND Chair in Labor Markets and Demographic Studies and was the Director of RAND's Labor and Population Studies Program from 1977 to 1994. He has led numerous projects, including studies of immigration, the economics of aging, Black-White wages and employment, the effects of economic development on labor markets, wealth accumulation and savings behavior, and the interrelation of health and economic status among the elderly.

**CAROL M. SWAIN** is Professor of Law and Professor, Political Science at Vanderbilt University. She is the author of *Black Faces, Black Interests: The Representation of African Americans in Congress,* which was selected by *Library Choice Journal* as one of the seven outstanding academic books of 1994, was the winner of the 1994 Woodrow Wilson prize given to "the best book published in the United States during the prior year on government, politics or international affairs," co-winner of the V.O. Key Award for the best book published on southern politics, and the winner of the 1995 D.B. Hardeman prize for the best scholarly work on the U.S. Congress during a biennial period.

**RUSSELL THORNTON** is Professor of Anthropology at the University of California at Los Angeles. Born and raised in Oklahoma, he is a registered member of the Cherokee Nation of Oklahoma. Since 1990 he has been chair of the Smithsonian Institution's Native American Repatriation

Review Committee. He has published six books and some 60 articles and book chapters.

**MORRIS WEINBERGER** is Director of Health Services Research at Roudebush Veterans' Affairs Medical Center. He is also a Professor of Medicine at the Indiana University School of Medicine and a Senior Investigator at the Regenstrief Institute for Health Care. His research interests include improved treatment of chronic medical conditions.

**DAVID R. WILLIAMS** is a Professor of Sociology, a Senior Research Scientist at the Institute for Social Research, and a Faculty Associate in the African American Mental Health Research Center and the Center for Afro-American and African Studies at the University of Michigan. His research focuses on socioeconomic status and health, and the health of the African American population. His publications examine how racism, social support, religious involvement, and health behaviors can affect health. His current research is examining the ways in which experiences of discrimination affect both physical and mental health.

**WILLIAM JULIUS WILSON** is Lewis P. and Linda L. Geyser University Professor at Harvard University. He is a member of the National Academy of Sciences, the American Academy of Arts and Sciences, the National Academy of Education, and the American Philosophical Society, and a fellow of the American Academy of Political and Social Science. Professor Wilson is a member of numerous national boards and commissions, including the President's Commission on White House Fellowships, The Center for Advanced Study in the Behavioral Sciences, and the Century Foundation. His book, *When Work Disappears: The World of the New Urban Poor*, was selected as one of the notable books of 1996 by the editors of the New York Times Book Review, and received the Sidney Hillman Foundation Award. He received the National Medal of Science in 1998.

**MIN ZHOU** is Professor of Sociology at the University of California, Los Angeles. Her main areas of research are immigration and immigrant adaptation, race/ethnicity, ethnic economies, the community, and urban sociology. Currently, she is doing research in immigrant communities in downtown Los Angeles examining how neighborhood environment influences parent-child and peer-group relations, children's after-school life, and their current academic and future occupational aspirations.

# Index

I and II indicate the respective volumes to
which the page numbers refer.

Firearms, II: 246, 328, 335, 338-339, 361, 362, 363, 364, 378
Florida
   I: 51, 107, 109, 206
   II: 402
Food stamps, II: 154-158 (passim), 160, 161, 163, 342
Ford, Gerald, I: 427
Foreign Assistance Act, II: 214
Foreign countries, *see* Immigrants and immigration; International perspectives; *specific countries*
Friends, *see* Peers and friends
Funding
   affirmative action,
      I: 320-321, 322, 325-326, 343-344, 426-427
      II: 76-77
   Asian/Pacific Islander election participation, I: 171, 172, 173, 192
   census counts and, I: 43
   drug abuse, treatment, II: 327
   housing, antidiscrimination, I: 426-427, 428
   housing subsidies,
      I: 445-446
      II: 156, 160-161, 163
   infant mortality, II: 364-365
   minority-owned businesses, II: 193
   school desegregation, I: 320-321
   veterans health care, II: 422, 424
   welfare, II: 342

## G

Gallop Poll data
   Blacks, criminal justice system, II: 1, 33
Gautreaux Demonstration Project
   I: 427
   II: 113
Gender factors
   affirmative action for women,
      I: 319, 321, 324, 325, 331, 334, 336, 337
      II: 113-114
   American Indians,
      I: 180
      II: 340
   Asians and Pacific Islanders,
      I: 180
      II: 102, 126, 128, 129, 130-132, 133, 134, 135, 141-143, 145

Blacks,
   I: 42, 180, 373
   II: 1, 22, 33, 42, 52-58, 158-160, 174, 179, 183, 323-328, 331, 336, 337, 341, 361-364 (passim), 378, 382-383, 384-385, 387-388
Blacks, employment,
   I: 27-30, 423, 424
   II: 52-55, 61-73, 75-76, 78-79, 81, 98-147, 174, 278, 326, 397-398
breast cancer, II: 383
businesses owned by minority men,
   I: 194-195
businesses owned by White women,
   II: 191-192, 193, 203
cardiovascular disease, II: 259
census undercounting, Blacks,
   I: 42
   II: 387-388
crimes and criminal justice system, II: 1, 22, 29-30, 323-326, 331, 378
employment, I: 14-15, 27-30, 224-227
   *see also "employment, gender factors" under* Blacks; Hispanics; and Whites
health risk factors, II: 272
Hispanics,
   I: 28, 29, 30, 39, 110, 130, 180, 224-227
   II: 53-59, 71-73, 81, 83, 102, 158-160, 261, 361, 362, 363, 364, 378
Hispanics, employment,
   I: 28, 29, 30, 39, 224-225
   II: 53-68, 71-73, 78, 81-87, 102, 124, 126, 129, 133, 135, 136, 141-143, 146-147
household structure,
   I: 24
   II: 352-353
immigrants, general, I: 206, 224-227
life expectancy,
   I: 86-87
   II: 372, 382-383, 384-385
marriage, Black *vs* White women's attitudes, I: 71, 74
military service by Black women, II: 174, 179, 183
mortality,
   I: 81, 82-83, 84, 86-87
   II: 259, 261, 363, 382-383, 384-385
prostate cancer, II: 393, 423
race, concept of,
   I: 254, 256, 259, 279
   II: 174

educational attainment, I: 181
electoral issues, I: 190
employment issues, II: 103, 128, 130, 131,
    132, 135
fertility, I: 66
health care, II: 282
health status, II: 263, 265, 266, 399
immigrants,
    I: 175, 176
    II: 399
marriage, I: 76
mortality,
    I: 81, 82, 83, 85, 86, 90
    II: 265, 266
regional demographics, I: 51
Jenkins, Renée R.
    I: 5, 18, 479
    II: 351-370, 441
Jews
    affirmative action, I: 328, 335
    immigrants, I: 212, 218
    political participation, I: 183, 191, 328
    racism and discrimination
        I: 163-164, 267, 335
        II: 89, 389, 390, 401
Jim Crow laws
    I: 6, 9, 13, 244-245, 292, 293, 294, 304,
        305, 306, 308-310, 314, 395, 402
    II: 281
    see also Apartheid
Job Training Partnership Act, II: 112
Johnson, Lyndon
    I: 321-322
    II: 204
Joint Center for Political and Economic
    Studies, I: 335, 336
Jurisprudence, see Crime and criminal
    justice; Litigation
Jury selection
    I: 319
    II: 2, 7-11, 33, 41

## K

Kennedy, John, I: 320
Kennedy, Randall
    I: 18-19, 479-480
    II: 1-21, 22, 24, 25, 32-48, 441-442
Kentucky, II: 8-9
Kerner Commission, see National Advisory
    Commission on Civil Disorders

Kidney disease, II: 393, 417
Kington, Raynard S.
    I: 17, 480
    II: 253-310, 442
Koreans
    Blacks, conflicts with, I: 222
    classification of, I: 41, 177
    educational attainment, I: 180, 181,
        209
    fertility, I: 66
    health care, II: 282
    immigrants, I: 51, 60, 175, 176, 177, 205,
        206, 209, 210, 216-217
    mortality,
        I: 81, 83
        II: 263
    political participation, I: 183
    regional demographics, I: 51, 60

## L

Language factors
    I: 267
    II: 144
    American Indians, I: 142, 149, 154
    Asians and Pacific Islanders, I: 178
    Blacks, II: 386
    English-language courses, I: 365-366
    Hispanics,
        I: 42, 118, 119, 122, 130, 208, 221, 224,
            349, 350, 354, 360
        II: 54, 142
    immigrants, general,
        I: 208, 229, 235
        II: 88, 102, 386
    reading ability,
        I: 149, 349-350, 352, 354, 356, 358, 359,
            360-362, 368, 369, 372
        II: 74, 313
Latino National Political Survey, I: 119
Latinos, see Hispanics
Lead poisoning, II: 289-290, 311, 315-318,
    339, 392
Legal issues, I: 6, 13
    American Indians,
        education, I: 149-150, 151
        litigation, I: 143-144, 145
        remains of dead, I: 154(n.10), 158-161,
            166
        tribal membership requirements,
            I: 139-140, 144

# M

## S